PASCAL plus
DATA STRUCTURES,
ALGORITHMS,
d ADVANCED
RAMMING

PASCAL plus
DATA STRUCTURES,
ALGORITHMS,
and ADVANCED
PROGRAMMING

Nell Dale
University of Texas at Austin

Susan C. Lilly

D.C. Heath and Company
Lexington, Massachusetts / Toronto

International Standard Book Number: 0-669-07239-7

Library of Congress Catalog Card Number: 84-82073

To the next generation of computer scientists
N.D.

To my father, Mason M. Lilly
S.L.

Preface

Until recently there has not been much consensus among educators on what formal education is necessary for a computer professional. It has always been considered essential to have a great deal of mathematical knowledge, as well as an understanding of computer hardware. Software education, however, often consisted of the teaching of a number of programming languages. The development of programming *techniques*, it was often assumed, was not a subject of formal education, but rather a matter of experience. This situation is analagous to an English department teaching only grammar without freshman composition, literature, or creative writing.

Today the shared experience of a generation of programmers has combined to form a body of practical and theoretical knowledge that can be taught along with computer languages. Software is now an area of study in its own right. The evolution of this situation can be clearly seen in the progression of computer science curricula advocated by the major computer professional organizations.

Three main professional organizations represent the spectrum of computer educators and professionals: the ACM (Association of Computing Machinery), the IEEE (Institute of Electronic and Electrical Engineers), and the DPMA (Data Processing Management Association). Each of these organizations has contributed greatly to computer science education over the years by publishing curriculum guidelines that identify what a student should know upon graduation from a four-year institution of higher learning.

The first curriculum guidelines were published in 1968 by the ACM. These guidelines assumed that only those students who had a broad mathematical background could possibly learn computer science. Programming was considered a skill that the student was to master on his or her own, perhaps within a laboratory setting. In 1976 the IEEE issued guidelines for a four-year program in Computer Engineering. Again programming was not a task to be mastered in its own right.

In 1978 the ACM revised its curriculum. For the first time, programming was mentioned as a topic of study. Another major change was that mathematics was considered a co-requisite, rather than a prerequisite, of the study of computing.

Three things happened in 1983–1984 which solidified the trends in computer-related education: the ACM approved the revision of CS1 (Curriculum '78) and presented a first draft of CS2, the IEEE revised its entire curriculum, and the curriculum for an Advanced Placement Exam in Computer Sciences was specified by the College Boards. The correlation between the ACM CS1 and (draft) CS2 and the AP curriculum was extraordinarily high, and this intersection mapped quite closely onto Subject Areas 1, 2, and 4 of the IEEE curriculum.

A consensus has evolved concerning what the curriculum should be for the first year of a computer science education—within engineering or elsewhere. To computer educators this is an exciting development. *Pascal Plus Data Structures, Algorithms, and Advanced Programming* covers the advanced topics in this consensus. It is designed to follow a one-semester course that is an introduction, or its equivalent, to top-down design and structured programming with Pascal.

WHY THIS TEXT IS DIFFERENT

Our presentation is unique in that we stress the leading edge of computer science theory and software engineering principles. These principles include modularization, data encapsulation, information hiding, data abstraction, top-down design of algorithms and data structures in parallel, testing strategies, program verification, and proper documentation.

We feel strongly that these principles can be stressed without resorting to complicated mathematical notation. Therefore, this book assumes no college-level mathematics. Even algorithm analysis and program verification are approached intuitively. Those students with a mathematics background can understand English presentations; those students with no mathematics cannot understand formalisms. We intend to reach both groups of students.

ORGANIZATION AND CONTENT

Chapter 1 reviews the basic principles of designing computer programs. We assume that the reader has a basic knowledge of Pascal programming. The goals for writing a good program are enumerated, and a number of tools for attaining these goals are described in detail. The techniques for the top-down design of both programs and data structures are reviewed with an emphasis on modularization and good documentation. Approaches for debugging and testing are also discussed. Detailed sample problems illustrate these points.

Chapter 2 describes how data structures will be studied throughout the rest of the book. One-dimensional arrays, two-dimensional arrays, and records—three structured data types with which the students should be familiar from their first course—are examined from three perspectives: the logical level, the application or usage level, and the implementation level.

The concept of an abstract data type is illustrated in an application that uses the one-dimensional array and the record to create a string data type. Utility routines to manipulate the string data type are designed, written, and tested. The string data type defined here is used in some of the applications in later chapters, illustrating the point that once a programmer has created a user-defined data type, subsequent problems may assume this type to be "built-in."

In Chapter 3 stacks are introduced to demonstrate the concept of data encapsulation in user-defined data structures. We develop, first, an understanding of the logical properties and operations on the structure (e.g., PUSH and POP), and second, one or more implementations of the structure and its operations in the Pascal programming language. Finally, stacks are used in two complete programs to illustrate the real-world application of this data structure.

Queues are discussed in a similar fashion in Chapter 4. In addition, this chapter examines in detail what design considerations must be given to the choice of a particular implementation. The chapter concludes with an application that illustrates a queueing system in a simulation problem.

Linked lists are presented in Chapters 5 and 6. The implementation level in Chapter 5 uses an array of records; in Chapter 6 the dynamic implementation of linked lists is discussed. We decided to present first the idea of linking the elements in a list in terms of structures that are already familiar (an array of records) before the introduction of a new, language-dependent syntax. After the concepts and this general solution are fully understood in Chapter 5, the syntax of the Pascal pointer type is presented in detail in Chapter 6, along with a discussion of dynamic allocation. To illustrate its use, the linked list structure is implemented again using pointer variables. Doubly-linked lists, circular lists, and lists with headers and trailers are also discussed.

We present recursion in Chapter 7 with two goals for the student—first, to give him or her an intuitive understanding of the concept and a belief that recursion actually works; and second, to convey how recursion can be used to solve programming problems. Guidelines for writing recursive functions and procedures are illustrated with many examples, and a simple technique for verifying the correctness of a recursive routine is presented. Since many students are wary of recursion (after having been warned to avoid its unintentional use in their first course), the presentation here is deliberately intuitive and nonmathematical.

In Chapter 8 the binary search tree is introduced as a way to arrange data that gives the flexibility of a linked structure without the liability of slow, sequential access. The insertion and deletion algorithms are developed in detail and implemented for a tree whose nodes are linked with pointer variables. A nonrecursive tree traversal is presented using a stack as a supplementary data structure. Then recursive tree traversals are presented, illustrating how recursion can greatly simplify some programming problems.

Chapter 9 is a collection of loosely related topics. We discuss expression trees, and point out the relationship between the different tree traversals and mathematical notation. The use of arrays to implement binary trees is presented as a lead-in to the discussion of heaps and heapsort. The final topic in the chapter is an introduction to graphs.

Chapter 10 is an introduction to program verification. This topic is on the leading edge of theoretical computer science. This is written as a stand-alone chapter, and may be omitted without losing continuity. However, program verification techniques will be employed by the next generation of computer professionals to produce reliable software. This chapter is intended to introduce students to a topic that they will encounter again in later courses.

Chapter 11 presents a number of sorting algorithms and asks the question: Which is best? To answer this question, we introduce the analysis of algorithms; and we compare the selection sort, bubble sort, quicksort, and heapsort. Chapter 12 continues the discussion of algorithm analysis in the context of searching. Various searching algorithms are presented and analyzed, including sequential and binary searches and hashing techniques. In both chapters the practical considerations in choosing appropriate sorting and searching techniques are balanced by the theoretical concepts behind the idea of measuring work.

Chapter 13 is a summary chapter that ties together the ideas introduced in this book in a discussion of the "real-world" programming environment. The concepts and techniques discussed throughout the previous chapters are developed to create the principles of software engineering practices that are in use today for solving large and complex programming problems.

ADDITIONAL FEATURES

Chapter Goals: At the beginning of each chapter the goals of that chapter are presented. These goals are then tested in the exercises and pretests at the end of the chapter.

Chapter Exercises: At the end of each chapter (except Chapter 13), there is a set of paper-and-pencil exercises to test whether the chapter goals have been attained. The complete exercise answers are in the back of the book.

Chapter Pretests: At the end of each chapter (except Chapter 13) there is a test for the student to measure his or her own progress. The answers to these questions are in the Instructor's Guide.

Applications: There are nine completely worked-out applications that illustrate the principles of good software design using the data structure under discussion in the particular chapter. Program reading is an essential skill for computer professionals, yet few books include programs of sufficient length for students to get experience in program reading. These applications provide students with practice in this skill.

Programming Assignments: A set of recommended programming assignments for each chapter is included at the end of the book. They were carefully chosen to illustrate the techniques described in the text. Sample input data are included for many of the problems.

Instructor's Guide: An Instructor's Guide is available with answers to the pretests, a test for each chapter, answers to the chapter tests, cumulative tests with answers, a final exam with answers, and transparency masters for each chapter.

Class Tested: This manuscript has been class tested with approximately 3,000 students over two years at the University of Texas at Austin. In addition, it has been reviewed and class tested at the following sites:

Southern Illinois University at Carbondale (Robert J. McGlinn)
University of Maryland (Richard H. Austing)
Broome Community College (Morton Goldberg)
National Cathedral School (Suzanne Golomb)

ACKNOWLEDGEMENTS

Thanking people who have contributed to a textbook is a little like saying thank-you at the Academy Awards: You thank a few and run the risk of missing someone important or you thank everyone and run the risk of losing the audience.

We cannot list all the students who helped so much by using and critiquing various manuscripts, but we can thank each of our fellow professionals who acted as reviewers:

Jeff Brumfield (The University of Texas at Austin)
Frank Burke (Middlesex County College)
Thomas E. Byther (University of Maine at Orono)
Henry A. Etlinger (Rochester Institute of Technology)
David L. Feinstein (University of South Alabama)
Gary Ford (University of Colorado at Colorado Springs)
George W. Heyworth (United States Military Academy)
Nancy Penney (University of Kansas)
Bruce Presley (Lawrenceville School)
Edwin D. Reilly (State University of New York at Albany)

David C. Rine (Western Illinois University)
David Stemple (University of Massachusetts)
Frank T. Vanecek (Norwich University)
Vicki Walker (Arizona State University)
Caroline Wardle (Boston University)
Bonnie Lynn Webber (University of Pennsylvania)
Chip Weems (University of Massachusetts)
Pat Woodworth (Ithaca College)

For this impressive list of reviewers, as well as her tremendous support, we must thank our editor, Pam Kirshen. She used to sign letters to us as "Your Coach," and indeed she was. Thanks, Pam! To all the others at D. C. Heath who contributed so much, especially Cathy Cantin and Ruth Thompson, we are indeed grateful.

We must also thank the faculty members and senior graduate students of the Computer Sciences Department at the University of Texas at Austin who have been involved over the years with the course for which this book was written: Rick Alterman, Bill Bulko, Joyce Brennan, Gael Buckley, Munjid Musallam, David Scott, and especially Jim Bitner.

Anyone who has ever written a book—or is related to anyone who has— knows the amount of time involved in such a project. To our families who learned this first-hand, all we can say is: "To Robert, David, Joshua, Al, Susy, Sarah, June, Judy, Pam, Bobby, Tim, and Phil, thanks for your tremendous support and indulgence."

Contents

Applications

Programming Tools 1

Goals

To be able to write a complete description of a programming problem.

To be able to write a top-down design for a given problem, using either pseudo-code or English.

To be able to list features that make a program readable and easily modified.

To be able to correct a segment of code that violates the rules of good style.

To be able to describe strategies to avoid various categories of program bugs.

To be able to suggest strategies to try to track down bugs, given the symptoms of the error.

To be able to describe several program testing strategies, and to indicate when each would be appropriate.

To be able to implement the top level of a command-driven system.

We don't hear much anymore about the "art of computer programming." Programmers, it seems, no longer need to be artists. We have become "computer scientists" as the body of scientific knowledge applied to programming has grown. And we have become "software engineers" as the tools of our trade have developed.

In the days when learning a computer language meant counting from zero to one, programming was a task better left to virtuosos. Nowadays it seems that everyone wants to be computer literate (whatever that means), and elementary school students are learning to program. Of course, that does not make them programmers. Many children take piano lessons also, though very few are considered pianists.

What differentiates a real programmer from someone who can write a computer program? The factors are the same ones that separate a concert pianist from someone who can play a song or two on the piano: practice and experience, a background of technical and theoretical knowledge, and expertise in the use of the tools of the trade.

THE PROGRAMMER'S TOOLBOX

What are the tools of the programmer's trade? There are several toolboxes, each containing tools that help to build and shape a program product.

One toolbox contains the hardware: the computers and their peripheral devices. A second toolbox contains various software items: operating systems to allocate the computer's resources, editors to simplify the input of programs, and compilers to translate high-level languages into something the computer can understand. You have already had the opportunity to use many of these tools and will surely learn more about them in advanced computer science courses.

A third toolbox is filled with the shared body of knowledge that programmers have collected over time. This box contains algorithms for solving common programming problems, as well as data structures for modeling the information processed by programs. It also contains some tools for measuring, evaluating, and proving the correctness of programs. We will explore the uses of many of these tools in the following chapters.

So far, we have been discussing power tools. The fourth toolbox contains the programmer's equivalent of a hammer and nails: a programming methodology. This tool is so basic that we will devote the entire first chapter of this book to it.

It might be argued that the use of these tools takes the creativity out of programming, that the design of software may become a cut-and-dried activity. We don't believe that to be true. Artists and musicians are creative; still, their creative works are based on a thorough grounding in basics. Similarly, the most talented and creative programmers build software through the disciplined use of basic programming tools.

THE GOAL

It is not enough to write a program that does something. A programmer must determine what the program is *supposed* to do and then write a *good* program that accomplishes the task.

A good program

(a)   works (that is, accomplishes its intended function),
(b)   can be read and understood,
(c)   can be modified if necessary without excruciating effort, and
(d)   is completed on time and within its budget.

We will not guarantee that simply by reading this chapter you will be able to write programs that will all run perfectly the first time. For all but small, trivial programs that is a rare occurrence. We will promise that the techniques described in this chapter will help you write programs that are easier to understand, to test and debug, and to modify. And, very likely, you will be able to write programs that are debugged and running before the deadline in class or at work.

The ideas in this chapter are not limited to Pascal. The techniques we will discuss are equally applicable to FORTRAN, PL/1, BASIC, and other programming languages.

If everything in this chapter is old hat to you, if the chapter is a review of your first programming course, congratulations! You were taught well the first time around. If all or most of this chapter is new to you, have patience. With a little practice and perseverance, you will learn good habits that will serve you all your programming life.

WHY BOTHER?

In your first Pascal course, you learned the vocabulary and the grammar of the language—the syntax of Pascal. You learned the reserved words and the constructs for selection (IF–THEN–ELSE) and looping (WHILE–DO). You learned the mechanism for declaring and manipulating the built-in data structures—the array and the record. And you learned how to define and use subprograms—procedures and functions.

You may or may not have learned a technique for putting it all together to solve problems. There are several popular approaches, including flow-charting, top-down, and bottom-up methods. Though all of these approaches have their fans and promoters, in this book we will use the top-down approach to designing computer programs.

Why is it important to have a technique for programming? Why not just sit down and write programs? Aren't we wasting a lot of time and paper, when we could just as easily write the program directly in Pascal or FORTRAN or assembly language?

If the degree of our programming sophistication never had to rise above the level of trivial problems (like summing a list of prices or averaging grades), we might get away with such a code-first technique (or, rather, lack of technique). Many new owners of personal computers program this way, hacking away at the code until the program works more or less correctly. However, if the problem is not small or not trivial, or if the program may need later modification (and most programs do), the need for a structured programming methodology becomes apparent.

GETTING STARTED

The First Step

No matter which programming design technique you use, the first steps will be the same. Imagine the following all-too-familiar situation: On the third day of class, you are given a twelve-page description of Programming Assignment One, which must be running perfectly and turned in by noon, a week from yesterday. You read the assignment and realize that this program will be three times as long as any program you've ever written before. Now, what is your first step?

The responses below are typical of those given by a class of computer science students in such a situation:

1. PANIC 39%
2. PICK UP A PENCIL AND START WRITING 26%
3. DROP THE COURSE 24%
4. COPY THE CODE FROM A SMART CLASSMATE 7%
5. STOP AND THINK...................................... 4%

Response 1 is a reasonable reaction from students who have not yet learned a good programming technique. Students who answered with response 3 will find their education coming along rather slowly. Response 4 will get you scholastic probation at most universities. Response 2 seems like a good idea, given the deadline looming ahead. But—resist the temptation to grab a pencil. The first step is to think.

Read the assignment. Read it again. Ask questions of the instructor (or manager or client). Think.

The problem with writing first is that it tends to lock you into one solution. The first approach that you come up with may not be the best. You can think of others. However, we all have the tendency to believe that once we've put anything in writing, we have too much invested in the idea to toss it out and start over. Resist the temptation to write first.

On the other hand, don't think about all the possibilities until the day before your deadline. (Invariably, the computer goes down that day.) For those of you who feel better with a pencil in hand, there is something that you can begin writing as you think. This leads us to the next hurdle.

The Terror of the Blank Page

A feeling of terror is familiar to artists standing before their blank canvases and writers staring at their typewriters (or, these days, at their word processors). Programmers, however, do not need to worry about where to begin. We can make the first mark and get on with the job by doing an important preliminary task.

Write a complete definition of the problem, including the input and output specifications, the goals, the requirements, and all the assumptions about the problem.

When you have finished this task, you have not only mastered your fear of the blank page, but also started the documentation for your program. In addition, you will become aware of any holes in the specifications. For instance, are embedded blanks in the input significant or can they be ignored? Do you need to check for errors in the input? By getting the answers to these questions at this stage, you can write the program correctly the first time.

At this point, you will probably appreciate your twelve-page assignment description. Chances are that in twelve pages most of the details are specified, and you will not be expected to divine them by ESP or by hanging around the professor's office. Of particular horror are "simple" program specifications, like the following:

Write a program to read in some student records (containing ID number, name, sex, department major, classification, and GPA), sort them according to GPA, and print out the students by class rank. Run your program on the class data set (on file DATA1).

The programming task described is not complicated; you can easily think of an approach to the problem. However, you are missing some pertinent information.

Input   How is the input formatted? Is it free format or within column delimiters? Is NAME one item or divided into first name and last name? Is sex denoted by MALE/FEMALE or M/F or 0/1? Is department major represented by a string or a character code or a number? How do you know when you have read in all the records? (Special character? EOF?) And so on.

Output   How should the output be formatted? Should you print out all the information in the student record or just the name and GPA? Should you list by class rank from highest to lowest or vice versa? And so on.

Special Requirements   Do you need to use the most efficient sort possible or can you use a slow but simple sorting routine?

You must know some details in order to write and run the program. Obviously, you cannot expect to input the data correctly if you do not know how it will be formatted. If the output will be written to a file and saved for use as input to another program, you must know the precise format required.

Other details, if not explicitly stated in the program description, may be handled according to the programmer's preference. Decisions about unstated or ambiguous specifications are called *assumptions*, and they should always be written explicitly in the program's documentation. In short, a complete description will both clarify the problem to be solved and serve as written documentation of the program.

Writing a complete description of the class rank problem is left as an exercise. A sample description is given in the Answer Key in the back of the book.

UNDERSTANDING THE PROBLEM

There is more than one good way to solve most problems. If you were asked for directions to Joe's Diner (Figure 1-1), you could give either of two equally correct answers:

1. "Go east on the big highway to the Y'all Come Inn and turn left."

or

2. "Take the winding country road to Honeysuckle Lodge and turn right."

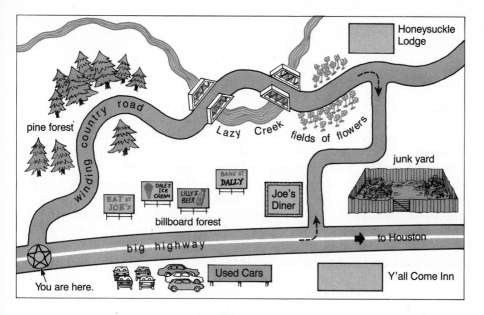

Figure 1-1.

Since following either route will get the traveler to Joe's, both answers are functionally correct.

However, if the request for directions had special requirements, one solution might be clearly preferable to the other. For instance, "I'm late to dinner. Tell me the quickest route to Joe's Diner" prompts the first response, whereas "Is there a pretty road to Joe's?" suggests the second. When no special requirements are known, the choice is a matter of personal preference: Which road do you like better?

In this book, we will present numerous *algorithms*. Choosing between two algorithms that do the same task often depends on the requirements of a particular application. If no such requirements exist, the choice depends on the programmer's own style.

ALGORITHM

A logical sequence of steps used to solve a problem in a finite amount of time.

If at all possible, determine the purpose of the program. This knowledge will help you choose between several competing solutions. For instance, SORT1 may be good for small data sets in nearly sorted order, whereas SORT2 is better for large data sets in completely random order. Both sorting routines will result in the correct answer. However, if computing speed is mentioned in the requirements, one routine may be preferable to the other.

TOP-DOWN DESIGN

Once you have fully clarified the goals of the program, you can begin to develop a strategy for meeting them. The method we will use is called *top-down design.* This method, also called *step-wise refinement,* takes the divide-and-conquer approach. First the problem is broken into several large tasks. Each of these in turn is divided into sections, the sections are subdivided and so on. The important feature is that *details are deferred as long as possible.*

This approach is probably familiar to you. Suppose you needed to write a comprehensive term paper on "Walt Whitman, His Poetry, and His Effect on American Literature." You could just sit down and start writing the paper. On the other hand, if you want to write a paper that sticks to the subject and presents an orderly discussion of the topic, you had better write an outline first. The main modules, denoted by large Roman numerals, might consist of

    I.   Biography of Walt Whitman
   II.   Whitman's poems
  III.   His effect on American literature

Within each main section, you would then add subsections. For instance, under Section I, you could add

    A.   Family history
    B.   Birth to early years
    C.   Newspaper years
    D.   The war years
    E.   The last years

Under each of these sections, you would add numbered subsections. Note that you have deferred as much detail as possible until the lower levels. For instance, I.A. does not tell the names of Whitman's parents and I.B. does not include the date of his birth. When the outline is complete down to the lowest level, it is a relatively simple task to write the paper. Note that the decisions on what to write are begun before the outline is written and continue through its development. By the time you actually begin writing the paper, these decisions have already been made.

The development of a computer program by top-down design proceeds in a similar way. You have already thought out the problem, defined it completely, and established your goals. You then devise a general strategy for solving the problem by dividing it into manageable units. Next, each of these large modules is subdivided into several tasks. The top levels of the

Idea	Top-down Design	Code
General strategy	Main module	Main program
↓	↓	↓
Development of each main subsection	Middle levels	Procedures/functions
↓	↓	↓
Details of each section	Lowest level	Individual lines of source code

Figure 1-2.

top-down design will not be written in source code (like Pascal or FOR-TRAN or BASIC), but rather in English or "pseudo-code." This divide-and-conquer activity goes on until, at the lowest level, you are down to individual lines of code.

Now the problem is simpler to code into a well-structured program. This approach encourages programming in logical units, using procedures and functions. The main module of the top-down design will become the main program, and subsections will develop into procedures. Figure 1-2 shows how the development of the top-down design parallels the thought process for solving the problem.

As an example, let's write part of the top-down design for the class rank problem. We have ascertained the input and output required, as well as the special requirements. The input is free format with each item separated by at least one blank. NAME consists of two character strings, LAST and FIRST, SEX is a one-character code, DEPT is a two- or three-letter abbreviation, and CLASS is an integer in the range 1–4. The last record is followed by a zero in place of the ID number.

MAIN MODULE   **Level 0**

```
GETDATA
SORTDATA
PRINTRESULTS
```

The program is now divided into three logical units, each of which will probably be developed into a procedure in the final program. In fact, we can already imagine what the main program will look like:

```
PROGRAM CLASSRANK (DATA1, OUTPUT);
  .
  .
  .
BEGIN   (* main program *)
  GETDATA(STUDENTS, NUMSTUDENTS);
  SORT(STUDENTS, NUMSTUDENTS);
  PRINTRESULTS(STUDENTS, NUMSTUDENTS)
END.     (* main program *)
```

Next, we develop each of these tasks by adding one layer of detail. Let's consider the first module:

GETDATA   **Level 1**

```
initialize NUMSTUDENTS to zero
WHILE more students DO
    GETRECORD
```

Initializing NUMSTUDENTS will translate directly into a Pascal assignment statement. "GETRECORD," however, will require more levels of development.

GETRECORD   **Level 2**

```
get IDNUM
IF IDNUM <> 0
    THEN
        increment NUMSTUDENTS
        store IDNUM
        GETWORD (LASTNAME)
        store LASTNAME
        GETWORD (FIRSTNAME)
        store FIRSTNAME
        get SEX
        store SEX
        GETWORD (DEPT)
        store DEPT
        get CLASS
        store CLASS
        get GPA
        store GPA
```

But where do we store all these data? We will discuss the process used to design data structures in the next section. For now, we will use an array of records.

Again, some lines of this module will convert directly into Pascal code. The storing tasks can be coded as

```
STUDENTS[I].IDNUM := IDNUM;
STUDENTS[I].LASTNAME := LASTNAME;
     .
     .
     .
STUDENTS[I].GPA := GPA
```

Lines like "get CLASS" and "get GPA" can also be coded directly as simple READ statements. Other lines, like "GETWORD," will require further breaking down.

GETWORD   **Level 3**

```
SKIPBLANKS—returns 1st nonblank character
WHILE CHARACTER <> BLANK DO
    put CHARACTER in WORD
    get next CHARACTER
pad WORD with blanks
```

Yet another level is required:

SKIPBLANKS   **Level 4**

```
REPEAT
    get CHARACTER
UNTIL CHARACTER not a blank
```

And so on. In the lowest level, the pseudo-code is directly convertible into Pascal code. The top-down design is complete when all the modules have been taken down to this level. It is like writing from a good outline; a good top-down design simplifies the job of coding.

The result of the top-down design process can be viewed as a big structure tree, with the general problem at the top and all the details branching out toward the bottom (Figure 1-3). From this tree, it is easy to see the relationships among the different modules of the program.

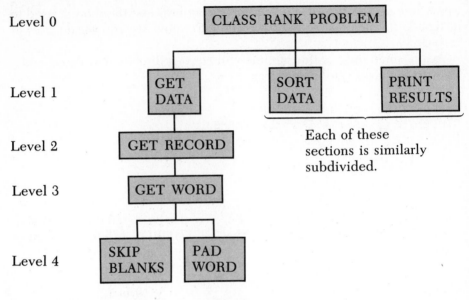

Figure 1-3.

Top-Down Design of Data Structures

Programs consist of both *algorithms* and *data*. At some point in the design process, it becomes apparent that we have to come up with appropriate data structures.

Just as we use a top-down approach to develop the algorithms for solving a problem, we can also design the structures to hold the program's data in a top-down manner. This means that we will defer details as long as possible. In general, it is better not to tie ourselves down to a particular implementation of a data structure too early. We have already seen that there are usually multiple functionally correct solutions to programming problems. Similarly, there are a number of possibilities for structuring the data used in a program.

Let's return to our class rank problem, and design its data structure in a top-down manner. At level 0, we see that we will need to get data. Since we will be required to process that data as a whole in order to sort it, we will need to create some kind of storage structure. At this high level, we do not need to specify the structure's precise implementation. (Defer detail!) We can envision it at a higher level merely as a list of student records. (Note that we are using *records* in its logical sense to mean a collection of related information, not to indicate a Pascal record.)

We do not need to decide specifically what we mean by *list* and *record* until we get to level 2, when it is necessary to assign values to the structure.

At this point we decide that an array of (Pascal) records would be a nice way to store the data.

It is important to note that this is not the only way we could have chosen to represent the data in memory. For instance, we could have chosen to use a series of parallel arrays. In terms of the program's correctness, these two implementations are equivalent.

How do you choose between two or more possible data structures? As with the choice between competing algorithms, you must first consider the program's requirements (for instance, the need to save space in memory or to be able to access a particular record quickly). If all things are equal, you then consider the relative elegance and clarity of the structures. Finally, the choice is left to the programmer's own style and creativity. The choice of appropriate data structures for various applications will be discussed throughout this book.

This data design process suggests a fourth column to be added to Figure 1-2:

Data Structures

"Abstract" data structures

↓

Intermediate development
of data structures

↓

Implementation in terms of
primitive data types in the
source language

Throughout this book we will discuss the need for data abstraction. The goal is to be able to manipulate the program's data with regard to its logical representation, rather than its physical storage. To a limited degree, programming languages provide built-in data structures that hide the physical placement of data in memory. For instance, you tend to picture a two-dimensional array as having rows and columns, though you know that its data is actually stored linearly in contiguous memory locations. A high-level programming language like Pascal allows you to access members of a two-dimensional array through their logical addresses, for instance:

TABLE[ROW, COLUMN]

(We will discuss the implementations of built-in data structures in Chapter 2.)

Why is it important to be able to hide the actual implementation of a data structure? We have already seen how this abstraction simplifies the program-design process. As we consider various programmer-defined data structures in the following chapters, we will discover other advantages to data abstraction.

My Smart Friend

One of the nice things about writing a top-down design is that when one task is especially difficult or complicated, it doesn't have to put a halt to the whole works. You merely make that task into a module and give it a name, thinking "I'll do the rest and my smart friend can take care of this part later." You can then return to the tricky module, working out its details and submodules at a later time. Even though you know that, eventually, you will have to come back to it yourself, it is very reassuring to think that your smart friend will take care of it.

WRITING EASILY MODIFIABLE CODE

In general, most of the effort involved during the lifetime of a large program is not spent in planning or writing it or even in debugging it, but in maintaining it. Features are added or taken out, specifications are modified, the format of the input is changed. It is not easy to remember all of the details of a program you wrote six months before. Often the modifications to a program are not made by the original authors, but by subsequent programmers. Although these concerns may not affect you directly as you write your student programs, it is important to form good programming habits from the start.

DOCUMENTATION

Documentation consists of the written descriptions, specifications, design, and actual code of a program.

We mentioned earlier that your complete description is an important piece of the program's documentation. The *external documentation* of a program is the written information that is outside of the body of executable code. In addition to the program specifications, the external documentation may include the history of the program's development and subsequent modifications, the top-down design, prologues to the program and its subprograms, and the user's manual.

The *internal documentation* includes comments, program formatting, and self-documenting code. The goal of all these features is to make the program readable, understandable, and easy to modify.

Comments

Comments can usually be taken directly from the pseudo-code in your top-down design. Although it is important to use comments to help the reader determine what the programmer is trying to do, it is not necessary to comment on every statement. Frequent use of comments like

```
SUM := 0;                                      (* sum is initialized to zero *)
```

or

```
I := I + 1;                                    (* increment the value of I *)
```

can clutter up your program, hiding the useful comments.

What constitutes the effective use of comments? In general, it is desirable to comment in the following places.

Declarations   Comment on the intended use of each variable. For example,

```
VAR NUMSTUDENTS : INTEGER;                     (* number of student records *)
```

Program Structures   Put a comment before or next to each branch (IF–THEN–ELSE or CASE statement) or loop in the program to explain its function. For example,

```
(* If value is found, return its index and stop processing; otherwise, check next value. *)
IF VAL = LIST[INDEX]
    THEN
       BEGIN
          LISTINDEX := INDEX;
          FOUND := TRUE
       END
    ELSE
       INDEX := INDEX + 1
```

Procedure or Function Calls   Put a comment before or next to each subprogram call to explain its function and effect on the data. For example,

```
(* SKIPBLANKS returns the first nonblank    *)
(* character encountered in the input stream. *)
SKIPBLANKS(LETTER);
```

Nonobvious Code   Place a comment with any confusing section of code. In general, of course, tricky code should be avoided completely. Comments concerning any particularly complicated or confusing code should be clear and precise.

Prettyprinting

Program formatting, known as *prettyprinting,* is encouraged by Pascal's relaxed rules about blank spaces and lines. By using blank spaces to indent, we can convey the logical structure of a program at a glance. In addition, blank lines can be used to separate the logical units of the program. Many systems have a prettyprinting program that will do much of the formatting for you. (In general, however, it is not a good idea to rely too much on such a tool.)

Self-documenting Code

Self-documenting code uses meaningful identifier names to convey the intended function of variables and constants. For instance,

```
CONST T = 0.042;
VAR   X, Y : REAL;
  .
  .
X := Y * T
```

doesn't tell us anything about the relationships and use of the constant and variables. On the other hand,

```
CONST  TAXRATE  = 0.042;
VAR    TAX, PRICE : REAL;
  .
  .
TAX := PRICE * TAXRATE
```

gives us much more information.

SELF-DOCUMENTING CODE

A program which uses meaningful identifiers to emphasize the function of the data.

The programs below illustrate how the use of comments, prettyprinting, and self-documenting code can increase the readability of a short program.

The first program is functionally correct, but it is difficult to read and understand.

```
PROGRAM MYSTERY(INPUT, OUTPUT);
VAR X,Y,Z:REAL;
BEGIN READLN(X,Y);IF(X<=0) OR (Y<=0) THEN
WRITELN('ERROR') ELSE BEGIN Z:=SQRT(SQR(X)+SQR(Y));
WRITELN(Z) END END.
```

The second program is functionally identical, but it is easier to read and understand.

```
PROGRAM HYPOTENUSE (INPUT, OUTPUT);

(* This program reads in two sides of a right triangle, calculates the length of the    *)
(* hypotenuse, and prints the result. The formula used is the Pythagorean Theorem:      *)
(* The square of the hypotenuse is the sum of squares of the other two sides.           *)

VAR     SIDE1,                                                (* known side 1 *)
        SIDE2,                                                (* known side 2 *)
        HYPOT : REAL;                                         (* hypotenuse *)

BEGIN    (* hypotenuse *)

  READLN (SIDE1, SIDE2);                                      (* get known sides *)

  (* If no input errors, calculate hypotenuse. *)
  IF (SIDE1 <= 0) OR (SIDE2 <= 0)
    THEN WRITELN('ERROR')
    ELSE
      BEGIN                                                   (* no errors in input *)
        HYPOT := SQRT(SQR(SIDE1) + SQR(SIDE2));
        WRITELN (HYPOT)
      END

END.     (* hypotenuse *)
```

Using Constants

The use of constants to represent "magic" numbers like pi, nonvariable tax rates, the maximum number of items in an array, and so on also makes code more readable and easily modifiable. Consider a program that reads numbers into an array DATA (ARRAY[1..100] OF INTEGER). Numerous operations will be performed on the values in the array throughout the program, each with a section of code beginning

```
FOR I := 1 TO 100 DO . . .
```

At some later time, if you need to increase the size of DATA to 200 elements, you must go back through the whole program to change every place that the size of the array is indicated:

```
FOR I := 1 TO 200 DO , , ,
```

However, if you had declared a constant

```
CONST  MAX = 100
```

and declared the array as ARRAY[1..MAX], the modifications of the array size would be trivial, involving only one line:

```
CONST  MAX = 200
```

Throughout the rest of the program, the references to the size of the array would not need modification:

```
FOR I := 1 TO MAX DO , , ,
```

DEBUGGING

The top-down design methodology will help you write better programs, but it will not guarantee that these programs will be correct on the first run. In fact, only the most trivial programs are likely to be written perfectly at first. By taking an aggressive approach to debugging, however, you can usually simplify the process of finding and removing errors from programs. The goal is to prevent as many types of errors as possible and to make the rest easy to detect and correct.

Errors in the Specifications

By writing a complete program description, you may avoid the worst kind of error: a program written to the wrong specifications. With such an error, much of the conceptual and design effort, as well as the coding, is wasted. Such a program may be completely useless, since it does not solve the problem. This type of error can be prevented by good communication between the programmer(s) and the party who originated the problem (the professor, manager, or customer).

Sometimes the specifications change during the design or coding of a program. In this case, the top-down design will help pinpoint the sections of the program that will have to be redone. For instance, a change in the input specifications of the class rank problem will not require the whole program to be rewritten. We can see, from the tree in Figure 1-3, that the offending sections are restricted to the modules below GET RECORD. Thus it is easy to locate the parts of the program that will require changes.

Errors in Syntax

"If worse comes to worst, read the manual."

Presumably, you learned the syntax of Pascal in your first programming course. In the process, you probably made a number of syntax errors, which resulted in compile-time program errors. That's par for the first course.

Now that you are more familiar with the Pascal programming language, save your debugging skills for really juicy logical errors. That is, *get the syntax right the first time.* It is not unreasonable to expect your first attempt to be free of syntax errors. A syntax error wastes computing time and money, as well as programmer time, and it is completely preventable.

In addition, don't make the classic error of the lazy programmer, assuming that the compiler will catch all your typos and syntax errors. Once in a blue moon, the compiler itself will be wrong (after all, it's just a program too), and a syntax error will escape it. This situation may cause very obscure, hard-to-locate errors.

A more common problem occurs when a variable name is mistyped. For instance, in the program segment

```
IF VALU > LIMIT
   THEN
      BEGIN
         LIMIT := VAL;
         WRITELN ('NEW LIMIT SET');
         .
         .
```

the typo (U left off VALU) should generate a syntax error (undeclared identifier). But what happens if VAL is an identifier declared elsewhere in the program? The assignment statement may succeed, and a hard-to-detect logical error will result. (For this reason, it is a good idea to avoid nearly identical identifiers.) In short, don't put your trust in the omnipotent compiler; check your own typing.

Programmers should also be familiar with the implementation of the language at their site, including all of its idiosyncrasies. A program written in the standard Pascal you learned in school may not run on the computer at your first job. When in doubt, check the manual!

Errors in Logic

In general, syntax errors are relatively easy to locate and correct. *Logical* errors, which occur during the execution of a program, are usually harder to detect.

There are two broad categories of logical errors encountered: those that stop execution of the program and those that allow execution to continue but produce the wrong results. The first type is often the result of the programmer's making too many assumptions. For instance,

```
X := Y / Z
```

will cause a run-time error if Z is zero. If X is declared INTEGER, the statement

```
READ(X)
```

will cause a run-time error (type conflict) when the input is a nonnumeric character.

These are situations where a defensive posture produces good results. You can check explicitly for error-creating conditions rather than letting them abort your program. For instance, it is generally unwise to make many assumptions about the correctness of input, especially input from a keyboard. A better approach is to check explicitly for the correct type and bounds of the input. The programmer can then decide how to handle the errors (request new input, go on to next record, print out error message, terminate program, and so on), rather than leaving the decision to the system.

Errors that do not stop execution but produce incorrect results are often harder to prevent and to locate. Our aggressive approach will take a dual focus.

First, don't use questionable code. Hand-check sections of code with paper and pencil. Look for loops that execute one time too many or too few. Make sure that all loops terminate. Check for variables that are incorrectly initialized or not initialized at all (but should be). Make sure that procedures that return values have VAR parameters, and that the order of the parameters in the heading and call matches up. See if the algorithm is correctly coded—no steps left out, all steps in the right order. Try out the lower and upper bounds of the algorithm.

Second, plan your debugging in the design phase of your program. When you write your top-down design, you will identify predictable trouble spots; anything left for your smart friend is surely suspect. Then, insert temporary "debug WRITELNs" into your code in the places where errors are likely to occur. If you want to trace the program's execution though a complicated sequence of nested procedures, add output statements that indicate when you are entering and/or leaving a procedure. A more useful debug output will also indicate the values of key variables, especially parameters of the procedure or function.

If hand-testing doesn't reveal all the bugs before you run the program, well-placed debug lines will at least help you to locate the rest of them at execution time. One popular technique is to make the debug WRITELNs dependent on a Boolean flag, which can then be turned off and on as necessary. For instance, one section of code known to be error-prone may be flagged in various spots for trace output using the Boolean variable DEBUGFLAG:

```
IF DEBUGFLAG
   THEN WRITELN(' SECTION A ENTERED ')
```

This flag may be turned off or on by assignment (e.g., DEBUGFLAG := TRUE to get the trace output) depending on the programmer's need. Usually, the debug lines are removed or "commented out" before the program is delivered to the customer (or turned in to the teacher).

One more piece of advice about debugging: Program bugs often travel in swarms. When you find a bug, don't be too quick to fix it and run your program again. Often, fixing one bug generates another one. A superficial guess about the cause of program error does not usually produce a complete solution. Don't experiment. Take your time and consider all the ramifications of the changes you are making.

PROGRAM TESTING

How do you know when you have found all the bugs in a program? You never know for sure. Running the program on sample data sets can reveal errors, but it does not guarantee that other errors do not exist. In all but the most limited cases, it is not practical to test the program on every possible set of data.

Many programmers are rather lax about program testing. It doesn't seem as interesting, challenging, or glamorous as writing the original program. Furthermore, after a large investment in a particular solution, who wouldn't be reluctant to see it fail? However, thorough testing is an integral part of the programming process, and it can be as challenging as writing the program itself.

Here is the challenge: Try to find data sets that will "break" the code in as many different ways as possible. This goal requires you to change roles—to become the adversary, rather than the creator, of the program. For this reason, it is often desirable to have someone else try to break the program. In fact, many software companies have separate staff for program design and program testing.

Developing a Testing Strategy

You can attempt program testing in a haphazard way, testing random data sets until you find one that causes the program to fail. You are likely to find some bugs this way, but you probably will not find all of them.

A more goal-oriented approach is to test general classes of data. Test at least one example of each category of inputs, as well as boundary and special cases. For instance, if the input consists of commands, each command must be tested. If the program stores a variable number of records in a fixed-size array, check to see what happens when the maximum number of records is used. Try one more than the maximum number. Can your program handle it?

A more structured approach requires that the test cases cause every possible *path* to be executed at least once. (A simple IF–THEN–ELSE statement has two paths.) This approach is more thorough. For a large program with many paths, however, it may not be a practical testing strategy.

Structured Testing

A large, complicated program can be tested in a structured way through a method very similar to the structured approach used to design the program. One method is top-down testing. Testing begins at the top levels, to see if the overall logical design works and if the interfaces between modules are correct. This approach assumes, at each level, that the lower levels will work correctly. To make this assumption, you replace the lower-level subprograms with dummy modules called *stubs*. A stub may consist of a single WRITELN statement, indicating that you have entered the procedure, or it may assign a value if the subprogram is supposed to return a value.

As a simple example, consider a program that reads in a command and a pair of values, executes the appropriate operation, and prints the result. To test the top level, run the main program:

```
BEGIN    (* main program *)
  GETCOMMAND(COMMAND);
  WHILE COMMAND <> STOPCOMMAND DO
    BEGIN
      READLN(X, Y);
      OPERATE(COMMAND, X, Y, RESULT);
      PRINTRESULT(COMMAND, X, Y, RESULT);
      GETCOMMAND(COMMAND)
    END
END.    (* main program *)
```

using stubs to stand in for GETCOMMAND, OPERATE, and PRINTRESULT. A stub for OPERATE might look like this:

```
PROCEDURE OPERATE (COMMAND : COMTYPE;
                   X, Y     : REAL    ;
                   VAR RESULT : REAL);

(* a stub for procedure OPERATE *)

BEGIN
  RESULT := 0.0
END;    (* operate *)
```

At the next level of testing, substitute the actual procedures for the stubs, creating new stubs to stand in for subprograms called from the second-level modules. For instance, Procedure OPERATE contains a CASE statement:

```
CASE COMMAND OF
   ADDCOM : ADD(X, Y, RESULT);
   SUBCOM : SUBTRACT(X, Y, RESULT);
   MULCOM : MULTIPLY(X, Y, RESULT);
   DIVCOM : DIVIDE(X, Y, RESULT)
END;     (* case *)
```

You can create stubs to stand in for the untested procedures ADD, SUB-TRACT, and so on.

Finally, at the lowest level, replace the stubs with the real procedures ADD, SUBTRACT, and so on.

```
PROCEDURE ADD (OP1, OP2 : REAL;
                   VAR SUM  : REAL);
(* returns the sum of OP1 and OP2 *)

BEGIN   (* add *)
   SUM := OP1 + OP2
END;     (* add *)
```

Although a program as simple as this one does not require such a structured testing strategy, it illustrates the approach.

A second program testing strategy is to test from the bottom up. This approach tests the lowest level subprograms first, using *driver* programs to call them. This is a useful approach in testing and debugging a critical module, where an error would have significant effects on other modules. It is also useful in a group-programming environment, where each program-mer writes and tests a separate module. This testing strategy is illustrated with an example at the end of the chapter.

TEST DRIVER

A program that sets up the testing environment by declaring and as-signing initial values to variables, then calls the procedure to be tested.

A third strategy is to combine the top-down and bottom-up approaches as necessary. Critical subprograms may be tested first, and then a top-down approach may be applied to put them together.

All these structured approaches require extra work in preparing the driv-ers and/or stubs. You must write and debug these extra programs, though chances are that they won't be turned in to your professor or delivered to the customer. These programs are part of a class of *software development tools*. Extra work is required to create these programs, but they may greatly simplify the programmer's job. Programs like this may be compared to the scaffolding that a contractor constructs around a building. It takes time and money to build the scaffolding, even though it will not be part of the final product. But without it, the building could not be constructed.

Program Verification Techniques

Thorough testing should uncover most of the bugs in a program, but it does not guarantee that no others exist, since checking every possible input is usually not feasible. Attempting to check all possible inputs is analogous to trying to prove the Pythagorean Theorem by showing that it works on every triangle; you can only say for sure that it worked on every triangle that you tried.

We can prove theorems in geometry mathematically. Can we do the same for computer programs?

The verification of program correctness, independent of data testing, is an important area of theoretical computer science research. This topic will be discussed in more detail in Chapter 10, Program Verification.

A WARNING

If, after you have gone through the whole top-down design process, your approach just doesn't work, don't be afraid to start over. If you think that you've already invested a lot of time in a solution that has become overly complicated, convoluted, and cumbersome, just think of what will be involved in trying to maintain the code.

Summary ━━━━━━━━━━━━━━━━━━━━━━━━━━━

The approach to program development discussed in this chapter may seem cumbersome at first. It pays off, however, in the long run.

- A complete program description ensures that you understand the problem in detail.
- The top-down design makes the actual coding trivial. It also makes the program easier to modify (by replacing some of the lower modules with new ones), to understand, and to test.
- External documentation makes the program easier to modify and to use.
- Internal documentation, including the use of comments, prettyprinting, constants, and meaningful identifiers, makes the program easier to read and understand, and thus simpler to debug and to modify.
- Planned, methodical debugging prevents many errors and makes others easier to locate and simpler to correct.
- A structured approach to program testing gives a more thorough test of the program and helps locate errors.

It is unwise to skimp on any of these tasks for the sake of speeding up the programming process. A program that is not well designed and coded will be expensive to maintain over its whole lifetime of use.

We can speed up the process of problem solving, however. It is not always necessary to solve every problem from scratch. As you go along, you will pick up some standard approaches to common programming tasks. For instance, in your first course, writing the code to keep a cumulative counter took some thought: first initialize the counter, then increment it on every iteration. Now you can write this kind of code in your sleep.

In this book, we will discuss many popular and useful algorithms. Familiarity with well-known algorithms can simplify the problem-solving process. It is not intended that the student memorize every algorithm. They are only included to show ways that others before you have solved common computing problems.

■ APPLICATION: COMMAND-DRIVEN PROBLEMS

Data Structures in Use
- ARRAYS

Software Techniques in Use
- USE OF TOP-DOWN DESIGN
- USE OF A COMMAND-DRIVEN PROGRAM

Let's look now at a type of problem that you will often encounter in programming assignments. This is a class of problems called *command-driven problems*, in which the input determines the program's task. Let's look at one such problem and implement the command level.

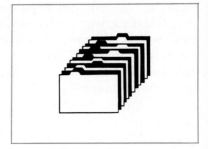

We are to implement a small file-handling system. The tasks that our system can perform are

1. sort a given file of integers
2. sort a given file of reals
3. merge two files of integers
4. merge two files of reals
5. print a file of integers
6. print a file of reals

Input: A series of commands: MERGE, SORT, PRINT, and STOP. Each command except STOP is followed by a type. The types are I (for integer) and R (for real). Each command begins on a separate line and is terminated by one or more blanks. The command STOP terminates processing.

Output: 'RUN IS FINISHED'.

Our job is not to write the code to sort, merge, or print. Our job is to write the top level of the program, which reads in a command, determines which task is to be done, and calls the proper subprogram to execute the task.

Our main module, then, is quite straightforward:

MAIN MODULE   **Level 0**

```
GET COMMAND
WHILE COMMAND 〈〉 STOP DO
    CASE COMMAND OF
        MERGE: DOMERGE;
        SORT  : DOSORT;
        PRINT : DOPRINT
    GET COMMAND
WRITE ('RUN IS FINISHED')
```

This main module is clearly self-documenting. We read in a command, and we use a CASE statement to determine which task to perform. The module is a classic example of a command-driven format.

In Pascal, however, it is not quite as straightforward as it looks. The obvious way to handle the input command is to store it in a character array. The CASE selector, however, must be an ordinal type. Therefore GET COMMAND must transform the command from an array into an ordinal value.

We will do this in a way that is transparent to the reader of the main module. We will hide this conversion within the GET COMMAND module.

The scheme we will use is as follows:

1. Define a user-defined data type made up of the four commands MERGE, SORT, PRINT, and STOP.
2. Create a table (COMTABLE) where the rows are the commands in character form and the index type is the user-defined data type we have created.
3. Store the command from the input file in a five-character array (COM-STRING).
4. Search the array COMTABLE for the character string COMSTRING. When we find a match, the index will be the correct command to use in the CASE statement.

Data Structures: User-defined data type (COMTYPE)
Packed-array type of five characters (STRING5)
A single variable of type STRING5 (COMSTRING)
An array whose index type is COMTYPE and whose elements are of type STRING5.

The Pascal declarations for this structure and a picture of this logical structure after it has been initialized are shown in the program below. (Note that the name for the type of the character array is STRING5. When dealing with strings of alphanumeric characters, we will call the type STRING followed by the number of characters in the string.)

```
TYPE   STRING5 = PACKED ARRAY[1..5] OF CHAR;
       COMTYPE = (MERGE, SORT, PRINT, STOP);
       TABLE   = ARRAY[COMTYPE] OF STRING5;


VAR    FIRSTCOM : COMTYPE;
       COMMAND  : COMTYPE;
       COMTABLE : TABLE;
```

COMTABLE

[MERGE]	'M'	'E'	'R'	'G'	'E'
[SORT]	'S'	'O'	'R'	'T'	' '
[PRINT]	'P'	'R'	'I'	'N'	'T'
[STOP]	'S'	'T'	'O'	'P'	' '

COMSTRING: used to store commands as read in

Now let's complete our top-down design:

GET COMMAND   **Level 1**

```
COMSTRING = '     '
SKIPBLANKS      (* Returns first nonblank character. *)
WHILE more characters DO
     get next letter into COMSTRING
CONVERT from STRING to COMTYPE
```

SKIPBLANKS   Level 2

```
REPEAT
      READ CH
UNTIL CH < > BLANK
```

CONVERT   Level 2

```
COMMAND ← FIRSTCOM
WHILE COMTABLE[COMMAND] < > COMSTRING
      COMMAND ← SUCC(COMMAND)
```

DOMERGE   Level 1

```
SKIPBLANKS(CH);
CASE CH OF
      'I' : (* Call integer merge routine. *)
      'R' : (* Call real merge routine. *)
```

DOSORT and DOPRINT are the same structure as DOMERGE.

What information must be passed back and forth among these modules? Let's examine them.

GET COMMAND has no input parameters, but must return a value of COMTYPE called COMMAND. SKIPBLANKS has no inputs, but returns the first nonblank character it encounters. CONVERT takes as input a command in character string form and returns the corresponding command in the user-defined type.

Should the name of the command table to be searched and the first element of the index type be passed as parameters or be accessed globally? Since these structures are only used in CONVERT, we could make them local to that procedure. However, this would require initializing them each time CONVERT is called. Passing these structures as parameters would mean that they would appear in the main program, and the transformation would not be transparent. Therefore it seems reasonable to access them globally.

Now let's code the main module and the procedures that are of interest to our discussion of command-driven systems. In addition to the procedures outlined, we will need an initialization routine.

```
PROCEDURE INITIALIZE;
(* Initializes the command table and sets FIRSTCOM. *)

BEGIN   (* initialize *)

  COMTABLE[MERGE] := 'MERGE';
  COMTABLE[SORT]  := 'SORT ';
  COMTABLE[PRINT] := 'PRINT';
  COMTABLE[STOP]  := 'STOP ';

  FIRSTCOM := MERGE

END;     (* initialize *)

(* ************************************************ *)

PROCEDURE SKIPBLANKS (VAR CH : CHAR);
(* Returns the first nonblank character from the input stream. *)

BEGIN   (* skipblanks *)
  REPEAT
    READ(CH)
  UNTIL CH <> ' '
END;     (* skipblanks *)

(* ************************************************ *)

PROCEDURE CONVERT (COMSTRING : STRING5,
              VAR COMMAND   : COMTYPE);
(* Takes a command in character string format and returns      *)
(* the appropriate command in the user-defined type COMTYPE.   *)
(* Assumes that COMSTRING is a valid command string.           *)

BEGIN   (* convert *)

  (* Start search with first command in COMTYPE. *)
  COMMAND := FIRSTCOM;

  (* Search COMTABLE until COMSTRING is found. *)
  WHILE COMTABLE[COMMAND] <> COMSTRING DO
    COMMAND := SUCC(COMMAND)

END;     (* convert *)

(* ************************************************ *)
```

```
PROCEDURE GETCOMMAND (VAR COMMAND : COMTYPE);
(* Reads in a string of characters representing a command and converts the string *)
(* into the proper user-defined command using Procedure CONVERT.          *)

VAR   INDEX      : INTEGER;                       (* index into string *)
      COMSTRING : STRING5;                 (* command as read in *)
      CH         : CHAR;                         (* character read in *)

BEGIN   (* getcommand *)

   COMSTRING := '        ';                    (* Start with blank string. *)
   SKIPBLANKS(CH);                 (* Get first nonblank character. *)
   INDEX := 1;
   REPEAT                                     (* Read COMSTRING. *)
     COMSTRING[INDEX] := CH;
     INDEX := INDEX + 1;
     READ(CH)
   UNTIL CH = ' ';

   (* Convert the string to COMTYPE. *)
   CONVERT(COMSTRING, COMMAND)

END;   (* getcommand *)

(* ******************************************************** )

BEGIN   (* main program *)
   INITIALIZE;                              (* Set up command table. *)
   GETCOMMAND(COMMAND);                        (* Get first command. *)
   WHILE COMMAND <> STOP DO
     BEGIN
         (* Process according to command. *)
         CASE COMMAND OF
           MERGE : DOMERGE;
           SORT  : DOSORT;
           PRINT : DOPRINT
         END;    (* case *)
         GETCOMMAND(COMMAND)                      (* Get next command. *)
     END;     (* while *)
   WRITELN(' RUN IS FINISHED  ')
END.    (* main program *)
```

We have not considered errors in this example. What happens if a command is misspelled? As it stands now, in Procedure CONVERT, an error would occur because the computer would try to find the successor of STOP that doesn't exist.

A built-in error check can be created by adding one more element to the defined type COMTYPE; call it ERROR. Add a condition to your WHILE loop that stops if the COMMAND becomes ERROR.

These additions are illustrated below.

```
COMTYPE = (MERGE, SORT, PRINT, STOP, ERROR);
 •
 •
 •
PROCEDURE CONVERT (COMSTRING   : STRING5;
                   VAR COMMAND : COMTYPE;
                   VAR   FOUND : BOOLEAN);

BEGIN   (* convert *)
   COMMAND := FIRSTCOM;
   FOUND := FALSE;
   WHILE NOT FOUND AND (COMMAND <> ERROR) DO
      IF COMTABLE[COMMAND] = COMSTRING
         THEN FOUND := TRUE
         ELSE COMMAND   := SUCC(COMMAND)
END;     (* convert *)

(* in main module *)
IF COMMAND = ERROR
    THEN (* whatever you want to do *)
    ELSE CASE COMMAND OF
       •
       •
       •
```

Test Driver

The command-driven program has many real-world applications. It is also useful as a programming tool—to build a driver for a bottom-up test strategy. The input command is used to determine which test to perform. For instance, if a program has several subprograms that may be independently tested, we can write a test driver that inputs a command that indicates which procedure is to be tested and its parameters, if any. An example follows:

```
PROGRAM TESTDRIVER (INPUT, OUTPUT);
(* Test driver for PROGRAM XXX. *)

TYPE COMMANDTYPE = (PROC1COM, PROC2COM, PROC3COM, OTHER);

VAR  COMMAND : COMMANDTYPE;

(* Code for PROC1 - PROC3, as well as supporting *)
(* subprograms like GETCOMMAND, goes here.       *)

BEGIN   (* test driver main program *)
   INITIALIZE;
   GETCOMMAND(COMMAND);
   CASE COMMAND OF
      PROC1COM  :  (* Set up calling arguments and call PROC1. *)
      PROC2COM  :  (* Set up calling arguments and call PROC2. *)
      PROC3COM  :  (* Set up calling arguments and call PROC3. *)
      OTHER     : ' WRITELN(' * * *  ILLEGAL COMMAND * * * ')
   END    (* case *)
END.    (* test driver main program *)
```

Note that many cases for each procedure may be tested using this driver, by replacing (* Set up calling arguments. . . . *) with code that reads in the calling arguments from the input stream. This allows us to use this program as a generalized test tool, as opposed to creating a separate driver for each procedure to be tested.

Exercises

1. Write a complete description of the class rank problem discussed in this chapter.

2. What are two uses for a complete program description?

3. What is the basic rule regarding details in a top-down design?

4. A top-down design is to a computer program what a(n) _____ is to a term paper.

5. Explain the term *step-wise refinement*.

6. Give a top-down design for getting up in the morning and going to an eight o'clock class.

7. What part of a program's code is analagous to the main module of the top-down design?

8. How does the top-down method encourage the use of procedures and functions?

9. The implementation of the data structures that will be used in a program should be decided before anything else.   T   F

10. There is usually only one good way to solve a problem and to structure its data.   T   F

11. In general, most of the effort involved over the lifetime of a program is spent in maintaining it.   T   F

12. How can the code of a program be considered part of its documentation?

13. When should the documentation of a program be started?

14. Use meaningful identifiers and constants to make sense out of the following code:

```
VAR X, Y, Z : REAL;
    .
    .
Z := X * 3.1417 * SQR (Y);
```

15. Differentiate between errors in logic and in syntax. When is each type of error likely to be found?

16. The compiler will always catch your typos and syntax errors.   T   F

17. This program has three separate errors, each of which causes an infinite loop. Can you find them?

```
PROGRAM LOOPTIME (INPUT, OUTPUT);

VAR COUNT : INTEGER;

PROCEDURE INCREMENT (X : INTEGER);

BEGIN  (* increment *)
   X := X + 1
END;  (* increment *)

(*  main  *)
BEGIN
   COUNT := 1;
   WHILE COUNT < 10 DO            (* Procedure INCREMENT adds
      WRITELN('HELLO');              1 to the value of COUNT      *)
      INCREMENT(COUNT);
      WRITELN('GOODBYE')
END.    (* main *)
```

18. What are stubs and drivers used for in program testing? Which testing stategy goes with each?

19. The following is a program description with some problems.

```
(*   ** THIS IS A PROGRAM TO TAKE SOME NAMES
     ** AND ALPHABETIZE THEM. INPUT : THE NAMES OF
     ** SOME PEOPLE, THEIR CITIES, AND ZIPCODES.
     ** OUTPUT : THE NAMES, CITIES AND ZIPCODES
     ** PRINTED OUT, ALPHABETIZED BY LAST NAMES.
*)
```

Write a COMPLETE program *description,* given the following sample input and output. (Don't write the program.)

Sample Input:

Col.	1 9	10	11 19	20	21 34	35	36 40
	FIRSTNAME	ʃ	LASTNAME	ʃ	CITY	ʃ	ZIPCODE
	TOM Q.		JONES		CHICAGO		30303
	MISS		SMITH		HOLLYWOOD		99999
	CAROLE		VAN KIRK		SWAMPCITY		00000
	SUSAN		MACMILLAN		AUSTIN,TX		78787
	NOMORE						
	(denotes						
	end of						
	input)						

Sample Output:

TOM Q. JONES	CHICAGO	30303
SUSAN MACMILLAN	AUSTIN,TX	78787
MISS SMITH	HOLLYWOOD	99999
CAROLE VAN KIRK	SWAMP CITY	00000

20. This is a program to read in 25 words, sort them, and print them out. The input is formatted one word per line, each word left-justified in the first 16 columns. As you can see, this program has a few style problems.

```
PROGRAM BADSTYLE (INPUT, OUTPUT);

TYPE X=PACKED ARRAY[1..16] OF CHAR;Y=ARRAY[1..25] OF X;
VAR A1,A2:INTEGER; B:CHAR; C:X; D:Y;

PROCEDURE SORT(VAR A:Y);

        (* CODE FOR SORT PROCEDURE HERE-ASSUME IT IS OKAY *)

                BEGIN (*MAINPROGRAM*) FOR A1 := 1 TO 25 DO
BEGIN    FOR A2 := 1 TO 16 DO BEGIN
READ(B);   C[A2] := B END;    READLN;
D[A1] := C   END;              SORT(D);
FOR A1 := 1 TO 25 DO WRITELN(D[A1]) END.
```

Rewrite this program as Program GOODSTYLE, using meaningful identifiers, constraints, comments, and prettyprinting.

Pre-Test

1. Well-designed programs are those that are easier to _____, _____, and _____.

2. Good programming practices dictate that

   (a) a procedure should be written before its specifications. T F

   (b) while doing top-down design, you should try to avoid changing the main program as you work on lower levels of your program. T F

   (c) when doing top-down design, you should first decide on the data structures that will be used. T F

3. Name two popular approaches to problem solving.

4. What is an algorithm?

5. Logical errors are easier to find and correct than syntax errors.   T   F

6. Two goals of internal program documentation are to make it _____ and _____.

7. Not all syntax errors will be caught by the compiler.   T   F

8. The first decision in designing a program is deciding what data structure to use.
   T   F

9. The top-down approach lends itself to programming in logical units.
   T   F

10. Two types of internal program documentation are _____ and _____.

11. What are two purposes of using constants in a program?

12. What is one popular technique for pinpointing hard-to-find logical errors?

13. What is the standard method of testing program limits?

14. Which of the following phases takes up the largest proportion of the lifetime of a program?

    (a)   coding

    (b)   debugging

    (c)   maintenance

    (d)   problem solving

    (e)   documentation

15. Dr. Robert gave a test to his class. The maximum score possible on the test was 19 points. But he wanted to know the grades as percentages of 100, so he wrote a program to convert the actual grades to percentage grades. A total of 117 students took the test. Each test grade is on a separate line in the input. As you can see, this program has some style problems.
    (a) Name the style problems.
    (b) Rewrite the program as Program GOODSTYLE.

```
PROGRAM BADSTYLE;
LABEL 10;
VAR A, B, C : INTEGER;
                     BEGIN (*MAINPROGRAM*) C :=0;
10:   READ(A);
WRITE(A:5); B := A * 100 DIV 19; WRITELN(B); C := C + 1;
    IF C < 117 THEN GOTO 10              END.
```

Built-in Data Structures 2

Goals

To be able to describe a data structure at the logical, implementation, and application levels.

To be able to define a one-dimensional array at the logical level.

To be able to calculate the accessing function for a given element in a one-dimensional array.

To be able to define a two-dimensional array at the logical level.

To be able to calculate the accessing function for a given element in a two-dimensional array.

To be able to define a record at the logical level.

To be able to calculate the accessing function for a given field in a record.

To be able to define a string at the logical level.

To be able to define operations on strings.

To be able to use an array and a record at the application level to implement a string.

To be able to implement the operations on strings.

To be able to define and implement your own abstract data type.

One of the tools that beginning programmers often take for granted is the high-level language in which they write their programs. Since most of us first learn to program in a language like Pascal, we do not appreciate its branching and looping structures and built-in data structures until we are later introduced to languages that do not have these features.

In the class rank example in Chapter 1, we decided to use an array of records to store our data. But what is an array? What is a record? Pascal, as well as many other high-level programming languages, provides arrays and records as built-in data structures. As a Pascal programmer, you can use these tools without concern about their implementation, much as a carpenter can use an electric drill without knowing about electricity.

However, there are many interesting and useful ways of structuring data that are not provided in general-purpose programming languages. The programmer who wants to use these structures must build them. In this book, we will look in detail at four very useful data structures: stacks, queues, lists, and binary trees. We will describe each of these structures and design algorithms to manipulate them. We will build (implement) them using the tools that are available in the Pascal language. Finally, we will examine applications where each is appropriate.

First, however, we will develop a definition of *data structure* and an approach that we can use to examine data structures. By way of example, we will apply our definition and approach to familiar Pascal data structures: the one-dimensional array, the two-dimensional array, and the record. In later chapters, we will extend this definition and approach to other user-defined data structures.

DATA STRUCTURE

A collection of data elements whose organization is characterized by accessing functions that are used to store and retrieve individual data elements.

This definition does not specify how the accessing is to be done, only that these functions return the desired element. For built-in data structures (those provided in a programming language), the programmer may never know how this accessing is done—it is transparent. For a data structure that is not provided in a language, a set of procedures and functions that carry out the accessing functions is specified by the programmer. In a job situation, the coding of these procedures and functions might well be done by someone else. In either case, how the accessing functions and procedures are coded would be immaterial to the program using them.

The definition of a data structure above doesn't say anything about what the data structure means. The physical or logical relationship of one element to another and the mode of access of each element are specified in the structure's definition, but the meaning of the relationships of one element to another is not. This meaning can be defined only when the structure is used in a program to represent the data in a particular problem. By way of analogy, let's look at Figure 2-1, which shows a floor plan with four rooms.

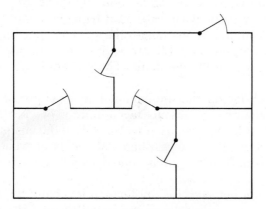

Figure 2-1. Anonymous Floor Plan

The doors (accesses) to each room are marked. Is this the plan for an apartment? An office suite? A doctor's office? There is no way to tell. We can see only a shell. Only when the rooms are occupied will we be able to tell what the plan represents.

What we are leading up to is that there are three distinct ways to look at a data structure: as an abstract collection of elements with a particular set of accessing functions, as a coding problem (i.e., how will the accessing functions be implemented?), and as a way of representing the data relationships in a specific context. We will analyze each data structure from these three perspectives.

1. *ABSTRACT OR LOGICAL LEVEL* At this level, we will picture the organization and specify general accessing procedures and functions.

2. *IMPLEMENTATION LEVEL* At this level, we will examine ways to represent the data elements in memory and to implement the accessing procedures and functions in Pascal. Each of the data structures we will examine can be implemented in more than one way. We will look at alternative representations.

3. *USAGE OR APPLICATION LEVEL* This level will be presented in short examples along with the other two levels and examined in detail in a case study in which the data structure accurately represents the relationships in the data.

A thorough understanding of the logical level is necessary in order both to use a data structure and to implement the accessing routines. However, a user does not need to know how the implementation is done, and someone writing the accessing routines does not need to know what the structure represents in a particular problem.

For example, when you go to a pharmacy, you give a prescription to a pharmacist at the window and she eventually gives the medicine to you. You don't know or particularly care what happens behind the window. If the pharmacist completely rearranges the stock to speed up the process of filling prescriptions, the only difference you should notice is that you don't have to wait as long for the medicine. The procedure *you* use remains the same.

The specifications for the implementation level are like that prescription. The prescription contains an exact definition of what the pharmacist is to prepare. How it is prepared is of no concern to the customer. Implementation level specifications are explicit statements of what the routines at this level are to do. How the job is done does not concern the calling module.

Communication between the application level and the implementation level should be done only through the specified interface of the accessing

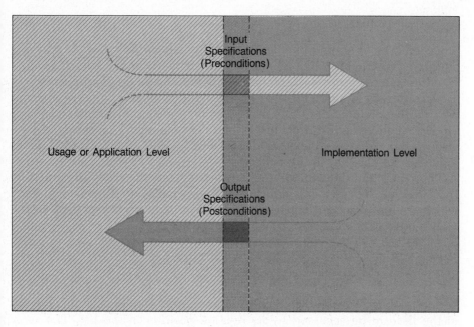

Figure 2-2. Application Level vs. Implementation Level

procedures and functions. This means that the implementation could be completely changed without affecting the program using the data structure, as long as the interfaces were maintained. Conversely, this structure and its accessing functions could be used by other programs for completely different purposes, as long as they maintain the correct interfaces.

Think of a wall separating the usage level from the implementation level. (See Figure 2-2.) The only communication into the implementation level is in terms of input specifications and allowable assumptions. These are sometimes called *preconditions* to the routines. The only output back to the usage level is the transformed data structure described in the output specifications of the routines. These are sometimes called *postconditions*.

In this book we will be asking you to move back and forth across this imaginary wall, alternately playing the role of the programmer (who uses these data structures to model the relationships among data elements in a particular problem) and the role of the coder or implementer of the accessing routines. In a job situation, you might not play both roles. However, it is good programming practice to separate these tasks within a program, limiting communication between these levels inside a program. The value of this technique, called *information hiding*, will be stressed throughout this book.

Now, lest you think all of this is new and terribly vague, let's take a data structure you are familiar with and look at it from these three levels.

ONE-DIMENSIONAL ARRAYS

Since almost all programming languages have a *one-dimensional array* as a built-in data structure, this is a good place to start. At the logical level, a one-dimensional array is a structured data type made up of a finite collection of ordered elements, all of which are of the same data type. (By *ordered* we simply mean that there is a first element, a second element, and so on. Since the collection is finite, there is also a last element.) Accessing is done through the use of an index that allows you to specify the desired element by giving its position in the collection.

The syntax and semantics of the language specify the accessing function. In Pascal you declare a data *type* that defines what a one-dimensional array will look like. You then create an array *variable* to be of that type in the VAR section. For example,

```
TYPE VECTOR = ARRAY[1..10] OF INTEGER;
VAR  DATA : VECTOR
```

defines a linearly ordered collection of ten integer elements. Each element in the list can be accessed by its relative position in the list. The array DATA can be pictured as follows:

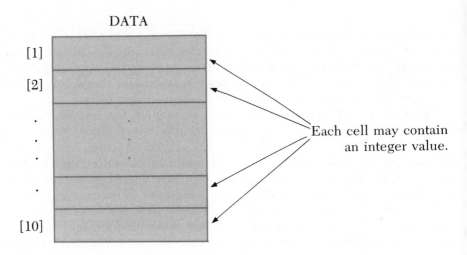

The syntax of the the accessing function is the name of the collection of elements, followed by an open bracket ('['), followed by an indexing expression whose value is between 1 and 10, concluded by a closed bracket (']'). The semantics of the accessing function is "locate the element associated with the indexing expression in the collection of elements whose name is DATA."

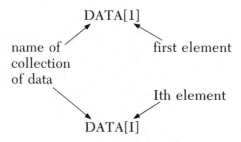

The accessing function is used in one of two ways: to specify a place into which a value is to be copied or to specify a place from which a value is to be extracted. As a user of arrays, you have probably not given much thought to how they are implemented. The implementation is transparent to you; the Pascal run-time support system took care of the accessing functions. However, someone somewhere wrote the code that actually accessed the correct place in the array. Let's change hats here and look at how arrays are actually represented and accessed.

Implementation of the One-Dimensional Array

Two things have to be done to achieve the implementation of any data structure: Memory cells have to be reserved for the data structure, and the accessing functions have to be coded. In the case of a one-dimensional array, the declaration statements tell the compiler how many cells are needed to represent the array. The name of the array is then associated with the characteristics of the array. These characteristics include:

1. the upper bound of the index range (UPBOUND).
2. the lower bound of the index range (LOBOUND).
3. the location in memory of the first cell in the array, called the *base address* of the array (BASE). (We will designate the base address of a specific array by using the name of the array with no index.)
4. the number of memory locations needed for each element in the array (SIZE).

The accessing function uses this information to determine the location of the desired element.

Before we go on to a concrete example, we will digress for a moment and look at memory. We have used the nonspecific term *cell* instead of *word* or *byte*. By *cell* we mean the unit of memory that will be assigned to hold a value. This unit is machine dependent. Figure 2-3 shows several different memory configurations. In practice, how memory is configured is a consideration for the compiler writer. In order to be as general as possible, however, we will continue to use the generic term *cell* to represent a location in memory.

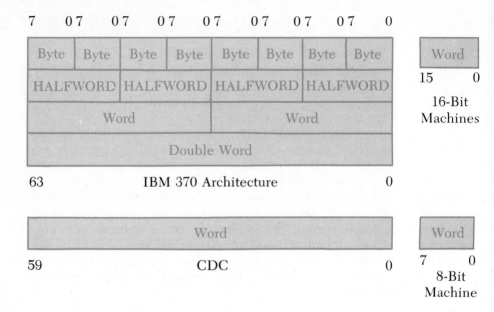

Figure 2-3.

We will demonstrate how the array characteristics are used to calculate the number of cells needed and to develop the accessing functions for the following arrays:

```
VAR DATA : ARRAY[1..10] OF INTEGER;
VAR VALUES : ARRAY[-3..2] OF REAL;
VAR LETTERCOUNT : ARRAY['A'..'Z'] OF INTEGER
```

These arrays have the following characteristics:

	DATA	*VALUES*	*LETTERCOUNT*
UPBOUND	10	2	Z
LOBOUND	1	−3	A
BASE	unknown	unknown	unknown
SIZE	1	1	1

We can look at the declaration for DATA and immediately see that ten cells will be required. However, the index type of VALUES is more complicated. To determine the number of cells needed by a particular index type, take the ORD of the upper bound of the index type, subtract the ORD of the lower bound of the index type, then add one. The following table applies this formula to the arrays above:

Index Type	ORD(UPBOUND)	–	ORD(LOBOUND)	+	1	=	Number of Cells
[1..10]	10	–	1	+	1	=	10
[−3..2]	2	–	(−3)	+	1	=	6
['A'..'Z']	('Z')	–	('A')	+	1	=	26

The compiler assigns memory cells to variables in sequential order. If the next memory cell available to be assigned is, let's say, 100 when the three declarations above are encountered, the memory assignments would be as shown. (We have used 100 to make the arithmetic easier.)

Location	DATA	Location	VALUES	Location	LETTERCOUNT
100	[1]	110	[−3]	116	['A']
101	[2]	111	[−2]	117	['B']
.	.	.	.	.	.
.	.	.	.	.	.
.	.	.	.	.	.
109	[10]	115	[2]	141	['Z']

Now we have determined the base address of each array: DATA is 100, VALUES is 110, and LETTERCOUNT is 116. The arrangement of these arrays in memory gives us the following relationships:

$$\text{Given} \begin{cases} \text{DATA[1]} \\ \text{DATA[9]} \\ \text{LETTERCOUNT ['A']} \\ \text{LETTERCOUNT ['C']} \\ \text{VALUES[−1]} \\ \text{VALUES[0]} \end{cases} \text{the program must access} \begin{cases} 100 \\ 108 \\ 116 \\ 118 \\ 112 \\ 113 \end{cases}$$

In our discussion so far we have assumed that the component type of the array requires only one memory cell. If the component type requires SIZE cells, the formula to determine the number of cells needed becomes

$$(\text{ORD(UPBOUND)} - \text{ORD(LOBOUND)} + 1) * \text{SIZE}$$

The accessing function that gives us the position of an element in a one-dimensional array associated with the expression INDEX is

Location(INDEX) = BASE + ORD(INDEX) − ORD(LOBOUND)

In the case where the index type is integer, we can simplify this for human purposes to

Location(INDEX) = BASE + INDEX − LOBOUND

Let's apply this formula and see if we do get what we have shown we should.

DATA[1]	100	+	1	−	1	=	100
DATA[9]	100	+	9	−	1	=	108
LETTERCOUNT['A']	116	+	0	−	0	=	116
LETTERCOUNT['C']	116	+	2	−	0	=	118
VALUES[−1]	110	+	(−1)	−	(−3)	=	112
VALUES[0]	110	+	0	−	(−3)	=	113

If the component type of the array takes more than one word in memory, we will again have to adjust the formula slightly. If each element takes SIZE words in memory, the formula becomes

Location(INDEX) = BASE + (ORD(INDEX) − ORD(LOBOUND)) * SIZE

The following table shows the calculations if SIZE is 3 and LETTERCOUNT is assigned to Location 50:

ADDRESS   INDEX   LETTERCOUNT

ADDRESS	INDEX	LETTERCOUNT	
50	['A']		LETTERCOUNT + (ORD('A') − ORD('A')) * 3 = 50
53	['B']		LETTERCOUNT + (ORD('B') − ORD('A')) * 3 = 53
. . .	. . .	. . .	
125	['Z']		LETTERCOUNT + (ORD('Z') − ORD('A')) * 3 = 125

In Pascal, the upper bound (UPBOUND) for each array is used in error checking. After an indexing expression has been calculated, this value is compared to the BASE + UPBOUND. If the calculated expression is greater than or equal to the BASE + UPBOUND, the address is not within the array. An error message is printed and execution halts.

TWO-DIMENSIONAL ARRAYS

In addition to one-dimensional arrays, most programming languages provide facilities for *two-dimensional arrays*. Two-dimensional arrays can be defined in two ways:

1. A two-dimensional array is a one-dimensional array where the data type of each component is itself a one-dimensional array.
2. A two-dimensional array is a structured data type made up of a finite collection of elements, all of which are of the same data type. Each element is ordered on two dimensions. Accessing is done through the use of a pair of indexes that allows you to specify which element in the collection you want to access. The first index refers to the element's position on the first dimension; the second index refers to the element's position on the second dimension.

Again the syntax and semantics of the programming language you are using specify the accessing function. In Pascal, you can declare a two-dimensional array in accordance with either of the definitions above. Let's look at an example:

```
TYPE   VECTOR = ARRAY[1..3] OF INTEGER;
       TABLETYPE = ARRAY[1..5] OF VECTOR;
VAR    TABLE : TABLETYPE
```

The accessing function is as follows:

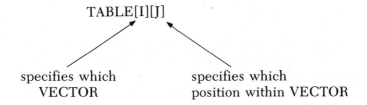

TABLE[I][J]

specifies which VECTOR · specifies which position within VECTOR

The second way of defining a two-dimensional array TABLE is as follows:

```
TYPE   TABLETYPE = ARRAY[1..5,1..3] OF INTEGER;
VAR    TABLE : TABLETYPE
```

The accessing function for the second definition is as follows:

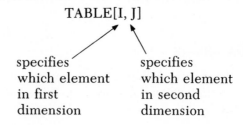

TABLE[I, J]

specifies
which element
in first
dimension

specifies
which element
in second
dimension

Although conceptually these structures are quite different, the data structures defined by these two methods are identical. The two accessing functions are interchangeable. The second form is usually referred to as the *abbreviated* form.

A two-dimensional array is the ideal data structure to represent data that is logically structured as a table with rows and columns. The first dimension represents rows and the second dimension represents columns. Each cell in the array can contain a value of some simple scalar type. Each dimension represents a relationship.

For example, we might want to keep track of the New York Stock Exchange over a period of four weeks. If we are interested in six stocks, the following data structure could be used to represent this information:

```
CONST NUMSTOCKS = 6;
      NUMWEEKS = 4;

TYPE  STOCKS = 1..NUMSTOCKS;
      WEEKS = 1..NUMWEEKS;
      TABLETYPE = ARRAY[STOCKS, WEEKS] OF REAL;

VAR   STOCK : STOCKS;
      WEEK : WEEKS;
      AVGPRICES : TABLETYPE;
```

The value in AVGPRICES[STOCK, WEEK] is the average price for a particular stock for a particular week. (See Figure 2-4.) All the values on a particular row represent prices for the same stock (one relationship). All the values in a particular column represent average prices for a particular week (second relationship).

Implementation of a Two-Dimensional Array

Let's change hats again and examine how the two-dimensional array is implemented. Remember that in the translation process, two things are done: Memory space is reserved for the structure, and the code to be generated for the accessing function must be determined.

AVGPRICES

Value in AVGPRICES[3, 2]
represents the average
price of the third stock
for the second week

Figure 2-4.

In the case of the one-dimensional array, the amount of memory space was calculated by subtracting the ORD of the lower bound of the index range from the ORD of the upper bound of the index range and adding one. This can be extended to the two-dimensional case by applying the same formula to both dimensions and multiplying the two results. To make the formula a little more manageable, let's use UB for upper bound of the index range and LB for lower bound of the index range.

(ORD(UB first dimension) − ORD(LB first dimension) + 1) *
    (ORD(UB second dimension) − ORD(LB second dimension) + 1)

Applying this formula to the stock example, we have

(ORD(6) − ORD(1) + 1) * (ORD(4) − ORD(1) + 1) = 6 * 4 = 24

If you count the number of cells in the table in Figure 2-4, you do indeed have 24.

Humans visualize a two-dimensional array as a table with rows and columns; in fact, we will call the first dimension ROW and the second dimension COLUMN in the balance of our discussion. Computer memory, however, is one long sequence of cells accessed by an address beginning at 0. Therefore, a two-dimensional array is stored with all the elements of a row (or column) in sequence, followed by all the elements of the next row (or column) in sequence, and so on. If the elements of a row are stored next to one another, the array is said to be stored in row-major order. If the elements of a column are stored next to one another, the array is in column-major order.

Some languages, such as FORTRAN, store arrays in column-major order. Pascal stores arrays in row-major order. Does this affect the FORTRAN or

Pascal application programmer? Not usually; the accessing mechanism is transparent. However, we are now wearing the hat of the systems programmer looking at the implementation level. To us, it does make a difference because the accessing function is different for the two methods of storage. We will first describe the accessing functions for row-major storage.

We will develop these functions using integer indexes (omitting the ORDs) because it is clearer. [Remember that ORD(1) is 1.] We will then convert it to the general case by inserting ORDs in the proper places.

Let's look again at the stock market example. Figure 2-4 shows how we visualize AVGPRICES. Figure 2-5 shows this table as it looks in memory. Remember, AVGPRICES is the identifier associated with the first cell in

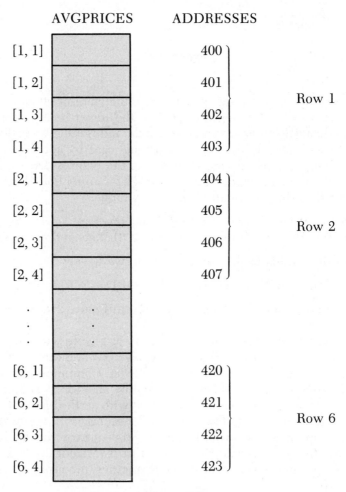

Figure 2-5.

the block of storage set aside for this table. Let's assume that the address is 400.

To access an element in the second row, you must skip over the elements in the first row. To access an element in row I, you must skip over I − 1 rows. How many elements are there in each row? The number of elements in the second dimension tells us. There is one element in a row for each column. Therefore,

$$UB\ COLUMN - LB\ COLUMN + 1$$

gives us the number of items in each row. Since there are four columns in AVGPRICES, there are four elements in a row.

The base address plus the number of elements in a row times the number of rows to be skipped gives us the first cell in the correct row. Consider this value to be the base address of the correct row. Now the same formula can be used to find the correct row item as was used to find the place in the one-dimensional case: the column index minus the lower bound of the column.

$$BASE + (UB\ COLUMN - LB\ COLUMN + 1) * (ROW\ INDEX - 1) + \\ (COLUMN\ INDEX - LB\ COLUMN)$$

Let's apply this to several references to AVGPRICES and see if we do indeed get the right cell. (Look back at Figure 2-4.) Since the number of elements in a row stays constant, we will calculate it only once.

Number of elements in a row of AVGPRICES: $(4 − 1) + 1 = 4$

AVGPRICES [1, 1]	:	400	+	4	×	(1 − 1)	+	(1 − 1)	=	400
AVGPRICES [3, 2]	:	400	+	4	×	(3 − 1)	+	(2 − 1)	=	409
AVGPRICES [4, 1]	:	400	+	4	×	(4 − 1)	+	(1 − 1)	=	412
AVGPRICES [6, 4]	:	400	+	4	×	(6 − 1)	+	(4 − 1)	=	423

Following is the complete general formula that is used to access an element in a two-dimensional array stored in row-major order. The index type can be any ordinal type, and the component type of the elements in the array can occupy SIZE cells.

Location(element at [I1, I2]) =

BASE + (ORD(UB2) − ORD(LB2) + 1)	(* elements per row *)
* SIZE	(* cells per element *)
* (ORD(I1) − ORD(LB1))	(* rows to be skipped *)
+ (ORD(I2) − ORD(LB2) * SIZE)	(* correct cell in row *)

where

UB1 = upper bound of first dimension
LB1 = lower bound of first dimension
UB2 = upper bound of second dimension
LB2 = lower bound of second dimension
I1 = first dimension index
I2 = second dimension index
BASE = base address of the array
SIZE = the number of cells each component type occupies

Before we look at the accessing formula for column-major order, we will take a breather and look at why this material is important. After all, if it is supposed to be transparent, why are we looking at it?

There are three important reasons for slugging through all these details. The first is that you, as a computer scientist, might have to write a compiler someday. This material is part of the theory that a computer scientist should know.

Second, we want to demonstrate how much detail can be hidden from the user. Later you will be implementing accessing routines for other data structures. Once these *utility* routines have been thoroughly debugged and documented, you may design and write your Pascal programs as if these data structures were built into Pascal. You can think of your Pascal compiler as having been enhanced to include these as built-in data types. This is another example of information hiding as discussed in Chapter 1. In case you still have any doubts about the value of information hiding, just imagine what it would be like if you had to use the long formula we discussed *every time* you wanted to access elements in a two-dimensional array!

Third, if you are writing programs at the assembly language level, you will have to use these techniques if you wish to use an array or a record. They are not built-in data types at the assembly language level.

Now we will derive the accessing formulas for column-major order. Remember, column-major order stores the elements of a column in consecutive memory cells as shown in Figure 2-6.

To access an element in row-major order, we found the correct row and then located the correct column. To access an element in column-major order, we have to find the correct column first and then locate the desired row element. Therefore,

BASE + (UB ROW − LB ROW + 1) ∗ (COLUMN INDEX − 1)

gives us the desired column and

ROW INDEX − LB ROW

gives us the item within the column. We will apply this formula to the same examples as we used when looking at row-major order and compare the results.

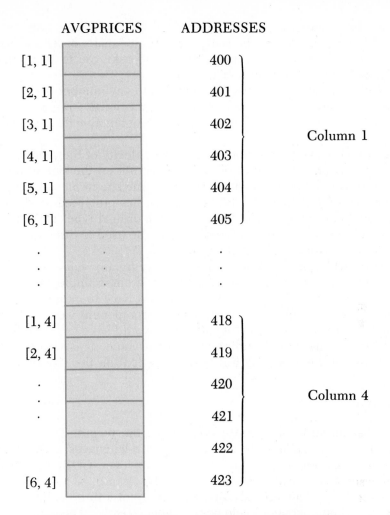

AVGPRICES   ADDRESSES

Figure 2-6. AVGPRICES : ARRAY[1..6, 1..4] OF REAL;
(Same structure as in Figure 2-5.)

Number of elements in a column of AVGPRICES: $(6 - 1) + 1 = 6$

		COLUMN-MAJOR	ROW-MAJOR
AVGPRICES [1, 1]	:	$400 + 6 \times (1 - 1) + (1 - 1) = 400$	400
AVGPRICES [3, 2]	:	$400 + 6 \times (2 - 1) + (3 - 1) = 408$	409
AVGPRICES [4, 1]	:	$400 + 6 \times (1 - 1) + (4 - 1) = 403$	412
AVGPRICES [6, 4]	:	$400 + 6 \times (4 - 1) + (6 - 1) = 423$	423

The first element, AVGPRICES[1, 1], and the last element, AVGPRICES[6, 4], are in the same place in row-major order and column-major order. The others are not. Exercise 15 asks you to summarize the accessing formula for column-major order.

The concept of an array can be extended to any number of dimensions. Exercise 16 asks you to define a three-dimensional array at the logical level. Exercise 17 asks you to give the accessing function for a three-dimensional array.

Before we leave arrays, note that the complexity of the accessing function depends on the number of dimensions, not on the size of the array. Array access must be fast because you use arrays to implement other data structures. It is this need for fast access that has prompted most language designers to limit the type of the index to an ordinal type. The ORD function is defined on all ordinal types, and can be used to directly access the element associated with a particular index.

It is possible, of course, to index an array by any value; however, the accessing function would be more complex. If, for example, you wished to index an array by a set of words, you would have to explicitly store the words in parallel with their corresponding component values. When you wished to retrieve a component value, you would have to search the set of words to find the corresponding component value. This would make the complexity of the accessing function dependent on the size of the array.

RECORDS

Pascal has an additional built-in data type: the record. This very useful structure is not available in all programming languages. FORTRAN, for example, does not support this structure. However, COBOL, a business-oriented language, uses records extensively.

A *record* is a structured data type made up of a finite collection of not necessarily homogeneous elements called *fields*. Accessing is done through a set of named field selectors.

Let's define the syntax and semantics of the accessing function within the context of the following Pascal declaration:

```
TYPE CARTYPE = RECORD
                 YEAR  : INTEGER;
                 COLOR : ARRAY[1..10] OF CHAR;
                 PRICE : REAL
               END;   (* record *)
VAR CAR : CARTYPE;
```

The record variable CAR is made up of three elements or components. The first is named YEAR and is of type INTEGER. The second component COLOR is an ARRAY data type. The third component PRICE is a REAL type. The names of the components make up the set of selectors.

The syntax of the accessing function is a record variable name, followed by a period, followed by a field selector.

CAR.YEAR

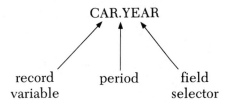

record   period   field
variable   selector

If this expression is on the right-hand side of an assignment operator, a value is being extracted from that place. If it is on the left-hand side, a value is being stored in that place.

CAR.COLOR refers to an array whose elements are of type CHAR. In Pascal you can access the array as a whole, as CAR.COLOR does, or you can access individual characters by using the array accessing function.

CAR.COLOR[2]

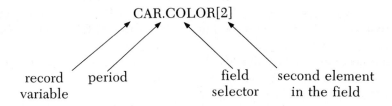

record   period   field   second element
variable   selector   in the field

The record data type allows us to collect together information about an object and to refer to the whole object by name, as well as to refer to the different attributes of the object by name. By this time in your career you should already be sold on the value of using records.

A record, like an array, occupies a consecutive block of cells in memory.* The array accessing function calculates the location of a particular cell from an index; the record calculates the location from a named field selector. The basic question, however, is the same: Which cell (or cells) in this consecutive block do you want?

The name of the record variable is associated with a location in memory. To access each field, all you need to figure out is how much of the record to skip to get to the desired field. This is done by calculating how many cells are needed for each field.

When a record is declared, a table is created that relates a field name to its position within the record. When a field selector is used in the program,

---

* In some machines this may not be exactly true, since boundary alignment (full or half word) may require that some space in memory be skipped so that the next field starts on a byte that is divisible by 2 or 4. This is true of the IBM 360/370. See Figure 2-3.

FIELD	LENGTH
YEAR	1
COLOR	10
PRICE	1

ADDRESS	
1000	(YEAR field)
1001	
1002	
.	(COLOR field)
.	
.	
1010	
1011	(PRICE field)

Figure 2-7. Cartype

this table is examined to see where the desired field is within the record variable. Figure 2-7 shows such a table for CARTYPE and what the record CAR would look like in memory if the base address of CAR were 1000 and each element took one cell.

If the accessing expression CAR.YEAR is encountered, the location is the base address of CAR plus the sum of the lengths of the fields in CARTYPE that precede the desired field YEAR.

$$CAR.YEAR = 1000 + 0 = 1000$$
$$CAR.COLOR = 1000 + 1 = 1001$$
$$CAR.PRICE = 1000 + 1 + 10 = 1011$$

Note that CAR.COLOR is the base address of an array. If an element within this array is to be accessed, this base address is used in the array accessing formula.

PACKED STRUCTURES

The structures we have examined so far have not been packed structures. In a packed structure, the elements may or may not map directly into an integral number of cells. The form of a packed structure is machine dependent. Figure 2-3 showed several different memory configurations. In a machine where the word size is eight bits, it takes eight bits to represent a character and a packed structure is identical to its unpacked version. In a machine where there are 60 bits in a word, each character requires six bits and ten characters can be packed into one word.

The accessing functions remain basically the same in packed structures.

You calculate how many places to skip from a base address to get to the one you want. However, in a packed structure the number of places may be in terms of binary digits (bits) or bytes rather than words.

ERROR CHECKING

In planning your programs, you should always build in a way to check for invalid data. This same principle applies to the implementation level of data structures.

Pascal has the error checking built into the accessing function. For instance, suppose the user tries to access DATA[11] where DATA is a ten-element ARRAY[1..10]. Since the calculated address is outside the range of cells assigned to DATA, a message is printed saying INDEX OUT OF RANGE and the program crashes.

In contrast, FORTRAN leaves error checking to the user. If the address calculated is outside of the range of addresses associated with DATA, a value is either stored into or extracted from the wrong place. In other words, the programmer is responsible for checking to make sure the value of the index is within range.

These two approaches illustrate different philosophies of error handling. Pascal checks for run-time errors and takes control away from the program if an error occurs. FORTRAN does very little run-time error checking.

There is a third philosophy that checks for errors but leaves the determination of what to do if an error condition arises to the programmer. That is, the accessing routines check for errors, but leave the error-handling decision to the programmer by setting an error flag. After each call to an accessing routine, the programmer can check the error flag to see if an error condition occurred. If so, the programmer makes the decision as to how to handle error conditions within the context of the semantics of the problem itself.

This third philosophy is used in the application at the end of this chapter. In the planning stage of each operation, possible error conditions are considered. An error flag is an output parameter from each procedure where an error condition is possible.

Summary

In this chapter we have examined two useful built-in data structures from three perspectives: the logical level, the application level, and the implementation level.

A data structure as defined at the logical level is called an abstract data type. A programmer should be able to use an abstract data type without being concerned about its implementation level. In your previous course you did use both the array type and the record type without having to know how they were implemented.

We will continue to study additional abstract data types that are not built into existing programming languages. We will not stop at the logical level; we will implement these structures in Pascal. Once you have an implementation for these structures, you can forget about that level. Subsequent programs can be written using these structures as if they were built-in.

This concept of augmenting or enhancing a programming language with your own structured data types is a very important one. Pascal does not have a mechanism for actually adding them to the compiler. You must declare them in each program and include accessing procedures and functions. There is no way to make them physically transparent to the user.

This concept has, however, been incorporated in the programming language ADA. The packaging feature of ADA that allows you to do this will be discussed in the last chapter.

■ APPLICATION: STRINGS

Data Structures in Use
- STRINGS
- RECORDS

Software Techniques in Use
- DESIGN FROM SPECIFICATIONS
- DATA ENCAPSULATION AND INFORMATION HIDING
- COMMAND-DRIVEN TEST DRIVER

You are the junior member of a programming team working for a software house (a company that writes and sells computer software). The sales staff has complained that your Pascal compiler doesn't support the string data type.

Some dialects of Pascal such as UCSD Pascal have a built-in data structure called a string. (A string is just what it sounds like: a string of alphanumeric characters.) The programming manager has turned over to your team the task of defining and implementing a set of procedures and functions that will implement a string data type. These will then be given to customers who want to use them.

Formally, a string is a finite sequence of alphanumeric characters, characterized by a property called *length*. The length of a string is the number of characters in the string. The operations defined on a string are:

1. LENGTH: determines the number of characters in a string
2. GETLINE: inputs a line of text
3. GETSTRING: inputs a word of text
4. PRINT: writes the contents of a string
5. SUBSTRING: returns a part of a string
6. CONCAT: makes a new string by putting two strings side by side
7. DELETE: deletes a substring from a string
8. INSERT: inserts a string into another string
9. SEARCH: searches a string for a given substring
10. COMPARE: compares two strings to determine if they are equal, or if the first is less than the second or the second less than the first
11. APPEND: appends a character to the end of a string

Your team's task will be to make each of these operations available to users as a standard procedure or function, just as READLN and SQRT are available in standard Pascal. Users will then have an enhanced version of Pascal.

The chief programmer in your team took the general descriptions listed, determined an appropriate data structure in which to represent a string, and wrote detailed specifications for each operation. You, as junior programmer, have been assigned to write the Pascal code to implement the operations according to these specifications.

Each string will be represented by two parts: the string of characters itself and an integer variable that indicates how many characters are in the string. Since Pascal doesn't allow variable-length arrays, a maximum length must be chosen. Each string will be represented as an array of the maximum length, but the string itself will constitute only that part of the array from position 1 to the position stated in the LENGTH field.

The declarations you are to use are:

```
CONST MAXLENGTH = ? ;

TYPE INDEXRANGE = 0..MAXLENGTH;

     STRINGTYPE = RECORD
                   LENGTH : INDEXRANGE;
                   CHARS : ARRAY[1..MAXLENGTH] OF CHAR
                 END;   (* record *)
```

You can picture a string like this:

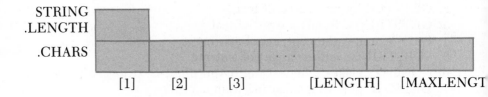

STRING.CHARS[1]..STRING.CHARS[LENGTH] is the string.

We will now take the specifications for each operation, develop its algorithm, and code it in Pascal.

LENGTH OPERATION

FUNCTION LENGTH (STRING : STRINGTYPE) : INDEXRANGE;
INPUT: STRING—a string
OUTPUT: the number of characters in the string
ASSUMPTIONS: none

Given our representation of a string, a function to return the length of a string consists of only one statement.

```
FUNCTION LENGTH (STRING : STRINGTYPE) : INDEXRANGE;
```

(* insert specification here for proper documentation *)

```
BEGIN   (* length *)
  LENGTH := STRING.LENGTH
END;    (* length *)
```

Isn't it inefficient to have a one-line function? Why not just replace the function invocation, LENGTH(STRING), in the calling program with STRING.LENGTH? Remember that the implementation is transparent to the user: *You* know this implementation takes only one line of code; the user sees this operation only from the logical level. If you let the user access the length directly, you have violated the concept of an abstract data type.

GETLINE OPERATION

```
PROCEDURE GETLINE (VAR DATA  : TEXT;
                   VAR LINE   : STRINGTYPE;
                   VAR ERROR  : BOOLEAN);

INPUT:    DATA  — name of a file
OUTPUT:   LINE  — the current line of text of the file DATA,
                  padded with blanks to MAXLENGTH
          ERROR — if the number of characters in the current line is greater
                  than MAXLENGTH, ERROR ← TRUE and skip to
                  new line, otherwise ERROR ← FALSE
ASSUMPTIONS: EOF will not be encountered
```

The algorithm to read in and store characters until end-of-line is a familiar one. Here we need to add a test to stop when MAXLENGTH characters have been read in.

GETLINE

```
WHILE more characters AND more space in string DO
    READ character
    PUT character in string
SET line length field
PAD line with blanks
SET error flag
READLN
```

We will need to keep track of the position within the string (POS) in order to store characters into LINE. The value of POS when we leave the WHILE loop will be the number of characters in the line. LINE[POS + 1] to LINE[MAXLENGTH] will contain blanks. How do we set the ERROR flag? IF EOLN is TRUE, all of the characters fit into the string and there has not been an error. Now the code can be written.

```
PROCEDURE GETLINE (VAR DATA : TEXT; VAR LINE : STRINGTYPE;
                   VAR ERROR : BOOLEAN);
(* insert specification for proper documentation *)

VAR POS : INDEXRANGE;                  (* LINE position pointer *)
    CH : CHAR;                   (* temporary character variable *)

BEGIN   (* getline *)
  POS := 0;
  (* Read and store characters until EOLN or maximum stored. *)
  WHILE NOT EOLN(DATA) AND (POS < MAXLENGTH) DO
    BEGIN
      POS := POS + 1;
      READ(DATA,CH);
      LINE.CHARS[POS] := CH
    END;

  LINE.LENGTH := POS;                      (* Set line length. *)

  (* Pad rest of LINE with blanks. *)
  FOR POS := POS + 1 TO MAXLENGTH DO
    LINE.CHARS[POS] := ' ';
  ERROR := NOT EOLN(DATA);
  READLN(DATA)
END;    (* getline *)
```

GETSTRING OPERATION

```
PROCEDURE GETSTRING (VAR DATA    : TEXT;
                     VAR STRING : STRINGTYPE;
                     ENDSTRING : SETOFPUNCT;
                     VAR ERROR  : BOOLEAN);

INPUT:   DATA         — name of an input file
         ENDSTRING — set of characters to be used as end-of-string
                      markers
OUTPUT:  STRING       — a string made up of the characters from the
                      current position on file DATA up to, but not
                      including, the first occurrence of a character
                      from the set ENDSTRING
         ERROR        — if no character in ENDSTRING is found before
                      MAXLENGTH characters are read,
                      ERROR ← TRUE and skip characters until
                      next character in ENDSTRING or EOLN,
                      otherwise ERROR ← FALSE
ASSUMPTIONS: EOF will not be encountered, and EOLN will be treated
             as a blank.
```

For those of you who have not used the built-in data type called SET, we will take a side trip and show you how to define and use a set. The following declaration statements will create a set type named SETOFPUNCT and a set variable named ENDSTRING.

```
TYPE PUNCTMARKS = ' '..'A';        (* This gets most of the punctuation *)
                                   (* marks in ASCII and EBCDIC.        *)

     SETOFPUNCT = SET OF PUNCTMARKS;

VAR  ENDSTRING : SETOFPUNCT;
```

The set variable ENDSTRING can contain any one of the characters listed. Like any variable, it doesn't have anything in it until you put something in it at run time. If you want ENDSTRING to contain a period, a comma, and a blank, you can use the following assignment statement:

```
ENDSTRING := ['.', ',', ' ']
```

If you only want blanks to mark the ends of words, you can use the following assignment statement:

```
ENDSTRING := [' ']
```

To determine if a character is in ENDSTRING, you can use the following expression:

```
IF CH IN ENDSTRING
    THEN    (* yes, it is *)
    ELSE    (* no, it is not *)
```

IN is an operator that returns TRUE if the variable named on its left contains one of the elements in the set named on its right. (See Appendix I for more information on the Pascal data type SET.)

Using a special character to end a word means that one character must be read outside of the loop. This is called a *priming read*. This technique is used frequently to solve problems dealing with EOF.

GETSTRING

```
READ a character
WHILE character not in ENDSTRING AND more room in word DO
    STORE character in string
    READ character
SET length of string
PAD word with blanks
SET error flag
IF error
    READ while character not in ENDSTRING
```

We need an index here to play the same role as POS in Procedure GETLINE. We can tell if there has been an error by checking to see if the last character read (CH) is in ENDSTRING. If not, we know that there is an error condition.

```
PROCEDURE GETSTRING (VAR DATA: TEXT; VAR STRING: STRINGTYPE
                     ENDSTRING: SETOFPUNCT; VAR ERROR : BOOLEAN);

(* Insert specification for proper documentation. *)

VAR POS : INDEXRANGE;                       (* position in string *)
    CH  : CHAR;                      (* temporary character variable *)

BEGIN   (* getstring *)
    POS := 0;
    READ(DATA,CH);                           (* Get first character. *)
```

```
(* Read and store characters until a character is found *)
(* that is in ENDSTRING or until maximum stored. *)
 WHILE NOT (CH IN ENDSTRING) AND (POS < MAXLENGTH) DO
    BEGIN
       POS := POS + 1;
       STRING.CHARS[POS] := CH;
       READ(DATA,CH)
    END;
 STRING.LENGTH := POS;                              (* Set length. *)

(* Pad rest of line with blanks. *)
 FOR POS := POS + 1 TO MAXLENGTH DO
    STRING.CHARS[POS] := ' ';

 ERROR := NOT (CH IN ENDSTRING);           (* Set error flag. *)
 WHILE NOT (CH IN ENDSTRING) DO
    READ(DATA,CH)    (* Word is longer than MAXLENGTH so read till end. *)
END;    (* getstring *)
```

PRINT OPERATION

> PROCEDURE PRINT (STRING : STRINGTYPE);
>
> INPUT: STRING — a string
> OUTPUT: STRING is printed on OUTPUT
> ASSUMPTIONS: no end-of-line is to be printed unless the number
>   of characters to be printed requires more than one line
>   — procedure does not use WRITELN

This operation is very simple. The string will be printed exactly as it is, character by character, using procedure WRITE. No WRITELN is issued.

```
PROCEDURE PRINT (STRING : STRINGTYPE);
(* Insert specification for proper documentation. *)

VAR POS : INDEXRANGE;                    (* loop control pointer *)

BEGIN   (* print *)
   FOR POS := 1 TO STRING.LENGTH DO
      WRITE(STRING.CHARS[POS])
END;    (* print *)
```

SUBSTRING OPERATION

PROCEDURE SUBSTRING (STRING : STRINGTYPE;
                                        VAR SUBSTR : STRINGTYPE;
                                        STARTPOS, NUM : INDEXRANGE;
                                        VAR ERROR : BOOLEAN);

INPUT: STRING   — the original string
                 STARTPOS — the starting position in the string
                 NUM   — the number of characters in the substring
OUTPUT: SUBSTR   — the substring of length NUM
                                       beginning at STRING.CHARS[STARTPOS]
                 ERROR   — if the substring is not part of
                                       the original string, then
                                       ERROR ← TRUE, otherwise
                                       ERROR ← FALSE
ASSUMPTIONS: SUBSTR is undefined if ERROR is TRUE

The SUBSTRING operation produces a substring of an original string, beginning at a designated character position (STARTPOS). We will take the characters one by one beginning at STRING.CHARS[STARTPOS] and put them into the new string beginning at SUBSTR.CHARS[1]. After we have copied NUM characters into SUBSTR.CHARS, we will pad the rest of the character positions in SUBSTR.CHARS with blanks.

SUBSTRING

SET error flag according to input values
IF not error
    FOR POS := 1 TO NUM
        SUBSTR.CHARS[POS] ← STRING.CHARS[STARTPOS + POS − 1]
    PAD rest of substring with blanks
    SET length of substring to NUM

To set the error flag, we must determine if the character positions to be copied are part of STRING. We need to calculate the last position to be copied and check whether that is greater than the length of STRING. We certainly don't want to copy past the end of the original string.

STARTPOS + NUM − 1

should give us this position. Let's try several values to convince ourselves that we are right. If NUM is 1, STARTPOS is the last (and only) character to move. If NUM is 3, STARTPOS + 2 is the last position to be copied. If

STARTPOS + 2 is not greater than STRING.LENGTH, everything is all right. If it is greater than STRING.LENGTH, an error has occurred.

We are now ready to code Procedure SUBSTRING.

```
PROCEDURE SUBSTRING (STRING : STRINGTYPE;
                     VAR SUBSTR : STRINGTYPE;
                     STARTPOS, NUM : INDEXRANGE;
                     VAR ERROR : BOOLEAN);

(* Insert specifications for proper documentation. *)

VAR POS : INDEXRANGE;                          (* loop counter *)

BEGIN   (* substring *)
  ERROR := STARTPOS + NUM - 1 > STRING.LENGTH;
  IF NOT ERROR
     THEN
       BEGIN
         FOR POS := 1 TO NUM DO                (* Copy characters. *)
           SUBSTR.CHARS[POS] :=
               STRING.CHARS[STARTPOS + POS - 1];
         FOR POS := NUM + 1 TO MAXLENGTH DO
           SUBSTR.CHARS[POS] := ' ';           (* Set balance to blanks. *)
         SUBSTR.LENGTH := NUM                   (* Set length. *)
       END (* not error *)
END;    (* substring *)
```

CONCAT OPERATION

PROCEDURE CONCAT (VAR STRING1 : STRINGTYPE;
                        STRING2 : STRINGTYPE;
                        VAR ERROR : BOOLEAN);

INPUT: STRING1—a string
            STRING2—a string
OUTPUT: STRING1—STRING1 concatenated with STRING2
            ERROR —if LENGTH(STRING1) + LENGTH(STRING2) >
                     MAXLENGTH, ERROR ← TRUE, otherwise
                     ERROR ← FALSE
ASSUMPTIONS: if ERROR is TRUE, STRING1 is not changed

The CONCAT operation "adds" one string to the end of a second string.

Note that we have only two strings as parameters, not three. We will leave the result in the first string. That is, we will copy the characters of the

second string, one at a time, into the first string beginning at position
STRING1.LENGTH + 1. (See Figure 2-8.)

CONCAT

```
CALCULATE length of new string
ERROR ← length of new string > MAXLENGTH
IF not error
    LASTPOS ← length of STRING1
    FOR POS = 1 TO length of STRING2
        increment LASTPOS
        STRING1.CHARS[LASTPOS] ← STRING2.CHARS[POS]
    SET length of STRING1 ← LASTPOS
```

There is nothing in this module that needs further decomposition. The code for the procedure to concatenate two strings is given below. Note that we don't have to pad the resulting string with blanks because STRING1 was already padded with blanks.

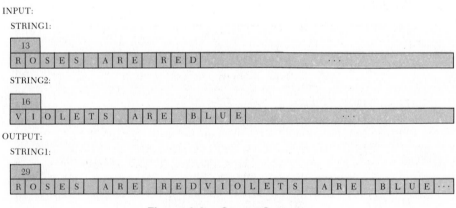

Figure 2-8. Concat Operation

```
PROCEDURE CONCAT (VAR STRING1 : STRINGTYPE;
                      STRING2 : STRINGTYPE;
                      VAR ERROR : BOOLEAN);
```

(* Insert specification for proper documentation. *)

```
VAR LEN,                                    (* length of new string *)
    LASTPOS,                          (* current last position in STRING1 *)
    POS : INDEXRANGE;                      (* position in STRING2 *)

BEGIN   (* concat *)
  LEN := STRING1.LENGTH + STRING2.LENGTH;
  ERROR := LEN > MAXLENGTH;
  IF NOT ERROR
     THEN
        BEGIN
          LASTPOS := STRING1.LENGTH;
          FOR POS := 1 TO STRING2.LENGTH DO
            BEGIN
              LASTPOS := LASTPOS + 1;
              STRING1.CHARS[LASTPOS] := STRING2.CHARS[POS]
            END;   (* for *)
          STRING1.LENGTH := LASTPOS                  (* Set length. *)
        END   (* not error *)
END;   (* concat *)
```

DELETE OPERATION

```
PROCEDURE DELETE (VAR STRING : STRINGTYPE;
                      POS, NUM : INDEXRANGE;
                      VAR ERROR : BOOLEAN);

INPUT:    STRING —the string from which some characters are to
                      be deleted
          POS      —the character position from which the first
                      character is to be deleted
          NUM      —the number of consecutive characters to be deleted
OUTPUT: STRING —the input string with NUM characters deleted
          ERROR  —if characters to be deleted are not within the
                      string, ERROR ← TRUE, otherwise
                      ERROR ← FALSE
ASSUMPTIONS: if ERROR is TRUE, STRING will not be changed
```

The DELETE operation removes a specified number of characters from a string, beginning at a given character position.

There are two distinct algorithms that we could use here. We could take that part of the original string on the right of the part to be deleted and move it down to fill in the deleted section. The part freed up could then be filled with blanks. Another approach would be to take advantage of two procedures we have already coded: CONCAT and SUBSTRING. We will use this second approach. We will use SUBSTRING to break the original string into two parts: the part before the deleted characters and the part following them. These two strings can then be concatenated to produce the string we want. Figure 2-9 shows a code walk-through of this algorithm.

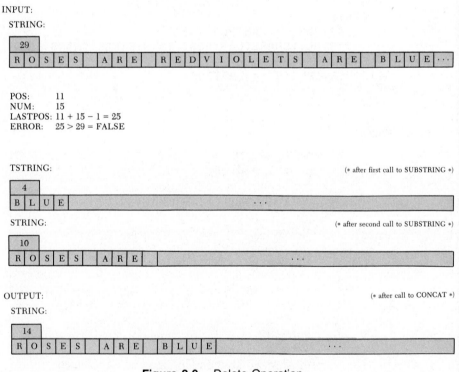

INPUT:

STRING:

29

| R | O | S | E | S | | A | R | E | | R | E | D | V | I | O | L | E | T | S | | A | R | E | | B | L | U | E | ··· |

POS: 11
NUM: 15
LASTPOS: 11 + 15 − 1 = 25
ERROR: 25 > 29 = FALSE

TSTRING: (* after first call to SUBSTRING *)

4

| B | L | U | E | ··· |

STRING: (* after second call to SUBSTRING *)

10

| R | O | S | E | S | | A | R | E | ··· |

OUTPUT: (* after call to CONCAT *)

STRING:

14

| R | O | S | E | S | | A | R | E | | B | L | U | E | ··· |

Figure 2-9. Delete Operation

DELETE

CALCULATE position of the last character to be deleted
ERROR is TRUE if last position is not within string
IF not error
    GET the substring to right of deleted section
    GET the substring to left of deleted section
    CONCAT two substrings together

The position of the last character to be deleted (LASTPOS) should be POS + NUM − 1. The substring to the right of the section to be deleted starts at LASTPOS + 1. The substring to the left of the section to be deleted goes from position 1 to position POS − 1. We will use a temporary string to hold the first substring.

Will this algorithm work if the characters to be deleted are the first characters or the last characters? If the characters to be deleted come at the very beginning of the string, the algorithm will work. SUBSTRING will simply return a string of length 0. If the characters come at the end of the string, the same thing will happen.

```
PROCEDURE DELETE (VAR STRING : STRINGTYPE;
                  POS, NUM : INDEXRANGE;
                  VAR ERROR : BOOLEAN);

  (* Insert specification for proper documentation. *)

VAR TSTRING : STRINGTYPE;             (* holds a string temporarily *)
    LASTPOS : INDEXRANGE;          (* position of last character to delete *)
    SUBERROR : BOOLEAN;        (* returned from SUBSTRING and CONCAT *)

BEGIN   (* delete *)
  LASTPOS := POS + NUM - 1;              (* last character to be deleted *)
  ERROR := LASTPOS > STRING.LENGTH;
  IF NOT ERROR
    THEN
      BEGIN
        (* Get the substring to the right of deleted section. *)
        SUBSTRING(STRING,TSTRING, LASTPOS + 1,
                  STRING.LENGTH - LASTPOS, SUBERROR);
        (* Get the substring to the left of deleted section. *)
        SUBSTRING(STRING, STRING, 1, POS - 1, SUBERROR);
        (* Build new string. *)
        CONCAT(STRING, TSTRING, SUBERROR)
      END
END;   (* delete *)
```

Note that it wasn't necessary to check the value of the error flag returned from SUBSTRING and CONCAT, since we know that we set up the parameters correctly.

INSERT OPERATION

PROCEDURE INSERT (VAR STRING : STRINGTYPE;
                INSTRING: STRINGTYPE;
                POS: INDEXRANGE; VAR ERROR : BOOLEAN);

INPUT: STRING   —a string into which a substring is to be inserted
            INSTRING —the substring to be inserted into the original string
            POS   —the character position in STRING where INSTRING
                        is to be inserted
OUTPUT: STRING   —the original string with the substring inserted
                        beginning at character position POS
            ERROR   —if POS is not within STRING or if the combined
                        lengths of STRING and INSTRING are greater
                        than MAXLENGTH, ERROR ← TRUE, otherwise
                        ERROR ← FALSE
ASSUMPTIONS: if ERROR is TRUE, STRING and INSTRING are unchanged

The mirror image of the DELETE operation is the INSERT operation. With INSERT, a substring is inserted into an original string, beginning at a specified character position. We can implement this operation the way we did the DELETE operation—by using CONCAT and SUBSTRING. We use SUBSTRING to get the substring that precedes the insertion point and the substring that begins at the insertion point. We concatenate the first substring with the substring to be inserted, and then concatenate this result with the last part of the original string.

INSERT

SET ERROR to TRUE if string to be inserted is too long
or if insertion point is not in STRING
IF not error
    GET SUBSTRING of STRING beginning at insertion point
        (use temporary string to contain it)
    GET SUBSTRING of STRING that precedes insertion point
        (put back into STRING)
    CONCATENATE STRING with string to be inserted
    CONCATENATE STRING with temporary string

A procedure to accomplish this algorithm can be written directly from this pseudo-code.

```
PROCEDURE INSERT (VAR STRING : STRINGTYPE;
                      INSTRING : STRINGTYPE;
                      POS : INDEXRANGE;
                      VAR ERROR : BOOLEAN);

   (* insert specification for proper documentation *)

VAR TSTRING  : STRINGTYPE;              (* to hold a string temporarily *)
    SUBERROR : BOOLEAN:        (* returned from SUBSTRING and CONCAT *)

BEGIN   (* insert *)
   ERROR := (STRING.LENGTH + INSTRING.LENGTH > MAXLENGTH)
             OR (POS > STRING.LENGTH);
   IF NOT ERROR
      THEN
         BEGIN
            (* Copy part to right of insertion point. *)
            SUBSTRING(STRING,TSTRING,POS,
               STRING.LENGTH-POS + 1, SUBERROR);
            (* Copy part to left of insertion point. *)
            SUBSTRING(STRING,STRING,1,POS - 1,SUBERROR);
            (* Concatenate left part with substring. *)
            CONCAT(STRING,INSTRING,SUBERROR);
            (* Concatenate right part back with the others. *)
            CONCAT(STRING,TSTRING,SUBERROR)
         END
END;   (* insert *)
```

Figure 2-10 shows a code walk-through of Procedure INSERT.

SEARCH OPERATION

```
PROCEDURE SEARCH (STRING, SUBSTR : STRINGTYPE;
                  VAR FOUND : BOOLEAN;
                  VAR POS : INDEXRANGE;
                  VAR ERROR : BOOLEAN);

INPUT:   STRING  —the string to be searched
         SUBSTR  —the substring to be searched for
OUTPUT: FOUND  —if SUBSTR is a substring of STRING,
                 FOUND ← TRUE, otherwise FOUND ← FALSE
         POS     —the character position in STRING where SUBSTR
                 begins if FOUND is TRUE, otherwise undefined
         ERROR  —if either STRING or SUBSTR is empty or if the
                 length of SUBSTR is greater than the length of
                 LINE, ERROR ← TRUE, otherwise ERROR ← FALSE
ASSUMPTIONS: we are only looking for the first match
```

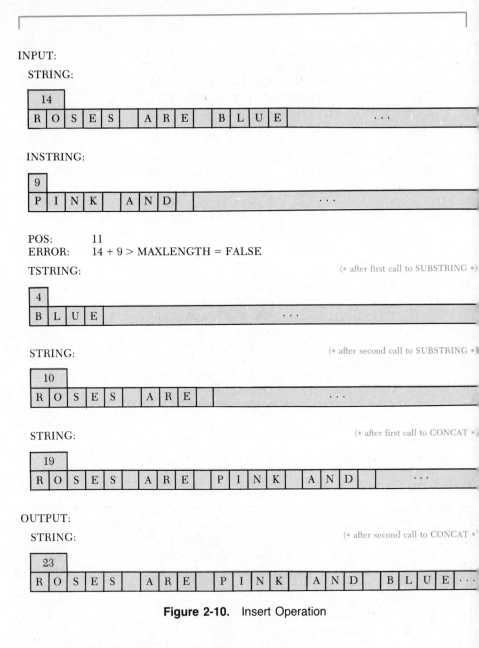

INPUT:

STRING:

| 14 |
| R | O | S | E | S | | A | R | E | | B | L | U | E | | | . . . |

INSTRING:

| 9 |
| P | I | N | K | | A | N | D | | | . . . |

POS: 11
ERROR: 14 + 9 > MAXLENGTH = FALSE

TSTRING: (* after first call to SUBSTRING *)

| 4 |
| B | L | U | E | | | . . . |

STRING: (* after second call to SUBSTRING *)

| 10 |
| R | O | S | E | S | | A | R | E | | | . . . |

STRING: (* after first call to CONCAT *)

| 19 |
| R | O | S | E | S | | A | R | E | | P | I | N | K | | A | N | D | | | . . . |

OUTPUT:

STRING: (* after second call to CONCAT *)

| 23 |
| R | O | S | E | S | | A | R | E | | P | I | N | K | | A | N | D | | B | L | U | E | . . . |

Figure 2-10. Insert Operation

The SEARCH operation is fairly complex. It takes a string and a sub-string and tries to find an occurrence of the substring within the string. However, not only do we want to know *if* the substring occurs, we also want to know *where*.

The algorithm has two parts. We will keep looking in the main string for an occurrence of the first letter in the substring. If we never find it, we know the substring is not there. If we find a match for the first character, we continue trying to match the next characters. If we match them all, the search is successful. If we find a character that does not match, we go back and begin looking for another match for the first character in the substring.

The process stops when the search is successful or when the number of characters left to check in the main string is less than the length of the substring.

SEARCH

```
ERROR ← TRUE if STRING is of length 0
        OR SUBSTR is longer than STRING
If not ERROR
    INITIALIZE FOUND ← FALSE,MORETOCHECK ← TRUE
                current position ← 1
    WHILE moretocheck AND we haven't found a match
        IF first character in SUBSTR = character in
                    current position in STRING
                THEN check rest of SUBSTR with next positions in STRING
                ELSE increment current position in STRING
            SET MORETOCHECK (TRUE if there is still a possibility
                of a match, FALSE if there are not enough characters
                left in STRING to be checked.
    IF search successful
            THEN POS ← position in STRING where SUBSTR begins
```

When a match for the first letter in SUBSTR has been found in STRING, we check the next letter in SUBSTR with the next position in STRING. This expands to a second loop nested inside the first:

CHECK REST OF SUBSTR

```
MATCH ← TRUE
WHILE more letters in SUBSTR AND MATCH
    IF the letter at this position of SUBSTR = the letter
        at the appropriate position of STRING
        THEN increment position
        ELSE MATCH ← FALSE
```

One line of the algorithm may require some explanation. How do we set MORETOCHECK, the Boolean variable that controls the outer loop? There is more to check when there are enough characters left in STRING to warrant continuing the search. That is, when the current line position in STRING plus the length of SUBSTR minus 1 exceeds the length of STRING, there is no possibility of a match. When this occurs, MORETOCHECK is FALSE, and the process ends.

```
PROCEDURE SEARCH (STRING, SUBSTR : STRINGTYPE;
                  VAR FOUND : BOOLEAN;
                  VAR POS : INDEXRANGE;
                  VAR ERROR : BOOLEAN);
```

(* Insert specification for proper documentation. *)

```
VAR STPOS,                            (* STRING position pointer *)
    SUBPOS : INDEXRANGE;              (* SUBSTR position pointer *)
    MATCH,                            (* temporary flag used in matching *)
    MORETOCHECK : BOOLEAN;            (* STRING still can contain SUBSTR *)

BEGIN  (* search *)
  ERROR := (STRING.LENGTH = 0) OR (SUBSTR.LENGTH = 0)
            OR (STRING.LENGTH < SUBSTR.LENGTH);
  IF NOT ERROR
     THEN
        BEGIN
           STPOS := 1;
           FOUND := FALSE;
           MORETOCHECK := TRUE;

           WHILE MORETOCHECK AND NOT FOUND DO
              BEGIN
                 IF SUBSTR.CHARS[1] = STRING.CHARS[STPOS]
                    THEN        (* first character in SUBSTR found in STRING *)
                       BEGIN
                          SUBPOS := 1;
                          MATCH := TRUE;
                       (* Check rest of word. *)
                          WHILE (SUBPOS < SUBSTR.LENGTH)
                                AND MATCH DO
                          (* If it matches, keep comparing, *)
                          (* otherwise increment STPOS.     *)
                             IF SUBSTR.CHARS[SUBPOS + 1] =
                                STRING.CHARS[STPOS + SUBPOS]
                                THEN SUBPOS := SUBPOS + 1
                                ELSE    (* doesn't match *)
                                   BEGIN
                                      MATCH := FALSE;
                                      STPOS := STPOS + 1
                                   END;
                          FOUND := MATCH;
                       END    (* first character match *)
```

```
            ELSE   (* first character doesn't match *)
                STPOS := STPOS + 1;

           MORETOCHECK := (STPOS + SUBSTR.LENGTH - 1)
                               <= STRING.LENGTH
        END;  (* while *)

        IF FOUND
            THEN POS := STPOS                  (* search succesful *)
       END      (* not error *)                (* Set POS. *)
END;   (* search *)
```

Figure 2-11 shows a code walk-through of the SEARCH operation.

STRING:

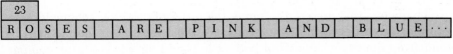

SUBSTR:

STRING is scanned character by character until there is a match for
  SUBSTR.CHARS[1].
Now : SUBSTR.CHARS[1] = STRING.CHARS[7]
We try to match SUBSTR.CHARS[2] with STRING.CHARS[8] and the
  match fails.
We go back to scanning STRING character by character until we find an-
  other match for SUBSTR.CHARS[1].
Now : SUBSTR.CHARS[1] = STRING.CHARS[16]
We try to match the next characters, and the following are the results:
  SUBSTR.CHARS[2] = STRING.CHARS[17]
  SUBSTR.CHARS[3] = STRING.CHARS[18]
Now : SUBPOS = SUBSTR.LENGTH (3 = 3)
MATCH = TRUE, FOUND = TRUE,   POS = 16

Figure 2-11. Walk-Through of Search Operation

COMPARE OPERATION

> FUNCTION COMPARE (SUBSTR1, SUBSTR2 : STRINGTYPE): RELATION;
>
> INPUT:　　SUBSTR1　—a string
> 　　　　　SUBSTR2　—a string
> OUTPUT: COMPARE　—LESS if SUBSTR1 comes before SUBSTR2 alphabetically (is less than)
> 　　　　　　　　　—EQUAL if SUBSTR1 is identical to SUBSTR2
> 　　　　　　　　　—GREATER if SUBSTR1 comes after SUBSTR2 alphabetically (is greater than)
> ASSUMPTIONS: RELATION is a user-defined data type consisting of (LESS, EQUAL, GREATER)

Since the strings we are concerned with here are not packed arrays, we will have to compare them character by character. The first time we find two characters that are not the same, the order of those two characters determines the order of the two strings. We must set up our loop to start by comparing the first character of both strings and then to continue comparing characters either until a pair of characters that do not match is found or until there are no more characters in the shorter string. If the two strings are of the same length and all of the characters match, they are equal. If all of the characters match and one string is shorter than the other, the shorter one comes before the longer one alphabetically.

COMPARE

```
WHILE more characters in shorter string AND STILLMATCH DO
    IF character at current position of SUBSTR1 = character at
        current position of SUBSTR2
        THEN increment current position
        ELSE STILLMATCH ← FALSE
            IF current character in SUBSTR1 < current character in SUBSTR2
                THEN COMPARE ← LESS
                ELSE COMPARE ← GREATER
IF STILLMATCH                          (* ran out of characters in shorter string;
    (* Use lengths to determine ordering. *)
    IF SUBSTR1.LENGTH = SUBSTR2.LENGTH
        COMPARE ← EQUAL
    ELSE IF SUBSTR1.LENGTH < SUBSTR2.LENGTH
        COMPARE ← LESS
    ELSE COMPARE ← GREATER
```

The COMPARE operation seems quite straightforward. We will need a counter that will run from 1 to the length of the shorter string. This counter will be used as a position pointer into the two strings. STILLMATCH is a BOOLEAN flag that will be TRUE as long as the characters in the two strings are identical. The WHILE loop will be terminated either when the position counter exceeds the length of the shorter string or when characters that do not match are encountered in the two strings.

```
FUNCTION COMPARE (SUBSTR1, SUBSTR2 : STRINGTYPE) : RELATION;

   (* insert specification for proper documentation *)

VAR POS : INDEXRANGE;              (* index for SUBSTR1 and SUBSTR2 *)
    STILLMATCH : BOOLEAN;          (* TRUE as long as characters match *)
    MINLENGTH : INDEXRANGE;                  (* length of shorter word *)

BEGIN    (* compare *)

   (* MINLENGTH ← length of shorter word. *)
   IF SUBSTR1.LENGTH < SUBSTR2.LENGTH
      THEN MINLENGTH := SUBSTR1.LENGTH
      ELSE MINLENGTH := SUBSTR2.LENGTH;

   POS := 1;
   STILLMATCH := TRUE;
   WHILE (POS <= MINLENGTH) AND STILLMATCH DO
      (* Search for characters that do not match. *)
      IF SUBSTR1.CHARS[POS] = SUBSTR2.CHARS[POS]
         THEN POS := POS + 1                 (* Keep comparing. *)
         ELSE
            BEGIN                     (* two strings do not match *)
               STILLMATCH := FALSE;
               IF SUBSTR1.CHARS[POS] < SUBSTR2.CHARS[POS]
                  THEN COMPARE := LESS
                  ELSE COMPARE := GREATER
            END;
   IF STILLMATCH (* ran out of characters in shorter string *)
      (* Use length to determine ordering. *)
      THEN IF SUBSTR1.LENGTH = SUBSTR2.LENGTH
              THEN COMPARE := EQUAL
      ELSE IF SUBSTR1.LENGTH < SUBSTR2.LENGTH
              THEN COMPARE := LESS
              ELSE COMPARE := GREATER
END;    (* compare *)
```

APPEND OPERATION

PROCEDURE APPEND (VAR STRING : STRINGTYPE; CH : CHAR;
VAR ERROR : BOOLEAN);

INPUT: STRING —a string to which a character is to be appended
         CH   —the character to be appended to STRING
OUTPUT: STRING —the original string with the character
                    appended (i.e., concatenated)
       ERROR —if STRING is originally at maximum length,
                  ERROR ← TRUE, otherwise ERROR ← FALSE
ASSUMPTIONS: none

The algorithm for the APPEND operation is very simple. If STRING.LENGTH is not equal to MAXLENGTH, we just increment STRING.LENGTH by one and store CH in STRING.CHARS [STRING.LENGTH]. In fact, we can code the procedure directly without a pseudo-code description.

```
PROCEDURE APPEND (VAR STRING : STRINGTYPE; CH : CHAR;
                  VAR ERROR : BOOLEAN);
   (* Insert specification for proper documentation. *)

BEGIN   (* append *)
   ERROR := STRING.LENGTH = MAXLENGTH;
   IF NOT ERROR
      THEN
         BEGIN   (* Append character. *)
            STRING.LENGTH := STRING.LENGTH + 1;
            STRING.CHARS[STRING.LENGTH] := CH
         END     (* not error *)
END;    (* append *)
```

We can create literal strings by initializing a string to EMPTYSTRING and appending characters, one by one. For example, we can create a string that contains a comma followed by a blank as follows:

```
STRING := EMPTYSTRING;                    (* a string of length 0 *)
APPEND(STRING, ',', ERROR);
APPEND(STRING, ' ', ERROR)
```

It would certainly be simpler if we could just use a constant string, such as

```
CONST

    STRING = ', '
```

Of course, we could create such a literal string, but we could not use it with our string operations, because it is of a different type than our strings. Pascal would create a packed array of two characters in this case. Since our strings are records, however, we have to create constant strings by using APPEND.

Remember, in our concatenation example we ended up with two words run together. We could have used APPEND to put a blank between those two words.

Testing: At this point, you have not yet finished coding the string operations in accordance with the specifications you were given. Before you can consider the job finished, you will have to demonstrate that these procedures and functions have been thoroughly tested. Since these routines are all low-level utility routines, you should use a bottom-up testing strategy.

You must write a driver program that will call or invoke each procedure and function with varying data values and print the results. Drivers of this type are so useful that we will digress here and describe a driver program called a *command-driven tester*.

The basic structure of the program is the same as the command-driven system discussed in Chapter 1. The names of the procedures and functions to be tested become the commands in the system. The task to be done for a particular command is to execute the procedure or function with the same name and print out the results.

Since each of the procedures and functions has a string as a parameter, we will have to read in which string the procedure or function is to manipulate. We will declare an array of strings. The input to the tester will be the name of the procedure or function to be executed followed by an integer number, which will be used as an index into the array of strings.

If the procedure to be executed needs additional parameters, they must also be read in. When GETSTRING and GETLINE are the input commands, the data to be read in are on the line immediately following the command. Therefore, the file name to be given GETSTRING and GETLINE will be whatever file the commands themselves are coming in on.

The syntax of the input for a command-driven tester for our string operations is summarized below.

Command lines for the command-driven testing program are as follows:

LENGTH, STRING
GETLINE, LINE   (* data are on next line *)
GETSTRING, STRING, CH, CH, ...   (* data are on next line *)
PRINT, STRING
SUBSTRING, STRING SUBSTR STARTPOS NUM
CONCAT, STRING1 STRING2
DELETE, STRING POS NUM
INSERT, STRING INSTRING POS
SEARCH, STRING SUBSTR
COMPARE, SUBSTR1 SUBSTR2
APPEND, STRING CH
STOP.

Each command is terminated by a comma, with the exception of STOP, which is terminated by a period. CH is a quote followed by a character followed by a quote. All other parameters are integer numbers. Each command line is terminated by EOLN.

The declaration section of the testing program might look like this:

```
CONST   MAXLENGTH = 80;

TYPE    STRING9 = PACKED ARRAY[1..9] OF CHAR;
        INDEXRANGE = 0..MAXLENGTH;
        STRINGTYPE = RECORD
                       LENGTH : INDEXRANGE;
                       CHARS : ARRAY[1..MAXLENGTH] OF CHAR
                     END;   (* record *)

VAR     STRINGS : ARRAY[1..10] OF STRINGTYPE;
        INDEX, POS, NUM : INDEXRANGE;
        CH : CHAR;
        COMTABLE : ARRAY[1..12] OF STRING9;
        DATA : TEXT;
        ERROR : BOOLEAN;
```

For example, the input

```
GETLINE, 1
GOOD MORNING AMERICA
```

would cause Procedure GETLINE to be called with STRINGS[1] as its second parameter (the first parameter would be the file from which the input is being read). Procedure GETLINE reads the next line of data and stores it in STRINGS[1].

Note that the heading of Procedure GETLINE is

```
PROCEDURE GETLINE (VAR DATA : TEXT; VAR LINE : STRINGTYPE;
                   VAR ERROR : BOOLEAN);
```

The invoking statement in the driver for this example is

```
GETLINE(DATA, STRINGS[1], ERROR);
```

Procedure GETLINE expects a string variable of STRINGTYPE as its second parameter. The driver passes it a row of an array variable, STRINGS. Is there any problem? No, each row in the array STRINGS is a string variable of STRINGTYPE. After GETLINE has been executed, the driver prints the contents of STRINGS[1].

The person who defined the test data would look at the printed output to see if 'GOOD MORNING AMERICA' was printed. If it was, the GET-LINE procedure worked correctly on this input string.

Testing using a command-driven tester is divided into two parts. The first part is to write and debug the command-driven tester. The second part is to create the input to the tester so that each procedure and function is thoroughly tested.

The first part requires a large investment of time when you first design the tester. If your tester is designed in good modular fashion, however, the second time you need to use it the time investment will be minimal. The basic structure of the program will remain the same; only the data, such as the contents of the command table, need to be changed. If you will be testing a second implementation of the same data type, nothing needs to be changed.

The second part—designing the test data—will vary from application to application. You have to make sure each boundary case, each error, and several general cases are tested. For example, to test the GETLINE operation thoroughly, we would have to do the following:

1. Input several strings whose lengths were between 1 and MAX-LENGTH. These are the general cases.
2. Input a string of length 0 and a string of length MAXLENGTH. These are the boundary cases.
3. Input a string of length greater than MAXLENGTH. This tests the error condition.

One of the programming assignments for this chapter asks you to finish the command-driven testing program for the string data type that we have outlined here. One of the exercises at the end of the chapter asks you to define the input data necessary to test several of these routines.

Exercises

1. Create a one-dimensional real array whose index type is 1..40.

2. Describe the Pascal accessing function of a one-dimensional array at the logical level.

Use the following declarations for 3 and 4:

```
TYPE NUMTYPE = ARRAY[1..5] OF INTEGER;
     LETTYPE = ARRAY['A'..'Z'] OF CHAR;
     FPTYPE = ARRAY[-4..6] OF REAL;
VAR NUM : NUMTYPE;
    LET : LETTYPE;
    FP : FPTYPE;
```

3. How much storage is set aside for
   - (a) NUM
   - (b) LET
   - (c) FP

4. If storage for NUM begins in location 0, and LET begins immediately after NUM, and FP begins immediately after LET, calculate the addresses of the following elements.

   NUM[1]
   NUM[3]
   NUM[5]
   LET['A']
   LET['N']
   LET['Z']
   FP[−4]
   FP[0]
   FP[6]

5. Create a two-dimensional array where the index type of the first dimension is 1..10, the index type of the second dimension is 'A'..'Z', and the component type is CHAR.

6. Create a two-dimensional array where the index type is 1..10, and the component type is an array whose index type is 'A'..'Z' and component type is CHAR.

7. Define the Pascal accessing function to a two-dimensional array at the logical level.

Use the following declarations for 8 and 9:

```
TYPE VALUTYPE = ARRAY[1..5, 1..6] OF INTEGER;
     TABLETYPE = ARRAY[1..3, -2..0] OF INTEGER;
     BOXTYPE = ARRAY['A'..'Z', 1..3] OF CHAR;
VAR VALU : VALUTYPE;
    TABLE : TABLETYPE;
    BOX : BOXTYPE;
```

8. How much storage is set aside for each of the following?

(a) VALU

(b) TABLE

(c) BOX

9. If the three arrays are assigned consecutively beginning at location 1000, calculate the addresses of the following elements (row major order).

VALU[1,1]
VALU[5,2]
VALU[5,6]
TABLE[1,−2]
TABLE[2,1]
TABLE[3,0]
BOX['A',1]
BOX['Z',2]
BOX['N',3]

10. Define a record at the logical level.

11. Define the Pascal accessing function to a record at the logical level.

Use the following declarations for 12, 13, and 14.

```
TYPE PEOPLE = RECORD
                NAME : ARRAY[1..20] OF CHAR;
                BDATE : INTEGER;
                AGE : INTEGER;
                ADDRESS : ARRAY[1..15] OF CHAR
              END; (* record *)
VAR PERSON : PEOPLE;
```

12. How much storage does each field require?

NAME
BDATE
AGE
ADDRESS

13. If PERSON is assigned beginning at location 50, calculate the addresses of the following elements.

PERSON.NAME
PERSON.BDATE
PERSON.ADDRESS
PERSON.AGE

14. If CROWD is an array of ten PEOPLE beginning at location 10, calculate the addresses of the following elements:

CROWD[1].NAME
CROWD[1].NAME[1]
CROWD[5].BDATE
CROWD[4].AGE
CROWD[10].ADDRESS[6]
CROWD[1].NAME[20]

15. Give the general formula for accessing an element in a two-dimensional array stored in column-major order.

16. Define a three-dimensional array at the logical level.

17. Give the general formula for accessing an element in a three-dimensional array.

18. Design the input data that will thoroughly test procedures SEARCH and SUBSTRING.

Pre-Test

1. Which of the following formulas is used to access an element LIST [I], where BASE is the address associated with the array LIST [1..100]?

    (a) BASE + I

    (b) BASE − I

    (c) BASE + I − 1

2. Name four data structures.

3. It is the responsibility of the person writing the code to modify specifications as necessary.   T   F

4. Limiting communication within a program is called _____.

5. Pascal stores arrays in _____ order, while FORTRAN uses _____ ordering.

6. CASE selectors must be of _____ type.

7. Pascal has the error checking built into the accessing functions.   T   F

8. At which level do you picture the organization and specify the general accessing procedures and functions—abstract, usage, or implementation?

9. Define *data structure*.

10. List the three distinct ways of looking at a data structure.

11. The formula that gives the Ith position in a one-dimensional array, each of whose elements is of size N, is _____.

12. Define a two-dimensional array using either of the two methods from the text.

13. Records, a built-in data type, are made up of a finite collection of _____ that are accessed by means of _____.

Use the following declarations for problems 14 and 15:

```
TYPE NUMTYPE  = ARRAY[1..6] OF INTEGER;
     LETTYPE  = ARRAY['A'..'F'] OF CHAR;
     REALTYPE = ARRAY[1..4, 1..3] OF REAL;
VAR  NUMBER   : NUMTYPE;
     LETTER   : LETTYPE;
     FPNUMBER : REALTYPE;
```

14. How much storage is set aside for

    (a) NUMBER

(b) LETTER

(c) FPNUMBER

15. If NUMBER begins at location 100, and LETTER and FPNUMBER immediately follow, calculate the addresses of the following elements:

(a) NUMBER[1]

(b) NUMBER[6]

(c) LETTER['D']

(d) FPNUMBER[1,1]

(e) FPNUMBER[2,2]

(f) FPNUMBER[4,3]

Use the following declarations for problems 16 and 17:

```
TYPE CARTYPE = RECORD
                    MAKE : ARRAY[1..20] OF CHAR;
                    MODEL : INTEGER;
                    COST : REAL;
                    PRICE : REAL
               END; (* record *)
VAR CAR : CARTYPE;
```

16. How much storage does each field require?

(a) MAKE

(b) MODEL

(c) COST

(d) PRICE

17. If MAKE is stored beginning at location 100, calculate the addresses of the following elements:

(a) CAR.MAKE

(b) CAR.MAKE[4]

(c) CAR.MODEL

(d) CAR.PRICE

Stacks

3

Goals

To be able to hand-simulate stack operations at the logical level.

To be able to hand-simulate the effect of stack operations on a particular implementation of a stack.

To be able to encode the basic stack operations given the implementation specifications.

To be able to determine when a stack is an appropriate data structure for a specific problem.

To be able to code the solution to a problem for which a stack is an appropriate data structure.

USER-DEFINED DATA STRUCTURES

In this chapter we will begin discussing data structures that are not built into programming languages like Pascal, but have to be created by the programmer in each program before they can be used. We will discuss the different structures at several levels, just as we discussed the Pascal array and record in Chapter 2. At one level, we will *define* the structures logically: What do they "look" like, and what are the logical operations on them? At the next level, we will *build* one or more possible implementations of the data structures, using Pascal declarations, and write subprograms to develop the accessing functions and other useful operations. At a third level, we will *use* the structures in various application examples.

Remember that we want to maintain walls between the different levels. Why is this important? First, as we saw in Chapter 1, this separation simplifies the design process, allowing us to put off deciding the implementation details as long as possible. This information hiding permits us to concentrate on the overall design of the data structure, without getting mired in details, in the top levels of program design.

Second, if we separate the procedures that use a data structure from the utility procedures and functions that implement it, we are free to change the implementation level without substantial modification of the higher levels of the program, perhaps with only a change in the declarations. This *encapsulation* of data structures makes our programs more easily modifiable.

DATA ENCAPSULATION

Separation of the representation of data from the applications that use the data at a logical level.

A third advantage of separating the implementation of data structures from their use is *portability*. If we want to use the same data structure in a different program, we can just lift out its implementation procedures and functions. We may be using the data structure for a completely different application, but the basic accessing functions and operations will remain the same.

Let's illustrate these important concepts with a simple data structure called the *stack*.

WHAT IS A STACK?

Consider the illustrations in Figure 3-1. Although the various pictures are very different, each illustrates a common concept: the stack.

> **STACK**
>
> A data structure in which elements are added and removed from only one end; a "last in, first out" (LIFO) structure.

At the logical level, a stack is an ordered group of elements. The removal of elements from the stack and the addition of new elements to it can take place only at the top of the stack. For instance, if your favorite blue shirt is in the stack of shirts underneath your ugly old red shirt, you must first remove the red shirt (the top element) from the stack. Only then can you remove the desired blue shirt, which is now the top element in the stack. The red shirt may then be replaced on the top of the stack or thrown away.

At any time, given any two elements in a stack, one element is higher than the other; that is, one is closer to the top of the stack. (The red shirt was higher in the stack than the blue shirt.) In this sense, the stack is an ordered group of items. Since the elements in a stack may constantly change, it is considered a dynamic structure.

Because items are added and removed from the top of the stack, the last element added is the first to be removed. There is a handy mnemonic to

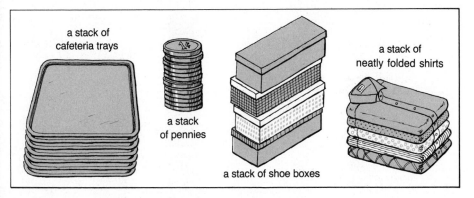

Figure 3-1. Real-Life Stacks

remember this rule of stack behavior: A stack is an LIFO (last in, first out) list.

To summarize, what is the accessing function for a stack? We retrieve elements only from the top of the stack. Assignment of new elements to the stack is also through the top.

OPERATIONS ON STACKS

You need to be familiar with a number of operations in order to use a stack. You must be able to create or clear a stack; that is, to initialize it to its empty state. (An empty stack is one that contains no elements.) As mentioned before, a stack is a dynamic structure, changing first when new elements are added to the top of the stack (called *pushing* an element onto the stack) and second when its top element is removed (called *popping* the stack). You must also be able to check whether a stack is empty before you attempt to pop it. Furthermore, although as a logical data structure a stack is never full, for a particular implementation you may need to test whether the stack is full before you try to push another element onto it.

For a moment, let's envision a stack as a stack of building blocks, and see how the basic PUSH and POP operations affect it.

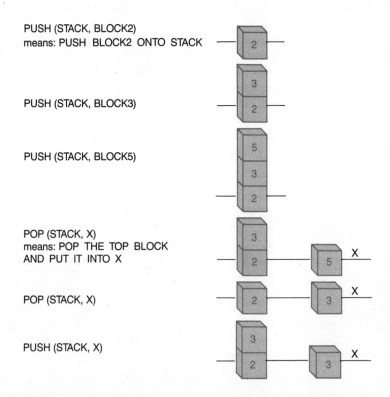

Let's look at an example of how these operations might be used in a program. Suppose that at some point in a program, you need to read in a string of characters, followed by a period, followed by the same characters in reverse order. You want to check whether the reversals are correct, so you write a function that will return TRUE if a string has been properly reversed, and FALSE otherwise. For example,

ABCD.DCBA returns TRUE

ABCD.ABCD returns FALSE

The algorithm for Function REVERSE is as follows.

```
clear the stack
read the first character
WHILE the character is not '.' DO
    push the character onto the stack
    read the next character
REVERSE ← TRUE
WHILE more elements in the stack DO
    read a character
    pop a character from the stack
    compare characters
        IF they are not the same
            THEN REVERSE ← FALSE
```

This algorithm codes easily into Function REVERSE, calling Procedures PUSH(STACK, ELEMENT), POP(STACK, ELEMENT), and CLEARSTACK(STACK) and Function EMPTYSTACK(STACK).

```
FUNCTION REVERSE : BOOLEAN;

   (* Returns true if the character string preceding the    *)
   (* period is the reverse of the string following the     *)
   (* period; false otherwise. Assumes the presence of the  *)
   (* period in the input and the same number of letters    *)
   (* preceding and following the period.                   *)

VAR    CH1, CH2 : CHAR;
       STACK    : STACKTYPE;

BEGIN  (* reverse *)
   CLEARSTACK(STACK);                         (* Set stack to empty. *)

   (* Read and PUSH all the characters up to the period. *)
   READ(CH1);
   WHILE CH1 <> '.' DO
     BEGIN
       PUSH(STACK, CH1);
       READ(CH1)
     END;   (* while *)
```

```
(* Read rest of string and compare characters to those in the stack. *)
  REVERSE := TRUE;
  WHILE NOT EMPTYSTACK(STACK) DO
    BEGIN
      READ(CH2);
      POP(STACK, CH1);
      IF CH1 <> CH2
        THEN REVERSE := FALSE
    END
END;  (* reverse *)
```

Note that we haven't yet considered how the stack will be implemented. The details of the implementation are hidden somewhere in the code of the Procedures PUSH, POP, and CLEARSTACK and the Function EMPTY-STACK. This observation illustrates *information hiding.* You don't need to know how the stack has been implemented to be able to use the PUSH and POP routines.

THE IMPLEMENTATION OF A STACK AS AN ARRAY

We must now consider the implementation of the stack data structure. PUSH and POP are not, like READ and WRITE, procedures that are magically available to the Pascal programmer. We will need to write them before we can call them in our program.

Since all the elements of the stack are of the same type, an array seems like a reasonable structure to contain a stack. We can place the elements in sequential slots in the array: the first element in the first array position, the second in the next array position, and so on. The floating "high-water mark" will be the top element.

Declarations for the Array Representation

We will need to decide the maximum size of our stack so that we can declare the array. Let's plan to use a stack of a maximum of 100 integer elements; we therefore declare

```
CONST MAXSTACK = 100;
TYPE  STACKTYPE = ARRAY[1..MAXSTACK] OF INTEGER;
VAR   STACK : STACKTYPE;
```

We need one more thing before we can implement our stack as an array. We need to know how to find the top element when we want to POP, and where to put our new element when we want to PUSH. Remember: Though we know that we can access any element of an array directly, we have agreed to the convention "last in, first out" for a stack. We will access the stack only through the top, not through the bottom or the middle. Recognizing this distinction from the start is important: Even though the implementation of the stack may be a random-access structure like an array, the stack itself as a logical entity is not randomly accessed.

There are a number of ways to keep track of the top position. We could have an integer variable TOP that would indicate the index of the current top position. However, this scheme would require us to pass TOP as an additional parameter to Procedures PUSH and POP. It would be better to find a way to bind both the elements and the top indicator into a single entity, STACK. This can be accomplished by extending the array to include one more position, STACK[0], in which we will store the index of the current top element. So we modify our declarations as follows:

```
CONST MAXSTACK = 100;
TYPE  STACKTYPE = ARRAY[0..MAXSTACK] OF INTEGER;
VAR   STACK : STACKTYPE;
```

Stack Operations with an Array Implementation

Now we can begin to write functions and procedures to implement our stack operations. Let's first consider how we will clear the stack. It isn't necessary to zero out the whole array. We only need to indicate that the stack is empty. This task is easily accomplished by setting STACK[0] (which holds the index of the top element) to 0, as in the following stack:

[0] [1] [2] [3] [4] [5] . . . [98] [99] [100]

It doesn't matter how much garbage is in the array. If the indicator of the top position says that the stack is empty, we cannot access any elements.

So our Procedure CLEARSTACK is short and simple:

```
PROCEDURE CLEARSTACK (VAR STACK : STACKTYPE);
    (* Initializes a stack to empty. *)

BEGIN   (* clearstack *)
    STACK[0] := 0
END;    (* clearstack *)
```

From this discussion, it is obvious that Functions EMPTYSTACK and FULLSTACK will also be very easy to write. Function EMPTYSTACK will return TRUE if the stack is empty, and return FALSE otherwise. Since we just cleared a stack to its empty state by setting its top indicator (STACK[0], in this case) to 0, we can test for EMPTYSTACK by checking to see if it is still 0.

```
FUNCTION EMPTYSTACK (STACK : STACKTYPE) : BOOLEAN;
   (* Returns true if stack is empty, false otherwise. *)

BEGIN   (* emptystack *)
   EMPTYSTACK := STACK[0] = 0
END;     (* emptystack *)
```

Note that the statement EMPTYSTACK := STACK[0] = 0 is functionally equivalent to the branching statement

```
IF STACK[0] = 0
   THEN EMPTYSTACK := TRUE
   ELSE EMPTYSTACK := FALSE
```

The expression STACK[0] = 0 evaluates to TRUE or FALSE, which can then be assigned to the Boolean variable EMPTYSTACK.

Similarly, we can test for a full stack by comparing our top indicator to MAXSTACK:

```
FUNCTION FULLSTACK (STACK : STACKTYPE) : BOOLEAN;
   (* Returns true if the stack is full, false otherwise. *)

BEGIN   (* fullstack *)
   FULLSTACK := STACK[0] = MAXSTACK
END;     (* fullstack *)
```

We said before that the stack as an abstract data structure cannot be full. Why then are we coding a function to test for a full stack? This function is made necessary by our choice of implementation, since the array has fixed bounds.

To add, or PUSH, an element onto the stack is a two-step task:

---

increment top indicator
STACK[top indicator] ← new element

Using the declarations above, this operation may be coded as a procedure as follows:

```
PROCEDURE PUSH (VAR STACK : STACKTYPE;
                    NEWELEMENT : INTEGER);
   (* Adds NEWELEMENT to the top of STACK; *)
   (* assumes that the stack is not full.        *)

BEGIN   (* push *)
   STACK[0] := STACK[0] + 1;
   STACK[STACK[0]] := NEWELEMENT
END;     (* push *)
```

Let's illustrate the effect of a PUSH operation on a particular stack. We begin with the following:

3	15	25	35	contains garbage
[0]	[1]	[2]	[3]	[4] $\cdots$ [100]

We want to PUSH(STACK, 65). We need to increment our top indicator from 3 to 4, then put our new element, 65, in the fourth element place. The result is

4	15	25	35	65	contains garbage
[0]	[1]	[2]	[3]	[4]	[5] $\cdots$ [100]

To use this operation in a program, we must make sure that the stack is not already FULL before we call PUSH.

```
IF NOT FULLSTACK(STACK)
   THEN PUSH(STACK, 65);
```

If the stack is already full when we try to PUSH, the result is called stack *overflow*. Error checking for overflow may be handled in different ways. We could test for overflow inside our PUSH procedure, instead of in the calling program. We might add a Boolean variable, OVERFLOW, to the formal parameter list. The revised algorithm would be

```
IF stack is full
    THEN OVERFLOW ← TRUE
    ELSE OVERFLOW ← FALSE
        increment top indicator
        STACK[top indicator] ← new element
```

Which version of PUSH you decide to use may depend on the specifications—especially if the utility procedures are being written by different programmers, as often happens on a large program. Since the interface differs in the number of parameters, it is important to establish whose responsibility it is to check for overflow.

Try writing Procedure TESTANDPUSH yourself.

To remove, or POP, an element from the stack, we do virtually the reverse of our PUSH operation. The algorithm is

> POPPEDELEMENT ← STACK[top indicator]
> decrement top indicator

The code is short and simple:

```
PROCEDURE POP (VAR STACK : STACKTYPE;
               VAR POPPEDELEMENT : INTEGER);
   (* Removes the top element from STACK and returns it in    *)
   (* POPPEDELEMENT; assumes that the stack is not empty. *)

BEGIN   (* pop *)
   POPPEDELEMENT := STACK[STACK[0]];
   STACK[0] := STACK[0] - 1
END;    (* pop *)
```

To illustrate the POP operation we start with the following stack:

3	16	42	38	garbage here
[0]	[1]	[2]	[3]	[4] . . . [100]

We want to POP the stack. The value in STACK[0] tells us that the top element is stored in STACK[3]. First the top element is popped from STACK[3]. Then the top indicator (STACK[0]) is decremented, giving us the following:

2	16	42	38	more garbage here
[0]	[1]	[2]	[3]	[4] . . . [100]

Note that after popping, 38 is still stored in the third element place in the array, but we cannot access it through our stack. The stack only contains two elements.

To execute the POP operation illustrated above, we must first test for an empty stack, and then call our POP procedure:

```
IF NOT EMPTYSTACK(STACK)
   THEN POP(STACK, X)
```

When the stack is empty and we try to POP it, the resulting condition is called stack *underflow*. Obviously, the test for underflow could also be written into the POP operation. The algorithm of POP would be modified slightly, to return a Boolean variable, UNDERFLOW, in addition to the popped element.

```
IF stack is empty
    THEN UNDERFLOW ← TRUE
    ELSE UNDERFLOW ← FALSE
            popped element ← STACK[top indicator]
            decrement top indicator
```

Try writing Procedure TESTANDPOP yourself.

You can imagine other operations that might be written for stacks. For example, you might want to find out the value of the top element, without changing the stack. To implement this operation, an integer function STACKTOP might be written. In effect, STACKTOP is simply a POP followed by a PUSH, but it can be written more directly than by calling these two procedures.

```
FUNCTION STACKTOP (STACK : STACKTYPE) : INTEGER;
    (* Returns the value of the top element of STACK. *)

BEGIN  (* stacktop *)
    STACKTOP := STACK[STACK[0]]
END;    (* stacktop *)
```

This operation is similar to POP, but it doesn't change the stack in any way. The top indicator is not modified. This function could also be written with an internal test for underflow.

A MORE GENERAL IMPLEMENTATION

Note that our implementation of a stack as an array with the top indicator in the first position takes advantage of the fact that the elements in the stack are of the same type (integer) as the top indicator. If the elements in the stack are to be of another type (real numbers, for instance), another method of keeping track of the top of the stack must be used. One such method is to make STACKTYPE a record with two fields: ELEMENTS (an array of elements) and TOP (an integer index to the array).

```
TYPE STACKTYPE = RECORD
                    ELEMENTS : ARRAY[1..MAXSTACK] OF REAL;
                    TOP : 0..MAXSTACK
                 END;    (* record *)
```

As we indicated earlier, changing the implementation of the stack will only affect the actual stack operation procedures and functions. The user, writing program segments that call these operations, will not need to be concerned about the change in implementation. Calls to Procedures PUSH(STACK, X) and POP(STACK, Y) are independent of the particular implementation. If we later decide to use the stack operations for keeping a stack of character, rather than real, elements, we need to change the ELEMENTS field in the declarations to

```
ELEMENTS : ARRAY[1..MAXSTACK] OF CHAR;
```

We will also have to change the headers of all the stack operation procedures and functions that specify the element type in the parameters. For instance,

```
PROCEDURE PUSH (VAR STACK : STACKTYPE;
                NEWELEMENT : REAL);
```

will need to be changed to

```
PROCEDURE PUSH (VAR STACK : STACKTYPE;
                NEWELEMENT : CHAR);
```

POP and STACKTOP will have to be modified in the same way. We can get around having to make these trivial changes throughout the program by adding a type ELTYPE (element type) in our declarations.

```
TYPE ELTYPE = CHAR;   (* or INTEGER or REAL or whatever *)
     STACKTYPE = RECORD
                    ELEMENTS : ARRAY[1..MAXSTACK] OF ELTYPE;
                    TOP : 0..MAXSTACK
                 END;   (* record *)
```

All of the procedure and function headings will use the type ELTYPE for stack elements; for example,

```
PROCEDURE PUSH (VAR STACK : STACKTYPE;
                NEWELEMENT : ELTYPE);
```

Now a change in element type will result in changes only to the declarations of the program. This feature makes our program more easily modifiable.

A stack represented with these declarations might have the following utility routines:

```
PROCEDURE CLEARSTACK (VAR STACK : STACKTYPE);
  (* Initializes stack to empty. *)

BEGIN   (* clearstack *)
  STACK.TOP := 0
END;    (* clearstack *)

(* ************************************************ )

FUNCTION EMPTYSTACK (STACK : STACKTYPE) : BOOLEAN;
  (* Returns true if the STACK is empty, false otherwise. *)

BEGIN   (* emptystack *)
  EMPTYSTACK := STACK.TOP = 0
END;    (* emptystack *)

(* ************************************************ )

FUNCTION FULLSTACK (STACK : STACKTYPE) : BOOLEAN;
  (* Returns true if the stack is full; false otherwise. *)

BEGIN   (* fullstack *)
  FULLSTACK := STACK.TOP = MAXSTACK;
END;    (* fullstack *)

(* ************************************************ )

PROCEDURE PUSH (VAR STACK : STACKTYPE;
                     NEWELEMENT : ELTYPE);
  (* Adds NEWELEMENT to the top of the stack; *)
  (* assumes that stack is not full.          *)

BEGIN   (* push *)
  STACK.TOP := STACK.TOP + 1;
  STACK.ELEMENTS[STACK.TOP] := NEWELEMENT
END;    (* push *)

(* ************************************************ )

PROCEDURE POP (VAR STACK : STACKTYPE;
                   VAR POPPEDELEMENT : ELTYPE);
  (* Removes the top element from the stack and returns it in *)
  (* POPPEDELEMENT. Assumes that STACK is not empty. *)

BEGIN   (* pop *)
  POPPEDELEMENT := STACK.ELEMENTS[STACK.TOP];
  STACK.TOP := STACK.TOP - 1
END;    (* pop *)
```

THE APPLICATION LEVEL

Our simple example in Function REVERSE hints at the type of application that uses a stack. A stack is the appropriate data structure when information must be saved and then later retrieved in reverse order. A situation that may require you to backtrack to some earlier position may be a good occasion to use a stack. For instance, in solving a maze, you may end up against a wall and need to backtrack to another exit. If you used a stack to save the alternative paths as you passed them, you could retrace your route to an earlier position. We will work through a sample maze problem at the end of this chapter.

Have you ever wondered how your program knew where to continue executing when it got to the end of a procedure or function? Many systems use a stack to keep track of the return addresses, parameter values or addresses, and other information used by subprograms. For instance, when Procedure A is called, its calling information is pushed onto the run-time stack. Then, when its nested Procedure B is called from A, B's calling information is pushed onto the top of the stack. B then calls Procedure C, and C's calling information is pushed onto the stack. When C finishes executing, the stack is popped to retrieve the information needed to return to Procedure B. Then B finishes executing, and its return address, and so forth, is popped from the stack. Finally, Procedure A completes, and the stack is popped again to get back to the main program. Since the order of procedure calls within a program is dynamic, the run-time stack that stores this data can grow and shrink throughout execution, according to the level of subprogram nesting. We will return to this topic later when we discuss recursion.

Stacks are also used extensively in the evaluation of arithmetic expressions. We will consider this application further in one of the examples that follow.

Summary

We have defined a stack at the logical level as an abstract data type and discussed two implementations that use arrays to contain the stack elements. The first used an extra slot in the array to store the index of the top element of a stack of integers. The second implementation used a record to separate the representations of the top indicator and the elements of the stack.

Which of these two implementations is better? Certainly the second one is more flexible, since it allows the type of the elements in the stack to be changed without affecting the code of the stack utility routines. This makes the utilities portable; they could be used in another program for a completely different purpose. The first implementation is rather rigid; we are limited to stacks whose elements are of the same type as the array index.

Overall, we would say that the second implementation is better. Note, however, that it uses a built-in data type, the record, that is not found in some programming languages (FORTRAN, for instance). In a FORTRAN program, you may very well see a stack represented within the top indicator in one of the array positions. Furthermore, we have not exhausted the possible stack implementations; in fact, we will discuss others later in this book.

The important point here is that by isolating the procedures and functions that operate on the implementation of the stack, we have encapsulated the data structure. No matter what implementation we select, we have kept the use of the data structure limited to the interfaces of a specified set of utility routines. A change in the implementation should not affect the user of the stack routines.

Can we enforce this encapsulation? That is, can we keep the user from accessing the middle element in the array that houses the stack? Unfortunately, Pascal does not have a mechanism to enforce data encapsulation. For now, we will have to depend on convention, an agreement that we will only manipulate the array that contains the stack through the set of stack utility routines.

■ APPLICATION: EXPRESSION EVALUATION

Data Structures in Use
- ■ STACKS

Software Techniques in Use
- ■ APPROACHES FOR EXPRESSION EVALUATION
- ■ DATA ENCAPSULATION AND INFORMATION HIDING
- ■ NEED FOR ERROR CHECKING

In grade school, you learned how to evaluate simple expressions that involve the basic binary operators: addition, subtraction, multiplication, and division. (These are called *binary* operators because they each operate on two operands.) It is easy to see how a child would solve the following problem:

$$X = 2$$
$$Y = 5$$
$$Z = X + Y$$
Solve for Z.

It is almost as easy to see how, given strings containing the three assignments, a computer program might evaluate the expression defining Z. First, it would save the values of X and Y; then it would add them to get the value of Z. (Of course, we would have to do a little parsing of the strings to get the values and then convert them from characters to integers, but this doesn't affect our basic approach.)

As expressions become more complicated, the pencil-and-paper solution requires a little more work. Given

$$X = 2$$
$$Y = 5$$
$$Z = (((Y - 1) / X) * (X + Y))$$
Solve for Z.

we see that there are a number of tasks to perform. First we solve for $Y - 1$, divide the result by X, and save this value. Then we evaluate $X + Y$ and save this value. Finally, we multiply the first saved value by the second to get the value of Z.

Designing a computer program to evaluate the expression is not so simple. There are a couple of decisions to make first. How do we know which part of the expression to evaluate first? And where do we save the intermediate values [like $(Y - 1) / X$] that contribute to the final result?

The first question is easy to answer if the expression to be evaluated is fully parenthesized (that is, if we do not depend on the relative precedence of the operators to tell us which part to evaluate first, but simply rely on the location of the parentheses). The innermost level of parentheses indicates which part of the expression must be evaluated first, and we work outward from there.

The second question, involving the storage of intermediate values, suggests that we must design an appropriate data structure for our solution. If we knew how many intermediate values would be produced, we could declare temporary variables to hold them (TEMP1, TEMP2, . . . TEMPN). But, obviously, the number of intermediate operands produced will vary from expression to expression. Luckily, we know of an ideal data structure for saving dynamically changing values for later processing—the stack. Let's consider how we can use a pair of stacks to evaluate the fully parenthesized expression

$$Z = (((Y - 1) / X) * (X + Y))$$

We will use one stack to store the operators and a second to store the operands. Assuming for now that the expression is fully and correctly parenthesized, we will ignore the left parentheses ("("). As we pass through the expression from left to right, we push each element onto the appropriate stack, until we come to a right parenthesis (")"). Figure 3-2 shows how the two stacks will look when we come to the first right parenthesis. At this point, we have reached the innermost level of parentheses (for this term, at least), and we can perform the first operation. Where are the two operands? They should be the last and next-to-last values pushed onto the operand stack. Where is the operator? It should be the top element on the operator stack. To evaluate the first intermediate operand, we pop the top two elements from the operand stack; these become OPERAND2 and OPERAND1, respectively. Then we pop the top element from the operator stack and perform the appropriate operation, $5 - 1$, producing the value 4. Note that $Y - 1 = 5 - 1 = 4$ is an intermediate step in the evaluation of the larger expression. The result of this step, 4, will be one of the operands in the next step, calculating $(Y - 1)/X$. Where do we put operands? That's right, on the operand stack, so we push 4 onto the operand stack.

$$X = 2$$
$$Y = 5$$
$$Z = (((Y - 1) / X) * (X + Y))$$

Figure 3-2.

Now we resume pushing operators and operands onto their respective stacks until we again come to a right parenthesis. Figure 3-3 shows the processing that occurs at this point. We pop OPERAND2 and OPERAND1 from the operand stack, pop the top element from the operator stack, and perform the operation, $4/2 = 2$. The result is pushed onto the operand stack, and we resume pushing elements onto the two stacks.

$$X = 2$$
$$Y = 5$$
$$Z = (((Y - 1) / X) * (X + Y))$$
$$\uparrow$$

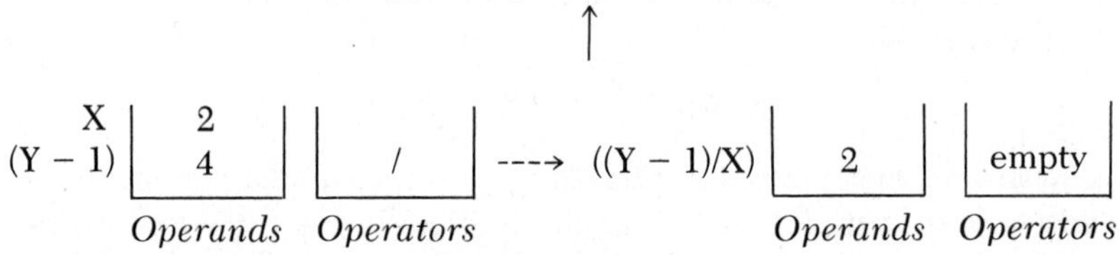

	X	2							((Y − 1)/X)	2		empty	
(Y − 1)		4				/	---→						

Operands   Operators   Operands   Operators

Figure 3-3.

Figure 3-4 shows the processing that occurs when we reach the next right parenthesis. This cycle is continued until we reach the end of the expression (Figure 3-5). At that point the operator stack should be empty, and the operand stack will contain only one value—the evaluated result of the whole expression.

Let's use this strategy to write a program for a very simple expression calculator.

$$X = 2$$
$$Y = 5$$
$$Z = (((Y - 1) / X) * (X + Y))$$
$$\uparrow$$

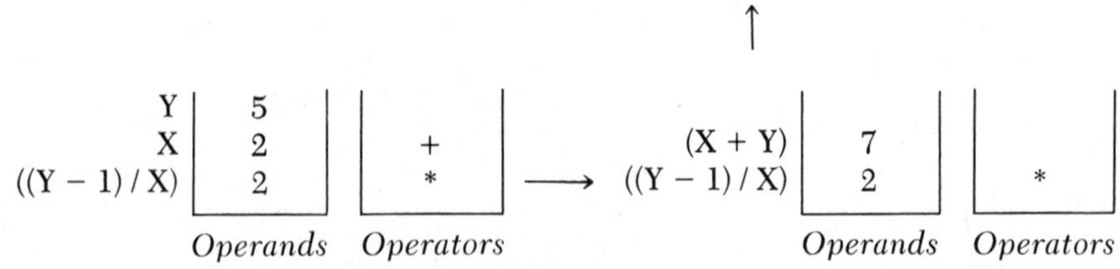

	Y	5							(X + Y)	7			
	X	2			+				((Y − 1) / X)	2			
((Y − 1) / X)		2			*		⟶					*	

Operands   Operators   Operands   Operators

Figure 3-4.

$$X = 2$$
$$Y = 5$$
$$Z = (((Y - 1) / X) * (X + Y))$$

(X + Y) ((Y − 1) / X)	7 2		*	⟶	(((Y − 1) / X) * (X + Y))	14		empty
Operands	*Operators*				*Operands*		*Operators*	

Figure 3-5.

Input: The input is a series of assignment statements, each in one of two possible forms:

⟨*varname*⟩ = ⟨*real number*⟩;

or

⟨*varname*⟩ : ⟨*expression*⟩;

where ⟨*varname*⟩ consists of a single letter, ⟨*real number*⟩ is a real number literal (like 3.5), and ⟨*expression*⟩ is a string representing a fully and correctly parenthesized expression made up of operators (the characters +, −, *, and /) and varnames. (Note that literal constants cannot be used in an expression in our simple example, only varnames like X and Y.)

At least one blank (maybe more) will separate each element of an assignment statement. Each assignment will terminate with a semicolon. Note that assignments of literal values to *varname* are indicated by the = operator, while assignments of expressions are indicated by a colon. We are using two different assignment operators to simplify the parsing (breaking into component parts) of the statement. There will be exactly one assignment statement per line, and the last line will contain only the character 0. Examples of valid assignment statements are

X = 5.0 ;
Y = 92.34 ;
Z : ((X − Y) * (X + Y)) ;

Examples of invalid assignment statements are

A = X ;   (Operator must assign literal constant.)
B = (X + Y) ;   (Should be : operator.)
C : X + Y ;   (Requires parentheses.)

Output: After each assignment statement, print

⟨*varname*⟩ IS ⟨*value*⟩

where ⟨*value*⟩ is the literal constant or the result of evaluating the expression, as appropriate. Use the previously assigned values of any variables in the expression (these will need to be stored somewhere).

When 0 is reached, print "GOODBYE. COME BACK SOON."

Assumptions: For the sake of simplicity, we will allow the following assumptions:

1. The expressions will be fully and correctly parenthesized.
2. The assignment statements will be valid forms.
3. The operations in expressions will be valid at run time. This means that we will not try to divide by 0. We will also assume that any varname that has not been defined before it is used as a term in an expression will be given the value of 0.0.

We have put these tremendous limitations on the input in order to concentrate on the processing of the expression evaluation using stacks. Since we will test and use this expression evaluator as an interactive tool (i.e., all the input will come from the keyboard), these assumptions are pretty unreasonable. We will come back to this point later. For now we will allow these restrictions so that we can develop the algorithms of interest to a stack user.

Data Structures: We have already seen that we will need to use a pair of stacks to hold intermediate values of operands and operators. Let's assume that someone was nice enough to prepare all the necessary stack utilities for our use. (We may not need to use all of them.)

For the operand stack:

```
PROCEDURE CLEARREAL (VAR STACK : REALSTACK);
   (* Sets stack of real numbers to empty state. *)

PROCEDURE PUSHREAL   (VAR STACK : REALSTACK;
                          ELEMENT : REAL);
   (* Adds ELEMENT to the top of the stack of real numbers. *)

PROCEDURE POPREAL    (VAR STACK : REALSTACK;
                          VAR ELEMENT : REAL);
   (* Removes the top element from a stack of real numbers; returns it in ELEMENT. *)

FUNCTION EMPTYREAL   (STACK : REALSTACK) : BOOLEAN;
   (* Returns TRUE if the stack of real numbers is empty, FALSE otherwise. *)

FUNCTION FULLREAL    (STACK : REALSTACK) : BOOLEAN;
   (* Returns TRUE if the stack of real numbers is full, FALSE otherwise. *)
```

For the operator stack:

```
PROCEDURE CLEARCHAR (VAR STACK : CHARSTACK);
    (* Sets stack of characters to empty state. *)

PROCEDURE PUSHCHAR   (VAR STACK : CHARSTACK;
                      ELEMENT : CHAR);
    (* Adds ELEMENT to the top of the stack of characters. *)

PROCEDURE POPCHAR    (VAR STACK : CHARSTACK;
                      VAR ELEMENT : CHAR);
    (* Removes the top element from a stack of characters and returns it in ELEMENT. *)

FUNCTION EMPTYCHAR   (STACK : CHARSTACK) : BOOLEAN;
    (* Returns TRUE if the stack of characters is empty, FALSE otherwise. *)

FUNCTION FULLCHAR    (STACK : CHARSTACK) : BOOLEAN;
    (* Returns TRUE if the stack of characters is full, FALSE otherwise. *)
```

We will need one other data structure for the processing of this program. We need a place to store the values assigned to various varnames, since these values will be required in the subsequent evaluation of expressions that use them. For our simple example, the range of varnames is limited to the characters of the alphabet, so we can use the varname itself as an index to an array of real values:

```
VALUES : ARRAY['A'..'Z'] OF REAL
```

Each time we want to make an assignment to a particular varname, we will put the value into VALUES[VARNAME].

Top-Down Design:

MAIN   Level 0

```
INITIALIZE
WHILE FLAG not stop DO
    PROCESSLINE
print final message
```

INITIALIZE will set the data structures to their starting values and set FLAG to some value other than stop.

INITIALIZE   Level 1

> set both stacks to empty
> INITVALUES — sets value of all varnames to 0.0
> FLAG ← ok

PROCESSLINE will process one line of input, a single calculator statement, unless the stop marker is encountered.

PROCESSLINE   Level 1

> GETVARNAME
> IF VARNAME is stop marker ('0')
>   THEN FLAG ← stop
>   ELSE GETVALUE

INITVALUES   Level 2

> FOR INDEX := 'A' TO 'Z' DO
>   VALUES[INDEX] ← 0.0

GETVARNAME   Level 2

> get first nonblank character

GETVALUE finds the value of the varname read in module PROCESSLINE, saves it in the list of values, and prints a message showing the result of the assignment.

GETVALUE   Level 2

> GETCHAR (ASSIGN) — gets assignment operator ('=' or ':')
> IF ASSIGN is '='
>   THEN READ real value
>   ELSE (* assign is ':' *)
>   EVALUATE expression to real value
> SAVEVALUE
> print assignment message
> go to next line (READLN)

GETVALUE has three lower level modules:

GETCHAR   Level 3

```
(returns first nonblank character)
REPEAT
    READ character
UNTIL character is not a blank
```

SAVEVALUE   Level 3

```
VALUES[VARNAME] ← value to be saved
```

EVALUATE   Level 3

```
GETCHAR (TOKEN)
WHILE TOKEN is not ENDEXPRESS (';') DO
    CASE TOKEN is
        'A'..'Z' : RETRIEVE value of VARNAME
                   push retrieved value onto stack of operands
        '+', '−',
        '*', '/'  : push TOKEN onto stack of operators
        '('       : do nothing
        ')'       : PERFORM appropriate operation
    END CASE
    GETCHAR (TOKEN)
pop operands stack to get final value of expression
```

EVALUATE requires two lower-level modules. RETRIEVE returns the current value of VARNAME.

RETRIEVE   Level 4

```
retrieved value ← VALUES[VARNAME]
```

PERFORM gets the next two operands and the next operator from their respective stacks, performs the indicated operation, and pushes the result back onto the operand stack.

PERFORM   **Level 4**

```
pop operands stack to get OPERAND2
pop operands stack to get OPERAND1
pop operator stack to get TOKEN
CASE TOKEN is
    '+' : NEWVALUE ← OPERAND1 + OPERAND2
    '−' : NEWVALUE ← OPERAND1 − OPERAND2
    '*' : NEWVALUE ← OPERAND1 * OPERAND2
    '/' : NEWVALUE ← OPERAND1 / OPERAND2
END CASE
push NEWVALUE onto operand stack
```

There are a couple of points worth noting in this top-down design. You may have wondered why we pushed the details of SAVEVALUE and RE-TRIEVE to lower levels in the design, even though they each "expanded" to only a single line. Why didn't we just put that line directly into the design? Note that these two tasks involve the manipulation of the array VALUES, the data structure in which we are storing the designated or calculated values of VARNAME. By separating this function into a lower level, we have tried to encapsulate the data structure. Why should we bother to do this, since we already decided how to implement this list of values? We are trying to make the design more easily modifiable. What happens if we decide to allow VARNAME to be a string of characters, instead of a single character? We cannot index the array of values by a string, and thus we will have to change the whole implementation of this list. By moving the part of the design that touches this data structure into a lower level, we can try to limit the changes that would result from a modification to the program.

We have accomplished this same flexibility by manipulating the various stacks through the stack utilities listed above. Do you know from the design how the stack of operators or the stack of operands has been implemented?

The algorithm and data structures are now sufficiently defined to allow us to write our calculator program. Because of the brevity of the top level, we have combined the Level 0 and Level 1 designs into the main program.

```
PROGRAM CALCULATOR (INPUT, OUTPUT);
(* Repeat specifications here. *)

CONST STOPMARKER = '0';              (* Indicates the end of input. *)
      ENDEXPRESS = ';';         (* Indicates the end of an expression. *)
      MAXSTACK   = 10;

TYPE  VALUELIST  = ARRAY['A'..'Z'] OF REAL;
      FLAGTYPE   = (OK, STOP);
      VARTYPE    = CHAR;

      REALSTACK  = RECORD
                      TOP : INTEGER;
                      ELEMENTS : ARRAY[1..MAXSTACK] OF REAL
                   END;  (* record *)

      CHARSTACK  = RECORD
                      TOP : INTEGER;
                      ELEMENTS : ARRAY[1..MAXSTACK] OF CHAR
                   END;  (* record *)

VAR   OPERANDS  : REALSTACK;              (* stack of operands *)
      OPERATORS : CHARSTACK;              (* stack of operators *)
      VALUES    : VALUELIST;         (* values of previously *)
                                     (* defined varnames *)

      FLAG      : FLAGTYPE;
      VARNAME   : VARTYPE;
```

(* **)

```
PROCEDURE CLEARREAL (VAR STACK : REALSTACK);
(* Sets stack of real numbers to empty state. *)

BEGIN   (* clearreal *)

   STACK.TOP := 0

END;   (* clearreal *)
```

(* **)

```
PROCEDURE PUSHREAL (VAR STACK: REALSTACK; ELEMENT: REAL);
(* Adds ELEMENT to the top of the stack of real numbers. *)

BEGIN  (* pushreal *)

  STACK.TOP := STACK.TOP + 1;
  STACK.ELEMENTS[STACK.TOP] := ELEMENT

END;  (* pushreal *)
```

(**)

```
PROCEDURE POPREAL (VAR STACK: REALSTACK;
                   VAR ELEMENT : REAL);
(* Remove the top element from a stack of real numbers; returns it in ELEMENT. *)

BEGIN  (* popreal *)

  ELEMENT := STACK.ELEMENTS[STACK.TOP];
  STACK.TOP := STACK.TOP - 1

END;    (* popreal *)
```

(**)

```
PROCEDURE CLEARCHAR (VAR STACK : CHARSTACK);
(* Sets stack of characters to empty state. *)

BEGIN  (* clearchar *)

  STACK.TOP := 0

END;  (* clearchar *)
```

(**)

```
PROCEDURE PUSHCAR (VAR STACK: CHARSTACK; ELEMENT : CHAR);
(* Adds ELEMENT to the top of the stack of characters. *)

BEGIN

  STACK.TOP := STACK.TOP + 1;
  STACK.ELEMENTS[STACK.TOP] := ELEMENT

END;
```

(***)

```
PROCEDURE POPCHAR (VAR STACK: CHARSTACK;
                   VAR ELEMENT : CHAR);
(* Removes the top element from a stack of characters; returns it in ELEMENT. *)

BEGIN    (* popchar *)

  ELEMENT := STACK.ELEMENTS[STACK.TOP];
  STACK.TOP := STACK.TOP - 1

END;     (* popchar *)
```

(***)

```
PROCEDURE GETVARNAME (VAR VARNAME : VARTYPE);
(* Skips leading blanks and returns VARNAME. *)

BEGIN    (* getvarname *)
  REPEAT
    READ(VARNAME)
  UNTIL VARNAME <> ' '
END;     (* getvarname *)
```

(***)

```
PROCEDURE GETCHAR (VAR CH : CHAR);
(* Returns first nonblank character. *)

BEGIN   (* getchar *)
  REPEAT
    READ(CH)
  UNTIL CH <> ' '   (* blank *)
END;   (* getchar *)
```

```
(******************************************************)
```

```
PROCEDURE INITVALUES (VAR VALUES : VALUELIST);
(* Initializes the value of every varname in list to zero. *)

VAR   INDEX : CHAR;

BEGIN   (* initvalues *)
  FOR INDEX := 'A' TO 'Z' DO
    VALUES[INDEX] := 0.0
END;   (* initvalues *)
```

```
(******************************************************)
```

```
PROCEDURE SAVEVALUE (NEWVALUE : REAL;
                     VARNAME  : VARTYPE;
                 VAR VALUES   : VALUELIST);
(* Saves the new value of VARNAME in the VALUES list. *)

BEGIN   (* savevalue *)
  VALUES[VARNAME] := NEWVALUE
END;   (* savevalue *)
```

```
(******************************************************)
```

```
PROCEDURE RETRIEVE (TOKEN  : VARTYPE;
                    VALUES : VALUELIST;
                VAR VAL    : REAL);
(* Returns the REAL value of TOKEN from the VALUES list. *)

BEGIN   (* retrieve *)
  VAL := VALUES[TOKEN]
END;   (* retrieve *)
```

```
(******************************************************)
```

```
PROCEDURE PERFORM;
(* Performs the next operation in the expression evaluation, and *)
(* leaves the result at the top of the operands stack.          *)

VAR     OP1, OP2 : REAL;
        TOKEN    : CHAR;
        NEWVALUE : REAL;

BEGIN   (* perform *)

  (* Get operands and operator. *)
  POPREAL(OPERANDS, OP2);
  POPREAL(OPERANDS, OP1);
  POPCHAR(OPERATORS, TOKEN);

  (* Perform the appropriate operation. *)
  CASE TOKEN OF
    '+' : NEWVALUE := OP1 + OP2;
    '-' : NEWVALUE := OP1 - OP2;
    '*' : NEWVALUE := OP1 * OP2;
    '/' : NEWVALUE := OP1 / OP2
  END;   (* case *)

  (* Put the result back on the operands stack. *)
  PUSHREAL(OPERANDS, NEWVALUE)

END;    (* perform *)

(* ************************************************** )
```

```
PROCEDURE EVALUATE (VAR NEWVALUE : REAL;
                        VALUES   : VALUELIST);
(* Evaluates expression using values in VALUES list; *)
(* result returned in NEWVALUE.                      *)

VAR    TOKEN : CHAR;
       VAL   : REAL;

BEGIN   (* evaluate *)

  GETCHAR(TOKEN);

  WHILE TOKEN <> ENDEXPRESS DO
    BEGIN
      CASE TOKEN OF
          'A','B','C','D',
          'E','F','G','H',
          'I','J','K','L',
          'M','N','O','P',
          'Q','R','S','T',
          'U','V','W','X',
          'Y','Z'          : BEGIN   (* it is an operand *)
                                RETRIEVE(TOKEN, VALUES, VAL);
                                PUSHREAL(OPERANDS, VAL)
                             END;

          '+','-','*','/' : (* it is an operator *)
                             PUSHCHAR(OPERATORS, TOKEN);

          ')'              : PERFORM;
                             (* leaves result at top of OPERANDS *)

          '('              : (* do nothing *)

      END;   (* case *)

  GETCHAR(TOKEN);                                  (* Get next token. *)
  END;   (* while *)

  (* Final result is at top of operands stack. *)
  POPREAL(OPERANDS, NEWVALUE);

END;   (* evaluate *)

(* *********************************************************** )
```

```
PROCEDURE GETVALUE (VARNAME : VARTYPE;
                    VAR VALUES  : VALUELIST);
(* Finds value to be assigned to VARNAME, saves it in VALUES, *)
(* and prints the assignment message.                         *)

VAR    ASSIGN   : CHAR;                    (* the assignment operator *)
       NEWVALUE : REAL;                (* the designated or calculated value *)

BEGIN    (* getvalue *)

   GETCHAR(ASSIGN);                        (* Get assignment operator. *)
   IF ASSIGN = '='
     THEN READ(NEWVALUE)
     ELSE EVALUATE(NEWVALUE, VALUES);     (* Assign operator is ':'. *)

   SAVEVALUE(NEWVALUE, VARNAME, VALUES);   (* Save the new value. *)

   READLN;
   WRITELN(VARNAME, ' IS ', NEWVALUE:8:2);   (* Print message. *)
   WRITELN

END;     (* getvalue *)

(* ******************************************************* )

BEGIN    (* main program *)

   (* Initialize. *)
   CLEARREAL(OPERANDS);                    (* Set the stacks to empty. *)
   CLEARCHAR(OPERATORS);
   INITVALUES(VALUES);                 (* Set values of all varnames to 0. *)
   FLAG := OK;

   WHILE FLAG <> STOP DO                (* Process assignment statements. *)
     BEGIN
       WRITELN('PLEASE INPUT NEXT STATEMENT: ');
       GETVARNAME(VARNAME);
       IF VARNAME = STOPMARKER          (* Check for stop condition. *)
         THEN FLAG := STOP
         ELSE GETVALUE(VARNAME, VALUES)
     END;  (* while *)

   WRITELN('GOODBYE, COME BACK SOON.')    (* Print final message. *)

END.     (* main program *)
```

Error Checking: As soon as we begin testing our calculator program, it becomes painfully clear that we have made some pretty unreasonable assumptions about the requirements for correct input. We cannot expect a person sitting at the keyboard to type every character perfectly. But what does our program do if there is an input error in an expression? In many cases, it just crashes. Furthermore, even if the input is typed correctly, there is the chance of stack overflow—a software error condition—that would also cause a run-time error.

As we said in Chapter 2, Pascal will check for many types of errors. But it is better to write the error-checking logic into the programs than to rely on the system to catch errors at run time. One reason for this is that you can then choose how to handle the error. In some cases, the system will do the same thing as you might choose to do. For instance, stack overflow might cause us to try to assign a value to a location outside the bounds of the array that contains the stack. Pascal examines the array bounds as part of its run-time error checking. When the error is detected, the program is aborted.

This may be the same action as we would choose if we detected the stack overflow condition in our program. However, there is an important difference: By doing the error checking ourselves, we can *control* the termination of the program. We may, for instance, want to print out an error message describing the problem before we stop executing. In other cases, we may not want the program to stop executing. For instance, if the user of our calculator program makes an error in typing the input line, we would probably want to reject that line with an error message and then go on to the next line. If we depend on the system to catch the error, it may result in the termination of the program or in incorrect results. Again, the reason for including the error checking in the design of the program is to keep control over the program's execution.

How do we decide what action to take when an error occurs? As always, we must first consider the requirements of the program. Sometimes the specifications will tell us explicitly what to do in case of each type of error. If not, the best course of action is to try to recover as gracefully as possible, with the least damage to the program's execution. Print out a message to warn the user that an error has occurred, then go on to the next processing that is not affected by the error. Sometimes, as we will see, this approach will require a little cleanup before we continue after an error; for instance, resetting the stacks to empty if they still contain values from the aborted processing. Of course, even if we do decide to terminate the program as the result of a particular error, we can still do so in a controlled manner, printing out a message to inform the user what went wrong.

Let's look at how we could incorporate error checking into the design of our calculator program. We first examine the top level of the program. To make this program as robust as possible, we will specify that if there is an input error anywhere in a line, we will stop processing that line, print an appropriate message, and go on to the next line. What is involved in recovering from an error within a line? First of all, we will want to get rid of the rest of the line. That's easy; a simple READLN will take care of it. What about the program's data, the stacks and the values list? Normally, if there are no errors, both stacks end up empty at the end of an expression evaluation. However, if we stop processing midway through the expression, there may be elements left over in the stacks. To get rid of these data, we will need to reset both stacks to their empty states, using the CLEAR routines. Should we also reinitialize the list VALUES? No, the values that are stored in this list have been assigned as the result of successful lines of input, so we will leave them alone.

ROBUSTNESS

The ability of a program to recover to a known state following an error.

We can rewrite the top level of the program with error checking by adding a third value, ERROR, to FLAGTYPE and letting Procedure GETVALUE return an additional parameter, FLAG.

What conditions in GETVALUE will set FLAG to ERROR? First of all, an error may result from bad input. In general, it is a good idea to check any input, especially when it comes from the keyboard. (The safest approach—although it is not particularly convenient—is to read in everything as CHAR data and to convert it yourself to the appropriate type.)

One kind of input situation that may cause errors is seen in Procedure GETVALUE. We check the assignment operator, a CHAR variable, to see if it is '='; if not, we assume that it is ':'. What if, in fact, ASSIGN is neither '=' nor ':'? Since it is not '=', we take the ELSE clause and process the rest of the line as an expression. It would be safer to check explicitly for each value; if assign is neither '=' nor ':', we set the error flag:

```
IF ASSIGN = '='
   THEN ...
   ELSE
      IF ASSIGN = ':'
         THEN ...
         ELSE FLAG := ERROR
```

Other input errors occur if the parentheses are not correct. Let's see what happens, for instance, if the expression is *not* fully parenthesized. The input lines

A = 5.0 ;
B = 3.0 ;
X : ((A + B) * (A − B) ;

will produce the result "X IS 2.00" instead of "X IS 16.00". The last operation is never performed. (Try it yourself.)

We can check for matching parentheses by keeping a counter, PARCOUNT. At the beginning of an expression evaluation we set PARCOUNT to 0, then add 1 to it each time we encounter a left parenthesis and subtract 1 each time we come across a right parenthesis. If PARCOUNT is not 0 when we get to the end of the expression, there has been an error in the input, and we must reject the line.

What about expressions like (A + B * C)? The parentheses match, but there aren't enough of them. Again, in this case, one of the operations would not be performed. We can check for this situation also: There should be as many sets of parentheses as there are operators; if there are not, an error has occurred.

We can't prevent errors in the input, especially input from a keyboard, but we can try to limit their effect on the continuing execution of the program.

A second source of run-time errors is software limitations like stack overflow. In this case, there is nothing really wrong with either the input or the logic of the program, but design decisions like the size of the data structures may impede the execution. We discussed in this chapter the need to check for stack overflow; in this program it might occur if the expression is complicated and requires the stacking of more values than the stack has been declared to hold. To implement the error checking in this program, we would use the FULLREAL and FULLCHAR functions that have been provided. If one of them returned a TRUE value, we would need to send an error message, reset the stacks to empty, and skip to the next line. What good would a "software error: stack overflow" message be to the user of this program? If the user consistently got this message, it would be clear that the software needed modification in order to be useful. A programmer might be called in to "tune" the size of the data structure to make it fit the needs of the user.

We have mentioned several ideas for making Program CALCULATOR a more reliable piece of software. When we add error checking, we decrease the likelihood that the program will fail at run time. By increasing the robustness of the program, we also increase the satisfaction of its user.

OTHER NOTATIONS FOR EXPRESSIONS

One of the things that made our calculator so clumsy to use was the need for parentheses to tell us the order of evaluation. The way that we are used to seeing expressions is called *infix* notation—the operator is *in* between the operands. Infix notation can be fully parenthesized or it can rely on a scheme of operator precedence, as well as the use of parentheses to override the rules, to express the order of evaluation within an expression. For instance, the multiplication operators * and / usually have a higher precedence than the addition operators + and −. The use of a precedence scheme like this reduces the need for parentheses to situations where we want to override the order imposed by the scheme. For example, if we want to multiply first,

$$A + B * C$$

is sufficient to express the correct order of evaluation of the expression. However, if we want to do the addition before the multiplication (breaking the rule), we must indicate this with parentheses:

$$(A + B) * C$$

For one of the programming exercises in this chapter you are asked to develop a program that incorporates a precedence scheme into the expression evaluation.

The problem with infix notation is its ambiguity. We must resort to an agreed-upon scheme to determine how to evaluate the expression. There are other ways of writing expressions, however, that do not require parentheses or such precedence schemes. We will briefly describe two of them here, and then show how we can convert from infix to another notation with the help of our new friend, the stack.

Prefix Notation

In *prefix* notation, the operator precedes the operands. For instance, we would write the infix expression "A + B" as "+ A B". The infix expression

$$(A + B) * C$$

which requires the use of parentheses to designate the order of evaluation, would be written as

$$* + A\ B\ C$$

Notice two features of the prefix expression:

- the operands maintain the same order as the equivalent infix expression, and
- we do not need to use parentheses to designate the expression unambiguously.

We evaluate a prefix expression by scanning from left to right until we find the first operator that is immediately followed by a pair of operands. This binary expression is evaluated and its result is put back into the expression to replace the operator/operands we used. This process continues until only a single value remains. Let's evaluate the expression

$$* + 5\ 2\ 4$$

to illustrate this process. The first symbol is an operator, *, so we save it and go on. The second symbol is also an operator, +, so we save it and go on. The third symbol, 5, is an operand, so we save it and look at the next symbol. It is also an operand, 2, so we perform the operation on the two operands. We have saved two operators. Which should we use? We want to use the operator that we *most recently* saw, that is, +.

$$5 + 2 = 7$$

so we substitute 7 back into the expression, replacing + 5 2. The next symbol is another operand, 4, so we perform the next operation, using the * that we first saved. Note that our first operand will be the 7 that we already calculated and the second will be 4.

$$7 * 4 = 28$$

Now we are at the end of the expression, and we are left with the single value 28 as the result of the expression evaluation.

Use this approach to show that the prefix expression

$$* - + 4\ 3\ 5\ / + 2\ 4\ 3$$

equals 4.

We will leave to the reader the development of this algorithm into a procedure. *Hint:* Note that using the most recent operator implies a last-in-first-out type of solution.

How can we convert an infix expression into a prefix expression? Our solution to this question will make use of the stack routines from this chapter and the string processing routines from Chapter 2.

For simplicity, we will again begin with a fully parenthesized infix expression of the same format used in the calculator program. Our output will be a string representing the equivalent prefix expression.

Our general approach will be to loop through the expression, reading a token (in this case, one character) and processing according to its type, until the end of the input expression. (The types are letters, symbols that represent operators, left parentheses and right parentheses.) If the token is a letter, representing an operand, we will push it onto a stack of operands. If the token represents an operator, we will push it onto a stack of operators. We will ignore left parentheses. So far, the processing looks just like the calculator program's EVALUATE module. However, the processing for a right parenthesis will be different. We will pop the last two operands and the most recent operator, convert them to a prefix expression, and push this expression back onto the operand stack. Note that the operand stack no longer contains real numbers; it is now a stack of *strings*.

How do we convert to prefix? If the operators, as well as the operands, are strings, we can use our string routines from Chapter 2 to create an expression that begins with an operator, followed by operand1 and operand2, respectively. This can be accomplished by using the CONCAT procedure. First, we concatenate the operator with operand1; then we concatenate the result with operand2.

When we reach the end of the input expression, we should find the complete prefix expression string as the top (and only) element in the operand stack.

We can use much of our design from the calculator program. The only changes to the EVALUATE module will be to make operands and operators into string type elements before they are pushed onto their respective stacks and to invoke module CONVERT, rather than module PERFORM, when a right parenthesis is encountered.

CONVERT

Pop operand2 from operands stack.
Pop operand1 from operands stack.
Pop operator from operators stack.
Concatenate operator with operand1.
Concatenate result with operand2.
Push the result onto the operands stack.

Since this module directly codes into a Pascal procedure, using PUSH, POP, and CONCAT, we will not include the code here.

Postfix Notation

In an alternative way of writing expressions, *postfix* notation, the operator follows the operands. For instance, the infix expression A + B would be written as the postfix expression A B +. The infix expression

$$(A + B) * C$$

which requires parentheses to indicate the order of evaluation, would be written as the postfix expression

$$A B + C *$$

You should note three features of postfix notation:

- like prefix notation, the relative order of the operands is maintained,
- parentheses are not necessary, since postfix expressions are by nature unambiguous, and
- the postfix notation is not merely the reverse of the equivalent prefix notation.

The algorithms to convert expressions into postfix notation and to evaluate postfix expressions, like those for prefix notation, make use of the stack data structure. For one of the programming assignments at the end of this chapter you are asked to develop and code algorithms for postfix expression notation.

So far, we have limited our discussion to expressions that are stored in strings. We will return to the topic of prefix and postfix notation for expressions in Chapter 9, when we will see a different way of representing expressions.

APPLICATION: MAZE

Data Structures in Use	Software Techniques in Use
■ TWO-DIMENSIONAL ARRAY OF RECORDS	■ USE OF THE STACK DATA STRUCTURE
■ STACK	

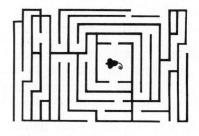

As a child, did you ever dream of playing in a maze? How fun and scary it would have been to get lost and then, just at sundown, find your way out.

If you had thought about it, you might have come up with the idea of marking your path as you went along. If you were blocked, you could then go back to the last crossing and take the other path.

This technique of going back to the last decision point and going the other way is called *back tracking*. Back tracking is a very useful technique in problem solving. Since it requires remembering where you have been in reverse, a stack is an appropriate data structure for backtracking.

We will now illustrate this technique in the context of trying to get out of a maze. The first step is to choose a data structure to represent the maze. We must be able to represent paths and dead ends. A two-dimensional array with symbols to represent where a path is and where a dead end is seems reasonable.

Figure 3-6 shows a maze and its representation in an array. Squares with a 0 in them represent paths. Squares with a 1 in them represent dead ends. The square with E represents the exit. Now we are in a position to state the problem.

EXIT

0	0	1	E	1	0	0	1	1	1
0	1	1	0	1	0	1	0	0	0
0	0	0	0	0	0	1	0	1	0
1	1	1	1	1	0	1	1	0	0
0	0	0	1	0	0	0	1	0	1
0	1	0	1	0	1	1	1	0	1
0	1	0	1	0	0	0	1	0	0
1	1	0	1	1	1	0	1	1	0
0	1	0	0	0	0	0	1	1	0
0	1	0	1	1	0	1	0	0	0

1's are hedges
0's are paths

Figure 3-6.

Problem: Given a starting point in a maze, you are to determine if there is a way out. The maze is represented by a 10 × 10 array of 1s and 0s. There is one exit from the maze. The door to the exit contains an E. You may move vertically or horizontally in any direction that contains a 0; you may not move to a cell with a 1. If you move into the cell with the E, you have exited. If you are in a cell with 1s on three sides, you must go back the way you came and try another path. You may not move diagonally.

Input: Input is a 10 × 10 array of characters (1, 0, E). Each data line consists of one row of the maze. Each succeeding line consists of pairs of values, representing starting points in the maze (i.e., row and column numbers). Process these entry points until EOF.

Output: For each entry into the maze, print the maze with an '*' in the entry square, followed by the message 'I AM FREE' if a way out exists from that point or 'HELP, I AM TRAPPED' if a way out does not exist from that point.

Processing: You begin at the entry point and continue moving until you find the way out or you have no more moves to try. Remember: You can move into any cell with a 0; cells with a 1 block you.

Discussion: What we need to simulate is "going back to the last crossing and going the other way." If you put the last crossing on a stack, when you pop the stack, you would get back the last crossing. How would you represent a crossing? You could put the row and column number of each square you pass through on the stack. When you pop the stack, you get back the last square you visited. From that point you could choose another direction.

An alternative approach would be to put all possible moves from the square you are in on the stack. When you have to backtrack, the square you pop off the stack would be the next one to try rather than the last crossing.

You decide to try the second alternative by hand to see how it would work. Figure 3-7 shows a simple 5 × 5 maze you use as an example.

You started with an entry point of [3, 1]; there are two ways to go, [4, 1] and [2, 1]. You put both moves on the stack. Figure 3-7(b) shows the stack at this point. You pop the stack and move into square [2, 1]. Note that you decide to put all possible alternatives from that point on the stack and then pop the stack to choose the next move. Your current position now is [2, 1]. This square does not contain an E, so you put the row and column number of each surrounding square that does not contain a "1" on the stack. Figure 3-7(c) shows the stack at this point.

You pop the stack and move into square [1, 1]. This square contains an E, so you are free. However, what would have happened if [1, 1] had con-

(a) MAZE [1] [2] [3] [4] [5]

	[1]	[2]	[3]	[4]	[5]
[1]	E	1	0	0	1
[2]	0	0	0	1	1
[3]	0	1	0	1	1
[4]	0	1	0	1	0
[5]	1	1	1	1	0

(b)

[2, 1]
[4, 1]

(c)

[1, 1]
[3, 1]
[2, 2]
[4, 1]

Figure 3-7.

tained a 1? The position [1, 1] would not have been put in the stack, so instead of moving into [1, 1], you would have moved into [3, 1]. You would have been in an infinite loop! Square [3, 1] was the starting square. You would have cycled from [3, 1] to [2, 1] to [3, 1] over and over and over. You will need to mark the squares you have visited so that you will not visit them again. You decide to mark them with a period (.). This means that you will put on the stack those squares that contain a 0 or E but not those squares that contain a 1 or a period.

There was one thing that you did automatically that will have to be made explicit in the program. When you put [4, 1] and [2, 1] on the stack, you knew by looking that there wasn't a square on the left of [4, 1]. These outside squares are a special case. The easiest way to handle them is to put a border of 1s around the whole maze. Then the borders of the actual maze are handled just like any other square.

Let's summarize this discussion with a list of the steps to take at each move.

1. At the beginning square we will examine the four adjacent squares (the one above, the one below, and the two on either side) and put the ones with a 0 or an E in them on the stack.
2. Mark the square we are in as having been visited by putting a period in the square. This will protect against infinite loops.

3. Get the next move from the stack. That is, pop the stack. Make the square whose coordinates have been popped the current square.
4. Repeat the process until you either reach the exit point or try to backtrack and the stack is empty. When you try to get an alternative path from the stack and it is empty, then there are no more possibilities. This means that there is no exit from the beginning square. You are surrounded by 1s and periods and the stack is empty.

Assumptions:

The entry point is within the maze.

Data Structures:

A two-dimensional array (MAZE) to represent the maze.
A record to hold a position in the maze represented by a row/column pair (MOVE).
A stack of possible moves (s).

To simplify the processing we will declare the maze to be (0..11, 0..11). Ones will be put in the borders. This will keep us from having to check for the edges at each move.

MAIN MODULE   Level 0

```
INITIALIZE
GETMAZE
WHILE more entry points DO
    GET START
    PROCESSMAZE(MAZE, MOVE)
```

INITIALIZE   Level 1

```
initialize rows 0 and 11 to 1s
initialize columns 0 and 11 to 1s
```

GETMAZE   Level 1

```
FOR ROW 1 THROUGH 10
    FOR COL 1 THROUGH 10
        READ MAZE[ROW, COL]
```

GETSTART   Level 1

```
READ MOVE.ROW, MOVE.COL
```

PROCESSMAZE(MAZE, MOVE)   Level 1

```
MAZE[MOVE.ROW, MOVE.COL] := '*'
PRINTMAZE
WHILE not trapped AND not free DO
     MARK(MOVE)
     STACKPOSSIBLES(MOVE, S)
     GETNEXTMOVE
IF trapped THEN WRITE 'HELP, I AM TRAPPED!'
     ELSE WRITE 'I AM FREE!'
```

PRINTMAZE(MOVE)   Level 2

```
FOR ROW 1 THROUGH 10
     FOR COL 1 THROUGH 10
          PRINT MAZE[ROW, COL]
```

MARK(MOVE)   Level 2

```
MAZE[MOVE.ROW, MOVE.COL] set to '.'
```

STACKPOSSIBLES   Level 2

```
IF MAZE[ROW + 1, COL] is a 0 or E
     PUT on stack (ROW + 1, COL)
IF MAZE[ROW − 1, COL] is a 0 or E
     PUT on stack (ROW − 1, COL)
IF MAZE[ROW, COL + 1] is a 0 or E
     PUT on stack (ROW, COL + 1)
IF MAZE[ROW, COL − 1] is a 0 or E
     PUT on stack (ROW, COL − 1)
```

PUTONSTACK(I, J)   Level 3

```
TMOVE.ROW ← I
TMOVE.COL ← J
PUSH(S, TMOVE)
```

Control Structures:

TRAPPED is set to TRUE (1) if the starting point contains a 1 or (2) if the stack is empty.

FREE is set to TRUE if current square contains an E.

Parameters:

GETMAZE and INITIALIZE will both need MAZE as a VAR parameter.

STACKPOSSIBLES will need MOVE as a value parameter and the stack S. Remember, MOVE contains the row and column of the current square. That is, by putting the coordinates of the desired square into MOVE, you are there; you have MOVEd.

PUTONSTACK takes a pair of integers that represent a row/column pair as parameters. They are put into a record and pushed onto the stack S.

MARK and GETSTART are only one line of code each and should just be coded inline.

PROCESSMAZE needs the maze and the beginning position. Note that this procedure changes the values in the maze by marking positions as it goes through them. Therefore the maze has to be restored before the next starting position is read and the process begins again. We can take care of this by passing MAZE as a value parameter to PROCESSMAZE. Therefore the changes are made to the copy passed to PROCESSMAZE, not the original. In order not to make a copy of the copy of MAZE, we will pass the maze as a VAR parameter to PRINTMAZE and STACKPOSSIBLES even though neither actually needs it as a VAR parameter.

```
PROGRAM MAZEEXIT (INPUT, OUTPUT);

CONST MAXSTACK  = 100;

TYPE  ETYPE     = RECORD
                     ROW, COL : 0..11
                  END; (* record *)

      MAZETYPE  = ARRAY[0..11,0..11] OF CHAR;

      STACKTYPE = RECORD
                     TOP : 0..MAXSTACK;
                     STACK : ARRAY[1..MAXSTACK] OF ETYPE
                  END; (* record *)

VAR   MAZE       : MAZETYPE;            (* array representing the maze *)
      FREE,                       (* TRUE if current square contains E *)
      TRAPPED    : BOOLEAN;               (* TRUE if there is no exit *)
      MOVE       : ETYPE;        (* represents a square in the maze *)

      S          : STACKTYPE;           (* S contains alternate moves *)
```

(*)

```
PROCEDURE PUSH (VAR S : STACKTYPE; X : ETYPE);
```
(* Adds X to the top of stack S. *)
```
BEGIN  (* push *)
  S.TOP := S.TOP + 1;
  S.STACK[S.TOP] := X
END;   (* push *)
```

(*)

```
PROCEDURE POP (VAR S : STACKTYPE; VAR X : ETYPE);
```
(* Removes the top element from stack S and returns it in X. *)
```
BEGIN  (* pop *)
  X := S.STACK[S.TOP];
  S.TOP := S.TOP - 1
END;   (* pop *)
```

(*)

```
PROCEDURE CLEARSTACK (VAR S : STACKTYPE);
(* Sets stack S to its empty state. *)

BEGIN  (* clearstack *)
  S.TOP := 0
END; . (* clearstack *)
```

(*)

```
FUNCTION EMPTYSTACK (S : STACKTYPE) : BOOLEAN;
(* Returns TRUE if stack S is empty, FALSE otherwise. *)

BEGIN  (* emptystack *)
  EMPTYSTACK := S.TOP = 0
END;    (* emptystack *)
```

(*)

```
PROCEDURE GETMAZE (VAR MAZE : MAZETYPE);
(* Reads values into array representing the maze. *)

VAR  I, J : 1..10;                              (* loop control variables *)

BEGIN  (* getmaze *)
  FOR I := 1 TO 10 DO
    BEGIN
      FOR J := 1 TO 10 DO                       (* Read a row. *)
        READ(MAZE[I, J]);
      READLN
    END
END;    (* getmaze *)
```

(*)

```
PROCEDURE PUTONSTACK (I, J : INTEGER);
(* Row and column of possible move are put into an *)
(* ETYPE record and pushed on the stack S.         *)

VAR  TMOVE : ETYPE;

BEGIN  (* putonstack *)
  TMOVE.ROW := I;
  TMOVE.COL := J;
  PUSH(S, TMOVE)
END;    (* putonstack *)
```

(*)

```
PROCEDURE STACKPOSSIBLES (MOVE : ETYPE;
                          VAR S: STACKTYPE;
                          VAR MAZE : MAZETYPE);

(* From the square MOVE, all adjacent squares containing *)
(* a 0 or an E are put on the stack.                      *)


(* ***************************************************** )

BEGIN   (* stackpossibles *)

  IF MAZE[MOVE.ROW + 1, MOVE.COL] IN ['0', 'E']
     THEN PUTONSTACK(MOVE.ROW + 1, MOVE.COL);
  IF MAZE[MOVE.ROW - 1, MOVE.COL] IN ['0', 'E']
     THEN PUTONSTACK(MOVE.ROW - 1, MOVE.COL);
  IF MAZE[MOVE.ROW, MOVE.COL + 1] IN ['0', 'E']
     THEN PUTONSTACK(MOVE.ROW, MOVE.COL + 1);
  IF MAZE[MOVE.ROW, MOVE.COL - 1] IN ['0', 'E']
     THEN PUTONSTACK(MOVE.ROW, MOVE.COL - 1)
END;    (* stackpossibles *)


(* ***************************************************** )

PROCEDURE PRINTMAZE (VAR MAZE : MAZETYPE);
(* Maze is printed with surrounding 1's. *)

VAR   I, J : 0..11;                      (* loop control variables *)

BEGIN   (* printmaze *)
  FOR I := 0 TO 11 DO
    BEGIN                                (* Print one row. *)
      FOR J := 0 TO 11 DO
        WRITE(MAZE[I, J], ' ');
      WRITELN
    END
END;    (* printmaze *)


(* ***************************************************** )
```

```
PROCEDURE INITIALIZE (VAR MAZE : MAZETYPE);
(* Sets the borders of the array to 1's. *)

VAR  ROW, COL : 0..11;                          (* loop control variables *)

BEGIN  (* initialize *)
   (* set right and left sides to 1's *)
   FOR ROW := 0 TO 11 DO
     BEGIN
        MAZE[ROW, 0] := '1';
        MAZE[ROW, 11] := '1'
     END;
   (* set top and bottom rows to 1's *)
   FOR COL := 1 TO 10 DO
     BEGIN
        MAZE[0, COL] := '1';
        MAZE[11, COL] := '1'
     END
END;   (* initialize *)


(* **************************************************** )

PROCEDURE PROCESSMAZE (MAZE : MAZETYPE; MOVE : ETYPE);
(* The maze is printed, and squares are visited until   *)
(* the square with the E is moved into or there are no  *)
(* more squares to try. The outcome is printed.         *)

VAR  S : STACKTYPE;

BEGIN  (* processmaze *)
   CLEARSTACK(S);
   FREE := MAZE[MOVE.ROW, MOVE.COL] = 'E';        (* initialize FREE *)
   TRAPPED := MAZE[MOVE.ROW, MOVE.COL] = '1';
                                                 (* initialize TRAPPED *)
   MAZE[MOVE.ROW, MOVE.COL] := '*';                (* set start to '*' *)
   PRINTMAZE(MAZE);


   (* Search for maze exit. *)
   WHILE NOT TRAPPED AND NOT FREE DO
     BEGIN
        MAZE[MOVE.ROW, MOVE.COL] := '.';  (* mark square as visited *)
        STACKPOSSIBLES(MOVE, S, MAZE);
        TRAPPED := EMPTYSTACK(S);
        IF NOT TRAPPED
          THEN POP(S, MOVE);
        FREE := MAZE[MOVE.ROW, MOVE.COL] = 'E'
     END;
```

```
(* Report result of search. *)
IF FREE
    THEN WRITELN('I AM FREE!')
    ELSE WRITELN('HELP, I AM TRAPPED!')

END;    (* processmaze *)


(* * * * * * * * * * * * * * * * * * * * * * * * * * * * * * * * * * * * * * * * * * * * * * * )

BEGIN   (* main program *)
  INITIALIZE(MAZE);
  GETMAZE(MAZE);
  WHILE NOT EOF DO
    BEGIN
      READLN(MOVE.ROW, MOVE.COL);
      PROCESSMAZE(MAZE, MOVE)
    END
END.    (* main program *)
```

Sample Output: The following output was created by running this program on six test cases.

```
1 1 1 1 1 1 1 1 1 1 1 1
1 0 0 1 E 1 0 0 1 1 1 1
1 0 1 1 0 1 0 1 0 0 0 1
1 0 0 0 0 0 0 1 0 1 0 1
1 1 1 1 1 1 0 1 1 0 0 1
1 0 0 0 1 0 0 0 1 0 1 1
1 0 1 0 1 0 1 1 1 0 1 1
1 0 1 0 1 0 * 0 1 0 0 1
1 1 1 0 1 1 1 0 1 1 0 1
1 0 1 0 0 0 0 0 1 1 0 1
1 0 1 0 1 1 0 1 0 0 0 1
1 1 1 1 1 1 1 1 1 1 1 1
I AM FREE!
1 1 1 1 1 1 1 1 1 1 1 1
1 0 0 1 * 1 0 0 1 1 1 1
1 0 1 1 0 1 0 1 0 0 0 1
1 0 0 0 0 0 0 1 0 1 0 1
1 1 1 1 1 1 0 1 1 0 0 1
1 0 0 0 1 0 0 0 1 0 1 1
1 0 1 0 1 0 1 1 1 0 1 1
1 0 1 0 1 0 0 0 1 0 0 1
1 1 1 0 1 1 1 0 1 1 0 1
1 0 1 0 0 0 0 0 1 1 0 1
1 0 1 0 1 1 0 1 0 0 0 1
1 1 1 1 1 1 1 1 1 1 1 1
I AM FREE!
```

```
1 1 1 1 1 1 1 1 1 1 1 1
1 0 0 1 E 1 0 0 1 1 1 1
1 0 1 1 0 1 0 1 0 0 0 1
1 0 0 0 0 0 0 1 0 1 0 1
1 1 1 1 1 1 0 1 1 0 0 1
1 0 0 0 1 0 0 0 1 0 1 1
1 0 1 0 1 0 1 1 1 0 1 1
1 0 1 0 1 0 0 0 1 0 0 1
1 1 1 0 1 1 1 * 1 1 0 1
1 0 1 0 0 0 0 0 1 1 0 1
1 0 1 0 1 1 0 1 0 0 0 1
1 1 1 1 1 1 1 1 1 1 1 1
I AM FREE!
1 1 1 1 1 1 1 1 1 1 1 1
1 0 0 1 E 1 0 0 1 1 1 1
1 0 1 1 0 1 0 1 0 0 0 1
1 0 0 0 0 0 0 1 0 1 0 1
1 1 1 1 1 1 0 1 1 0 0 1
1 0 0 0 1 0 0 0 1 0 1 1
1 0 1 0 1 0 1 1 1 0 1 1
1 0 1 0 1 0 0 0 1 * 0 1
1 1 1 0 1 1 1 0 1 1 0 1
1 0 1 0 0 0 0 0 1 1 0 1
1 0 1 0 1 1 0 1 0 0 0 1
1 1 1 1 1 1 1 1 1 1 1 1
HELP, I AM TRAPPED!
1 1 1 1 1 1 1 1 1 1 1 1
1 0 0 1 E 1 0 0 1 1 1 1
1 0 1 1 0 1 0 1 0 0 0 1
1 0 0 0 0 0 0 1 0 1 0 1
1 1 1 1 1 1 0 1 1 0 0 1
1 0 0 0 1 0 0 0 1 0 1 1
1 0 1 0 1 0 1 1 1 0 1 1
1 0 1 0 1 0 0 0 1 0 0 1
1 1 1 0 1 1 1 0 1 1 0 1
1 0 1 * 0 0 0 0 1 1 0 1
1 0 1 0 1 1 0 1 0 0 0 1
1 1 1 1 1 1 1 1 1 1 1 1
I AM FREE!
```

```
1 1 1 1 1 1 1 1 1 1 1 1
1 0 0 1 E 1 0 0 1 1 1 1
1 0 1 1 0 1 0 1 0 0 0 1
1 * 0 0 0 0 0 1 0 1 0 1
1 1 1 1 1 1 0 1 1 0 0 1
1 0 0 0 1 0 0 0 1 0 1 1
1 0 1 0 1 0 1 1 1 0 1 1
1 0 1 0 1 0 0 0 1 0 0 1
1 1 1 0 1 1 1 0 1 1 0 1
1 0 1 0 0 0 0 0 1 1 0 1
1 0 1 0 1 1 0 1 0 0 0 1
1 1 1 1 1 1 1 1 1 1 1 1
I AM FREE!
```

The algorithm we have used in this program keeps track of possible moves by putting them in a stack. When we need to move, we take the top one in the stack, which represents the most recent alternative. If the stack is empty and we have not found the exit, we know there is no path to the exit point from the given entry point. If we reach the square with the E, we know there is a path from the given entry point because we have taken it. However, our scheme has not recorded that path.

A simple alteration to our algorithm could give us this path. After a square has been marked as visited (contains a '.'), put its position in the stack. When you need to pop the stack to get the next move, test the new move to see if that position contains a '.' or a '0'. If it contains a '.', that position did not lead to a successful path. Just pop it off to get another possible move. Now if the exit point is reached, the path is represented in the stack along with the untried (and unneeded) alternative branch points. To list the path, you pop the stack and print each position whose value is a '.'.

Another way to keep track of the path is to use a second stack. As a square is marked as visited, put it in this second stack. When you must backtrack through that square, pop it off the path stack. How do you know when this has occurred? When STACKPOSSIBLES does not put any possible moves on the stack, it means a dead end has been reached, and you must backtrack through a marked position to a previous branching point.

Exercises

1. Show what is written by the following segments of code. (S is a stack of integer elements; X, Y, and Z are integer variables.)

   (a)
   ```
   X := 3;
   Y := 5;
   Z := 2;
   CLEARSTACK(S);
   PUSH(S, X);
   PUSH(S, 4);
   POP(S, Z);
   PUSH(S, Y);
   PUSH(S, 3);
   PUSH(S, Z);
   POP(S, X);
   PUSH(S, 2);
   PUSH(S, X);
   WHILE NOT EMPTYSTACK(S) DO
     BEGIN
       POP(S, X);
       WRITELN(X)
     END;
   ```

   (b)
   ```
   Y := 1;
   CLEARSTACK(S);
   PUSH(S, 5);
   PUSH(S, 7);
   POP(S, X);
   X := X + Y;
   POP(S, X);
   PUSH(S, X);
   PUSH(S, Y);
   PUSH(S, 2);
   POP(S, Y);
   POP(S, X);
   WHILE NOT EMPTYSTACK(S) DO
     BEGIN
       POP(S, Y);
       WRITELN(Y)
     END;
   WRITELN('X = ', X);
   WRITELN('Y = ', Y);
   ```

2. Show what is written by the following segments of code. (S1 and S2 are stacks of

integer elements; I, J, and K are integer variables.)

(a)
```
CLEARSTACK(S1);
CLEARSTACK(S2);
FOR I := 1 TO 10 DO
   PUSH(S1, I);
WHILE NOT EMPTYSTACK(S1) DO
   BEGIN
      POP(S1, I);
      IF I MOD 2 = 0
         THEN PUSH(S2, I)
   END;
WHILE NOT EMPTYSTACK(S2) DO
   BEGIN
      POP(S2, I);
      WRITELN(I)
   END;
```

(b)
```
I := 1;
CLEARSTACK(S1);
CLEARSTACK(S2);
WHILE I * I < 50 DO
   BEGIN
      J := I * I;
      PUSH(S1, J);
      I := I + 1
   END;
FOR I := 1 TO 5 DO
   BEGIN
      POP(S1, J);
      PUSH(S2, J)
   END;
POP(S1, I);
FOR J := 1 TO I DO
   BEGIN
      POP(S2, K);
      PUSH(S1, K)
   END;
WHILE NOT EMPTYSTACK(S1) DO
   BEGIN
      POP(S1, I);
      WRITELN(I)
   END;
```

Use the following information for Exercises 3, 4, 5, and 6: A stack, S, is implemented by an ARRAY[1..5] OF CHAR; TOP is an integer variable (0..5); C is a character variable. For each example below, show the result of the operation on the stack. If overflow or underflow occurs, check the appropriate box; otherwise show the new contents of the array, TOP, and C. (*Note:* Some values in the array may *not* be in the stack.)

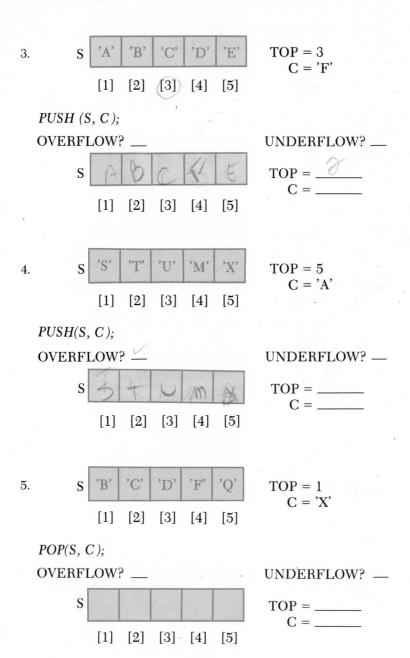

3. S | 'A' | 'B' | 'C' | 'D' | 'E'

        [1]   [2]   [3]   [4]   [5]

    TOP = 3
    C = 'F'

    PUSH (S, C);

    OVERFLOW? __   UNDERFLOW? __

    S | A | B | C | X | E

        [1]   [2]   [3]   [4]   [5]

    TOP = _0_
    C = _____

4. S | 'S' | 'T' | 'U' | 'M' | 'X'

        [1]   [2]   [3]   [4]   [5]

    TOP = 5
    C = 'A'

    PUSH(S, C);

    OVERFLOW? ✓   UNDERFLOW? —

    S | S | T | U | M | X

        [1]   [2]   [3]   [4]   [5]

    TOP = _____
    C = _____

5. S | 'B' | 'C' | 'D' | 'F' | 'Q'

        [1]   [2]   [3]   [4]   [5]

    TOP = 1
    C = 'X'

    POP(S, C);

    OVERFLOW? __   UNDERFLOW? —

    S | | | | |

        [1]   [2]   [3]   [4]   [5]

    TOP = _____
    C = _____

6.   S 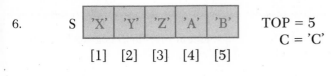   TOP = 5
                                    C = 'C'

POP(S, C);

OVERFLOW? ___   UNDERFLOW? ___

     S 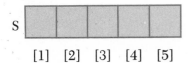   TOP = _____
                                    C = _____

7. Use Procedures POP and PUSH and Functions EMPTYSTACK and STACK-TOP to do the following:

   (a) Set I (an integer variable) to the third element in the stack, leaving the stack without its top two elements.

   (b) Set I to the value of the third element in the stack, leaving the stack unchanged.

   (c) Given an integer N, set I to the Nth element in the stack, leaving the stack without its top N elements.

   (d) Given an integer N, set I to the Nth element in the stack, leaving the stack unchanged. (*Hint:* Use a second stack.)

   (e) Set I equal to the bottom element in the stack, leaving the stack empty.

   (f) Set I equal to the bottom element in the stack, leaving the stack unchanged.

8. Show what is wrong with the following segment of code. (S is a stack of integer elements; X, Y, and Z are integer variables.)

```
CLEARSTACK(S);
X := 5;
Y := X + 3;
PUSH(S, Y);
PUSH(S, X - 2);
POP(S, X);
POP(S, Y - 2);
POP(S, Z);
```

9. Read in a string of characters and determine if they are a palindrome. (A palindrome is a sequence of characters that reads the same forward and backward.) The character '.' ends the string. *Example:*

   ABLE WAS I ERE I SAW ELBA.

   Write 'yes' if the string is a palindrome, and 'no' otherwise. This does not need to be a complete program, only a program fragment. You may assume that the data are correct and that the maximum number of characters is 100.

Pre-Test

1. Show what is written by the following segment of code. S is a stack of integer elements; X, Y, and Z are integer variables.

(a)
```
CLEARSTACK(S);
X := 0;
Y := 5;
Z := Y DIV 2;
PUSH(S, X);
PUSH(S, Y);
POP(S, Z);
PUSH(S, X + 1);
PUSH(S, Y);
PUSH(S, 3);
WHILE NOT EMPTYSTACK(S) DO
  BEGIN
    POP(S, Z);
    WRITELN(Z)
  END;
WRITELN(' X = ', X);
WRITELN(' Y = ', Y);
WRITELN(' Z = ', Z);
```

(b)
```
CLEARSTACK(S);
A := 0;
B := 5;
C := 4;
PUSH(S, A);
PUSH(S, B);
POP(S, C);
A := A + 1;
PUSH(S, A);
PUSH(S, C);
PUSH(S, 8);
B := A + B;
PUSH(S, B);
PUSH(S, 7);
WHILE NOT EMPTYSTACK(S) DO
  BEGIN
    POP(S, A);
    WRITE(A)
  END;
```

2. Stack S is represented by an array [1..5] of CHAR. TOP is an integer variable (0..5). CH is a CHAR variable. For each example below, show the result of the operation on the stack. If overflow or underflow occurs, check the appropriate box; otherwise show the array, TOP, and CH. *Note:* Some values in the array may not be in the stack.

(a)

'B'	'C'	'D'	'F'	'O'
[1]	[2]	[3]	[4]	[5]

TOP = 1
CH = 'X'

POP(S, CH)

[1]	[2]	[3]	[4]	[5]

TOP = _____
CH = _____

OVERFLOW? ___ UNDERFLOW? ___

(b)

'X'	'Y'	'Z'	'A'	'B'
[1]	[2]	[3]	[4]	[5]

TOP = 5
CH = 'C'

PUSH(S,'A')

[1]	[2]	[3]	[4]	[5]

TOP = _____
CH = _____

OVERFLOW? ___ UNDERFLOW? ___

3. What is the output produced by the following segment of code?

```
N := 1;
CLEARSTACK(STACK);
REPEAT
    IF N <= 7
        THEN BEGIN
                PUSH(STACK, N);
                N := 2 * N
             END
        ELSE BEGIN
                POP(STACK, N):
                WRITE(N);
                N := 2 * N + 1
             END
UNTIL EMPTYSTACK(STACK) AND N > 7;
WRITELN;
```

Hint: The REPEAT-UNTIL loop will repeat 14 times, in 7 of these 14 iterations the WRITE(N) statement will execute.

Advice: Keep track of the values of STACK and N at the end of each iteration.

4. Suppose that TEST is some Boolean function that takes any given integer and returns either TRUE or FALSE. Consider the following segment of code:

```
CLEARSTACK(STACK);
FOR I := 1 TO 3 DO
    IF TEST(I) THEN WRITE(I)
                ELSE PUSH(STACK, I);
WHILE NOT EMPTYSTACK(STACK) DO
    BEGIN
      POP(STACK, I);
      WRITE(I)
    END;
WRITELN;
```

Which of the following are possible outputs of the above code? Circle one: P (for possible) or I (for impossible).

(a)	1	2	3			P	I
(b)	1	3	2			P	I
(c)	2	1	3			P	I
(d)	3	1	2			P	I
(e)	2	3	1			P	I
(f)	3	2	1			P	I

5. Write a procedure REPLACES which takes as arguments a stack and two variables. If the first variable (OLDEL) is found anywhere in the stack, replace it with the second variable (NEWEL). If OLDEL is not found in the stack, return the stack unchanged. You may assume the following stack operations have been defined and coded. You do not know what implementation has been used, however.

```
CLEARSTACK (VAR S : STACKTYPE)
PUSH (VAR S : STACKTYPE; CH : CHAR)
POP (VAR S : STACKTYPE; VAR CH : CHAR)
EMPTYSTACK (S : STACKTYPE): BOOLEAN
```

Queues 4

Goals

To be able to hand-simulate the queue operations at the logical level.

To be able to determine the contents of an array that contains the elements of a queue after a series of queue operations, given the implementation specifications.

To be able to explain the design decisions made in the development of the queue implementation in this chapter.

To be able to code the basic queue routines using an array to contain the queue's elements.

To be able to design and code the solution to a problem for which a queue is an appropriate data structure.

THE LOGICAL LEVEL: WHAT IS A QUEUE?

We have already discussed the stack, a LIFO (last in, first out) structure. We know from experience that many lists operate in quite the reverse manner. A *queue* (pronounced like the letter *Q*) is an ordered group of elements in which new elements are added at one end (the *rear*) and elements are removed at the other end (the *front*). Consider a line of students at a university bookstore, waiting to pay for their textbooks. In theory, if not in practice, each new student gets in line at the rear. When the cashier is ready for a new customer, she takes the student at the front of the line. This is an example of a queue. We will discuss other examples of queues later in this chapter. Queues are also known as FIFO (first in, first out) lists.

Example of a QUEUE

What is the accessing function for a queue? For adding elements, we access the rear of the queue; for removing elements, we access the front. The middle elements are logically inaccessible, even if we physically store the queue in a random-access structure like an array.

OPERATIONS ON QUEUES

The bookstore example suggests two operations that can be applied to a queue. First, new elements are added to the queue, an operation that we will call ENQ (en-queue). ENQ(Q, X) means "add item X at the rear of queue Q." We also take elements off the front of the queue, an operation that we will call DEQ (de-queue). DEQ(Q, X) means "remove the front element from queue Q, and return its contents in X." Unlike the stack operations PUSH and POP, whose names are fairly standard, the adding and deleting operations on a queue have no standard names. ENQ is sometimes called ADD or INSERT; DEQ can also be called REMOVE or DE-LETE.

Another useful queue operation is checking whether the queue is empty. EMPTYQ(Q) returns TRUE if queue Q is empty and FALSE otherwise. We can only DEQ when the queue is not empty. Theoretically, we can *always* ENQ, since in principle a queue is not limited in size. We know from our experience with implementing stacks, however, that certain implementations (an array representation, for instance) require that we test whether the structure is full before we add another element. This real-world consideration applies to queues as well.

Finally, we need to be able to initialize a queue to an empty state, an operation that we will call CLEARQ(Q).

In terms of program design, what we have just described are the *interfaces* to the queue. We don't know anything at this point about the insides of these queue routines; we only know that to use them we must have the correct interface, or calling sequence—the name of the procedure or function, and the parameter list.

An Illustration of Queue Operations

Let's see how a series of these operations would affect a queue:

	REAR			FRONT
CLEARQ(Q)				
ENQ(Q, 2)	REAR		(2)	FRONT
ENQ(Q, 5)	REAR	(5)	(2)	FRONT

ENQ(Q, 7)	REAR	(7) (5) (2)	FRONT		
DEQ(Q, X)	REAR	(7) (5)	FRONT	X = 2	
ENQ(Q, X)	REAR	(2) (7) (5)	FRONT	X = 2	
DEQ(Q, X)	REAR	(2) (7)	FRONT	X = 5	

A Simple Problem

Suppose a string contains character information in the form

substring1.substring2

where substring1 and substring2 are the same length, and are separated by a period. We want to write a function to see if the two substrings are the same. If so, function MATCH returns TRUE; otherwise, it returns FALSE. For instance, MATCH(STRING1), where STRING1 is

'ABCDEFG.ABCDEFG'

returns TRUE, while MATCH(STRING2), where STRING2 is

'ABCDEFG.ABCDEFQ'

returns FALSE.

The algorithm for this function is as follows:

```
Initialize the queue to empty
ENQ all the characters, up to the '.'
MATCHING ← TRUE
WHILE more elements in queue AND still MATCHING DO
    Remove an element from the queue
    Get the next character from the string
    Compare
    IF they don't match
        THEN MATCHING ← FALSE
        ELSE keep testing
MATCH ← MATCHING
```

This algorithm can be coded into Function MATCH, using procedures CLEARQ(Q), ENQ(Q, X), and DEQ(Q, X) and function EMPTYQ(Q). We don't care about the representation of the string; let's assume that we have a function GETCHAR that returns the next character from a string.

```
FUNCTION MATCH (STRING : STRINGTYPE) : BOOLEAN;
(* Takes a string containing two substrings of equal length, separated by a *)
(* period. Returns TRUE if the substrings are the same; FALSE otherwise.*)

VAR       CH1, CH2  : CHAR;
          QUEUE     : QTYPE;
          MATCHING  : BOOLEAN;

BEGIN    (* match *)

  (* Initialize the queue to empty. *)

  CLEARQ(Q);
  (* Get the first character. *)
  CH1 := GETCHAR(STRING);

  (* Queue all the characters in the first substring, up to the period. *)
  WHILE CH1 <> '.' DO
    BEGIN
      ENQ(QUEUE, CH1);
      CH1 := GETCHAR(STRING)
    END;

  (* Compare the queued substring to the second substring, one character at a *)
  (* time, until there is a mismatch or the end of the substring.          *)
  MATCHING := TRUE;
  WHILE NOT EMPTYQ(QUEUE) AND MATCHING DO
    BEGIN
      (* Get a character from each substring. *)
      CH2 := GETCHAR(STRING);
      DEQ(QUEUE, CH1);

      (* Compare the two characters. *)
      IF CH1 <> CH2
         THEN MATCHING := FALSE
         (* else keep testing *)
    END;   (* while *)
  MATCH := MATCHING                        (* Assign result to function. *)

END;     (* match *)
```

IMPLEMENTING THE QUEUE

In our discussion of a queue as a logical structure, we have not mentioned how the queue is to be implemented. As with stacks, by "pushing down" the details of the implementation into the lower-order subroutines, we can write programs that use the queue operations without concern about how the queue is actually stored. Eventually, of course, we have to sit down and write ENQ, DEQ, and other queue operations as subprograms.

Like a stack, a queue can be stored in a record, with the elements in an array (ARRAY[1..MAXQUEUE] OF ELTYPE) and other information in separate fields. Since the representation of a queue is slightly more complicated than that of a stack, we will use this implementation to illustrate the types of considerations that come up in the design of a data structure and its operations. In Chapter 5, we will discuss a quite different implementation of a queue.

The first question to consider is how we will keep the elements in the array. We began inserting stack elements in the first array position, and let the top float with subsequent PUSH and POP operations. The bottom of the stack, however, was fixed at the first slot in the array. Can we use a similar solution for a queue, keeping the front of the queue fixed in the first slot in the array and letting the rear move down as we add new elements?

Let's see what happens after a few ENQs and DEQs. We insert the first element in the first array position, the second element in the second position, and so on. After four calls to ENQ, the queue would look as pictured below:

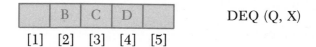

ENQ (Q, 'A');
ENQ (Q, 'B');
ENQ (Q, 'C');
ENQ (Q, 'D');

The front of the queue is fixed, remember, at the first slot in the array, while the rear of the queue moves down with each ENQ. Now we DEQ the front element in the queue:

DEQ (Q, X)

This deletes the element in the first array slot and leaves a hole. To keep the front of the array fixed at the top of the array, we will need to move every element in the queue up one slot:

Let's summarize the queue operations using this representation. The ENQ operation would be the same as PUSH. The DEQ operation would be more complicated than POP, for all the remaining elements of the queue would need to be shifted up in the array in order to move the (new) front of the queue up to the first slot. The CLEARQ, EMPTYQ, and FULLQ operations could be the same as the equivalent stack operations.

Before we go any further, let's make one observation: This design would work. It may not be the best design for a queue, but it could be successfully implemented. We must stress that there are multiple *functionally correct* ways to implement the same abstract data structure. A poor design may use more space in memory or take longer to execute, yet still execute correctly. Though we don't advocate the use of poor designs of programs or their data structures, it must be said that the *first* requirement must always be program correctness. A design that seems to be clever but doesn't work is useless.

Now, let's evaluate this design. What is its strength? Its simplicity—it is almost exactly like the collection of stack routines that we wrote in the previous chapter. Though the queue involves access to both ends, rather than only one (like the stack), we only have to keep track of the rear, since the front is fixed. Only the DEQ routine is more complicated. What is the weakness of this design? The need to move all the elements up every time we remove an element from the queue will reduce the performance level of the DEQ procedure.

How serious is this weakness? To make this judgment, we have to know something about the use and requirements of the queue. If the queue will be used for storing large numbers of elements at one time, or if the elements in the queue are large (records with many fields, for instance), the processing required to move all the other elements up after removing the front element will make this a poor solution. On the other hand, if the queue generally only contains a few elements and the elements are small (integers, for instance), all this moving may not amount to much processing. Further, we need to consider whether performance is of critical importance to the application that will use the queue. Thus the complete evaluation of the design depends on the requirements of the program.

In the real programming world, however, you don't always know the exact use or complete requirements. For instance, you may be programming on a very large project with over a hundred other programmers. Some programmers are writing the specific application programs for the project, while you are producing the utilities used by all the different applications. You may not know the requirements of the various users of your package of queue routines. Therefore, you must design general-purpose utilities. In this situation, the design we discussed above is not the best we can do.

ANOTHER QUEUE DESIGN

The need to move up elements in the array was caused by our decision to keep the front of the queue fixed in the first array slot. If we keep track of the index of the front, as well as the rear, of the queue, we can let both ends of the queue float in the array.

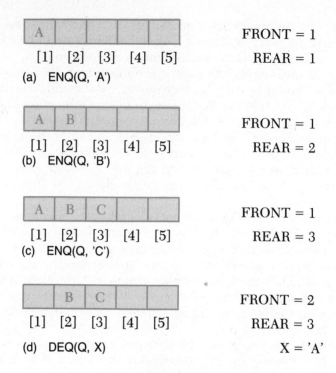

Figure 4-1.

Figure 4-1 shows how several ENQs and DEQs would affect the queue. The ENQ operations have the same effect as before; they add elements to subsequent slots in the array and increment the index of the REAR indicator. The DEQ operation is simpler, however. Instead of moving elements up to the beginning of the array, it merely increments the FRONT indicator to the next slot. For simplicity, in these figures, we only show the elements that are in the queue. The other slots may contain garbage; including values that have been DEQed.

Letting the elements in the queue float within the array will create a

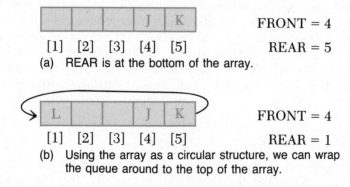

Figure 4-2.

new problem when the REAR gets to the end of the array. In our first design, this situation told us that the queue was full. Now, however, it is possible for the rear of the queue to reach the end of the (physical) array when the (logical) queue is not yet full [Figure 4-2(a)].

Since there may still be space available at the beginning of the array, the obvious solution is to let the queue "wrap around" the end of the array. That is, the array can be treated as a circular structure, in which the last slot is followed by the first slot [Figure 4-2(b)]. To get the next position for REAR, for instance, we can use an IF statement:

```
IF REAR = MAXQUEUE
   THEN REAR := 1
   ELSE REAR := REAR + 1
```

(Alternatively, if our array of elements begins at 0 instead of 1, we can use the MOD operator to get the next value; e.g., REAR := (REAR + 1) MOD MAXQUEUE.)

This solution leads us to a new problem: how do we know whether a queue is empty or full? In Figure 4-3, we remove the last element, leaving the queue empty. In Figure 4-4, we add an element to the last free slot in

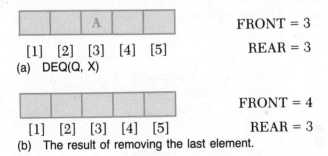

(a) DEQ(Q, X)
FRONT = 3
REAR = 3

(b) The result of removing the last element.
FRONT = 4
REAR = 3

Figure 4-3.

(a) ENQ(Q, 'E')
FRONT = 4
REAR = 2

(b) The result of adding the last element,
     making the queue full.
FRONT = 4
REAR = 3

Figure 4-4.

the queue, leaving the queue full. The values of FRONT and REAR, however, are identical in the two situations.

The first solution that comes to mind is to add another field to our queue record, in addition to FRONT and REAR—a count of the elements in the queue. When the count is 0, the queue is empty; when the count is equal to the maximum number of array slots, the queue is full. Note that keeping this count adds processing to the ENQ and DEQ routines. If the queue user frequently needed to know the number of elements in the queue, however, this would certainly be a good solution. We will leave the development of this design as a homework assignment.

Another common, but less intuitive, approach is to let FRONT indicate the index of the array slot *preceding* the front element in the queue, not the front element itself. (The reason for this will not be immediately clear; keep reading.) REAR will still indicate the index of the rear element in the queue. In this case, a queue is empty when FRONT = REAR. Before we DEQ [Figure 4-5(a)], we first check for the empty condition. Since the queue is not empty, we can DEQ. FRONT is incremented to indicate the true first queue element, and the value of that slot is assigned to X. (Note that updating the FRONT index *precedes* assigning the value in this design, since FRONT does not point to the actual front element at the beginning of DEQ.) After this DEQ, EMPTYQ will find that FRONT is now equal to REAR, indicating that the queue is empty [Figure 4-5(b)].

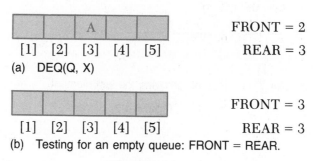

(a) DEQ(Q, X)   FRONT = 2   REAR = 3

(b) Testing for an empty queue: FRONT = REAR.   FRONT = 3   REAR = 3

Figure 4-5.

An additional convention that we must establish to implement this scheme is that the slot indicated by FRONT (the slot preceding the true front element) will be reserved. It cannot contain a queue element. That is, if there are 100 array positions, the maximum size of the queue is 99 elements.

To test for a full queue, we look to see if the next space available (after REAR) is the special reserved slot indicated by FRONT:

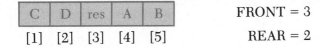

C	D	res	A	B	FRONT = 3
[1]	[2]	[3]	[4]	[5]	REAR = 2

To ENQ, we must first increment the REAR indicator, so that it contains the index of the next free slot in the array. We can then insert the new element into this space.

Using this scheme, how do we initialize a queue to its empty state? We want FRONT to indicate the array index that precedes the front of the queue. In this case, when we first ENQ, the front of the queue will be in the first slot of the array. What is the position that *precedes* the first array slot? Since the array is circular, the first slot is preceded by the last slot. So we initialize FRONT to MAXQUEUE. Since our test for an empty queue is FRONT = REAR, we will initialize REAR to FRONT, or MAXQUEUE.

We can now write the declarations and queue operation routines for this design:

```
CONST      MAXQUEUE = 100;

TYPE       ELTYPE      = INTEGER;
           INDEXTYPE   = 1..MAXQUEUE;
           QTYPE       = RECORD
                            ELEMENTS : ARRAY[INDEXTYPE]
                                           OF ELTYPE;
                            FRONT,
                            REAR      : INDEXTYPE
                         END;   (* record *)

VAR        Q  : QTYPE;

(* ***************************************************** )

PROCEDURE CLEARQ (VAR QUEUE : QTYPE);
   (* Initialize QUEUE to empty condition. *)

BEGIN   (* clearq *)
   QUEUE.FRONT := MAXQUEUE;
   QUEUE.REAR  := MAXQUEUE
END;   (* clearq *)

(* ***************************************************** )
```

```
FUNCTION FULLQ (QUEUE : QTYPE) : BOOLEAN;
   (* Returns TRUE if QUEUE is full; FALSE otherwise. *)

VAR    NEXTREAR : INDEXTYPE;

BEGIN   (* fullq *)

   (* Find the next rear position. *)
   IF QUEUE.REAR = MAXQUEUE
      THEN NEXTREAR := 1
      ELSE NEXTREAR := QUEUE.REAR + 1;

   (* QUEUE is full if the next rear position is equal to QUEUE.FRONT. *)
   FULLQ := NEXTREAR = QUEUE.FRONT

END;   (* fullq *)
```

(*)

```
FUNCTION EMPTYQ (QUEUE : QTYPE) : BOOLEAN;
   (* Returns TRUE if QUEUE is empty; FALSE otherwise. *)

BEGIN   (* emptyq *)

   (* QUEUE is empty if QUEUE.REAR = QUEUE.FRONT. *)
   EMPTYQ := QUEUE.REAR = QUEUE.FRONT

END;   (* emptyq *)
```

(*)

```
PROCEDURE ENQ (VAR QUEUE  : QTYPE;
                   NEWVAL : ELTYPE);
   (* Add NEWVAL to the rear of the queue. The queue may wrap around the *)
   (* end of the array. Assumes that the queue is not already full.       *)

BEGIN   (* enq *)

   (* Find the next rear position. QUEUE.REAR is *)
   (* the index of the current rear of the queue. *)
   IF QUEUE.REAR = MAXQUEUE
      THEN QUEUE.REAR := 1
      ELSE QUEUE.REAR := QUEUE.REAR + 1;

   (* Add new element to the rear of the queue. *)
   QUEUE.ELEMENTS[QUEUE.REAR] := NEWVAL

END;   (* enq *)
```

(*)

```
PROCEDURE DEQ (VAR QUEUE   : QTYPE;
                   VAR DEQVAL : ELTYPE);
```
   (* Remove the front element from QUEUE, and return it in DEQVAL. *)
   (* QUEUE.FRONT is the index of the array slot preceding the front   *)
   (* element in the queue. Assumes that the queue is not empty.   *)

```
BEGIN   (* deq *)
```

   (* Update QUEUE.FRONT to the front of the queue. *)
   (* The queue may wrap around the end of the array.   *)
```
   IF QUEUE.FRONT = MAXQUEUE
      THEN QUEUE.FRONT := 1
      ELSE QUEUE.FRONT := QUEUE.FRONT + 1;
```

   (* Assign the front element to DEQVAL. *)
```
   DEQVAL := QUEUE.ELEMENTS[QUEUE.FRONT]
```

```
END;    (* deq *)
```

(*)

Note that DEQ, like POP, does not actually remove the value of the element from the queue. The value that has just been DEQed still exists physically in the array, but cannot be accessed because of the change in QUEUE.FRONT.

This solution is not nearly as simple or intuitive as our first queue design. What did we gain by adding some amount of complexity to our design? We wanted to achieve better performance; specifically, we needed a more efficient DEQ algorithm. In the design of data structures and program algorithms, we will find that there are often tradeoffs—a more complex algorithm may give more efficient performance, a less efficient solution may allow us to save much memory space. As always, we must make design decisions according to what we know of the requirements of the problem.

QUEUE APPLICATIONS

One application in which queues figure as the prominent data structure is the computer simulation of a real-world situation. The sample program at the end of this chapter describes this type of application in more detail.

Queues are also used in many ways by the operating system, the program that schedules and allocates the resources of a computer system. One of these resources is the CPU (central processing unit) itself. If you are working on a multi-user system and you tell the computer to run a particular program, the operating system adds your request to its "job queue." When your request gets to the front of the queue, the program you requested is executed. Similarly, the various users of the system must share the I/O devices (printers, disks, tapes, card readers, and so forth). Each device has its own queue of requests to print, read, or write to these devices.

Summary

In this chapter, we have examined the definition and operations of a queue at the logical level. The queue is a first in, first out (FIFO) data structure; that is, its accessing functions involve only the first (front) and last (rear) elements.

We have also examined some of the design considerations encountered when an array is used to contain the elements of a queue. Though the array is a random-access structure, our logical view of the queue limits us to accessing only the elements in the front and rear positions of the queue stored within it.

We have seen that there may be more than one functionally correct design for the same data structure. Given multiple correct solutions, the choice of the best design is related to the requirements and specifications of the problem. Often, improving performance requires some sacrifice in simplicity of design.

■ APPLICATION: SIMULATION

Data Structures in Use
- QUEUES

Software Techniques in Use
- TOP-DOWN DESIGN
- TIME-DRIVEN SIMULATION
- TESTING AND EVALUATION

Before astronauts go up in space, they spend many hours in the spaceship simulator, a physical model of a space vehicle where astronauts can experience all the things that will happen to them in space.

This spaceship simulator is a physical model of another object. The technique being used is called *simulation*. In computing we use the same technique to build computer models of objects and events rather than physical models.

A model can be thought of as a series of statements or rules that describe the behavior of a real-world system. We change the rules and watch the effect of these changes on the behavior we are observing.

In a computer simulation, each object in the real world system is usually represented as a data object. Actions in the real world are represented as operations on the data objects. The rules that describe the behavior determine what the actions should be.

Let's look at a very useful type of simulation that uses queues as the basic data structures. In fact, the real-world system is called a *queueing system*. A queueing system is made up of servers and queues of objects to be served. The behavior we are examining is wait time.

The objectives of a queueing system are to utilize the servers as fully as possible and to keep the average wait time within a reasonable limit. These goals usually require a compromise between cost and customer satisfaction.

To put this on a personal level, no one likes to stand in line! If there were one checkout counter for each customer in your local supermarket, you—the customer—would be delighted. However, the supermarket would not be in business very long. So a compromise is made: the number of checkers is within the budget of the store and the average customer is not kept waiting too long. A computer simulation is one way to examine this compromise.

When doing a computer simulation of a queueing system, there are four things that we need to know:

1. number of events and how they affect the system
2. number of servers
3. distribution of arrival times
4. expected service time

The program uses these parameters to predict average wait time. The interactions of these parameters are the rules of the model. The rules are changed by changing these parameters. The average wait times are then examined to determine what a reasonable compromise would be.

For example, consider the case of a drive-in bank. There is one teller at the local drive-in bank, and the average transaction takes 5 minutes. A car arrives about every 5 minutes. How long does the average car have to wait? If business gets better and cars start arriving more often, what effect does this have on the average wait time? When will a second drive-in window be necessary?

This is clearly a queueing problem. There is a server (the teller) and objects being served (the customer or the car—which ever way you think of it), and the average wait time is what we are interested in observing. Let's determine the parameters and write a program to simulate this one-teller operation.

The events are the arrival and departure of customers (or cars). Since the people are arriving and departing in cars, let's just think of cars as the objects. The number of servers is one. The distribution of arrival times is "about every 5 minutes." We can quantify this by using probabilities. Saying that the probability of a car arriving each minute is 0.20 would give us the same thing in 1-minute time intervals. We want to turn the distribution time into minutes, because we will be calculating the average wait time in minutes. The expected service time is the average transaction time, which is 5 minutes.

We will solve this problem as a time-driven simulation. That means that the program will have a counter which represents a clock. Each time the counter is incremented, a minute has passed. The things that can happen each minute that we must keep track of are: a car can arrive, a car can go, people can still be waiting in line.

Let's make a list of these actions and what we should do when they occur.

1. If a car arrives, it gets in line.
2. If the teller is free, a car advances to the window. The service time is set to 5 minutes.
3. If a customer is at the window, the time remaining for that customer to be serviced must be decremented.
4. If there are cars in line, we must record that they have remained in the queue an additional minute.

How do we know whether or not a car has arrived? We have converted our "about every 5 minutes" to "the probability of a car arriving each minute is 0.20." Since each increment of our clock represents 1 minute, we can simulate the arrival of a customer by using a random number generator. Many Pascal systems have a built-in function that returns a random number between 0.0 and 1.0. We can simulate the arrival of a car by generating a random number each minute and applying the following rules.

1. If the random number is between 0.0 and 0.2, a car has arrived.
2. If the random number is greater than 0.2 and less than 1.0, no cars arrived.

If a car does arrive, it is put in line (i.e., it is put in the queue).

We can simulate a free teller by considering the teller to be free when the time remaining for the car at the window is 0. To move a car up to the window, we simply remove the first car in the queue and reset the time left to be served to 5, the service time.

If a customer is at the window, the time remaining for service will be nonzero and we just decrement the time remaining by 1. Note that the time remaining for service may now be 0. If so, the teller will be considered free in the next minute interval.

Now that we understand the actions, we can design the representation of the objects. We can represent the teller as a simple variable, which will be set to 5 when a car moves to the teller, and will be decremented by 1 each minute that a car remains. When this counter reaches 0, the teller is free.

What do we need to know about each car? Only how long it has been waiting. Therefore, each car can also be represented by a simple integer counter. This counter is set to 0 when the car enters the queue and is incremented each minute it remains there.

In order to find the average wait time, we must keep track of how many cars have been serviced and what the total wait time is for all the cars.

We described the problem in terms of a specific arrival rate and service time. Actually these values should be varied to see what effect the changes have on the average wait time. Therefore, the probability of a car arriving each minute and the average transaction time will be read as input, along with the number of minutes the simulation should run.

A time-driven simulation may vary its parameters, but the events are determined by the clock and (usually) a random number generator. An event-driven simulation, in contrast, is a simulation in which the operations on the objects—the events—are read in as data. In the programming assignments you are asked to solve this problem using an event-driven simulation.

We are now ready to write the top-down design for our time-driven simulation of the one teller drive-in bank.

Input: Length of the simulation in minutes (TIMELIMIT)
Probability of a car arriving each minute (ARRIVALPROB)
Average length of each transaction in minutes (SERVICETIME)
Each arrival probability and service time pair will be on a separate
line

Output: Echo system parameters
Average wait time for each ARRIVALPROB/SERVICETIME pair
(AVERAGE)

Data Structures: A queue (Q)
Simple variables

Assumptions: None

MAIN   Level 0

```
READ and echo print number of minutes
WHILE more variations DO
    READ and echo print ARRIVALPROB and SERVICETIME
    INITIALIZE
    WHILE more time DO
        IF CARARRIVES
            put in queue
        IF TELLERFREE
            THEN CARTOTELLER         (* Move car to teller. *)
        Increment time
    CALCULATE AVERAGE
    PRINT
```

INITIALIZE   Level 1

```
set number of cars, total waiting time, teller and clock to 0
CLEAR queue
```

CARARRIVES   Level 1

```
IF random number <= probability of arrival
    THEN car has arrived
```

CALCULATE AVERAGE   Level 1

> AVERAGE is total waiting time divided by number of cars

CARTOTELLER   Level 1

> IF car in queue
>   get car
>   increment number of cars
>   add time spent in queue to total time
>   set TELLER to SERVICETIME

To increment the time of each car in the queue, we must access each element in the queue. The queue itself must remain unchanged. We can do this by dequeueing a car, incrementing it, and enqueueing it again. Remember that the car is being represented in the queue by a simple variable that keeps track of how many minutes the car has been in the queue. DEQ(Q, CAR) returns the counter for the car which is at the front of the line in the variable CAR. You add 1 to CAR and then ENQ(Q, CAR). Now the counter for that car is at the end of the line. You continue this process until you are back at the point where you began.

The problem is to determine when we are back where we started. We can solve this by putting a dummy element or flag in the queue. When we dequeue this flag element, we have accessed each element in the queue. Since our elements are just positive integers in this case, we can use −1 as a flag.

INCREMENT TIME   Level 1

```
Increment CLOCK
set FLAG to −1            (*  −1 is entered at the rear of      *)
IF TELLER <> 0           (*  the queue. Elements are removed   *)
    decrement TELLER     (*  from the front, incremented, and  *)
ENQ(Q, FLAG)             (*  put back on the rear of the queue. *)
DEQ(Q, CAR)             (*  When the −1 is dequeued, each      *)
WHILE CAR <> FLAG       (*  element of the queue has been      *)
    increment CAR        (*  incremented and the original order *)
    ENQ(Q, CAR)         (*  of the queue has been restored.    *)
    DEQ(Q, CAR)
```

CONTROL STRUCTURES

TELLERFREE should be TRUE when TELLER = 0
'more time' is TRUE when CLOCK is less than TIMELIMIT

Before we start coding our modules, we need to consider possible error conditions. Have we neglected to put in tests at places where errors could occur? Let's look at each module.

In the main module we read in three values. If the number of minutes is negative, the whole outer loop will be skipped and no damage is done. The number of minutes is echo printed so the cause of the failure is obvious.

The length of time that the program will run is directly related to the number of minutes the simulation should run. Should this be checked to make sure it is not too large? What is too large? It is not within the scope of this text to answer that question. However, if you are writing a simulation program of this type in a job setting, you should discuss this with a statistician and put in a test.

If the probability of arrival is negative, no car will ever arrive. This value should be checked. If a negative value is entered, an error message should be printed and another arrival probability and service time should be read. If the service time is negative, the teller will never be free. So this value should be checked as well. Is there a relationship between the arrival probability and the service time which we should check? Yes, there is. We will demonstrate this by looking at actual output later.

These checks imply that the reading of the arrival probability and the service time should be moved into a GET PARAMETERS module. There should be an output flag from this module which lets the main program know whether a good set of input values has been found.

GET PARAMETERS   Level 1

```
READ and echo print ARRIVALPROB, SERVICETIME
WHILE either one is negative DO
    IF ARRIVALPROB <= ZERO
       PRINT error MESSAGE
    IF SERVICETIME <= ZERO
       PRINT error MESSAGE
    READ and echo print ARRIVALPROB, SERVICETIME
```

An examination of the other modules turns up no other possible errors. So we can now code our program.

NOTE: Since not all Pascal systems provide a random number generator, we have coded one in the program listed below. By tradition, random number generators have been coded as functions. We do so here, although it goes against current thinking about good style because the function must access (and change) a global variable called a *seed*. This variable is set to any integer value to initialize the function and is changed each time the function is called.

The output shown from this program, however, was from a run that used a built-in random number generator, not the function coded below.

```
PROGRAM BANK (INPUT, OUTPUT);

CONST   ZERO = 0;
        MAXQUEUE = 100;

TYPE INDEXTYPE = 1..MAXQUEUE;
     QUEUETYPE = RECORD
                      ELEMENTS : ARRAY[INDEXTYPE] OF INTEGER;
                      FRONT,
                      REAR : INDEXTYPE
                 END;   (* record *)

VAR TIMESUM,                             (* sum of waiting times *)
    NUMCARS,                           (* number of cars served *)
    TIMELIMIT,                  (* length of simulation in minutes *)
    SERVICETIME,                   (* average transaction time *)
    CLOCK,                          (* simulation time counter *)
    TELLER,               (* time remaining for customer at window *)
    NEWVAL,
    DEQVAL : INTEGER;

    TELLERFREE : BOOLEAN;              (* TRUE when the teller is free *)
    AVERAGE, SEED,
    ARRIVALPROB : REAL;     (* probability of a car arriving each minute *)
    Q : QUEUETYPE;
    DATAOK : BOOLEAN;            (* DATAOK is FALSE if no good input *)
                                     (* values are found. *)

(* ************************************************************** *)
```

```
PROCEDURE CLEARQ (VAR Q : QUEUETYPE);
(* See text for complete documentation. *)

BEGIN   (* clearq *)
  Q.FRONT := MAXQUEUE;
  Q.REAR := MAXQUEUE
END;   (* clearq *)

(* ********************************************** *)

FUNCTION EMPTYQ (Q : QUEUETYPE) : BOOLEAN;
(* See text for complete documentation. *)

BEGIN   (* emptyq *)
  EMPTYQ := Q.REAR = Q.FRONT
END;   (* emptyq *)

(* ********************************************** *)

PROCEDURE ENQ (VAR Q : QUEUETYPE; NEWVAL : INTEGER);
(* See text for complete documentation. *)

BEGIN   (* enq *)
  IF Q.REAR = MAXQUEUE
     THEN Q.REAR := 1
     ELSE Q.REAR := Q.REAR + 1;
  Q.ELEMENTS[Q.REAR] := NEWVAL
END;   (* enq *)

(* ********************************************** *)

PROCEDURE DEQ (VAR Q : QUEUETYPE; VAR DEQVAL : INTEGER);
(* See text for complete documentation. *)

BEGIN   (* deq *)
  IF Q.FRONT = MAXQUEUE
     THEN Q.FRONT := 1
     ELSE Q.FRONT := Q.FRONT + 1;
  DEQVAL := Q.ELEMENTS[Q.FRONT]
END;   (* deq *)

(* ********************************************** *)
```

```
FUNCTION RANDOM : REAL;
(* RANDOM returns a pseudo random number between 0 and 1. *)

CONST PI = 3.14159;

VAR TEMP : REAL;                              (* temporary variable *)

BEGIN  (* random *)
  TEMP := SEED + PI;                  (* SEED is a global variable. *)
  TEMP := EXP(5.0 * LN(TEMP));
  SEED := TEMP - TRUNC(TEMP);
  RANDOM := SEED
END;   (* random *)

(* ********************************************** *)

PROCEDURE INITIALIZE;
(* Initialize all simulation variables. *)

BEGIN  (* initialize *)
  TIMESUM := 0;
  NUMCARS := 0;
  CLOCK := 0;
  TELLER := 0;
  CLEARQ(Q);
  TELLERFREE := TRUE
END;   (* initialize *)

(* ********************************************** *)

PROCEDURE GETPARAMETERS (VAR ARRIVALPROB : REAL;
                         VAR SERVICETIME : INTEGER;
                         VAR DATAOK : BOOLEAN);
(* ARRIVALPROB and SERVICETIME are read until a pair where *)
(* both are positive is found. DATAOK is FALSE if no good      *)
(* pair of values for ARRIVALPROB and SERVICETIME is found. *)

BEGIN  (* getparameters *)
  READLN(ARRIVALPROB, SERVICETIME);
  WRITELN('PROBABILITY OF ARRIVAL IS : ', ARRIVALPROB);
  WRITELN('TIME TO SERVICE IS : ', SERVICETIME);
  DATAOK := (ARRIVALPROB > ZERO) AND (SERVICETIME > ZERO);
```

```
                  (* If this input is incorrect, read until a correct pair is found. * )
                  WHILE NOT DATAOK DO
                    BEGIN
                        (* Print error message.* )
                        IF ARRIVALPROB <= ZERO
                          THEN
                             WRITELN('ARRIVAL PROBABILITY IS INCORRECT');
                        IF SERVICETIME <= ZERO
                          THEN
                             WRITELN('SERVICE TIME IS INCORRECT');

                        (* Read new pair of values. * )
                        READLN(ARRIVALPROB, SERVICETIME);
                        WRITELN('PROBABILITY OF ARRIVAL IS : ', ARRIVALPROB);
                        WRITELN('TIME TO SERVICE IS : ', SERVICETIME);
                        DATAOK := (ARRIVALPROB > ZERO) AND (SERVICETIME > ZERO
                    END
                  END;    (* getparameters *)


(* ************************************************* )


PROCEDURE CARTOTELLER (VAR Q : QUEUETYPE; VAR NUMCARS,
                       TIMESUM, TELLER : INTEGER);
(* If a car is waiting, it is moved to the window and       *)
(* the time the car spent in the queue is added to total    *)
(* wait time and the total number of cars is incremented.   *)

VAR CAR : INTEGER;                              (* temporary variable *)

BEGIN   (* cartoteller *)
  IF NOT EMPTYQ(Q)
     THEN
        BEGIN
           DEQ(Q, CAR);                         (* Remove car from queue. *)
           NUMCARS := NUMCARS + 1; (* Increment number of cars served. *)
           TIMESUM := TIMESUM + CAR;            (* Add time in queue   *)
                                                (* to total wait time. *)
           TELLER := SERVICETIME              (* Reset time of car at teller. *)
        END
END;    (* cartoteller *)


(* ************************************************* )
```

```
PROCEDURE INCREMENT (VAR Q : QUEUETYPE;
                        VAR TELLER, CLOCK : INTEGER);
(* One time unit has passed — increment all simulation variables. *)

CONST FLAG = -1;                              (* end of queue marker *)

VAR    CAR: INTEGER;

BEGIN   (* increment *)

   CLOCK := CLOCK + 1;
   IF TELLER <> 0
      THEN
         TELLER := TELLER - 1;

   ENQ(Q, FLAG);                    (* Mark end of the queue. *)
   DEQ(Q, CAR);                     (* Get first CAR from queue. *)
   WHILE CAR <> FLAG DO          (* Entire queue will be accessed. *)
      BEGIN   (* one car at a time *)
         CAR := CAR + 1;
         ENQ(Q, CAR);                (* Replace CAR in queue. *)
         DEQ(Q, CAR)                 (* Get next car from queue. *)
      END

END;    (* increment *)

( * * * * * * * * * * * * * * * * * * * * * * * * * * * * * * * * * * * * * * * * * * * * * * * * * )

FUNCTION CARARRIVES: BOOLEAN;
(* CARARRIVES is TRUE if the number generated by function RANDOM *)
(* is greater than or equal to the arrival probability.          *)

BEGIN   (* cararrives *)
   CARARRIVES := RANDOM <= ARRIVALPROB

END;    (* cararrives *)

( * * * * * * * * * * * * * * * * * * * * * * * * * * * * * * * * * * * * * * * * * * * * * * * * * )
```

```
BEGIN   (* main *)
  SEED := 4.0;                    (* Initialize seed of random number generator. *)
  READ (TIMELIMIT);
  WRITELN('SIMULATION WILL RUN FOR ', TIMELIMIT:4,
          ' MINUTES.');
  WHILE NOT EOF DO
    BEGIN
      GETPARAMETERS (ARRIVALPROB, SERVICETIME, DATAOK);
      IF DATAOK
        THEN
          BEGIN
            INITIALIZE;
            WHILE CLOCK < TIMELIMIT DO
              BEGIN
                IF CARARRIVES
                  THEN
                    ENQ(Q, ZERO);
                IF TELLERFREE
                  THEN
                    CARTOTELLER(Q, NUMCARS, TIMESUM,
                    TELLER);
                INCREMENT(Q, TELLER, CLOCK);
                TELLERFREE := TELLER = ZERO
              END;   (* while* )
            (* Report simulation result. *)
            AVERAGE := TIMESUM / NUMCARS;
            WRITELN('AVERAGE WAIT TIME WAS ', AVERAGE,
                    ' MINUTES')
          END    (* if dataok *)
    END     (* while *)
END.    (* main *)
```

The data for the first run of this program were as follows:

$$
\begin{array}{rr}
120 & \\
0.4 & 5 \\
0.3 & 4 \\
0.5 & 7 \\
0.5 & -3 \\
-0.1 & 5 \\
-0.1 & -2 \\
\end{array}
$$

Note that the first three lines of arrival probabilities and service times are correct. The fourth line has a negative service time, the fifth line has a negative arrival probability, and the sixth line has negative values for both of these items. This should test the error-checking routine.

However, it doesn't work. We get a TRIED TO READ PAST EOF error. Can you find the cause?

Table 4-1. Average Wait Time in Minutes

Arrival probability	Transaction time	Length of simulation in minutes				
		120	240	360	480	1540
0.4	5	36.83	71.23	100.78	130.22	392.12
	4	22.87	46.38	64.24	92.26	255.38
	3	11.45	23.06	44.83	28.69	87.68
	2	0.93	2.06	1.64	1.68	2.47
0.3	5	15.50	48.60	70.85	81.26	278.53
	4	12.83	16.27	14.07	34.84	114.51
	3	3.73	7.18	13.58	3.94	4.83
	2	0.26	0.54	0.49	0.44	0.86
0.25	4	17.30	30.63	4.33	6.82	50.82
	3	0.79	2.25	1.76	4.19	3.07
	2	0.45	0.48	0.32	0.56	0.54
0.2	5	10.73	4.39	6.29	5.31	78.64
	4	1.75	2.76	9.05	2.16	3.71
	3	1.86	0.36	1.15	1.37	1.31
	2	0.17	0.17	0.46	0.28	0.31
0.1	5	2.43	0.96	0.66	1.29	1.80
	4	1.00	0.69	0.39	0.87	1.20
	3	0.38	0.25	0.29	0.37	0.41
	2	0.00	0.08	0.07	0.13	0.12

Procedure GETPARAMETERS goes back and tries to read a good line of data without checking for end of file. We need to rewrite the assignment statement which sets DATAOK as follows:

DATAOK : = (ARRIVALPROB > ZERO) AND (SERVICETIME > ZERO)
AND NOT EOF

This program was run five times with varying simulation times. Table 4-1 shows the output from the five runs, condensed for comparison purposes. The numbers 120, 240, 360, 480, and 1540 are the lengths of the simulations in minutes.

The results of this very simple simulation illustrate two important facts about simulations. Notice that some of the wait times just keep getting bigger and bigger, while others stay approximately the same.

The numbers which keep increasing represent cases where the queue is unstable. This means that the probability of arrival is greater than the transaction time. For example, the largest wait time occurs when the probability of arrival is 0.4 and the transaction time is 5 minutes. The probability of a car arriving each minute multiplied by the number of minutes required for each transaction tells us the probability of a car arriving during the transaction time. If the probability is greater than 1.0, then the queue will be unstable.

If two cars arrive every 5 minutes but only one leaves, the queue just keeps getting longer and longer and longer! (You have probably experienced this situation.) In each of the cases where the wait time just keeps increasing, you will see that the probability of a car arriving within the transaction time is greater than 1.0.

In the cases where the probability of a car arriving within the transaction time is equal to 1.0, you will note the highest fluctuations (i.e., 0.25 with a transaction time of 4 minutes and 0.20 with a transaction time of 5 minutes).

When we were discussing error conditions, we indicated that there would be a case where the relationship between the arrival probability and the service time should be checked. If the queue is known to be unstable from the beginning, the numbers are meaningless. You should consider putting in such a check in a job situation. In the case where the probability multiplied by the service time is greater than 1, we could print a message and read in another pair of arrival probabilities and service times.

We have used a random number generator or function to simulate the arrival of a car. The idea here is that each time a random number generator is called, it will give us a particular value depending purely on chance. Much theoretical work has gone into the development of algorithms to produce random numbers. However, given a particular function to produce random numbers and the current output from the function, the next value is completely predictable—not random at all!

Therefore, the numbers from such a function are called *pseudo-random*. For simulation purposes, however, pseudo-random numbers are sufficient. If a simulation is run for a long enough period of time, the theory of random numbers says that the wait time will converge no matter what random (or pseudo-random) number generator you use.

This is illustrated in Table 4-1. The average wait times for cases where the probability of a car arriving during a transaction time is less than 1.0 fluctuates over time but stays within the same general range.

Now let's answer our original questions. With the probability of 0.2 of a car arriving each minute (i.e., the probability of 1.0 that a car will arrive every 5 minutes) and a transaction time of 5 minutes, the average wait times vary from 4 minutes to 1 hour and 19 minutes. The wait time is already too long. The bank had better either lower the average transaction time or add a new drive-in window immediately.

In the programming assignments you will be asked to further extend this simulation by varying the transaction times among customers as follows: 20% of the people take 2 minutes, 50% of the people take 4 minutes, and 30% of the people take 7 minutes. How do you determine how many minutes a particular customer will take? You guessed it. Use a random number generator!

Note that the elements in the queue were just integer numbers representing minutes in the queue. Another way of keeping track of the length of time a car is in the queue would be to represent each car as the value of the clock when it entered the queue. When a car is dequeued the difference between its value and the value of the clock tells how long the car was in the queue.

This technique, called "time stamping," would be faster than incrementing the queue elements in this program. However, we were illustrating the use of a queue in this example; incrementing the values in a queue illustrates a useful technique for accessing each element in a queue sequentially, leaving the queue as it was originally.

In the programming assignments you will be asked to redo this same simulation using time stamping.

Exercises

Use the following information for Exercises 1 and 2. Q is a queue that contains integer elements. X, Y, and Z are integer variables. Show what is written by the following segments of code:

1.
```
CLEARQ(Q);
ENQ(Q, 5);
ENQ(Q, 6);
ENQ(Q, 7);
ENQ(Q, 8);
DEQ(Q, X);
DEQ(Q, Y);
ENQ(Q, X);
ENQ(Q, Y+1);
DEQ(Q, X);
ENQ(Q, Y);
WHILE NOT EMPTYQ(Q) DO
   BEGIN
      DEQ(Q, X);
      WRITELN(X)
   END
```

2.
```
CLEARQ(Q);
X := 5;
Y := 7;
ENQ(Q, X);
ENQ(Q, 5);
ENQ(Q, Y);
DEQ(Q, Y);
ENQ(Q, 2);
ENQ(Q, X);
ENQ(Q, Y);
Z := X - Y;
IF Z = 0
   THEN WHILE NOT EMPTYQ(Q) DO
      BEGIN
         DEQ(Q, X);
         WRITELN(X)
      END
   ELSE WRITELN('THE END')
```

3. Give an example of an application for which the array implementation with FRONT fixed at the top of the array (the one with the inefficient DEQ) might be acceptable.

4. Using the final implementation discussed in this chapter, show the result of the following operations on the queues indicated. If overflow or underflow results, mark the appropriate spot; otherwise, show any changes to the array and indicate the resulting values of FRONT and REAR. (*Warning*: Some of the values in the array may not be elements in the queue.)

(a)

A	B	C	D	E
[1]	[2]	[3]	[4]	[5]

FRONT = 1
REAR = 4

ENQ(Q, 'F')

OVERFLOW? ___   UNDERFLOW? ___

FRONT = _1_   REAR = _5_

(b)

A	B	C	D	E
[1]	[2]	[3]	[4]	[5]

FRONT = 5
REAR = 4

ENQ(Q, 'G')

OVERFLOW? _✓_   UNDERFLOW? ___

FRONT = ___   REAR = ___

(c)

A	B	C	D	E
[1]	[2]	[3]	[4]	[5]

FRONT = 4
REAR = 5

ENQ(Q, 'H')

OVERFLOW? ___   UNDERFLOW? ___

FRONT = _4_   REAR = _1_

(d)

A	B	C	D	E
[1]	[2]	[3]	[4]	[5]

FRONT = 2
REAR = 1

DEQ(Q, X)

OVERFLOW? ___   UNDERFLOW? ___

FRONT = _3_   REAR = _1_   X = _C_

(e)

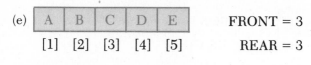

A	B	C	D	E
[1]	[2]	[3]	[4]	[5]

FRONT = 3

REAR = 3

DEQ(Q, X)

OVERFLOW? __   UNDERFLOW? __

FRONT = __   REAR = __   X = __

(f)

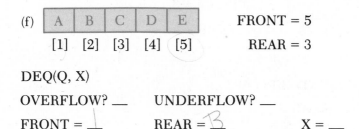

A	B	C	D	E
[1]	[2]	[3]	[4]	[5]

FRONT = 5

REAR = 3

DEQ(Q, X)

OVERFLOW? __   UNDERFLOW? __

FRONT = _1_   REAR = _3_   X = __

5. You have been assigned the task of testing the set of general-purpose utility routines. You decide to use a bottom-up approach, and you write a test-driver to read in a series of commands to manipulate the queue. The commands are

CLEAR (* Clears the queue. *)
ENQ element
DEQ (* Dequeues an element and prints it. *)
PRINTALL (prints the current elements in the queue without changing the queue)

Assuming that ELTYPE is INTEGER and MAXQUEUE = 5, create a set of test data (commands) that would adequately test the queue routines. The driver is written to test for empty and full before dequeing and enqueing.

6. Using the final implementation discussed in this chapter, write procedures with the following interfaces:

(a) PROCEDURE TESTENQ (VAR QUEUE : QTYPE;
                            NEWVAL : ELTYPE;
                       VAR OFLOW : BOOLEAN);
    (* Tests QUEUE for overflow condition before *)
    (* trying to add NEWVAL to the rear of the   *)
    (* queue.   *)

```
(b)   PROCEDURE TESTDEQ (VAR QUEUE  : QTYPE;
                         VAR DEQVAL : ELTYPE;
                         VAR UFLOW  : BOOLEAN);
```

(* Tests QUEUE for underflow condition before *)
(* removing the front element from the queue   *)
(* and assigning it to DEQVAL.   *)

7. The user of the queue routines will have frequent need for a count of the elements in the queue, so we add another Function QCOUNT(Q). We decide to add a field COUNT to the record that contains the queue. Rewrite the queue routines using the following declaration for QTYPE:

```
TYPE  QTYPE = RECORD
                    ELEMENTS = ARRAY[INDEXTYPE] OF ELTYPE;
                    COUNT : INTEGER;
                    FRONT, REAR : INDEXTYPE

              END;   (* record *)
```

Note that we no longer need to reserve an unused slot in the array to differentiate between an empty and full queue.

8. A *deque* is what you get when you cross a stack with a schizophrenic queue. You can add to and delete from either end of a deque. It's sort of a FLIFLO (first or last in, first or last out) structure. Using an array to contain the elements of the deque, write

(a)   the declarations for DEQUETYPE

(b)   PROCEDURE INDEQUEFRONT

(c)   PROCEDURE INDEQUEREAR

(d)   PROCEDURE OUTDEQUEFRONT

(e)   PROCEDURE OUTDEQUEREAR

(f)   a description (25 words or less) of some application of this data structure.

9. A (fictional) operating system queues jobs waiting to execute according to the following scheme:

- Users of the system have relative priorities according to their user ID number:

users 100–199	highest
users 200–299	next highest
users 300–399	.
.	.
.	.
users 800–899	next to lowest
users 900–999	lowest (their jobs only run at 3 A.M. on weekends)

- Within each priority group, the jobs execute in the same order that they arrive in the system.
- If there is a highest-priority job queued, it will execute before any other job; if

'not, if there is a next-to-highest-priority job queued, it will run before any lower-priority jobs, and so on. That is, a lower-priority job will only run when there are no higher-priority jobs waiting.

- The system has an array of queues (JOBS : ARRAY[1..9] OF QTYPE) to hold the queues for the various priority levels.

You may call any of the queue procedures (ENQ, DEQ, etc.) from this chapter in the following:

(a) Write a procedure ADDJOB that receives a user ID and a token (representing the job to be executed), and adds the token to the appropriate queue for this user's priority level.

(b) Write a procedure GETNEXTJOB that returns the token for the highest-priority job queued for execution.

(c) The system is going down for maintenance. All jobs waiting for execution will be purged from the job queues. However, this is a very friendly system that notifies users when their jobs are being killed, so they know to resubmit the jobs later. Procedure NOTIFY(TOKEN, MESSAGEID) takes care of this notification.

Write a procedure CLEANUPJOBS that sends Message 7 to all the users with queued jobs. (Call Procedure NOTIFY.) Of course, send messages to the highest-priority users first.

Pre-Test

1. Show what is written by the following segment of code. Q is a queue of integer elements; X, Y, and Z are integer variables.

```
CLEARQ(Q);
X := 2;
ENQ(Q, 4);
ENQ(Q, X);
DEQ(Q, Y);
ENQ(Q, Y + 3);
ENQ(Q, 0);
DEQ(Q, Z);
X := Y + Z;
ENQ(Q, X);
ENQ(Q, X - 1);
ENQ(Q, X);
WHILE NOT EMPTYQ(Q) DO
   BEGIN
      DEQ(Q, X);
      WRITELN(X)
   END;
```

2. S and Q are a stack and a queue, respectively, of integers. A, B, and C are integer variables. Show what is written by the following segment of code:

```
CLEARSTACK(S);
CLEARQ(Q);
A := 0;
B := 1;
C := A + B;
WHILE C < 10 DO
   BEGIN
      IF (C MOD 2) = 0
         THEN PUSH(S, C)
         ELSE ENQ(Q, C);
      A := B;
      B := C;
      C := A + B
   END;
WHILE NOT EMPTYSTACK(S) DO
   BEGIN
      POP(S, C);
      WRITE(C)
   END;
WHILE NOT EMPTYQ(Q) DO
   BEGIN
      DEQ(Q, C);
      WRITE(C)
   END
```

3. Write a segment of Pascal code to create a copy of a given queue. Let QA be the given queue and QB the copy of QA. Before your segment of code, the value of QB is undefined, but after this segment of code, QA and QB must have equal values.

Note: Assume that the appropriate queue type declaration and all the queue utility routines are already written.

4. A *palindrome* reads the same backward as forward. For example,

ABLE WAS I ERE I SAW ELBA.

One way to determine if a string of characters is a palindrome is to use one stack and one queue and to apply the following algorithmic strategy: Put the input string on the stack and the queue simultaneously; removing the stack elements is thereby equivalent to reading the string backward, while removing the queue elements is equivalent to reading the string forward.

Write a segment of Pascal code to determine if an input string of characters, terminated with a '.', is a palindrome. Print out 'YES' if the string is a palindrome and 'NO' otherwise. You must implement the above strategy. *Note:* Assume that the appropriate stack type and queue type declarations and all the stack and queue utility routines are already written.

5.

X	Y	A	Z	S
[1]	[2]	[3]	[4]	[5]

FRONT = 4

REAR = 1

A queue is implemented as a circular array of CHAR. REAR and FRONT are integer variables (1..5). Show the contents of the array after each queue operation. Note that some characters will remain in the array but not be in the queue.

(a) ENQ(Q, 'W')   REAR ____   FRONT ____

(b) ENQ(Q, 'B')   REAR ____   FRONT ____

(c) DEQ(Q, ELEMENT)   ELEMENT ____   REAR ____   FRONT ____

Linked Lists 5

Goals

To understand the concept of levels of data abstraction.

To be able to implement the following algorithms using a singly linked list represented as an array of records:

- *creating a linked list*
- *inserting an element as the first element in a linked list*
- *inserting an element into its proper place in an ordered linked list*
- *copying a linked list*
- *deleting an element from a linked list.*

To be able to demonstrate understanding of the memory allocation scheme used by doing the following:

- *encoding GETNOTE, FREENODE, and INITIALIZE*
- *showing the state of memory after certain operations.*

To be able to implement stack operations using a linked list.

To be able to implement queue operations using a linked list.

LEVELS OF DATA ABSTRACTION

In Chapter 1, we introduced the idea of the top-down design of data structures. Just as you can begin the functional design of a program at a very high level, you can also start the design of the program's data structures by specifying those structures at a very abstract level. As you gradually develop the program through the step-wise refinement of its algorithms, you add levels of detail in the definition of the data structures. It is important to stress that this can be a gradual process; there can be multiple levels of data abstraction.

For instance, at the highest level, you may decide that you will need an ordered list of data elements. At this point, it doesn't matter how this data will be organized in the physical memory of the computer; you are only considering the list as an abstraction. You can define certain characteristics about a list (for example, that its elements will be ordered from smallest to largest); you can also determine a number of operations that you may need to manipulate the list. For instance, to use a list, you might need operations to

- determine if the list is empty
- add new elements to the list
- locate a particular element in the list
- delete a particular element from the list
- print all the elements in the list

At this high level, these are logical operations on a list. At a low level, these operations will be implemented as Pascal procedures or functions that manipulate an array or other data structure that contains the list's elements. In between, there are intermediate design decisions.

LIST REPRESENTATIONS

In this chapter, we will begin our discussion at the intermediate level of abstraction. We have decided that we need to use a list. How will we represent the list? There are two ways that you will usually see lists represented: sequentially and linked.

In a sequential list representation, the physical arrangement of the elements is the same as their logical ordering. For instance, the abstract ordered list

(BOB, MARY, NELL, SUSAN)

would be represented as

1: BOB
2: MARY
3: NELL
4: SUSAN

The first element is in the first slot, the next element is in the second slot, and so on. Given any element in the list, the identity of the next element is implicitly defined: it is the element in the next slot.

You are probably already familiar with sequential representations of lists. No doubt you have written a program in which the data items in a list were stored one after another in an array. In this chapter and the following one, we will discuss the linked representation of lists. In a linked list, the logical order of the elements is not necessarily equivalent to their physical arrangement. The elements in our list

(BOB, MARY, NELL, SUSAN)

may be physically ordered as

1: MARY
2: NELL
3: BOB
4: SUSAN

How then can the original order be maintained? How do we know which element comes first and which comes next? In a linked list, the identity of the next element must be explicitly defined. We will spend the rest of this chapter and all of the next one examining how—and why—linked lists are used.

A RATIONALE FOR LINKED LISTS

Suppose that a large corporation is having a stockholders' meeting. There will be 500 people attending, staying at five different hotels. The meeting organizers need to keep lists of attendees by hotel, and have asked us to write a program for this purpose. We could use an array for each hotel, but this arrangement would necessitate the use of five arrays, each declared to hold the maximum number of attendees; even though each stockholder might choose any of the five hotels, it is possible that they would all elect to stay at a particular one. Using an array for each hotel wastes a lot of space because 5 hotels × 500 stockholders = 2500. Space for 2000 array entries would be wasted. (See Figure 5-1.) Ideally, the information about each stockholder would be stored in such a way that we only need to declare a structure and request space that we are actually going to use.

We could keep one hotel list in sequential spaces in the array, with the first element in LISTARRAY[1], the second in LISTARRAY[2], and so forth. A second list could be kept sequentially from the other end of the array, with the first element in LISTARRAY[500], the second in LISTAR-RAY[499], the third in LISTARRAY[498], and so forth. But storing the third, fourth, and fifth hotel lists presents a problem. There is no simple, practical

Hilton	Holiday Inn	Sheraton	SleepInn	Y'all Come Inn
1	1	1	1	1
2	2	2	2	2
3	3	3	3	3
.	.	.	.	.
.	.	.	.	.
.	.	.	.	.
500	500	500	500	500

Figure 5-1. Total space for 2500 records, of which 2000 will be wasted.

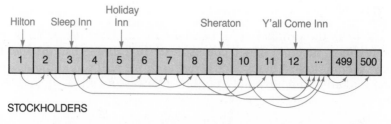

Figure 5-2. Total space for 500 records, with no waste.

way to keep them in sequential order. However, if we could find a way to connect the elements in each list, we could then determine which elements go together. The links between elements in a particular list would hold the list together without depending on sequential contiguity in memory. Memory space for 500 attendees could be declared, and the hotel lists could be linked lists. Even considering the extra space necessary to store the links, much space would still be saved. (See Figure 5-2.)

AN ABSTRACT VIEW OF A LINKED LIST

You can picture a linked list as a collection of elements, or *nodes*, each containing some data, as well as the link (or *pointer*) to the next node in the list. An external pointer to the first node in the list is also needed so that you can access the whole list. You don't access nodes in a linked list directly or randomly. Rather, you access the first node through the external pointer, the second node through the first node's pointer, the third node through the second node's pointer, etc., to the end of the list. (See Figure 5-3.)

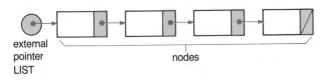

external
pointer
LIST
nodes

Figure 5-3. Abstract view of a linked list.

ANATOMY OF A NODE

Each node in a linked list must contain at least two fields. The first is the data field. This field may be a simple integer, a character, a string, or even a large record containing many other fields. In the following discussion, we will refer to this field as the INFO field. The second field is the pointer, or link, to the next node in the list. We will refer to this field as the NEXT field. This is one node:

INFO	NEXT

value(s) of any type   pointer to
next node in
the list

The NEXT field of the last node in the list contains a special value that is not a valid address. This value tells us that we have reached the end of the list.

SOME NOTATION

Until we begin talking about a particular implementation of a linked list, we will need some way of indicating the parts of a node. Note that this notation is only being used in describing algorithms; it is not Pascal code.

LIST is an external pointer to the first node in a linked list.
P is a pointer to a node in the list.
NODE(P) refers to the whole node pointed to by P.
INFO(P) refers to the data field of the node pointed to by P.
NEXT(P) refers to the pointer field of the node pointed to by P (points to the node that follows this node in the list).

Using this notation, let's write an algorithm for printing the elements (the INFO fields) of a linked list. We will need to use a temporary pointer, P, to traverse the list.

```
(1) P ← LIST
(2) WHILE the list is not empty DO
(3)     print (INFO(P))
(4)     P ← NEXT(P)
```

Let's examine this algorithm. In line (1), P is initialized to the beginning of the linked list. In line (2), we see the loop control "WHILE the list is not empty DO." If the list is empty, we stop. How do we know when the list is empty? When P is equal to the special value in the NEXT field of the last node, we know that we have reached the end of the list. In line (3), we write the information field of the node pointed to by P. In line (4), we advance P by setting it to the value of the NEXT field of the current node.

SOME OPERATIONS ON A LINKED LIST

How did the information get into the linked list? Consider a list whose nodes were inserted, one node at a time, at the beginning of the list. (See Figure 5-4.) After three nodes were added, the list looked like Figure 5-4(a). Now, to insert a new node containing the data value 5 to the front of the list, we must first get an empty node from somewhere. Let's assume

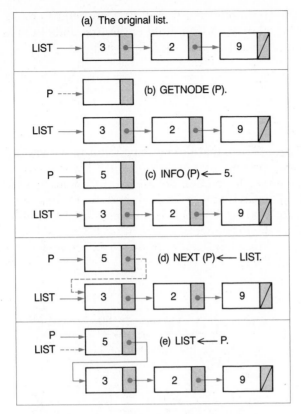

Figure 5-4.   Insert-first-node algorithm.

that all the nodes not currently in use are in a pool of available nodes. Whenever we need one, we call the procedure GETNODE (whose coding we will discuss shortly), which will return the pointer to an empty node (the INFO and NEXT fields of this new node may actually contain some values, but we will consider them to be garbage). Now that we have a free node, we can put the value 5 in its INFO field and insert the node into the list by manipulating the relevant pointers.

```
GETNODE (P)          [Figure 5-4(b)]
INFO(P) ← 5          [Figure 5-4(c)]
NEXT(P) ← LIST       [Figure 5-4(d)]
LIST ← P             [Figure 5-4(e)]
```

To delete the first node of a linked list, we need to make the external pointer LIST equal to the NEXT field of the first node in the list. This task is easily accomplished (see Figure 5-5) as follows:

LIST ← NEXT(LIST)

Note, in Figure 5-5(b), that the node containing the value 1 is no longer pointed to by any pointers. We no longer have a way to access this node at all. After many nodes have been deleted in this manner, a large amount of space will be taken up by these unused, and unusable, nodes. It would be better to put each node deleted back into the pool of available nodes. To do this, let's assume the existence of a procedure FREENODE (which we will write later) that takes a temporary pointer to an unneeded node to put that

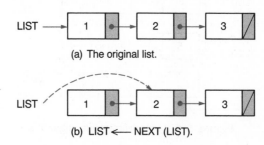

(a) The original list.

(b) LIST ← NEXT (LIST).

Figure 5-5. Delete-first-node algorithm.

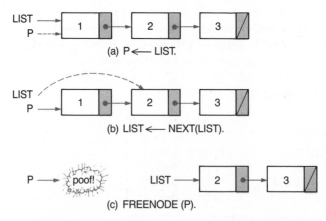

(a) P ← LIST.

(b) LIST ← NEXT(LIST).

(c) FREENODE (P).

Figure 5-6. Delete-first-node with FREENODE.

node back into the pool of available nodes. We can rewrite our delete-first-node algorithm, using a temporary pointer P to hold onto the node that will be deleted. (See Figure 5-6.)

```
P ← LIST                [Figure 5-6(a)]
LIST ← NEXT(LIST)       [Figure 5-6(b)]
FREENODE(P)             [Figure 5-6(c)]
```

GETNODE AND FREENODE OPERATIONS

To write our GETNODE and FREENODE operations, we must first understand that the pool of available nodes is represented as a second linked list. We will call the external pointer to this list AVAIL:

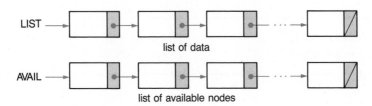

To get a node from the list of available nodes, we will use our delete-first-node algorithm. NEWNODE is the pointer to the node returned by GETNODE. (See Figure 5-7.)

```
IF the list of available nodes is not empty
    THEN NEWNODE ← AVAIL            [Figure 5-7(a)]
         AVAIL ← NEXT(AVAIL)        [Figure 5-7(b)]
```

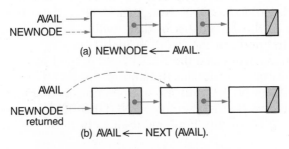

Figure 5-7. The GETNODE algorithm.

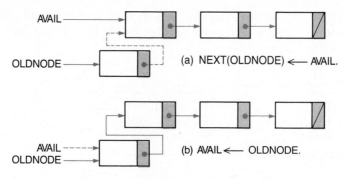

Figure 5-8. The FREENODE algorithm.

The algorithm for **FREENODE** is simply our insert-first-node operation. OLDNODE is the pointer to the node being returned to the list of available nodes. (See Figure 5-8.)

NEXT(OLDNODE) ← AVAIL   [Figure 5-8(a)]
AVAIL ← OLDNODE   [Figure 5-8(b)]

IMPLEMENTATION OF A LINKED LIST AS AN ARRAY OF RECORDS

We haven't yet discussed how the linked list will be implemented. One way to represent a linked list in storage is as an array of records. We can picture each node of a linked list as a record with two fields, INFO and NEXT. These records can be stored in any physical order in an array of records, and are linked together through their NEXT fields. Both the list of data elements (pointed to by LIST) and the list of available nodes (pointed to by AVAIL) can be stored in the same array. Figure 5-9 shows how a list containing the ordered elements 13, 16, 27, and 32 might be stored in an array of records called NODES. Note that LIST contains the array index of the first node in the linked list of data, while AVAIL contains the array index of the first node in the list of available nodes.

We mentioned earlier that the NEXT field of the last node must contain an invalid address to designate the end of the list. This special value is often called NIL or NULL. Since our array indexes begin at 1, the value 0 is not a valid index; that is, there is no NODES[0]. Therefore, 0 makes an ideal value for NIL in this implementation. In most Pascal implementations, NIL is a reserved word. We will see the reason for this in the next chapter. Therefore, we will declare a constant NULL = 0 to use with our array representation of a linked list.

A linked list implemented as an array of records could use the following declarations:

```
CONST NULL = 0;
      MAX  = maximum nodes in list;

TYPE  POINTERTYPE = 0..MAX;
      INFOTYPE = declarations for infotype;
      NODETYPE = RECORD
                      INFO : INFOTYPE;
                      NEXT : POINTERTYPE
                 END;   (* record *)

VAR   NODES : ARRAY[1..MAX] OF NODETYPE;
      LIST, AVAIL : POINTERTYPE
```

NODES	.INFO	.NEXT
[1]	13	5
[2]	X	6
[3]	32	0
[4]	X	7
[5]	16	8
[6]	X	4
[7]	X	9
[8]	27	3
[9]	X	10
[10]	X	0

LIST   1

AVAIL   2

} one node = one record

X indicates garbage in the INFO field of the available space list.

The list of available space includes NODES[2], NODES[6], NODES[4], NODES[7], NODES[9], and NODES[10].

Figure 5-9.

In the sample declarations, the INFO field is declared to be of type INFOTYPE. We will use this generic declaration to represent any type: INTEGER, CHAR, REAL, or BOOLEAN, a packed array, or a whole record in itself.

For example, in the hotel problem from Figure 5-1, we might use the following declarations:

```
CONST NULL = 0;
      MAX  = 500;

TYPE  POINTERTYPE = 0..MAX;
      STRING20 = PACKED ARRAY[1..20] OF CHAR;

      DATETYPE = RECORD
                      DAY, MONTH, YEAR : INTEGER
                 END;   (* datetype *)

      INFOTYPE = RECORD
                      NAME, ADDRESS, CITY : STRING20;
                      ARRIVAL : DATETYPE;
                      LENGTHSTAY : INTEGER;
                      ROOMCODE : CHAR;
                      CREDITCODE : CHAR;
                      CREDITNO : INTEGER;
                      CHARGE : REAL
                 END;   (* infotype *)

      NODETYPE = RECORD
                      GUEST : INFOTYPE;
                      NEXT : POINTERTYPE
                 END;   (* nodetype *)

VAR   NODES : ARRAY[1..MAX] OF NODETYPE;
      AVAIL, HILTON, HOLIDAYINN, SHERATON,
      SLEEPINN, YALLCOMEINN : POINTERTYPE;
```

We can print the name of the first guest in the Hilton list by the statement

```
WRITELN(NODES[HILTON].GUEST.NAME);
```

We will always access a field of a given node by its array index (a pointer) and field specification. For instance, in the following list, the INFO field of the first node in the list is referenced by NODES[LIST].INFO. The INFO field of NODE(P) can be referenced by NODES[P].INFO. The

INFO field of the following node (containing 'C') can be referenced by NODES[NODES[P].NEXT].INFO, and so on.

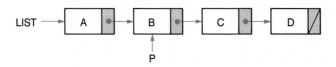

GETTING STARTED

Let's consider the simplest situation: We plan to keep one list of data and one list of available nodes in the array NODES. Each node record has two fields: INFO and NEXT. When we first begin, the linked list of data will be empty, so LIST = 0 (or NULL). AVAIL will point to a list containing *all* of the nodes in the array (see Figure 5-10). The nodes can be linked together in any order, of course, but it is simplest to string them together sequentially, as in the procedure, INITIALIZE.

NODES	.INFO	.NEXT
[1]		2
[2]		3
[3]		4
[4]		5
[5]		6
[6]		7
[7]		8
[8]		9
[9]		10
[10]		0

LIST   0

AVAIL   1

Figure 5-10. Initializing the AVAIL list to contain all the nodes in the array.

```
PROCEDURE INITIALIZE (VAR AVAIL, LIST : POINTERTYPE);
   (* Link all nodes into the list of available nodes. *)

VAR    P : POINTERTYPE;

BEGIN   (* initialize *)

   (* Make AVAIL point to the first node. *)
   AVAIL := 1;

   (* Make each node point to the next node. *)
   FOR P := 1 TO (MAX - 1) DO
      NODES[P].NEXT := P + 1;

   (* Set last pointer to null. *)
   NODES[MAX].NEXT := NULL;

   (* Set list to empty. *)
   LIST := NULL

END;   (* initialize *)
```

IMPLEMENTING THE LIST OPERATIONS

Converting our general pointer algorithms into this Pascal implementation
is simple. Consider the print-all-the-elements algorithm we discussed earlier:

```
P ← LIST
WHILE the list is not empty DO
     print (INFO(P))
     P ← NEXT(P)
```

With our array-of-records implementation, this algorithm can be coded as

```
P := LIST;
WHILE P <> NULL DO
   BEGIN
      WRITE(NODES[P].INFO);
      P := NODES[P].NEXT
   END;
```

NODES	.INFO	.NEXT
[1]	J	8
[2]	P	7
[3]	D	6
[4]	R	0
[5]	A	2
[6]	G	1
[7]	E	0
[8]	M	4
[9]	Q	10
[10]	B	5

LIST   3

AVAIL   9

Prints:
   D   G   J   M   R

Figure 5-11.

Using the array shown in Figure 5-11, let's see what is written by this segment of code. P is originally set to 3 (the value of the external pointer, LIST), and the value of NODES[3].INFO is printed. Then P is advanced to NODES[3].NEXT, or 6. Since 6 <> NULL, the loop is repeated. NODES[6].INFO is printed, and P is advanced to NODES[6].NEXT, or 1. Again P <> NULL, so the loop is repeated.

This cycle continues until P = 4. Then NODES[4].INFO is printed, and P is advanced to NODES[4].NEXT, or 0 (our NULL value). This 0 signifies the end of the list, and we exit the loop.

Why are there two NULL values in the NEXT field? Simply because two linked lists are being stored in the array, each with its own external pointer (LIST and AVAIL) and each with a final pointer value (NODES[P].NEXT = 0). In Figure 5-10, there is only one list stored in the array, the list of available nodes, so only one NULL value is seen in the NEXT field.

Coding GETNODE and FREENODE is also simple. Since all of our nodes are coming from the same source, NODES, we will access this array and the external pointer AVAIL globally.

```
PROCEDURE GETNODE (VAR P : POINTERTYPE);
    (* Returns a pointer to a free node in P, or NULL if no free nodes exist. *)

BEGIN  (* getnode *)
    IF AVAIL <> NULL
        THEN                                    (* If free nodes exist, get a node. *)
            BEGIN
                P := AVAIL;
                AVAIL := NODES[AVAIL].NEXT
            END
        ELSE                                    (* No free nodes; set P to NULL. *)
            P := NULL

END;   (* getnode *)
```

(**)

```
PROCEDURE FREENODE (P : POINTERTYPE);
    (* Puts the node pointed to by P into the list of available nodes. *)

BEGIN (* freenode *)
    NODES[P].NEXT := AVAIL;
    AVAIL := P
END;  (* freenode *)
```

INSERTING INTO AN ORDERED LINKED LIST

Presumably, we want to use a linked list to store some sort of ordered list of elements. If our elements are employee records and they are to be ordered by seniority (based on the order the records come in), then our insert-first-node algorithm is sufficient.

Records are inserted into the list in the order in which they come in, as new employees are hired. The list is ordered from lowest to highest seniority:

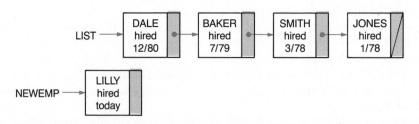

However, if our employee records are to be ordered alphabetically, by employee name, we will need to use a different kind of insert algorithm.

Let's use a simpler example to develop our algorithm. Given a linked list of positive integer elements (see Figure 5-12), ordered from smallest to largest, we will get a value and insert it into the linked list.

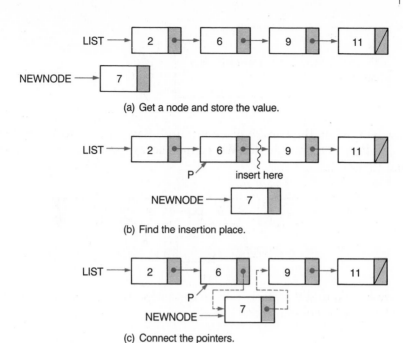

(a) Get a node and store the value.

(b) Find the insertion place.

(c) Connect the pointers.

Figure 5-12.

First, we will need to get a node to put the value, NEWVALUE, into. We will call the pointer to this node NEWNODE.

```
GETNODE(NEWNODE)          [Figure 5-12(a)]
INFO(NEWNODE) ← NEWVALUE
Insert NODE(NEWNODE)
```

The first two lines of the algorithm can be coded directly. The insert task can be broken into two parts:

> Find the place to insert   [Figure 5-12(b)]
> Connect the pointers   [Figure 5-12(c)]

The first task involves comparing the new value to the INFO field of each successive node in the list (using a temporary pointer P to traverse the list) until NEWVALUE < INFO(P). This task may be seen as a WHILE loop:

```
P ← LIST
WHILE NEWVALUE >= INFO(P) DO
    advance P
```

However, when the correct place is found, P is pointing to the node that should *follow* the new node. We cannot access the preceding node to change its pointer.

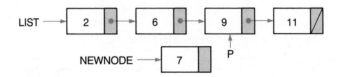

Here we have found the place, but we cannot get back to change the NEXT field of the node containing 6.

Let's modify our algorithm slightly, to "peek ahead" one node:

```
P ← LIST
WHILE NEWVALUE >= INFO(NEXT(P)) DO
    advance P
```

Working through the example in Figure 5-12, we quickly notice that the first node is skipped in the comparison. Further, it is clear that if NEWVALUE < INFO(LIST) (the first node), we have a special case. The reason this case is special becomes apparent when we do the second task of the insert algorithm: connecting the pointers. In the general case [Figure 5-12(c)], we need to change two pointers:

```
NEXT(NEWNODE) ← P(NEXT)
P(NEXT) ← NEWNODE
```

In our special case, NODE(NEWNODE) becomes the first node in the list:

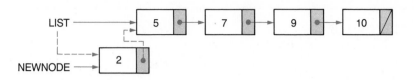

We must now change our external pointer, LIST:

NEXT(NEWNODE) ← LIST
LIST ← NEWNODE

We can modify our algorithm to test for this case before entering the WHILE loop:

P ← LIST
IF NEWVALUE < INFO(P)
    THEN change the pointers to insert NODE(NEWNODE) as the 1st node
    ELSE
        WHILE. . .

We have considered the general case of inserting into the middle of the list and the special case of inserting at the beginning of the list. What about the case when NEWVALUE is greater than all the values in the list? We will then need to insert at the end of the list. Our loop control

WHILE NEWVALUE >= INFO(NEXT(P)) DO

will always be satisfied, leading us, erroneously, to try to move P past NULL. To avoid this situation, we can use a Boolean variable PLACEFOUND in our search loop.

There is one other special condition: when we are inserting into an empty list. In this case, we simply want to set LIST to point to the new node. Our whole algorithm becomes

```
IF LIST = NULL
   THEN LIST ← pointer to new node
   ELSE
      P ← LIST
      IF NEWVALUE < INFO(P)
         THEN change the pointers to insert NODE(NEWNODE)
              as the 1st node
         ELSE PLACEFOUND ← FALSE
              WHILE NEXT(P) <> NULL
                    AND NOT PLACEFOUND DO
                 IF NEWVALUE >= INFO(NEXT(P))
                 THEN advance P
                 ELSE PLACEFOUND ← TRUE
              Change pointers to insert NODE(NEWNODE)
```

Figure out for yourself why we needed to use PLACEFOUND. Why couldn't we have used the following loop control:

```
WHILE (NEXT(P) <> NULL) AND (NEWVALUE >= INFO(NEXT(P))) DO
```

Hint: Remember that Pascal evaluates *all* of the conditions of the WHILE clause. What happens when NEXT(P) = NULL? This consideration is language-dependent; some other programming languages stop evaluating compound Boolean expressions as soon as the result is determined (e.g., after the first FALSE when expressions are ANDed together).

IMPLEMENTING THE INSERT ALGORITHM

Consider the linked list in Figure 5-13(a). (The INFO fields of nodes in the AVAIL list are represented by X to simplify our view of the list.) Following the insert algorithm given above, we will insert a node with an INFO value of 8. (This is the general case of inserting into the middle of the list.) First, the value is put into the INFO field of the first available node (NODES[4].INFO). Next, the value of AVAIL is incremented to NODES[4].NEXT, or 6. Then, the linked list pointed to by LIST is traversed until the insertion place is found [when NEWVALUE < INFO(NEXT(P))]. This situation occurs when P = 9 and INFO(NEXT(P)) = 11. The two pointers are changed (NODES[4].NEXT and NODES[9].NEXT), and our insertion is complete. In all, we have changed 4 values: AVAIL, NODES[4].INFO, NODES[4].NEXT, and NODES[9].NEXT. [See Figure 5-13(b).]

(a)

NODES	.INFO	.NEXT
[1]	18	8
[2]	11	5
[3]	4	9
[4]	X 8	6 2
[5]	13	1
[6]	X	7
[7]	X	0
[8]	22	10
[9]	7	2 4
[10]	25	0

LIST 3

AVAIL 4

(b)

NODES	.INFO	.NEXT
[1]	18	8
[2]	11	5
[3]	4	9
[4]	8	2
[5]	13	1
[6]	X	7
[7]	X	0
[8]	22	10
[9]	7	4
[10]	25	0

LIST 3

AVAIL 6

Figure 5-13.

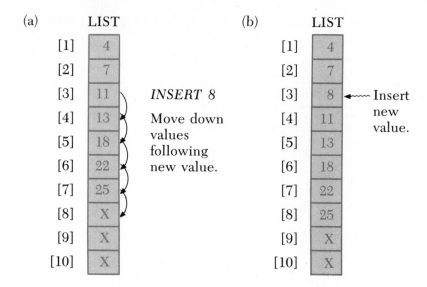

Figure 5-14.

Compare this to a sequential array implementation of the same ordered list (Figure 5-14). In this case, the insertion place is found, and then all the values following it are moved down before a place is made to insert the new value.

Which of these two implementations of a list is more efficient will depend on several factors. The sequential representation uses less space (since we do not need the NEXT field), and a binary search (faster than a sequential search) can be used to find the place to insert or the node to delete. Generally, if the insertions and deletions are primarily toward the beginning of the list, the linked list may be more efficient.

The code to implement the insert algorithm as a Pascal procedure is given below.

```
PROCEDURE INSERT (VAR LIST : POINTERTYPE;
                      NEWVALUE : INTEGER);
   (* Inserts NEWVALUE into the linked list pointed to *)
   (* by LIST. Assumes that there is available space   *)
   (* in the list. NODES is accessed globally.         *)

VAR    NEWNODE     : POINTERTYPE;        (* pointer to new node *)
       P           : POINTERTYPE;        (* temporary pointer *)
                                         (* used for search   *)

       PLACEFOUND : BOOLEAN;
```

```
BEGIN    (* insert *)

  (* Put NEWVALUE into a node. *)
  GETNODE(NEWNODE);
  NODES[NEWNODE].INFO := NEWVALUE;
  NODES[NEWNODE].NEXT := NULL;

  (* Insert the new node into the list. *)
  IF LIST = NULL                              (* inserting into empty list *)
    THEN LIST := NEWNODE
    ELSE
      BEGIN    (* insert into nonempty list *)
        P:=LIST;
        (* Check for special case inserting to front of list. *)
        IF NEWVALUE < NODES[P].INFO
          THEN
            BEGIN    (* insert before first node *)
              NODES[NEWNODE].NEXT := LIST;
              LIST := NEWNODE
            END      (* insert before first node *)

          ELSE
            BEGIN    (* general case *)
              (* Find insertion place. *)
              PLACEFOUND := FALSE;
              WHILE (NODES[P].NEXT <> NULL) AND
                      NOT PLACEFOUND DO
                  IF NEWVALUE >= NODES[NODES[P].NEXT].INFO
                    THEN P := NODES[P].NEXT
                    ELSE PLACEFOUND := TRUE;

              (* Connect the pointers. *)
              NODES[NEWNODE].NEXT := NODES[P].NEXT;
              NODES[P].NEXT := NEWNODE
            END      (* general case *)
      END    (* insert into nonempty list *)
END;    (* insert *)
```

DELETING FROM A LINKED LIST

Another essential operation on a linked list is deletion of nodes that are no longer needed. In our employee list, we may have the situation that Baker retires, and her employee record will need to be removed from the list.

Let's return to our linked list of ordered integers, and develop an algorithm for removing the node with value DELETEVAL from the list. We will assume, for simplicity, that we know that the value is actually in the list and appears only once.

We know from our experience with the insert algorithm that various cases (first, middle, or last node) required different treatments. We developed that algorithm by trial and error. Now that we know to watch out for these different cases, let's use a more structured approach to developing the delete algorithm. The basic tasks for the delete algorithm are

```
Find the node containing DELETEVAL
Modify the pointer(s) to delete the node
Free the node
```

Since we know that the value DELETEVAL will be in the list, we can find the node with a simple WHILE loop:

```
WHILE INFO(P) <> DELETEVAL DO
    advance pointer
```

When INFO(P) = DELETEVAL, P will be pointing to the node that we wish to delete, and we drop out of the loop. At this point, we need to be concerned with the different cases of node position in the list.

The case of deleting the first node is straightforward. The external pointer LIST needs to be modified to point to the second node in the list; then the first node must be freed. [See Figure 5-15(a).]

```
LIST ← NEXT(LIST)
FREENODE(P)
```

The other cases are more complicated. When P is pointing to the node we want to delete, we don't have a pointer to its predecessor in the list, which we would normally use in order to change its NEXT field. We could use the method of peeking ahead from the insert algorithm. However, another simple way to deal with this problem is to keep a *pair* of pointers, CURRENTNODE and BACKNODE, to traverse the list. When CURRENTNODE is pointing to the node we want to delete, BACKNODE is pointing to its predecessor. Deleting NODE(CURRENTNODE) becomes simple [Figure 5-15(b)]:

```
NEXT(BACKNODE) ← NEXT(CURRENTNODE)
FREENODE (CURRENTNODE)
```

Is the case of deleting the last node different? Executing NEXT(BACK-NODE) ← NEXT(CURRENTNODE) puts NULL into NEXT(BACK-NODE), which is exactly what we want to do. Then the last node is freed. [See Figure 5-15(c).] This case is the same as the case of the middle node.

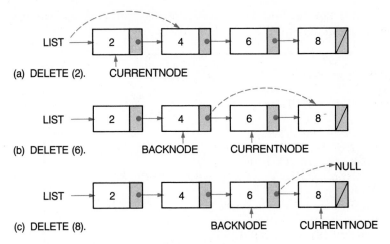

(a) DELETE (2).

(b) DELETE (6).

(c) DELETE (8).

Figure 5-15.

Using a second pointer will complicate our search loop slightly. We can initialize CURRENTNODE to LIST, and BACKNODE to NULL. Then, WHILE INFO(CURRENTNODE) <> DELETEVAL, we increment both pointers, like an inchworm inching his way. BACKNODE (the tail of the inchworm) catches up with CURRENTNODE (the head), then CURRENTNODE advances (Figure 5-16).

How do we know if we are deleting the first node? If BACKNODE is still equal to NULL when we drop out of the search loop, we know that the

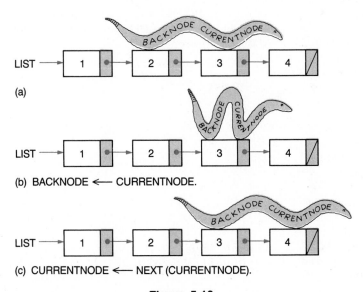

(a)

(b) BACKNODE ⟵ CURRENTNODE.

(c) CURRENTNODE ⟵ NEXT (CURRENTNODE).

Figure 5-16.

pointers have not been advanced and that we need to delete the first node. The whole algorithm:

```
(* initialize pointers *)
CURRENTNODE ← LIST
BACKNODE ← NULL

(* search for node to delete *)
WHILE INFO(CURRENTNODE) <> DELETEVAL DO
    BACKNODE ← CURRENTNODE
    CURRENTNODE ← NEXT(CURRENTNODE)

(* check if we are deleting first node *)
IF   BACKNODE = NULL
        THEN LIST ← NEXT (LIST)
        ELSE NEXT(BACKNODE) ← NEXT(CURRENTNODE)

FREENODE(CURRENTNODE)
```

IMPLEMENTING THE DELETE ALGORITHM

Coding the delete algorithm as a procedure, using the array-of-records implementation, is fairly direct:

```
PROCEDURE DELETENODE (VAR LIST : POINTERTYPE;
                           DELETEVAL : INTEGER);
   (* Delete the node containing the value of DELETEVAL from the linked list *)
   (* pointed to by LIST. NODES is accessed globally.                        *)

VAR   CURRENTNODE,
         BACKNODE       : POINTERTYPE;

BEGIN   (* deletenode *)

   (* Initialize pointers. *)
   CURRENTNODE := LIST;
   BACKNODE := NULL;

   (* Search for node to delete. *)
   WHILE NODES[CURRENTNODE].INFO <> DELETEVAL DO
      BEGIN
         BACKNODE := CURRENTNODE;
         CURRENTNODE := NODES[CURRENTNODE].NEXT
      END;
```

```
(* Check if we are deleting first node. *)
IF BACKNODE = NULL
    THEN LIST := NODES[LIST].NEXT
    ELSE NODES[BACKNODE].NEXT := NODES[CURRENTNODE].NEXT;

FREENODE(CURRENTNODE)

END;    (* deletenode *)
```

Consider the linked list in Figure 5-17(a). We want to delete the node containing the value 9. CURRENTNODE is initialized to 2, the index of

(a) NODES	.INFO	.NEXT
[1]	X	0
[2]	6	5
[3]	11	7
[4]	X	1
[5]	7	8
[6]	X	4
[7]	14	0
[8]	9	3
[9]	X	10
[10]	X	6

LIST   2

AVAIL   9

(b) NODES	.INFO	.NEXT
[1]	X	0
[2]	6	5
[3]	11	7
[4]	X	1
[5]	7	3
[6]	X	4
[7]	14	0
[8]	9	9
[9]	X	10
[10]	X	6

LIST   2

AVAIL   8

Figure 5-17.

the first node in the list, and BACKNODE is initialized to zero (NULL). The search loop begins.

When CURRENTNODE is pointing to the node containing 9 (CURRENTNODE = 8), BACKNODE is pointing to its immediate predecessor in the list (BACKNODE = 5). We are not deleting the first node in the list, so NODES[BACKNODE].NEXT is set to NODES[CURRENTNODE].NEXT, effectively skipping NODE(CURRENTNODE). Then FREENODE(CURRENTNODE) is called, adding NODE(CURRENTNODE) to the beginning of the AVAIL list. Freeing NODE(CURRENTNODE) necessitates changing NODES[CURRENTNODE].NEXT and AVAIL.

KEEPING A STACK IN A LINKED LIST

When we discussed implementing a stack as an array, we pointed out that the particular implementation should not affect the code in the higher levels of the program. Only low-level routines, like PUSH and POP, and the declarations for the data structure will need to be modified. We can also represent the stack as a linked list with an external pointer that points to the top of the stack:

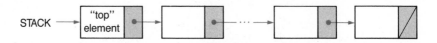

Using the declarations for the array NODES and an external pointer STACK, let's write the basic routines needed for stack operations. Note that type STACKTYPE is now equal to POINTERTYPE.

It can be readily seen that the PUSH and POP operations are analogous to our insert-first-node and delete-first-node algorithms.

```
PROCEDURE PUSH (VAR STACK : STACKTYPE;
                    NEWELEMENT : INFOTYPE);
   (* Add NEWELEMENT to the top of the stack. *)
   (* NODES is accessed globally.              *)

VAR   NEWNODE : POINTERTYPE;

BEGIN   (* push *)
   (* Get a node and store new element. *)
   GETNODE(NEWNODE);
   NODES[NEWNODE].INFO := NEWELEMENT;

   (* Insert new node. *)
   NODES[NEWNODE].NEXT := STACK;
   STACK := NEWNODE
END;   (* push *)
```

```
PROCEDURE POP (VAR STACK : STACKTYPE;
                  VAR POPPEDELEMENT : INFOTYPE);
```
(* Delete the top element from STACK, and return it in POPPEDELEMENT. *)
(* Assumes the stack is not empty. NODES is accessed globally.   *)

```
VAR    TEMP : POINTERTYPE;

BEGIN   (* pop *)
   (* Get the value of the top element. *)
   POPPEDELEMENT := NODES[STACK].INFO;

   (* Delete the top node. *)
   TEMP := STACK;
   STACK := NODES[STACK].NEXT;
   FREENODE(TEMP)
END;   (* pop *)
```

Writing a routine to test for an empty stack is a simple task. When the stack is empty, its external pointer will equal NULL.

```
FUNCTION EMPTYSTACK (STACK : STACKTYPE) : BOOLEAN;
```
(* Returns true if the stack is empty, false otherwise. *)

```
BEGIN   (* emptystack *)
   EMPTYSTACK := STACK = NULL
END;    (* emptystack *)
```

Do we need to test for a full stack? If all the stacks we are using share the same pool of available nodes and we have declared NODES to be large enough to hold the maximum number of elements in all the stacks combined, we will never have to test whether a particular stack is full. If we do not have this assurance, we will have to write a function FULL. (Try this yourself.)

KEEPING A QUEUE IN A LINKED LIST

A queue can be implemented in a linked list by keeping two external pointers to the list—one to the node on each end:

The two pointers may be joined into a single record:

```
TYPE QTYPE = RECORD
                FRONT, REAR : POINTERTYPE
             END;   (* record *)

VAR Q : QTYPE;
```

We can access the front of the queue through the pointer Q.FRONT and the rear of the queue through Q.REAR.

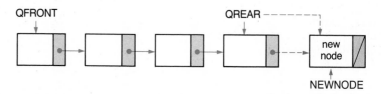

We can remove elements from the queue using an algorithm similar to our delete-first-node algorithm, where QFRONT points to the first node. But since we add new elements to the list by inserting after the *last* node, we need a new ENQ algorithm:

```
(*  get a new node for the new element  *)
GETNODE(NEWNODE)
INFO(NEWNODE) ← new element value
NEXT(NEWNODE) ← NULL

(*  insert the new node  *)
IF  the queue is empty
    THEN QFRONT ← NEWNODE
    ELSE NEXT(QREAR) ← NEWNODE

(*  update pointer to rear of queue  *)
QREAR ← NEWNODE
```

Note the relative positions of QFRONT and QREAR. Had they been reversed (Figure 5-18), we could have used our insert-first-node algorithm for ENQ, but how could we DEQ? To delete the last node of the linked list, we need to be able to reset QFRONT to point to the node preceding the deleted node. Since our pointers all go forward, we can't get back to the preceding node. To accomplish this task, we would have to either traverse the whole list (very inefficient, especially if the list is long) or keep a list with pointers in both directions. Such a *doubly linked list* is not necessary if we set up our queue pointers correctly to begin with.

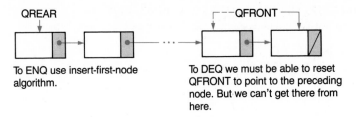

To ENQ use insert-first-node algorithm.

To DEQ we must be able to reset QFRONT to point to the preceding node. But we can't get there from here.

Figure 5-18. A bad queue design.

Note in the insert algorithm that inserting into an empty queue is a special case, since we need to make QFRONT point to the new node also. Similarly, in our delete algorithm, we will need to allow for the case of deleting when the list only contains one node, leaving the list empty. If, after we have deleted the front node, QFRONT is NULL, we know that the queue is now empty. In this case, we will need to set QREAR to NULL also. The algorithm for deleting the front element from a queue is illustrated as follows:

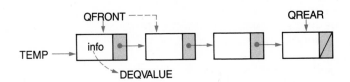

This algorithm assumes that the test for EMPTYQ is made before entering the delete routine—that is, that we know that the queue has at least one node.

```
TEMP ← QFRONT
DEQVALUE ← INFO(QFRONT)
QFRONT ← NEXT(QFRONT)
IF QFRONT = NULL  (* queue is now empty *)
    THEN QREAR ← NULL
FREENODE(TEMP)
```

We know that when the queue is empty, both QFRONT and QREAR will equal NULL. Testing for an empty queue simply involves checking either of these pointers for NULL.

```
FUNCTION EMPTYQ (Q : QTYPE) : BOOLEAN;
(* Returns true if the queue is empty; false otherwise. *)

BEGIN   (* emptyq *)
  EMPTYQ := Q.REAR = NULL
          (* or *)
  (* EMPTYQ := Q.FRONT = NULL *)
END;     (* emptyq *)
```

As in the case of the stack, if we have declared our array NODES to be large enough to hold the maximum number of elements in all the queues we are using, we need not check whether a particular queue is full. The code for ENQ and DEQ is

```
PROCEDURE ENQ (VAR Q : QTYPE;
               NEWELEMENT : INFOTYPE);
  (* Add NEWELEMENT to the rear of the queue. NODES is globally accessed. *)
  (* Assumes that there is space available in NODES.                       *)

VAR   NEWNODE : POINTERTYPE;

BEGIN   (* enq *)
  (* Create a node for new element. *)
  GETNODE(NEWNODE);
  NODES[NEWNODE].INFO := NEWELEMENT;
  NODES[NEWNODE].NEXT := NULL;

  (* Insert new node at rear of the queue. *)
  IF Q.REAR = NULL                                  (* if list is empty *)
     THEN Q.FRONT := NEWNODE
     ELSE NODES[Q.REAR].NEXT := NEWNODE;

  Q.REAR := NEWNODE                   (* Update pointer to rear of queue. *)
END;     (* enq *)
```

(**)

```
PROCEDURE DEQ (VAR Q : QTYPE;
               VAR DEQVALUE : INFOTYPE);
(* Remove the front element from the queue, and return it in DEQVALUE. *)
(* Accesses NODES globally. Assumes that the queue is not empty.       *)

VAR   TEMP : POINTERTYPE;

BEGIN   (* deq *)
  TEMP := Q.FRONT;
  DEQVALUE := NODES[Q.FRONT].INFO;
  Q.FRONT := NODES[Q.FRONT].NEXT;
  IF Q.FRONT = NULL                                 (* if list is empty *)
     THEN Q.REAR := NULL;
  FREENODE (TEMP)
END;   (* deq *)
```

CIRCULAR LINKED LISTS

There is a common problem with using linear linked lists: Given a pointer to a node somewhere in the list, we can access all of the nodes that follow, but none of the nodes that precede it. With a linear singly linked list structure, we must always have the pointer to the beginning of the list to access all of the nodes in the list.

We can, however, change the linear list slightly by making the pointer in the NEXT field of the last node point back to the FIRST NODE instead of NULL:

Now our list is *circular*, rather than linear. We can start at any node in the list and traverse the whole list. For this reason, we can make our external pointer to the list point to *any* node and still access all the nodes in the list. It is convenient, but not necessary, to let the external pointer to a circular list point to the last node in the list. In this way, we can easily access both ends of the list, since the NEXT field of the last node contains a pointer to the first node. (See Figure 5-19.) Note that an empty circular list has been represented by a NULL value for the external pointer to the list.

Using a circular, rather than a linear, linked list makes one obvious change in our list traversal algorithm: We no longer stop traversing the list when the pointer becomes NULL. Instead, we look for the external pointer as a stop sign. Let's write a procedure that will print out the elements of a circular linked list.

We can initialize a temporary pointer, P, to LIST, the external pointer. Then we can print one node ahead of the pointer, until P comes full circle—when P = LIST. Note that this algorithm works even when there is only one node in the list—when P, LIST, and NODES[P].NEXT are all equal [Figure 5-19(b)].

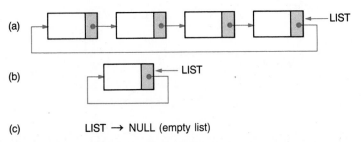

(a)

(b)

(c)   LIST → NULL (empty list)

Figure 5-19. Some circular linked lists, with external pointer to rear element.

```
P ← LIST
REPEAT
    Print INFO(NEXT(P))
    P ← NEXT(P)
UNTIL P = LIST
```

We do run into problems, however, when the list is empty [Figure 5-19(c)]. References to NEXT(P) are illegal when P is NULL. We can check for this possibility ahead of time, and print out an appropriate message if the list is empty.

```
PROCEDURE PRINTLIST (LIST : POINTERTYPE);
    (* Print out all the elements in the list. *)

VAR    P : POINTERTYPE;

BEGIN (* printlist *)
    P := LIST;
    (* Check for empty list. If not empty, print the elements. *)
    IF P = NULL
        THEN WRITELN('THE LIST IS EMPTY')
        ELSE
          REPEAT
            WRITELN(NODES[NODES[P].NEXT].INFO);
            P := NODES[P].NEXT
          UNTIL P = LIST
END;    (* printlist *)
```

A CIRCULAR LIST APPLICATION—THE QUEUE

We mentioned one convention of having the external pointer to a circular linked list point to the last node. In this way, we can easily access both ends of the list at once. This feature makes it possible to implement queue operations using one pointer to the queue, rather than separate pointers to the front and the rear:

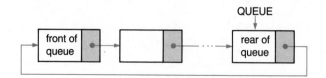

We can access the rear node, in order to ENQ, through the external pointer, QUEUE, and the front node, in order to DEQ, through NEXT(QUEUE). An empty queue would be represented by QUEUE = NULL.

Coding the ENQ and DEQ procedures for this implementation of a queue is left as a homework exercise.

Summary

A list of items is something that most people use often in their everyday lives. Thus we are already familiar with the concept of storing the elements of a list sequentially, as if we were writing them down one after another on a piece of paper. An array is often used to fill this role in computer solutions to problems that use lists. The elements of the list are stored in subsequent locations of the array.

In this chapter, we introduced the concept of *linking* the elements in a list, allowing us to keep them physically in any convenient order. The links preserve the logical order of the elements.

At an implementation level, we can use an array to store the elements and their links. An external pointer to the list indicates where in the array we can find the first element. Although the array itself is a random-access data structure (we can locate any element directly through its index), we can only access the elements of the linked list stored there through the pointer scheme we have imposed. That is, if the linked list is stored in an array called DATA, we do not know anything about the relative position of a list element by accessing its array position directly. DATA[5] may be the first, fifth, or any other element in the list, or it may not be in the list at all. We only give meaning to the structure by using the external pointer to access the beginning of the list and then following the pointers from element to element.

Using an array representation for a linked list, we are responsible for creating our own GETNODE and FREENODE operations. In the next chapter, we will see how Pascal provides a mechanism for letting the system allocate and free nodes for us. The basic list operations at a logical level remain the same. The changes we will describe occur at the implementation level.

■ APPLICATION: MAGAZINE CIRCULATION

Data Structures in Use
- LINKED LISTS
- STRINGS
- EXTERNAL FILE OF RECORDS

Software Techniques in Use
- PORTABILITY OF UTILITY ROUTINES (THIS PROGRAM USES SEVERAL ROUTINES DEVELOPED IN EARLIER CHAPTERS.)
- PASSING FUNCTIONS AS PARAMETERS
- WRITING PROGRAMS WITH RETAINED DATA
- USING TOP-DOWN DESIGN

The circulation department of a magazine has hired you as a contract programmer to automate the production of mailing labels. Since the description "automate production of mailing labels" is not very precise, you start by asking questions. After much discussion, you write the following revised job description and ask your new boss to sign off on it, that is, approve it.

Input: Current date.

The Sales Department will provide the original master list of subscribers, one subscriber per 80-character line, alphabetized by last name, in the following format:

> Positions 1–10: the first name or initial
> Positions 12–25: the last name
> Positions 27–44: the address
> Positions 46–56: the city
> Positions 58–65: the state abbreviation
> Positions 67–71: the zip code
> Positions 73–77: the expiration date of the subscription

All the entries except the expiration date are just strings of characters. The date is in the form mm/yy (the month followed by the year). For example, 11/85 would be November 1985; 02/87 would be February 1987. The missing columns between fields will contain blanks.

After the original input, in each succeeding month, there will be new subscriptions entered in the same format.

Output: Three sets of mailing labels, ordered by zip code:

1. those people whose subscriptions have expired
2. those people whose subscriptions will expire in the current month
3. those people whose subscriptions will expire sometime after the current month

An alphabetical list of all subscribers whose subscriptions have not yet expired (i.e., lists 2 and 3 above) must be printed and saved to use for the next month's processing.

A diagram illustrating the contents of the data base of subscribers is shown below.

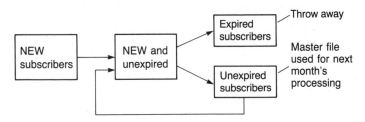

The data for the subscribers whose subscriptions have not expired is saved to be used the next time the program is run. It is called the *retained data* of the program.

The output labels must have the following format.

⟨FIRST NAME⟩ ⟨LAST NAME⟩ (with exactly one blank between)
⟨STREET ADDRESS⟩
⟨CITY⟩, ⟨STATE⟩ ⟨ZIP⟩ (one blank between state and zip)

Management agrees that this description is exactly what they want. The input format looks strange but is correct. It comes from the old days of computing, when information had to be in particular columns on a line or card. The blanks were inserted between each field of information for clarity when printing since the entire field may be filled with characters. These blanks may actually be useful when you write your input routines.

Several questions concerning input and output processing occur to you immediately. Should you keep the subscription records as they are given to you from sales, converting them to the proper format for printing on each run, or should you convert them to a format for easy printing once and save them in that format? Saving them in a format for easy printing seems reasonable, but just what should that format be?

The precise printing specification would imply that you know the length of each first name, city, and state so that the appropriate commas and blanks can be inserted. Perhaps the STRINGTYPE data type defined in Chapter 2 would be appropriate.

If you decide to keep the data in a format for easy printing, another question arises: Should you write a special-purpose program to convert the original input to the printing format? Since each monthly run will contain new subscriptions in the sales format, maybe the program can be organized so that the first run has no master file and all subscribers are treated as new subscribers.

You decide to keep these questions in mind while you do a first pass at the top level of your design. You also decide to save the subscription data in a format designed for easy printing, which you will call the *label format*.

MAIN   **Level 0**

```
READ current date              (* read current date from the terminal *)
WHILE more subscribers DO                      (* read master list *)
    GET label
WHILE more new subscribers DO                     (* read new list *)
    GET person
    CREATE label
COMBINE old and new labels
BREAK into three lists ordered by zip code    (* call them EXPIRED, *)
PRINTLISTS (the 3 sets of labels)          (* EXPIRING, and OKAY *)
COMBINE EXPIRING and OKAY
SORT by last name
PRINT sorted list
SAVE for next month's run
```

The exact format of the labels themselves can be decided later, but the data structures to be used to hold the three sets of labels must be determined before any further development can be done. Since the sizes of the three lists to be printed may vary from 0 to the whole subscription list, a linked representation seems appropriate for EXPIRED, EXPIRING, and OKAY. In contrast, the master lists of labels could be read into an array of records, putting new subscriptions into the bottom of the same array. This data structure is shown below.

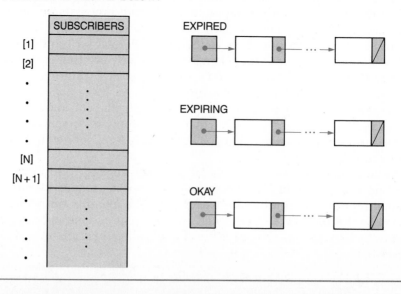

The problem with this representation is that each label is represented twice: once in the SUBSCRIBERS array and once in a list for printing. Is the array of subscribers actually necessary? Why not put the labels immediately into their respective lists for printing? This would surely save space.

Later, when the EXPIRING and OKAY lists are combined into a single list for printing and saving, each label can be removed from whichever list it is in and inserted into a linked list ordered by last name. Therefore, only one copy of each label is needed. Space will be needed in each label record for a pointer, but this field is small relative to the size of the label. This consideration will, however, change the top-down design.

MAIN   **Level 0**

```
READ current date
WHILE more labels DO
    GET label
    INSERT into proper list ordered by zip code
WHILE more new subscribers DO
    GET person
    CREATE label
    INSERT into proper list ordered by zip code
PRINTLISTS
COMBINE EXPIRING AND OKAY ordered by last name
PRINT
SAVE
```

One objective was to have the program itself handle the conversion of the original file. The first time the program is run, the first WHILE loop will be skipped because the file containing the master list of subscribers will be empty. All the subscribers will be treated as new. This should take care of the conversion problem. In succeeding months, the file of labels will be the file written by the program itself. This has a distinct advantage. The file can be treated as a nontext file. You can read and write each label as a complete record, rather than writing and reading each field separately. This makes the input/output routines much easier to write and faster to execute.

For those of you who have not used nontext files before, we will make a slight digression and describe how they operate.

The built-in data type for files is TEXT. A file of type TEXT is actually a FILE OF CHAR. READ(LN) and WRITE(LN) are procedures provided to handle input and output with TEXT files. If a file is declared to be of some other type, READ(LN) and WRITE(LN) cannot be used. The built-in procedures to be used with non-TEXT files are GET and PUT, which read and write one element of the component type of the file at a time.

For example, we can declare the master file of subscriber labels to be made of label records as shown:

```
TYPE       LABELTYPE = RECORD
                          FNAME,                                       (* first name *)
                          LNAME,                                       (* last name *)
                          ADDRESS,        (* street address or box number *)
                          CITY,                                             (* city *)
                          STATE,                                          (* state *)
                          ZIP,                                     (* zip code *)
                          DATE: STRINGTYPE        (* expiration date *)
                        END   (* record *)


           FILETYPE = FILE OF LABELTYPE;

VAR        MASTER : FILETYPE;              (* all current subscriptions *)
           SUBSCRIBER : LABELTYPE;            (* a temporary label *)
           NEWFILE : TEXT;           (* new subscriptions on text file *)
```

RESET and REWRITE have their usual meanings—they open the file for reading or writing. Remember that RESET also defines the file buffer variable. The file buffer variable is the name of the file (e.g., MASTER) followed by an up-arrow. To get the next component of a file, you use built-in Procedure GET. The parameter of GET is a file name. GET-(FILE1) puts into FILE1 the next component of FILE1. Let's summarize the terminology referring to files:

MASTER ↑ refers to the current record on file MASTER called the file buffer variable. (See Appendix H.)

MASTER ↑.FNAME refers to the FNAME field of the current record on file MASTER.

GET(MASTER) advances the file to the next record.

MASTER ↑ := SUBSCRIBER copies the record SUBSCRIBER into file buffer variable for file MASTER.

PUT(MASTER) writes the record on file MASTER.

EOF(MASTER) is TRUE if MASTER ↑ is the last record on file MASTER.

Again the top level of the design will have to be revised.

MAIN   Level 0

```
READ current date
RESET MASTER file              (* define MASTER ↑ first time   *)
WHILE more labels DO
    INSERTPROPER(MASTER ↑ )     (* MASTER ↑ is a subscriber label *)
    GET(MASTER)                      (* get next subscriber record *)
WHILE more new subscriptions DO
    CREATELABEL(SUBSCRIBER)          (* new subscriber returned in *)
                                     (* same format as old subscriber *)

    INSERTPROPER(SUBSCRIBER)
PRINTLISTS                        (* EXPIRING, EXPIRED, OKAY *)
COMBINE EXPIRING and OKAY
PRINTMASTER
SAVE MASTER FILE
```

INSERTPROPER   Level 1

```
IF current date < LABEL.DATE
    THEN INSERT(OKAY, LABEL)
ELSE IF current date = LABEL.DATE
    THEN INSERT(EXPIRING, LABEL)
    ELSE INSERT(EXPIRED, LABEL)
```

PRINTLISTS   Level 1

```
PRINTLABEL(EXPIRED)
PRINTLABEL(EXPIRING)
PRINTLABEL(OKAY)
```

In order to combine the two lists in alphabetical order to be printed and then saved for the next run, you will remove the labels one at a time from EXPIRING and insert them in order by last name into the linked list called LIST. When EXPIRING is empty, you remove the labels from OKAY one at a time and insert them into LIST.

In our discussion of linked lists, we showed how a stack could be implemented as a linked list. The operation of popping a stack was simply removing the first in the list. The operation of testing for empty was just checking to see if the list was empty. You can use these two operations here. To remove a label, you can use POP. To tell us when the list is empty, you can use EMPTY.

COMBINE Level 1

```
WHILE NOT EMPTY(EXPIRING) DO
    POP label
    INSERT label into LIST ordered by LNAME
WHILE NOT EMPTY(OKAY) DO
    POP label
    INSERT label into LIST ordered by LNAME
```

PRINTMASTER Level 1

```
WHILE more labels DO
    GET label
    PRINT label.fname
    PRINT label.lname
    PRINT label.address
    PRINT label.city
    PRINT label.state
    PRINT label.zip
    PRINT label.date
```

SAVE Level 1

```
WHILE more labels DO
    GET label
    MASTER ↑ ← label
    PUT MASTER
```

The level 2 routines will all require that you know exactly what the label records look like. The type declarations on page 224 showed all the fields as STRINGTYPE. This seems an appropriate representation for everything except the zip code and the date. The zip code could be carried as an integer number. This would make the insertion into the three lists more efficient, since numeric comparisons are much faster than string comparisons using our COMPARE function. However, a five-digit integer is greater than MAXINT on some machines. Therefore, for consistency across machines, it is safer to represent the zip code as a string. This will make your program more portable.

Since you will be comparing dates to determine relative magnitude, it would be convenient if the date could be treated as a single number. You can indeed transform a date into a number that can be compared. You input the month and the date as distinct integer values and then convert them to one number as follows:

$$\text{DATE} := \text{YEAR} * 100 + \text{MONTH}$$

DATE will be stored in the label records as an integer value that was calculated in this fashion from the original sales information. The current date will also be input and saved in this format. The following table shows several dates in the original format and the converted format, and indicates into which list the label containing that date would be put.

Original Format	Converted Format	List
01/85	8501	current date
02/87	8702	OKAY
12/84	8412	EXPIRED
11/85	8511	OKAY
12/88	8812	OKAY
01/85	8501	EXPIRING

To input the fields of STRINGTYPE, you have two choices: You can use either GETLINE or GETSTRING. GETSTRING reads a string until a delimiter character is read. What character could be used here? The first name field may have initials and/or names, so a blank won't work as a delimiter. In fact, the same is true of all of the fields.

You could instead input the entire line using GETLINE, and break the line into the proper fields using SUBSTRING and DELETE. However, there is a different problem here. The strings would be the length of the field in the original line. There may be trailing blanks that you would need to remove. Again you could use other string operations such as SEARCH, SUBSTRING, and DELETE to get rid of these trailing blanks.

Yet, if you look at the input description, you will see that the routine to input the proper columns into each field is really quite easy. Likewise, removing trailing blanks only requires beginning at the end of the string and moving up until a nonblank character is found.

This, then, is a case where you should write a special-purpose input routine for the variables of STRINGTYPE. This routine would store the characters directly into the proper field and remove trailing blanks.

CREATELABEL Level 1

GETFIELD first name from column 1–11
GETFIELD last name from column 12–26
GETFIELD address from column 27–45
GETFIELD city from column 46–57
GETFIELD state from column 58–66
GETFIELD zip code from column 67–72
READLN month, year
DATE ← year * 100 + month

GETFIELD will need three parameters: the string in which it will store the characters and the beginning and ending column numbers, which will indicate how many characters should be read.

GETFIELD Level 2

INDEX ← 0
FOR CT from FIRST to LAST
   READ CH
   increment INDEX
   STR.CHARS[INDEX] ← CH

REPEAT   (* trailing blank column will *)
   INDEX ← INDEX − 1   (* be part of the field *)
UNTIL (STR.CHARS[INDEX] <> ' ') OR (INDEX = 1)

IF STR.CHARS[INDEX] = ' '
   THEN STR.LENGTH ← 0
   ELSE STR.LENGTH ← INDEX

All of the design has now been completed except for INSERT and PRINTLABEL. You should be able to use Procedure INSERT from page 206. All you need to do is change the variable names in the comparison statement. When inserting into the three separate mailing lists, you will compare on zip code. When inserting into LIST, you will compare on last name.

Unfortunately, Pascal does not let you pass a field name as a parameter. You could write two insert procedures, one for the zip code field and one for the last name field. Another alternative, which will be illustrated here, is to pass the name of the function to use in the comparison as a parameter. (Yes, you can pass function or procedure names as parameters.)

You will have to write two functions, COMNAME and COMZIP. COMNAME will call function COMPARE with the name fields. COMZIP will call function COMPARE with the zipcode fields. Procedure INSERT will have an added formal parameter which is a function name. The function will be called when the insert algorithm needs to make a comparison.

When you are inserting into the three lists by zipcode, the actual parameter for Procedure INSERT will be COMZIP. When you are inserting into the list kept in alphabetical order by last name, the actual parameter to Procedure INSERT will be COMNAME.

PRINTLABEL   **Level 2**

```
WHILE more labels DO
     GET label
     PRINT label.fname
     WRITE a blank
     PRINT label.lname
     WRITELN               (* skips to next line *)
     PRINT label.address
     WRITELN               (* skips to next line *)
     PRINT label.city
     WRITE a comma
     PRINT label.state
     WRITE zip in 6 fields (* puts in a leading blank *)
```

As you look back over this design in preparation for coding it, you may see an inconsistency in the notation. The statement

GET label

has been used in several modules. In COMBINE, it was defined to be POP, i.e., remove the first node in the linked list. In the MAIN module, it refers to the built-in procedure GET. In PRINTMASTER, PRINTLABEL, and SAVE, it means to cycle through the list without removing the node.

Although it was clear what was meant at each point, we should be more precise with our language even when we are creating our top-down designs. A more precise formulation of "GET label" in the cases where we are cycling would be "label ← next label."

An improvement shows up at this stage. There is a great deal of duplication in PRINTMASTER and SAVE. Both of these modules cycle through the list of subscribers to be used for next month's processing. PRINTMASTER prints the list, and SAVE writes each label out to external storage. These two modules could be combined into one PRINTANDSAVE module.

PRINTANDSAVE   Level 1

```
Label ← first label
WHILE more labels DO
        MASTER ↑ ← label
        PUT(MASTER)
        PRINT label.fname
        PRINT label.lname
        PRINT label.address
        PRINT label.city
        PRINT label.state
        WRITELN label.zip, label.date
        label ← next label
```

The MAIN module needs to be revised one more time to reflect the combination of the modules PRINTMASTER and SAVE into one module, PRINTANDSAVE.

MAIN   Level 0

```
READ date
WHILE more labels DO
        INSERTPROPER(MASTER ↑ )
        GET(MASTER)
WHILE more new subscriptions DO
        CREATELABEL(SUBSCRIBER)
        INSERTPROPER(SUBSCRIBER)
PRINTLISTS
COMBINE EXPIRING and OKAY
PRINTANDSAVE
```

The code for this program appears below:

```
PROGRAM LABELS (INPUT, OUTPUT, MASTER, NEWFILE);

CONST MAXLENGTH = 20;                      (* maximum string length *)
      MAXNODES = 100;                      (* maximum subscribers *)
      NULL = 0;

TYPE  INDEXRANGE = 0..MAXLENGTH;
      POINTERTYPE = 0..MAXNODES;

      STRINGTYPE = RECORD
                     LENGTH : INDEXRANGE;
                     CHARS  : ARRAY[1..MAXLENGTH] OF CHAR
                   END;   (* record *)

      LABELTYPE = RECORD
                    FNAME ,                        (* first name *)
                    LNAME ,                        (* last name *)
                    ADDRESS ,                   (* street address *)
                    CITY ,                              (* city *)
                    STATE ,                            (* state *)
                    ZIPCODE : STRINGTYPE;            (* zip code *)
                    DATE : INTEGER              (* expiration date *)
                  END;   (* record *)

      NODETYPE = RECORD
                   SLABEL : LABELTYPE;          (* address label *)
                   NEXT : POINTERTYPE
                 END;   (* record *)

      RELATION = (LESS, EQUAL, GREATER);
                   (* result of string compare *)
      FILETYPE = FILE OF LABELTYPE;

VAR   NODES : ARRAY[1..MAXNODES] OF NODETYPE;
      AVAIL ,                     (* available space external pointer *)
      NODE ,                         (* temporary pointer variable *)
      EXPIRING ,                 (* labels which expire this month *)
      EXPIRED ,                  (* labels which expired last month *)
      OKAY ,                        (* labels expiring in the future *)
      LIST : POINTERTYPE;        (* EXPIRING combined with OKAY *)
      MONTH, YEAR,
      CURRENTDATE : INTEGER;     (* date of run to be read from console *)
      MASTER : FILETYPE;      (* file of labels kept from month to month *)
      NEWFILE : TEXT;              (* file of new subscriptions *)
      SUBSCRIBER : LABELTYPE;    (* temporary label for new subscriber *)
```

(***)

```
PROCEDURE INITIALIZE;
(* Initialize available space list to contain all nodes; *)
(* initialize list pointers to NULL.                     *)

VAR  P : POINTERTYPE;

BEGIN    (* initialize *)
  AVAIL := 1;
  FOR P := 1 TO (MAXNODES - 1) DO
    NODES[P].NEXT := P + 1;
  NODES[MAXNODES].NEXT := NULL;

  (* Set external pointers to linked lists to NULL. *)
  LIST := NULL;
  EXPIRING := NULL;
  EXPIRED := NULL;
  OKAY := NULL;
END;     (* initialize *)
```

(**)

```
PROCEDURE GETNODE (VAR P : POINTERTYPE);
(* See text for proper documentation. *)

BEGIN   (* getnode *)
  IF AVAIL <> NULL
      THEN
        BEGIN
          P := AVAIL;
          AVAIL := NODES[AVAIL].NEXT
        END
      ELSE
        P := NULL
END;    (* getnode *)
```

(**)

```
PROCEDURE FREENODE (P : POINTERTYPE);
(* See text for complete documentation. *)

BEGIN   (* freenode *)
  NODES[P].NEXT := AVAIL;
  AVAIL := P
END;    (* freenode *)
```

(**)

```
PROCEDURE GETFIELD (VAR STR : STRINGTYPE;
                        FIRST, LAST : INTEGER);
(* LAST - FIRST + 1 characters are moved from the input to STRING. *)
(* LENGTH is set to the actual length of the left-justified string.    *)
(* FILE NEWFILE is accessed globally.                                   *)

VAR  CH : CHAR;
     INDEX : INDEXRANGE;
     CT : INTEGER;

BEGIN   (* getfield *)
  INDEX := 0;
  (* Read in and store characters in field, which includes trailing blank. *)
  FOR CT := FIRST TO LAST DO
    BEGIN
      READ(NEWFILE, CH);
      INDEX := INDEX + 1;
      STR.CHARS[INDEX] := CH
    END;   (* for loop *)

  (* Move index from right to first nonblank character. *)
  REPEAT
    INDEX := INDEX - 1
  UNTIL (STR.CHARS[INDEX] <> ' ') OR (INDEX = 1);

  (* Set length field. *)
  IF STR.CHARS[INDEX] = ' '
     THEN STR.LENGTH := 0
     ELSE STR.LENGTH := INDEX
END;    (* getfield *)

(* ********************************************** )

PROCEDURE PRINT (STRING : STRINGTYPE);
(* See chapter 2 for proper documentation. *)

VAR  POS : INDEXRANGE;

BEGIN   (* print *)
  FOR POS := 1 TO STRING.LENGTH DO
    WRITE(STRING.CHARS[POS])
END;    (* print *)

(* ********************************************** )
```

```
PROCEDURE CREATELABEL (VAR SUBSCRIBER : LABELTYPE);
(* Procedure GETFIELD is called to read in each field of the new subscriber record. *)
(* FILE NEWFILE is accessed globally.                                              *)

VAR  MONTH, YEAR : INTEGER;                        (* date in month/year *)

BEGIN   (* create label *)
  GETFIELD(SUBSCRIBER.FNAME, 1, 11);
  GETFIELD(SUBSCRIBER.LNAME, 12, 26);
  GETFIELD(SUBSCRIBER.ADDRESS, 27, 45);
  GETFIELD(SUBSCRIBER.CITY, 46, 57);
  GETFIELD(SUBSCRIBER.STATE, 58, 66);
  GETFIELD(SUBSCRIBER.ZIPCODE, 67, 72);
  READ(NEWFILE, MONTH);
  READLN(NEWFILE, YEAR);
  SUBSCRIBER.DATE := YEAR * 100 + MONTH
END;    (* createlabel *)

(* ************************************************************ )

FUNCTION COMPARE (SUBSTR1, SUBSTR2 : STRINGTYPE) : RELATION
(* See chapter 2 for proper documentation. *)

VAR  POS : INDEXRANGE;
     STILLMATCH : BOOLEAN;
     MINLENGTH : INDEXRANGE;

BEGIN   (* compare *)
  IF SUBSTR1.LENGTH < SUBSTR2.LENGTH
    THEN MINLENGTH := SUBSTR1.LENGTH
  | ELSE MINLENGTH := SUBSTR2.LENGTH;
  POS := 1;
  STILLMATCH := TRUE;

  WHILE (POS <= MINLENGTH) AND STILLMATCH DO
    IF SUBSTR1.CHARS[POS] = SUBSTR2.CHARS[POS]
      THEN POS := POS + 1
      ELSE
        BEGIN
          STILLMATCH := FALSE;
          IF SUBSTR1.CHARS[POS] < SUBSTR2.CHARS[POS]
            THEN COMPARE := LESS
            ELSE COMPARE := GREATER
        END;
```

```
    IF STILLMATCH
       THEN
          IF SUBSTR1.LENGTH = SUBSTR2.LENGTH
             THEN COMPARE := EQUAL
       ELSE
          IF SUBSTR1.LENGTH < SUBSTR2.LENGTH
             THEN COMPARE := LESS
             ELSE COMPARE := GREATER
END;    (* compare *)
```

(***)

```
FUNCTION COMNAME (NEWLABEL, OLDLABEL : LABELTYPE) : RELATION;
```
(* Function COMPARE is called with the LNAME fields as parameters. *)

```
BEGIN
  COMNAME := COMPARE(NEWLABEL.LNAME, OLDLABEL.LNAME)
END;
```

(***)

```
FUNCTION COMZIP (NEWLABEL, OLDLABEL : LABELTYPE) : RELATION;
```
(* Function COMPARE is called with the ZIPCODE fields as parameters. *)

```
BEGIN
  COMZIP := COMPARE(NEWLABEL.ZIPCODE, OLDLABEL.ZIPCODE)
END;
```

(***)

```
PROCEDURE INSERT (VAR LIST : POINTERTYPE;
                  NEWLABEL  : LABELTYPE;
                  FUNCTION XCOMPARE(NEWLABEL, OLDLABEL :
                                    LABELTYPE) : RELATION);
```
(* See text for proper documentation. *)
(* Insertion is by zip or name based on Function XCOMPARE. *)

```
VAR  NEWNODE, P : POINTERTYPE;
     PLACEFOUND : BOOLEAN;
```

```
BEGIN   (* insert *)
  GETNODE(NEWNODE);
  NODES[NEWNODE].SLABEL := NEWLABEL;
  NODES[NEWNODE].NEXT := NULL;
  IF LIST = NULL
     THEN LIST := NEWNODE
  ELSE
     BEGIN
        P := LIST;
        IF (XCOMPARE(NEWLABEL, NODES[P].SLABEL) = LESS)
           THEN
             BEGIN
               NODES[NEWNODE].NEXT := LIST;
               LIST := NEWNODE
             END
        ELSE
           BEGIN
             PLACEFOUND := FALSE;
             WHILE (NODES[P].NEXT <> NULL)
                   AND NOT PLACEFOUND DO
               IF (XCOMPARE(NEWLABEL,
                   NODES[NODES[P].NEXT].SLABEL) = GREATER)
                  THEN P := NODES[P].NEXT
                  ELSE PLACEFOUND := TRUE;
             NODES[NEWNODE].NEXT := NODES[P].NEXT;
             NODES[P].NEXT := NEWNODE
           END
     END
END;   (* insert *)

(* ************************************************* *)

PROCEDURE POP (VAR LIST : POINTERTYPE;
               VAR SLABEL : LABELTYPE);
(* See chapter 3 for proper documentation. *)

VAR  TEMP : POINTERTYPE;

BEGIN   (* pop *)
  SLABEL := NODES[LIST].SLABEL;
  TEMP := LIST;
  LIST := NODES[LIST].NEXT;
  FREENODE(TEMP)
END;   (* pop *)
```

```
( ************************************************* )

FUNCTION EMPTY (LIST : POINTERTYPE) : BOOLEAN;

BEGIN  (*  empty  *)
  EMPTY := LIST = NULL
END;    (*  empty  *)

( ************************************************* )

PROCEDURE INSERTPROPER (SLABEL : LABELTYPE; CURRENTDATE : INTEGER;
           VAR EXPIRED, EXPIRING, OKAY : POINTERTYPE);
(* Date of expiration of subscription is compared with current date *)
(* and label is put into the proper list.                          *)

BEGIN  (* insertproper *)
  IF CURRENTDATE < SLABEL.DATE
     THEN
        INSERT(OKAY, SLABEL, COMZIP)
  ELSE IF CURRENTDATE = SLABEL.DATE
     THEN
        INSERT(EXPIRING, SLABEL, COMZIP)
  ELSE INSERT(EXPIRED, SLABEL, COMZIP)
END;    (* insertproper *)

( ************************************************* )

PROCEDURE COMBINE (VAR LIST, EXPIRING, OKAY : POINTERTYPE);
(* Labels for subscriptions which will be used next month are *)
(* combined into a list ordered by LASTNAME.                 *)

VAR  TLABEL : LABELTYPE;                    (* temporary label *)

BEGIN  (* combine *)
  WHILE NOT EMPTY(EXPIRING) DO
    BEGIN
      POP(EXPIRING, TLABEL);
      INSERT(LIST, TLABEL, COMNAME)
    END;

  WHILE NOT EMPTY(OKAY) DO
    BEGIN
      POP(OKAY, TLABEL);
      INSERT(LIST, TLABEL, COMNAME)
    END
END;    (* combine *)
```

```
(* * * * * * * * * * * * * * * * * * * * * * * * * * * * * * * * * * * * * * * * * * * * * *)

PROCEDURE PRINTLABEL (LIST : POINTERTYPE);
(* Labels are printed according to specification. *)

VAR  TLABEL : LABELTYPE;                                    (* temporary label *)

BEGIN   (* printlabel *)
  WHILE LIST <> NULL DO
    BEGIN
      TLABEL := NODES[LIST].SLABEL;
      PRINT(TLABEL.FNAME);
      WRITE(' ');
      PRINT(TLABEL.LNAME);
      WRITELN;
      PRINT(TLABEL.ADDRESS);
      WRITELN;
      PRINT(TLABEL.CITY);
      WRITE(', ');
      PRINT(TLABEL.STATE);
      WRITE(' ');
      PRINT(TLABEL.ZIPCODE);
      LIST := NODES[LIST].NEXT;
      WRITELN
    END
END;   (* printlabel *)

(* * * * * * * * * * * * * * * * * * * * * * * * * * * * * * * * * * * * * * * * * * * * * *)

PROCEDURE PRINTLISTS (OKAY, EXPIRING, EXPIRED : POINTERTYPE
(* Invokes PRINTLABEL to print three sets of labels. *)

BEGIN   (* printlists *)
  WRITELN('OKAY LIST');
  PRINTLABEL(OKAY);
  WRITELN('EXPIRING');
  PRINTLABEL(EXPIRING);
  WRITELN('EXPIRED');
  PRINTLABEL(EXPIRED)
END;   (* printlists *)

(* * * * * * * * * * * * * * * * * * * * * * * * * * * * * * * * * * * * * * * * * * * * * *)
```

```
PROCEDURE PRINTANDSAVE (LIST : POINTERTYPE);
(* Print subscribers in alphabetical order.           *)
(* Save labels in alphabetical order for next month's run. *)
(* File MASTER is accessed globally.                  *)

VAR  TLABEL : LABELTYPE;

BEGIN   (* printandsave *)
  REWRITE(MASTER);
  WRITELN('SAVED FOR NEXT MONTH');
  WHILE NOT EMPTY(LIST) DO
    BEGIN
      POP(LIST, TLABEL);
      PRINT(TLABEL.LNAME);
      WRITE(', ');
      PRINT(TLABEL.FNAME);
      WRITELN;
      MASTER↑ := TLABEL;
      PUT(MASTER)
    END
END;    (* printandsave *)
(* ********************************************** )
BEGIN   (* main *)
  WRITELN('MAIN PROGRAM BEGUN');
  RESET(NEWFILE);
  RESET(MASTER);
  INITIALIZE;
  READ(CURRENTDATE);

  WHILE NOT EOF(MASTER) DO                    (* Read master file. *)
    BEGIN
      WRITELN('READING MASTER');
      INSERTPROPER(MASTER↑, EXPIRED, EXPIRING, OKAY);
      GET(MASTER)
    END;

  WHILE NOT EOF(NEWFILE) DO
    BEGIN                                     (* Read new subscribers. *)
      WRITELN('READING NEWFILE');
      CREATELABEL(SUBSCRIBER);
      INSERTPROPER(SUBSCRIBER↑, EXPIRED, EXPIRING, OKAY)
    END;

  PRINTLISTS(OKAY, EXPIRING, EXPIRED);        (* Print labels. *)
  COMBINE(LIST, OKAY, EXPIRING);
  PRINTANDSAVE(LIST)                          (* Create new master list. *)

END.    (* main *)
```

Your program has been running now for several months. There have been no major problems, but it seems to take a long time to execute. The company is concerned that as the number of subscribers increases, the amount of machine time (and cost) required will be excessive. They ask you to analyze the program and see if you can find ways to speed it up.

Several thoughts occur to you immediately. You could change the data structure of the fields from strings to packed arrays of a fixed length. This would speed up the comparison operation when labels are inserted into the master list ordered alphabetically. Of course, the print routine would also take longer, since you would have to check for trailing blanks as you printed.

Before doing anything drastic like changing the data structure, you decide to analyze the processing. You were able to save processing during the original design by noticing that PRINTMASTER and SAVE both cycled through the same list. You were able to cut out one traversal of the linked list by combining those two modules. Perhaps there are other places where some of the processing is duplicated.

The first loop in the main module gets a label from the master file and inserts it into its list for printing. The second loop in the main module gets a new subscriber, creates a label and inserts it into its list for printing. There is no duplication here.

Procedure PRINTLIST calls Procedure PRINTLABEL three times with three different lists to print; no duplication here. Procedure COMBINE removes labels from the lists that are to be kept and inserts them into the master list. There is no duplication here. PRINTLABEL cycles through the three lists, printing them. Wait! PRINTLABEL and COMBINE both cycle through EXPIRING and OKAY.

The control structure in Procedure PRINTLABEL can be moved up into Procedure PRINTLISTS. As you cycle through the lists, labels can be removed. After the labels from EXPIRED are printed, nothing more will be done to them. As the labels from EXPIRING and OKAY are being printed, they can be inserted into LIST. Procedure COMBINE can now be deleted completely. The design for PRINTLISTS becomes as follows.

PRINTLISTS   **Level 1**

```
WHILE NOT EMPTY(EXPIRED) DO
    POP label
    PRINTLABEL label

WHILE NOT EMPTY(EXPIRING) DO
    POP label
    INSERT label into LIST
    PRINTLABEL label

WHILE NOT EMPTY(OKAY) DO
    POP label
    INSERT label into LIST
    PRINTLABEL label
```

Programming assignment 3 asks you to rewrite Program CIRCULATION incorporating this change.

Exercises

1. Show how the linked list would be affected by the following operations:

(a)   **INSERT 17.**

NODES	.INFO	.NEXT
[1]	12	0
[2]	19	5
[3]	~~17~~	~~2~~ 6
[4]	6	10
[5]	14	1
[6]	32	7
[7]	67	9
[8]	95	0
[9]	68	8
[10]	11	~~6~~ 3

LIST   4

AVAIL   ~~3~~

7

(b)   **DELETE 105.**

NODES	.INFO	.NEXT
[1]	65	9
[2]	85	5
[3]	95	~~10~~ 0
[4]	25	7
[5]	35	8
[6]	15	4
[7]	45	1
[8]	55	0
[9]	75	3
[10]	105—	~~0~~

LIST   6

AVAIL   ~~2~~

10

(c) INSERT 42; DELETE 11.

NODES	.INFO	.NEXT
[1]	5	0
[2]	17	3
[3]	35	6 8
[4]	92	0
[5]	76	4
[6]	43	9
[7]	11	2 10
[8]	12 42	10 6
[9]	57	5
[10]	42	1

LIST 7 2

AVAIL 8

10

2. (a) Write a segment of code to print out the INFO (char) portion of a linked list pointed to by LIST. (NULL is represented by 0.)

   (b) Show what would be printed out by applying the above code to the following list:

NODES	.INFO	.NEXT
[1]	A	3
[2]	D	4
[3]	Z	10
[4]	G	8
[5]	K	7
[6]	B	2
[7]	V	9
[8]	I	5
[9]	W	0
[10]	H	0

LIST 6

AVAIL 1

Use the following declarations in answering questions 3–8.

```
TYPE  PTR = 0..MAX;
      NODE = RECORD
                  INFO : INTEGER;
                  NEXT : PTR
            END;  (* record *)

VAR   NODES : ARRAY[1..MAX] OF NODE;
      START, AVAIL : PTR;
```

3. Write a segment of code to delete the first element of the linked list pointed to by START.

4. Write a segment of code to insert a value N after the last node in the linked list.

5. Given an integer I, delete the Ith element from the list. [*Hint:* Find the (I − 1)th element, then delete the node following it.]

6. Write a procedure, INSERT, that takes the pointer to a sorted list and a pointer to a node, and inserts the node into its correct ordered position in the list.

7. Assuming that START points to a list of unordered nodes, write a segment of code to order the list from lowest to highest value. (*Hint:* Use a temporary list.) You can use your INSERT procedure from the preceding question.

8. Given two ordered lists, pointed to by START1 and START2, merge them into a single ordered linked list, pointed to by NEWLIST.

9. What is wrong with the following linked list?

NODES	.INFO	.NEXT
[1]	32	5
[2]	12	9
[3]	17	1
[4]	101	2
[5]	46	6
[6]	57	7
[7]	98	0
[8]	12	7
[9]	12	8
[10]	14	3

LIST 10

AVAIL 4

10. Why are there two 0s (NULL values) in the NEXT field of the array?

NODES	.INFO	.NEXT
[1]	11	3
[2]	41	6
[3]	60	5
[4]	2	7
[5]	9	0
[6]	63	8
[7]	16	9
[8]	85	0
[9]	32	2
[10]	22	1

LIST   4

AVAIL   10

11. A circular linked list contains integer elements. LIST points to the last node in the list. Write a procedure to print the positive (not including 0) elements in the list. If there are none, print NO POSITIVE ELEMENTS.

12. Using the description of a queue implemented as a circular list (see the figure on page 218), write PROCEDURE ENQ (VAR Q : PTR; X : ELTYPE). You do not have to test for FULLQ.

13. Write PROCEDURE DEQ (VAR Q : PTR; VAR X : ELTYPE) for a queue implemented as a circular list. You do not have to test for EMPTYQ.

Pre-Test

For this test use the following declarations where appropriate. You may use GET-NODE without defining it.

```
CONST MAX = 7;
      NULL = 0;

TYPE PTR = 0..MAX;
     NODE = RECORD
                  INFO : INTEGER;
                  NEXT : PTR
            END  (* record *)

VAR NODES : ARRAY[1..MAX] OF NODE;
    LIST, AVAIL, P : PTR;
```

1. Fill in the contents of the array NODES after the following numbers have been inserted into their proper place in the list pointed to by LIST. The list has been initialized and is empty to begin with. These operations are the first executed following the execution of Procedure INITIALIZE. Show also the contents of LIST and AVAIL. Numbers: 17, −23, 42, −17 (the list should be in ascending order).

NODES	.INFO	.NEXT
[1]		
[2]		
[3]		
[4]		
[5]		
[6]		
[7]		

LIST ☐

AVAIL ☐

2. Given the situation shown above, show the values of the variables that have been changed by the following insertion and deletion. The list should remain in order.

INSERT: 7
DELETE: 42

NODES	.INFO	.NEXT
[1]		
[2]		
[3]		
[4]		
[5]		
[6]		
[7]		

LIST ☐

AVAIL ☐

3.

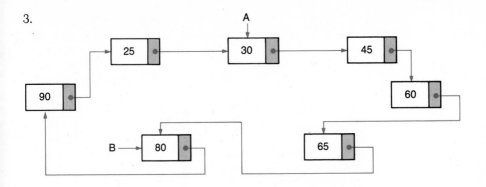

(a) NODES[NODES[NODES[B].NEXT].NEXT].INFO is   ——

(b) NODES[NODES[B].NEXT].INFO is   ——

(c) NODES[NODES[NODES[NODES[B].NEXT].NEXT].NEXT].INFO
is   ——

(d) NODES[NODES[NODES[A].NEXT].NEXT].INFO is   ——

4.

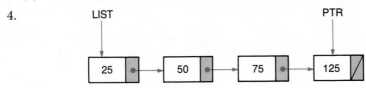

Write one Pascal statement for each of the following three tasks. Each time restart with the original data structure as shown above.

(a) Make PTR point to the first block in the list.

(b) Print out the value in the block pointed to by PTR.

(c) Make the block pointed to by PTR point to the first block in the list (creating a circle).

5. Write a procedure to sum the elements of a linked list pointed to by LIST.

6. Write a procedure, NEXTOP, that inserts a node with the value VAL into the linked list pointed to by LIST immediately before NODE(P). (P is a pointer, not a value.) The formal parameters should be LIST, P, and VAL.

Pointer Variables 6

Goals

To be able to explain what is meant by "dynamic allocation."

To be able to define a Pascal pointer type.

To be able to declare a Pascal pointer variable.

To be able to use the built-in functions NEW and DISPOSE.

To be able to implement all the linked list algorithms using Pascal pointer variables.

To be able to define and use list headers and trailers.

To be able to implement all the linked list algorithms using doubly linked lists.

In the previous chapter, we discussed the use of pointers to link together the nodes of a list. By *pointer* we meant the address of a node. Since the nodes were kept in an array, our pointer type was an index into the array. Pascal, like a number of other high-order languages, also provides a built-in pointer type. The use of these pointer-type variables requires both a knowledge of their special syntax and an understanding of a concept called *dynamic allocation*. Therefore, we will work with two different tool boxes in this chapter. One will contain the nuts and bolts of the syntax that allows us to implement data structures using Pascal pointer variables. The other tool box will contain the concepts that are behind the choice to use dynamically allocated structures. As always, we will consider the concepts before their implementation.

THE RATIONALE FOR DYNAMIC ALLOCATION

In the declaration of an array, the specification of the index range is a type, and thus it cannot vary. In other words, the compiler must know how many locations to assign to the array. Arrays are *static* variables—their size is fixed at compile time.

A static variable is around as long as the part of the program (block) in which it was declared is executing. Those variables declared in the VAR section of the main Pascal program are always there; that is, they exist during execution of the whole program. Local variables declared in the VAR section of a procedure or function exist from the time the subprogram is called until control is passed back to the invoking routine.

Pascal also has a mechanism for creating *dynamic* variables. That is, you can *define* a type at compile time, but not actually *instantiate* it (create any variables of that type) until run time. We refer to this process as *dynamic storage allocation*. These dynamic variables can be created or destroyed at any time during the execution of the program. They can be defined as being of any simple or structured type.

> **DYNAMIC ALLOCATION**
>
> Creation of a variable's storage space in memory during the execution (rather than compilation) of the program.

Previously, we used static variables, such as arrays and records, to structure our data. These work very well for many applications, but they do have some disadvantages. For instance, using an array-of-records implementation of linked lists, you must guess the length of the list(s) to be stored in the array in order to declare the array type. The compiler needs to know how much space in memory to reserve for the array. If the guess is too large, memory space will be wasted. If the guess is too small and the array space is inadequate to store all the nodes in the list, the program will fail at execution time.

Dynamic variables can be used to overcome these problems of a static variable such as the array. You can create new components (nodes) for a list as you need them by using dynamic variables. You don't need to know in advance how long the list will be. The only limitation is the amount of available memory space.

Let's apply this idea to the implementation of a familiar data structure. In this chapter, we will use the linked list as a convenient example of the use of dynamic storage allocation. We will see later that other data structures may be similarly implemented. Note that our discussion will center now on the lowest level of design considerations, the implementation level. At the level of logical operations on the list, it shouldn't make any difference whether the space for the list is allocated statically or dynamically.

USING PASCAL POINTER VARIABLES

Our algorithms for creating and manipulating a linked list accessed the nodes in the list through pointers—variables that gave us the address of the node we wished to access. In the array-of-records implementation, a pointer referred to an address in the array, the array index of a certain record (node).

Similarly, using pointer variables, we will access a node through its pointer. In this case, the pointer variable contains the *address in memory* of the node. In most machines, this is an integer value, since memory locations have addresses ranging from 0 to the size of the memory. However, we must differentiate between pointer types and integers. In Pascal, we cannot assign an integer value to a pointer variable. Rather than using the actual addresses, it is convenient to picture pointer variables graphically as arrows connecting one node to another.

The following discussion refers to Pascal syntax. A Pascal pointer type is denoted by the symbol, ↑, followed by the name of the type of data structure that the pointer will access. Let's consider the following declarations as an example of how pointer variables can be used to implement a linked list:

```
TYPE  POINTERTYPE = ↑NODETYPE;

      NODETYPE = RECORD
                    INFO : INFOTYPE;
                    NEXT : POINTERTYPE
                 END;  (* record *)

VAR   LIST,                        (* the external pointer to the list *)
      P    : POINTERTYPE
```

There are several things to note in the preceding declarations:

1. We used the symbol ↑ (read "up-arrow"), followed by a type name (NODETYPE), to denote a pointer type. Any variable of type POINTERTYPE that we declare will be a pointer to a record of type NODETYPE and only of that type. The type identifier following the ↑ does *not* have to be previously defined. For instance, NODETYPE has not yet been defined when POINTERTYPE is declared to be ↑NODETYPE. This situation is an exception in Pascal, where types normally need to be defined before they are used.
2. We declare a pointer variable as an external pointer to access the list (e.g., LIST). This is similar to the array-of-records implementation. Note, however, that we did *not* declare an array of nodes. This point must be stressed: We did not declare any variables of type NODETYPE in the VAR section of the declarations. At the beginning of the program's execution, no space has been allocated for the nodes. We will create the variables dynamically as we need them during the execution of the program.
3. Note that we did not declare an external pointer to a list of available nodes. Pascal provides a special built-in procedure, NEW, to allocate space as needed. We will discuss this in greater detail below.
4. We can assign pointers of the same type, and only of the same type, to each other. For instance, we can initialize a temporary pointer, P, to point to the beginning of the list by the statement

```
P := LIST
```

If, however, we decided to keep another list with nodes of a different type (e.g., ↑XNODETYPE), we could not assign values of type ↑NODETYPE (as defined above) to pointer variables of the second type. Therefore, after adding these declarations to the ones above

```
TYPE XPOINTERTYPE = ↑XNODETYPE;

     XNODETYPE = RECORD
                      DATA : INTEGER;
                      NEXT : XPOINTERTYPE
                 END;   (* record *)

VAR  XLIST, Q : XPOINTERTYPE;
```

the following statements would be illegal (type conflicts):

```
XLIST := LIST;
LIST := Q;
P := XLIST;
```

These variables are all pointers, but LIST and P point to records of type NODETYPE, while XLIST and Q point to records of type XNODETYPE. We could, however, make the assignment

```
Q := XLIST;
```

since Q and XLIST are of the same type.

5. We could have left out the declaration of POINTERTYPE = ↑NODETYPE. Our resulting declarations would be

```
TYPE NODETYPE = RECORD
                    INFO : INFOTYPE;
                    NEXT : ↑NODETYPE
                END;   (* record *)

VAR  LIST, P : ↑NODETYPE;
```

Defining the variables LIST and P by the type description ↑NODETYPE is analogous to defining an array variable in the VAR declarations, as in

```
VAR WORD : ARRAY[1..10] OF CHAR;
```

The definition of types in the VAR section is legal but bad style. These variables cannot subsequently be used as actual parameters for procedures and functions. That is, we cannot write

```
PROCEDURE READWORD (VAR WORD : ARRAY[1..10] OF CHAR);
```

Similarly, we cannot write

```
PROCEDURE DOSOMETHING (VAR POINTER : ↑NODE);
```

UP-ARROW SYNTAX

We have already seen that the symbol ↑, followed by a type identifier, defines a pointer type. This up-arrow symbol is also used in other ways.

Pointer-variable-name ↑ denotes the variable to which the pointer variable is pointing. For example, using the declarations of POINTERTYPE and NODETYPE above, LIST ↑ refers to the node of the linked list pointed to by the pointer variable LIST. Note the difference between LIST and LIST ↑ —the first is a pointer variable (an address), while the second is the actual data it points to (a record).

LIST   LIST ↑

Where the variable being pointed to is a record type (like NODETYPE), we can refer to individual fields of the record.

Pointer-variable-name ↑ **.field** denotes the *contents of the field* of the node to which the pointer variable points. For example, WRITE (LIST ↑ .INFO) prints the contents of the INFO field of the node pointed to by LIST. Note the difference between LIST ↑ and LIST ↑ .INFO—LIST ↑ is a whole record, while LIST ↑ .INFO is the data in one field of that record.

Important: You *cannot* print the value of a Pascal pointer variable. That is, WRITE(LIST) is not a legal statement. Similarly, WRITE(LIST ↑ .NEXT) is not a legal statement, since the NEXT field of the node contains a pointer. This restriction will have implications in the debugging of your programs.

Manipulating Pointer Variables

Given the diagram of a linked list in Figure 6-1(a), we can manipulate the pointers to do a number of tasks:

- Make P point to the next node [Figure 6-1(b)]:

```
P := P↑ .NEXT
```

Both P and P ↑ .NEXT are of type POINTERTYPE, so this is a legal assignment statement.

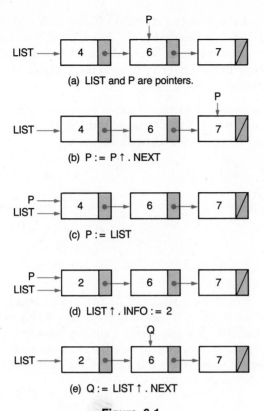

(a) LIST and P are pointers.

(b) P := P ↑ . NEXT

(c) P := LIST

(d) LIST ↑ . INFO := 2

(e) Q := LIST ↑ . NEXT

Figure 6-1.

- Make P point to the beginning of the list [Figure 6-1(c)]:

```
P := LIST
```

P and LIST are both of type POINTERTYPE.

- Set the value of the INFO field of the first node in the list to 2 [Figure 6-1(d)]:

```
LIST↑.INFO := 2
```

Both LIST. ↑ INFO and 2 are of type INTEGER. (This could also have been accomplished, in this example, by the statement P ↑ .INFO : = 2.)

- Set another pointer, Q, to point to the second node in the list [Figure 6-1(e)]:

```
Q := LIST↑.NEXT
```

To see how this works, follow the arrows in Figure 6-1(e). LIST points to the first node. LIST ↑ is the first node. LIST ↑.NEXT is the NEXT field of the first node. It contains a pointer to the second node. The NEXT field is of type POINTERTYPE, as is the variable Q, so we can make the assignment.

As you can see, it is possible to make some very complicated pointer expressions. For instance, to print the value of the INFO field of the third node of the linked list in Figure 6-2(a), we can write

```
WRITE(LIST↑.NEXT↑.NEXT↑.INFO)
```

Use the diagrams in Figure 6-2 to convince yourself that the statement is correct.

Traversing the List

Of course, we don't have to write a series of increasingly complex pointer expressions every time we need to traverse the whole list (for instance, to print all the values in the list). We can write a simple loop to traverse the list, using a temporary pointer to point to each successive node. We first initialize P (our temporary pointer) to the beginning of the list with the statement

```
P := LIST
```

We can then print the value of the node pointed to by P,

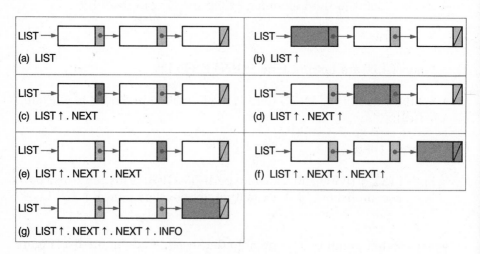

Figure 6-2.

```
WRITELN(P↑.INFO)
```

and move P along to the next node

```
P := P↑.NEXT
```

This process is repeated until the end of the list is reached. How do we know when we have reached the end? The last node in the list has a special value, called NIL, in its NEXT field. In the array-of-records implementation, we created a special constant called NULL to indicate an impossible address (index) in the array. Similarly, the Pascal reserved word NIL is an impossible address for a pointer variable. We can control our print loop with the statement

```
WHILE P <> NIL DO
```

(Note that we *cannot* substitute the value 0 for the word NIL in this implementation.) We can represent the value NIL graphically by placing a slash across the field whose value is NIL.

A procedure that would print all the values in a linked list might look like this:

```
PROCEDURE PRINTLIST (LIST : POINTERTYPE);
    (* Print out the value of the INFO field of each *)
    (* node in the linked list.                      *)

VAR P : POINTERTYPE;

BEGIN  (* printlist *)

    (* Process all nodes until end of list. *)
    P := LIST;
    WHILE P <> NIL DO
      BEGIN
        (* Print data and advance pointer. *)
        WRITELN(P↑.INFO);
        P := P↑.NEXT
      END   (* while *)

END;    (* printlist *)
```

Creating New Nodes

Up until now, we have been manipulating pointers of a list that already exists. We need to be able to create new nodes, in order to create the nodes of the original list and to add nodes to an existing list.

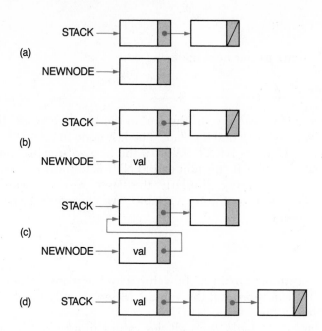

Figure 6-3. The PUSH operation.

In the array-of-records implementation, all of the nodes available existed in a list pointed to by an external pointer, AVAIL. To access one of these nodes, we wrote a procedure GETNODE that returned a pointer to an available node. Using dynamic storage allocation, nodes are created from free memory space as we need them, using the built-in Pascal procedure, NEW. This procedure takes one parameter: the name of the pointer to the new node.

For instance, to create a new node, pointed to by P, we can write

```
NEW(P)
```

This is analogous to the call GETNODE(P) in the array-of-records implementation. However, since the programmer no longer needs to be concerned with managing the available storage, there is no longer a need for the pointer, AVAIL. The system now manages the allocation of available space.

To see how the procedure NEW may be used, let's look at a procedure that inserts a new node with a specified value at the beginning of a linked list. (See Figure 6-3.) Does this task sound familiar? If the linked list represents a stack, this procedure would be our PUSH routine:

```
PROCEDURE PUSH (VAR STACK : POINTERTYPE;
                    VAL   : INFOTYPE);
```
   (* Add VAL to the top of the stack. *)

```
VAR NEWNODE : POINTERTYPE;
```

```
BEGIN   (* push *)
```

 (* Get a new node and put VAL into the INFO field. *)
```
   NEW(NEWNODE);                              (* Figure 6-3(a) *)
   NEWNODE↑.INFO := VAL;                      (* Figure 6-3(b) *)
```

 (* Attach the new node into the stack. *)
```
   NEWNODE↑.NEXT := STACK;                    (* Figure 6-3(c) *)
   STACK := NEWNODE                           (* Figure 6-3(d) *)
```

```
END;    (* push *)
```

Freeing Old Nodes

Most Pascal compilers also provide a procedure analogous to FREENODE. The DISPOSE procedure takes one parameter—a pointer to the node you wish to dispose of. It is important to note that the statement

```
DISPOSE(P)
```

makes future reference to P illegal, until P has been redefined by an assignment statement (e.g., P := LIST) or a subsequent call to NEW(P).

What happens when DISPOSE is called? There is no standard treatment in the Pascal language; each implementation of Pascal has its own version of the DISPOSE procedure. In some implementations, P is set to NIL; in others, P is left unchanged, with a valid address stored in P. Therefore, it is the programmer's responsibility to make sure that references to P never follow a call to DISPOSE.

A simple example of the use of the DISPOSE procedure can be seen in the following procedure (see Figure 6-4), which removes the first node from the list and returns the value of its INFO field to the calling program. (This should also sound familiar by now.)

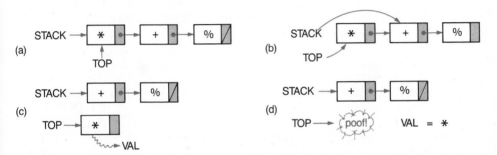

Figure 6-4. The POP operation.

```
PROCEDURE POP (VAR STACK : POINTERTYPE;
                VAR VAL    : INFOTYPE);
```
(* Remove the top element from the stack, and return *)
(* its value in VAL. Assumes the stack is not empty. *)

```
VAR TOP   : POINTERTYPE;

BEGIN   (* pop *)
```
    (* Take the top node off the stack. *)
```
   TOP := STACK;                                      (* Figure 6-4(a) *)
   STACK := STACK↑.NEXT;                              (* Figure 6-4(b) *)
```
    (* Put the top value in VAL. *)
```
   VAL := TOP↑.INFO;                                  (* Figure 6-4(c) *)
```
    (* Free the old node. *)
```
   DISPOSE(TOP)                                       (* Figure 6-4(d) *)

END;    (* pop *)
```

It is important to remember to use the DISPOSE procedure when you will be deleting many nodes from a list. This will return the memory cells occupied by the node to available space for later use. In a large program, if you do not DISPOSE properly, you might run out of memory.

List Operations Using Pointer Variables

By examining the PRINTLIST, PUSH and POP procedures above, you can see that we are only making changes at the implementation level; the algorithms for the various list operations remain the same. Changing from the array-of-records implementation to the pointer-variable implementation is a simple and direct conversion. (See Figure 6-5.)

Using the algorithms in the previous chapters, you should be able to write procedures and functions for list, stack, and queue operations using pointer variables. Writing the code for INSERT and DELETE procedures has been left as an exercise.

DEBUGGING HINTS

Pointer variables contain memory addresses. These values cannot be printed out. Even if they could, they might not tell you what you need to know to debug a program. For this reason, programs using pointer variables are often more difficult to debug.

Array of records	Pointer variables
GETNODE(P)	NEW(P)
FREENODE(P)	DISPOSE(P)
NODES[P].INFO	P ↑ .INFO
NODES[P].NEXT	P ↑ .NEXT
NODES[NODES[P].NEXT].INFO	P ↑ .NEXT ↑ .INFO
WHILE P <> NULL DO	WHILE P <> NIL DO

Figure 6-5. Two implementations of linked lists.

It is hard to tell whether or not pointer variables contain valid values. The values of the variable *referenced by* the pointer, however, can be printed out [for instance, by using a debug WRITELN statement like WRITELN(P ↑ .INFO)]. This assumes, of course, that the pointer is pointing to something, not NIL.

Use the following hints for testing and debugging your programs using pointer variables:

Compile-Time Problems

- Pascal pointer variables are *typed* pointers. That is, they point to data of a particular type and only that type. Remember that pointers must be of the same type in order for them to be compared or assigned to each other.
- Don't confuse the pointer with the variable it points to. If P and Q are both type PTRTYPE = ↑ NODETYPE [where NODETYPE is a record with two fields, INFO and NEXT (type PTRTYPE)], P := Q ↑ .NEXT is legal, since P and the NEXT field of Q are both type PTRTYPE, but P := Q ↑ is illegal, since P is a pointer and Q ↑ is a node.
- Be careful when using complex pointer expressions. Some compilers limit the complexity of pointer expressions, requiring the programmer to rewrite the expression using a temporary variable. For instance, if your compiler will not accept

```
DATA1 := P↑.NEXT↑.NEXT↑.NEXT↑.INFO
```

the statement can be rewritten by breaking up the pointer expression as follows:

```
TEMPPTR := P↑.NEXT↑.NEXT;
DATA1   := TEMPPTR↑.NEXT↑.INFO
```

Run-Time Problems

- Be sure that a pointer is not NIL before accessing its referenced variable. If the pointer P is either NIL or undefined, accessing P ↑ will give you a run-time error.
- Be especially careful with compound expressions in a WHILE loop. Most Pascal compilers evaluate both sides of a compound expression (one using AND or OR), regardless of the outcome of the first expression. For instance,

```
WHILE (P <> NIL) AND (P↑.INFO > VAL) DO
```

will cause an error when P is NIL.

- Remember that DISPOSE(P) leaves P undefined; trying to access P afterward will cause a run-time error.
- Return nodes to available space when you are finished with them. When deleting nodes from a linked list, use DISPOSE to return those nodes to available space for later use. In a large program, failure to DISPOSE may cause you to run out of memory. If you have used DISPOSE properly and you still run out of memory space, check to be sure that you do not have an inadvertent recursive call or an infinite loop. It is also possible to run out of memory space if you are passing large data structures as value parameters.
- Keep track of pointers. Changing pointer values prematurely may cause problems when you try to get back to the referenced variable.

MORE ON LISTS

Now that you are familiar with the syntax of the Pascal pointer type, let's look at some other things we can do with linked lists.

Headers and Trailers

We have seen, in writing insert and delete algorithms for ordered linked lists, that special cases arise when we are dealing with the first and the last nodes. It may be desirable in some applications to use simpler algorithms for inserting and deleting, and just make sure that you never insert before the first node or after the last node and that you never delete the first node.

How can this be accomplished? A linked list is usually ordered according to the value in some field—numerically by identification number, alphabetically by last name, and so forth. If you can determine the range of possible values for this field, it is a simple matter to set up dummy nodes with values outside this range. For instance, if a list of students is ordered by last name, we can assume that there will be no student named AAAAAAAAAA or ZZZZZZZZZZ. We can therefore initialize our linked list to contain *header* and *trailer* nodes with these values in the key field.

A sample procedure to initialize the header and trailer nodes of a list that is linked with pointer variables is given below:

```
PROCEDURE INITIALIZE (VAR LIST : POINTERTYPE);
    (* Initialize a header and a trailer node for the list. The list is ordered *)
    (* alphabetically with respect to the NAME field.                          *)

VAR TEMPPTR : POINTERTYPE;

BEGIN   (* initialize *)
```

```
(* Set up trailer node. *)
NEW(TEMPPTR);
TEMPPTR↑.NAME := 'ZZZZZZZZZZ';
TEMPPTR↑.NEXT := NIL;

(* Set up header node. *)
NEW(LIST);
LIST↑.NAME := 'AAAAAAAAAA';

(* Link trailer node to header node. *)
LIST↑.NEXT := TEMPPTR

END;     (* initialize *)
```

Now, when we insert into or delete from the list, there will be only one case to consider—the case of inserting or deleting in the middle of the list. No value for the key field will be "smaller" than that in the header node or "larger" than that in the trailer node. (See Figure 6-6.)

A header node may also be used for a quite different purpose. There may be times when you wish to carry some special information about the list, data that you will need often. For example, you may frequently want to know how many nodes there are in the list. You could keep count of the number of elements in the list in a separate variable, LISTCOUNT. Alternatively, you could bind the count information to the list itself by storing the count in the INFO field of a header node, incrementing and decrementing the count as you insert into and delete from the list.

Depending on the particular application, you may want to use a header, a trailer, both, or neither.

Doubly Linked Lists

We have discussed using circular linked lists to enable us to reach any node in the list from any starting point. While this structure has advantages over a simple linear linked list, it is still limited for certain types of applications. Suppose we want to be able to delete a particular node in a list, given *only* a pointer to that node (Figure 6-7). This task involves changing the pointer in the NEXT field of the node preceding NODE(P). However, we have not been given a pointer to that node. Another difficult task to perform on a linear linked list is traversing the list backwards.

Figure 6-6. Linked list with header and trailer.

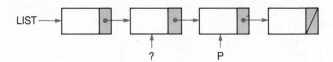

Figure 6-7. We want to delete NODE(P), but we can't get to its predecessor node.

In cases like these, we can facilitate these operations by using *doubly linked lists*—lists linked in both directions.

Each node of a doubly linked list contains three basic fields:

INFO—the data stored in the node
NEXT—pointer to the following node
BACK—pointer to the preceding node

A linear doubly linked list can be pictured as follows:

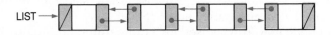

Such a list might have the following declarations:

```
TYPE POINTERTYPE = ↑NODE;

     NODE = RECORD
               INFO : INFOTYPE;
               NEXT, BACK : POINTERTYPE
            END;   (* record *)

VAR  LIST : POINTERTYPE;
```

Note that in a linear doubly linked list, the BACK field of the first node, as well as the NEXT field of the last node, contains NIL.

Operations on Doubly Linked Lists The algorithms for operations on doubly linked lists are somewhat more complicated than those for singly linked lists. The reason for this is clear: There are more pointers to modify.

For example, to insert a new node [NODE(P)] after a given node [NODE(Q)] in a singly linked list, we need to change two pointers: P ↑ .NEXT and Q ↑ .NEXT [Figure 6-8(a)]. The same operation on a doubly linked list requires four pointer changes [Figure 6-8(b)].

Because of this complexity, it is important to be careful about the order in which you change the pointers. For instance, when inserting NODE(P) after NODE(Q), if we change the pointer in Q's NEXT field first, we lose

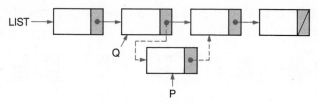

(a) Inserting into a singly linked list.

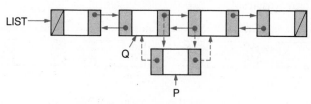

(b) Inserting into a doubly linked list.

Figure 6-8.

our pointer to Q's successor. A correct order for the pointer changes would be

```
P↑.BACK  := Q;
P↑.NEXT  := Q↑.NEXT;
Q↑.NEXT↑.BACK  := P;
Q↑.NEXT  := P;
```

Writing a procedure to insert a node into a doubly linked list is left as an exercise.

One of the useful operations that can be performed on a doubly linked list is the deletion of a given node without requiring a pointer to its predecessor. The following procedure deletes the node pointed to by P from the list. The list has a header and a trailer node (that means that we will never be trying to delete the first or last node).

```
PROCEDURE DELETENODE (P : POINTERTYPE);
   (* Delete the node pointed to by P from the list. *)

BEGIN   (* deletenode *)

   (* Change pointers to skip NODE(P). *)
   P↑.BACK↑.NEXT  := P↑.NEXT;
   P↑.NEXT↑.BACK  := P↑.BACK;

   (* Free the node pointed to by P. *)
   DISPOSE(P)

END;   (* deletenode *)
```

Variations on a Doubly Linked List   As seen above, doubly linked lists can also have headers and trailers:

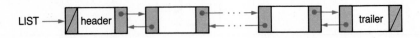

With or without headers and trailers, a doubly linked list may be circular, rather than linear:

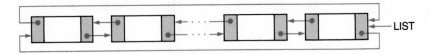

Given a circular doubly linked list, let's write a procedure to traverse the list backwards, printing all the elements in the list. (We will assume that the external pointer LIST points to the *last* node in the list, as discussed in the previous chapter. Note, however, that since the list is doubly linked, it is completely symmetrical. We could just as well have LIST point to the first node.)

```
PROCEDURE PRINTBACK (LIST : POINTERTYPE);
   (* Print the data in the list in reverse order. *)

VAR P : POINTERTYPE;

BEGIN   (* printback *)
   (* Set P to the end of the list. *)
   P := LIST;

   (* Check first for an empty list. *)
   IF P = NIL
      THEN                              (* Issue empty list message. *)
         WRITELN('THE LIST IS EMPTY')
      ELSE                              (* Print the list backwards. *)
         REPEAT
            WRITELN(P↑.INFO);
            P := P↑.BACK
         UNTIL P = LIST
END;      (* printback *)
```

Array Implementation of Doubly Linked Lists   Though our discussions of doubly linked lists have been illustrated with examples using pointer variables, we can change to an array-of-records implementation fairly directly. New GETNODE and FREENODE routines must be written, of course. Note that the list of available nodes does not have to be doubly linked. It can be linked through either the NEXT or BACK pointer field, as long as the linking is consistent.

APPLICATIONS OF LINKED LISTS

Linked lists are used in a wide variety of applications. We will discuss a few of them here. Some others will be discussed in the exercises at the end of this chapter and the program assignments at the end of the book.

One interesting use of linked lists is a line editor. You can keep a linked list of line nodes, each containing a line number, a line of text, and a pointer to the next line information node. Since you cannot predict how many lines will be needed, this would be an appropriate application to implement with dynamically created nodes.

In Chapter 2 we saw how strings can be implemented with arrays. Variable-length strings can also be represented as linked lists. A string may be declared as a record that contains a string count and a pointer to the linked list of characters. In one simple representation, each character node contains a single character and a pointer to the next character node. Character manipulation is very simple with this string implementation. Unfortunately, with this representation much more space is used for the pointers than for the characters. If space is limited, each node can contain several characters, as well as a pointer to the next node. This representation saves space at the cost of increasing the complexity of the algorithms that manipulate the characters in the strings.

Linked lists are often used to implement sparse matrices. A *sparse matrix* is a table with relatively few nonzero elements. Consider a table of company sales in which the rows represent the different salespeople and the columns represent the various products sold by the company. Each element in the table contains the total number of a particular object that has been sold by one of the salespeople. If the various salespeople specialize, each selling only a small range of the different products, it is likely that many or most of the numbers in the table will be 0 (Figure 6-9). This is an

| | 0 0 3 | 0 0 4 | 0 2 6 | 0 5 6 | 0 7 2 | 1 2 4 | 1 5 5 | 2 3 7 | 2 7 4 | 2 8 7 | ... | 8 2 2 | 8 5 3 | 9 3 3 | 9 4 5 | 9 4 9 |
Salesperson																
Addams	0	36	91	0	0	0	0	0	0	28	...	0	0	0	0	0
Baker	93	0	0	33	59	0	0	0	0	0	...	0	0	56	0	0
Cole	39	0	0	26	55	0	0	0	0	33	...	0	0	39	0	5
Dale	0	0	0	0	0	0	0	0	0	0	...	0	76	47	98	45
.																
.																
.																
Xavier	0	20	23	33	64	0	0	0	0	0	...	36	0	0	0	0
Young	0	0	0	0	0	54	46	78	36	0	...	71	0	0	0	0
Zorro	48	0	0	0	0	0	0	0	0	69	...	0	87	0	67	0

Figure 6-9. In a sparse matrix, most of the elements are zero.

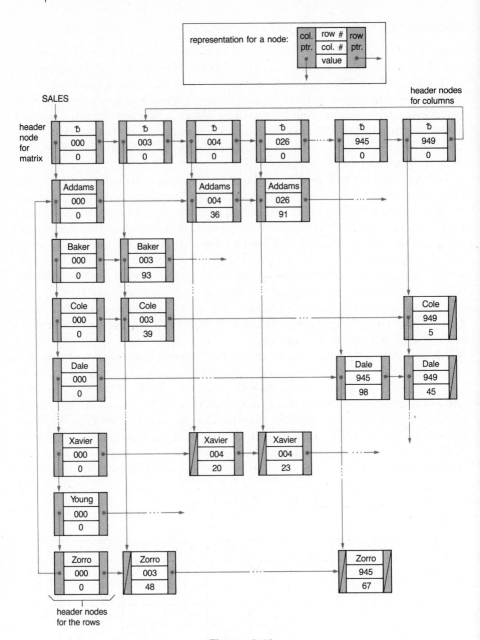

Figure 6-10.

example of a sparse matrix. Though it is natural to think of implementing a matrix as a two-dimensional array, a sparse matrix may be more efficiently implemented (with regard to space use, not time) as a linked-list structure. A sparse matrix represented as linked lists with header nodes is pictured in Figure 6-10.

An operating system is a program that manages and allocates the resources of a computer system. Operating systems use linked lists in many ways. The allocation of memory space may be managed using a doubly linked list of variably sized blocks of memory. Doubly linking the list facilitates removal of blocks from the middle of the list. In a multi-user system, the operating system may keep track of user jobs waiting to execute through linked queues of control blocks.

Summary

The Pascal pointer type, coupled with dynamic storage allocation, gives us another way to implement linked lists. In general, applications that use linked lists can be coded with either an array or pointer-variable implementation. Therefore, the applications discussed in the previous chapter are also appropriate to this one.

There are, however, situations in which the ability to allocate more space dynamically makes the pointer-variable implementation a better choice. In a program in which the amount of data to be stored is very unpredictable or may vary widely, the dynamic implementation has major advantages. Pointer variables provide efficient access to nodes. The actual address of the node is stored in the pointer. In an array implementation, the address of NODES[P] must be computed by adding P (an index) to the base address of the array NODES, as we saw in Chapter 2.

Pointer variables also present a problem when we need to retain the data in the data structure between runs of the program. For instance, we may want to write all the nodes in the list to a file, and then use this file as input the next time we run the program. An array index would still be valid on the next run of the program, while a pointer variable—an actual address—would be meaningless.

Finally, there are a number of languages which do not have pointer types. If you were programming in FORTRAN, for instance, you would have to represent pointers as array indexes. In fact, since FORTRAN also doesn't support record types, you would need to set up a parallel array of pointers (indexes).

Exercises

Use these declarations in the following questions:

```
TYPE POINTER =  ↑NODE;
     NODE = RECORD
               INFO : INTEGER;
               NEXT : POINTER
            END; (* record *)
VAR  P, Q, R : POINTER;
```

1. Show what the following commands do to the schematic diagram of a linked list.

(a) `P := P↑.NEXT`

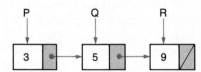

(b) `Q := P`

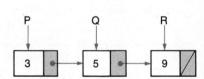

(c) `R := P↑.NEXT`

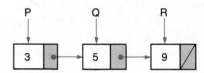

(d) `P↑.INFO := Q↑.INFO`

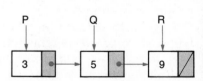

(e) `P↑.INFO := Q↑.NEXT↑.INFO`

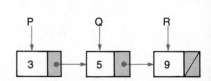

(f) `R↑.NEXT := P`

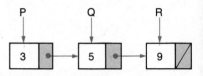

2. Write one statement (using the ↑ notation) to effect the change indicated by the dotted line.

   (a)

   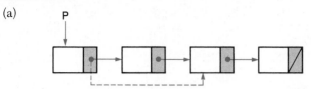

   (b)

   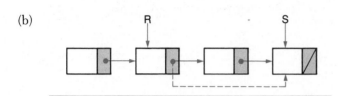

   (c)

   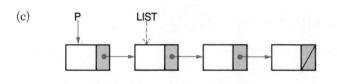

   (d)

   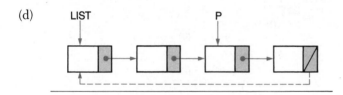

3. Show what is written by the following segments of code:

   (a)
   ```
   NEW(P);
   NEW(Q);
   P↑.INFO  := 5;
   Q↑.INFO  := 6;
   P := Q;
   P↑.INFO  := 1;
   WRITELN(P↑.INFO, Q↑.INFO);
   ```

   (b)
   ```
   NEW(P);
   P↑.INFO  := 3;
   NEW(Q);
   Q↑.INFO  := 2;
   NEW(P);
   P↑.INFO  := Q↑.INFO;
   Q↑.INFO  := 0;
   WRITELN(P↑.INFO, Q↑.INFO);
   ```

4. The following type declaration is illegal, since PTR = ↑NODE is a forward reference to an undefined type called NODE.   T   F

```
TYPE STRING = PACKED ARRAY[1..10] OF CHAR;
     PTR = ↑NODE;
     NODE = RECORD
                NAME : STRING;
                NEXT : PTR
            END;
```

5. Show what is written by the following segment of code.

```
NEW(P);
NEW(Q);
P↑.INFO := 0;
P↑.NEXT := Q;
Q↑.NEXT := NIL;
Q↑.INFO := 5;
P↑.NEXT↑.NEXT := P;
Q↑.INFO := Q↑.NEXT↑.INFO;
P := Q;
P↑.NEXT↑.INFO := 2;
WRITELN(P↑.INFO, Q↑.INFO);
```

6. Given these declarations for a linked list of company employees:

```
TYPE PTR = ↑EMPLOYEE;
     EMPLOYEE = RECORD
                   NAME : PACKED ARRAY[1..25] OF CHAR;
                   DEPTNO : 1..20;
                   EMPNO : 0..1000;
                   SALARY : INTEGER;
                   NEXT : PTR
                END; (* record *)
VAR  P, EMPLOYEES : PTR;
```

(a) Initialize EMPLOYEES, a pointer to a company list, with a header node. Assume that the list will be ordered by employee number.

(b) Write a segment of code to read in information about an employee and store it in a node (to be later inserted into the linked list of employees). Assume that the information about each employee is located on a separate line of input in the format:

col.	1–25	27–28	30–33	35–40
	NAME	DEPTNO	EMPNO	SAL

Feel free to use any additional variables you need.

(c) Write a procedure to insert a new employee node into the list you initialized in (a). The procedure will take EMPLOYEES (a pointer to the list) and EMP [a pointer to the new employee's node, filled with information in (b)].

7. Debug the following. Assume these declarations:

```
TYPE NODE = RECORD
                INFO : INTEGER;
                NEXT : ↑NODE
            END;
```

(a) FUNCTION EVEN (P : ↑NODE) : BOOLEAN;

```
    BEGIN
      IF P↑.INFO MOD 2 = 0
          THEN EVEN := TRUE
          ELSE EVEN := FALSE
    END;
```

(b) PROCEDURE SUCCESSOR(P : PTR);

```
    BEGIN
      WHILE P <> NIL DO
        WRITELN(P↑.INFO, ' IS FOLLOWED BY ',
                   P↑.NEXT↑.INFO);
    END;
```

(c) PROCEDURE POP (VAR LIST : PTR; VAR VAL : INTEGER);

```
    BEGIN
      VAL := LIST↑.INFO;
      DISPOSE(LIST);
      LIST := LIST↑.NEXT
    END;
```

8. Write a procedure to delete a node from a doubly linked linear list that does not have a header or a trailer node.

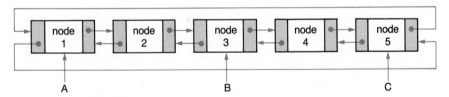

9. For the circular doubly linked list above:
   (a) Express the INFO field of node 1 referenced from pointer A.
   (b) Express the INFO field of node 1 referenced from pointer C.
   (c) Express the NEXT field of node 4 referenced from pointer B.
   (d) Express the NEXT field of node 4 referenced from pointer C.
   (e) Express node 1 referenced from pointer B.
   (f) Express the BACK field of node 3 referenced from pointer B.
   (g) Express the BACK field of node 2 referenced from pointer B.

10. Given a list pointed to by EMPLIST, with the following declarations:

```
TYPE STRING = PACKED ARRAY[1..20] OF CHAR;
     PTR = ↑NODE;
     NODE = RECORD
                NAME : STRING;
                EMPNUM : INTEGER;
                DEPTCODE : CHAR;
                WEEKHRS : INTEGER;
                SAL : REAL;
                NEXT : PTR
            END;   (* record *)

VAR  EMPLIST : PTR;
```

Write a procedure to delete from the list all the employees who work less than forty hours a week. (This information is stored in the WEEKHRS field.)

11. Assuming that the declarations for NODE in problem 10 include the field BACK (type PTR) (the list is doubly linked) and the list has a header and a trailer node, write a procedure to insert an employee record into the list. The list is ordered by EMPNUM.

Pre-Test

1. The following procedure counts the number of elements in a list pointed to by LIST. This list has a header node. The procedure leaves the total number in the INFO portion of the header node. Fill in the portions of the code indicated by blanks.

```
PROCEDURE COUNT (LIST : PTR);

VAR P   : PTR;
    CT  : INTEGER;

BEGIN  (* count *)
   CT := 0;
   P := _____ ;
   WHILE _____ DO
      BEGIN
         CT := CT + 1;
         P := _____
      END;
   _____ := CT
END;   (* count *)
```

2. Fill in the values indicated by the pointer variable expressions below, based on the following linked list:

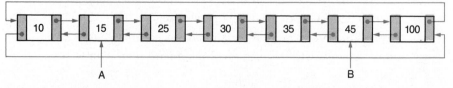

(a) A↑.NEXT↑.NEXT↑.INFO _____

(b) B↑.NEXT↑.INFO _____

(c) B↑.NEXT↑.BACK↑.BACK↑.INFO _____

(d) A↑.BACK↑.NEXT↑.INFO _____

```
3. TYPE PTRTYPE = ↑BLOCK;
        BLOCK = RECORD
                    SCORE : INTEGER;
                    NAME : PACKED ARRAY[1..20] OF CHAR;
                    NEXT : PTRTYPE
                END;   (* record *)
```

Write a code fragment to take a list of blocks (as defined above) pointed to by START and create two new lists pointed to by PASS and FAIL, respectively, in which the first list contains all blocks having scores >= 50 and the second contains all blocks having scores < 50. It is required that the blocks in the two new lists occur in *exactly the same order* as in the original list.

4. Write a function, MEMBER, that returns TRUE if a value VAL occurs anywhere in the linked list pointed to by LIST. This function returns FALSE otherwise. Use the following function heading:

```
FUNCTION MEMBER (VAL : INTEGER; LIST : PTRTYPE)
                 : BOOLEAN;
```

```
5. TYPE   PTRTYPE = ↑NODETYPE;
          NODETYPE = RECORD
                        INFO : CHAR;
                        NEXT : PTRTYPE
                     END;   (* record *)
```

Write a nonrecursive Pascal procedure, REVERSE, that takes one input parameter, CIRCLE, of type PTRTYPE. Assume that CIRCLE points to the "first" node in a singly linked nonempty circular list. The purpose of this procedure is to print out the characters in the list CIRCLE in reverse order. For instance, the output for the following example would be ZYX:

CIRCLE

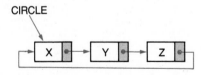

Hint: Use a stack of pointers. You may assume that the appropriate STACK-TYPE declaration and all stack utility routines are already written.

Recursion 7

Goals

To be able to do the following given a recursive routine:

- *determine whether the routine will halt.*
- *determine the base case(s).*
- *determine the general case(s).*
- *determine whether the routine is correct and correct it if it is not.*
- *determine what the routine does.*

To be able to take a simple recursive problem and do the following:

- *determine the base case.*
- *determine the general case.*
- *code the algorithm.*

To be able to compare and contrast dynamic storage allocation and static storage allocation.

To be able to explain how recursion works internally by showing the contents of the run-time stack.

To be able to hand simulate the quicksort algorithm.

To be able to encode the quicksort algorithm.

As a beginning programmer, you may have been told never to use a function name within the function on the right-hand side of an assignment statement, as in the following program:

```
FUNCTION SUM (LIST : ARRAYTYPE;
                NUMITEMS : INTEGER) : INTEGER;
(* Sums the elements in the array LIST. *)

VAR I : INTEGER;

BEGIN   (* sum *)
    SUM := 0;
    FOR I := 1 TO NUMITEMS DO
        SUM := SUM + LIST[I]
END;    (* sum *)
```

You were probably told that using a function name this way would cause something mysterious and undesirable to occur—the function would try to call itself *recursively*. You may also have been told that you would learn how to use recursion as a powerful programming tool in a later course. In this chapter we will explore how to understand and to write recursive functions and procedures, as well as how recursion works in a high-level language like Pascal.

AN EXAMPLE OF RECURSION

Mathematicians often define concepts in terms of the process used to generate them. For instance, one mathematical description of n! (read "n factorial"—this value is equal to the number of permutations of n elements) is

$$n! = \begin{cases} 1, & \text{if } n = 0 \\ n * (n - 1) * (n - 2) * \cdots * 1, & \text{if } n > 0 \end{cases}$$

Consider the case of 4! Since n > 0, we use the second part of the definition:

$$4! = 4 * 3 * 2 * 1 = 24$$

This definition essentially provides a different definition for each value of n, since the three dots stand in for the intermediate factors. That is, the definition of 2! is 2 * 1, while the definition of 3! is 3 * 2 * 1, and so forth.

We can also express n! with a single definition for *any* nonnegative value of n:

$$n! = \begin{cases} 1, & \text{if } n = 0 \\ n * (n - 1)!, & \text{if } n > 0 \end{cases}$$

This definition is recursive, since we express the factorial function in terms of itself.

Let's consider the recursive calculation of 4! intuitively. Four is not equal to 0, so we use the second half of the definition:

$$4! = 4 * (4 - 1)! = 4 * 3!$$

Of course, we can't do the multiplication yet, since we don't know the value of 3!. So we call up our good friend Sue Ann, who has a Ph.D in math, to find the value of 3!.

$$4! = 4 * 3!$$

Sue Ann has the same formula that we have for calculating the factorial function, so she knows that

$$3! = 3 * (3 - 1)! = 3 * 2!$$

She doesn't know that value of 2! however, so she puts you on hold and calls up her friend Max, who has an M.S. in math.

Max has the same formula that Sue Ann has, so he quickly calculates that

$$2! = 2 * (2 - 1)! = 2 * 1!$$

But Max can't complete the multiplication because he doesn't know the value of 1!. He puts Sue Ann on hold and calls up his mother, who has a B.A. in math education.

Max's mother has the same formula that Max has, so she quickly figures out that

$$1! = 1 * (1 - 1)! = 1 * 0!$$

Of course, she can't perform the multiplication, since she doesn't have the value of 0!. So Mom puts Max on hold and calls up her colleague Bernie, who has a B.A. in English literature.

Bernie doesn't need to know any math to figure out that $0! = 1$ because he can read that information in the first clause of the formula ($n! = 1$, if $n = 0$). He reports the answer immediately to Max's mother. She can now complete her calculations:

$$1! = 1 * 0! = 1 * 1 = 1$$

and she reports back to Max. Max now performs the multiplication in his formula, and learns that

$$2! = 2 * 1! = 2 * 1 = 2$$

He reports back to Sue Ann, who can now finish her calculation:

$$3! = 3 * 2! = 3 * 2 = 6$$

Sue Ann calls you with this exciting bit of information. You can now complete your calculation:

$$4! = 4 * 3! = 4 * 6 = 24$$

PROGRAMMING RECURSIVELY

Of course, use of recursion is not limited to mathematicians with telephones. Computer languages like Pascal that support recursion give the programmer a powerful tool for solving certain kinds of problems by reducing the complexity or hiding the details of the problem.

We will consider recursive solutions to several simple problems. In our initial discussion, you may wonder why a recursive solution would ever be preferred to an iterative, nonrecursive one, since the iterative solution often seems simpler and more efficient. Don't worry. There are, as we will see later, situations in which the use of recursion gives you a much simpler—and more elegant—program.

Coding the Factorial Function

A recursive function or procedure is one that calls itself. In the previous section, we mentioned that Sue Ann, Max, Max's mom, and Bernie all had the same formula for solving the factorial function. When we construct a recursive Pascal function NFACT for solving n!, we know where we can get the value of (n − 1)! that we need in the formula. We already have a function for doing this calculation: NFACT. Of course, the actual parameter (N − 1) in the recursive call will be different from the parameter in the original call (N). (The recursive call is the one within the function.) As we will see, this is an important and necessary consideration.

A Pascal function for calculating n! for a nonnegative integer N may be coded as follows:

```
FUNCTION NFACT (N : INTEGER) : INTEGER;
(* Calculates the value of N! recursively. *)

BEGIN    (* nfact *)
   IF  N = 0                            (* line 1 *)
      THEN NFACT := 1                   (* line 2 *)
      ELSE NFACT := N * NFACT(N - 1)    (* line 3 *)
END;     (* nfact *)
```

Notice the two uses of NFACT in the ELSE clause. On the left side of the assignment statement, NFACT is the function name receiving a value. This use is the one that we are accustomed to seeing. On the right side of the assignment statement, NFACT is a recursive call to the function, with the parameter N − 1.

Let's walk through the calculation of 4! using function NFACT. The original value of N is 4.

Line	Action
1	4 is not equal to 0, so skip to ELSE clause.
3	NFACT := 4 * NFACT(4 − 1)
	First recursive call returns us to the beginning of the function, with N = 3.
1	3 is not equal to 0, so skip to ELSE clause.
3	NFACT := 3 * NFACT(3 − 1)
	Second recursive call returns us to the beginning of the function, with N = 2.
1	2 is not equal to 0, so skip to ELSE clause.
3	NFACT := 2 * NFACT(2 − 1)
	Third recursive call returns us to the beginning of the function, with N = 1.
1	1 is not equal to 0, so skip to ELSE clause.
3	NFACT := 1 * NFACT(1 − 1)
	Fourth recursive call returns us to the beginning of the function, with N = 0.

1	$0 = 0$, so go to line 2.
2	NFACT := 1
	The value of NFACT(0) is returned to the calling statement, the fourth recursive call.
3	NFACT := $1 * $ NFACT(0) $= 1 * 1 = 1$
	The value of NFACT(1) is returned to the calling statement, the third recursive call.
3	NFACT := $2 * $ NFACT(1) $= 2 * 1 = 2$
	The value of NFACT(2) is returned to the calling statement, the second recursive call.
3	NFACT := $3 * $ NFACT(2) $= 3 * 2 = 6$
	The value of NFACT(3) is returned to the calling statement, the first recursive call.
3	NFACT := $4 * $ NFACT(3) $= 4 * 6 = 24$
	The function now returns a value of 24 to the original calling statement, e.g., WRITE(NFACT(4)).

This kind of walk-through to check the validity of a recursive function or procedure is time consuming, tedious, and often confusing. Furthermore, simulating the execution of NFACT(4) tells us that the function works when N = 4, but it doesn't tell us if it is valid for *all* nonnegative values of N. It would be useful to have a technique that would help us determine inductively whether the procedure or function will work.

Verifying Recursive Procedures and Functions

Consider the following three questions. For a recursive procedure or function to work, you must be able to answer "yes" to all three.

1. *Is there a nonrecursive way out of the procedure or function, and does it work correctly in this case?* There must be some trivial or base case where the calculations end; otherwise you would have an infinite series of recursive calls. For instance, in the function NFACT, this base case occurs when N = 0. NFACT is then assigned a value of 1, the correct value for 0!, and no further calls to NFACT are made.

2. *Does each recursive call to the procedure or function involve a smaller case of the problem?* "Smaller" means that there is a diminished part of the problem left to examine. To answer this question, look at the parameters passed in the recursive call(s). For instance, in Function NFACT, the recursive call passes N − 1. Each subsequent recursive call sends a smaller value of the parameter, until the value sent is 0. At this point, as we verified in Question 1 above, we have reached the smallest case, and no further recursive calls are made.

3. *Assuming that the recursive call(s) works correctly, does the whole procedure or function work correctly?* In the case of a function like NFACT, we need to verify that the formula that we are using will actually

result in the correct solution. Assuming that the recursive call NFACT(N − 1) will give us the correct value of (n − 1)!, we get the assignment of N * (N − 1)! to NFACT. Since this is the definition of a factorial, we know that the function works for all positive integers. We have already ascertained, in Question 1 above, that the function works for 0. (N! is only defined for nonnegative integers.)

Those of you who are familiar with inductive proofs will recognize what we have done. Having made the assumption that the function works for some base case (N − 1), we can now show that applying the function to the next value, (N − 1) + 1, or N, results in the correct formula for calculating n factorial.

Writing Recursive Procedures and Functions

It should be obvious that the questions used for verifying recursive procedures and functions can also be used as a guide for *writing* recursive procedures and functions.

You can use the following approach for writing any recursive routine:

- First, get an exact definition of the problem to be solved. (This, of course, is the first step of any programming problem.)
- Next, determine the size of the whole problem to be solved. This will determine the value(s) of the parameter(s) in the initial call to the procedure or function.
- Third, solve the base case(s) in which the problem can be expressed nonrecursively. This will assure that you have a "yes" response to Question 1 of the validity test.
- Last, solve the general case(s) correctly, in terms of a smaller case of the same problem (a recursive call). This will assure "yes" answers to Questions 2 and 3.

FUNCTION SUM REVISITED

Remember Function SUM from page 278? How would we write it recursively? We want to write a function that will sum the elements in an array. Our task is to add the value of the first element in the array to the sum of all the elements in the rest of the array.

SUM ← LIST[1] + the sum of the rest of array LIST

If only we had a function that would sum all the rest of the elements in the array . . . . But we *do* have one! Function SUM sums elements in an array; we just need to start at the second, instead of the first, element (a smaller case). This indicates that we will need to pass the starting place (an array index) to the function as a parameter, rather than keeping the index as a local variable.

```
FUNCTION SUM (LIST : ARRAYTYPE;
              I, NUMITEMS : INTEGER) : INTEGER;
```

We will call the function with a statement like WRITE(SUM(LIST, 1, NUMITEMS)), where LIST is an array, 1 indicates that we want to start summing at LIST[1], and LIST[NUMITEMS] is the last element in the array.

Our general case is therefore

```
SUM := LIST[I] + SUM(LIST, I + 1, NUMITEMS);
```

Note that by incrementing I in the parameter list, we have diminished the size of the problem to be solved. LIST[I + 1]..LIST[NUMITEMS] is a smaller array than LIST[I]..LIST[NUMITEMS].

What is the base case? When I = NUMITEMS, we have reached the end of the array, and no further recursive calls should be made. At this point, SUM should be set to the last element in the array.

We can now summarize the tasks discussed in the previous section and write Function SUM.

FUNCTION SUM

Definition of problem: sum all the elements in the array.
Size of problem: the whole array LIST, from LIST[1] to
        LIST[NUMITEMS].
Base case: when I = NUMITEMS, SUM ← LIST[I].
General case: when I < NUMITEMS, SUM ← LIST[I] + SUM(rest
        of LIST).

The code for a recursive function SUM is given below.

```
FUNCTION SUM (LIST : ARRAYTYPE;
              I, NUMITEMS : INTEGER) : INTEGER;
(* Sums the elements in the array recursively. *)
(* Assumes that I <= NUMITEMS.                  *)

BEGIN   (* sum *)
   IF I = NUMITEMS
      THEN   (* base case *)
         SUM := LIST[I]
      ELSE   (* general case *)
         SUM := LIST[I] + SUM(LIST, I + 1, NUMITEMS)
END;    (* sum *)
```

The user of this function would invoke it with the name of the array, and the upper and lower indexes of the array to be summed. For instance, to print the sum of the first 100 elements in the array INVENTORY, we would state

```
WRITELN(SUM(INVENTORY, 1, 100))
```

It is important to note that the initialization of the counter, I, is effected through the choice of the value of the second argument in the calling sequence. That is, on the initial invocation of the function, the counter I will have the value of the first index. I is then incremented through the calling sequence of the recursive invocation within the function.

Let's verify the function inductively, using our three questions.

1. *Is there a nonrecursive case, and does this base case work?* Yes, when I = NUMITEMS, we are at the end of the array, so we want the sum returned to be equal to the last element in the array.
2. *Does the recursive call involve a smaller version of the problem to be solved?* Yes, SUM(LIST, I + 1, NUMITEMS) sums a smaller array than SUM(LIST, I, NUMITEMS)—one element smaller.
3. *Assuming that the recursive call SUM(LIST, I + 1, NUMITEMS) actually returns the sum of all the rest of the elements in the array, does the function work?* Yes, SUM is assigned the value of the first element plus the sum of the rest of the elements in the array, which should total the sum of all the elements in the array.

Problem: Try to write a recursive function, SUM, that sums the array from the bottom up. You will only need two parameters. Verify your answer using the inductive method above.

A BOOLEAN FUNCTION

Our next problem is to write a Boolean function, SEARCH, that searches an array, LIST (ARRAY[1..MAXLIST] OF INTEGER), for the value, VAL. Using the approach discussed above, we generate the following information:

FUNCTION SEARCH

Definition of problem: search array LIST from LIST[1] to LIST[MAXLIST]. Return TRUE if VAL is found, FALSE otherwise.

Size of problem: size of the array (MAXLIST).

Base cases: (1) when LIST[I] = VAL, SEARCH ← TRUE;
(2) when I = MAXLIST (whole array searched) and LIST[I] <> VAL, SEARCH ← FALSE.

General case: SEARCH the rest of the array.

We know from the definition and size of the problem that we will need to pass several pieces of information to the function. Of course, we need to pass the array (LIST), its size (MAXLIST), and VAL. This information would be required by an iterative solution as well. For a recursive solution, the function needs an additional parameter—the index (I) of the lower limit of the array to be searched. Obviously, in our initial function call, this value will be 1. In our general case (SEARCH the rest of the array), this parameter will have to be incremented, effectively diminishing the size of the problem solved by the recursive call. That is, searching the array from I + 1 to MAXLIST is a smaller task than searching from I to MAXLIST. Following is the Function SEARCH frozen in mid-execution:

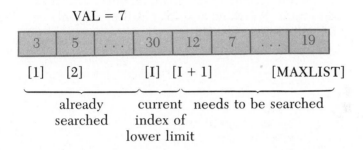

Finally, we need to know when to stop searching. In this problem we have more than one base case: (1) when the value is found (return TRUE) and (2) when we have reached the end of the array without finding the value (return FALSE). In either case, we stop making recursive calls to SEARCH.

The code for Function SEARCH is given below.

```
FUNCTION SEARCH (LIST : ARRAYTYPE;
                 I, MAXLIST, VAL : INTEGER) : BOOLEAN;
(* Searches LIST recursively to find the value VAL.       *)
(* If VAL is found, returns TRUE; otherwise, returns FALSE. *)

BEGIN     (* search *)
   IF LIST[I] = VAL
      THEN                                        (* base case 1 *)
         SEARCH := TRUE
      ELSE
         IF I = MAXLIST
            THEN                                  (* base case 2 *)
               SEARCH := FALSE
            ELSE                               (* general case *)
               SEARCH := SEARCH(LIST, I + 1, MAXLIST, VAL)
END;     (* search *)
```

Note again that the index that acts as a counter through the array, I, is initialized outside of the function in the original calling sequence. A sample use of the function is given below.

```
(* Execute this if NUMBER is found in the array. *)
IF SEARCH(LISTARRAY, 1, MAXARRAY, NUMBER)
   THEN , , ,
```

Problem: Use the three-question method to verify this function yourself.

A RECURSIVE PROCEDURE

So far we have written several recursive functions. Now let's try to write a recursive procedure. We want to print out the elements of a linked list implemented with pointer variables.

Use the following declarations:

```
TYPE PTR = ↑NODE;

     NODE = RECORD
              INFO : INFOTYPE;
              NEXT : PTR
            END; (* record *)

VAR  LIST : PTR;
```

By now, you are probably protesting that this task is so easy to accomplish nonrecursively that it doesn't make any sense to write it using recursion. So let's make the task more fun: Write a procedure, REVPRINT, to print out the elements of a linked list backwards. This problem is somewhat more challenging to write nonrecursively, but simple to solve recursively.

What is the task to be performed? First, we want to print out the second through last elements in the list, in reverse order. Then, we need to print the first element in the list (Figure 7-1).

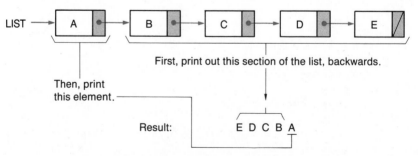

Figure 7-1. The algorithm for the recursive REVPRINT.

We know how to do the second part of this task. If P points to the first node in the list, we can print its contents with the statement WRITE(P↑.INFO). The first part of the task is not much more complicated, since we already have a procedure for printing out the second through last elements of the list—REVPRINT. Of course, we have to adjust the parameter somewhat: REVPRINT(P↑.NEXT). This says: print, in reverse order, the linked list pointed to by P↑.NEXT. Of course, this task is also accomplished recursively in two steps:

> REVPRINT the rest of the list (third through last elements)
> WRITE the second element in the list

And—of course—the first part of this task is accomplished recursively. Where does it all end? We need a base case. We can stop calling REVPRINT when we have completed its smallest case: REVPRINTing a list of one element. Then the value of P↑.NEXT will be NIL, and we stop making recursive calls.

Let's summarize our problem:

PROCEDURE REVPRINT

Definition: print out the list in reverse order.
Size: number of elements in the list pointed to by P.
Base case: when list is empty, do nothing.
General case: REVPRINT the list pointed to by P↑.NEXT, then
print P↑.INFO.

We can now write Procedure REVPRINT.

```
PROCEDURE REVPRINT (P : PTR);
(* Prints out the elements in the list in reverse *)
(* order. This is a recursive procedure.          *)

BEGIN   (* revprint *)
   IF  P <> NIL
      THEN   (* general case *)
         BEGIN
            REVPRINT(P↑.NEXT);
            WRITE(P↑.INFO)
         END
END;   (* revprint *)
```

An initial call to REVPRINT might be REVPRINT(LIST).

Let's verify this procedure according to our inductive method.

1. *Is there a base case, and does it work correctly?* Yes, the trivial case is implied. When P = NIL, we return to the statement following the last

recursive call to REVPRINT, and no further recursive calls are made.

2. *Does the recursive call involve a smaller version of the problem to be solved?* Yes, the list pointed to by P ↑ .NEXT is one element shorter than the list pointed to by P.

3. *Assuming that REVPRINT(P ↑ .NEXT) works correctly, does the whole procedure work?* Yes, REVPRINT(P ↑ .NEXT) will print the second through last elements in the list, in reverse order. Then, WRITE(P ↑ .INFO) will print the first element, giving our desired result.

We will return to procedure REVPRINT later, when we discuss how recursive routines are implemented in Pascal.

Problem: How would you change REVPRINT to make it print out the list in order?

A FEW MORE POINTS

These examples illustrate a couple of interesting differences between recursive and iterative procedures and functions. First, where an iterative routine uses a WHILE statement (or FOR or REPEAT..UNTIL), a recursive routine uses IF..THEN to control the looping. In addition, recursive procedures and functions often have more parameters, and fewer local variables, than equivalent iterative routines. For instance, in functions SUM and SEARCH, the index (I) of the lower limit of the array is passed as a parameter. This is necessary in order to permit its value to be modified in each successive recursive call. The value is initialized in the calling statement, outside of the function. Iterative versions of the same problems might use local variables for this purpose, initialized at the beginning of the function and incremented in each iteration.

REVPRINT REVISITED

Let us, at this point, write a nonrecursive version of Procedure REVPRINT. Why? First of all, because many programming languages (like FORTRAN and COBOL) do not support recursion. Second, because recursive programs are generally less efficient than their nonrecursive equivalents. Third, because such an exercise will help us understand how recursion works, and what tasks must be done by the computer, hidden from the programmer, to support recursion in a programming language.

Now, how would we write Procedure REVPRINT nonrecursively? As we traverse the list, we need to keep track of the pointer to each node, until we reach the end of the list (when our traversing pointer equals NIL). We then need to "back up," accessing the last pointer and printing the value of the INFO field of the last node. Then, we back up again and print again, and so on.

We know of a data structure in which we can store the pointers and retrieve them in reverse order—the stack. Our general task for REVPRINT then is

```
PUSH all the pointers onto the stack
POP and WRITE, until the stack is empty
```

A nonrecursive REVPRINT may be coded like this:

```
PROCEDURE REVPRINT (LIST : PTR);
(* Prints out the elements in the list in reverse *)
(* order. This is a nonrecursive procedure.      *)

VAR STACK : STACKTYPE;
     P       : PTR;

BEGIN   (* revprint *)
   (* Push pointers to all nodes onto stack. *)
   CLEARSTACK(STACK);
   P := LIST;
   WHILE P <> NIL DO
      BEGIN
         PUSH(STACK, P);
         P := P↑.NEXT
      END;   (* while P <> nil *)

   (* Retrieve pointers in reverse order and *)
   (* print elements.                        *)
   WHILE NOT EMPTYSTACK(STACK) DO
      BEGIN
         POP(STACK, P);                       (* get next pointer *)
         WRITELN(P↑.INFO)                      (* print the data *)
      END   (* while not empty *)
END;   (* revprint *)
```

Notice that our nonrecursive version of REVPRINT is quite a bit longer than its recursive counterpart, especially if we add in the code for the stack routines PUSH, POP, CLEARSTACK and EMPTYSTACK. This verbosity is caused by our need to stack and unstack the pointers explicitly. In the recursive version, we just called REVPRINT again, and let the computer keep track of the pointers. Of course, the computer must have some structure, hidden from the programmer, to keep all those pointers in. In fact, it uses the same structure that we used—a stack. The key word is *hidden*. The beauty of recursion lies in its capacity to hide details that are not germane to the application problem, like the pointer stacking in the nonrecursive version of REVPRINT. The application programmer is free to solve the problem at a higher level, and the system takes care of the rest. This assumes that the system is prepared to handle the task. As we shall see in the following section, there are features of programming languages that determine whether a language can support recursion.

HOW RECURSION WORKS

In order to understand how recursion works and why some programming languages allow it and some do not, we will have to take a detour and look at how languages associate places in memory with variable names. The association of a memory address with a variable name is called *binding*. The point in the compile/execute cycle where binding occurs is called the *binding time*.

Programming languages are usually classified as having either static storage allocation or dynamic storage allocation. Static storage allocation associates variables with memory locations at *compile* time; dynamic storage allocation associates variables with memory locations at *execution* time. We know from our discussion of pointer variables that Pascal is a language that uses dynamic storage allocation. Let's look at how each type of allocation might work, and examine the implications for recursion.

Static Storage Allocation

As a program is being translated, the compiler creates a table called a *symbol table*. When a variable is first defined, it is entered into the symbol table, and a memory location is then assigned to it. When a statement that accesses the variable is translated, the symbol table is searched, and the memory location associated with that symbol (the variable name) is entered into the translated version of the instruction. For example, let's look at the following Pascal fragment and translate it using static storage allocation:

```
VAR X, Y, Z : INTEGER;
   .
   .
   .
Z := X + Y;
```

The VAR statement causes entries to be made in the symbol table

SYMBOL	LOCATION
X	0000
Y	0001
Z	0002

Another way of saying this is:

X is bound to Location 0000
Y is bound to Location 0001
Z is bound to Location 0002

Whenever X, Y, or Z is encountered later, the actual address is substituted.

For example, the assignment statement (Z := X + Y;) is translated into the following actions:

- take the contents of Location 0000
- add it to the contents of Location 0001
- put the result into Location 0002

The code itself is then stored in a different part of memory. For example, the translated instructions might begin in Location 1000. When execution begins, control would then be transferred to Location 1000. The instruction stored there would be executed; then the instruction in 1001 would be executed; and so on.

Subprograms are usually translated in the following way: The formal parameters of a subprogram are assumed to be left in a particular place, usually directly preceding the code for each subprogram. For instance, if a subprogram whose code begins at Location CODE has three formal parameters (simple variables), A, B, and C, they would be found at Locations CODE − 1, CODE − 2, and CODE − 3. Given the procedure head

```
PROCEDURE EXAMPLE (A, B, C : INTEGER);
```

the statement A := B * C in the body of the procedure would generate the following actions:

- take the contents of location CODE − 2
- multiply it by the contents of CODE − 3
- store the result in location CODE − 1

The representation of a program with two subprograms is shown in Figure 7-2 on the following page.

We can compare the static allocation scheme to one way of allocating seats in an auditorium where a lecture is to be held. A finite number of invitations are issued for the event, and the exact number of chairs needed are set up before the lecture. If anyone brings friends, there will be nowhere for them to sit.

What is the implication of binding variables to memory locations before the program executes? If each parameter and local variable has but a single location assigned to it at compile time, where is the storage for the multiple versions of these variables generated by recursive calls? Since the intermediate values of the parameters and local variables must be retained, the recursive call cannot store its arguments in the fixed number of locations that were set up at compile time. This would cause the values from the previous recursive call to be overwritten and lost. Therefore, a language that is implemented with static storage allocation does not support recursion.

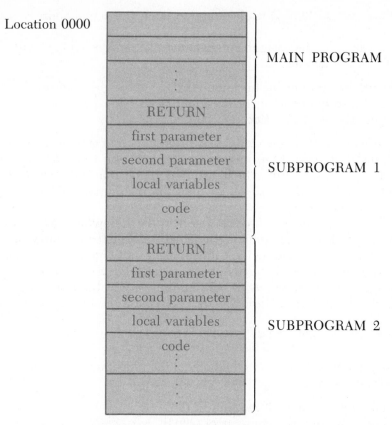

Location 0000

MAIN PROGRAM

RETURN

first parameter

second parameter

local variables

code

SUBPROGRAM 1

RETURN

first parameter

second parameter

local variables

code

SUBPROGRAM 2

Figure 7-2. Static allocation of space for a program with two subprograms.

Dynamic Storage Allocation

In dynamic storage allocation, all variables are accessed relatively, not to any code, but to a particular variable.

Let's look at a simplified version of how this actually works in Pascal. Since Pascal requires that all variables be declared before they are used (as opposed to FORTRAN, where the use of a name suffices to declare it), all global variables (variables declared in the outermost block) are assigned relative positions in the order in which they are declared. The actual location of the first is stored in a pointer called the base pointer (BASE).

For example,

```
TYPE LISTTYPE = ARRAY[0..9] OF INTEGER;

VAR  A, B, C : INTEGER;
     ANS : REAL;
     LIST : LISTTYPE;
```

would create the following memory assignments:

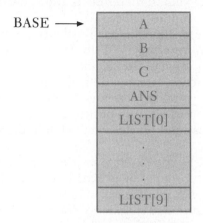

The location of A would be the contents of BASE; B would be found in BASE + 1. LIST[0] would be BASE + 4; LIST[3] would be BASE + 4 + 3. LIST[I] would be stored in BASE + 4 + I.

The contents of BASE, the base pointer, is set at the beginning of execution and does not change.

When a procedure or function is translated, each formal parameter and local variable is also assigned memory space relative to a position. They are then accessed backwards from a position pointed to by a pointer called TOP. For example,

```
PROCEDURE ONE (X, Y : REAL);

VAR I : INTEGER;
```

would look as follows:

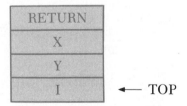

X would be TOP − 2; Y would be TOP − 1; I would be TOP. The place to return to at the end of the execution of the subprogram would be found in TOP − 3.

Note that in static allocation each formal parameter and local variable is accessed through a fixed memory location. In dynamic allocation, each formal parameter and local variable is accessed indirectly through the *contents* of a fixed location in memory.

When a procedure or function is called, the actual parameters are assigned the next free spaces immediately below the global variables, and

TOP is set to the address of the last parameter or local variable. The space required to store these values, therefore, is allowed to grow along with the level of nesting of procedure calls.

After the procedure or function has finished executing, it returns these locations for reuse by resetting TOP to TOP minus the locations being returned. Storage allocation of data connected with a particular invocation of a procedure or function is supported by a run-time stack, with all the parameters and local variables accessed by their positions relative to the top of the stack. These variables are pushed onto the stack at the entrance to a subprogram, then popped off the stack when the procedure or function completes execution.

This scheme might be compared to another way of allocating seats in an auditorium where a lecture has been scheduled. A finite number of invitations are issued, but each guest is asked to bring a chair. In addition, each guest can invite an unlimited number of friends, as long as they all bring their own chairs. Of course, if the number of extra guests gets out of hand, the space in the auditorium will run out, and there will not be enough room for any more friends or chairs. Similarly, the level of recursion in a program must eventually be limited by the amount of memory available in the run-time stack.

NFACT—ONE MORE TIME

Let's do a code walk-through of the factorial function discussed at the beginning of this chapter.

```
FUNCTION NFACT (N : INTEGER) : INTEGER;

BEGIN     (* nfact *)
   IF N = 0
      THEN NFACT := 1
      ELSE NFACT := N * NFACT(N - 1)
END;      (* nfact *)
```

R2   (* the recursive call *)

The initial invocation is

```
ANS := NFACT(5)
```

R1   (* the original call *)

When NFACT is called the first time from the statement

```
ANS := NFACT(5)
```

three locations are put in the run-time stack: one for the return address, one for the formal parameter N, and one for the function identifier, which is in essence a VAR parameter. The return address will be the place in the translated code where the result is stored into ANS. Let's call it R1. The value of the actual parameter N is stored in the second place (N's relative place), and the third place will still be undefined, since we have not yet made any assignments to NFACT.

	global variables
(RETURN)	R1
(N)	5
(NFACT)	? ← TOP

The code is now executed. Is N (the value in location TOP − 1) equal to 0? No, it is 5, so the ELSE branch is taken:

```
NFACT := N * NFACT(N - 1)
```

So the function NFACT is called again from a different place—the place where, when we have a value for NFACT, we will store it in the function identifier. Let's mark this place R2.

Three locations are again assigned: one for the return address, R2; one for the parameter, N; and one for the function identifier, NFACT.

	global variables
(RETURN)	R1
(N)	5
(NFACT)	?
(RETURN)	R2
(N)	4
(NFACT)	? ← TOP

Again the code is executed. Is N (the value in TOP − 1) equal to 0? No, N is 4, so the ELSE branch is taken:

```
NFACT := N * NFACT(N - 1)
```

So the function NFACT is called again from the place within the function that we called R2. This process continues until the situation looks like

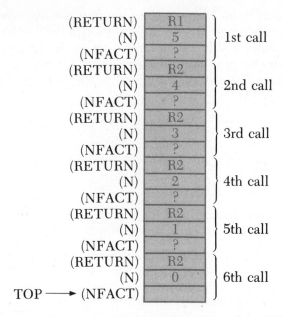

Figure 7-3. The run-time stack during the execution of NFACT.

Figure 7-3. Now, as the code is being executed, we again ask the question: Is N (the value in TOP − 1) equal to 0? Yes! Now we take the THEN branch, which stores the value 1 in NFACT (located in TOP). This time the function has executed to completion. The value in NFACT is returned to the place of the call (R2) and the stack is popped. (That is, TOP becomes TOP − 3.)

The place of the call is where the returned value is multiplied by N (the value in TOP − 1) and stored in NFACT (in location TOP). This is done, and the function has been completed. The value in NFACT is then re-turned to the place of the call, and TOP is reset to TOP − 3.

This process continues until we are back to the first call:

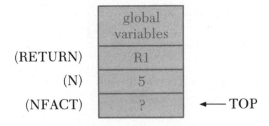

and 24 has just been returned as the value of NFACT(N − 1). This value is multiplied by N (that is, 5) and the result, 120, is stored in NFACT (location TOP). This assignment completes the execution of Function NFACT. The value in location TOP (that is, NFACT) is returned to the place of the original call and TOP is reset to TOP − 3. Now, 120 is stored in ANS and the statement following the original call is executed.

Summary

There are several factors to consider in deciding whether or not to use a recursive solution to a problem. In general, the nonrecursive solution is more efficient in terms of both computer time and space. The recursive solution may require considerable overhead for multiple procedure or function calls, since the return addresses and copies of local and temporary variables must be saved. If a program is to be run frequently (like a compiler) and/or it must be very efficient, the use of recursive programming may not be a good choice.

For some problems, however, a recursive solution is more natural and simpler for the programmer to write. We can picture the total amount of work required to solve a problem as an iceberg. By using recursive programming, the applications programmer may limit his or her view to the tip of the iceberg. The system will take care of the great bulk of the work below the surface. Compare, for example, the recursive and nonrecursive versions of REVPRINT. In the recursive version, we let the system take care of the stacking that we had to do explicitly in the nonrecursive procedure. Thus recursion is a tool that can help reduce the complexity of a program by hiding some of the implementation details. As the cost of computer time and memory space decreases, and the cost of programmer time rises, it may be worthwhile to use recursive solutions to such problems.

In general, if the nonrecursive solution is not much longer than the recursive version, use the nonrecursive one. According to this rule, NFACT, SUM, and SEARCH are not good examples of recursive programming. While they serve well to illustrate how to understand and write recursive procedures and functions, they would be more efficiently and just as simply written iteratively. In the following chapter, we will see how recursion can greatly simplify the design and coding of operations on another data structure, the binary tree.

■ APPLICATION: QUICKSORT — AN EXAMPLE OF A RECURSIVE ALGORITHM

Data Structure in Use
- ARRAY

Software Techniques in Use
- AN EFFICIENT SORTING ALGORITHM
- RECURSION

Quicksort is a sorting algorithm that is based on the fact that it is faster and easier to sort two small lists than one larger one. (We will quantify the idea of *faster* in a later chapter.) This algorithm is called Quicksort because, in general, it can sort a list of data elements significantly faster than any of the common simple sorts. The basic strategy of Quicksort is divide and conquer.

If you were given a large stack of final exams to sort by name, you might use the following approach: Pick a splitting value, say L, and divide the stack of tests into two piles, A–L and M–Z. (Note that the two piles will not necessarily contain the same number of tests.) Then take the first pile and subdivide it into two piles, A–F and G–L. The A–F pile can be further broken down into A–C and D–F. This division process goes on until the piles are small enough to sort easily. The same process is applied to the M–Z pile.

Eventually, all the small sorted piles can be stacked one on top of the other to produce an ordered set of tests. (See Figure 7-4.)

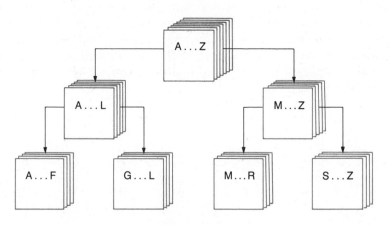

Figure 7-4.

This strategy is based on recursion—each attempt to sort a stack of tests divides the stack and then uses the same approach to sort each of the smaller stacks (a smaller case). This process goes on until the small stacks do not need to be further divided (the base case).

Let's develop a procedure, QSORT, that uses this strategy to sort an array of elements of any type that allows comparisons.

```
TYPE ARRAYTYPE = ARRAY[1..N] OF ELEMENT;
     INDEXTYPE = 0..N + 1;
```

The basic algorithm is

```
IF not finished
    THEN select a splitting value V
         SPLIT on V
         QSORT the elements less than or equal to V
         QSORT the elements greater than V
```

What information will we need to supply QSORT? Certainly we will need to specify the name of the array, as well as its size (FIRST index and LAST index). Our procedure heading will be

```
PROCEDURE QSORT (VAR LIST : ARRAYTYPE;
                 FIRST, LAST : INDEXTYPE);
```

If we want to sort the whole array, our initial call will be

```
QSORT(LIST, 1, N);
```

Let's use the value in LIST[FIRST] as the splitting value, V. After the call to SPLIT, all the elements less than or equal to V will be on the left side of the array and all those greater than V will be on the right side of the array:

FIRST   SPLITPOINT   LAST

| V | | | . . . | | | . . . | |

[1]   [2]   [N]

The two "halves" meet at SPLITPOINT, the index of the last element that is less than or equal to V. Note that we don't know the value of SPLITPOINT until the splitting process is complete. We can then swap V with the value at SPLITPOINT:

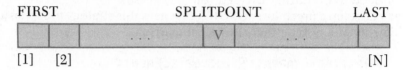

Our recursive calls to QSORT will use this index (SPLITPOINT) to reduce the size of the problem in the general case.

QSORT(LIST, FIRST, SPLITPOINT − 1) sorts the bottom "half" of the array. QSORT(LIST, SPLITPOINT + 1, LAST) sorts the top half of the array. The value in LIST[SPLITPOINT] is already in its correct position.

What is the base case? When the segment being examined has less than two elements, we do not need to go on. So "IF not finished" can be translated into "IF FIRST < LAST".

We can now code Procedure QSORT.

```
PROCEDURE QSORT (VAR LIST : ARRAYTYPE;
                 FIRST, LAST : INDEXTYPE;

VAR SPLITPOINT : INDEXTYPE);

BEGIN    (* qsort *)
   IF FIRST < LAST
      THEN
         BEGIN
            SPLIT(LIST, FIRST, LAST, SPLITPOINT);
            (* Procedure SPLIT chooses the splitting value, V, *)
            (* and rearranges the array so that                *)
            (* LIST[FIRST]..LIST[SPLITPOINT − 1] <= V          *)
            (* LIST[SPLITPOINT] = V                            *)
            (* LIST[SPLITPOINT + 1]..LIST[LAST] > V            *)


            QSORT(LIST, FIRST, SPLITPOINT − 1);
            QSORT(LIST, SPLITPOINT + 1, LAST)
         END
END;     (* qsort *)
```

Let's verify QSORT according to our three questions.

1. *Is there a nonrecursive base case?* Yes. When FIRST >= LAST (there is at most one element in the segment), QSORT does nothing.

2. *Does each recursive call involve a smaller case of the problem?* Yes. SPLIT divides the segment into two not-necessarily-equal pieces, and each of these smaller pieces is then QSORTed. Note that even if V is the largest or smallest value in the segment, the two pieces will still be smaller than the original one:

FIRST   LAST
SPLITPOINT

QSORT(LIST, FIRST, SPLITPOINT − 1) will terminate immediately, since FIRST > SPLITPOINT − 1. QSORT(LIST, SPLITPOINT + 1, LAST) will QSORT a segment one element smaller than the original.

3. *Assuming that the recursive calls succeed, does the whole procedure work?* Yes. We assume that QSORT(LIST, FIRST, SPLITPOINT − 1) actually sorts the first SPLITPOINT − 1 elements, whose values are less than or equal to V. LIST[SPLITPOINT], containing V, is in its correct place. By the assumption we know that QSORT(LIST, SPLITPOINT + 1, LAST) has correctly sorted the rest of the list, whose values are all greater than V. So we know that the whole list is sorted.

In good top-down fashion we have shown that our algorithm will work if Procedure SPLIT works. Now we must develop our splitting algorithm. We must find a way to get all of the elements equal to or less than V on one side of V and the elements greater than V on the other side.

We will do this by using a pair of indexes, RIGHT and LEFT. RIGHT will be initialized to FIRST + 1 and LEFT will be initialized to LAST. [See Figure 7-5(a).] We then move RIGHT toward the middle, comparing LIST[RIGHT] to V. If LIST[RIGHT] <= V, we keep incrementing RIGHT; otherwise, we leave RIGHT and begin moving LEFT toward the middle. [See Figure 7-5(b).]

Now LIST[LEFT] is compared to V. If it is greater than V, we continue decrementing LEFT; otherwise, we leave LEFT in place. [See Figure 7-5(c).]

At this point, it is clear that LIST[LEFT] AND LIST[RIGHT] are each on the wrong side of the array. Note that the elements to the left of LIST[RIGHT] or to the right of LIST[LEFT] are not necessarily sorted;

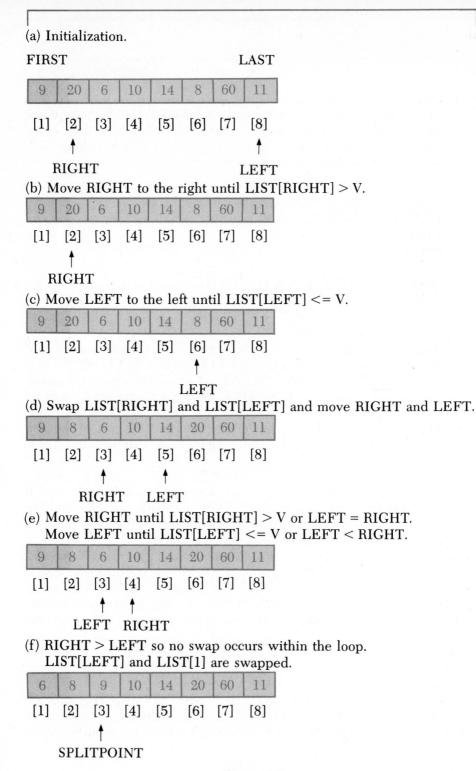

(a) Initialization.

FIRST   LAST

9	20	6	10	14	8	60	11
[1]	[2]	[3]	[4]	[5]	[6]	[7]	[8]

     ↑   ↑

RIGHT   LEFT

(b) Move RIGHT to the right until LIST[RIGHT] > V.

9	20	6	10	14	8	60	11
[1]	[2]	[3]	[4]	[5]	[6]	[7]	[8]

↑

RIGHT

(c) Move LEFT to the left until LIST[LEFT] <= V.

9	20	6	10	14	8	60	11
[1]	[2]	[3]	[4]	[5]	[6]	[7]	[8]

↑

LEFT

(d) Swap LIST[RIGHT] and LIST[LEFT] and move RIGHT and LEFT.

9	8	6	10	14	20	60	11
[1]	[2]	[3]	[4]	[5]	[6]	[7]	[8]

↑   ↑

RIGHT   LEFT

(e) Move RIGHT until LIST[RIGHT] > V or LEFT = RIGHT.
Move LEFT until LIST[LEFT] <= V or LEFT < RIGHT.

9	8	6	10	14	20	60	11
[1]	[2]	[3]	[4]	[5]	[6]	[7]	[8]

↑ ↑

LEFT   RIGHT

(f) RIGHT > LEFT so no swap occurs within the loop.
LIST[LEFT] and LIST[1] are swapped.

6	8	9	10	14	20	60	11
[1]	[2]	[3]	[4]	[5]	[6]	[7]	[8]

↑

SPLITPOINT

Figure 7-5.

they are just on the correct side with respect to V. To put LIST[RIGHT] and LIST[LEFT] onto their correct sides, we merely swap them, then increment RIGHT and decrement LEFT. [See Figure 7-5(d).]

Now we repeat the whole cycle, moving RIGHT to the right until it encounters a value that is greater than V, then moving LEFT to the left until it encounters a value that is less than or equal to V. [See Figure 7-5(e).]

When does the process stop? When RIGHT and LEFT pass each other, no further swaps are necessary. Now we just exchange LIST[FIRST] and LIST[LEFT], and the SPLIT procedure is finished. [See Figure 7-5(f).]

```
PROCEDURE SPLIT (VAR LIST : ARRAYTYPE;
                 FIRST, LAST : INDEXTYPE;
                 VAR SPLITPOINT : INDEXTYPE);
(* Chooses a splitting value V and arranges LIST so that *)
(* LIST[FIRST]..LIST[SPLITPOINT − 1] <= V            *)
(* and LIST[SPLITPOINT + 1]..LIST[LAST] > V          *)

VAR RIGHT, LEFT : INDEXTYPE;
    V : ELEMENT;

BEGIN    (* split *)
  V := LIST[FIRST];
  RIGHT := FIRST + 1;
  LEFT := LAST;

  REPEAT

    WHILE (RIGHT < LEFT) AND (LIST[RIGHT] <= V) DO
        THEN RIGHT := RIGHT + 1;
                        (* LIST[FIRST]..LIST[RIGHT] <= V *)

    WHILE (RIGHT <= LEFT) AND (LIST[LEFT] > V) DO
        LEFT := LEFT − 1;        (* LIST[LEFT]..LIST[LAST] > V *)

    IF RIGHT <= LEFT
       THEN
         BEGIN
           SWAP(LIST[RIGHT], LIST[LEFT]);
           RIGHT := RIGHT + 1;   (* move RIGHT once to the right *)
           LEFT := LEFT − 1;     (* move LEFT once to the left *)
         END             (* LIST[RIGHT]..LIST[LEFT] is unexamined *)
  UNTIL RIGHT > LEFT;

  SWAP(LIST[FIRST], LIST[LEFT]);
  SPLITPOINT := LEFT
END;    (* split *)
```

What happens if our splitting value is the largest or the smallest value in the segment? The algorithm will still work correctly, but because of the lopsided splits it will not be quick.

Is this situation likely to occur? It depends on how we choose our splitting value and on the original order of the data in the array. If we use LIST[FIRST] as the splitting value and the array is already sorted, then every split will be lopsided. One side will contain one element, while the other side will contain all but one of the elements. Thus our Quicksort will not be a quick sort. This splitting algorithm favors an array in random order.

It is not unusual, however, to want to sort an array that is already in nearly sorted order. If this is the case, a better splitting value would be the middle value,

```
LISTC(FIRST + LAST) DIV 2]
```

This value could be swapped with LIST[FIRST] at the beginning of the procedure.

There are many possible splitting algorithms. One that is a slight variation of the one we have just developed is given below. It uses the value in the middle of the array as the splitting value without moving it to the first slot. The result is that the value in LIST[SPLITPOINT] may or may not be in its permanent place.

```
PROCEDURE SPLIT   (VAR LIST : ARRAYTYPE;
                   FIRST, LAST : INDEXTYPE;
                   VAR SPLITPT1, SPLITPT2 : INDEXTYPE);
   (* Chooses a splitting value V and  arranges LIST so that *)
   (* LIST[FIRST]..LIST[SPLITPT2] <= V                        *)
   (* and LIST[SPLITPT1 + 1]..LIST[LAST] > V                  *)

VAR RIGHT, LEFT : INDEXTYPE;
    V : ELEMENT;

BEGIN   (* split2 *)

   (* Let V be the middle value. *)
   V := LISTC(FIRST + LAST) DIV 2];
   RIGHT := FIRST;
   LEFT  := LAST;
```

```
REPEAT
   WHILE LIST[RIGHT] < V DO
      RIGHT := RIGHT + 1;              (* LIST[RIGHT] < V *)
   WHILE LIST[LEFT] > V DO
      LEFT := LEFT - 1;               (* LIST[LEFT] > V *)

   IF RIGHT <= LEFT
      THEN
         BEGIN
            SWAP(LIST[RIGHT], LIST[LEFT]);
            RIGHT := RIGHT + 1;
            LEFT  := LEFT - 1;
         END
   UNTIL RIGHT > LEFT;

   SPLITPT1 := RIGHT;
   SPLITPT2 := LEFT
END;    (* split2 *)
```

If this algorithm is used, Procedure QSORT will have to be adjusted slightly.

```
PROCEDURE QSORT2 (VAR LIST : ARRAYTYPE;
                  FIRST, LAST : INDEXTYPE);
   (* Sorts LIST from index FIRST to index LAST. *)

VAR SPLITPT1, SPLITPT2: INDEXTYPE;

BEGIN    (* qsort2 *)
   IF FIRST < LAST
      THEN
         BEGIN
            SPLIT2(LIST, FIRST, LAST, SPLITPT1, SPLITPT2);
            IF SPLITPT1 < LAST
               THEN QSORT(LIST, SPLITPT1, LAST);
            IF FIRST < SPLITPT2
               THEN QSORT(LIST, FIRST, SPLITPT2)
         END;
END;    (* qsort2 *)
```

Notice that QSORT2 checks to see how many elements are in a segment and does not recurse if there is only one. This makes the code more efficient.

Exercises

1. Write a recursive function that takes as parameters two elements of a set, and returns TRUE if the first element is less than the second and FALSE otherwise. You can assume that both elements are actually in the set and the last element is called LASTEL. You may assume that EL1 and EL2 are not LASTEL.

    Example: Given the enumerated type

    ETYPE = (DOG, FOX, COYOTE, HYENA, WOLF, LASTEL);

    if EL1 is FOX and EL2 is WOLF, then Function LESSTHAN will return TRUE. If EL1 is HYENA and EL2 is DOG, then LESSTHAN will return FALSE.

    Hint: Use the SUCC function.

2. How would Procedure REVPRINT from this chapter be changed to make it print out a list in order?

Use these declarations for Problem 3.

```
TYPE PTR = ↑NODE;
     NODE = RECORD
              INFO : INTEGER;
              NEXT : PTR
            END;  (* record *)

VAR  LIST : PTR;
```

3. Some statistical operations need the value of the sum of the squares of a group of numbers. Assume that the set of numbers is stored in a linked list, pointed to by LIST. Write a recursive function SUMSQRS that takes the pointer to the list, and returns the value of the sum of the squares.

    Example:

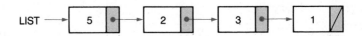

$$\text{SUMSQRS} = (5 * 5) + (2 * 2) + (3 * 3) + (1 * 1) = 39$$

4. For each of the following recursive functions, tell whether or not the function will "work" and if so, what does it do? If not, why not?

    (a) `FUNCTION MYSTERY (LIST, TEMP : PTR) : INTEGER;`

```
BEGIN  (* mystery *)
  TEMP := LIST
  IF TEMP = NIL
    THEN MYSTERY := 0
    ELSE MYSTERY := TEMP↑.INFO +
           MYSTERY(LIST, TEMP↑.NEXT)
  END;    (* mystery *)
```

(b) `FUNCTION PUZZLE (LIST : PTR) : INTEGER;`

```
BEGIN  (* puzzle *)
  IF LIST <> NIL
     THEN IF LIST↑.INFO > 0
             THEN PUZZLE := LIST↑.INFO *
                    PUZZLE(LIST↑.NEXT)
             ELSE PUZZLE := PUZZLE(LIST↑.NEXT)
        ELSE PUZZLE := 1
  END;    (* puzzle *)
```

(c) `FUNCTION BRAINLESS (LIST : PTR) : BOOLEAN;`

```
BEGIN  (* brainless *)
  IF LIST = NIL
     THEN BRAINLESS := FALSE
     ELSE BRAINLESS := (1 + 1 = 2) AND
                BRAINLESS(LIST↑.NEXT)
  END;    (* brainless *)
```

(d) `FUNCTION HEADACHE (LIST : PTR) : INTEGER;`

```
BEGIN  (* headache *)
  IF LIST <> NIL
     THEN HEADACHE := 1 + HEADACHE(LIST↑.NEXT)
     ELSE HEADACHE := HEADACHE(LIST)
  END;    (* headache *)
```

5. Show what would be returned by the following recursive function after the given calls.

```
FUNCTION QUIZ (BASE, LIM : INTEGER) : INTEGER;

BEGIN  (* quiz *)
  IF BASE = LIM
     THEN QUIZ := 1
     ELSE IF BASE > LIM
             THEN QUIZ := 0
             ELSE QUIZ := BASE + QUIZ(BASE + 1, LIM)
  END;    (* quiz *)
```

(a) X := QUIZ(0, 3)   X is _____

(b) Y := QUIZ(10, −7)   Y is _____

(c) Z := QUIZ(5, 5)   Z is _____

6. In each of the following, identify

- the trivial case(s).
- a recursive call to a smaller version of the function or procedure.

(a) FUNCTION POWER (M, N : INTEGER) : INTEGER;

```
BEGIN   (* power *)
  IF N = O
    THEN POWER := 1
    ELSE POWER := M * POWER(M, N - 1)
END;   (* power *)
```

(b) PROCEDURE PRINT (P : PTR);

```
BEGIN   (* print *)
  IF P <> NIL
    THEN BEGIN
           WRITELN(P↑.INFO);
           PRINT(P↑.NEXT)
         END;
END;   (* print *)
```

(c) FUNCTION FACT (N : INTEGER) : INTEGER;

```
BEGIN   (* fact *)
  IF N > O
    THEN FACT = N * FACT(N - 1)
    ELSE IF N = O
           THEN FACT := 1
           ELSE WRITELN('ERROR')
END;   (* fact *)
```

(d) PROCEDURE SORT (A : ARY; LL, UL : INTEGER);

```
VAR J : INTEGER;

BEGIN   (* sort *)
  IF LL <> UL
    THEN BEGIN
           J := MAXPOS(A, LL, UL);
           SWAP(A, J, UL);
           SORT(A, LL, UL - 1)
         END
END;   (* sort *)
```

Pre-Test

1. Consider the following recursive Pascal procedure that prints and permutes characters in a peculiar fashion:

```
PROCEDURE PANDP (X, Y, Z : CHAR; N : INTEGER);
```

```
BEGIN
   IF N > 0
      THEN
         BEGIN
            WRITE(X);
            PANDP(Y, Z, X, N - 1);
            WRITE(Z)
         END      (* if *)
END;   (* pandp *)
```

Show the output produced by each of the following three procedure calls:

(a) PANDP('A', 'B', 'C', 1)

(b) PANDP('A', 'B', 'C', 2)

(c) PANDP('A', 'B', 'C', 3)

2. Let COMM(N, K) represent the number of different committees of K people that can be formed given N people to choose from. For example, COMM(4, 3) = 4, since, given four people A, B, C, and D, there are four possible three-member committees: ABC, ABD, ACD, and BCD. It is well known that

   COMM(N, 1) = N
   COMM(K, K) = 1
   COMM(N, K) = COMM(N − 1, K − 1) + COMM(N − 1, K) for N > K > 1

   Write a recursive Pascal function to compute COMM(N, K) for N >= K and K >= 1.

3. Consider the following TYPE declaration:

```
PTRTYPE = ↑NODETYPE;
NODETYPE = RECORD
               INFO : CHAR;
               NEXT : PTRTYPE
           END;
```

   Recall that a palindrome is a list that has the same sequence of elements when read from right to left as it does when read from left to right. Define a recursive Pascal procedure, PALINDROMIZE, that takes a pointer to a linked list of characters as its input parameter and prints out a palindrome twice as long as the linked list. For instance, the following PALINDROMIZE(P) prints out ABCCBA:

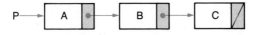

4. Write a recursive function, POSCT, to calculate the number of cells that contain positive values in the list pointed to by LIST.

5. Consider the following recursive function that calculated X − Y. (The two written statements are only to help you trace the function execution.)

```
FUNCTION DIFF (X, Y : INTEGER) : INTEGER;

BEGIN    (* diff *)
   IF  Y = 0
      THEN
         BEGIN
            WRITELN(X);
            DIFF := X
         END
      ELSE
         BEGIN
            WRITELN(PRED(X), PRED(Y));
            DIFF := DIFF(PRED(X), PRED(Y))
         END
END;    (* diff *)
```

(a) Trace the execution of this function when it is invoked by DIFF(7, 4) (i.e., show what is printed out and in what order).

(b) What necessary assumption(s) should be included in the parameter specifications of the function DIFF?

Binary Search Trees 8

Goals

To be able to define and use the following terminology:

- *root*
- *parent*
- *child*
- *sibling*
- *ancestor*
- *descendant*
- *level*
- *subtree*

To be able to describe the properties of a binary search tree.

To be able to show what a binary search tree would look like after a series of insertions and deletions.

To be able to code the following binary search tree algorithms in Pascal:

- *inserting an element into the tree*
- *deleting an element from the tree*
- *searching for an element in the tree*
- *preorder, inorder, and postorder traversals of the tree.*

We have discussed some of the advantages of using a linear linked list to store ordered information. One of the drawbacks of using this data structure is the problem of searching a long list. Consider the list in Figure 8-1. To find the value 10, we must make a sequential traversal of all the nodes in the whole list. Is there a searching technique that is more efficient for a linked structure? The binary search tree provides us with a structure that retains the flexibility of a linked list, while allowing quicker access to any node in the list.

AT THE LOGICAL LEVEL: A BINARY SEARCH TREE

Each node in a singly linked list may point to one other node: the one whose value follows it. It is basically a linear structure. The binary search tree gets its tree structure by allowing each node to point to *two* other nodes: one that precedes it in the list, and one that follows it. Unlike a node

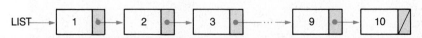

Figure 8-1. A singly linked list with ten nodes.

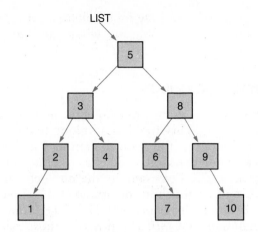

Figure 8-2. A binary search tree with ten nodes.

in a doubly linked list, a node in a binary search tree does not necessarily point to the nodes whose values immediately precede and follow it. The nodes pointed to may be any nodes in the list, as long as they satisfy the basic rule: the node to the "left" contains a value smaller than the node pointing to it, and the node to the "right" contains a larger value. (We will assume that the nodes in the tree are ordered with respect to some key field.)

Figure 8-2 shows a binary search tree that could be created from the nodes in Figure 8-1. Notice that, for any given node, the nodes to its left contain smaller values and the nodes to its right contain larger values. As in a linear linked list, the first node in the tree is pointed to by an external pointer. To access the node containing the value 10, we look in the first node (called the *root* of the tree). The value in the root node is smaller than 10, so we know by the basic rule that the node we seek is located somewhere to its right. Now we check the node immediately to its right and compare the value there to 10. It is smaller, so we move again to the right. This process continues until we arrive at the node that contains 10. Note, by following the path from the root to the node containing 10, that our search only required four comparisons. By contrast, the search for the value 10 in the linear linked list required ten comparisons.

How should duplicate nodes be handled? In some applications, it may be desirable to ignore them. In another situation, occurrences of duplicates may be noted by checking a special flag field or incrementing a counter field in the node. Or new nodes with duplicate values may be inserted to the right or left of the original node. The choice of how to handle duplicates is dependent on the nature of the problem. In our discussion of binary tree algorithms in this chapter, we will assume, for the sake of simplicity, that the nodes are ordered with respect to some unique value.

In this chapter we will learn the basic tree vocabulary, and then develop the algorithms and implementations of some of the procedures needed to use a binary search tree—searching for an element, inserting an element, deleting an element, and traversing the whole tree (to print out all the elements, for example).

SOME BINARY TREE VOCABULARY

Figure 8-3 illustrates the relationships among the nodes in a binary tree. As we have indicated, each binary tree has a unique first element called the root of the tree. In the figure, the node containing J is the root of the tree. The root may have a node to its left, called its *left child,* and/or a node to its right, called its *right child.* For example, the node containing J has a left child containing D and a right child containing Q. The node containing J is called the *parent* of the nodes containing D and Q. (Some people use the terms *left son, right son,* and *father* to describe these relationships.) Any node in a binary tree may have 0, 1, or 2 children. A node with no children is called a *leaf.* For instance, the nodes containing B, E, I, and S are leaves.

Two nodes are *siblings* (or *brothers*) if they have the same parent. The nodes containing B and G are both children of the node containing D; thus, they are siblings. A node is an *ancestor* of another node if it is the parent of the node, or the parent of some other ancestor of that node. The ancestors of the node containing E are the nodes containing J, D, and G. Obviously, the root is an ancestor of every other node in the tree. Similarly, a node is a *descendant* of another node if it is the child of the node or the child of some other descendant of that node. The descendants of the node containing D are the nodes containing B, G, E, and I. All the nodes in the tree are descendants of the root. The descendants to the left of a node comprise its *left subtree,* whose root is the left child of the node. Similarly, the descendants to the right of a node comprise its *right subtree,* whose root is the right child of the node.

The *level* of a node refers to its distance from the root. If we designate the level of the root as 0, the nodes containing D and Q are level 1 nodes, the nodes containing B, G, and T are level 2 nodes, and the nodes containing E, I, and S are level 3 nodes. The maximum number of nodes at any level N is 2^N.

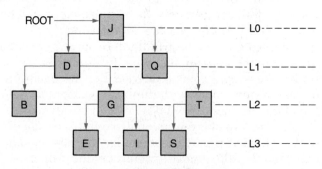

Figure 8-3.

We will access the whole tree through an external pointer (e.g., ROOT). As with linear linked lists, we can access nodes through their pointers. We will refer to three basic fields in each node of a tree:

- INFO(P)—contains the data stored in the node pointed to by P. Like the INFO fields of linked list nodes, it may contain an integer, character, record, or any other data type.
- LEFT(P)—a pointer to the left child of the node pointed to by P.
- RIGHT(P)—a pointer to the right child of the node pointed to by P.

SEARCHING THE TREE

Executing a binary search on the tree simply involves moving a pointer to the left or right until the desired value is found. Let's construct the algorithm for a search routine that returns a pointer to the node containing a given value known to be in the tree. We will use a temporary pointer, P, to search the tree.

Since we access the tree through its root, we first set P equal to the pointer, ROOT. We then begin comparing the INFO field of the nodes in the tree to the value we are searching for. If a node's INFO field is equal to this value, we have found the desired node, and we exit the routine, returning the current value of P. If the INFO field of the node is greater than the searched-for value, we set P equal to the left pointer [LEFT(P)]; otherwise, we set P equal to the right pointer [RIGHT(P)]. We continue comparing until the correct node is found. The whole algorithm is

```
P ← ROOT
WHILE INFO(P) <> VAL DO
    IF INFO(P) > VAL
        THEN P ← LEFT(P)
        ELSE P ← RIGHT(P)
(* Assuming that VAL is in the tree, P will point to the  *)
(* node containing the desired value when we exit         *)
(* from the loop.                                         *)
```

As the algorithm makes clear, the maximum number of comparisons in a binary search on a tree equals the level of the lowest node on the tree (farthest from the root) plus 1 (for the root—level 0). Thus, for the tree in Figure 8-3, the maximum number of comparisons needed to find any node on the tree is four. For the same information ordered in a linear linked list, the maximum number of comparisons equals the number of nodes in the list.

We will leave a detailed discussion of the relative efficiency of linear versus binary searches until Chapter 12. But to illustrate the improvement in searching that a binary search tree may provide, we will give an example. In the worst case, searching for the last node in a linear linked list, you must look at every node in the list. If the list contains 1000 nodes, you must make 1000 comparisons. If the 1000 nodes were arranged in a binary search tree (and the tree was evenly balanced), you would never make more than *11* comparisons, no matter what node you were seeking!

INSERTING INTO A BINARY SEARCH TREE

To create and maintain a binary search tree, it is necessary to have a routine that will insert new nodes into the tree. A new node will always be inserted into its appropriate position in the tree *as a leaf.* Figure 8-4 shows a series of insertions into a binary tree.

(a) ROOT → NULL

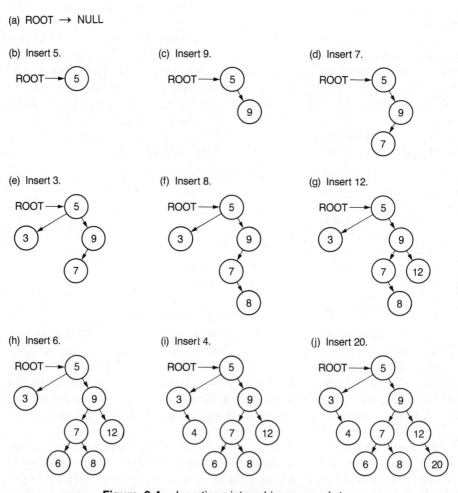

Figure 8-4. Insertions into a binary search tree.

Given the root of a binary search tree and a value to be added to the tree, we have several tasks to perform:

1. Create a node for the new value.
2. Search for the insertion place.
3. Fix pointers to insert the new node.

How we will allocate a new node will depend on whether our implementation of the tree is static or dynamic. For now, let's just say that we have allocated a new node, pointed to by NEWNODE. Since the new node will be a leaf in the tree, we can set both its pointer fields to NULL:

```
LEFT(NEWNODE) ← NULL
RIGHT(NEWNODE) ← NULL
```

Then the new value is stored in the INFO field:

```
INFO(NEWNODE) ← VAL
```

Now that the new node has been created, we can search for its insertion point. After initializing a temporary pointer, P, to point to the root node, we can move P left and right through the tree, as if we were searching for VAL in the tree. When P equals NULL, we will have found the insertion point. Of course, once P is NULL, we cannot link the new node to the node P was pointing to just before it became NULL. We have "fallen out" of the tree and need to climb back into it. In Figure 8-5, P is equal to NULL when we have found the insertion point. We need the pointer P' to be able to access the node containing 13, in order to set its right link to point to node 14.

Our solution will be to have a second pointer trail P as it moves through

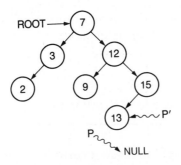

Figure 8-5.

the tree. When P becomes NULL, this back pointer allows us to access the leaf node to which we will link the new node.

The algorithm for the search for the insertion point is

```
(* Initialize the pointers. *)
P ← ROOT
BACK ← NULL

(* Loop until P falls out of the tree. *)
WHILE P <> NULL DO

        (* BACK catches up to P. *)
        BACK ← P

        (* Advance P. *)
        IF INFO(P) > VAL
            THEN move P left
            ELSE move P right
```

At the end of the loop, BACK will point to the node to which we want to link the new node.

The third task is to fix the pointers to attach the new node. In the general case, we can compare the new value to the value in the node pointed to by BACK. We then set either the left or right pointer field of NODE(BACK) to NEWNODE.

```
IF INFO(BACK) > VAL
    THEN LEFT(BACK) ← NEWNODE
    ELSE RIGHT(BACK) ← NEWNODE
```

However, in the case of inserting into an empty tree, when P equals NULL, BACK also equals NULL and references to NODE(BACK) are illegal. We need to make a special case for inserting the first node into the tree. We can test for BACK = NULL to determine if the tree is empty. If so, we will want to change ROOT to point to our new node:

```
IF BACK = NULL
    THEN ROOT ← NEWNODE
    ELSE attach new node to NODE(BACK)
```

From our discussion of the insert algorithm, it can be seen that the order in which nodes are inserted determines the shape of the tree. Figure 8-6 illustrates how the same data, inserted in different orders, will produce very differently shaped trees. If the values are inserted in order (or in re-

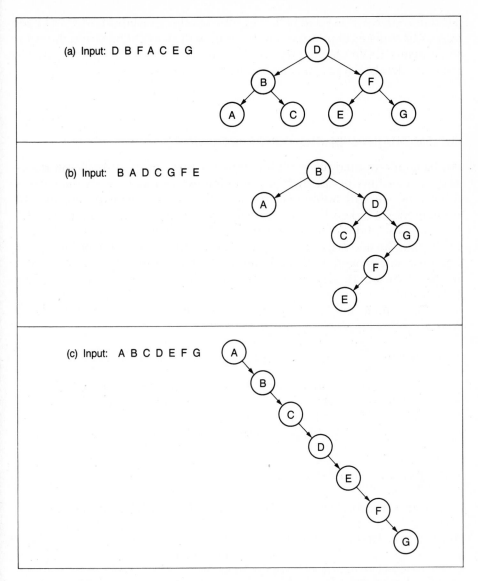

(a) Input: D B F A C E G

(b) Input: B A D C G F E

(c) Input: A B C D E F G

Figure 8-6. The input order determines the shape of the tree.

verse order), the resulting tree will be very skewed. A random mix of the elements will produce a shorter, "bushy" tree. Since the height of the tree (the maximum level of nodes in the tree) determines the maximum number of comparisons in a binary search, the tree's shape is very important. Obviously, minimizing the height of the tree will maximize search efficiency. There are algorithms to adjust a tree to make its shape more desirable, but these schemes are subject matter for more advanced courses.

Taken together, these pieces of the insert algorithm can be coded as a procedure, INSERT. What is the interface to this procedure? We will need to pass two pieces of information: the root of the tree (ROOT) and the value to be inserted (VAL). Note that ROOT must be a VAR parameter, since its value is changed when we insert into an empty tree.

IMPLEMENTATION OF THE INSERT ALGORITHM

We have determined the function of the insertion procedure, its interfaces, and an algorithm for effecting it. But before we can write it, we must determine how we will implement the structure. From our experiences with implementing linked lists, two possibilities come to mind. One possibility is to keep the nodes of the tree as records in an array. A second possibility is to allocate the nodes dynamically and then to link them using pointer variables. We will expand on this second implementation in this chapter. Note, however, that all the algorithms we discuss here can be coded using either implementation.

To implement the binary search tree using pointer variables, we could use the following declarations:

```
TYPE INFOTYPE = the type of the data to be stored

     PTRTYPE  = ↑NODETYPE;
     NODETYPE = RECORD
                     INFO : INFOTYPE;
                     LEFT, RIGHT : PTRTYPE
                END;  (* record *)

VAR  ROOT : PTRTYPE;
```

The insert algorithm could be coded as the following procedure:

```
PROCEDURE INSERT (VAR ROOT : PTRTYPE;
                      VAL : INFOTYPE);
(* Inserts a node containing VAL into the binary *)
(* search tree pointed to by ROOT.               *)

VAR    NEWNODE,
       P,
       BACK : PTRTYPE;

BEGIN   (* insert *)

  (* Create a new node. *)
  NEW(NEWNODE);
  NEWNODE↑.LEFT := NIL;
  NEWNODE↑.RIGHT := NIL;
  NEWNODE↑.INFO := VAL;
```

```
(* Search for insertion place. *)
P := ROOT;
BACK := NIL;
WHILE P <> NIL DO
  BEGIN
    BACK := P;
    IF P↑.INFO > VAL
       THEN P := P↑.LEFT
       ELSE P := P↑.RIGHT
  END;   (* while *)

(* Insertion place is found—connect *)
(* pointers to add new node.        *)
IF BACK = NIL
    THEN                          (* Case of adding to an empty tree. *)
       ROOT := NEWNODE
    ELSE                          (* Case of adding to an existing tree;  *)
                                  (* link new node to appropriate field of *)
                                  (* NODE(BACK).                           *)

       IF BACK↑.INFO > VAL
          THEN BACK↑.LEFT := NEWNODE
          ELSE BACK↑.RIGHT := NEWNODE

END;   (* insert *)
```

DELETING FROM A BINARY SEARCH TREE

Another operation that would be useful in maintaining a binary search tree is the deletion of a specific node from the tree. It can be easily seen that this operation varies depending on the position of the node in the tree. Obviously, it is simpler to delete a leaf than to delete the root of the tree. In fact, we can break down our delete algorithm into three cases, depending on the number of children linked to the node we want to delete:

1. *Deleting a leaf (no children).* As shown in Figure 8-7, deleting a leaf is simply a matter of setting the appropriate link of its parent to NULL, then disposing of the unnecessary node.

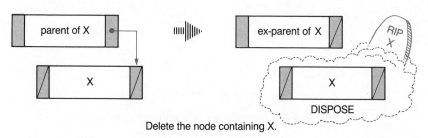

Delete the node containing X.

Figure 8-7. Deleting a leaf.

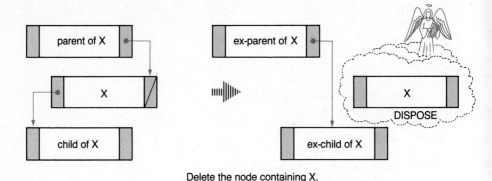

Delete the node containing X.

Figure 8-8. Deleting a node with one child.

2. *Deleting a node with only one child.* The simple solution for deleting a leaf will not suffice for deleting a node with children, since we don't want to lose all of its descendants from the tree. We want to make the pointer from the parent skip over the deleted node and point instead to the child of the node we intend to delete. We then dispose of the unneeded node (Figure 8-8).

3. *Deleting a node with two children.* This case is the most complicated, as we cannot make the parent of the deleted node point to *both* of the deleted node's children. In fact, there are several ways to accomplish this deletion. One common method is to replace the node we wish to delete with the node that is closest in value to the deleted node. This node can come from either the left or the right subtree. In this example, we will replace the node to be deleted with the node of closest

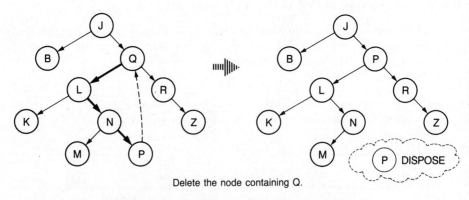

Delete the node containing Q.

Figure 8-9. Deleting a node with two children.

value from the left subtree. This value will be the value in the tree which immediately precedes the one we are deleting. If we had chosen the value from the right subtree, the value would be the one which immediately succeeds the value being deleted. Problem 9 in the Exercises at the end of the chapter asks you to develop the delete algorithm using the immediate successor of the value to be deleted.

To find the immediate predecessor, we move *once* to the *left*, and then as far as we can to the *right*. (If the left child of the node we want to delete has no right child, then the left child itself is used as the replacement node.) Next, we replace the value to be deleted with the value from the replacement node. Then we can delete the *replacement node* (which has either 0 or 1 child) by changing one of its parent's pointers (Figure 8-9).

Examples of all of these types of deletions are shown in Figure 8-10.

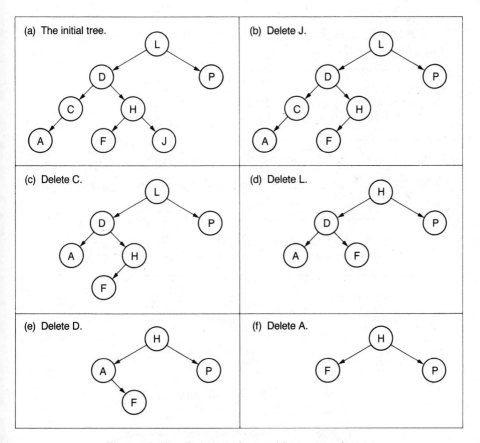

Figure 8-10. Deletions from a binary search tree.

IMPLEMENTING THE DELETE ALGORITHM

When we developed the algorithm for deleting from a linear linked list, we used a back pointer to avoid losing access to the node that pointed to the node we wished to delete. A similar need arises in the case of deletions from binary search trees: when the search pointer indicates the node to be deleted, we no longer have access to its parent node. To remedy this situation, we will keep two pointers: one to the node to be deleted and one to its parent.

Let's develop the algorithm case by case. Let P be a pointer to the node to be deleted and let BACK be the pointer to P's parent. The first case involves deleting a leaf (Figure 8-11):

```
IF (RIGHT(P) = NULL) AND (LEFT(P) = NULL)
    THEN change the appropriate field of NODE(BACK) to NULL
```

Which field of NODE(BACK) gets changed? We check to see which pointer field points to NODE(P):

```
IF  RIGHT(BACK) = P
    THEN RIGHT(BACK) ← NULL
    ELSE LEFT(BACK) ← NULL
```

If NODE(P) is not a leaf, we need to determine how many children it has:

```
IF (RIGHT(P) <> NULL) AND (LEFT(P) <> NULL)
    THEN we know that NODE(P) has two children
```

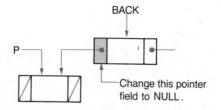

Figure 8-11. Node to be deleted is a leaf.

This is the most complicated case; let's come back to it.

ELSE . . . We know that NODE(P) has one child (Figure 8-12). Left or right? Let's check first for a right child, then for a left. (We already know that it cannot have both from the previous case.)

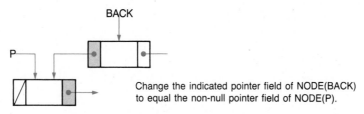

Change the indicated pointer field of NODE(BACK) to equal the non-null pointer field of NODE(P).

Figure 8-12. Node(P) has one child.

```
IF RIGHT(P) <> NULL
    THEN change the appropriate field of
        NODE(BACK) to RIGHT(P)
    ELSE  (* LEFT(P) <> NULL *)
        change the appropriate field of
        NODE(BACK) to LEFT(P)
```

Which is the "appropriate" field of NODE(BACK)? As in the case of deleting a leaf, we can examine the fields of NODE(BACK) to find which pointer field points to NODE(P):

```
IF RIGHT(BACK) = P
    THEN set RIGHT(BACK)
    ELSE set LEFT(BACK)
```

Deleting a node with two children involves searching the tree for the value that is closest to the value in the node to be deleted (immediately before or immediately after). We will not actually delete NODE(P). Instead, we will delete its *contents* by putting this closest value in its place. Then we can delete the node whose value we moved. Our algorithm guarantees that the node we are now deleting has at most one child, so its deletion is relatively simple.

As we said in the previous section, we will use the value immediately *preceding* the value to be deleted. That is, we will search for the replacement value in the left subtree. This value will be in one of two places. If the node to the left of NODE(P) has no right child, then this node contains the replacement value [Figure 8-13(a)]. Otherwise, the replacement value is found in the rightmost descendant of the node to the left of NODE(P) [Figure 8-13(b)].

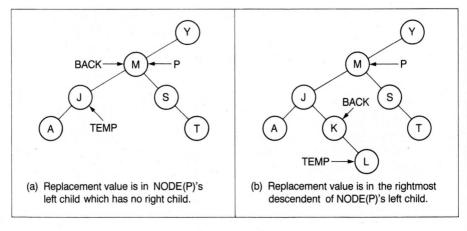

(a) Replacement value is in NODE(P)'s left child which has no right child.

(b) Replacement value is in the rightmost descendent of NODE(P)'s left child.

Figure 8-13.

The following algorithm will find this value, copy it into NODE(P), and delete the unneeded node. We will let P act as a placeholder, and use TEMP and BACK to find and delete the replacement node.

```
BACK ← P
TEMP ← LEFT(P)
WHILE RIGHT(TEMP) <> NULL DO
    BACK ← TEMP
    move TEMP to the right
Replace info in deleted node
Delete NODE(TEMP)
```

Deleting NODE(TEMP) is simple, since at the termination of the loop, RIGHT(TEMP) is NULL. Therefore, we know that NODE(TEMP) has at most one child. Deleting this node requires only a simple pointer manipulation:

```
IF BACK = P   (*  Node to left of NODE(P) has no right child.  *)
    THEN LEFT(BACK) ← LEFT(TEMP)
    ELSE RIGHT(BACK) ← LEFT(TEMP)
```

This design has one serious problem: If we try to delete the root node, difficulties will result. Particularly, if the root has no children or one child, it will be necessary to change the value of the external pointer to the tree, ROOT. In addition, the references to BACK ↑ .LEFT and BACK ↑ .RIGHT will cause run-time errors, since BACK = NIL.

There are a couple of solutions to this problem. We could keep a header node in the tree, so that we need never attempt to delete the root. Alternatively, we could write the delete routine with the additional VAR parameter ROOT, checking for this case separately with a few more IFs.

Procedure DELETENODE below incorporates the second approach. Note that we do not have to do any special processing for deleting the root node when it has two children, since the actual node is not deleted.

```
PROCEDURE DELETENODE (VAR ROOT : PTRTYPE;
                          P, BACK : PTRTYPE);
(*  Deletes the node pointed to by P from the binary *)
(*  search tree with the root pointer ROOT.          *)

VAR  TEMP : PTRTYPE;

BEGIN   (* deletenode *)

    (*  If NODE(P) is a leaf *)
    IF (P↑.RIGHT = NIL) AND (P↑.LEFT = NIL)
        THEN
            IF BACK = NIL                  (* NODE(P) is the last node in tree. *)
                THEN ROOT := NIL
                ELSE
                    IF BACK↑.RIGHT = P
                        THEN BACK↑.RIGHT := NIL
                        ELSE BACK↑.LEFT  := NIL
```

```
    ELSE                                    (* if NODE(P) has two children *)
 IF (P↑.RIGHT <> NIL) AND (P↑.LEFT <> NIL)
    THEN
       BEGIN
            (* Initialize pointers for search *)
            (* for replacement value.       *)
            BACK := P;
            TEMP := P↑.LEFT;
            (* Locate node containing closest value *)
            (* less than the one being deleted.     *)
            WHILE TEMP↑.RIGHT <> NIL DO
              BEGIN
                 BACK := TEMP;
                 TEMP := TEMP↑.RIGHT
              END;   (* while *)
            (* Put the replacement value into the node *)
            (* whose value is being deleted.           *)
            P↑.INFO := TEMP↑.INFO;
            (* Delete the node from which replacement *)
            (* value was taken.                       *)
            IF BACK = P
               THEN BACK↑.LEFT := TEMP↑.LEFT
               ELSE BACK↑.RIGHT := TEMP↑.LEFT;
            P := TEMP                     (* Set P to be DISPOSED. *)
       END   (* if NODE(P) has two children *)

       ELSE                                 (* if NODE(P) has one child *)


 (* Reset one of the pointer fields of NODE(BACK) *)
 (* according to whether P has a right or left child. *)
 IF P↑.RIGHT <> NIL
    THEN                                    (* NODE(P) has a right child. *)
       IF BACK = NIL
          THEN ROOT := P↑.RIGHT             (* delete root node *)
          ELSE                              (* delete nonroot node *)
             IF BACK↑.RIGHT = P
                THEN BACK↑.RIGHT := P↑.RIGHT
                ELSE BACK↑.LEFT := P↑.RIGHT
    ELSE                                    (* NODE(P) has a left child. *)
       IF BACK = NIL
          THEN ROOT := P↑.LEFT              (* delete root node *)
          ELSE                              (* delete nonroot node *)
             IF BACK↑.RIGHT = P
                THEN BACK↑.RIGHT := P↑.LEFT
                ELSE BACK↑.LEFT := P↑.LEFT;

 DISPOSE(P)                                 (* Free NODE(P). *)

END;   (* deletenode *)
```

ALTERNATE DELETION ALGORITHM

The deletion algorithm as presented makes heavy and confusing use of nested IFs. The main reason for this situation is the need to determine which pointer field in NODE(BACK) must be modified. Consider the source of P and BACK. Perhaps the calling code made a search of the tree for a particular value to be deleted, using external pointers P and BACK to work through the tree. This code may appear in a routine like the following procedure, FINDANDKILL.

```
PROCEDURE FINDANDKILL (VAR ROOT : PTRTYPE;
                           VAL  : VALTYPE);
   (* The node with the value VAL will be found *)
   (* and deleted from the binary search tree.   *)
   (* Assumes that the node exists in the tree.  *)

VAR    BACK, P : PTRTYPE;

BEGIN (* findandkill *)

   (* Search tree for node containing VAL. *)
   P := ROOT;
   BACK := NIL;
   WHILE P↑.INFO <> VAL DO
      BEGIN
         BACK := P;
         IF P↑.INFO > VAL
             THEN P := P↑.LEFT
             ELSE P := P↑.RIGHT
      END;   (* while *)

   (* Delete the node pointed to by P. *)
   DELETENODE(ROOT, P, BACK)
END;   (* findandkill *)
```

As an example, in Figure 8-14, the search for the value B ends with P pointing to the node containing B and BACK pointing to the node containing J. *Copies* of these two pointers are sent to procedure DELETENODE. (Remember, they are value parameters.) When the delete routine wants to

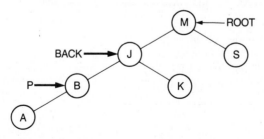

Figure 8-14. Pointers P and BACK are external to the tree.

modify the appropriate field of the parent node, it has no information regarding the relative position of NODE(P)—right or left? We must explicitly check for this information.

It would be nice if, instead of an external pointer to NODE(P), we could send the delete routine the *actual pointer in the tree* (see Figure 8-15). In this case, the delete routine no longer needs to have a back pointer at all, since the pointer to the node to be deleted (a VAR parameter) can be modified directly. As a matter of fact, we know the name of this pointer. If NODE(P) is the root node, we call DELETENODE(ROOT). If BACK↑.LEFT = P, then we call DELETENODE(BACK↑.LEFT). Otherwise, we call DELETENODE(BACK↑.RIGHT). Note that, in any case, we are sending an actual pointer in the tree to the delete routine. Since we will make this pointer a VAR parameter, we can make changes in the tree directly.

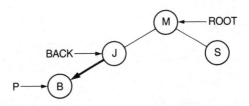

Figure 8-15. Pointer BACK is external to the tree, but BACK↑.LEFT is an actual pointer in the tree.

Let's look at the changes to our algorithm on a case-by-case basis. Remember (again!) that P is the *actual pointer* from the parent node to the node to be deleted.

```
IF NODE(P) is a leaf
    THEN P ← NULL
```

That was easy.

```
    ELSE
IF NODE(P) has one child
    THEN IF RIGHT(P) = NULL
            THEN P ← LEFT(P)
            ELSE P ← RIGHT(P)
```

Actually, the cases of no children and one child can be considered together. In either case, if RIGHT(P) = NULL, we want to set P to LEFT(P). [When NODE(P) is a leaf, LEFT(P) will be NULL, but that's okay.] Otherwise, if LEFT(P) = NULL, we set P to RIGHT(P). Let's start again:

```
IF RIGHT(P) = NULL
    THEN P ← LEFT(P)
    ELSE IF LEFT(P) = NULL
            THEN P ← RIGHT(P)
```

ELSE . . . we know that NODE(P) has two children. We will leave P in place, and use a local pointer variable, TEMP, to search for the replacement value. A local back pointer, BACK, is also used.

```
(* Move TEMP once to the left, then as far as  *)
(* possible to the right to locate the         *)
(* replacement value.                          *)
TEMP ← LEFT(P)
BACK ← P
WHILE RIGHT(TEMP) <> NULL DO
      BACK ← TEMP
      TEMP ← RIGHT(TEMP)
```

When the node containing the replacement value is found, the values are copied into NODE(P); then the replacement node is deleted.

```
INFO(P) ← INFO(TEMP)
IF BACK = P
    THEN LEFT(BACK) ← LEFT(TEMP)
    ELSE RIGHT(BACK) ← LEFT(TEMP)
```

The only thing left to do is to dispose of the deleted node. In the case of the node with two children, we can now delete NODE(TEMP). But in the other two cases, we have "jumped over" the deleted node without saving its pointer. This problem is easily remedied by setting TEMP to P at the beginning of the procedure. Now in all cases we finish with a call to DISPOSE(TEMP).

The complete procedure is given below.

```
PROCEDURE DELETENODE2 (VAR P : PTRTYPE);
   (* Deletes the node pointed to by P from the *)
   (* binary search tree. P is the real pointer  *)
   (* in the tree, not an external pointer.       *)

VAR   BACK, TEMP : PTRTYPE;

BEGIN   (* deletenode2 *)

   (* Save the value of P for disposal. *)
   TEMP := P;

   (* Case of 0 or 1 child. *)
   IF P↑.RIGHT = NIL
      THEN P := P↑.LEFT
      ELSE
         IF P↑.LEFT = NIL
            THEN P := P↑.RIGHT
            ELSE
               (* Case of 2 children. *)
               BEGIN
                  (* Initialize pointers for search for the *)
                  (* replacement value.                      *)
                  TEMP := P↑.LEFT;
                  BACK := P;

                  (* Locate the node containing the largest *)
                  (* value smaller than the value in the    *)
                  (* node being deleted.                     *)
                  WHILE TEMP↑.RIGHT <> NIL DO
                     BEGIN
                        BACK := TEMP;
                        TEMP := TEMP↑.RIGHT
                     END;   (* while *)

                  (* Replace value to be deleted. *)
                  P↑.INFO := TEMP↑.INFO;

                  (* Delete replacement node. *)
                  IF BACK = P
                     THEN BACK↑.LEFT  := TEMP↑.LEFT
                     ELSE BACK↑.RIGHT := TEMP↑.LEFT
               END;   (* case of 2 children *)

   DISPOSE(TEMP)                          (* Free the deleted node. *)

END;   (* deletenode2 *)
```

To complete Procedure FINDANDKILL, we can replace the last line with

```
IF  P = ROOT
    THEN DELETENODE2(ROOT)
    ELSE
       IF BACK↑.LEFT = P
       THEN DELETENODE2(BACK↑.LEFT)
       ELSE DELETENODE2(BACK↑.RIGHT)
```

TREE TRAVERSALS

Traversing a tree means to visit all of its nodes—for example, to print all of the values in the tree. In traversing a linear linked list, we set a temporary pointer equal to the start of the list, and then follow the links from one node to the next until we reach a node whose pointer value is NIL. Similarly, to traverse a binary tree, we initialize our pointer to the root of the tree. But where do we go from there? To the left or to the right? Do we print the root first, or should we print the leaves first?

Suppose we decide to print out the values in the tree in order, from smallest to largest. We first need to print the root's *left* subtree—the values in the tree that are smaller than the value in the root node. Then we print the value in the root node. Finally, we print the values in the root's *right* subtree—values that are larger than the value in the root node (Figure 8-16).

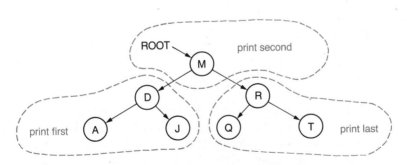

Figure 8-16. Printing all the nodes in order.

Some considerations become immediately apparent. As we move our pointer, P, to the left in order to begin traversing the left subtree, we lose our access to the root. We can't get back up. In fact, this problem is a general one as we move through the tree. When P points to the node to the left of the root (Figure 8-17), we need to repeat the whole procedure—print the nodes to the left, print NODE(P), then print the nodes to the right. We will move our pointer again to the left, not yet printing anything, but again we won't be able to get back to nodes we have passed. We need some way of keeping track of these nodes as we pass them. Later we will want to re-trieve them, beginning with the node that was most recently saved and proceeding backwards.

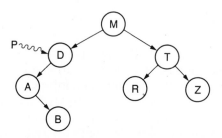

Figure 8-17. When you have finished with the left subtree, how can you get back up to print the root and the right subtree?

Luckily we know of a data structure that is just perfect for this backtrack-ing task—a stack. As we travel down the left branch as far as possible, we push the pointers to the nodes we have passed onto the stack:

```
WHILE P <> NULL DO
    PUSH(STACK, P)
    P ← LEFT(P)
```

When P is NULL, we know the left subtree is empty, and we can climb back into the tree by popping the stack. We print the value in the node pointed to by P. Then we traverse that node's right subtree by setting P to RIGHT(P) and repeating the whole routine.

How do we know when we are finished? In traversing a linear linked list, we need only note when P is equal to NULL. When we are traversing a binary tree, this condition is not sufficient; we also need to look at the status of the stack. When P is NULL *and* the stack is empty, we are fin-ished.

Using our pointer-variable representation of a binary search tree, we come up with the following procedure. We will assume that the declarations for STACKTYPE, as well as the stack utility routines, exist elsewhere in the program.

```
PROCEDURE INORDER (ROOT : PTRTYPE);
    (* Prints out the elements in the binary tree pointed *)
    (* to by ROOT in order from smallest to largest.      *)

VAR   STACK : STACKTYPE;    (* stack of pointers used to keep track of nodes *)
                            (* as they are passed, until they are printed    *)

      P : PTRTYPE;                         (* used to traverse the list *)

BEGIN    (* inorder *)
    (* Start with an empty stack. *)
    CLEARSTACK(STACK);

    (* Start at the root of the tree. *)
    P := ROOT;
    REPEAT
        (* Go to the left as far as possible, pushing the *)
        (* pointers to nodes as they are passed. Stop      *)
        (* when P falls out of the tree.                   *)
        WHILE P <> NIL DO
            BEGIN
                PUSH(STACK, P);              (* Push node pointer on stack. *)
                P := P↑.LEFT                 (* Keep moving to the left. *)
            END;

        (* If there's anything left in the stack, pop the  *)
        (* top element, print the value of the node, and   *)
        (* move once to the right.                         *)
        IF NOT EMPTYSTACK(STACK)
            THEN
                BEGIN
                    POP(STACK, P);           (* Climb back into tree. *)
                    WRITELN(P↑.INFO);        (* Print value of node. *)
                    P := P↑.RIGHT            (* Move to the right. *)
                END    (* if not empty *)
    UNTIL (P = NIL) AND (EMPTYSTACK(STACK))
END;    (* inorder *)
```

Figure 8-18 traces through this procedure, using a tree with only four nodes.

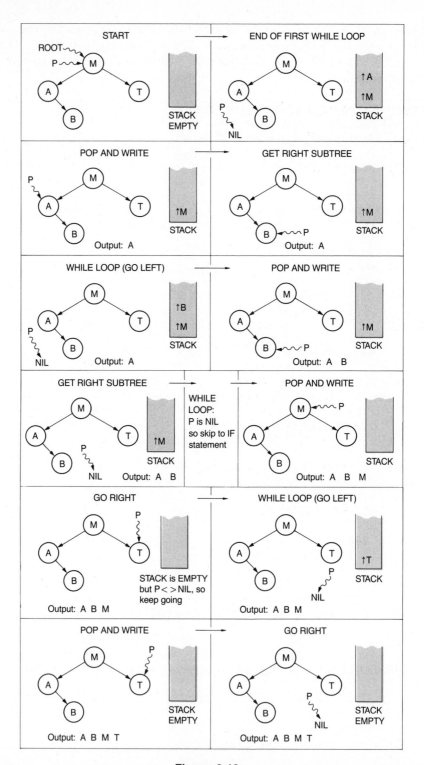

Figure 8-18.

Recursive Tree Traversals

The procedure given in the previous section is not exactly intuitive, and only an example of a walk-through like the one in Figure 8-18 makes it really clear how the tree is traversed. As we said in Chapter 7, the binary search tree provides us with an example of a more elegant use of recursion.

Pascal offers us a way of performing the necessary stacking to keep track of the nodes in the tree through its support of recursive programming. We can write a very short recursive procedure to do this in-order printing operation.

Let's use the technique we developed in Chapter 7 to describe the problem in detail:

PROCEDURE INORDER

Definition: Print out all the elements in the binary search tree in order from smallest to largest.

Size: Nodes in the whole tree.

Base case: When P = NULL, do nothing.

General case: Traverse the left subtree in order.
Print INFO(P)
Traverse the right subtree in order.

This description can be coded into Procedure INORDER2:

```
PROCEDURE INORDER2 (P : PTRTYPE);
(* Prints out the elements in a binary search tree       *)
(* in order from smallest to largest. This is a recursive solution. *)

BEGIN    (* inorder2 *)

    (* Base case: if P is NIL, do nothing. *)
    IF P <> NIL
        THEN    (* general case *)
            BEGIN
                (* Traverse the left subtree to print the smaller values. *)
                INORDER2(P↑.LEFT);

                (* Print the value of this node. *)
                WRITELN(P↑.INFO);

                (* Traverse the right subtree to print the larger values. *)
                INORDER2(P↑.RIGHT)
            END    (* general case *)

END;    (* inorder2 *)
```

To print out the whole tree, we initially call this procedure with the statement INORDER2(ROOT). Note that the initialization of P to the root of the tree is effected through the original calling argument.

As an exercise, use the three-question method to verify this procedure.

Other Tree Traversal Orders

We may want to traverse the nodes of a binary tree in other orders. Two other orders that are commonly used are preorder and postorder traversals. The traversal we first discussed was called inorder because each node was visited in between its left and right subtrees. Preorder visits each node before its left and right subtrees and postorder visits each node after its left and right subtrees.

A *preorder traversal* of a binary tree

1. visits the root
2. traverses the left subtree preorder
3. traverses the right subtree preorder.

Given the tree in Figure 8-19 on the following page, a preorder traversal would print

```
P F B H G S R Y T W Z
```

The preorder print procedure can be written recursively by changing the order of the statements in the inorder routine:

```
PROCEDURE PREORDER (P : PTRTYPE);
(* Prints out the elements in a binary tree in preorder. *)

BEGIN   (* preorder *)

   (* Base case: if P is NIL, do nothing. *)
   IF P <> NIL
      THEN   (* general case *)
         BEGIN
            (* Print the value of this node. *)
            WRITELN(P↑.INFO);

            (* Traverse its left subtree. *)
            PREORDER(P↑.LEFT);

            (* Traverse its right subtree. *)
            PREORDER(P↑.RIGHT)
         END   (* general case *)

END;   (* preorder *)
```

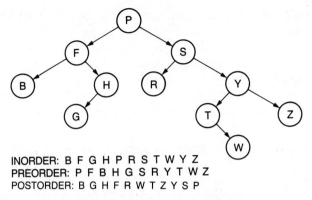

INORDER: B F G H P R S T W Y Z
PREORDER: P F B H G S R Y T W Z
POSTORDER: B G H F R W T Z Y S P

Figure 8-19. Three tree traversals.

We will see in the following chapter how a preorder traversal can be used to produce the prefix notation of an expression stored in a binary tree.

A *postorder traversal* of a binary tree

1. traverses the left subtree postorder
2. traverses the right subtree postorder
3. visits the root.

A postorder traversal of the tree in Figure 8-19 would print

B G H F R W T Z Y S P

A procedure to print out the elements in a binary tree in postorder is given below. Like procedure PREORDER, it rearranges the order of the three statements in the general case to change the order of printing.

```
PROCEDURE POSTORDER (P : PTRTYPE);
(* Prints out the elements in a binary tree in postorder. *)

BEGIN   (* postorder *)
   (* Base case: if P is NIL, do nothing. *)
   IF P <> NIL
      THEN   (* general case *)
         BEGIN
            (* Traverse the left subtree. *)
            POSTORDER(P↑.LEFT);

            (* Traverse the right subtree. *)
            POSTORDER(P↑.RIGHT);

            (* Print the value of this node. *)
            WRITELN(P↑.INFO)
         END   (* general case *)
END;   (* postorder *)
```

When might one want to use a postorder traversal of a binary search tree? Consider the following situation: We want to traverse the tree and delete all the nodes that meet some criteria. In this case, we could use any of the traversal orders with the same final results. However, we know that deleting a leaf is simpler than deleting a node with children. If we can start our traversal at the bottom of the tree (where the leaves are) using a postorder traversal, we will increase the likelihood of deleting leaves.

APPLICATIONS OF BINARY SEARCH TREES

A binary search tree is an appropriate structure for many of the same applications that we have previously discussed for other list structures. The special advantage to its use is that it facilitates searching. While it is not a random-access structure like a simple array, it provides faster and more constant access to individual nodes than does a linked list. Thus it is particularly suitable for applications in which search time must be minimized or the nodes will not necessarily be processed in order.

For instance, suppose we have 1000 customer records in a list. If our main activity is to send out updated monthly statements to the customers and the statements are printed in the same order as the list is ordered, a linked list would be suitable. But suppose we decide to keep a terminal available to give out account information to the customers whenever they ask. If our data are kept in a linked list, the first customer on the list can be located almost instantly, but the last customer will have a long wait. In this case, where fast, random access to the records is needed, the binary search tree is a more appropriate structure.

As usual, there is a trade-off. The binary search tree, with its extra pointer, will take up more memory space than a singly linked list. In addition, as we have seen, the algorithms for manipulating the tree are somewhat more complicated. For instance, the inorder traversal of a binary tree is much more expensive than the sequential traversal of a linked list containing the same data.

Summary

In this chapter we have seen how the binary tree may be used to structure ordered information in a way that reduces the search time for any particular element. (We are measuring search time as a function of the number of comparisons needed to locate the element.) We developed the operations to insert and delete elements of such a tree.

The tree structure is very useful and versatile. As we will discuss in Chapter 9, there are binary trees that are not binary search trees, and there are trees that are not binary trees. The operations on these structures will be highly dependent on the purpose for which the structure is used.

■ APPLICATION: INDEX

Data Structures in Use
- BINARY SEARCH TREES
- QUEUE
- STRINGS

Software Techniques in Use
- USE OF BINARY SEARCH ON A TREE
- USE OF DEBUGGING TECHNIQUES

The set of notes that you have been using all semester needs an index. Your job is to write a program to create one.

There are two ways to create an index. One way is to use two passes. A list of all the different words used in the text is created on the first pass. A human goes over this list and chooses the words that are to be in the index. The second pass takes this list of words as input and scans the text again, noting where each word occurs in the text.

Dale/Lilly

This is called a two-pass process because the entire text of the manuscript is read twice. You actually have two separate programs. The output from the first program is the list of all the words in the text. This is edited for input to the second program, which creates the index.

The other way to create an index is to create your list of words and keep track of where they occur at the same time, in a single pass. You decide to use this second algorithm, which requires only one program.

The problem here, of course, is that your index becomes cluttered with words that don't belong in an index: "the," "and," "but," and so on. How do you recognize these words, in order to avoid putting them in the index? One way is to use a dictionary of words that you do *not* want in your index. A word is entered into the index only if it is not on this list.

Another problem involves words like "tree" and "computer," which occur so often that you only want to list the first few references. A way to handle this problem is to keep track of how many pages you have for each word and, when this count reaches a certain limit, remove that word from the index and add it to the list of words you do not want in the index.

Input:
The dictionary of words not to include in the index on file WORDS. These words are not in alphabetical order.

The text to be indexed on file BOOK. Pages are separated by the symbol # surrounded by blanks. This end-of-page marker may appear anywhere in the text between words.

Output:
Words and page references for any word deleted from the index because of frequency. If a word appears twice on the same page, the page number should be listed only once.

An alphabetical list of words in the index and their page references.

Discussion: The general processing seems straightforward. We read in the dictionary of words that we do not want to include in our index. We then read in the text, one word at a time, and check each word to see if it is in the dictionary of words to skip. If it is not a word to skip, we update the index; otherwise, we just go back to get another word of the text.

Updating the index requires two processes: one if the word is already in the index and one if the word must be inserted into the index. If the word is there, we look at the last page on the list of pages associated with the word to see if it is the same as the current page. If it is, we return and get another word since we only want to enter a page number once; otherwise we must update the list of pages on which this word appears by adding the current page to the list. If the number of pages associated with this word is now at the limit, we must delete this word from the index, print it with its page list, and insert the word into the dictionary of words not to include in the index.

That last paragraph reads like a nested IF statement. We now have a basic understanding of the flow of the problem. It is time to write the top levels of our top-down design.

MAIN   **Level 0**

```
GET DICTIONARY of words not to index
WHILE more words DO
    GET A WORD from BOOK
    PROCESS WORD
PRINT INDEX
```

GET DICTIONARY will read a list of words from file WORDS and save them in the dictionary of words to reject.

GET DICTIONARY   **Level 1**

```
WHILE more words DO (* not EOF *)
    GET A WORD
    INSERT in dictionary
```

To cut down on space used by the dictionary, you decide to eliminate words of less than 3 letters.

GET A WORD   Level 1

```
REPEAT
    GETWORD(WORD, BOOK)
    IF WORD = ENDOFPAGE
        increment CURRENTPAGE
UNTIL length(WORD) >= MINLENGTH
```

PROCESS WORD   Level 1

```
IF WORD not in DICTIONARY
    THEN
        IF WORD in INDEX
            THEN
                UPDATE PAGELIST
            ELSE (* word not yet in INDEX *)
                INSERT WORD in INDEX
```

Before we can go on to the next level of our design, we must decide what data structures to use. There are two decisions to be made here. We must decide how to represent words and how to represent the index and the dictionary of words to omit from the index.

There are two ways that we can represent words: as packed arrays of characters or as the stringtype defined in Chapter 2. Before determining which representation to use, let's review what processing we will do to words. They are to be read, compared, and printed. Each operation can be applied to either representation. However, we will need to know the number of characters in a word. If we use the stringtype, determining the number of characters is a predefined function. We could, of course, write such a function on our packed arrays.

Which then is the better representation? The comparison operation is the operation that will be applied the most often as we search both the dictionary and the index. The comparison operation defined on the stringtype is slow because it is done character by character. Since we are working with words only, not lines, we can determine a maximum number of characters we wish to carry for each word and define the packed array to be of this size. We can pad the shorter words with blanks and truncate the longer words. We save space because we don't need to have a length field, and the comparison operation is much faster because we can compare the words directly. For these reasons, we decide to use a packed array of characters to represent a string.

The index and the dictionary will be searched frequently, so the data structure we choose should allow for rapid searching. A binary search tree seems a logical choice for both the index and the dictionary. The question is whether or not both trees can have the same type of node. It would certainly simplify processing if they could.

Each tree will need a field for a word, but the dictionary will also need a place to keep page numbers. One possible structure would be the following:

```
CONST  MAXLENGTH = 15;                        (* max string length *)
       LIMIT = 5;                             (* max page references *)
       MINLENGTH = 3;              (* minimum length of word in INDEX *)

TYPE   NODEPTR = ↑NODE;

       STRINGTYPE = PACKED ARRAY[1..MAXLENGTH] OF CHAR;

       NODE = RECORD
                  WORDFIELD : STRINGTYPE;
                  PAGELIST  : RECORD
                                  INDEX : 0..LIMIT;
                                  PAGE  : ARRAY[1..LIMIT]
                                              OF INTEGER
                              END; (* record *)
                  RIGHT, LEFT : NODEPTR
              END; (* record *)
```

The INDEX field indicates the number of pages associated with a word and PAGE[INDEX] contains the last page number entered in the list of pages.

However, if we used the same node type to represent the dictionary, there would be a lot of wasted space. One alternative would be to store a pointer to the PAGELIST record in the node, rather than the record itself. This pointer would contain NIL when the node is used to represent the words in the dictionary. This way the only wasted space in the dictionary node would be for the pointer, not the whole record containing the page list. Another alternative would be to represent the page list as a linked list. This would save space in the index because a cell would only be assigned for a page if it were needed. The processing would be a little slower, however, because of repeated calls to NEW.

Which is best? Or rather, which is better? The answer depends on your requirements. If space is the resource you need to conserve, you should use two different node types, one for the dictionary and one for the index. This would minimize the use of space, but the processing would be more complicated. We would have to have two sets of tree operations, one for each node type.

Let us assume that programmer time is the resource we are conserving and use one node type containing a pointer to the page list. We will not make a decision on the representation of the page list. Instead, we will treat the page list as a queue. Our operations on the page list will be in terms of queue operations. Our nodes will simply contain a field of type QPTR, a pointer to a queue. The only queue operation that we will have to change is FULL. We will have FULL return TRUE when the number of elements in the queue is equal to the limit on the number of pages.

Data Structures: Words will be represented as packed arrays of characters. The dictionary will be represented by a binary tree (DICTIONARY). The index will be represented by a binary tree (INDEX). The declarations for our structures will be as follows:

```
CONST MAXLENGTH = 15;                        (* max string length *)
      LIMIT = 5;                             (* max page references *)
      MINLENGTH = 3;              (* minimum length of word in INDEX *)

TYPE  NODEPTR = ↑NODE;
      STRINGTYPE = PACKED ARRAY[1..MAXLENGTH] OF CHAR;
      QPTR = ↑QUEUETYPE
      NODE = RECORD
                WORDFIELD : STRINGTYPE;
                QUEUE : QPTR;                (* ptr to queue of pages *)
                RIGHT,LEFT : NODEPTR;
             END; (* record *)
```

Now we can continue with the next levels of our design.

GETWORD   Level 2

```
WORD ← blanks
COUNTER ← 0
Skip to first character (CH) that is not blank or punctuation.
WHILE CH NOT a punctuation mark or a blank
    AND COUNTER < MAXLENGTH
        increment COUNTER
        WORD[COUNTER] ← CH
        READ(DATA, CH)
Skip to next punctuation or blank if not already there.
```

Since we decided to save space by automatically eliminating all words of less than three characters, we need a function to determine the length of a word.

LENGTH   Level 2

```
IF WORD = blanks
    LENGTH ← 0
ELSE
    COUNTER ← MAXLENGTH
    WHILE WORD[COUNTER] = blank DO
        COUNTER ← COUNTER − 1
    LENGTH ← COUNTER
```

This algorithm to determine the length of a string will work with any string. However in this particular case, we can actually replace this algorithm with a simple Boolean expression. We really don't need to know the length; we just need to know if the word is at least MINLENGTH characters. Since our words do not contain any embedded blanks, we can simply ask if WORD[MINLENGTH] is a blank. If it isn't, then the word is at least MINLENGTH characters long. Therefore our terminating expression in the REPEAT-UNTIL in GETWORD will be a Boolean function, LENGTHOK. Function LENGTHOK is simply the one line

```
LENGTHOK := WORD[MINLENGTH] <> ' '
```

INSERT   Level 2

We can use the INSERT algorithm we developed in this chapter directly. The element to be inserted into the tree is of type NODE.

Checking whether WORD is in the dictionary tree requires us to search the tree. If the search pointer becomes NULL before we find the word we are looking for, we know that the word is not in the tree.

NODE FOUND   Level 2

```
CURRENT pointer ← root of tree
FOUND ← FALSE
WHILE (CURRENT <> NULL) AND NOT FOUND DO
    IF WORDFIELD(CURRENT) = word we are searching for
        THEN FOUND ← TRUE
        ELSE advance CURRENT
NODEFOUND ← FOUND
```

We could also use Function NODEFOUND to determine if WORD is in the INDEX. However, this function just tells us if the word is there. Here we wish to access the node if it's in the tree, or insert it if it is not in the tree. In addition we may need to delete the word from the index if its page list is full. This means that as output parameters we need the entry where the word is, if it is there, and the pointer to where it should go, if it is not there. Let's call this procedure FINDPLACE and rewrite PROCESS WORD reflecting this change.

PROCESS WORD   Level 1

```
IF NOT NODEFOUND(DICTIONARY, WORD)
    FINDPLACE(WORD, INDEX, BACK, ENTRY, FOUND)
    IF FOUND
        THEN                (* WORD is in INDEX *)
            UPDATE PAGELIST(BACK, ENTRY, INDEX, DICTIONARY)
        ELSE                (* WORD is not in INDEX *)
            INSERT WORD in INDEX
```

FIND PLACE   Level 2

```
(* Find WORD's place in INDEX. *)
FOUND ← False
ENTRY ← INDEX
BACK ← NULL
WHILE ENTRY <> NULL AND NOT FOUND DO
    IF WORDFIELD(ENTRY) = WORD
        THEN FOUND ← True
        ELSE (* advance BACK and ENTRY *)
            BACK ← ENTRY
            IF WORDFIELD(ENTRY) < WORD
                THEN ENTRY ← RIGHT(ENTRY)
                ELSE ENTRY ← LEFT(ENTRY)
```

UPDATE PAGELIST   Level 2

```
IF CURRENTPAGE not listed
    ENQ(ENTRY ↑ .QUEUE ↑ , CURRENTPAGE)
    IF FULLQ(ENTRY ↑ .QUEUE ↑ )
        THEN  (* number of pages has reached the limit *)
            PRINT WORD and PAGELIST
            DELETE WORD from INDEX
            INSERT WORD in DICTIONARY
```

"CURRENTPAGE not listed" expands to CURRENTPAGE<>QUEUE-REAR(ENTRY↑.QUEUE↑). QUEUEREAR will be a special purpose function that returns the last element put in the queue without changing the queue.

To print out the INDEX in alphabetical order, we can use a recursive inorder tree traversal.

PRINT INDEX   Level 1

```
IF INDEX <> NULL
    THEN PRINTINDEX(LEFT(INDEX))
        PRINTQUEUE of page numbers
        PRINTINDEX(RIGHT(INDEX))
```

PRINTQUEUE   Level 2

```
WRITE(P↑.WORDFIELD)
WHILE NOT EMPTYQ(P↑.QUEUE↑) DO
    DEQ(P↑.QUEUE↑, PAGE)
    WRITE(PAGE:4, ',')
```

We have not yet considered error conditions. What will happen to GET A WORD if the last word in either file is less than three characters long? We will get a TRIED TO READ PAST END OF FILE message. Since one of the marks of a good program is robustness, we must take care of this situation. Remember that robustness means that the program will not crash. That is, all abnormal conditions are taken care of within the program itself.

We will therefore have to add EOF to the terminating condition of our REPEAT loop in GET A WORD. PROCESS WORD must be skipped if EOF is TRUE.

```
PROGRAM CONSTRUCTINDEX (BOOK, WORDS, BOOKINDEX,
                        DEBUGFILE);

CONST LIMIT = 5;                        (* maximum number of page references *)
      MAXQUEUE = 6;                          (* maximum size of queue *)
      BLANKS = '        ';                        (* blank word *)
      MAXLENGTH = 15;                  (* maxlength of a string data type *)
      ENDOFPAGE = '#      ';      (* end of page marker *)
      MINLENGTH = 3;              (* min length of word included in index *)
      DEBUG = TRUE;                   (* used for output during debug stage; *)
                             (* when program goes into production, debug is set *)
                                    (* to false to cancel intermediate prints *)


TYPE  NODEPTR = ↑NODE;
      PAGETYPE = 1..999;                              (* page numbers *)
      STRINGTYPE = PACKED ARRAY[1..MAXLENGTH] OF CHAR;
      INDEXRANGE = 0..MAXLENGTH;
      INDEXTYPE = 1..MAXQUEUE;                (* size of queue of pages *)
      QPTR = ↑QUEUETYPE;                (* pointer to stack of page numbers *)

      NODE = RECORD
               WORDFIELD : STRINGTYPE;
               QUEUE : QPTR;        (* pointer to queue of page numbers *)
               RIGHT, LEFT : NODEPTR
             END;  (* record *)

      SETOFPUNC = SET OF CHAR;          (* maximum size of a set type is *)
                                        (* implementation dependent; *)
                                   (* check before using SET OF CHAR *)

      QUEUETYPE = RECORD
               ELEMENTS : ARRAY[INDEXTYPE] OF
                 PAGETYPE;
               FRONT,
               REAR : INDEXTYPE
             END;  (* record *)

VAR   DICTIONARY,                       (* words not to include in index *)
      INDEX : NODEPTR;                        (* words in the index *)
      WORD : STRINGTYPE;
      DEBUGFILE,                     (* output file for debug information, *)
                                     (* used during testing phase only *)

      BOOKINDEX,                       (* output file containing index *)
      WORDS,                           (* file containing dictionary *)
      BOOK : TEXT;                       (* file containing text *)
      CURRENTPAGE : PAGETYPE;           (* current page number *)
      PUNCTUATION : SETOFPUNC;          (* end of word markers *)

(* ******************************************************* )
```

```
PROCEDURE TESTPRINTTREE (ROOT : NODEPTR);
(* This print routine prints a binary tree in preorder. It is used here to print the *)
(* index and dictionary during testing since the regular print routine also prints *)
(* the queue of page numbers.                                                       *)

BEGIN  (* testprinttree *)
  IF ROOT <> NIL
    THEN
      BEGIN
        TESTPRINTTREE(ROOT↑.LEFT);
        WRITE(DEBUGFILE, ROOT↑.WORDFIELD);
        TESTPRINTTREE(ROOT↑.RIGHT)
      END
END;  (* testprinttree *)

(* ********************************************** )

PROCEDURE CLEARQ (VAR Q : QUEUETYPE);
(* Initialize Q to empty condition. *)

BEGIN  (* clearq *)
  Q.FRONT := MAXQUEUE;
  Q.REAR  := MAXQUEUE
END;   (* clearq *)

(* ********************************************** )

FUNCTION EMPTYQ (Q : QUEUETYPE) : BOOLEAN;
(* Returns TRUE if Q is empty; FALSE otherwise. *)

BEGIN    (* emptyq *)
  EMPTYQ := Q.REAR = Q.FRONT
END;     (* emptyq *)

(* ********************************************** )

FUNCTION FULLQ (Q : QUEUETYPE) : BOOLEAN;
(* Returns TRUE if Q is full; FALSE otherwise. *)

VAR  NEXTREAR : INDEXTYPE;

BEGIN  (* fullq *)
  IF Q.REAR = MAXQUEUE
    THEN NEXTREAR := 1
    ELSE NEXTREAR := Q.REAR + 1;
  FULLQ := NEXTREAR = Q.FRONT
END;     (* fullq *)

(* ********************************************** )
```

```
PROCEDURE ENQ (VAR Q : QUEUETYPE; NEWPAGE : PAGETYPE);
(* Insert NEWPAGE into Q. Assumes queue is not full. *)

BEGIN    (* enq *)
   IF Q.REAR = MAXQUEUE
      THEN Q.REAR := 1
      ELSE Q.REAR := Q.REAR + 1;
   Q.ELEMENTS[Q.REAR] := NEWPAGE
END;      (* enq *)
```

(************* ***)

```
PROCEDURE DEQ (VAR Q : QUEUETYPE; VAR NEXTPAGE :
                   PAGETYPE);
(* Removes NEXTPAGE from the Q. Assumes queue is not empty. *)

BEGIN   (* deq *)
   IF Q.FRONT = MAXQUEUE
      THEN Q.FRONT := 1
      ELSE Q.FRONT := Q.FRONT + 1;
   NEXTPAGE := Q.ELEMENTS[Q.FRONT]
END;     (* deq *)
```

(**)

```
FUNCTION QUEUEREAR (Q : QUEUETYPE) : PAGETYPE;
(* QUEUEREAR returns the last element inserted into the queue, *)
(* leaving the queue unchanged. Assumes that Q is not empty.   *)

BEGIN   (* queuerear *)
   QUEUEREAR := Q.ELEMENTS[Q.REAR]
END;    (* queuerear *)
```

(**)

```
PROCEDURE PRINTQUEUE (P : NODEPTR);
(* Prints an entry in the dictionary, followed by the pages on which the entry *)
(* occurs. Pages are printed in numeric order on file BOOKINDEX.              *)
(* Queue of pages is DISPOSED. P↑.QUEUE is set to NIL.                         *)

VAR  PAGE : PAGETYPE;

BEGIN   (* printqueue *)
   WRITE(BOOKINDEX, P↑.WORDFIELD:16);
```

```
    WHILE NOT EMPTYQ(P↑.QUEUE↑) DO
      BEGIN
        DEQ(P↑.QUEUE↑, PAGE);
        WRITE(BOOKINDEX, PAGE : 4)      (* print page number in 4 spaces *)
      END;

    WRITELN(BOOKINDEX);
    DISPOSE(P↑.QUEUE);
    P↑.QUEUE := NIL
END;      (* printqueue *)

(* * * * * * * * * * * * * * * * * * * * * * * * * * * * * * * * * * * * * * * * * * * *)

PROCEDURE INSERT (VAR ROOT : NODEPTR; WORD : STRINGTYPE);
(* Insert node representing new word into the tree. *)

VAR   NEWNODE,                                    (* node to be inserted *)
      CURRENT,                                    (* moving node pointer *)
      BACK : NODEPTR;                             (* trailing node pointer *)

BEGIN  (* insert *)
  IF DEBUG (* debug is true during testing *)
     THEN WRITELN(DEBUGFILE, WORD,
         ' BEING INSERTED IN DICTIONARY');

  (* Get and initialize new node. *)
  NEW(NEWNODE);
  NEWNODE↑.WORDFIELD := WORD;
  NEWNODE↑.QUEUE := NIL;
  NEWNODE↑.LEFT := NIL;
  NEWNODE↑.RIGHT := NIL;

  (* Look for insertion point. *)
  CURRENT := ROOT;
  BACK := NIL;
  WHILE CURRENT <> NIL DO
    BEGIN
      BACK := CURRENT;
      IF CURRENT↑.WORDFIELD > WORD
         THEN CURRENT := CURRENT↑.LEFT
         ELSE CURRENT := CURRENT↑.RIGHT
    END;   (* while *)
```

```
    (* Check for insertion into empty tree. *)
    IF BACK = NIL
       THEN ROOT := NEWNODE
       ELSE IF BACK↑.WORDFIELD > WORD
               THEN BACK↑.LEFT := NEWNODE
               ELSE BACK↑.RIGHT := NEWNODE
END;    (* insert *)
```

(*)

```
PROCEDURE DELETE (VAR ENTRY : NODEPTR);
(* Delete NODE(ENTRY) from tree. Entry is assumed to be a *)
(* pointer within the tree, not an external pointer.      *)
(* See chapter for complete internal documentation.       *)

VAR   BACK,
      TEMP : NODEPTR;

BEGIN  (* delete *)
   TEMP := ENTRY;
   IF ENTRY↑.RIGHT = NIL                          (* zero or one child *)
      THEN ENTRY := ENTRY↑.LEFT
   ELSE IF ENTRY↑.LEFT = NIL
      THEN ENTRY := ENTRY↑.RIGHT
      ELSE
         BEGIN  (* 2 children *)
            TEMP := ENTRY↑.LEFT;
            BACK := ENTRY;
            WHILE TEMP↑.RIGHT <> NIL DO
               BEGIN
                  BACK := TEMP;
                  TEMP := TEMP↑.RIGHT
               END;  (* while *)

            ENTRY↑ := TEMP↑;
            IF BACK = ENTRY
               THEN BACK↑.LEFT := TEMP↑.LEFT
               ELSE BACK↑.RIGHT := TEMP↑.LEFT
         END;  (* 2 children *)

   DISPOSE(TEMP)

END;   (* delete *)
```

(*)

```
FUNCTION NODEFOUND (TREE : NODEPTR; WORD : STRINGTYPE) :
                       BOOLEAN;
(* Returns TRUE if WORD is in the tree; FALSE otherwise. *)

VAR FOUND : BOOLEAN;
    CURRENT : NODEPTR;

BEGIN   (* nodefound *)
  CURRENT := TREE;
  FOUND := FALSE;
  WHILE (CURRENT <> NIL) AND NOT FOUND DO
    IF CURRENT↑.WORDFIELD = WORD
       THEN FOUND := TRUE
       ELSE IF CURRENT↑.WORDFIELD < WORD
               THEN CURRENT := CURRENT↑.RIGHT
               ELSE CURRENT := CURRENT↑.LEFT;
  NODEFOUND := FOUND;

  IF DEBUG                              (* debug is true during testing *)
     THEN
        IF FOUND
           THEN WRITELN(DEBUGFILE, WORD,
             ' IS FOUND IN DICTIONARY')
           ELSE WRITELN(DEBUGFILE, WORD,
             ' IS NOT IN DICTIONARY')

END;   (* nodefound *)

(* ********************************************************* )
```

```
PROCEDURE FINDPLACE (WORD : STRINGTYPE;
                     INDEX : NODEPTR;
                     VAR BACK : NODEPTR;
                     VAR ENTRY : NODEPTR;
                     VAR FOUND : BOOLEAN);
```

(* FINDPLACE searches the index for an occurrence of WORD. If WORD is in   *)
(* the index, FOUND is TRUE, ENTRY points to the node containing WORD, and   *)
(* BACK points to the parent of this node. If WORD is not in the index, FOUND *)
(* is FALSE, and BACK points to the node in the index to which WORD's node   *)
(* should be attached.   *)

```
BEGIN   (* findplace *)
  ENTRY := INDEX;
  BACK := NIL;
  FOUND := FALSE;

  (* Search for WORD in index. *)
  WHILE (ENTRY <> NIL) AND NOT FOUND DO
    IF ENTRY↑.WORDFIELD = WORD
        THEN FOUND := TRUE
        ELSE
          BEGIN
            BACK := ENTRY;
            IF ENTRY↑.WORDFIELD < WORD
                THEN ENTRY := ENTRY↑.RIGHT
                ELSE ENTRY := ENTRY↑.LEFT
          END;

  IF DEBUG                          (* debug is true during testing *)
      THEN
        IF FOUND
            THEN WRITELN(DEBUGFILE, WORD,
              ' IS FOUND IN INDEX')
END;   (* findplace *)
```

(*)

```
PROCEDURE UPDATEPAGELIST (BACK : NODEPTR;
                          ENTRY : NODEPTR;
                          VAR INDEX : NODEPTR;
                          VAR DICTIONARY : NODEPTR);
```

(* If CURRENTPAGE is on page list, nothing is done. Otherwise page is put *)
(* on page list. If number of pages is at the limit, the ENTRY is deleted *)
(* from the INDEX and the word is printed along with its page list.   *)
(* The word is then inserted into the DICTIONARY of words not to be indexed. *)

```
BEGIN   (* updatepagelist *)
  IF CURRENTPAGE <> QUEUEREAR(ENTRY↑.QUEUE↑)
    THEN                                  (* add page to page list *)
      BEGIN    (* update page *)
        ENQ(ENTRY↑.QUEUE↑, CURRENTPAGE);
        IF FULLQ(ENTRY↑.QUEUE↑)
          THEN                            (* page list is full *)
            BEGIN
              PRINTQUEUE(ENTRY);       (* Print word and page list. *)
              IF BACK = NIL              (* Delete word from index. *)
                THEN DELETE(INDEX)
                ELSE IF BACK↑.RIGHT = ENTRY
                  THEN DELETE(BACK↑.RIGHT)
                  ELSE DELETE(BACK↑.LEFT);
              INSERT(DICTIONARY, WORD)      (* Insert word *)
                                            (* into dictionary. *)
            END
      END
END;   (* updatepagelist *)

(* ************************************************** )

PROCEDURE INSERTWORD (BACK : NODEPTR;
                      WORD : STRINGTYPE;
                      VAR INDEX : NODEPTR);
(* WORD is inserted into the INDEX at the place pointed to by BACK. *)

VAR NEWNODE : NODEPTR;
    Q : QPTR;

BEGIN    (* insertword *)
  IF DEBUG                              (* debug is true during testing *)
    THEN WRITELN(DEBUGFILE, WORD,
      ' IS BEING INSERTED IN THE INDEX ');

  NEW(NEWNODE);                         (* Build node for WORD. *)
  NEW(Q);
  NEWNODE↑.QUEUE := Q;
  NEWNODE↑.WORDFIELD := WORD;
  CLEARQ(NEWNODE↑.QUEUE↑);
  ENQ(NEWNODE↑.QUEUE↑, CURRENTPAGE); (* Put first page occurrence in queu
  NEWNODE↑.LEFT := NIL;
  NEWNODE↑.RIGHT := NIL;
```

```
    IF BACK = NIL                                    (* check for empty tree *)
        THEN INDEX := NEWNODE
        ELSE IF BACK↑.WORDFIELD < WORD
          THEN BACK↑.RIGHT := NEWNODE
          ELSE BACK↑.LEFT := NEWNODE
    END;    (* insertword *)


(* ********************************************** )


PROCEDURE PROCESSWORD (WORD : STRINGTYPE;
                       VAR INDEX, DICTIONARY : NODEPTR);
(* If WORD is in the dictionary, the procedure is exited.    *)
(* If WORD is in the index, its page list is updated.        *)
(* If WORD is not in the index, it is inserted into the index. *)


VAR   ENTRY : NODEPTR;
      FOUND : BOOLEAN;
      BACK : NODEPTR;


BEGIN    (* processword *)
  IF NOT NODEFOUND(DICTIONARY, WORD)
      THEN                                   (* WORD not in the dictionary *)
        BEGIN
          FINDPLACE(WORD, INDEX, BACK, ENTRY, FOUND);
          IF FOUND
              THEN                                  (* WORD in index *)
                UPDATEPAGELIST(BACK, ENTRY, INDEX,
                    DICTIONARY)
              ELSE                              (* WORD not in index *)
                INSERTWORD(BACK, WORD, INDEX)
        END
END;    (* processword *)


( * ********************************************** )
```

```
PROCEDURE INORDER (INDEX : NODEPTR);
(* Prints the tree rooted at index in order. *)
(* This is a recursive procedure.            *)
BEGIN   (* inorder *)
  IF INDEX <> NIL
    THEN
      BEGIN
        INORDER(INDEX↑.LEFT);
        PRINTQUEUE(INDEX);
        INORDER(INDEX↑.RIGHT)
      END
END;    (* inorder *)
```

(*)

```
PROCEDURE GETWORD (VAR DATA : TEXT;
                   VAR WORD : STRINGTYPE);
(* Stores into word characters beginning at the next character NOT IN    *)
(* PUNCTUATION and continues until either a character IN PUNCTUATION     *)
(* is found or MAXLENGTH characters have been stored.                    *)

VAR  CH : CHAR;                    (* temporary character variable *)
     COUNTER : INTEGER;                    (* index into WORD *)

BEGIN   (* getword *)
  WORD := BLANKS;
  COUNTER := 0;

  (* Skip to next character which is not IN PUNCTUATION. *)
  REPEAT
    READ(DATA, CH)
  UNTIL NOT (CH IN PUNCTUATION) OR EOF(DATA);

  (* Read and store characters until a character IN PUNCTUATION    *)
  (* is encountered or until MAXLENGTH characters have been stored. *)
  WHILE NOT (CH IN PUNCTUATION) AND (COUNTER < MAXLENGTH) DO
    BEGIN
      COUNTER := COUNTER + 1;
      WORD[COUNTER] := CH;
      READ(DATA, CH)
    END;

  (* Read until a character IN PUNCTUATION is found, in case WORD *)
  (* was longer than MAXLENGTH.                                    *)
  WHILE NOT (CH IN PUNCTUATION) DO
    READ(DATA, CH)

END;    (* getword *)
```

(*)

```
FUNCTION LENGTHOK (WORD : STRINGTYPE) : BOOLEAN;
(* Returns TRUE if the number of characters in WORD is *)
(* greater than or equal to MINLENGTH.                 *)

BEGIN    (* lengthok *)
  LENGTHOK := WORD[MINLENGTH] <> ' '
END;     (* lengthok *)

( * * * * * * * * * * * * * * * * * * * * * * * * * * * * * * * * * * * * * * * * * * * * * * * * * )

PROCEDURE GETAWORD (VAR WORD: STRINGTYPE;
                    VAR DATA : TEXT);
(* Invokes GETWORD and checks to see if WORD returned is an *)
(* end of page marker, increments CURRENTPAGE if it is.     *)
(* Checks to be sure WORD is at least minimum length and    *)
(* returns to get another WORD if it is not minimum length. *)

BEGIN    (* getaword *)
  REPEAT
    GETWORD(DATA, WORD);
    IF WORD = ENDOFPAGE
       THEN CURRENTPAGE := CURRENTPAGE + 1
  UNTIL LENGTHOK(WORD) OR EOF(DATA)
END;     (* getaword *)

( * * * * * * * * * * * * * * * * * * * * * * * * * * * * * * * * * * * * * * * * * * * * * * * * * )

PROCEDURE GETDICTIONARY (VAR DICTIONARY : NODEPTR;
                         VAR WORDS : TEXT);
(* Words not to be included in the index are read from file WORDS *)
(* and stored into a binary search tree DICTIONARY.              *)

VAR  WORD : STRINGTYPE;

BEGIN         (* getdictionary *)
  WHILE NOT EOF(WORDS) DO
    BEGIN
      GETAWORD(WORD, WORDS);
      IF NOT EOF(WORD)
         THEN
           INSERT(DICTIONARY, WORD)
    END
END;         (* get dictionary *)

( * * * * * * * * * * * * * * * * * * * * * * * * * * * * * * * * * * * * * * * * * * * * * * * * * )
```

```
BEGIN    (* main *)
  (* Initialize. *)
  DICTIONARY := NIL;
  INDEX := NIL;
  CURRENTPAGE := 1;
  IF DEBUG                                    (* debug is true during testing *)
      THEN REWRITE(DEBUGFILE);

  REWRITE(BOOKINDEX);
  RESET(BOOK);
  RESET(WORDS);
  PUNCTUATION := [',', '.', '!', ';', ':', ' '];

  (* Input dictionary of words not to include in the index. *)
  GETDICTIONARY(DICTIONARY, WORDS);

  IF DEBUG
                                              (* debug is true during testing *)
      THEN TESTPRINTTREE(DICTIONARY);

  (* Read the text of the manuscript on file BOOK processing       *)
  (* each word individually. If a word is not in the dictionary    *)
  (* of words to be skipped, it is entered into the index and the  *)
  (* pages on which it occurs are recorded. When the number        *)
  (* of pages on which a word occurs reaches a predetermined limit,*)
  (* the word is removed from the index, its page list is printed, *)
  (* and the word is entered into the dictionary of words to skip. *)
  WHILE NOT EOF(BOOK) DO
    BEGIN
      GETAWORD(WORD, BOOK);
      IF NOT EOF(BOOK)
          THEN
              PROCESSWORD(WORD, INDEX, DICTIONARY)
    END;

  (* Print each word in the index along with the page numbers *)
  (* on which it occurs.                                      *)
  INORDER(INDEX)

END.    (* main *)
```

Testing and Debugging: There were two major logic errors in the first version of this program that we wrote. The function to check the last element entered into the queue was coded to check the front of the queue instead of the rear. (This error has been corrected for the top-down design shown here.) The second error was that the index was passed as a value parameter to the INSERT procedure. Therefore the external pointer to the index was never changed; it remained nil.

We tracked down these errors in our testing by inserting intermediate prints which were activated by a Boolean variable called DEBUG. DEBUG was set to TRUE in the CONST section and the DEBUG output was written to a file called DEBUGFILE. We have given the code for this program exactly as it was on the final test run, including all the debugging aids used. The text input and the two output files follow in the next section.

In a small program like this, it would be easy to go through and remove the debugging print statements. However, in a large project they should be left in the program. The DEBUG constant would be changed to FALSE so that the testing output would not be generated during production runs. If the program were altered at a later date, the debugging output would be turned on again for further testing.

The testing of this program also uncovered an omission in the design. The program treats lower and upper case letters as different characters. Therefore, "Run" and "run" are considered to be different words. Unless our input text consists only of upper case letters, we must do something to equate the upper and lower case versions of the alphabetical characters. The easiest solution is to convert all letters, as they are read in, to either the upper or the lower case representation, depending on which way you would like to print out the text.

This conversion requires knowledge of the character set for the machine on which the program will be run. Note that this modification to the program has a major software implication. Since character sets differ, your program will no longer be *portable;* it will only run on machines that have the same character set.

File: BOOK

This is a story of Dick and Jane. # Dick and Jane are friends. # Dick and Jane like to run. # See Dick run. Dick can run very fast. # See Jane run. # Run, Dick and Jane. # At the end of the day, Dick and Jane are tired. # You would be tired if you ran like Dick and Jane.

File: WORDS

```
This
and
are
like
the
thiswordistoolong
would
you
```

File: BOOKINDEX

Dick	1	2	3	4	6
Jane	1	2	3	5	6
Run	6				
See	4	5			
You	8				
can	4				
day	7				
end	7				
fast	4				
friends	2				
ran	8				
run	3	4	5		
story	1				
tired	7	8			
very	4				

File: DEBUGFILE

```
This                 BEING INSERTED IN DICTIONARY
and                  BEING INSERTED IN DICTIONARY
the                  BEING INSERTED IN DICTIONARY
thiswordistooloBEING INSERTED IN DICTIONARY
are                  BEING INSERTED IN DICTIONARY
you                  BEING INSERTED IN DICTIONARY
would                BEING INSERTED IN DICTIONARY
like                 BEING INSERTED IN DICTIONARY
This           and                are             like
the            thiswordistoolowould               you
This           IS FOUND IN DICTIONARY
story          IS NOT IN DICTIONARY
story          IS BEING INSERTED IN THE INDEX
```

```
Dick              IS NOT IN DICTIONARY
Dick              IS BEING INSERTED IN THE INDEX
and               IS FOUND IN DICTIONARY
Jane              IS NOT IN DICTIONARY
Jane              IS BEING INSERTED IN THE INDEX
Dick              IS NOT IN DICTIONARY
Dick              IS FOUND IN INDEX
and               IS FOUND IN DICTIONARY
Jane              IS NOT IN DICTIONARY
Jane              IS FOUND IN INDEX
are               IS FOUND IN DICTIONARY
friends           IS NOT IN DICTIONARY
friends           IS BEING INSERTED IN THE INDEX
Dick              IS NOT IN DICTIONARY
Dick              IS FOUND IN INDEX
and               IS FOUND IN DICTIONARY
Jane              IS NOT IN DICTIONARY
Jane              IS FOUND IN INDEX
like              IS FOUND IN DICTIONARY
run               IS NOT IN DICTIONARY
run               IS BEING INSERTED IN THE INDEX
See               IS NOT IN DICTIONARY
See               IS BEING INSERTED IN THE INDEX
Dick              IS NOT IN DICTIONARY
Dick              IS FOUND IN INDEX
run               IS NOT IN DICTIONARY
run               IS FOUND IN INDEX
Dick              IS NOT IN DICTIONARY
Dick              IS FOUND IN INDEX
can               IS NOT IN DICTIONARY
can               IS BEING INSERTED IN THE INDEX
run               IS NOT IN DICTIONARY
run               IS FOUND IN INDEX
very              IS NOT IN DICTIONARY
very              IS BEING INSERTED IN THE INDEX
fast              IS NOT IN DICTIONARY
fast              IS BEING INSERTED IN THE INDEX
See               IS NOT IN DICTIONARY
See               IS FOUND IN INDEX
Jane              IS NOT IN DICTIONARY
Jane              IS FOUND IN INDEX
run               IS NOT IN DICTIONARY
run               IS FOUND IN INDEX
Run               IS NOT IN DICTIONARY
Run               IS BEING INSERTED IN THE INDEX
Dick              IS NOT IN DICTIONARY
Dick              IS FOUND IN INDEX
Dick              BEING INSERTED IN DICTIONARY
```

```
and              IS FOUND IN DICTIONARY
Jane             IS NOT IN DICTIONARY
Jane             IS FOUND IN INDEX
Jane             BEING INSERTED IN DICTIONARY
the              IS FOUND IN DICTIONARY
end              IS NOT IN DICTIONARY
end              IS BEING INSERTED IN THE INDEX
the              IS FOUND IN DICTIONARY
day              IS NOT IN DICTIONARY
day              IS BEING INSERTED IN THE INDEX
Dick             IS FOUND IN DICTIONARY
and              IS FOUND IN DICTIONARY
Jane             IS FOUND IN DICTIONARY
are              IS FOUND IN DICTIONARY
tired            IS NOT IN DICTIONARY
tired            IS BEING INSERTED IN THE INDEX
You              IS NOT IN DICTIONARY
You              IS BEING INSERTED IN THE INDEX
would            IS FOUND IN DICTIONARY
tired            IS NOT IN DICTIONARY
tired            IS FOUND IN INDEX
you              IS FOUND IN DICTIONARY
ran              IS NOT IN DICTIONARY
ran              IS BEING INSERTED IN THE INDEX
like             IS FOUND IN DICTIONARY
Dick             IS FOUND IN DICTIONARY
and              IS FOUND IN DICTIONARY
Jane             IS FOUND IN DICTIONARY
```

Exercises

1. Use the following tree to answer each question independently. (Answer each question for the original tree.)

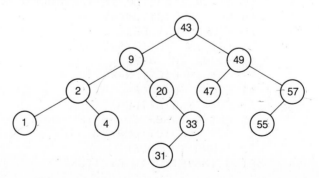

(a) Show what the tree would look like after adding node 3.

(b) Show what the tree would look like after adding node 90.

(c) Show what the tree would look like after adding node 56.

(d) Show what the tree would look like after deleting node 20.

(e) Show what the tree would look like after deleting node 43.

(f) Show what the tree would look like after deleting node 55.

(g) What are the ancestors of node 33?

(h) What are the descendents of node 20?

(i) Show what would be printed by a postorder traversal of the tree.

(j) Show what would be printed by a preorder traversal of the tree.

(k) Show what would be printed by an inorder traversal of the tree.

(l) What is the maximum possible number of nodes in the tree at the level of node 55?

(m) What is the maximum possible number of nodes in the tree at the level of node 31?

(n) How many nodes would be in the tree if it were completely full down to the level of node 31?

2. The information field of the nodes of a binary tree contains three-letter words. Show how the tree will look after the following words are read in (in this order). Assume the tree is empty before you begin adding nodes.

      fox   dog   leg   hoe   egg   elf   boy   box   zoo

3. How would a binary tree look if the information were already ordered when it was read in?

Use these declarations in problems 4 and 5.

```
TYPE TPTR = ↑TNODE;
     SEXTYPE = (MALE, FEMALE);
     STRING20 = PACKED ARRAY[1..20] OF CHAR;
     TNODE = RECORD
                 LASTNAME, FIRSTNAME : STRING20;
                 IDNUM : INTEGER;
                 SEX : SEXTYPE;
                 GPA : REAL;
                   .
                   .
                   .
                 LEFT, RIGHT : TPTR
             END; (* record *)
```

4. A binary search tree contains information about the senior class. It is ordered by GPA. You want to print a listing of the GPAs from highest to lowest, in order to show class standing. Write a procedure to print the GPA and student name. (Do *not* re-order the values in the tree.)

Sample Output:

```
4.00    SUSIE     BRAINCHILD
3.56    JOHNNY    SMART
2.75    JOHN Q.   DOE
0.02    FRED      JONES
```

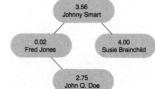

5. The binary search tree is ordered according to student number. Print the names of all the women, ordered from smallest to largest ID number. (Write a recursive procedure.)

6. A binary tree contains integer values in the INFO field of each node. Write a function, SUMSQRS, that returns the sum of the squares of the values in the tree.

7. Write a nonrecursive procedure, ANCESTOR, that prints the ancestors of a given node whose INFO field contains a value NUM. NUM only occurs once in the tree. Do not print NUM. You may assume that ROOT is not empty. Use the following procedure heading:

```
PROCEDURE ANCESTOR (ROOT : PTR; NUM : INTEGER);
```

8. (a) Write a recursive procedure, ANCESTOR. Use the following heading:

```
PROCEDURE ANCESTOR (P : PTR; NUM : INTEGER);
```

   (b) Write a call to Procedure ANCESTOR in Exercise 8a to print the ancestors of the node containing the value 14.

9. Develop the delete algorithm using the immediate successor of the value to be deleted for the case of deleting a node with two children.

Pre-Test

Use the following tree for problems 1 and 2.

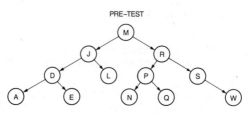

PRE–TEST

1. (a) List all of the nodes in PREORDER.
   (b) List all of the nodes in INORDER.
   (c) List all of the nodes in POSTORDER.
   (d) List all of the ancestors of node P.
   (e) List all of the descendants of node J.
   (f) List all of the nodes in level 3.
   (g) Draw the tree that will be obtained after inserting K.
   (h) Draw the tree that will be obtained after deleting M.

Use the following TYPE declarations for problems 2 and 3.

```
TYPE    TREEPTR = ↑TREENODE;
        TREENODE = RECORD
                     DATA : CHAR;
                     LEFT, RIGHT : TREEPTR
                   END;   (* record *)

VAR    ROOT : TREEPTR;
```

2. Using the tree in problem 1, complete the following WRITE statements.

(a) WRITE(ROOT_____)
so that an L will be printed.

(b) WRITE(ROOT_____)
so that an S will be printed.

Use the following tree for problem 3.

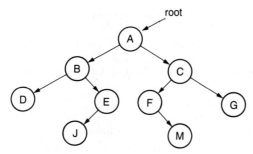

3. Consider the following two procedures:

```
PROCEDURE DOUBLEORDER (P : TREEPTR);

BEGIN   (* doubleorder *)
   IF P <> NIL
      THEN BEGIN
              WRITE(P↑.DATA);
              DOUBLEORDER(P↑.LEFT);
              DOUBLEORDER(P↑.RIGHT);
              WRITE(P↑.DATA)
           END   (* if *)
END;      (* doubleorder *)

PROCEDURE PRINT (P : TREEPTR);

BEGIN   (* print *)
   IF P <> NIL
      THEN BEGIN
              PRINT(P↑.LEFT);
              IF (P↑.LEFT=NIL) AND (P↑.RIGHT=NIL)
                 THEN
                    WRITE(P↑.DATA);
              PRINT(P↑.RIGHT)
           END   (* if *)
END;      (* print *)
```

(a) What output will be printed when DOUBLEORDER(ROOT) is invoked?
(b) What output will be printed when PRINT(ROOT) is invoked?

4. Write a Pascal procedure that takes the root of a binary tree as an input parameter and traverses this tree level by level (starting with the root node and then from left to right on each level). The data field of each node is printed when that node is visited.

   Example: This procedure should print the data fields of the tree given in problem 3 in the following (alphabetical) order: ABCDEFGJM.

Hint: Use a queue of tree pointers. You may assume that all queue utility routines are given and that queuetype is appropriately declared as a TYPE of queue of tree pointers.

Advice: Think iteratively NOT recursively.

5. Fill in the blank (less than, equal to, more than). The maximum number of nodes that can be on level i of a binary tree is _____ the sum of all the nodes in the tree from the root through level i-1.

6. You are writing a program which uses a binary tree as the basic data structure. For generality you decide to use an array of records instead of Pascal pointer variables. Given the following declarations, show how the tree would look in memory after it has been loaded in the order shown in the INFO field. Be sure to fill in all spaces. Available space is linked in the LEFT field. If you do not know the contents of a space, insert a "?".

```
TYPE NODE = RECORD
              INFO : CHAR;
              LEFT, RIGHT : 0..100
            END;   (* record *)
VAR NODES : ARRAY[1..100] OF NODE;
```

NODES	.INFO	.LEFT	.RIGHT	TREE☐
[1]	Q			AVAIL☐
[2]	L			
[3]	W			
[4]	F			
[5]	M			
[6]	R			
[7]	N			
[8]	S			
[9]				

7. Show the contents of NODES after B has been inserted and R has been deleted. You may fill in all spaces or only those that have changed.

NODES	.INFO	.LEFT	.RIGHT	TREE☐
[1]				AVAIL☐
[2]				
[3]				
[4]				
[5]				
[6]				
[7]				
[8]				
[9]				

Trees Plus 9

Goals

To be able to show how an arithmetic expression may be stored in a binary tree.

To be able to build and evaluate a binary expression tree.

To be able to show how a binary tree may be stored in a nonlinked representation in an array.

To be able to define the following terms:

- *full binary tree*
- *complete binary tree*
- *heap*

To be able to explain the strategy used in the heapsort algorithm.

To be able to define the following terms related to graphs:

- *directed graph*
- *undirected graph*
- *vertex*
- *edge*
- *path*
- *complete graph*
- *weighted graph*
- *adjacency matrix*
- *adjacency list*

To be able to explain the difference between a depth-first and a breadth-first search, and to describe how stacks and queues can be used to implement these searching strategies.

So far, we have examined several basic data structures in depth, discussing their uses and operations, as well as one or more implementations of each. As we have constructed these programmer-defined data structures out of the built-in types provided by our high-level language, we have noted variations that adapt them to the needs of different applications. In Chapter 8, we saw how a tree structure—the binary search tree—could facilitate searching data stored in a linked structure. In this chapter, we will see how this familiar tree structure may be extended and varied to fit other application needs.

BINARY EXPRESSION TREES

The two words *binary* and *tree* suggest that binary trees have something in common with arithmetic expressions:

Binary Expressions are made up of values, on which binary operations (like addition, subtraction, multiplication, and division) may be performed. Each node of a binary tree may have at most two children; therefore, we can represent a simple binary expression as a two-level binary tree. The root node contains the operator, and the two children contain the two operands. Following are tree representations of four such expressions:

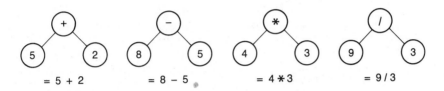

= 5 + 2   = 8 − 5   = 4 ∗ 3   = 9 / 3

Note that the values are in the leaf nodes, while the operator is in their parent node.

Tree The various parts of a complicated expression have lower and higher precedence of evaluation. For instance, when we see the expression (A + B) ∗ C, we know that (A + B) is evaluated before the multiplication is performed. When we write the expression in infix notation, with the operator between the operands, we must depend on some operator precedence scheme and the use of parentheses to describe an expression precisely. When we use a binary tree to represent an expression, parentheses are not needed to indicate precedence. The levels of the nodes in the tree indicate the relative precedence of evaluation implicitly.

The following binary tree represents the expression (12 − 3) ∗ (4 + 1).

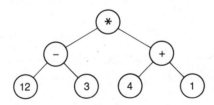

Let's start at the root node and evaluate the expression. The root contains the operator, ∗, so we look at its children to get the two operands. The *subtrees* to the left and right of the root contain the two operands. Since the node to the left of the root contains another operator, −, we know that the left subtree itself consists of an expression. We must evaluate the subtraction of the value in that node's right child from the value in its left child before we can do the multiplication. Similarly, in the node on the right of the root, we find another operator, +. Therefore, we know that we must evaluate the addition of the operands in that node's left and right children before we can do the multiplication. This example illustrates that the operations at higher levels of the tree are evaluated later than those below them.

The operation at the root of the tree will always be the last operation performed.

See if you can determine the expressions represented by the following binary trees:

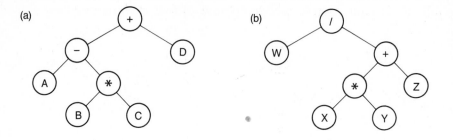

(a)   (b)

Expression Evaluation

Let's develop a function to evaluate a binary expression tree. We know that the value of the complete tree is equal to

$$\langle \text{operand1} \rangle \quad \langle \text{bin operator} \rangle \quad \langle \text{operand2} \rangle$$

where ⟨bin operator⟩ is one of the binary operators (+, −, *, or /) in the root node, ⟨operand1⟩ is the value of its left subtree, and ⟨operand2⟩ is the value of its right subtree. What is the value of the left subtree? If the left subtree consists of a single node containing a value, operand1 is that value itself. If the left subtree consists of an expression, we must evaluate it. Of course, we can use our same expression evaluation function to calculate its value. That is, our function will be a recursive one. The right subtree is evaluated similarly.

Let's summarize the recursive solution,

FUNCTION EVAL

Definition of problem: Evaluate the expression represented by the binary tree.

Size of problem: The whole tree pointed to by TREE.

Base case: If the content of the node is an operand, THEN

$$\text{EVAL} \leftarrow \text{the value of the operand}$$

General case: If the contents of the node is an operator, THEN

$$\text{EVAL} \leftarrow \text{EVAL(left subtree)} \ \langle \text{bin operator} \rangle \ \text{EVAL(right subtree)}$$

This description leads us to the following algorithm for Function EVAL:

```
IF INFO(TREE) is an operand
   THEN EVAL ← INFO(TREE)
   ELSE                                    (* It is an operator. *)
        CASE INFO(TREE) OF
           '+' : EVAL ← EVAL(LEFT(TREE))  + EVAL(RIGHT(TREE))
           '−' : EVAL ← EVAL(LEFT(TREE))  − EVAL(RIGHT(TREE))
           '*' : EVAL ← EVAL(LEFT(TREE))  * EVAL(RIGHT(TREE))
           '/' : EVAL ← EVAL(LEFT(TREE))  / EVAL(RIGHT(TREE))
        END CASE
```

When you try to code this function, you notice that we are using the INFO field of the tree node to contain two different types of data— sometimes a character representing an operator, and other times a numeric value. How can we represent two data types in the same field of the node? Pascal and several other high-level languages provide a data type that is ideal for this situation: the variant record. This data type allows us to use record variables for multiple purposes. (See Appendix G for a review of the syntax of the Pascal variant record type.) We can declare each tree node as a record, with the INFO field varying according to the data type that will be stored in it, either operator or operand.

```
TYPE INFOTYPE = (OPERATOR, OPERAND);
     TREEPTR   = ↑TREENODE;
     TREENODE = RECORD
                  LEFT, RIGHT : TREEPTR;
                  CASE CONTENTS : INFOTYPE OF
                    OPERATOR : (OPER : CHAR);
                    OPERAND : (VAL : REAL)
                END;  (* record *)
```

The declaration of the variant record type TREENODE has two parts:

- A fixed part, consisting of LEFT and RIGHT, the pointers to left and right children. These fields will be included in every variable of type TREENODE.
- A variant part, which begins with the keyword CASE. The field CONTENTS is called the *tag field,* and its type, INFOTYPE, is the *tag type.* The value in the tag field will determine which set of additional fields will be part of the record variable. In this case, we see from the declaration of INFOTYPE that the CONTENTS field may take on the values OPERATOR and OPERAND. When CONTENTS has the value of OPERATOR, the TREENODE-type record includes a character field OPER, in addition to LEFT and RIGHT; this field will be used to contain a character that represents an operator. When CONTENTS has the value of OPERAND, the TREENODE-type record

includes the real number field VAL, in addition to LEFT and RIGHT; this field will be used to contain the value of an operand.

Using these declarations, we can now write the function.

```
FUNCTION EVAL (TREE : TREEPTR) : REAL;
  (* Evaluates the expression represented by the binary *)
  (* expression tree pointed to by TREE.              *)

BEGIN   (* eval *)

  IF TREE↑.CONTENTS = OPERAND
    THEN EVAL := TREE↑.VAL

    ELSE                              (* contents is operator *)
      CASE TREE↑.OPER OF
        '+' : EVAL := EVAL(TREE↑.LEFT) + EVAL(TREE↑.RIGHT);
        '-' : EVAL := EVAL(TREE↑.LEFT) - EVAL(TREE↑.RIGHT);
        '*' : EVAL := EVAL(TREE↑.LEFT) * EVAL(TREE↑.RIGHT);
        '/' : EVAL := EVAL(TREE↑.LEFT) / EVAL(TREE↑.RIGHT)
      END. (* case *)

END;   (* eval *)
```

Printing a Binary Expression Tree

We said in the Applications for Chapter 3 that prefix notation and postfix notation provide us with ways of writing an expression without using parentheses to denote precedence. It's very simple to print out the prefix and postfix representations of an expression stored in a binary tree. The preorder and postorder tree traversals that we discussed in Chapter 8 will accomplish the task. Figure 9-1 shows an expression stored in a binary tree and its

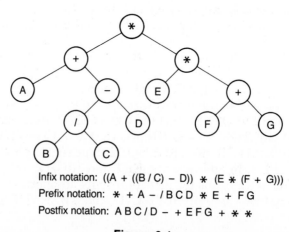

Infix notation: ((A + ((B / C) − D)) * (E * (F + G)))
Prefix notation: * + A − / B C D * E + F G
Postfix notation: A B C / D − + E F G + * *

Figure 9-1.

corresponding prefix, infix, and postfix notations. Note that we cannot write the infix notation directly from the tree because of the need to add parentheses.

Building a Binary Expression Tree

By now you have probably already asked the obvious question: How did the expression get into the tree? We will now develop an algorithm for building a binary expression tree from an expression in prefix notation.

The basic format of the prefix expression is

⟨bin operator⟩ ⟨operand1⟩ ⟨operand2⟩

We know that for a simple prefix expression like + AB, the operator, +, will go in the root node, and the operands, A and B, will go into its left and right child nodes, respectively. What happens if one of the operands is also an expression? For instance, how would we represent + * A Y B [equivalent to (A * Y) + B] in a tree? Again, the first operator, +, will go in the root node. The second operator, *, will go in the node to the left of the root, since it is part of operand1. The operands of *, A and Y, will be the children of this node. To put B into the tree, we must backtrack up to the root, in order to place its node as the right child of the root node:

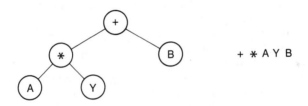

The general approach that we will use to put nodes into the tree is as follows: insert new nodes, each time moving to the *left* until we have put in an operand. Then backtrack to the last operator, and put the next node to its *right*. We continue in the same pattern: if we have just inserted an operator node, we put the next node to its left; if we have just inserted an operand node, we backtrack and put the next node to the right of the last operator.

In addition to the tree we are creating, we will need a temporary data structure in which to store pointers to the operator nodes, to support the backtracking we just described. Did you guess from the word *backtrack* that we would use a stack? We will also use a flag, NEXTMOVE, to indicate whether our next node should be attached to the left or the right, based on whether the current node contains an operator or an operand. (We are assuming the presence of some special character to denote the end of the expression. In the figures, we are representing this character as a semicolon; however, its identity is not relevant to the processing.)

Here is a more detailed version of the algorithm we will use:

```
(* Build root node. *)
get SYMBOL
GETNODE(NEWNODE)
put SYMBOL (the first operator) into NODE(NEWNODE)
ROOT ← NEWNODE
(* Prepare for loop. *)

NEXTMOVE ← LEFT
CLEAR stack
get next SYMBOL

(* Add SYMBOLS to the tree. *)
WHILE SYMBOL is not LASTSYMBOL DO
    LASTNODE ← NEWNODE            (* Keep pointer to previous node. *)
    GETNODE(NEWNODE)
    put SYMBOL into NODE(NEWNODE)

    (* Attach new node to tree. *)
    IF NEXTMOVE is LEFT
        THEN attach NODE(NEWNODE) to the left of NODE(LASTNODE)
            PUSH pointer LASTNODE onto pointer stack
        ELSE                       (* NEXTMOVE is RIGHT. *)
            POP pointer stack to get pointer LASTNODE
            attach NODE(NEWNODE) to the right of NODE(LASTNODE)

    (* Reset NEXTMOVE according to type of symbol. *)
    IF SYMBOL is an operator
        THEN NEXTMOVE ← LEFT
        ELSE                       (* SYMBOL is an operand. *)
        set both child fields of NODE(NEWNODE) to NULL
            NEXTMOVE ← RIGHT

    get next SYMBOL
(* end of loop *)
```

This algorithm is a little complicated, so let's trace it through a simple expression: * + A − B C D. [This is the same as ((A + (B − C)) * D).] We begin by getting the first symbol, *, and building the root node. At the point, before the loop, when we get the next symbol, our tree looks as shown in Figure 9-2. We then get the next symbol, +, and since it is not the last symbol, we enter the loop.

In the loop, we first set LASTNODE (a back pointer) to NEWNODE. Then we allocate a new node, and put SYMBOL into it. NEXTMOVE is still equal to LEFT, so we attach the new node to the left of

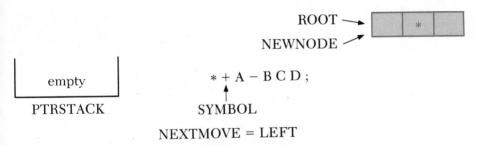

ROOT →

NEWNODE ↗

empty

PTRSTACK

* + A − B C D ;
↑
SYMBOL

NEXTMOVE = LEFT

Figure 9-2. Before first iteration of loop.

NODE(LASTNODE). At this point it is obvious why we are keeping the pointer LASTNODE: we must have this pointer in order to access the node whose left child pointer will be set to NEWNODE. We do one more task when NEXTMOVE = LEFT; we push LASTNODE onto the stack. This will allow us to return to this node eventually, in order to attach its right child node (the other operand). Before we exit the loop, we reset NEXTMOVE, according to the symbol type. SYMBOL (+) is another operator, so NEXTMOVE is reset to LEFT. This means that we will attach the next node to the left of NODE(NEWNODE). Since this node contains an operator, it must have first a left and then a right child containing its operands, so LEFT is the correct value for NEXTMOVE at this point. Then we get the next symbol. At this point, the data look as shown in Figure 9-3.

The new value of SYMBOL (A) is not the last symbol, so we reenter the loop. We build a new node to contain A, and since NEXTMOVE is still equal to LEFT, we attach this node to the tree exactly as we did before, saving the pointer LASTNODE in the stack. Now we must reset

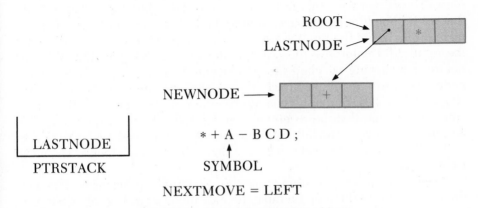

ROOT ↘

LASTNODE ↗

NEWNODE ⟶   +

LASTNODE

PTRSTACK

* + A − B C D ;
↑
SYMBOL

NEXTMOVE = LEFT

Figure 9-3. End of first iteration of loop.

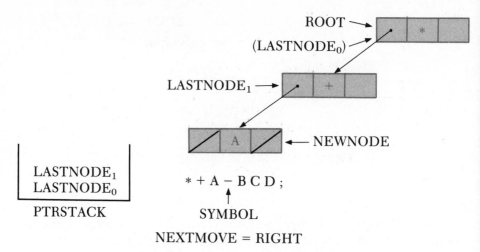

Figure 9-4. End of second iteration of loop.

NEXTMOVE. The symbol is an operand, so we take the ELSE clause, setting both child fields of the new node to NULL (remember, operands always live in leaf nodes), and set NEXTMOVE to RIGHT. We just attached the first operand to the left of the last operator; now we must get the second operand to put on its right, so RIGHT is the correct value for NEXTMOVE at this point. Then we get the next symbol. At this point, the data look as shown in Figure 9-4. (Note that we continue to show previous values of LASTNODE, indicated by subscripts and in parentheses, so that it will be apparent later how these values correspond to the values being popped from the stack.)

Since the next symbol $(-)$ is not the last symbol, we reenter the loop. We build a new node to contain the symbol, and then we attach it to the tree. NEXTMOVE is now equal to RIGHT, so we take the ELSE clause. Note that we will be linking the new node to the last *operator* node, not the last node built. To get the pointer to this node, we pop the stack. Then we set the right child pointer of the last operator node to NEWNODE. We said before that, having attached the first operand to the left of the operator node, we were ready to attach the second operand to its right. But NODE(NEWNODE) doesn't contain an operand; it contains another operator. (This means that the second operand will itself be an expression.) We will need to move to the left of this new node, so we reset NEXTMOVE to LEFT. We then get the next symbol. At this point, the data look as shown in Figure 9-5.

Trace through the algorithm yourself to see how it progresses. The next three iterations of the loop produce the data pictured in Figures 9-6 to 9-8.

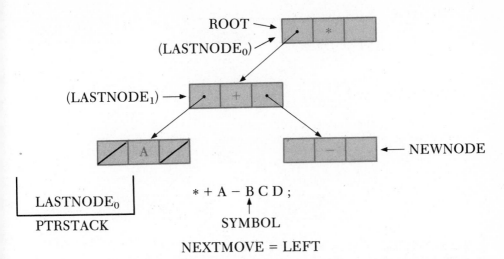

NEXTMOVE = LEFT

Figure 9-5. End of third iteration of loop.

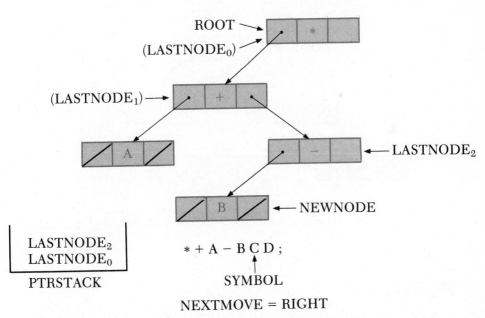

NEXTMOVE = RIGHT

(Next node will be attached to the RIGHT of NODE(LASTNODE$_2$).)

Figure 9-6. End of fourth iteration of loop.

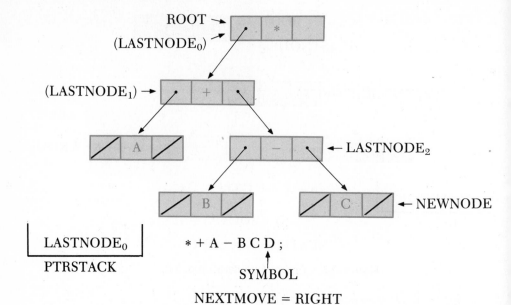

NEXTMOVE = RIGHT

(Next node will be attached to the RIGHT of NODE(LASTNODE$_0$).)

Figure 9-7. End of fifth iteration of loop.

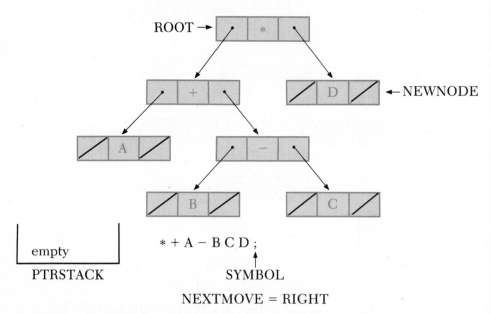

NEXTMOVE = RIGHT

(Next symbol is last symbol, so we quit.)

Figure 9-8. End of sixth (last) iteration of loop.

Did you get the same result? Do a preorder traversal of the resulting tree to see if it indeed matches the original prefix expression.

Before we write Procedure BUILDTREE, let's specify clearly what the input will look like. It will be a valid prefix expression, made up of single-letter operands and the binary operators +, *, −, and /. The expression will be followed by some delineating character, which we will know as LASTSYMBOL. We will have available the lower-level procedure GET-SYM, which takes a prefix expression (TYPE = PREFIXTYPE) and returns the next character in the expression. We will not worry about how GET-SYM does this. We will also be able to call the CLEARSTACK, PUSH, and POP procedures for using the stack of pointers.

Procedure BUILDTREE takes a prefix expression and returns the pointer to the root of the equivalent binary expression tree.

```
PROCEDURE BUILDTREE (PRESTRING : PREFIXTYPE;
                     VAR ROOT : TREEPTR);
   (* Builds the binary expression tree that corresponds to the *)
   (* valid prefix expression PRESTRING, and returns a          *)
   (* pointer to it in ROOT.                                     *)

TYPE   MOVETYPE = (LEFT, RIGHT);

VAR    PTRSTACK : STACKTYPE;          (* stack of pointers *)
       NEXTMOVE : MOVETYPE;           (* direction in which next node *)
                                      (* will be attached *)

       LASTNODE,
       NEWNODE  : TREEPTR;
       SYMBOL   : CHAR;

BEGIN  (* buildtree *)

   GETSYM(PRESTRING, SYMBOL);               (* Get first symbol. *)

   NEW(NEWNODE);                            (* Build root node. *)
   NEWNODE↑.INFO := SYMBOL;
   ROOT := NEWNODE;
   NEXTMOVE := LEFT;
   CLEARSTACK(PTRSTACK);                    (* Initialize for loop. *)
   GETSYM(PRESTRING, SYMBOL);               (* Get next symbol. *)

   (* Add the next symbol to the tree. *)
   WHILE SYMBOL <> LASTSYMBOL DO
      BEGIN
         LASTNODE := NEWNODE;               (* Save pointer to previous node. *)

         NEW(NEWNODE);                      (* Build the new node. *)
         NEWNODE↑.INFO := SYMBOL;
```

```
(* Attach the new node to the tree. *)
IF NEXTMOVE = LEFT
    THEN                      (* Attach to the left of NODE(LASTNODE). *)
        BEGIN
          LASTNODE↑.LEFT := NEWNODE;
          PUSH(PTRSTACK, LASTNODE)    (* Save LASTNODE ptr. *)
        END
    ELSE                      (* Attach to the right of last operator node. *)
        BEGIN
          POP(PTRSTACK, LASTNODE);
          LASTNODE↑.RIGHT := NEWNODE
        END;

(* Reset NEXTMOVE according to symbol type. *)
IF SYMBOL IN ['+', '-', '*', '/']
                              (* SYMBOL is an operator. *)
    THEN NEXTMOVE := LEFT
    ELSE                      (* SYMBOL is an operand. *)
        BEGIN
          NEWNODE↑.LEFT := NIL;
          NEWNODE↑.RIGHT := NIL;
          NEXTMOVE := RIGHT
        END;

GETSYM(PRESTRING, SYMBOL)              (* Get next symbol. *)

    END     (* while loop *)

END;    (* buildtree *)
```

Now that we know how to put a prefix expression into a binary tree, what can we do with the tree? We have already seen that we can evaluate it or print it in several different notations. We can also use the tree format to do more complicated processing, like differentiating the expression with respect to one of its variables. This problem is included in the programming assignments for this chapter. Don't panic—this task is much easier than it sounds, once the expression is in a binary expression tree. As a matter of fact, you don't even need to know any calculus to write the program, since all the processing is described in the program's specifications.

A NONLINKED
REPRESENTATION OF BINARY TREES

Our discussion of the implementation of binary trees has so far been limited to a scheme in which the pointers from parent to children are explicit in the data structure. A field is declared in each node for the pointer to the left child and the pointer to the right child.

There is a way to store a binary tree in an array in which the relationships in the tree are not physically represented by link fields, but are implicit in the algorithms that manipulate the tree stored in the array. The code is, of course, much less self-documenting, but we save memory space because there are no pointers.

Let's take a binary tree and store it in an array in such a way that the parent-children relationships are not lost. We will store the tree in the array level by level, left to right. This mapping is as follows:

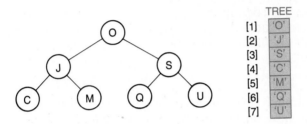

The number of nodes in the tree is NUMNODES. The tree is stored with the root in TREE[1] and the last node in TREE[NUMNODES].

If we can take the array representation and redraw the tree, the relationships have been maintained. We can then write algorithms to manipulate the tree in this form. An examination of where in the array a node's children reside will give us the information we need to reconstruct the tree.

> TREE[1]'s children are in TREE[2] and TREE[3]
> TREE[2]'s children are in TREE[4] and TREE[5]
> TREE[3]'s children are in TREE[6] and TREE[7]

Do you see the pattern? For any node TREE[I],

> TREE[I]'s left child is in TREE[I * 2]
> TREE[I]'s right child is in TREE[I * 2 + 1]

Another way of saying this is that the root of the tree is stored in TREE[1], and for a node stored in TREE[I], the root of its left subtree will be in TREE[I * 2] and the root of its right subtree will be in TREE[I * 2 + 1], provided I * 2 is less than NUMNODES. Notice that the nodes in the array from

> TREE[NUMNODES DIV 2 + 1] to TREE[NUMNODES]

are leaf nodes.

In fact, we can take any arbitrary array and create a binary tree. Whether it means anything as a tree is another matter. We will use this fact in the discussion of the heapsort algorithm later in this chapter.

Let's write a procedure to print the elements in the tree in preorder using the array representation of the tree. Rather than reinvent the wheel, let's see if we can't simply adapt Procedure PREORDER written for the dynamic storage representation.

```
PROCEDURE PREORDER (P : PTRTYPE);
    (* Recursive procedure to print out the elements in a *)
    (* binary tree. The tree is represented by dynamically *)
    (* allocated nodes accessed through pointer variables. *)

BEGIN    (* preorder *)
  IF P <> NIL
     THEN
        BEGIN
          WRITE(P↑.INFO);              (* Print this element. *)
          PREORDER(P↑.LEFT);           (* Print the left subtree. *)
          PREORDER(P↑.RIGHT)           (* Print the right subtree. *)
        END
END;    (* preorder *)
```

Let's go through this procedure line by line and see if we can make the switch to the new representation. The parameter will be an index rather than a pointer. What does P <> NIL actually tell us? If this condition is false (if P is equal to NIL), the last node we visited was a leaf node. In the array representation, if the index into the array is outside of the array bound, the last node visited was a leaf node. Now we simply replace the pointer reference with the corresponding array reference and we have finished changing the procedure.

```
PROCEDURE PREORDER (I : INDEXTYPE);
    (* Recursive procedure to print out the elements in a *)
    (* binary tree. The tree is represented in an array,  *)
    (* where the links are implicit in the array indexes.  *)

BEGIN    (* preorder *)
  IF I <= NUMNODES
     THEN
        BEGIN
          WRITE(TREE[I]);              (* Print this element. *)
          PREORDER(I * 2);             (* Print the left subtree. *)
          PREORDER(I * 2 + 1)          (* Print the right subtree. *)
        END
   (* ELSE last node visited was a leaf *)
END;    (* preorder *)
```

What happens if the tree is not completely filled out? For example, the whole right subtree of the node whose value is O might not be there. To use this representation, we must store a dummy value in those positions in the array in order to maintain the proper parent-child relationship. What that dummy value might be would depend on what the information represented in the tree actually is. If the tree represented data that could not logically contain a number, we could use a number as a dummy value. If it is possible that your tree might not be completely filled out, the algorithms to manipulate the tree have to reflect this possibility. For example, to determine if the last node visited was a leaf, you would have to compare the value in DATA[I] to that dummy value, after checking to see if I is within the array bounds.

In the next section we will discuss a sorting technique that is based on a binary tree represented in an array.

HEAPSORT

The heapsort sorting algorithm sorts an array of values that represent a tree with a special property: the *heap* property. We will need several formal definitions in order to develop this algorithm.

A *full binary tree* is a binary tree in which all the leaves are on the same level and every nonleaf node has two children. The tree in Figure 9-8 (page 385) is a full binary tree.

A *complete binary tree* is a binary tree that is either full or full through the next-to-last level, with the leaves on the last level as far left as possible. Figure 9-9 shows some examples.

A complete binary tree is a *heap* if, for every node, the value stored in

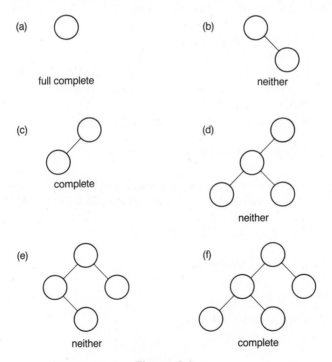

Figure 9-9.

that node is greater than or equal to the value in each of its children. If a heap is stored in an array representation as described earlier, the heap property means that, for every nonleaf node TREE[I],

$$(\text{TREE}[I] >= \text{TREE}[I * 2]) \text{ AND } (\text{TREE}[I] >= \text{TREE}[I * 2 + 1])$$

The figure that follows is a tree with the heap property and its representation in an array. Take a good look and see what it is about this representation that should help us in sorting the array.

We know where the maximum value in the array is: it will always be in TREE[1] if the tree is a heap. We will make use of this fact in the following strategy. The values we wish to sort are stored in the array, DATA, which contains MAXDATA elements.

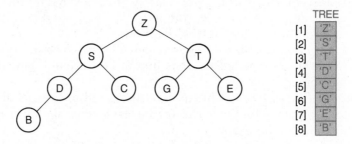

1. We build a heap out of the values in

   DATA[1] .. DATA[MAXDATA]

2. We swap the values in DATA[1] and DATA[MAXDATA]. Now the maximum value in the array DATA is in its proper place, which is (DATA[MAXDATA]).
3. We build a heap out of the values in

   DATA[1] .. DATA[MAXDATA - 1]

4. We swap the values in DATA[1] and DATA[MAXDATA − 1]. Now the two largest values are in their proper places (DATA[MAXDATA] and DATA[MAXDATA − 1]).
5. We build a heap out of the values in

   DATA[1]..DATA[MAXDATA - 2]

   and so on.

This process is pictured as follows:

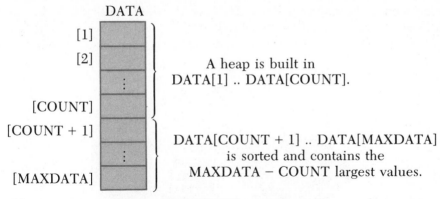

DATA

[1]
[2]

[COUNT]

[COUNT + 1]

[MAXDATA]

A heap is built in
DATA[1] .. DATA[COUNT].

DATA[COUNT + 1] .. DATA[MAXDATA]
is sorted and contains the
MAXDATA − COUNT largest values.

Now we can write the HEAPSORT procedure. Yes, we have not yet shown how to build a heap. But in good top-down fashion, we will give this task a name, BUILDHEAP, and come back to it later.

```
PROCEDURE HEAPSORT (VAR DATA : ARRAYTYPE;
                         MAXDATA : INDEXTYPE);
   (* Sorts the elements in the array DATA from index 1 *)
   (* to index MAXDATA in increasing order.              *)

VAR   COUNT : INDEX;

BEGIN    (* heapsort *)

   (* Build a heap containing the first MAXDATA *)
   (* elements of the array DATA.                *)
   BUILDHEAP(DATA, 1, MAXDATA);

   (* Sort the heap by swapping the first element in *)
   (* the array with the last unsorted element, then *)
   (* reheaping. Continue until array sorted from     *)
   (* index 1 to index MAXDATA.                       *)
   FOR COUNT := MAXDATA DOWNTO 2 DO
      BEGIN
         SWAP(DATA[1], DATA[COUNT]);
         BUILDHEAP(DATA, 1, COUNT - 1)
      END
END;    (* heapsort *)
```

If BUILDHEAP works correctly, Procedure HEAPSORT will put the first MAXDATA elements in the array DATA into ascending order. Now, we cannot put BUILDHEAP off any longer. It is called from two places in HEAPSORT, but clearly we know more about the state of the elements in DATA at the time BUILDHEAP is called within the loop. Let's begin our discussion at the point that BUILDHEAP is called the first time through the loop. We know that the left subtree and the right subtree of the root are still heaps, because only the root node, DATA[1], has been changed.

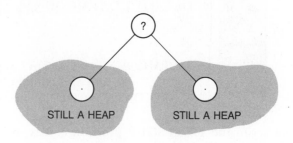

When BUILDHEAP is called within the loop, there are two possibilities. If the value in DATA[1] is greater than or equal to the values of its children, the heap property is intact and we don't have to do anything. In the other case, we know that the maximum value that we need to put into DATA[1] is either in its left child, DATA[2], or in its right child, DATA[3].

We will determine which of the children has the larger value and swap that value with the value in DATA[1]. Now we know that either the subtree whose root value was swapped with DATA[1] is a heap, in which case we are through, or its root value must be swapped with the maximum of the values of *its* children.

Yes, this is a recursive process. We are working with smaller and smaller subtrees until

1. the value in the root of the subtree being examined is greater than the values of its two children, or
2. the root of the subtree being examined is a leaf node.

Since this is a recursive process, a recursive solution seems logical.

```
PROCEDURE BUILDHEAP (VAR DATA : ARRAYTYPE;
                         ROOT,
                         COUNT : INDEXTYPE);
(* Restores the heap property to the subtree whose root *)
(* is ROOT. At the invocation of this recursive         *)
(* procedure, it is assumed that only the root node      *)
(* violates the heap property.                           *)

VAR    MAXCHILD : INDEXTYPE;       (* index of the child with larger value *)
```

```
BEGIN       (* buildheap *)

   IF ROOT * 2 <= COUNT
       THEN                               (* DATA[ROOT] is not a leaf *)
          BEGIN

                 (* DATA[COUNT + 1] .. DATA[MAXDATA] is sorted. *)
                 (* Calculate MAXCHILD. *)
             IF ROOT * 2 = COUNT
                 THEN MAXCHILD := ROOT * 2          (* only one child *)
                 ELSE                 (* Compare values of the two children. *)
                    IF DATA[ROOT * 2] > DATA[ROOT * 2 + 1]
                       THEN MAXCHILD := ROOT * 2
                       ELSE MAXCHILD := ROOT * 2 + 1;

             IF DATA[ROOT] < DATA[MAXCHILD]
                 THEN                                     (* not yet a heap *)
                    BEGIN
                       SWAP(DATA[ROOT], DATA[MAXCHILD]);
                       BUILDHEAP(DATA, MAXCHILD, COUNT)
                    END

                 (* ELSE it already is a heap, so stop. *)
          END

   (* ELSE DATA[ROOT] is a leaf, so stop. *)
END;   (* buildheap *)
```

Although this is clearly a recursive process, a look at the code shows us that the recursion is *tail recursion;* that is, there is only one recursive call and it is the last statement in the procedure. As we will discuss in more detail in Chapter 11, a recursive solution may reduce the efficiency of the program, and efficiency is often a major goal in sorting problems. However, tail recursion can be easily removed.

When we change from a recursive solution to an iterative one, the outer control structure will change from a selection structure to a looping structure. The missing ELSE branch from the inner IF takes care of the case in which the heap property is now restored. This is done implicitly by ending the procedure. In the iterative solution we will need a Boolean variable to tell us whether the tree is now a heap. The ELSE branch of this IF will then set the Boolean variable to TRUE.

```
PROCEDURE IBUILDHEAP (VAR DATA : ARRAYTYPE;
                          ROOT,
                          COUNT : INDEXTYPE);
```
(* Restores the heap property to the subtree whose root is ROOT. *)
(* It is assumed that on invocation of the procedure, the heap   *)
(* property is violated only by the root node.   *)

```
VAR    ISAHEAP : BOOLEAN;
       MAXCHILD : INDEXTYPE;

BEGIN   (* ibuildheap *)
  ISAHEAP := FALSE;
  WHILE (ROOT * 2 <= COUNT) AND NOT ISAHEAP DO
    BEGIN
```
        (* Calculate the index of the child with the larger value. *)
```
      IF ROOT * 2 = COUNT
        THEN MAXCHILD := ROOT * 2              (* only one child *)
        ELSE                          (* Pick greater of the two children. *)
          IF DATA[ROOT * 2] > DATA[ROOT * 2 + 1]
            THEN MAXCHILD := ROOT * 2
            ELSE MAXCHILD := ROOT * 2 + 1;
```
        (* If heap property is violated, swap values. *)
```
      IF DATA[ROOT] < DATA[MAXCHILD]
        THEN
          BEGIN                                (* not yet a heap *)
            SWAP(DATA[ROOT], DATA[MAXCHILD]);
            ROOT := MAXCHILD
          END
        ELSE ISAHEAP := TRUE                   (* already is a heap *)
    END   (* while loop *)

END;   (* ibuildheap *)
```

Both versions of the routine to build a heap take a tree represented by the index of the root node, in which you know that the two subtrees (if they exist) are heaps. If the value of the root node is not greater than the maximum value in its children, a swap occurs and the process repeats on the subtree whose root value was changed.

We can actually use this same procedure to build the original heap from any given set of values stored in an array. Rather than starting with the whole tree and working down, we will start with the lowest level subtrees and work up.

We know that all leaf nodes are heaps. We will start with the first nonleaf node, consider it the root of a tree whose subtrees are heaps, and apply the BUILDHEAP procedure to it. Now that subtree is a heap. We will do this to all the subtrees on that level. Then we will move up a level and start the process over again. This is illustrated in picture form in Figure 9-10, and in an array representation in Figure 9-11.

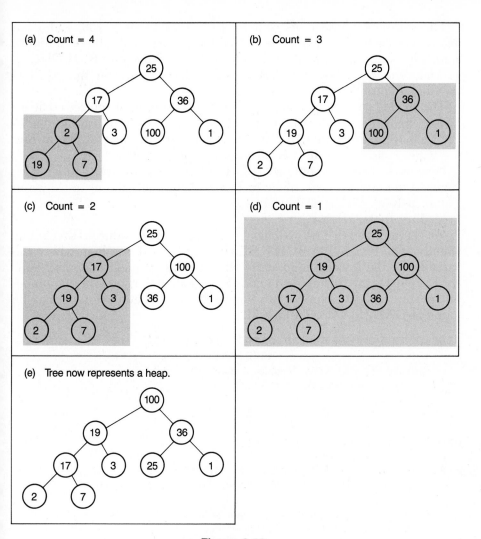

Figure 9-10.

	[1]	[2]	[3]	[4]	[5]	[6]	[7]	[8]	[9]
ORIGINAL DATA	25	17	36	2	3	100	1	19	7
AFTER BUILDHEAP COUNT = 4	25	17	36	19	3	100	1	2	7
AFTER COUNT = 3	25	17	100	19	3	36	1	2	7
AFTER COUNT = 2	25	19	100	17	3	36	1	2	7
AFTER COUNT = 1	100	19	36	17	3	25	1	2	7

Tree is a heap.

Figure 9-11.

The subtrees whose roots contain the values 19, 7, 3, 100, and 1 are heaps because they are leaf nodes. Therefore, the shaded subtree in Figure 9-10(a) has left and right subtrees that are heaps. Procedure BUILDHEAP will take the tree whose root has the value 2 and return the tree as illustrated in Figure 9-10(b).

The shaded subtree in Figure 9-10(b) has left and right subtrees that are heaps. Procedure BUILDHEAP will take that tree and return the one in Figure 9-10(c). Procedure BUILDHEAP will take the shaded tree in Figure 9-10(c) and return the tree in Figure 9-10(d).

Now we just have to apply BUILDHEAP to the whole tree and we have changed the original tree shown in Figure 9-10(a) into the heap shown in Figure 9-10(e). We have done this conversion by successively applying Procedure BUILDHEAP.

We can now see that we will have to change our Procedure HEAPSORT slightly. The first call to BUILDHEAP must be within a loop where the variable for the lower bound starts with the first nonleaf node and ends with 1. What is the first nonleaf node? Since half of the nodes of a complete binary tree are leaves (prove this yourself), the first nonleaf node may be found at DATA[MAXDATA DIV 2].

```
PROCEDURE HEAPSORT (VAR DATA : ARRAYTYPE;
                         MAXDATA : INDEXTYPE);
   (* Sorts the first MAXDATA elements of array DATA in *)
   (* ascending order, using the heapsort algorithm.    *)

VAR   COUNT : INTEGER;

BEGIN   (* heapsort *)
   (* Build the original heap. *)
   FOR COUNT := (MAXDATA DIV 2) DOWNTO 1 DO
     BUILDHEAP(DATA, COUNT, MAXDATA);

   (* Sort the heap by swapping the first element in *)
   (* the array with the last unsorted element, then *)
   (* reheaping. Continue until array sorted from 1  *)
   (* to MAXDATA index.                              *)
   FOR COUNT := MAXDATA DOWNTO 2 DO
     BEGIN
       SWAP(DATA[1], DATA[COUNT]);
       BUILDHEAP(DATA, 1, COUNT - 1)
     END    (* for loop *)

END;    (* heapsort *)
```

Figure 9-12 takes the heap created in Figure 9-11 (the last line) and shows the changes in the array that occur as a result of each iteration of the sorting loop. The elements that are sorted are underlined.

	[1]	[2]	[3]	[4]	[5]	[6]	[7]	[8]	[9]
HEAP	100	19	36	17	3	25	1	2	7
SWAP	7	19	36	17	3	25	1	2	100
BUILDHEAP	36	19	25	17	3	7	1	2	100
SWAP	2	19	25	17	3	7	1	36	100
BUILDHEAP	25	19	7	17	3	2	1	36	100
SWAP	1	19	7	17	3	2	25	36	100
BUILDHEAP	19	17	7	1	3	2	25	36	100
SWAP	2	17	7	1	3	19	25	36	100
BUILDHEAP	17	3	7	1	2	19	25	36	100
SWAP	2	3	7	1	17	19	25	36	100
BUILDHEAP	7	3	2	1	17	19	25	36	100
SWAP	1	3	2	7	17	19	25	36	100
BUILDHEAP	3	1	2	7	17	19	25	36	100
SWAP	2	1	3	7	17	19	25	36	100
BUILDHEAP	2	1	3	7	17	19	25	36	100
SWAP	1	2	3	7	17	19	25	36	100
BUILDHEAP	1	2	3	7	17	19	25	36	100
EXIT FROM SORTING LOOP	1	2	3	7	17	19	25	36	100

Figure 9-12.

GRAPHS

Binary trees provide a very useful way of representing relationships in which a hierarchy exists. That is, a node is pointed to by at most one other node, and each node points to at most two other nodes. If we remove the restriction that each node can point to at most two other nodes, we have a nonbinary tree, as pictured on the next page.

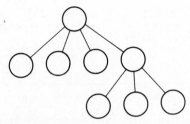

If we remove the restriction that each node can be pointed to by at most one other node, we have a data structure called a *directed graph*. If we replace the words *pointed to* by *is related to,* we have a data structure called an *undirected graph*.

A graph is made up of a set of nodes (also called *vertices*) and a set of lines called *edges* (or *arcs*) that connect the different nodes. The set of nodes is specified by listing the nodes in set notation (within brackets). The set of edges is specified by listing a sequence of edges. Each edge is denoted by writing the names of the two nodes that the edge connects in parentheses, with a comma between them.

If the graph is a directed graph, the direction of the line is indicated by which node is listed first. If the graph is an undirected graph, the relation between the two nodes is unordered. That is, one node doesn't point to the other; they are simply connected.

Formally, a graph is defined as follows:

$$G = (V, E)$$

where

    V(G) is a finite, nonempty set of vertices
    E(G) is a set of pairs of vertices

Let's look at some examples of graphs in Figure 9-13. (The picture of G2 may look familiar; it is the tree we looked at earlier in connection with nonlinked representation of a binary tree.) We can see that a tree is a special case of a directed graph. Note that in the pictures of the directed graphs (often called *digraphs*), the arrows indicate the direction of the relationship.

There is a great deal of formal mathematics associated with graphs. In fact, there is an area of mathematics called graph theory. In later computing courses, you will probably analyze graphs and prove theorems about them. Our objective here, however, is merely to introduce you to the graph as a data structure, give you a little terminology, indicate how a graph might be implemented, and describe how graph search algorithms make use of our old friends, the stack and the queue.

More Terminology

If (Vi, Vj) is an edge in E(G), Vi and Vj are said to be *adjacent*. If (Vi, Vj) is a directed edge, you say Vi is adjacent to Vj, and Vj is adjacent from Vi.

A *path* from vertex Vi to vertex Vj is a sequence of vertices that connects

(a) G1 is an undirected graph.

$V(G1) = \{A, B, C, D\}$
$E(G1) = \{(A, B), (A, D), (B, C), (B, D)\}$

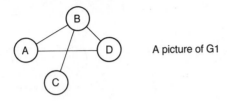

A picture of G1

(b) G2 is a directed graph.

$V(G2) = \{O, J, S, C, M, Q, U\}$
$E(G2) = \{(O, J), (O, S), (J, C), (J, M), (S, Q), (S, U)\}$

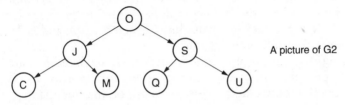

A picture of G2

(c) G3 is a directed graph.

$V(G3) = \{1, 3, 5, 7, 9, 11\}$
$E(G3) = \{(1, 3), (3, 1), (5, 7), (5, 9), (9, 11), (9, 9), (11, 1)\}$

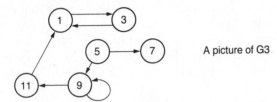

A picture of G3

Figure 9-13.

Vi to Vj. For a path to exist from Vi to Vj, there must be edges (Vi, Vk_1), (Vk_1, Vk_2), . . . , (Vk_n, Vj). That is, there must be an uninterrupted sequence of lines from Vi through any number of nodes to Vj. In the following graph there is a path from vertex A to vertex G, but not from vertex A to vertex C.

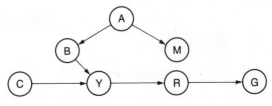

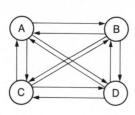

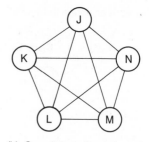

(a) Complete directed graph.   (b) Complete undirected graph.

Figure 9-14.

A *complete graph* is one in which every node is connected to every other node. Figure 9-14 shows two complete graphs. If there are N nodes, there will be N(N − 1) edges in a complete, directed graph and N(N − 1)/2 edges in a complete, undirected graph.

A *weighted graph* is a graph in which each edge carries a value. Weighted graphs can be used to represent situations in which the *value* of the connection between the vertices is important, not just the *existence* of a connection. For instance, in the weighted graph pictured in Figure 9-15, the vertices represent cities, and the edges indicate the bus routes that connect the cities. The weights attached to the edges represent the bus fare for service between pairs of cities. To see if we can get from Sommertown to Myrtle Falls, we look for a path between them. Note that there may be multiple paths between two vertices. If the cost of a bus trip is determined by the sum of the fares between each pair of cities along the way, we can calculate the cost of a ticket from Sommertown to Myrtle Falls by adding the weights attached to the edges that constitute the path between them. (It might be cheaper to fly!)

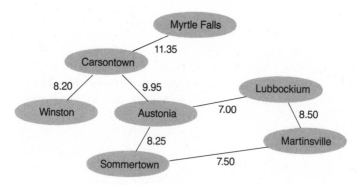

Figure 9-15.

Representing Graphs

A graph can be represented by either an adjacency matrix or adjacency lists. If there are N nodes in a graph, an *adjacency matrix* is a table with N rows and N columns. The value in the [i, j] position in the table is 1 if (Vi, Vj) is an edge in E and 0 otherwise. If the graph is a weighted graph, the [i, j] cell can contain the weight on that edge if the edge is in E and a 0 otherwise.

   Adjacency lists are linked lists, one for each node, containing the names of the nodes to which it is connected. The heads of each of these lists are held in an array of pointers. Figure 9-16 shows graph G2 represented both as an adjacency matrix and as adjacency lists.

   With all data structures, we need a systematic way to reach or search for each element. To access each element in a one-dimensional array, we use a count-controlled loop going from the index of the first element to the index of the last element. For a two-dimensional array, we use a pair of nested count-controlled loops. For a stack, we pop each element until the stack becomes empty. For a queue, we remove each element until the queue becomes empty.

   For a tree, three traversals are commonly used, each of which goes to the deepest level of the tree and works up. This strategy of going down a branch to its deepest point and moving up is called a *depth-first* strategy. To systematically visit each node in a tree, we could visit each node on level 0 (the root), then each node on level 1, then each node on level 2, etc. Visiting each node by level in this way is called a *breadth-first* strategy. With graphs, both a depth-first strategy and a breadth-first strategy are useful. We will outline both algorithms within the context of an example.

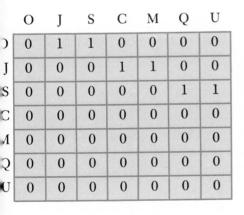

	O	J	S	C	M	Q	U
O	0	1	1	0	0	0	0
J	0	0	0	1	1	0	0
S	0	0	0	0	0	1	1
C	0	0	0	0	0	0	0
M	0	0	0	0	0	0	0
Q	0	0	0	0	0	0	0
U	0	0	0	0	0	0	0

a) Adjacency matrix of G2.

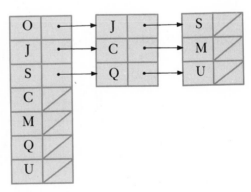

(b) Adjacency lists of G2.

Figure 9-16.

Using Graphs

Graphs are useful structures for representing physical relationships such as roads between cities or airline routes. Let's assume that we are interested in airline routes between seven cities: Austin, Dallas, Houston, Denver, Atlanta, Chicago, and Washington, D.C.

Our favorite airline flies the following routes:

Atlanta to Houston
Atlanta to Washington
Austin to Dallas
Austin to Houston
Chicago to Denver
Dallas to Austin
Dallas to Chicago
Dallas to Denver
Denver to Atlanta
Denver to Chicago
Houston to Atlanta
Washington to Atlanta
Washington to Dallas

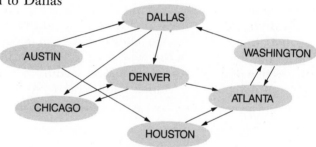

(a) Picture of graph.

	ATL	AUS	CHI	DAL	DEN	HOU	WASH
ATLANTA	0	0	0	0	0	1	1
AUSTIN	0	0	0	1	0	1	0
CHICAGO	0	0	0	0	1	0	0
DALLAS	0	1	1	0	1	0	0
DENVER	1	0	1	0	0	0	0
HOUSTON	1	0	0	0	0	0	0
WASHINGTON	1	0	0	1	0	0	0

(b) Adjacency matrix.

Figure 9-17.

The seven cities are the nodes or vertices in the graph. The directed pairs of cities that describe the routes are the edges in the graph. Figure 9-17 shows a picture of this graph and its adjacency matrix.

The question we can answer with this data structure is "Can I get from city X to city Y on my favorite airline?" This is equivalent to asking whether a path exists in the graph from city X to city Y.

The strategy we will use is first to take our starting city and see if we can reach our destination directly. If we can't, we will take each of the places we can reach directly and see if we can reach our destination directly from any one of them (i.e., in one stop). If we can't, we repeat the process to see if we can reach our destination from any of the next level of cities (i.e., in two stops). The process continues until we find our destination or determine that we can't get there from here.

We need a systematic way to keep track of the cities as we investigate them. If we can't reach our destination in one stop, we need to remember all the cities we can reach in one stop so we can fan out from them if we don't find our destination at the one-stop level.

Does this problem of remembering alternative branching points sound familiar? Remember the maze problem in Chapter 3? We kept track of alternative routes by using a stack. We can do the same thing here. Rather than put the row number and column number of a square on the stack, we will put the cities we need to fan out from on the stack.

We will begin by looking at each city we can reach directly. If we find our destination, the search is over. Otherwise, each city is put on the stack. When we have looked at all the cities we can reach directly and have not found our destination, we will pop the stack and start looking for our destination from the city that we have taken from the stack.

Let's apply this algorithm to our sample airline route data. We want to go from Austin to Washington. The places we can reach directly from Austin are Dallas and Houston. Neither is our destination, so they are pushed onto the stack. [See Figure 9-18(a).] When we determine that there are no other flights from Austin, we pop the stack and start searching from Houston. Atlanta can be reached from Houston, but that isn't our destination, so Atlanta goes on the stack. [See Figure 9-18(b).] There are no more flights out of Houston on this airline, so we pop the stack and begin our search from Atlanta.

There is a flight from Atlanta to Houston, but since that isn't our destination, Houston goes on the stack. [See Figure 9-18(c).] There is also a flight from Atlanta to Washington. Washington is indeed our destination, so our question has been answered. Yes, we can take our favorite airline from Austin to Washington.

However, if there were only one flight from Atlanta and it were to Houston, our algorithm would be in trouble. In fact, it would be an infinite

(a)	(b)	(c)
Houston	Atlanta	Houston
Dallas	Dallas	Dallas

Figure 9-18.

loop—we've been to Houston before! We have to take care of cycling in this algorithm just as we did in the maze problem. There we marked a square as having been visited by putting a period in the square. Here, we must also mark a city as having been visited so that it will not be investigated a second time.

This search is called a depth-first search because all the paths beginning at Houston are examined before we come back to Dallas to try from there. (The maze problem used a depth-first search also.) When you have to backtrack, you take the branch closest to where you dead ended. That is, you go as far as you can down one path before you take alternative choices at earlier branches.

A breadth-first search looks at all possible paths at the same depth before it goes to a deeper level. In our flight example, a breadth-first search would mean that we would check all possible one-stop connections before checking any two-stop connections, which would be preferable in this context. How do we change a depth-first search into a breadth-first search? A stack keeps track of things or events in the order opposite that of their occurrence. What we want here is to keep track of things in the order in which they happened. What data structure will do this for us? A queue, of course! We must put the cities we need to come back to on a queue instead of a stack.

Let's do the same algorithm using a queue instead of a stack. Dallas and Houston get ENQed instead of pushed at the first step. [See Figure 9-19(a).] Instead of popping Houston, we remove (DEQ) Dallas. There are direct flights from Dallas to Austin, Chicago, and Denver. Austin has been visited, so it does not go on the queue, but Chicago and Denver do go on the queue. [See Figure 9-19(b).] Since our destination has not been found, we remove Houston and begin our search from there. There is only one flight out of Houston, to Atlanta. Since it is not our destination, Atlanta is ENQed. [See Figure 9-19(c).]

Now we know that we cannot reach Washington with one stop, so we start examining the two-stop connections. We remove Chicago, which has a flight to Denver. Since Denver is not our destination, it is put into the queue. [See Figure 9-19(d).] Now this points out a problem. Do we mark a city as visited when we put it in the queue or stack, or when we have looked at its outgoing flights? If you mark it only after investigating its outgoing flights, a city may have its outgoing flights investigated while another copy of the city name is in the queue or stack. Therefore, when a city is removed from the stack or queue, a check must be made to see if the

Figure 9-19.

city has been visited before and discard it if it has.

The alternative approach is to mark the city as visited when it is put into the stack or queue. Which is better? It depends on the processing. You may want to know if there are alternative routes, in which case you would want to put a city into the queue or stack more than once.

Back to our example. We have Denver put into the queue in one step and removed (a previous entry) at the next step. There are direct flights from Denver to Atlanta and Chicago. Chicago has been visited, but Atlanta is ENQed (second Atlanta entry). [See Figure 9-19(e).] The first entry of Atlanta is removed. There are flights from Atlanta to Houston and Washington. Houston does not go into the queue because it has already been visited. Washington is then compared with our destination, and our processing is complete.

Figure 9-20 illustrates these two searching approaches. (The arrows indicate arcs investigated.)

There are a few paper-and-pencil exercises on graphs at the end of this chapter to test your understanding of depth-first and breadth-first searching. This section is meant only to introduce graphs, not to cover them in detail. We leave that to an advanced course in data structures. However, you should have a feel for the role of the stack in depth-first searching and the queue in breadth-first searching.

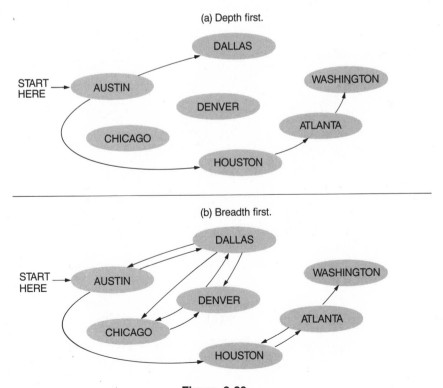

Figure 9-20.

Summary

In this chapter we have discussed several applications that require modifications to the data structures we are already familiar with, as well as a new structure, the graph. These topics will probably be covered in detail in more advanced computer science courses; it is our intention only to introduce them here, in order to show the wide variety of applications for which programmers must create data structures.

Exercises

1. Show the preorder, inorder, and postorder notation of the following binary expression trees. (Note that you must supply parentheses for the inorder notation.)

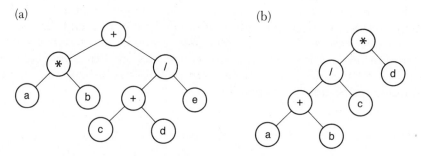

(a)

(b)

2. Evaluate the following binary expression tree:

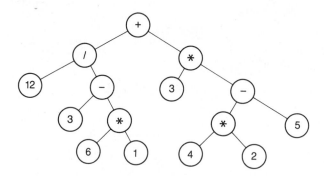

3. Show the binary expression tree that represents the following preorder expression:

$$/ - + a b c + d - e * f + g h$$
$$[\text{infix} = (((a + b) - c)/(d + (e - (f * (g + h)))))]$$

4. Write a recursive procedure to print the preorder representation of a binary expression tree. (Use the variant record implementation of the nodes in the tree.)

5. Tell whether the following trees are complete, full, or neither.

(a)

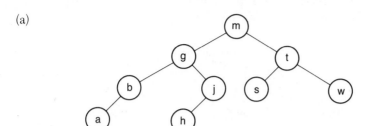

(b)

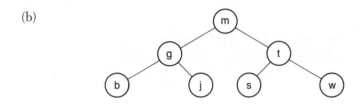

(c)

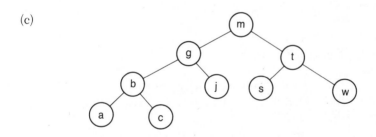

6. Show how the following heap would look in an array implementation.

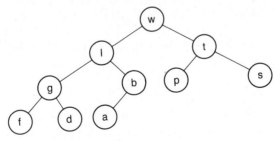

7. Show the heap that this array represents.

95	86	37	52	61	12	13	35
[1]	[2]	[3]	[4]	[5]	[6]	[7]	[8]

8. (a) Show how the representation of a complete binary tree as an array can be modified to represent any binary tree.

   (b) Implement your representation on the following tree.

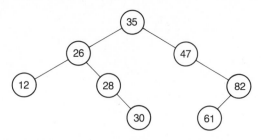

9. Given an array with the following values, show how the original heap would be arranged.

| 14 | 27 | 23 | 45 | 10 | 20 | 55 | 31 | 29 | 80 |

[1] [2] [3] [4] [5] [6] [7] [8] [9] [10]

10. Show how the heap in Problem 6 would look after three values were in place, before reheaping.

11. Draw a picture of the undirected graphs specified below.

   (a) G1 = (V, E)
   V(G1) = {X, Y, Z, W}
   E(G1) = {(X, Y), (X, Z), (Z, Z), (Z, W)}

   (b) G2 = (V, E)
   V(G2) = {RED, PURPLE, WHITE, PINK, BLUE}
   E(G2) = {(RED, PURPLE), (RED, WHITE), (PINK, PINK), (BLUE, PINK)}

12. Draw a picture of the directed graphs specified below.

   (a) G1 = (V, E)
   V(G1) = {MARY, JOSH, SUSAN, GEORGE, BILL, SARAH}
   E(G1) = {(MARY, BILL), (SUSAN, JOSH), (SARAH, JOSH), (SARAH, BILL), (JOSH, SUSAN), (GEORGE, SUSAN), (MARY, GEORGE), (BILL, MARY), (GEORGE, SARAH)}

   (b) G2 = (V, E)
   V(G2) = {0, 1, 2, 3, 5, 8, 13, 21}
   E(G2) = {(0, 1), (1, 2), (2, 3), (3, 5), (5, 8), (8, 13), (13, 21)}

13. Draw the adjacency matrix for G1 and G2 in Problem 12.

14. Using the adjacency matrix for G1 developed in Problem 13, describe the path from SARAH to SUSAN using

   (a) a breadth-first strategy.

   (b) a depth-first strategy.

Pre-Test

1. Use the tree to answer the following questions:

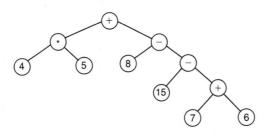

(a) Evaluate the expression represented by the binary expression tree.
(b) Show the inorder notation of the expression.
(c) Show the preorder notation of the expression.
(d) Show the postorder notation of the expression.

2. Show how the following binary tree containing positive integer data might be represented in an array without the need for pointers:

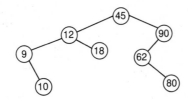

3. Given an array with the following values, show how the original heap would look:

14	27	52	10	45	97	20	27	10	4
[1]	[2]	[3]	[4]	[5]	[6]	[7]	[8]	[9]	[10]

4. Show how the heap produced by Problem 3 would look after three values were in place, after reheaping.

5. Define the graphs pictured:
   (a)

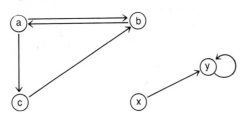

G1 is a directed graph.
G1 = (V, E)
V(G1) = {   }
E(G1) = {   }

(b)

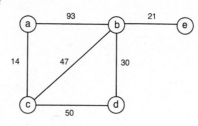

G2 is a weighted, undirected graph.
G2 = (V, E)
V(G2) = {   }
E(G2) = {   }

6. Draw the adjacency list for Problem 5(a).

7. Draw the adjacency matrix for Problem 5(b), storing the weights if an edge exists, zero otherwise.

Verification 10

Goals

To be able to apply verification rules to assignment statements.

To be able to apply verification rules to selection statements.

To be able to determine a loop invariant.

To be able to apply verification rules to loops.

How many times have you corrected "one last bug" only to find another? How many "only one more run" runs have you made? If you are human, far too many.

Debugging gets rid of known bugs. Good testing helps you to find more bugs. Unless the test data checks every possible combination of branches with every possible input, however, testing cannot really prove conclusively that the program is correct. In a large program, the number of possible combinations of branches makes this approach unfeasible.

For this reason, one of the theoretical areas of computer science research involves *program verification*. The goal of this research is to establish a method of proving programs correct that is analogous to the method of proving theorems in geometry. The techniques exist to do this, but the proofs of the programs are long and often more complicated than the programs themselves. So the proofs must be proved correct, and the proofs of the proofs, and so on.

Therefore, the major thrust of verification research is building automatic program provers. That is, computer scientists would like to build a verifiable program that verifies other programs.

Why is this subject being mentioned in a text to be used for a second or third programming course? Program verification is discussed here for two reasons. First, to stress the point that computer science is indeed a science. There *is* a body of mathematical theory that can be used to help us construct good programs. Second, program verification is discussed to demonstrate how some of its techniques can be useful now to you, a beginning computer science student.

THE VERIFICATION TECHNIQUE

The essence of the verification technique is to say, "If the input satisfies some condition P, and S (a program segment) is executed, then if S terminates, the output condition Q is satisfied." Formally we say:

$$\{P\}\ S\ \{Q\}$$

This notation comes from propositional calculus, which is not a prerequisite for this course, so we will define our notation intuitively as we go along.

{P} and {Q} are statements about the state of the machine (the computer). They are called *assertions*. Formally, {P} S {Q} is interpreted as "If P is true and S is executed, then (if S terminates), Q is true." P is called the *precondition* for S, and Q is called the *postcondition* of S.

To verify a program, you have to verify each statement and use the rule for sequences to collect the statements into larger and larger proved units. The rule for sequences is as follows:

$$(\{P\}\ S1\ \{R\})\ AND\ (\{R\}\ S2\ \{Q\}) \rightarrow \{P\}\ S1;S2\ \{Q\}$$

The final step in verifying a program is to show

$$\{P\}\ S\ \{Q\}$$

initial state   program   final state

In addition to this rule for sequences, there are rules for assignment statements, selection statements, and iteration statements. We will give examples of each to give you a flavor of what can be done, but the techniques applied to loops will be looked at in more detail because they are immediately useful in writing correct loops.

Assignment Statement

The general rule for assignment statements is as follows:

$$\{P_e^v\}\ v := e\ \{Q\}$$

This means that within {Q}, every occurrence of v has been replaced with e.

The following table gives some illustrations of this rule:

$\{P_e^v\}$	S	$\{Q\}$
{J = 6}	J := J + 1	{J = 7}
{K = 3}	L := K + 3	{K = 3 AND L = 6}
{DATA[I] = J}	J := J + 1	{DATA[I] = J − 1}

If we look at the output assertion {Q}, we can see that every occurrence of v (the left side of the assignment) in {Q} is really e (the right side of the assignment) before the assignment is done. That is what this rule is saying.

Selection (IF statements)

The rule for selection or branching is

$$\{P \text{ AND } E\} \text{ S1 } \{Q\}, \{P \text{ AND NOT } E\} \text{ S2 } \{Q\} \rightarrow$$
$$\{P\} \text{ IF } E \text{ THEN S1 ELSE S2 } \{Q\}$$

This rule says that we want {Q} to be true eventually. Now if E is true initially, S1 will be executed with {P AND E} as the initial condition. If E is not true, S2 will be executed with {P AND NOT E} as the initial condition.

This can be pictured as follows:

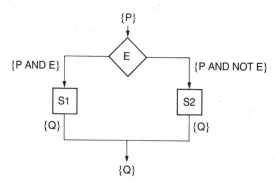

Note that if there is no ELSE clause, S2 is the identity function; that is, everything keeps its previous identity.

The following example to set MAX to the maximum of X and Y demonstrates how the verification of the selection statement works.

{P}	{true}	(* no preconditions exist *)
	IF X > Y	
	THEN	{X > Y} {X = maximum(X, Y)}
{S1}	MAX := X	{MAX = maximum(X, Y)} is TRUE
	ELSE	{X <= Y} {Y = maximum(X, Y)}
{S2}	MAX := Y	{MAX = maximum(X, Y)} is TRUE
{Q}	{MAX = maximum(X, Y)}	

In the THEN branch we know that X is greater than Y, and thus maximum(X, Y) equals X. In the ELSE branch we know that X is not greater than Y, and thus maximum(X, Y) equals Y.

The next example shows a case where the verification fails. The segment of code is supposed to set MAX to the maximum of X and Y.

{P}	{true}	(* no preconditions exist *)
	IF X > Y	
{S1}	THEN	{X > Y} {X = maximum(X, Y)}
	MAX := X	{MAX = maximum(X, Y)} is TRUE
	(* no else *)	{X <= Y} {MAX = MAX}
{S2}	(* identity *)	{MAX = maximum(X, Y)} is undefined
{Q}	{MAX = maximum(X, Y)} is FALSE.	

In the THEN branch we know that X is greater than Y, and thus maximum(X, Y) equals X. In the ELSE branch, we know that X is not greater than Y. However, because there is no action, maximum is unchanged and it is probably left containing an incorrect or undefined value.

Iteration (WHILE statements)

The rule for loops is

$$\{P \text{ AND } B\} S \{P\} \rightarrow$$
$$\{P\} \text{ WHILE } B \text{ DO } S \{P \text{ AND NOT } B\}$$

Let's rewrite this rule adding an additional assertion, {I}. The backward C means *implies*.

$$\{P\} \supset \{I\}, \{I \text{ AND } B\}, \{I \text{ AND NOT } B\} \supset \{Q\}$$

{I} is called the *invariant* of the loop. {I} must be true before the loop is entered, and the loop must maintain the truth of {I} at the end of each iteration. When condition B becomes FALSE, the loop is terminated, and {I} is still true.

In order to make use of the important principles here, let's rewrite this as a chart showing where certain things must be shown to be true.

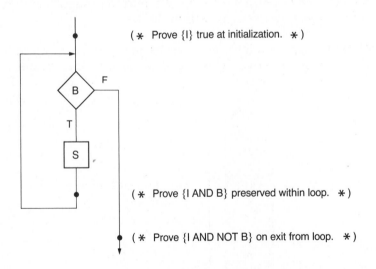

(* Prove {I} true at initialization. *)

(* Prove {I AND B} preserved within loop. *)

(* Prove {I AND NOT B} on exit from loop. *)

Just what is this loop invariant {I} that we are trying to prove? It is a statement about the relationships of the variables involved in the loop. It expresses the semantics of the loop, as opposed to the mechanics. The expression B, which controls the loop repetition, is used to tell when the semantics of the loop would be violated if another repetition were performed.

Let's tie all this together by looking at an example: summing the N integer values in an array, DATA.

```
SUM := 0;
I := 1;
WHILE I <= N DO
   BEGIN
     SUM := SUM + DATA[I];
     I   := I + 1
   END
```

To prove this section of code, we must do the following:

1. Define the loop invariant (actually, this should be done before the code is written).
2. Show that the loop invariant is true before entering the loop.
3. Show that the invariant is preserved within the loop.
4. Show that the loop halts and that the invariant and the terminating condition on the loop imply {Q}.

The loop invariant is "SUM contains the sum of all the elements in the array up to (but not including) DATA[I] as long as I is less than or equal to one more than the number of elements in DATA." The last part of the invariant can more easily be expressed as $I <= N + 1$. Figure 10-1 is a picture of the relationships in the loop.

To verify this loop, we must prove the invariant is true at the initialization point and at the exit from the loop. We must then show that the code of the loop maintains the invariant within the loop.

Initialization The loop invariant says that at the end of any iteration, the area of the array before DATA[I] is already summed. Substituting 1 for I in

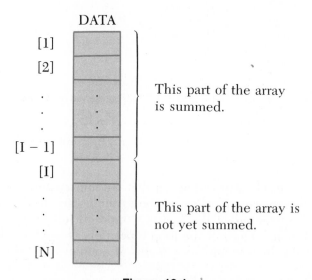

DATA

[1]

[2]

·
·
·

This part of the array
is summed.

[I − 1]

[I]

·
·
·

This part of the array is
not yet summed.

[N]

Figure 10-1.

the loop invariant, we get "SUM contains the sum of all the elements in the array up to but not including DATA[1]," which is correct, since SUM = 0.

Termination When we reach this point, we know that the condition of the WHILE (I <= N) is not true. Since our loop invariant says that I <= N + 1 and we know that I > N, I must be N + 1.

Substituting N + 1 for I in the loop invariant gives "SUM contains the sum of all the elements in the array up to but not including DATA [N + 1]"—that is, the sum of the whole array.

How do we know that we actually reach this point? That is, how do we know that the section of code actually terminates? We don't. We have proved partial correctness. If this section of code terminates, the results are correct. To prove termination, we have to add a precondition that N, the number of elements, is greater than or equal to 1. I begins at 1 and is incremented by 1 each time. N is not changed within the loop. Therefore I will eventually be greater than N, and the loop will terminate.

Preservation We know from the loop invariant that SUM contains the sum of the values from DATA[1] up to and including DATA[I − 1]. The first statement in the loop adds the value in DATA[I] to SUM. So now SUM contains the values from DATA[1] up to and including DATA[I]. The next statement increments I. Applying the rule for assignment statements, we replace the I with I − 1 in the previous statement. We have that SUM contains the sum of the values from DATA[1] up to and including DATA [I − 1], which is our loop invariant.

This seems like an awful lot of work to show something that is obvious anyway: the code *is* correct. It may be obvious in this small example, but the technique can be used to verify much more complicated examples.

How can this technique be immediately useful? If you think about your loop in terms of the loop invariant first (i.e., in terms of the semantics of your loop), you can choose the correct initialization and termination conditions the first time. Substituting them into the invariant, you can show that the initialization is correct and that the termination is correct. Second, if the invariant is added to the code as a comment, a reader can immediately tell the meaning of the loop, not just the code to accomplish it.

THE CASE AGAINST GOTO

We have discussed the verification of the assignment statement and the three basic program structures: the sequence, the branch, and the loop. Those of you who have previous programming experience in FORTRAN or BASIC, or who like to read the fine print in the Pascal manual, may be familiar with another kind of statement that determines program control: the GOTO statement. The GOTO statement means just what it says: go to the line in the program indicated by the label following GOTO. It is an unconditional branch to another place in the program.

How can program segments that include GOTO statements be verified? A GOTO statement within one of the basic program structures—sequence, selection, or loop—can take control away so that the structure does not terminate normally. A GOTO inside a WHILE loop, for instance, may make the loop terminate while the condition is still true. The following example sets PLACE to the location of VALUE1 in an array called LIST:

```
LABEL 10;
CONST MAX = 100;
VAR   LIST : ARRAY[1..MAX] OF INTEGER;
      VALUE1 ,
      PLACE : INTEGER;
      .
      .
      .
PLACE := 1;
WHILE PLACE <= MAX DO
   IF LIST[PLACE] = VALUE1
      THEN GOTO 10
      ELSE PLACE := PLACE + 1
      .
      .
      .
10: WRITELN('PLACE = ',PLACE);
```

The invariant of this loop is "VALUE1 is not contained in the array LIST up to but not including LIST[PLACE]," and the terminating condition on the loop control is PLACE< = MAX. But if VALUE1 is found in the array, the terminating condition will still be true at the exit of the loop. Note that the code is functionally correct; it works. However, it is very difficult to verify programs that include GOTO statements.

The difficulty of verification is not the only problem with the GOTO statement. The use of GOTO leads to unstructured programs with multiple entries into and exits from control structures. This is sometimes called "spaghetti code" because trying to read it can be like trying to untangle a bowl of spaghetti. Programs with GOTO statements are harder to read, understand, modify, and debug.

Summary

It is obvious from the examples in this chapter that program verification is very time consuming and, in a job environment, expensive. Why then would you ever want to use these techniques? Certainly, not every program is worthy of such cost and effort. There are, however, three situations in which formal program verification would be indicated.

First, formal verification should be done when it has been specified in the program's requirements. In the class environment, this is when your professor has specified verification as part of your programming assignment. In the work environment, verification may be specified by a customer in the contract for a particular programming job.

Second, formal verification may be indicated for sections of a program that are particularly complicated and error-prone. It may be wise in this case to start the verification procedure in the design stage of the program, to try to avoid costly errors.

A third place where verification should be used is in programs whose correct execution is critical to human life. For instance, a program that is responsible for the safe return of astronauts from a space mission would be worthy of verification. For a more down-to-earth example, consider the potential for disaster if a hospital's patient data base system has a bug that makes it lose information about patients' allergies to medications.

■ APPLICATION: THE INSERTION SORT

Data Structure in Use
- Array

Software Technique in Use
- Use of a loop invariant to develop correct loops

In this section, we will illustrate the verification technique again in a more complicated example—a procedure to implement the insertion sort algorithm. This will be our third sorting algorithm. We have already discussed quicksort and heapsort.

In Chapter 11, we will develop a way to compare sorting algorithms. Since looking at different algorithms to do the same task can be boring, we have spread different sorting algorithms throughout the text.

The principle of the insertion sort is quite simple: Each successive element in the array to be sorted is inserted into its proper place with respect to the other, already sorted elements. We start with the first element. There is only one element in the part of the array being examined, so it must be in its place. Now we take the second element in the array, and put it into its correct place, so that DATA[1] and DATA[2] are in order. Now the value in DATA[3] is put into its proper place. Now DATA[1]..DATA[3] are in order. This process continues until all the elements have been sorted. An example of this process is shown below:

DATA		DATA		DATA		DATA		DATA	
[1]	20	[1]	15	[1]	15	[1]	3	[1]	3
[2]	15	[2]	20	[2]	18	[2]	15	[2]	9
[3]	18	[3]	18	[3]	20	[3]	18	[3]	15
[4]	3	[4]	3	[4]	3	[4]	20	[4]	18
[5]	9	[5]	9	[5]	9	[5]	9	[5]	20
(a)		(b)		(c)		(d)		(e)	

An examination of the way the values in the array DATA are changing reveals the following pattern:

(a) DATA[1]..DATA[1] is sorted.
(b) DATA[1]..DATA[2] is sorted.
(c) DATA[1]..DATA[3] is sorted.
(d) DATA[1]..DATA[4] is sorted.
(e) DATA[1]..DATA[5] is sorted.

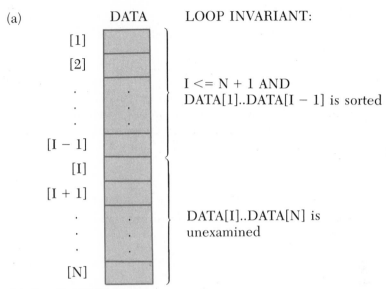

(a)   DATA   LOOP INVARIANT:

[1]

[2]

I <= N + 1 AND
DATA[1]..DATA[I − 1] is sorted

[I − 1]

[I]

[I + 1]

DATA[I]..DATA[N] is
unexamined

[N]

(b) Put DATA[I] in its proper slot.
(c) Increment I by 1 and you are back at (a).

Figure 10-2.

Since there are five elements, the entire array has been sorted.

Earlier we discussed the concept of a loop invariant. Can you see what the loop invariant is in this algorithm? Figure 10-2 shows the data structure, the loop invariant, and the accompanying algorithm.

"Put DATA[I] in its proper slot" must now be defined. There are three possibilities to consider. Remember that the first I − 1 elements are already sorted with respect to one another (but not necessarily to the rest of the array).

1. DATA[I] > DATA[I − 1]. DATA[I] is greater than all the sorted elements. In this case DATA[I] is in its proper place, and we don't need to do anything.

2. DATA[I] = DATA[I − 1]. DATA[I] is equal to the largest sorted element. Now there is a choice: We can interchange them or leave them as they are. If we leave them as they are, we preserve the order in which duplicate values occur in the original data. If we are talking about integer values, the order of duplicates isn't important. However, if we are actually sorting an array of records using an integer value field to order them, we might *want* to preserve the original order. A sort that preserves this original order is a *stable* sort. We will

choose to preserve the order here by combining this case with the one above. That is, we will do nothing if DATA[I] is equal to DATA [I − 1].

3. DATA[I] < DATA[I − 1]. DATA[I] is less than the largest sorted element, so we swap them. Now DATA[I − 1] becomes the DATA[I] in this analysis, and we are back to our original choices. Clearly this implies an inner loop which will run from I down to the place where situation (1) or (2) occurs or the loop counter reaches 1. Figure 10-3 shows a picture of the data structure during this processing.

The Inner Loop

To verify the algorithm, we must prove (that is, argue logically about) each of the loops. Let's begin with the innermost loop (Figure 10-3). The algorithm is as follows:

```
J ← I
WHILE (J > 1) AND (DATA[J] < DATA[J − 1]) DO
    swap DATA[J] and DATA[J − 1]
    decrement J
```

Let's look at each of the four parts of the loop invariant in detail:

J >= 1 will be used to determine the value of J at the end of the loop. "DATA[1]..DATA[J − 1] is sorted" says that the first J − 1 elements of the array are sorted with respect to each other.

"DATA[J]..DATA[I] is sorted" says that the elements from index J to index I are sorted with respect to each other.

The fourth part of the invariant ties the two halves of the array together. It says that if J is greater than 1 but less than I, then DATA[J − 1] is less than or equal to DATA[J + 1]. This will be used to show that when a swap is made between DATA[J − 1] and DATA[J], the second half is still sorted.

Initialization We know that the elements from DATA[1] up to and including DATA[I − 1] are sorted, because this is the invariant of the outer loop. Since J is initialized to I, the statement that DATA[1] up to and including DATA[J − 1] is sorted is true. DATA[I]..DATA[I] is sorted because there is only one element in this set. In order to show that J >= 1, we must know that I >= 1. For this part of our discussion, we will assume that I >= 1 is a precondition for this code segment. Such assumptions should be written in as comments.

We do not need to prove the last part of the invariant, since it only holds if J < I. So we have now shown that our invariant is true at initialization.

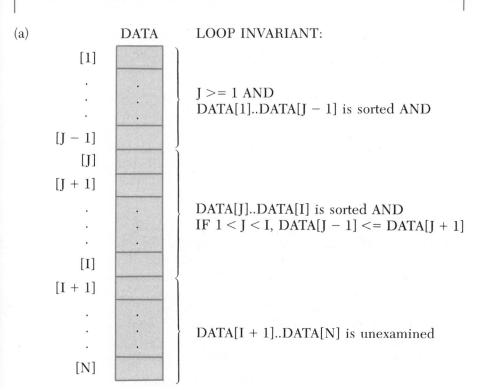

(a) DATA LOOP INVARIANT:

[1]

J >= 1 AND
DATA[1]..DATA[J − 1] is sorted AND

[J − 1]
[J]
[J + 1]

DATA[J]..DATA[I] is sorted AND
IF 1 < J < I, DATA[J − 1] <= DATA[J + 1]

[I]
[I + 1]

DATA[I + 1]..DATA[N] is unexamined

[N]

(b) If DATA[J] < DATA[J − 1], swap them.
(c) Decrement J by 1 and you are back at (a).

Figure 10-3.

Termination   There are two cases here: either J is not greater than 1 or DATA[J] is not less than DATA[J − 1]. Let's look at each case separately.

1. Our loop invariant says that J >= 1, and the conditional expression (J > 1) is false. Therefore, J must be equal to 1. Substituting 1 for J in the relevant parts of our loop invariant, we have

    DATA[1]..DATA[0] is sorted.
    DATA[1]..DATA[I] is sorted.

   The first statement is true because there are no elements in this set. The second statement is just what we wanted to prove.

2. The second terminating condition says that DATA[J] is not less than DATA[J − 1]. Therefore we know the following facts:

    DATA[1]..DATA[J − 1] is sorted.
    DATA[J]..DATA[I] is sorted.
    DATA[J − 1] <= DATA[J].

The first two lines state that the two halves are each sorted. The third states that the largest in the first half is less than the smallest in the second half. Hence, DATA[1]..DATA[I] is sorted.

Notice that in this discussion we say that the set of values from DATA[1] to DATA[0] is empty. This is not like a FOR loop, in which you can go both TO and DOWNTO. We are discussing values that are in an array from position I + 1 up to and including position I, and this set of values is empty. Therefore, anything general we want to say about all elements in that array segment is true. For example, they are sorted, summed, examined, and unexamined.

Preservation   After the swap, we know that DATA[J − 1] is now less than DATA[J]. If this is the first time through the loop, J is equal to I, and DATA[J − 1]..DATA[I] is sorted. If it is not the first time through the loop, we know that DATA[J] is less than DATA[J + 1] from our loop invariant. Therefore DATA[J − 1]..DATA[I] is sorted. We also know that DATA[J − 2] is less than DATA[J], because they were in a sorted segment of the array. DATA[1] to DATA[J − 2] is still sorted because it hasn't been changed.

Before we go on, let's summarize what it is we now know:

DATA[1]..DATA[J − 2] is sorted.
DATA[J − 1]..DATA[I] is sorted.
DATA[J − 2] <= DATA[J].

Applying the rule of assignment statements, we substitute J for J − 1:

DATA[1]..DATA[J − 1] is sorted.
DATA[J]..DATA[I] is sorted.
DATA[J − 1] <= DATA[J + 1].

Now let's code the whole algorithm as a procedure.

```
PROCEDURE INSSORT (VAR DATA : ARRAYTYPE; N : INTEGER);

VAR I, J : INTEGER;
    PLACEFOUND : BOOLEAN;

BEGIN   (* inssort *)
  I := 2;
  WHILE I <= N DO
    BEGIN
      (* Put DATA[I] in its proper place relative to DATA[1]..DATA[I − 1]. *)
      PLACEFOUND := FALSE;
      J := I;
      WHILE (J > 1) AND NOT PLACEFOUND DO
        IF DATA[J] < DATA[J − 1]
          THEN
            (* Swap and decrement J. *)
            BEGIN
              SWAP(DATA[J], DATA[J − 1]);
              J := J − 1
            END
          ELSE
            PLACEFOUND := TRUE;

      I := I + 1
    END   (* outer loop *)
END;   (* inssort *)
```

The Outer Loop

Now let's prove the outer loop. Remember our invariant says that DATA[1] to DATA[I − 1] is sorted and I is less than or equal to N + 1.

Initialization   I is initialized to 2. Substituting 2 for I in the invariant, we have that DATA[1] to DATA[2 − 1] is sorted. Since this range contains only one value, it is sorted.

Termination   On termination of the loop, I is equal to N + 1 by the same logic we have used before. Substituting this back into the loop invariant, we have that DATA[1] to DATA[N] is sorted, which is just what we set out to prove.

We should note here that we have proved partial correctness. We must also demonstrate that the loops actually do terminate. If the precondition states that N is greater than 1, we can show that the outer loop does terminate. We add 1 to I each time through the loop without changing N; therefore, I will eventually be incremented beyond N, and the loop condition will become false.

In the inner loop, J is set to I, which is initialized to 2 and only increases. Since J is decremented by 1 each time through the loop, J will eventually reach 1, and the loop will terminate.

Preservation   The body of the loop consists of two parts: the inner loop and the statement that increments the loop counter I. We have already proved the inner loop. Therefore we can use the terminating condition of the inner loop as an assertion here. We know that DATA[1] to DATA[I] is sorted. After I is incremented, we apply the assignment rule and get that DATA[1] to DATA[I − 1] is sorted.

You will note that the code for the inner loop in the final procedure is slightly different from the algorithm we proved. This is because Pascal evaluates both sides of a conditional expression regardless of the outcome of the first part. That is, even if the result of the first part gives the answer directly, the second part is still evaluated. This means that even though J is equal to 1, the second half of the condition, the expression DATA[J] < DATA[J − 1] will be evaluated. Since trying to access DATA[0] will cause a run-time error, this test must be made within the loop, where we know this condition cannot occur, and the result returned through a Boolean flag.

Exercises

1. Fill in the $\{P_e^v\}$ column.

$\{P_e^v\}$	S	$\{Q\}$
	I := I + 2	$\{I = 6\}$
	K := K − 3	$\{K = 6\}$
	J := N + 2	$\{N = 1 \text{ AND } J = 3\}$
	J := J − 1	$\{DATA[I] = J + 1\}$

2. Write the code to find the minimum of two numbers, X and Y, and verify the code.

3. Write the code that implements the following loop invariant.

$$1 <= I <= N + 1 \text{ AND } VALU = \pi DATA[1]..DATA[I − 1]$$

4. Where must the loop invariant be shown to be true?

5. Prove:

```
{(A = 5) AND (B = 4)}
BEGIN
   TEMP :=   A;
   A :=   B;
   B :=   TEMP
END;
{(A = 4) AND (B = 5)}
```

Pre-Test

1. Fill in the $\{P_e^v\}$ column in the following table:

$\{P_e^v\}$	S	$\{Q\}$
	J := 2 * J	$\{J = 18\}$
	J := K DIV 2	$\{(J = 12) \text{ AND } (K = 24)\}$
	J := J + K − L	$\{(J = 0) \text{ AND } (K = 5) \text{ AND } (L = 10)\}$

2. Prove the following segment of code by filling in the missing assertions on the side.

```
{X >= 0 AND Y >= 0}
     IF X > Y
         THEN            {                    }
             Z := Y − X  {                    }
         ELSE            {                    }
             Z := X − Y  {                    }
{X >= 0 AND Y >= 0 AND Z <= 0}
```

3. A loop invariant:
   (a) is false just before the loop is executed the first time.   T   F
   (b) may or may not be true after the execution of each statement within the loop.   T   F
   (c) is true at the top of the loop prior to each execution of the loop body.   T   F
   (d) is always true.   T   F
   (e) is false after the loop execution is complete.   T   F

4. Prove the following segment of code by filling in the missing assertions on the side.

```
{TRUE}
{(A - B) * (A + B) = A² - B² }
BEGIN
    X := A + B;              {                    }
    Y := A - B;              {                    }
    C := X * Y;              {                    }
END;
{C = A² - B²}
```

Sorting Algorithms and Efficiency Considerations

11

Goals

To be able to encode and hand-simulate the sorting algorithms:

- *straight selection sort*
- *bubble sort (two versions)*

To be able to determine the order of the following sorting algorithms using Big-O notation:

- *straight selection sort*
- *insertion sort*
- *bubble sort (two algorithms)*
- *quicksort*
- *heapsort*

To be able to outline other efficiency considerations.

To be able to sort on several keys.

At many points in this book, we have gone to great trouble to keep lists of elements in sorted order: student records sorted by ID number, integers sorted from smallest to largest, words sorted alphabetically. The goal of keeping sorted lists, of course, is to facilitate searching them. Given an appropriate data structure, a particular list element can be found faster if the list is sorted.

Putting an unordered list of data items into order—sorting—is a very common and useful operation. Whole books have been written about various sorting algorithms, as well as algorithms for searching an ordered list to find a particular element. The goal, of course, is to come up with better sorts. Since the efficiency of a sort may in large part determine the efficiency of the whole program, a good sorting routine is very desirable. This is one area in which programmers are sometimes encouraged to sacrifice clarity in favor of speed of execution. For this reason, we will use the subject of sorting algorithms to illustrate the considerations involved in measuring efficiency.

This chapter then will have a dual focus: (1) to introduce several sorting algorithms and some terminology used to describe sorts, and (2) to talk about efficiency considerations, using the comparison of sorting algorithms as an example.

First, however, we must decide what we mean by efficiency.

WHAT IS "GOOD"?

In Chapter 7, we said that quicksort is a good sorting algorithm. What do we mean by *good*? How can we compare two algorithms that do the same task?

To make such a comparison, we must first define a set of objective measures that can be applied to each algorithm. The analysis of algorithms is an important area of theoretical computer science; in advanced courses, you will undoubtedly see extensive work in this area. We will look at a small part of this topic—only enough to let us determine which of two algorithms requires less work to accomplish a particular task.

How do we measure the work that two algorithms perform? The first solution that comes to mind is simply to code the algorithms and then compare the execution times for running the two programs. The one with the shortest execution time is clearly the better algorithm. Or is it? We can really only say that Program A is more efficient than Program B *on this computer.* Execution times are specific to a particular computer. Of course, we could test the algorithms on all possible computers, but we want a more general measure.

A second possibility is to count the number of instructions or statements executed. This measure, however, varies with the programming language used, as well as with the style of the individual programmer. To standardize this measure somewhat, we could count the number of passes through a critical loop in the algorithm. If each iteration involves a constant amount of work, this measure will give us a meaningful yardstick of efficiency.

These musings lead to the idea of isolating a particular operation fundamental to the algorithm and counting the number of times that this operation is performed. Suppose, for example, that we are searching an array for a certain value. We might count how many comparisons between the target value and the elements in the array are necessary to locate the value. If we were summing the elements in an integer array, we could count the integer addition operations needed. (Note that this count is a function of the number of elements in the array. For an array of N elements, there will be N − 1 addition operations. So we can compare the algorithms for the general case, not just for a specific array size.) If we want to compare algorithms for multiplying two real matrices together, we can come up with a measure that combines the real multiplication and addition operations required for matrix multiplication.

This last example brings up an interesting consideration: Sometimes an operation will so dominate the algorithm that the other operations fade into the background "noise." If we want to buy elephants and goldfish, for example, and we are considering two pet stores, we really only need to compare the prices of elephants; the cost of the goldfish is trivial by comparison. Similarly, real multiplication is so much more expensive than addition in terms of computer time that the addition operation is a trivial factor in the efficiency of the whole matrix multiplication algorithm; we might as well count only the multiplication operations, ignoring the addition. In analyzing algorithms, we can often find one operation that dominates the algorithm, effectively relegating the others to the noise level.

From our examination of the insertion sort in Chapter 10, we can see that the dominant operation in the loop is the comparison operation—which element is bigger? In our study of other sorting algorithms, we will use the number of comparisons as a measure of the efficiency of each algorithm.

Each sort takes the same input—an unordered array—and produces the same output—an ordered array containing the same elements. We will consider Sort A to be more "efficient" than Sort B if it can accomplish its task with a smaller amount of work. That is, a more efficient sort, according to our measure, will require fewer comparisons. (There are other ways to measure the efficiency and cost of an algorithm, which will be discussed later.)

As in the case of summing the elements in an array, we do not actually have to count the number of critical operations on an array of a particular size. The number of comparisons will be some function of the number of elements (N) in the array. Therefore, we can express the number of comparisons in terms of N (like N + 5 or N^2) rather than as an integer value (like 52).

NOTE: In all the examples that follow, DATA is an ARRAY[1..N] OF INTEGER, and all sorting is in order of increasing value.

STRAIGHT SELECTION SORT

If you were handed a list of names and asked to put them in alphabetical order, you might use this general approach:

1. Find the name that comes first in the alphabet and write it on a second sheet of paper.
2. Cross the name out on the original list.
3. Continue this cycle until all the names on the original list have been crossed out and written onto the second list, at which point the second list is sorted.

This algorithm is simple to translate into a computer program, but it has one drawback: It requires space in memory to store two complete lists. Although we have not talked about memory space considerations, this duplication is clearly wasteful. However, a slight adjustment to this manual approach does away with the need to duplicate space. As you cross a name off the original list, a free space opens up. Instead of writing the minimum value on a second list, you can exchange it with the value currently in its correct place in the original list.

Let's look at the example in Figure 11-1.

1. The smallest value in DATA is in location [4]. Therefore, we swap the contents of DATA[1] and DATA[4]. Now the smallest value is in its correct position in the array.
2. The smallest value in the unordered part of the array (DATA[2] ..DATA[5]) is in location [3], so we swap DATA[2] and DATA[3]. Now the first two positions in the array are sorted.
3. The smallest value in the unsorted part of the array is in DATA[3], its correct position, so we do nothing. (Actually, the algorithm merely

	DATA		DATA		DATA		DATA
[1]	126	[1]	1	[1]	1	[1]	1
[2]	43	[2]	43	[2]	26	[2]	26
[3]	26	[3]	26	[3]	43	[3]	43
[4]	1	[4]	126	[4]	126	[4]	113
[5]	113	[5]	113	[5]	113	[5]	126
(a) Initial		(b) First iteration		(c), (d) Second, third iteration		(e) Fourth iteration	

Figure 11-1. An example of the straight selection sort.
(The sorted elements are shaded.)

swaps the value with itself, rather than checking for the special case.)

4. The smallest value in the unsorted part of the array (DATA[4] ..DATA[5]) is in position [5]; we swap DATA[4] and DATA[5].

5. DATA[5] now must contain the largest value in the array. The values in DATA are now sorted. The algorithm for the selection sort is shown in Figure 11-2.

(a)

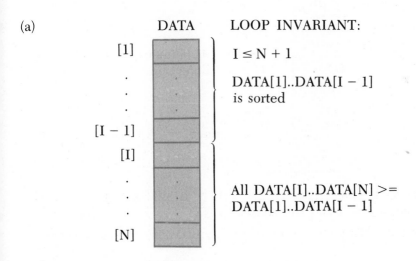

DATA   LOOP INVARIANT:

$I \leq N + 1$

DATA[1]..DATA[I − 1] is sorted

All DATA[I]..DATA[N] $>=$ DATA[1]..DATA[I − 1]

(b) Find the smallest value in DATA[I]..DATA[N].
(c) Exchange it with DATA[I].
(d) Increment I by 1 and you are back at (a).

Figure 11-2. The algorithm for the straight selection sort.

Let's break down step (b) of the algorithm further. Our task is to find the index of the minimum value in the unsorted section of the array. We will need a loop that starts with I and compares the values in the subarray DATA[I]..DATA[N], returning the index of the smallest value (MINDEX). The loop control variable, J, representing the cursor moving through the unordered part of the array, will begin at I + 1. In each iteration we will ask: Is the value in DATA[J] less than the value in DATA[MINDEX]? If so, we update MINDEX. We increment J and keep checking until we reach the end of the array (when J > N). MINDEX is now the index of the smallest value in the unordered part of the array. The algorithm is illustrated in Figure 11-3.

(a)

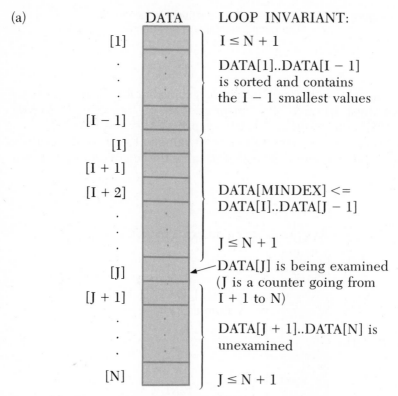

DATA   LOOP INVARIANT:

I ≤ N + 1

DATA[1]..DATA[I − 1]
is sorted and contains
the I − 1 smallest values

DATA[MINDEX] <=
DATA[I]..DATA[J − 1]

J ≤ N + 1

DATA[J] is being examined
(J is a counter going from
I + 1 to N)

DATA[J + 1]..DATA[N] is
unexamined

J ≤ N + 1

(b) IF DATA[J] < DATA[MINDEX] THEN MINDEX := J
(c) Increment J by 1 and you are back at (a).

Figure 11-3. The algorithm for finding the location of the minimum element.

You will note that each loop is expressed in terms of the relationship of the variables within the loop. What is such a description called? That's right—a loop invariant. We will define these loop invariants in words, and leave the proofs of them as an exercise. Try them yourself, using the technique from Chapter 10.

The invariant for the algorithm in Figure 11-2 is "The elements from DATA[1] up to and including DATA[I − 1] are sorted, and all the values in DATA[I] up to and including DATA[N] are greater than or equal to any of the values in DATA[1]..DATA[I − 1]."

The invariant for the inner loop (Figure 11-3) is "DATA[MINDEX] is less than or equal to any values from DATA[I] up to and including DATA[J − 1]."

The code for Procedure SELECTSORT is given below.

```
PROCEDURE SELECTSORT (VAR DATA : ARRAYTYPE;
                          N : INTEGER);
(* Sorts array DATA from index 1 through N *)
(* in order of increasing value.          *)


VAR    I, J, MINDEX : INTEGER;

BEGIN   (* selectsort *)
   I := 1;

   (* Loop through whole array. *)
   WHILE I <= N DO
      BEGIN   (* outer loop *)
         (* Initialize. *)
         MINDEX := I;
         J := I + 1;

         (* Find index of minimum unsorted element. *)
         WHILE J <= N DO
            BEGIN   (* inner loop *)
               IF DATA[J] < DATA[MINDEX]
                  THEN MINDEX := J;
               J := J + 1
            END;   (* inner loop *)

         (* Swap first unsorted element with minimum *)
         (* unsorted element.                        *)
         SWAP(DATA[MINDEX], DATA[I]);
         I := I + 1
      END   (* outer loop *)
END;   (* selectsort *)
```

Note that the loops have been written as WHILE, rather than FOR, loops. FOR loops would shorten the code, but they leave the loop control variable undefined at the end of the loop. Because of this fact, we could not prove that the loop invariants hold. Therefore, the algorithm is coded using the more general WHILE loop. Of course, in practice either construct will work.

Now let's get back to the business of measuring the amount of work required by this algorithm in terms of the number of comparisons made.

There are two loops, one nested within the other, and the comparison is in the inner loop. The first time through the inner loop, there are N − 1 comparisons, the next time N − 2 comparisons, and so on until there is 1 comparison in the last iteration. This totals up to

$$(N - 1) + (N - 2) + (N - 3) + \cdots + 1 = (N(N - 1)/2)$$

To accomplish our goal of sorting an array of N elements, the straight selection sort requires $N(N - 1)/2$ comparisons. For an array of 10 elements, for instance, 45 comparisons are needed. Note that doubling the array size more than quadruples the number of comparisons. Also note that the particular arrangement of values in the array does not affect the amount of work done at all. Even if the array is in sorted order before the call to SELECTSORT, the procedure will still make $N(N - 1)/2$ comparisons.

BUBBLE SORT

The identifying feature of a selection sort is that, on each pass through the loop, one element is put in its proper place. In the straight selection sort, each iteration found the smallest unsorted element and put it in its correct place. If we had made the inner loop find the *largest* value, instead of the smallest, the algorithm would have sorted in descending order. We could also have made the loop go down from N to 1, putting the elements in the bottom of the array first. All these are variations on the straight selection sort. The variations do not change the basic way that the minimum (or maximum) element is found.

The bubble sort is a selection sort that uses a different scheme for finding the minimum (or maximum) value. Each iteration puts the smallest unsorted element in its correct place, but it also makes changes in the location of the other elements in the array. The first iteration will put the smallest element in the array in the first position. We start with the element in the Nth position, and compare successive pairs of elements, swapping whenever the bottom element of the pair is smaller than the one above it. In this way, the smallest element "bubbles" up to the top of the array. The next iteration puts the smallest element in the unsorted part of the array into the second position, using the same technique. As we walk through the example in Figure 11-4, note that in addition to putting one element in its proper place, each iteration causes some intermediate changes in the array.

The first iteration puts 6 in DATA[1]. Unlike the straight selection sort, which would make only the single swap between 6 and 36, the bubble sort causes two additional intermediate swaps. It first compares the values in DATA[5] and DATA[4]. Since 12 >= 6, no swap occurs. Then DATA[4] and DATA[3] are compared; 6 < 10, so the two are swapped. The new value in DATA[3], which is 6, is compared to DATA[2]; 6 < 24, so they are swapped. Finally, the new value in DATA[2] (6 again) is compared to DATA[1]; 6 < 36, so a swap occurs. Now, the smallest value (6) is in the top position in the array. The second iteration will put the next smallest value (10) in the second position, causing one additional swap, and so on. Note

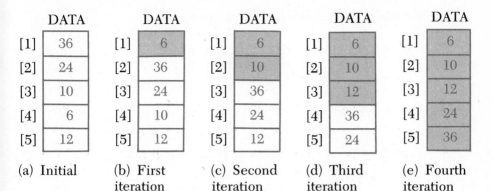

(a) Initial   (b) First   (c) Second   (d) Third   (e) Fourth
                  iteration   iteration   iteration   iteration

Figure 11-4. Example of the bubble sort.

that each iteration stops comparing values at the Ith position; the first $I - 1$ values are already sorted, and all the elements in the unsorted part of the array are greater than or equal to the sorted elements. A snapshot picture of this algorithm is shown in Figure 11-5.

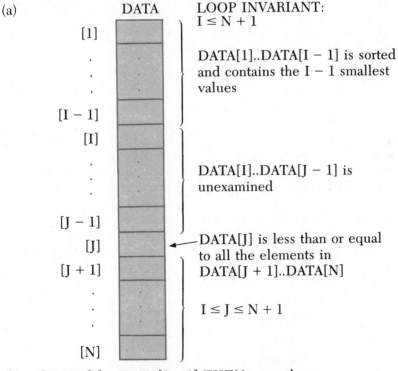

(a)   DATA   LOOP INVARIANT:
                $I \leq N + 1$

DATA[1]..DATA[I − 1] is sorted and contains the I − 1 smallest values

DATA[I]..DATA[J − 1] is unexamined

DATA[J] is less than or equal to all the elements in DATA[J + 1]..DATA[N]

$I \leq J \leq N + 1$

(b)   If DATA[J] < DATA[J − 1] THEN swap them
(c)   Decrement J by 1 and you are back at (a).
(d)   When J = I, the unexamined portion is empty.

Figure 11-5. The algorithm for the bubble sort.

One version of the bubble sort is given below.

```
PROCEDURE BUBBLE1 (VAR DATA : ARRAYTYPE;
                        N : INTEGER);
(* Sorts DATA from index 1 through N in ascending order. *)

VAR  I, J : INTEGER;

BEGIN    (* bubble1 *)
   (* Loop through the whole array. *)
   I := 1;
   WHILE I < N DO
     BEGIN
        (* Bubble up the smallest unsorted value. *)
        J := N;

        WHILE J > I DO
          BEGIN
             (* If the bottom value is smaller than *)
             (* its predecessor, swap them.         *)
             IF DATA[J] < DATA[J - 1]
                 THEN SWAP(DATA[J], DATA[J - 1]);
             J := J - 1
          END;      (* while J > I *)

        I := I + 1
     END    (* while I < N *)
END;   (* bubble1 *)
```

Analysis of the work required by BUBBLE1 is easy. It is the same as for the straight selection sort algorithm. There are $N - 1$ comparisons the first time through the outer loop, $N - 2$ comparisons the second time, etc. Therefore, BUBBLE1 and SELECTSORT require the same amount of work.

Note that this version of the bubble sort makes no provision for the possibility that the array will be completely sorted long before the procedure is finished. For example, in the following case the array is sorted after the first iteration of the outer loop, yet the procedure continues to execute—changing nothing—for three more passes:

	DATA			DATA
[1]	14		[1]	12
[2]	16		[2]	14
[3]	35		[3]	16
[4]	12		[4]	35
[5]	50		[5]	50

original   after one iteration

Let's add a Boolean flag, SWAPPED, to tell us when the array is sorted before the maximum number of iterations. We set SWAPPED to FALSE inside the outer loop. If any elements are swapped in the inner loop, we reset SWAPPED to TRUE. If no elements have been swapped, we know that the array is already in order. Now we only need to make one extra pass through the outer loop when the array is in order. This procedure is coded below as BUBBLE2.

```
PROCEDURE BUBBLE2 (VAR DATA : ARRAYTYPE;
                        N : INTEGER);
(* Sorts DATA from index 1 through N in ascending *)
(* order; stops sorting when the array is sorted.     *)

VAR    I, J    : INTEGER;
        SWAPPED : BOOLEAN;

BEGIN     (* bubble2 *)
   (* Initialize. *)
   I := 1;
   SWAPPED := TRUE;

   (* Loop through array; stop when sorted. The array is sorted when there are no *)
   (* values swapped in the inner loop.                                            *)
   WHILE (I < N) AND SWAPPED DO
      BEGIN
         (* Initialize. *)
         J := N;
         SWAPPED := FALSE;

         (* Bubble up the smallest unsorted value. *)
         WHILE J > I DO
            BEGIN
               (* If the bottom value is smaller than its      *)
               (* predecessor, swap them. Note that the swap   *)
               (* took place by setting Boolean flag SWAPPED. *)
               IF DATA[J] < DATA[J - 1]
                  THEN
                     BEGIN
                        SWAPPED := TRUE;
                        SWAP(DATA[J], DATA[J - 1])
                     END;   (* if *)

               J := J - 1
            END;   (* while J > I *)

         I := I + 1
      END   (* while I < N *)
END;   (* bubble2 *)
```

The analysis of BUBBLE2 is more difficult. Clearly, if the array is already sorted, one pass through the outer loop will tell us so. In that case, only N − 1 comparisons are required for the sort—the best possible case.

What if the original array were actually sorted in descending order before the call to BUBBLE2? This is the worst possible case. In this case, BUBBLE2 requires as many comparisons as BUBBLE1 and SELECTSORT. Note that we are still defining work as the number of comparisons required. This measure does not include such overhead as setting the Boolean flag in each iteration of BUBBLE2, or all the extra swaps in both the bubble sorts. So, is BUBBLE2 more efficient than BUBBLE1 or SELECTSORT?

It depends on the data. That is, the amount of work needed will vary, depending on the order of the original data. Can we calculate an average case? Note that the number of comparisons in iteration i is $N - i$. Let K indicate the number of iterations executed before BUBBLE2 finishes its work. The total number of comparisons required is

$$(N - 1) + (N - 2) + (N - 3) + \cdots + (N - K)$$

A little algebra changes this to

$$(2KN - K - K^2)/2$$

Since K is not greater than N, $(2KN - K - K^2)/2$ is less than or equal to $N(N - 1)/2$. Therefore, BUBBLE2 is better than either BUBBLE1 or SELECTSORT, right? Well, maybe. Remember that the overhead in BUBBLE2 is greater. So even though we have a quantitative measure of how much work is done, we are still having trouble actually comparing the various algorithms. We have hedged by saying that efficiency is data dependent. Can't we do better than that?

THE BIG-O

Our interest in efficiency mainly involves a concern about solving a problem of large size. If the array to be sorted contains only 10 elements, whether or not the sort is efficient doesn't matter, since the problem is small and the number of comparisons is reasonably small. But as the size of the array grows, the number of comparisons grows even faster.

We can express an approximation of the relationship between the size of the job and the amount of work required to do it using a mathematical notation called *order of magnitude* or *Big-O* notation. (Note that this is a letter O, not a zero.) The order of magnitude of a function is the same as the order of the term in the function that increases *fastest* relative to N (the size of the job). For instance, if

$$f(N) = N^4 + 100N^2 + 10N + 50$$

then f(N) is of order N^4 [in Big-O notation, $O(N^4)$]. That is, for large values of N, N^4 will dominate the function. (Remember the elephants and goldfish?)

A constant computing time is referred to as $O(1)$. Since it is our goal to minimize work, $O(1)$ is better than $O(N)$ (linear time), which in turn is better than $O(N^2)$ (quadratic time). $O(N^3)$ (cubic time) is worse, and $O(2^N)$ (exponential) is awful. One other frequently seen computing time is $O(log_2N)$, which is better than $O(N)$.

N	log_2N	$N log_2N$	N^2	N^3	2^N
1	0	1	1	1	2
2	1	2	4	8	4
4	2	8	16	64	16
8	3	24	64	512	256
16	4	64	256	4096	65536
32	5	160	1024	32768	2147483648
64	6	384	4096	262144	About 5 years worth of instructions on a super computer
128	7	896	16384	2097152	About 600,000 times greater than the age of the universe in nanosecs (for a 6-billion-year estimate)
256	8	2048	65536	16777216	don't ask

Figure 11-6.

As you can see in Figure 11-6, some of the computing times increase very dramatically in relation to the size of N. In particular, note that $Nlog_2N$ grows much more slowly than N^2. (It is also interesting to note that the values in the last column grow so quickly that the computation time required for problems of this order may exceed the estimated life span of the universe.)

THE BIG-O COMPARISON OF SORTS

We determined that the number of comparisons in the straight selection sort and BUBBLE1 is $N(N - 1)/2$, or, in expanded form, $0.5N^2 - 0.5N$. In Big-O notation, we only consider the first term (the elephant), since it increases faster relative to N. Further, we can ignore the constant 0.5, making the notation for these algorithms $O(N^2)$. This means that, for large values of N, the computation time will be approximately proportional to N^2.

To compare BUBBLE2 we need to find the order of magnitude of $(2KN - K - K^2)/2$ (the number of comparisons). The term which is increasing the fastest relative to N is $2KN$. We know that K is less than N, so K is $O(N)$ and, of course, N is $O(N)$. Therefore, the order of magnitude of $2KN$ is N^2. So BUBBLE2 is also $O(N^2)$. Note, however, that in the best case (the array is already sorted), only one iteration is needed. So, only $N - 1$ comparisons are made, giving us $O(N)$. In the best case, then, BUBBLE2 is $O(N)$.

The analysis of the insertion sort (described in Chapter 10) is similar to that of BUBBLE2. In the best case, when the initial array is already sorted, only one comparison is made on each pass, so the sort is O(N). In the worst case (the array is sorted in reverse order), the number of comparisons is the same as in the straight selection sort and BUBBLE1, namely, N(N − 1)/2, or O(N²). On the average, the insertion sort is O(N²). It is better than the straight selection sort, however, if the original file approaches sorted order.

Since the straight selection sort, both bubble sorts, and the insertion sort are all on the order of N², for large values of N there is no difference between their performances. BUBBLE2 may require somewhat fewer comparisons, but the difference, on the average, is not significant.

ANALYZING QUICKSORT

Now that we have a measure (number of comparisons) and a way of saying "much more efficient," let's analyze Quicksort.

On the first call, every element in the array is compared to the dividing value, so the work done is O(N). The array is divided into two pieces, which are then examined.

Each of these segments is then divided, making four pieces. This analysis is illustrated in Figure 11-7. At each level, the number of pieces doubles. At what level have we finished dividing the elements? If we split each segment into approximately one half each time, it will take up log₂N splits. At each split, we make O(N) comparisons.

So quicksort is O(N log₂N) on the average, which is quicker than O(N²). When is quicksort not quick? Consider a quicksort routine whose splitting algorithm uses the first element of the array (or the segment of the array

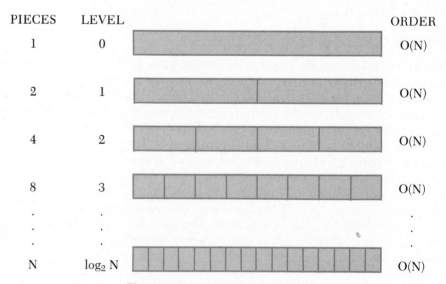

Figure 11-7. Analysis of quicksort.

under consideration) as a splitting value. What would happen if the array were already sorted? The splits would be very lopsided, and the subsequent calls to quicksort would sort into a segment of one element and a segment containing all the rest of the array (or segment of the array). Clearly, this situation would produce a sort that is not at all quick. In fact, in this case quicksort would be $O(N^2)$. The possibility of this situation occurring by chance is very unlikely. By analogy, consider the odds of shuffling a deck of cards and coming up with an ordered deck. On the other hand, in some applications you may know that the original array is likely to be sorted or nearly sorted. In such cases, you would want to use either a different sort or a different splitting algorithm for quicksort.

ANALYZING HEAPSORT

It is hard to believe, from our small-sized example in Chapter 9, that heapsort is really very efficient. It seems odd to move the largest value all the way to the top before putting it in its place at the bottom. And, in fact, for small values of N, heapsort is not very efficient.

For large arrays, however, heapsort can be very efficient indeed. Consider that a complete binary tree with N nodes has log $(N + 1)$ levels. Even if each element were a leaf and had to pass through the entire tree, the sort would still be $O(N \log_2 N)$. So heapsort, unlike quicksort, is $O(N \log_2 N)$ regardless of the initial order of its elements.

OTHER EFFICIENCY CONSIDERATIONS

When N Is Small

As we have stressed throughout this chapter, our analysis of efficiency has been based on the number of comparisons made by a sorting algorithm. This number gives us a rough estimate of the computation time involved, since a comparison is made on each iteration of the inner loop of the algorithm. The other activities that accompany the comparison (swapping, keeping track of Boolean flags, and so forth) contribute to the *constant of proportionality* of the algorithm.

In comparing Big-O evaluations, we ignored these constants, since we wanted to know how the algorithm would perform on large values of N. In general, $O(N^2)$ sorts require few extra activities in addition to the comparisons, so their constant of proportionality is fairly small. On the other hand, an $O(N \log_2 N)$ sort may be more complex, with more overhead and thus a larger constant of proportionality. This situation may cause anomalies in the relative performances of the algorithms when the value of N is small. In this case, N^2 is not much greater than $N \log_2 N$, and the constants may dominate instead, causing an $O(N^2)$ sort to run faster than an $O(N \log_2 N)$ sort.

Eliminating Calls to Procedures and Functions

We mentioned at the beginning of this chapter that it may be desirable, for efficiency considerations, to streamline the code as much as possible, even at the expense of readability. For instance, we have consistently written

```
SWAP(X, Y)
```

instead of the expanded version

```
TEMP := X;
X := Y;
Y := TEMP
```

Though the call to SWAP is clearer, in the actual coding it would be better to use the in-line expansion. Procedure and function calls require extra overhead that you may prefer to avoid in a sorting routine.

Similarly, the recursive quicksort procedure requires the extra overhead involved in implementing the recursive calls. You may want to avoid this overhead by coding a nonrecursive quicksort procedure.

Programmer Time

Why then would you ever decide to use a recursive version of the sort? The decision involves a choice between types of efficiency desired. Up until now, we have only been concerned with minimizing computer time. However, while computers are becoming faster and cheaper, it is not at all clear that computer *programmers* are following that trend. Therefore, in some situations programmer time may be an important consideration in choosing a sort algorithm and its implementation. In this respect, the recursive version of quicksort is more desirable than its nonrecursive counterpart, which requires the programmer to simulate the recursion explicitly.

Space Considerations

Another efficiency consideration is the amount of memory space required. In general, this is not a very important factor in choosing a sorting algorithm, since the space needed is usually closer to $O(N)$ than to $O(N^2)$. The usual time versus space tradeoff applies to sorts—more space means less time, and vice-versa.

Since processing time is the factor that applies most often to sorting algorithms, we have considered it in detail here. Of course, as in any application, the programmer must determine goals and requirements before selecting an algorithm and starting to code.

MORE ABOUT SORTING IN GENERAL

Keys

In our descriptions of the various sorts, we showed examples of sorting arrays of integers. In reality we are more likely to be sorting arrays of records that contain several fields of information. A sort *key* is the field in such a record whose value is used to order the records. Each record must contain some unique identifying key, such as an IDNUMBER field. In addition, a record may contain secondary keys, which may or may not be unique. For instance, a student record may contain the following fields:

STUDENTNUMBER   Primary unique key
NAME ⎫
ADDRESS   ⎬   Secondary keys
MAJOR ⎭

If the data contain only single integers, it doesn't matter whether the original order of duplicate values is kept. As we will see, preserving the original order of records with identical key values may be desirable. If a sort preserves this order, it is said to be *stable*.

Consider the following declarations for personnel records:

```
CONST MAX = 200;

TYPE  STRING10 = PACKED ARRAY[1..10] OF CHAR;
      STRING20 = PACKED ARRAY[1..20] OF CHAR;

      ADDRESSTYPE = RECORD
                      NUMBER : INTEGER;
                      STREET,
                      CITY,
                      STATE : STRING10;
                      ZIP : INTEGER
                    END;  (* record *)

      PERSONTYPE = RECORD
                     NAME : STRING20;
                     ADDRESS : ADDRESSTYPE;
                      .
                      .
                   END;  (* record *)

      PEOPLE = ARRAY[1..MAX] OF PERSONTYPE;

VAR   EMPLOYEES : PEOPLE
```

For some purposes, we might want to see a listing in order by name. In this case, our sort key would be the field

```
EMPLOYEES[I].NAME
```

To sort by city, the key would be

```
EMPLOYEES[I].ADDRESS.CITY
```

To sort by zip code, the key would be

```
EMPLOYEES[I].ADDRESS.ZIP
```

If the sort is stable, we can get a listing by zip code, with the names in alphabetical order within each zip code, by sorting twice: the first time by name and the second time by zip code. A stable sort preserves the order of the records when there is a match on the key. The second sort, by zip code, will produce many such matches, but the alphabetical order imposed by the first sort will be preserved.

To get a listing by city, with the zip codes in order within each city and the names alphabetically ordered within each zip code, we would sort three times, on the following keys:

```
EMPLOYEES[I].NAME
EMPLOYEES[I].ADDRESS.ZIP
EMPLOYEES[I].ADDRESS.CITY
```

The file would first be put into alphabetical order by name. The output from the first sort would be input to a sort on zip code. The output from this sort would be input to a sort on city name. If the sorting algorithms used were stable, the final sort would give us what we are looking for.

Sorting Pointers

Sorting large records using some kind of exchange sort may require much computer time just to move sections of memory from one place to another every time we make a swap. This move time can be reduced by setting up an array of pointers to the records and then sorting the pointers instead of the actual records. This scheme is illustrated in Figure 11-8.

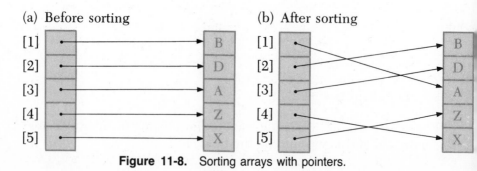

Figure 11-8. Sorting arrays with pointers.

EMPLOYEEDATA		NAMEORD	

<table>
<tr><td>[1]</td><td>15
JONES
20000</td><td>[1]</td><td>3</td></tr>
<tr><td></td><td></td><td>[2]</td><td>4</td></tr>
<tr><td>[2]</td><td>20
SMITH
40000</td><td>[3]</td><td>1</td></tr>
<tr><td></td><td></td><td>[4]</td><td>5</td></tr>
<tr><td>[3]</td><td>34
ABLE
29246</td><td>[5]</td><td>2</td></tr>
</table>

SALORD

EMPLOYEEDATA	SALORD
[4] 100 BAKER 20000	[1] 5
	[2] 1
	[3] 4
[5] 144 OWENS 6000	[4] 3
	[5] 2

Figure 11-9.

Note that, after the sort, the records are still in the same physical arrangement, but they may be accessed in order through the sorted array of pointers.

This scheme may also be extended to allow us to keep a large array of data sorted on more than one key. For instance, with the declarations

```
TYPE EMPLOYEETYPE = RECORD
                    IDNUM : INTEGER;
                    NAME : STRING20;
                    SALARY : INTEGER
                  END; (* record *)

     EMPLOYEES = ARRAY[1..MAX] OF EMPLOYEETYPE;

VAR  EMPLOYEEDATA : EMPLOYEES
```

the data in Figure 11-9 are physically stored according to the primary key, IDNUM. The arrays NAMEORD and SALORD contain pointers (indexes) to the records in the large array, EMPLOYEEDATA. In this way, we can keep the array ordered with respect to the secondary keys, NAME and SALARY, as well.

Summary

We have not attempted in this chapter to give every known sorting algorithm. We have presented a few of the popular sorts, for which many variations exist. It should be clear from this discussion that no single sort is best for all applications. The simpler, generally $O(N^2)$ sorts work as well, and sometimes better, for fairly small files. Since they are simple, they require relatively little programmer time to write and maintain. As you add features to improve these sorts, you also add to the complexity of the algorithms, increasing both the work required by the routines and the programmer time needed to maintain them.

Another consideration in choosing a sort algorithm is the order of the original data. If the data are already ordered (or almost ordered), a simple insertion sort or BUBBLE2 will only be $O(N)$, while some versions of quicksort will be $O(N^2)$.

As always, the first step in choosing an algorithm is to determine the goals of the particular application. This step will usually narrow down the options considerably. After that, knowledge of the strong and weak points of the various algorithms will assist you in making a choice.

Exercises

1. Write the proofs of the loop invariants given for the loops in SELECTSORT (shown in Figure 11-2 and 11-3), using the technique from Chapter 10.

2. Which sorts are $O(N^2)$? Which sorts are $O(N \log_2 N)$?

3. What conditions can make an $O(N^2)$ sort run faster than an $O(N \log_2 N)$ sort?

4. Given the array, DATA, containing the elements

19	23	2	4	99	1

[1]   [2]   [3]   [4]   [5]   [6]

determine which sort produced the results shown below. (*Iteration* refers to the execution of the outer loop.)

(a) 1   2 23 4 99 19 (after 2nd iteration)
(b) 1 19 23 2   4 99 (after 1st iteration)
(c) 2 19 23 4 99   1 (after 2nd iteration)

5. Given the array, DATA, containing the elements

41	56	20	31	59	15

[1]   [2]   [3]   [4]   [5]   [6]

show the contents of the array after each sort below.

(a) INSERTION (after 3rd iteration)
(b) BUBBLE (after 4th iteration)
(c) SELECTION (after 3rd iteration)

6. Sooey County is about to have its annual Big Pig Contest, and since the sheriff's son, Wilbur, is majoring in computer science, the county hires him to computerize the Big Pig judging. Each entry is to be read in the format

PIGNAME (string10)   PIGWEIGHT (integer)
columns 1–10   columns 12–15

The county expects 250 entries this year.

The required output is a listing of the top 10 pigs from biggest to smallest. Since Wilbur has just learned some sorts at school, he feels up to the task of producing the needed output. He writes a program to read all the entries into an array of records, then uses the insertion sort to put the array in order according to the PIGWEIGHT field. Can you think of a better way to write the program?

7. Show how the sorts that we have discussed are affected by the order of the original data in the following cases. (Mark B [best case], W [worst case], or DM [doesn't matter].)

	Data are in completely random order	Data are ordered from lowest to highest	Data are ordered from highest to lowest
INSSORT			
SELECTSORT			
BUBBLE1			
BUBBLE2			
QUICKSORT*			
HEAPSORT			

* Using the first position as a split value.

8. Big State U. needs a listing of the overall SAT percentiles of all the students it has accepted in the past year (13,438 students). The data are in a file that contains the student ID number, SAT overall percentile, math score, English score, and high school GPA, one student to a line. There is at least one blank between each value. The required output is a listing of all the percentile scores, one per line, ordered from highest to lowest. (Duplicates should be printed.) Write a procedure to produce the listing. The procedure should be O(N).

9. Procedure A does a particular task in a "time" of $N^3 + 100$, where N is the number of elements processed. Procedure B does the same task in a time of $3N^2 + N + 500$. What are the Big-O requirements of each task? Which task is more efficient according to its Big-O notation? When does the less efficient procedure (by Big-O standards) execute faster than the more efficient one?

10. Give arguments for and against using procedures to encapsulate frequently used code (like SWAP) within a sorting routine.

11. What is meant by *programmer time* as an efficiency consideration?

Pre-Test

1. Show what the array would look like after the Ith iteration using the given sort. The Ith iteration means that the Ith element is in its proper place.

94	1	27	32	2	7	4	101
[1]	[2]	[3]	[4]	[5]	[6]	[7]	[8]

   (a) bubble sort (2nd iteration)
   (b) insertion (3rd iteration)
   (c) heap (0th iteration, i.e., 1st heap)
   (d) heap (2nd iteration, before reheaping)
   (e) selection (2nd iteration)
   (f) quick (before 1st recursive call) Use [4] as SPLITPOINT.

2. Given the following file and the state of the file at the indicated point, tell what sort is being used.

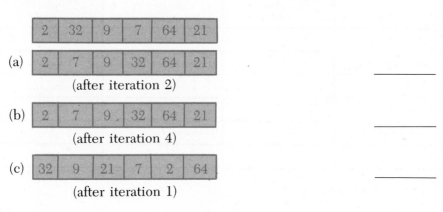

2	32	9	7	64	21

   (a) | 2 | 7 | 9 | 32 | 64 | 21 | _____
   (after iteration 2)

   (b) | 2 | 7 | 9 | 32 | 64 | 21 | _____
   (after iteration 4)

   (c) | 32 | 9 | 21 | 7 | 2 | 64 | _____
   (after iteration 1)

3. Fill in the following table by putting a B (best case) or a W (worst case) in the appropriate column if that original order describes either the best case or the worst case for that sort. For example, if the best case for a selection sort is when the input data are in ascending order, put a B under the *ascending* column beside *selection*. If the order makes no difference, put DM (doesn't matter).

	Ascending	Descending	Random
SELECTION			
INSERTION			
SIMPLE BUBBLE			
BUBBLE W/CUT OFF			
QUICK			

4. You are asked to print a list of the 100 best students in alphabetical order. Since the file of students contains 49,000 records (ordered by Social Security number), it is not feasible to read them all in and sort them. You must devise another strategy. The records are described as follows:

```
TYPE
   STURECORD = RECORD
                  LAST,
                  FIRST : PACKED ARRAY[1..10] OF CHAR;
                  SSNUM : INTEGER;
                  GPA : REAL
               END
```

You may use the following routines without writing the code for them. Just give the *formal* and *actual* parameter lists.

Procedure READDATA, which reads in one student record.

Procedure SORT, which sorts a list, as specified by the parameter list. (If you want this to be a specific sort algorithm, just state which one in comments.)

Searching 12

Goals

To be able to hand-simulate and to encode a sequential search.

To be able to hand-simulate and to encode an ordered sequential search.

To be able to hand-simulate and to encode a binary search.

To be able to define hashing and collisions.

To be able to implement a hashing algorithm.

To be able to implement a collision resolution algorithm.

As we discussed in Chapter 2, for each particular structure used to hold data, the functions that allow access to elements in the structure must be defined. In some cases, access is limited to the elements in particular positions in the structure, like the top element in a stack or the front element in a queue. Generally, however, when data are stored in a list, you can access any element.

Sometimes the retrieval of a certain element can be performed directly. For instance, the fifth element of the list stored sequentially in ARRAY1 is found in ARRAY1[5]. Often you want to access an element according to some *key* value. For instance, if a list contains student records, you may want to find the record of the student named Suzy Brown (the key field is STUDENTNAME) or the record of the student whose ID number is 203557 (the key field is IDNUM). In cases like these, some kind of searching technique is needed to allow retrieval of the desired record.

In the preceding chapters, we have discussed some of the algorithms that allow you to search particular data structures for a given element. In this chapter, we will describe several algorithms for searching lists. We will discuss which representations (sequential array, linked lists, and so forth) are appropriate for each search technique, as well as the efficiency of each method according to the criteria used in Chapter 11 on sorting. As in our discussion of sorting, we will only consider the case of data structures that are stored completely in main memory. The topic of external searching, while important, is outside the scope of this book.

SEQUENTIAL SEARCHING

The simplest search technique is the sequential search. You begin at the head of the list and search for the desired record by examining each subsequent record, until either the search is successful or the list is exhausted. This technique is appropriate for both sequential lists and linked lists. The list does not have to be ordered, although the efficiency of the search may be improved if the list is ordered.

The general algorithm for finding the record containing the key value, KEYVAL, is

---

Start with the first element in the list
WHILE more elements in list AND KEYVAL not found DO
    Get next element in list
IF KEYVAL not found
    THEN return record not found
    ELSE return record

We will code this algorithm for searching an array of records that contain a field called KEY. The records in the array are not necessarily ordered with respect to the KEY field.

```
PROCEDURE SEQFIND1 (LIST : ARRAYTYPE;
                    NUMELEMENTS : INTEGER;
                    KEYVAL : KEYTYPE;
                    VAR LOCATION : INTEGER);
(* This procedure locates the record whose KEY field contains the value *)
(* KEYVAL. The index of the record is returned in LOCATION. If the      *)
(* record is not found, 0 is returned in LOCATION.                      *)

VAR   FOUND : BOOLEAN;
      I : INTEGER;

BEGIN   (* seqfind1 *)
   (* Initialize. *)
   I := 1;
   FOUND := FALSE;

   (* Search until element is found or array exhausted. If element is found, *)
   (* the index I will contain its location.                                 *)
   WHILE NOT FOUND AND (I <= NUMELEMENTS) DO
      IF LIST[I].KEY = KEYVAL
         THEN FOUND := TRUE              (* I is desired index *)
         ELSE I := I + 1;

   (* Set the value of LOCATION. *)
   IF FOUND
      THEN LOCATION := I
      ELSE LOCATION := 0
END;    (* seqfind1 *)
```

Based on the number of comparisons, it should be obvious that this search is $O(N)$, where N is the number of elements. In the worst case, in which we are looking for the last record in the list or for a nonexistent record, we will have to make N comparisons. On the average, assuming that there is an equal probability of searching for any item in the list, we will make N/2 comparisons; that is, on the average we will have to search half the list.

High-Probability Ordering

The assumption of equal probability for every record in the list is not always valid. Sometimes certain list elements are in much greater demand than others. This observation suggests a way to improve the search: Put the most often desired elements at the beginning of the list. For instance, given a command-driven program, you can order the elements in the command table according to the frequency of their use. Using this scheme, you are more likely to make a hit in the first few tries, and rarely will you have to search the whole table.

If the elements in the list are not static as in a command table, or if you cannot predict their relative demand, you need some scheme to keep the most frequently used records at the front of the list. One way to accomplish this goal is to move each record accessed to the front of the list. Of course, there is no guarantee that this record will later be frequently used. However, if the record is not retrieved again, it will drift toward the end of the list, as other records are moved to the front. This scheme is easy to implement for linked lists, requiring only a couple of pointer changes, but it is less desirable for lists kept sequentially in arrays.

A second algorithm, which causes records to move toward the front of the list gradually, is appropriate for either linked or sequential–array list representations. As each element is accessed, it is swapped with the element that precedes it. Over many list retrievals, the most frequently desired elements will tend to be grouped at the front of the list.

Keeping the most active records at the front of the list will not affect the worst case; it will still take N comparisons. However, the average performance should be better. Both of these algorithms depend on the assumption that some elements in the list are used much more often than others. If this assumption is not applicable, a different ordering strategy is needed to improve the efficiency of the search technique.

KEY ORDERING

Ordering a list according to the key value, as discussed in Chapter 11, can greatly improve the efficiency of a searching scheme. In the case of a sequential search, it is no longer necessary to search the whole list to discover that a record does not exist. You only need to search until you have passed its logical place in the list—that is, until you come across a record with a larger key value. If the list is stored in a linked representation, you can add a trailer node with an impossibly large key value (e.g., a NAME field of 'ZZZZZZZZZZ') to ensure that there will always be some value larger than the one for which you are searching.

Procedure SEQFIND2 in the following program searches a linked list implemented with pointer variables for the value KEYVAL. The list contains a trailer node.

```
PROCEDURE SEQFIND2 (LIST : LISTPOINTER;
                    KEYVAL : KEYTYPE;
                    VAR LOCATION : LISTPOINTER);
(* This procedure searches the linked list pointed to by LIST for the *)
(* value KEYVAL. If found, the pointer LOCATION is set to point to *)
(* the node. If not found, LOCATION is set to NIL.              *)

VAR    FOUND : BOOLEAN;

BEGIN   (* seqfind2 *)
  FOUND := FALSE;

    (* Search until element found, or its logical place *)
    (* in the list is passed.                           *)
    WHILE NOT FOUND AND (LIST↑.KEY <= KEYVAL) DO
       IF LIST↑.KEY = KEYVAL
          THEN FOUND := TRUE
          ELSE LIST := LIST↑.NEXT;

    (* Set value of LOCATION. *)
    IF FOUND
       THEN LOCATION := LIST
       ELSE LOCATION := NIL
END;    (* seqfind2 *)
```

The advantage to sequentially searching an ordered list is the ability to stop searching before the list is exhausted if the record does not exist. Again, the search is O(N). The worst case, searching for the largest element, still requires N comparisons. However, the average number of comparisons for a nonexistent record is now N/2, instead of a guaranteed N.

As we are about to see, there are other ways to improve our search time if the list is ordered.

BINARY SEARCHING

The advantage of the sequential search is its simplicity. In the worst case, you will have to make N comparisons, since you only examine one record at a time and you might be searching for the last record in the list. If the list is sorted and stored in an array, however, you can improve the search time to a worst case of $O(\log_2 N)$. Of course, we improve efficiency at the expense of simplicity.

The idea of a binary search is best described recursively.

Examine the middle element in the list
IF the middle element contains the desired key
    THEN stop searching
    ELSE IF the middle element is larger than the desired key
        THEN binary search the first half of the list
        ELSE (* middle element is smaller than the key *)
            binary search the second half of the list

Consider how this algorithm could be used to find the page with the name "Dale" in the phone book. We open the phone book to the middle and see that the names there begin with M. M is larger than D, so we binary search from A to M. We turn to the midpoint and see that the names there begin with G. G is larger than D, so we binary search from A to G. We turn to the middle page, and find that the names there begin with C. C is smaller than D, so we binary search the second half—that is, from C to G. And so on, until we are down to the single page that contains the name "Dale."

Although the recursive description is conceptually simpler, we know that a nonrecursive solution will be more efficient. The Procedure BINARYFIND performs a binary search on array LIST, returning the index of the desired element in LOCATION (or 0 if the element is not found).

```
PROCEDURE BINARYFIND (LIST : ARRAYTYPE;
                      KEYVAL : KEYTYPE;
                      NUMELEMENTS : INTEGER;
                      VAR LOCATION : INTEGER);
```
(* This procedure does a binary search for the record containing KEYVAL. *)
(* If it is found, its index is returned in LOCATION; if not, 0 is returned. *)

```
VAR FOUND : BOOLEAN;
    MIDPOINT,                        (* index of midpoint of search *)
    FIRST,                           (* first index in search area *)
    LAST  : INTEGER;                 (* last index in search area *)

BEGIN   (* binaryfind *)
  (* Initialize. *)
  FOUND := FALSE;
  FIRST := 1;
  LAST := NUMELEMENTS;

  (* Search until element found or there are no more elements. *)
  WHILE (FIRST <= LAST) AND NOT FOUND DO
    BEGIN
      (* Compare middle element in search area to *)
      (* the key value.                           *)
      MIDPOINT := (FIRST + LAST) DIV 2;
```

```
      IF LIST[MIDPOINT] = KEYVAL
          THEN FOUND := TRUE
          ELSE (* Move first and last indexes to cut search area in half. *)
              IF LIST[MIDPOINT] > KEYVAL
                  THEN LAST := MIDPOINT - 1
                  ELSE FIRST := MIDPOINT + 1
      END;    (* while *)

  (* Sets value of LOCATION. *)
  IF FOUND
      THEN LOCATION := MIDPOINT
      ELSE LOCATION := 0
END;     (* binaryfind *)
```

Figure 12-1 (page 458) illustrates how Procedure BINARYFIND is used to locate the record with the key value 25.

Note that each iteration of the loop halves the size of the list left to be searched. In the worst case, we no longer need to look at every element in the list; only $\log_2 N$ elements. This is quite an improvement over the sequential search, especially as the list gets larger. For instance, if the original list contains 1024 records, the sequential search will require 512 comparisons on the average, and 1024 comparisons to retrieve the last record in the list. A binary search of the same list will only require, in the worst case, 10 comparisons.

The binary search, however, is not guaranteed to be faster for searching very small lists. Notice that even though the binary search generally requires fewer comparisons, each comparison requires more computation. When N is very small, the constant of proportionality may dominate. While fewer comparisons are required, each involves more processing. For instance, in one assembly language program, the sequential search required 5 time units per comparison, while the binary search took 35. For a list size of 16 elements, therefore, the worst case sequential search would require 5 * 16 = 80 time units. The worst case binary search would only require 4 comparisons, but at 35 time units each, the comparisons would take 140 time units. In cases where the number of elements in the list is small, a sequential search is certainly adequate and sometimes faster than a binary search.

As the number of elements increases, however, the disparity between the sequential search and the binary search grows very quickly. For instance, given the time unit requirements described above, consider the worst cases for a list of 1024 records. The sequential search would require 1024 comparisons at 5 time units each, for a total of 5120 time units. The binary search would take, at the worst, 10 comparisons at 35 time units each. Thus the total time requirement would be 350—less than 7% of the sequential search time. Figure 12-2 (page 459) illustrates the relative growth of the sequential and binary searches, measured in number of comparisons.

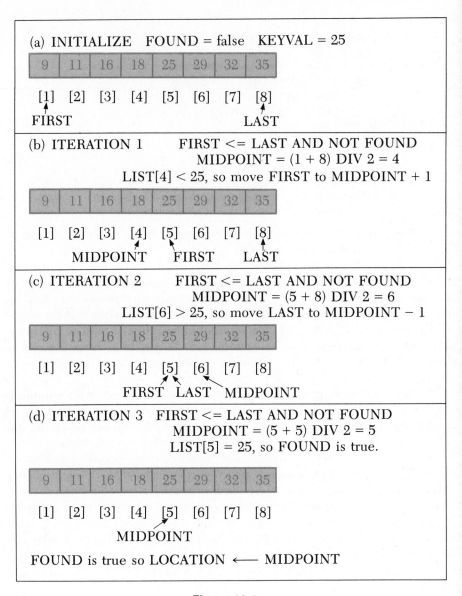

Figure 12-1.

Note that the binary search discussed here is only appropriate for lists stored in a sequential array representation. After all, how can you find the midpoint of a linked list? But you already know of a structure that allows you to perform a binary search on a linked data representation—the binary search tree. The operations used to search a binary tree are discussed in Chapter 8.

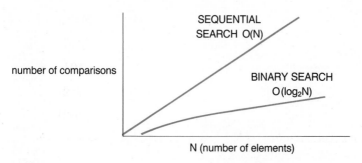

Figure 12-2. Comparison of sequential and binary searches.

HASHING

So far, we have succeeded in paring down our O(N) search to O(log$_2$N) by keeping the list ordered with respect to the value of the key field—that is, the key in the first record is less than (or equal to) the key in the second record, which is less than the key in the third, and so on. Can we do better than that? Is it possible to design a search of O(1)—that is, one that takes the same search time to find any element in the list?

In theory, this is not an impossible dream. Consider a list of employees of a fairly small company. Each of the 100 employees has an ID number in the range 1 to 100. In this case, we can store the records in an array that is indexed from 1 to 100, allowing us direct access to the record of any employee.

In practice, this perfect relationship between the key value and the address of a record is not easy to establish or maintain. Consider a similar company that uses its employees' Social Security numbers (SSN) as the primary key. Now the range of key values is from 000000000 to 999999999. Obviously, it is impractical (impossible) to set up an array of a billion records, of which only one hundred will be needed, just to make sure that each employee's record will be in a perfectly unique and predictable location.

What if we keep the array size down to the size that we actually need (ARRAY[0..99]) and just use the last two digits of the key field to identify each employee? For instance, the record of employee 467353374 will be in EMPLOYEELIST[74], while the record of employee 587421235 will be in EMPLOYEELIST[35]. Note that the records will not be ordered according to the values in the key field, as they were in our earlier discussion; the record of employee 587421235 precedes that of employee 467353374 in this scheme. Instead, the records are ordered with respect to some *function* of the key value.

The function has two uses. First, the result of the function is used as a kind of key on which the list is sorted. That is, the function is used to

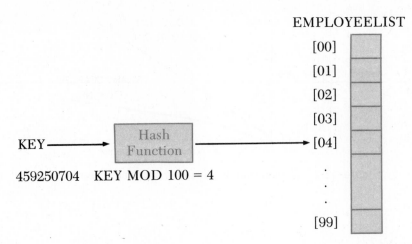

EMPLOYEELIST

KEY ⟶ Hash Function ⟶ [04]

459250704   KEY MOD 100 = 4

Figure 12-3. Using a hash function to determine the location of the element in the array.

determine where in the array to store the record. Second, the function is used as a method of accessing the record.

This function is called a *hash function*. In the case of the employee list above, the hash function is KEY MOD 100. The key (SSN) is divided by 100, and the remainder is used as an index into the array of employee records. This scheme is illustrated in Figure 12-3.

Collisions

By now you are probably objecting to this scheme on the grounds that it does *not* actually guarantee unique addresses. SSN 000001234 and SSN 999991234 both "hash" to the same address: EMPLOYEELIST[34]. The problem of avoiding these *collisions* is the biggest challenge in designing a good hash function. A good hash function minimizes collisions by spreading the records uniformly throughout the table. Note that we say "minimizes collisions," for it is extremely difficult to avoid them completely.

Assuming that there will be some collisions, where do you store the records that produce them? We will briefly describe several popular collision-handling algorithms in the next sections. Note that the scheme that is used to find the place to store a record determines the method of subsequently retrieving it.

Hash and Search

A simple approach to resolving collisions is to store the colliding element in the next available space. In the situation in Figure 12-4, we want to add

EMPLOYEELIST

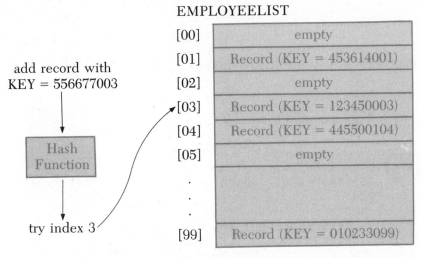

Figure 12-4. Hash and search: the new record will go in the first free space, EMPLOYEELIST[5].

the employee record with key SSN 556677003. This key is hashed into the address (index) 03. But there is already a record stored in this slot in the array. We increment the index and examine the next slot. EMPLOYEELIST[4] is also in use, so we increment the index again. This time we find a slot that is free, so we store the new record in EMPLOYEELIST[5]. (Of course, all of the unused slots have been initialized to a null or dummy key value, so it is easy to tell if the slot is free.) What happens if the key hashes to the last index in the array and that space is in use? We can consider the array as a circular structure and continue looking for an empty slot at the beginning of the array.

Procedure HASHSTORE uses this algorithm to store a new element in a list.

```
PROCEDURE HASHSTORE (VAR LIST : ARRAYTYPE;
                         NEWVALUE : INFOTYPE;
                         VAR PLACEFOUND : BOOLEAN);
(* Uses function HASH to determine the location in which to store the new element   *)
(* NEWVALUE. If the index supplied by the hash function indicates a slot that is not *)
(* available, a sequential search is performed to find the next free slot. If all the slots *)
(* are already filled, PLACEFOUND will return FALSE to the calling program;         *)
(* otherwise, PLACEFOUND will be TRUE, and LIST will contain NEWVALUE in            *)
(* the first free slot. MAXLIST is a global constant indicating the maximum number of *)
(* elements in the array. (The array indexes run from 0 to MAXLIST − 1.)            *)
(* DUMMYVAL is a global constant indicating a dummy value to which all empty         *)
(* slots in the list were initialized.                                              *)

VAR    STARTPLACE,          (* starting location returned from HASH function *)
       TRYPLACE   : INDEXTYPE;
```

```
BEGIN   (* hashstore *)
   (* HASH is a function that returns the result of *)
   (* a hash function applied to NEWVALUE.      *)
   STARTPLACE := HASH(NEWVALUE);

   (* Initialize for search. *)
   TRYPLACE := STARTPLACE;
   PLACEFOUND := FALSE;

   (* Search for place to insert NEWVALUE. *)
   REPEAT
     IF LIST[TRYPLACE] = DUMMYVAL
        THEN (* place found *)
           BEGIN
              LIST[TRYPLACE] := NEWVALUE;
              PLACEFOUND     := TRUE;
           END
        ELSE (* try next place *)
           TRYPLACE := (TRYPLACE + 1) MOD MAXLIST
   UNTIL PLACEFOUND OR (TRYPLACE = STARTPLACE)

END;    (* hashstore *)
```

To search for a record using this collision-handling technique, we perform the hash function on the key, then compare the desired key to the actual key in the record at the designated location. If the keys do not match, we do a sequential search, beginning at the next slot in the array. Try writing PROCEDURE HASHFIND (LIST, ELEMENT, FOUND) as an exercise.

Rehashing

Another common technique for resolving collisions is rehashing. If the first computation of the hash function produces a collision, you use the hash address as the input to the rehash function and compute a new address. For instance, if our original hash function is KEY MOD 100, we may use the rehash function (KEY + 1) MOD 100 to produce a new address. (This particular choice is, in effect, hash and search.) Our original address (Figure 12-4), 556677003, produces the address 03, which is already in use. So we apply the rehash function, using the first hash address as input: (03 + 1) MOD 100 = 04. This address, EMPLOYEELIST[4], is also in use, so we reapply the rehash function until we get an available slot. Each time, we use the address computed from the previous rehash as input (KEY) to the rehash function.

In fact, you can use any function (KEY + <constant>) MOD <number of slots>, as long as <constant> and <number of slots> are relatively prime—that is, not evenly divisible by any integer except 1. These functions will produce successive rehashes that will eventually cover every index in the array.

To access a record, use the hashing function to get an index into the array. Compare the key of the record in this location to the desired key. If it is not a match, rehash and compare again. Continue this cycle until you find the desired record.

Chaining

A third technique for handling collisions uses the hash address not as the actual location of the record, but as the index into an array of pointers called *buckets*. Each bucket consists of a *chain* of records that share the same hash address. Figure 12-5 illustrates this solution to the situation discussed in the previous section. Rather than searching the array or rehashing, we simply allow both records to share hash address 03. The entry in the array at this location contains a pointer to a chain that includes both records.

To search for a given record, first apply the hash function to the key, then search the chain for the bucket indicated by the hash address. Note that you have not eliminated searching, but you have limited the search to records that actually share a hash address. Using the first hash and search technique we discussed, you may have to search through many additional records if the slots following the hash address are filled with records from collisions on other addresses.

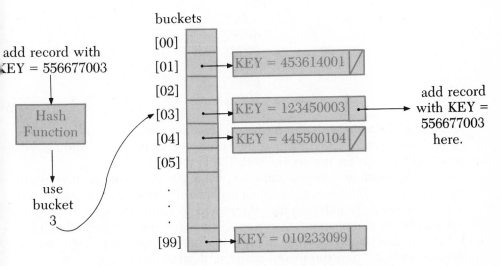

Figure 12-5. Hashing with buckets for handling collisions.

HASH-ADDRESS = KEY MOD 100

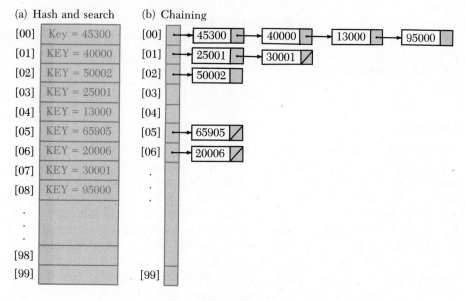

Figure 12-6.

Figure 12-6 illustrates a comparison of the two schemes. The records were added in the following order:

45300
20006
50002
40000
25001
13000
65905
30001
95000

Figure 12-6(a) represents the hash and search approach to collision handling, while Figure 12-6(b) shows the result of chaining the colliding records. Let's search for the record with the key 30001.

Using the hash and search approach, we apply the hash function to get the index 1. LIST[1] does not contain the record with the key 30001, so we search sequentially until we find the record in LIST[7].

Using the chaining approach, we apply the hash function to get the index 1. LIST[1] directs us to a chain of records whose keys hash to 1. We search this list until we find the record with the desired key.

Choosing a Good Hash Function

One way to minimize collisions is to use a data structure that has more space than is actually needed for the number of records, in order to increase the range of the hash function. For instance, if you keep the employee records in an array with twice as many slots as employees, you should only have half as many collisions. In practice, it is desirable to have the array size somewhat larger than the number of records requires (though not double) to reduce the number of collisions.

More importantly, you can design your hash function to minimize collisions. The goal is to distribute the records as uniformly as possible throughout the array. Therefore, you want your hash function to produce unique addresses as often as possible. Once you admit collisions, you must introduce some sort of searching, either through array or chain searching or through rehashing. The access to each record is no longer direct, and the search is no longer O(1). In fact, if the collisions cause very disproportionate chains, the worst case may be almost O(N)!

To avoid such a situation, you need to know something about the distribution of keys. Imagine a company whose employee records each have a company ID six digits long. There are 500 employees, and we decide on a chained approach to handling collisions. We set up 100 buckets (planning on an average of five records per bucket chained together) and use the hash function:

```
HASHADDRESS := ID MOD 100;
```

That is, we will use the last two digits of the six-digit ID as our bucket index. The planned hash scheme is shown in Figure 12-7(a).

Figure 12-7(b) shows the result after the hash scheme was implemented. What happened? How could the distribution of the records have come out so skewed? It turns out that the company's ID number is a concatenation of three fields:

X X X	X	X X
3 digits	1 digit	2 digits
unique number	department number	year hired
(000–999)	(0–9)	(e.g., 81)

Our hash scheme depended solely on the year hired to produce unique addresses. Since the company was founded in 1981, all the records were crowded very disproportionately into a small subset of the hash addresses. A search for an employee record, in this case, is O(N). Although this is an exaggerated example, it illustrates the need to understand as completely as possible what are the domain and predicted values of keys in a hash scheme.

(a)

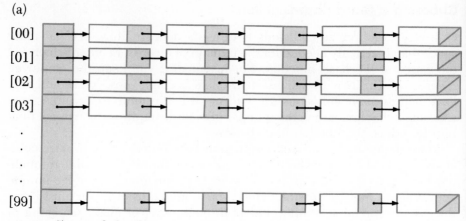

average 5 records/bucket
5 records × 100 buckets = 500 employees

expected search—O(5)

(b)

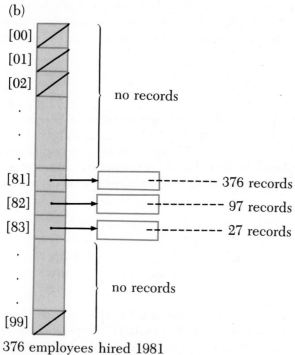

376 employees hired 1981
 97 employees hired 1982
 27 employees hired 1983
500 employees

real search—almost O(N)

Figure 12-7.

Division Method

The most common hash functions use the division method (MOD) to compute hash addresses. This is the type of function used in the preceding examples. The general function is

```
HASHADDRESS := KEY MOD TABLESIZE
```

(or HASHADDRESS := KEY MOD TABLESIZE + 1 to index the table beginning at 1, rather than 0). We have already mentioned the idea of making the table somewhat larger than the number of records requires, in order to increase the range of hash addresses. In addition, it has been found that better results are produced with the division method when the table size is prime.

The advantage of the division hash function is simplicity. However, sometimes it is necessary to use a more complicated (or even exotic) hash function to get a good distribution of hash addresses.

Other Hash Methods

A hash method called *folding* breaks the key into several pieces and concatenates or "exclusive OR"s some of them to form the hash address. Another method squares the key and then uses some of the digits (or bits) of the key as a hash address. There are a number of other techniques, all of which are intended to make the hash address as unique and random (within the allowed range) as possible.

For instance, suppose we want to devise a hash function that will result in an index between 0 and 255, and the internal representation of the key is a string of 32 bits. We know that it takes 8 bits to represent the 256 index values ($2^8 = 256$). A folding algorithm to create a hash function might

1. break the key into 4 strings of 8 bits each,
2. exclusive OR the first and last bit strings,
3. exclusive OR the two middle bit strings,
4. and finally, exclusive OR the results of Steps 2 and 3 to produce the 8-bit index into the array.

This scheme is illustrated using the key 618403. The binary representation of this key is 00000000000010010110111110100011. We break this bit string into 4 8-bit strings:

$$00000000 \text{ (leftmost 8 bits)}$$
$$00001001 \text{ (next 8 bits)}$$
$$01101111 \text{ (next 8 bits)}$$
$$10100011 \text{ (rightmost 8 bits)}$$

The next step is to exclusive OR the first and last bit strings. (The exclusive OR of two bits is 0 if the two bits are the same, and 1 if they are different. To exclusive OR—XOR—bit strings, we apply this rule to successive pairs of bits.)

$$
\begin{array}{r}
00000000 \\
\text{(XOR)}\ 10100011 \\
\hline
10100011
\end{array}
$$

Then we exclusive OR the middle 2-bit strings:

$$
\begin{array}{r}
00001001 \\
\text{(XOR)}\ 01101111 \\
\hline
01100110
\end{array}
$$

Finally, we exclusive OR the results of the preceding two steps:

$$
\begin{array}{r}
10100011 \\
\text{(XOR)}\ 01100110 \\
\hline
11000101
\end{array}
$$

This binary number is equivalent to the decimal number 197. So the key 618403 hashes into the index 197.

The relationship between the key and the index is not intuitively obvious, but the indexes produced are likely to be randomly distributed through the range of possible values.

When using an exotic hash function, you should keep two considerations in mind. First, the efficiency of calculating the function should be considered. Even if a hash function always produces unique addresses, it is not a good hash function if it takes longer to calculate the address than to search half the list. Second, an extremely exotic function that somehow produces unique addresses for all the known key values may fail if the domain of possible key values changes in a later modification. The programmer who has to modify the program may then waste a lot of time trying to find another hash function that is just as clever (and that may not exist). Programmer time should be considered.

Summary

Searching, like sorting, is a topic that is closely tied to the goal of efficiency. We speak of a sequential search as an O(N) search, since it may require up to N comparisons to locate an element. (N refers to the number of records in the list.) Binary searches are considered $O(\log_2 N)$ and are appropriate only for arrays. A binary search tree may be used to allow binary searches on a linked structure. The goal of hashing is to produce a search that approaches O(1). Because of collisions of hash addresses, some searching or rehashing is usually necessary. A good hash function minimizes collisions and distributes the records randomly throughout the table.

For programmers, it is usually more interesting to create a new procedure to solve some problem than to review someone else's solution. Why then have we devoted the past two chapters to a discussion of well-known sorting and searching algorithms? First, it is important to be familiar with several of the basic sorting and searching techniques. These are tools that you will use over and over again in a programming environment, and you will need to know which ones are appropriate solutions to different problems. Second, a review of sorting and searching techniques has supplied us with an opportunity to examine another tool—a measuring tool that helps us determine how much work is required by a particular algorithm. Both building and measuring tools are needed to construct sound program solutions.

Exercises

1. Fill in the following table, showing the number of comparisons necessary to either find a value in the array DATA or determine that the value is not in the array.

DATA

26	42	96	101	102	162	197	201	243
[1]	[2]	[3]	[4]	[5]	[6]	[7]	[8]	[9]

KEYVAL   NUMBER OF COMPARISONS

KEYVAL	Sequential Ordered Search	Sequential Unordered Search	Binary Search
26			
2			
96			
98			
103			
243			
244			

2. The following values are to be stored in a hash table.

$$25, 42, 96, 101, 102, 162, 197, 201$$

Use the division method of hashing with a table size of 11. Use the sequential method of resolving collisions.

3. Rewrite your solution to Problem 2 using rehashing as the method of collision resolution. Use (KEY + 3) MOD TABLESIZE as the rehash function.

4. Complete the following procedure using the given specifications.

```
PROCEDURE MOVE1 (VAR DATA : ARRAYTYPE; (* array to be searched *)
                 NUMEL,                  (* number of elements *)
                 KEYVAL : INTEGER;       (* value searched for *)
                 VAR FOUND : BOOLEAN);   (* TRUE if KEYVAL *)
                                         (* in DATA *)
(* Array DATA is searched for KEYVAL. If found, FOUND is set to    *)
(* TRUE and KEYVAL is put into DATA[1]. Other values in DATA are   *)
(* shifted down appropriately. Otherwise FOUND is FALSE.           *)
```

5. Write the search routine, Procedure HASHFIND, that finds an element that was stored by Procedure HASHSTORE described in this chapter.

Pre-Test

1. Fill in the following table, showing the number of comparisons necessary to either find a value in the array DATA or determine that the value is not in the array.

DATA

6	32	86	91	202	262	397	501	843
[1]	[2]	[3]	[4]	[5]	[6]	[7]	[8]	[9]

KEYVAL NUMBER OF COMPARISONS

KEYVAL	Sequential Ordered Search	Sequential Unordered Search	Binary Search
5			
6			
96			
202			
261			
843			
944			

2. The following values are to be stored in a hash table.

25, 42, 96, 101, 102, 162, 197

Use the division method of hashing with a table size of 7. Use the sequential method of resolving collisions.

3. Rewrite your solution to Problem 2 using chaining as the method of collision resolution.

4. Complete the following procedure using the given specifications.

```
PROCEDURE MOVE2 (VAR DATA : ARRAYTYPE; (* array to be searched *)
                 NUMEL,                        (* number of elements *)
                 KEYVAL : INTEGER;                 (* value searched for *)
                 VAR INDEX : INDEXRANGE);    (* index where *)
                                          (* KEYVAL is found, else 0 *)
(* Array DATA is searched for KEYVAL. If found, DATA[INDEX] *)
(* is swapped with DATA[INDEX - 1], else INDEX is set to 0.    *)
```

Welcome to the Real World

13

Goals

To be able to trace some of the stages in the life cycle of a software project.

To be able to describe two kinds of situations that lead to program modification.

To be able to discuss four goals for a good program.

To be able to describe software-engineering principles that relate to attaining these goals.

To be able to construct a schedule for completing a programming assignment on time.

To be able to name and describe a technique used in this book for designing a program through multiple levels of abstraction.

To be able to explain what is meant by data encapsulation and why it is an important principle of software engineering.

To be able to show how Pascal cannot enforce data encapsulation, and to name a language that can.

To be able to show how a programmer can effect data encapsulation in a Pascal program.

To be able to describe several guidelines for choosing an appropriate data structure.

We have said that, over the life cycle of a computer program, the largest effort is expended not in its design or coding, but in its maintenance after the coding is finished. To understand this assertion, you must look past your immediate student programming experience into the real-world programming environment. In the university, you typically write a program of some several hundred lines of source code, debug it, run it on a few test cases, and then leave it. In this situation, your greatest effort is spent on the design and coding of the program. Understanding the code is clearly not a problem, since it was written by one person over a short interval of time; maintaining it is usually unnecessary, since programming assignments are generally discrete activities.

In your professional computing career, you will probably engage in a wide variety of activities in addition to coding. In fact, the act of coding is one of the least time consuming (and least creative) aspects of program development and maintenance. Unlike your student program, which usually ceases to have a function after it is delivered to your professor, the professionally produced program really *begins* its active life at the time of delivery to the customer. Thus program maintenance is a significant part of the program's life cycle.

THE ACME AUTOMATION COMPANY (A FICTION)

The idea that a product needs to be maintained over the course of its life cycle is more obvious in the realm of hardware. Take, for instance, the case of the Acme Automation Company and its automatic cookie-making machine. The New Business Department had the original idea: Bakeries would be interested in buying a machine that automated the mixing, cutting, baking, and bagging of their cookies. The idea was passed to the New Product Development Department, which made up a detailed description of the proposed machine. The department determined, for instance, that the machine should have a set of digital controls to determine how much of each ingredient should be added, as well as a dial for controlling how long the cookies should bake. The department also decided that the machine should have interchangeable cookie cutters. Finally, New Product Development determined that the whole process should produce 10 dozen cookies per minute.

The specifications were passed to a group of engineers in the Product Design Department. The engineers designed a machine and built a prototype for testing. When they had a working design, the Factory Division began building the automated cookie-making machines. Sales were good, and soon several hundred of the machines were in use in bakeries.

But the story does not end here. Over time, some of the machines needed servicing, and the company had to send out field engineers to repair them. In addition, modifications to the original design were found to be necessary. First, after a period of use in bakeries, it was found that, in practice, the machines did not actually meet their advertised claim of producing 10 dozen cookies a minute. The engineers were brought back in to evaluate the problem and discovered a design flaw that made certain parts of the machine wear down quickly, eroding the production rates. This problem was solved with some clever redesign work; the machines were modified accordingly, and the customers were happy. Second, after several important customers had expressed a desire for an enhanced cookie-making machine, the Acme Automation Company had its engineers make additional modifications to the original design. The new machine made 25 dozen cookies a minute, allowed a greater range of packaging options (boxes as well as bags), and required fewer operators.

Note that modifications to the design were prompted by two situations: first, when the design did not meet its specifications, and second, when the specifications changed.

THE SOFTWARE SITUATION

Obviously in the production of a piece of hardware, the actual building of the item in the factory is but one step in the product's total life cycle. Similarly, the production of a computer program involves a great deal more than just writing code. Computer programs are developed for a wide variety of applications and customers, from word-processing programs that will be reproduced many times for commercial distribution to massive programs developed for the exclusive use of a single customer (the software to control a spacecraft, for example). However, the general activities of software production are common to different applications.

First, from the concept stage, a set of detailed specifications is determined. On a large project, the specifications are often not created by the programmers, but by a separate group that acts as an intermediary between the customer and the programmers. These specifications are used by software designers (programmers) as a sort of contract that delineates what is expected from the resulting program. If the specification says, "The program shall support Function A," then the final program must do so. The relationship of a program to its specifications is already familiar to you as a student: If the programming assignment from your professor stipulates that the output data should be listed in sorted order, your grade on the assignment will reflect, in part, whether or not your program correctly sorts the data.

The development from specifications to deliverable product is therefore the part of the software life cycle most familiar to the student programmer. You get the specifications from your professor; you deliver a listing of the completed program some short time later. We have spent most of this book discussing strategies for the design and implementation of computer programs.

Aside from a limited number of test runs, most student programs are never used; their life cycle ends upon delivery. In a professional environment, however, the development from conception to delivery is analogous to the development of a baby before its birth. It is only after birth that a baby truly begins living its life. And, just as the mother's role does not end with the birth of her child, the software professional's role extends beyond the delivery of the program. This extended role is what we referred to as program maintenance.

To get a feel for what is involved in the next step—program maintenance—go back to your first program of the semester and change some aspect of the specifications. Now try to implement the resulting changes in your program. Do you remember all the details of the program's original design? Can you read and make sense of your own program several months later? Will a minor change (e.g., an increase in the size of a table or the addition of a new command to be processed) require massive changes throughout the program, or are the modifications localized to a small portion of the program?

We saw that there were two sources of modifications to the Acme cookie-making machine: correction of design errors when the design did not meet the specifications, and redesign when the specifications changed. Software requires modifications for exactly the same reasons.

For instance, users of commercially developed word-processing software occasionally find that the software does not perform as indicated in the manual. Once in a while, some bugs escape even rigorous testing and only show up when the user attempts something that the testers never tried. For example, as we prepared this manuscript on a commercial word-processing program, we discovered a bug in the text-printing function. According to the manual, the printing process may be paused in the middle and resumed either in place or at the beginning of the text. However, when we tried to restart the printing from the beginning, we found that the program confused the paging of the text; it started printing in the middle of the page and ran off the end. This is an example of a program not meeting its specifications: The program does not correctly support a stated function.

The company that produced the word processor should assign programmers to correct the printing function of the program. Of course, the programmers who originally wrote this section of the program may no longer work at the company or may now be busy with other assignments. In either case, the program would need to be modified by other programmers. It is important, therefore, that the original program be written clearly and be well documented, using the elements of good style discussed in Chapter 1.

Now let us consider an example of program modifications introduced when changes are made to the specifications. The specifications of one system provide for certain data to be archived (a copy of the data written to tape for safekeeping) upon the command of the operator. To meet this specification, an archival function is designed and implemented. It is tested, found to work correctly, and delivered as part of the system. One customer using the system needs to archive crucial data every half hour. It is clearly risky, as well as inconvenient, to leave this responsibility to the operator, who, after all, is only human. So the customer asks the company that designed the system to modify it to support automatic archival as a function of the computer's internal clock. Note that there is nothing wrong with the original system, according to its specifications. The customer, in this case, wants to change the specifications to support an additional function.

For the managers of the software project, it is important to differentiate between the sources of program modifications, since this factor determines who pays for the change. An error in the software will require correction at no charge to the customers, while subsequent changes in the specifications by the customers will generally involve extra charges. From the programmer's perspective, however, the source of the modification does not usually matter. For the maintenance programmer, the more important issue is whether the original program is clearly written and easily modifiable. A small change that requires the modification of ten lines of a program may take an hour to correct if the programmer can easily understand the program. The same change may take the programmer ten times as long if the program is hard to read or full of tricky code.

SOFTWARE ENGINEERING

The term *programming* emphasizes the act of writing a program for a computer to execute—the generation of code in a computer language. As programmers, you know that this act also includes the design phase that precedes coding and the testing and maintenance phases that follow it. But the stress of the term *programming* is on the act of coding.

The term *software engineering* may more adequately reflect the set of activities that control a program through its whole life cycle. As we said in Chapter 1, the development of computer programs requires more than artistry, especially as the size and complexity of software products skyrocket.

> **SOFTWARE ENGINEERING**
>
> A disciplined approach to the design and maintenance of computer programs, utilizing tools that help one to manage the size and complexity of the resulting software products.

You cannot depend on artistry or wizardry to control the design, implementation, testing, and maintenance of a program a million lines long that involves the efforts of 200 programmers. You need the application of serious tools, including design methodologies (like top-down design), principles of program and data abstraction and a way to implement them, modern programming languages that enforce abstraction and information hiding, verification techniques, and so on. Smaller projects as well benefit from the use of a disciplined approach to development. We have emphasized several of the basic principles of software engineering in this book. Let's restate the goals for good programs, and we will then review the principles that can help you attain them.

THE GOALS FOR GOOD PROGRAMS

In Chapter 1, we stated several goals for a good program:

(a) *A good program works.* A good program correctly incorporates all its specifications; that is, it does everything it is supposed to. Further, a good program should be reliable, since the cost of software failure may range from customer disgruntlement and the monetary expense of correction to the danger of loss of life and property. Another word for this reliability factor is the program's *robustness*. In addition to being complete and reliable, a program that works uses the computer's resources efficiently, according to the needs and specifications of the program. Generally, this means efficient use of computing time or memory space or both, although you usually have to trade off one for the other.

(b) *A good program can be read and understood.* Imagine yourself as a newly hired junior programmer on a large project. You will be responsible for maintaining some section of the program, and must become familiar with its design and code. You hope that it is clearly written and well documented. If it isn't, your new job may be more frustrating than challenging.

Many software companies have programming standards that relate to matters ranging from the formatting of the code to the allowable choice of variable identifiers to documentation requirements. A program that is functionally correct (that works) may still be unacceptable if it does not meet these standards. Sometimes customers (the military, for instance) have their own set of standards. Such standardization is used to make programs more consistent, readable, and understandable.

(c) *A good program can be modified, if necessary, without excruciating effort.* The ability to control and limit the repercussions of changes in programs is a primary goal, given the fact that maintenance is the greatest part of the software life cycle.

(d) *A good program is completed on time and within its budget.* Budget may refer to the expected size of the program (e.g., 5000 lines of source code), as well as the financial cost of its development.

THE PRINCIPLES OF CREATING GOOD PROGRAMS

Progress Management

Let us first discuss how to achieve the last goal. You know what happens in school when you turn your program in late. You have probably grieved over an otherwise perfect program that was given only half credit because you turned it in one day late. "But the computer was down five hours last night!" you protest.

Although the consequences of tardiness may seem arbitrary in the academic world, they are significant in the business world. First, time is money. This assertion sounds trite, but it is usually true. A company budgets a certain amount of time and money to the development of a piece of software. As a programmer, you are paid a salary or an hourly wage. If, when the deadline passes, your part of the project is only 80% complete, the company must pay you—or another programmer—to finish it. The extra expenditure in salary is not the only cost, however. Other workers may be waiting for your part of the project to integrate it into the system for testing. If the program is part of a contract with a customer, there may be monetary penalties for missing deadlines. If the program is being developed for commercial sales, the company may lose money when another firm puts a similar product on the market first. If you were managing a software project, would you reward programmers who consistently finished their work long after their deadlines passed?

Thus you must learn to schedule your work. Software development must be paced. Most programmers complain that the hardware is unreliable. This is not true: You can *always* count on the computer to go down for five hours on the last day before your deadline. The problem is to avoid being the victim of this situation; the solution is to make a schedule of milestones in your progress and stick to it. Given a deadline to deliver a program, work backwards and set goals for completing the various milestones. Let's look at an example: On October 5, you are given an assignment that must be completed and turned in three weeks later on October 26. Since October 26 is a Monday and since you don't like to spend weekends working, schedule your completion date as Friday, October 23. This leaves you room to over-run your own schedule without missing the assignment's deadline. Given this new completion date, you can make up the following schedule of milestones:

Oct. 5   Assignment received. THINK.

Oct. 7   Specifications completely understood. Get answers to any questions about requirements, input, output, etc.

Oct. 9   Level 0 of top-down design completed.

Oct. 15 All levels of top-down design completed. (Save for external documentation.) All data structures determined.

Oct. 18 Coding completed.

Oct. 19 Code clean compiled. (All syntax errors out.) Begin testing.

Oct. 22 Testing completed. Make sure that program meets all standards for delivery, and that external and internal documentation are complete.

Oct. 23 Program ready for delivery.

If you schedule your progress from the start, you will avoid being surprised on the night before the program is due when the hardware fails. Your schedule will also give you a greater appreciation for the relative time requirements of the various programming activities.

Abstraction and Information Hiding

Throughout this book we have discussed the desirability of the abstraction of program and data design. With multiple levels of abstraction, the programmer sees only the details that are relevant at a particular level of the design. In addition, we stated that information hiding makes certain details inaccessible to the programmer at higher levels. Why is this desirable? Shouldn't the programmer know everything?

No. This is one situation in which a certain amount of ignorance is advantageous. As designer of a utility function, for instance, you don't want the high-level application programmers to have any special knowledge that allows them to violate the logical abstraction of the design. Information hiding prevents the high levels of the design from becoming dependent on low-level design details that are more likely to be changed. Further, you don't want to require a complete understanding of the complicated details of low-level routines for the design of higher ones. This would introduce a much greater risk of errors spreading throughout the whole program.

Implementing Abstraction in Program Design   The concept of information hiding is implemented in algorithm development through modular, top-down design techniques. The implementation of the Pascal procedure READ, for instance, is completely invisible to the user of the procedure. When the program says READ(REALNUMBER), this procedure somehow gets the characters that represent a real number from the input stream (a file or a keyboard), converts the characters to the representation of a real number for this particular machine, and stores that value in REAL-NUMBER. Even this very high-level explanation of the procedure is inconsequential to the programmer who uses Procedure READ. What is important for the user is the knowledge that READ will assign a value of the appropriate type to the designated variable. If the internal logic of this standard procedure changes, it will be transparent to the application that calls it. This information is hidden from the calling program.

The top-down design technique encourages the incorporation of information hiding into the application by separating the program's function into clear-cut levels of abstraction. Once you have stated the function of a low-level procedure and its interface specifications—the calling sequence and any assumptions—you should be able to forget *how* the low-level module accomplishes this function. The details are hidden at the higher levels.

Implementing Abstraction in Data Design   Abstraction and information hiding are implemented in the data design through *data encapsulation.* By emphasizing the development of a set of utility procedures and functions for each data structure that we described in this book, we have tried to show how the implementation of the structure may be encapsulated from the user applications. The user doesn't need to know how the structure is represented in memory; he or she only needs to be aware of a set of logical functions that operate on the structure.

The Abstract Integer   The idea of using a data type without knowing how it is physically represented is not new to you. You have, for instance, been using integers since your first program. The integer is a *primitive* type; that is, it needs no further definition for program use. But what is an integer? There is no single implementation of even this low-level data type. It may be represented in the memory of one machine as a binary-coded decimal, on a second as a sign and magnitude binary, and on a third computer in one's-complement or two's-complement notation. All this time you've probably been using integers without even knowing what any of these terms mean.

Does the representation make any difference? Of course it does! The implementation of all the operations on integers is directly dependent on their machine representation. As Pascal programmers, you don't usually get involved in matters at this level; you simply *use* integers. You know how to define an integer variable in the syntax of the source language, and you know what operations are allowed on integers: addition, subtraction, multiplication, division, and modulo. In fact, in a sense, the expression

$$X + Y$$

can be considered analogous to the subprogram call

```
ADDINT(X, Y)
```

where the operator, +, has been defined in the lowest level of data abstraction. All you need to know is how to use the operator: + is an infix binary operator that takes two integer-type operands. You also know that there is another + that is used in an identical way (binary infix) with operands of type REAL. What is invisible to the users is the fact that the REAL + is actually implemented in a completely different way.

In fact, both + operators are usually implemented in the machine's hardware. How they work is transparent to the programmer. It would be intolerable if, every time you wanted to add two numbers, you had to get down to the machine-representation level. Your code would be completely weighted down with low-level detail and very prone to error. Furthermore, if you wanted to use the program on a different machine, you would have to change every use of the + operator to fit the new representation of numbers. Your program would not be portable.

Clearly, then, the bit level of data representation needs to be hidden from the programmer. So we draw a "black box" around the type that has been defined (e.g., INTEGER). On the outside of the black box is the name of the type and a list of its operations. Inside the black box are the details of the representation of the data element and the implementation of the operations on it. The user can only see the outside of the box.

Figure 13-1 shows how a black box for type INTEGER might look to the Pascal user.

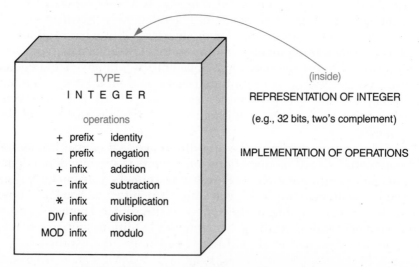

Figure 13-1. Black box representing an integer.

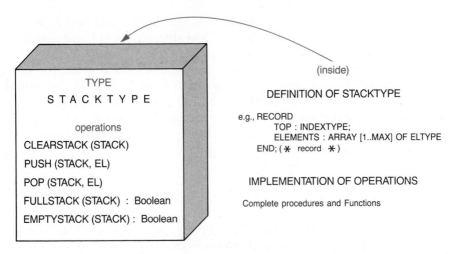

Figure 13-2. Black box representing a stack.

In fact, this idea can be carried further, generating a hierarchy of data elements in black boxes, with bits at the lowest level (we won't even consider how bits are implemented) and other data types built on top. We have already discussed how primitive types like INTEGER and REAL are created. In Chapter 2, we discussed how the built-in aggregate types (arrays and records) add another level of data abstraction. In the chapters on stacks, queues, linked lists, and trees, we have carried the idea even further.

The goal in this concept is *to reduce complexity through abstraction*. Drawing a black box around high-level data structures indicates that they can be used without consideration of their representation. Figure 13-2 illustrates such a black box for a stack.

The Problem of Enforcement   Hiding data elements in a black box is another way to describe data encapsulation. Simply put, data encapsulation permits programmers to use a data object by *naming* it (e.g., STACKTYPE) without knowledge of its implementation. The data are accessed through the operations interfaces [for instance, PUSH(STACK, X)] and *only* through these interfaces.

Unfortunately, in Pascal it is difficult to enforce this rule. We define a stack and its operations. We agree to access the data in the stack only through the operations PUSH and POP. But we cannot really keep someone from writing

```
X := STACK.ELEMENTS[5]
```

in the main program. Though we have conceptually encapsulated the stack's data and provided the interface to access it properly, we have no way to enforce the use of the interface. Accessing the data in the middle of a stack completely denies its whole logical abstraction, but will not cause a compile-time or a run-time error.

A truly abstract data type can be manipulated *only* through the operations defined for it. The user is unaware of its implementation. As such, the abstract data type can only be simulated in Pascal, since there is no way to enforce the prohibition against direct access of the implementation. The ability to create enforceably abstract data types has been included in the design of the programming language Ada.

Ada   In the early 1970s, the U.S. Department of Defense (DoD) experienced a significant increase in its computer systems expense, even though hardware costs were greatly decreasing. It was determined that software technology (or its lack) was responsible for much of this increasing cost, and great effort was expended to develop solutions to the problem. One solution was the decision to select a single language in which to implement the numerous DoD projects. At that time, more than 500 different high-level and assembly languages were in use in DoD systems. A number of these languages were considered, including Pascal, and it was determined that none of them met the criteria that DoD had established. Therefore, an international design competition took place.

The details of this competition are, to say the least, very colorful; eventually, the designs from four contractors were picked as semifinalists, and were nicknamed Blue, Yellow, Red, and Green. It is interesting that all four of these competing groups based their designs on the Pascal language. In the end, the Green language, designed by Honeywell/Honeywell Bull, was selected as the winner of the design competition. The resulting language was renamed *Ada*, in honor of Augusta Ada Byron, Countess of Lovelace. Ada Lovelace, the daughter of the poet Lord Byron, was a mathematician who worked with Charles Babbage on his computing machines in the mid–nineteenth century. She had suggested how Babbage's machines might be programmed to do different tasks and for this reason is considered by some to be the world's first programmer. (She was not, however, the world's first software engineer.)

One of the things the Ada programming language does that Pascal does not do is enforce data encapsulation. The Ada *package* enforces data encapsulation by letting the programmer put a black box around the data type definitions. The package is split into two parts: the *package specification* that gives the interface (the outside of the black box), and the *package body* that contains the hidden implementation (the contents of the black box).

You can declare a stack using an Ada package and then allow use of the stack only through the interface in the package specification. An example of an Ada package specification is shown below.

```
package STACKPACK is

  --STACKPACK encapsulates the representation and
  --implementation of a stack of integer elements.

  type STACKTYPE is private;

procedure PUSH (STACK : in out STACKTYPE;
                X      : in      INTEGER);
  --Adds X to the top of the stack.
  --Assumes that the stack is not full.

procedure POP (STACK : in out STACKTYPE;
               X      :     out INTEGER);
  --Removes the top element from the stack
  --and returns it in X.
  --Assumes that the stack is not empty.

procedure CLEARSTACK (STACK : in out STACKTYPE);
  --Sets the stack to its empty state.

function EMPTYSTACK (STACK : in STACKTYPE)
  return BOOLEAN;
  --Returns true if the stack is empty;
  --false otherwise.

function FULLSTACK (STACK : in STACKTYPE)
  return BOOLEAN;
  --Returns true if the stack is full;
  --false otherwise.

private
  MAXSTACK : constant INTEGER := 100;
  type STACKTYPE is
      record
        TOP      : INTEGER range 0..MAXSTACK;
        ELEMENTS : array(1..MAXSTACK) of INTEGER;
      end record;

end STACKPACK;
```

Note first of all that, because of its Pascal base, the Ada syntax seems very familiar and is readable to a Pascal programmer who has no Ada training. The double dashes (--) precede a comment, and there is the unfamiliar use of the words *is*, *in*, and *out*, but on the whole, the package specification is understandable.

The package specification, which is available to the stack user, gives the interface to each of the stack utilities. However, the declaration of STACK-TYPE itself is in a special section called the *private* part. This section of the specification, unlike the procedure and function declarations that precede it, is not visible to the stack user. That is, this private information about the stack's implementation cannot be used in programs that use the stack package. Why was it necessary to put this information in the specification at all? The information is included in the specification, even though it is not visible to the user, because the type STACKTYPE is used in the interfaces to the procedures and functions. If a type is completely internal to the package, it may be declared within the package body instead of the specification, in which case it will be invisible to the package user.

The private declaration of STACKTYPE is visible, of course, to the package body associated with this package specification. The package body for STACKPACK is shown below.

```
package body STACKPACK is

  --Contains the implementation of the utility
  --procedures and functions that operate on a
  --stack of integer elements.

  procedure PUSH (STACK : in out STACKTYPE);
                  X      : in       INTEGER) is
    --Adds X to the top of the stack.
    --Assumes that the stack is not full.

  begin
    STACK.TOP := STACK.TOP + 1;
    STACK.ELEMENTS(STACK.TOP) := X;
  end PUSH;


  .
  .            --code for the other procedures and functions
  .            --goes here.

  function FULLSTACK (STACK : in STACKTYPE)
     return BOOLEAN is
     --Returns true if the stack is full;
     --false otherwise.
  begin
     return STACK.TOP = MAXSTACK;
  end FULLSTACK;

end STACKPACK;
```

The implementation of the stack utilities is in the package body, which may even be compiled separately from the package specification. The package body, combined with the private part of the specification, is analogous to the inside of the black box, the part that is hidden from the stack user. This enforces the encapsulation of the data; the language will not permit a user of package STACKPACK to reference the implementation of the stack.

How does an application use the package? One way is to preface all the calls to its subprograms with the package name. For instance, to push NUM onto STACK1, you would write

```
STACKPACK.PUSH(STACK1, NUM);
```

A simpler way to use the stack routines is to tell the calling program that you want to use this package. This is accomplished through the *use* clause:

```
use STACKPACK;

begin
   .
   .
   PUSH(STACK1, NUM);
   .
   .
end;
```

Either way, the user has access only to the visible part of the package specification, which contains the interfaces to the stack routines.

Effecting Data Abstraction in Pascal How can you make Pascal programs enforce abstract data types? One way is to make programs look more like pseudo-code. You can, for example, code a low-level procedure to insert an element in a linked list that has been implemented with Pascal pointer variables. This procedure may include references to PTR ↑ .INFO and PTR ↑ .NEXT. The procedure that calls this insertion routine is a higher-level subprogram, and shouldn't include the details of the list implementation. Instead of using such statements as

```
IF PTR↑.INFO > VALUE2
   THEN INSERT(PTR)
```

you could say

```
IF INFO(PTR) > VALUE2
   THEN INSERT(PTR)
```

Note that INFO(PTR) is the notation that we used in our pseudo-code to describe the data field of the node pointed to by the designated pointer. Now, in the higher-level procedure, it doesn't matter how the list is implemented. What is INFO(PTR)? It looks like a function call, and in fact INFO is simply a lowest-level subprogram that gives a real value to the logical one.

```
FUNCTION INFO (P : PTRTYPE) : INFOTYPE;
   (* Sets INFO to the INFO field of NODE(P). *)

BEGIN  (* info *)
   INFO := P↑.INFO
END;  (* info *)
```

If the implementation of the linked list is changed to an array of records, the change could be contained in this low-level function, rather than affecting every list access. The modified Function INFO would be

```
FUNCTION INFO (P : PTRTYPE) : INFOTYPE;
   (* Sets INFO to the INFO field of NODE(P). *)

BEGIN    (* info *)
   INFO := NODES[P].INFO
END;     (* info *)
```

The higher-level procedures that access list items still reference INFO(PTR), since the implementation change is transparent at that level. Similarly, NEXT and BACK pointer fields may be accessed through such accessing functions. We discussed in Chapter 2 how the set of accessing functions defines a data structure.

Such a scheme seems very inefficient because of the tremendous overhead of procedure and function calls. In fact, a greater degree of data encapsulation will likely be somewhat inversely related to the (time) efficiency of the program. As always, the identification of the goals of the program is paramount. Does the program require fast execution above all, or is ease of maintenance and modification a primary need? In most cases, ease of maintenance and modification will be more important, which means data encapsulation is the appropriate choice.

FULFILLING OUR GOALS

How are our good-program goals met by this strategy of abstraction, information hiding, and data encapsulation? When details are hidden at each level, the code becomes simpler and more readable. This makes the program easier to maintain. The top-down design process also produces modular units that are easier to test, debug, and maintain.

One side effect of modular design is that modifications tend to be *localized* in a small set of modules. This reduces the cost of modifications. Remember that whenever a module is modified, it must be retested to make sure that it still works correctly in the program. By localizing the modules affected by changes to the program, we limit the extent of this *regression testing*.

REGRESSION TESTING

Reexecuting tests of programs after modifications have been made to ensure that the programs still work correctly.

Finally, reliability is increased by making the design conform to the logical picture and by limiting error-causing details to lower levels of the program.

CHOOSING A DATA STRUCTURE

You are given a problem that requires you to get and store some input data, process the data, and print out or save the results. How do you know what conceptual structure is appropriate for the data? Where do you begin? One place to start is suggested by the question "How would you do it by hand?" The answer to this question can lead you to first drafts (top levels) of both the problem solution and the data structures.

The choice of data structures is just as important as the choice of algorithms. In fact, you need a knowledge of the algorithms to be applied to the data in order to make a wise choice of data structures. Conversely, the choice of good algorithms requires knowledge of the data structures used. One of the advantages of a top-down design approach over flowcharting is that the data structures for the program can be developed in an analogous fashion and are integral to the design. Flowcharting tends to be more preoccupied with the flow of control, and there is less emphasis on the data that are retained through the program.

Throughout this book, we have discussed the basic logical operations that you would expect to apply to each data structure. The advantages and disadvantages of different data organizations and implementations should be considered with respect to the operations required by the current problem. For instance, one of the disadvantages of using linked lists instead of simple sequential lists in an array is the limitation to a sequential search; however, if the current program requires many insertions at the beginning of the list, this disadvantage is irrelevant. If you decide to use a linked representation of a list, you must decide whether it should be linear or circular, singly or doubly linked. Double links are more expensive (an extra pointer field to be set), but if the program requires many deletions from the list, it may be worth the expense. Should the linked list be implemented in an array of records or in dynamically allocated nodes with pointer variables (assuming that the source language has pointer variables)? For this decision you may take into consideration whether or not you can predict how many records will be needed. If you cannot, an array may be either risky (estimate too small) or wasteful (estimate too large).

We will not attempt to answer the question "Which data structure?" in this chapter; the answer depends on the factors to be considered for each specific problem. We hope that you are now aware of many of the design considerations involved in using each structure, as discussed in the previous chapters. Here we will list as guidelines a few criteria for making a choice:

> The data structure should reflect the requirements of the operations to be performed on the data.

If one of the built-in data types (e.g., the primitive types, array, or record in Pascal) fits the problem solution, it should be used.

If not, the data structure designed should mirror the conceptual picture of the data. Think about how you would solve the problem by hand.

The implementation should be deferred to lower-level subprograms, transparent to the application part of the program. This makes the code more easily readable, as well as modifiable.

If efficiency is a major consideration, the choice of data structure and implementation should reflect the source of the limiting factor. Limited memory may require a less complicated data structure—for example, fewer link fields in a linked list. Stringent time requirements, on the other hand, may call for data structures that are more complicated (take more space) to speed the algorithm. Usually, time and space requirements cannot both be completely satisfied. In many cases, however, programmer efficiency may be the limiting factor, requiring the data structure to support the simplification of the program design.

Finally, resist the temptation to over-design. In student programs, it is tempting to want to use everything at once. If the program really only requires a simple linear linked list, don't use a doubly linked list, with headers and trailers for good measure. That clearly wastes space, time, and your efforts. Always design your data structures, as well as your algorithms, to reflect the specifications of the program.

Summary

In this chapter, we have tried to bring together the many ideas presented throughout this book. The tools we have discussed have varied greatly, from style and formatting considerations to data structures to techniques for using recursion and for sorting and searching. We hope that the presentation has stressed that these are all pieces of a larger, growing body of knowledge that programmers—software engineers—share. The judicious use of these tools leads to a goal that we all share as well: the production of high-quality computer software.

Appendixes*

APPENDIX A RESERVED WORDS

AND	END	MOD	REPEAT
ARRAY	FILE	NIL	SET
BEGIN	FOR	NOT	THEN
CASE	FORWARD	OF	TO
CONST	FUNCTION	OR	TYPE
DIV	GOTO	PACKED	UNTIL
DO	IF	PROCEDURE	VAR
DOWNTO	IN	PROGRAM	WHILE
ELSE	LABEL	RECORD	WITH

(EXTERN, FORTRAN, GLOBAL, LOCAL, OTHERWISE, VALUE and others may be reserved words in some implementations.)

---

* Some of these Appendixes are taken from *Introduction to Pascal and Structured Design,* by Nell Dale and David Orshalick. Copyright © 1983.

APPENDIX B STANDARD IDENTIFIERS

Standard Constants

FALSE   TRUE   MAXINT

Standard Types

INTEGER   BOOLEAN   REAL   CHAR   TEXT

Standard Files

INPUT   OUTPUT

Standard Functions

	Parameter type	Result type	Returns
ABS(X)	INTEGER or REAL	Same as parameter	Absolute value of X
ARCTAN(X)	INTEGER or REAL	REAL	Arctangent of X in radians
CHR(X)	INTEGER	CHAR	Character whose ordinal number is X
COS(X)	INTEGER or REAL	REAL	Cosine of X (X is in radians)
EOF(F)	FILE	BOOLEAN	End-of-file test of F
EOLN(F)	FILE	BOOLEAN	End-of-line test of F
EXP(X)	REAL or INTEGER	REAL	e to the X power
LN(X)	REAL or INTEGER	REAL	Natural logarithm of X
ODD(X)	INTEGER	BOOLEAN	Odd test of X
ORD(X)	Ordinal (scalar except REAL)	INTEGER	Ordinal number of X
PRED(X)	Ordinal (scalar except REAL)	Same as parameter	Unique predecessor of X (except when X is the first value)
ROUND(X)	REAL	INTEGER	X rounded
SIN(X)	REAL or INTEGER	REAL	Sine of X (X is in radians)
SQR(X)	REAL or INTEGER	Same as parameter	Square of X
SQRT(X)	REAL or INTEGER	REAL	Square root of X
SUCC(X)	Ordinal (scalar except REAL)	Same as parameter	Unique successor of X (except when X is the last value)
TRUNC(X)	REAL	INTEGER	X truncated

Standard Procedures

	Description
DISPOSE(P)	Destroys the dynamic variable referenced by pointer P by returning it to the available space list.
GET(F)	Advances the current position of file F to the next component and assigns the value of the component to F ↑.
NEW(P)	Creates a variable of the type referenced by pointer P, and stores a pointer to the new variable in P.
PACK(U, I, P)	Copies the elements beginning at subscript position I of array U into packed array P beginning at the first subscript position of P.
PAGE(F)	Advances the printer to the top of a new page before printing the next line of text file F.
PUT(F)	Appends the value of the buffer variable F ↑ to the file F.
READ(F,variable list)	Reads data values from text file F (if F is not specified, default is INPUT) and assigns these values to the variable(s) in the variable list in order until the list is satisfied.
READLN(F,variable list)	Same as READ except advances the file pointer past the end-of-line after satisfying its variable list.
RESET(F)	Resets file F to its beginning for reading.
REWRITE(F)	Resets file F to its beginning for writing; old contents of F are lost.
UNPACK(P, U, I)	Copies the elements beginning at the first subscript position of packed array P into array U beginning at subscript position I.
WRITE(F,parameter list)	Writes the data in the order specified in the parameter list to text file F (if F is not specified, default is OUTPUT).
WRITELN(F,parameter list)	Same as WRITE except generates an end-of-file after satisfying its parameter list.

(Some compilers provide additional types, files, functions and/or procedures. Check the manual for your specific implementation to see what is available.)

APPENDIX C PASCAL OPERATORS AND SYMBOLS

+		plus or set union
−		minus or set difference
*		times or set intersection
/		divide
DIV		integer divide
MOD		remainder from integer divide (modulus)
<		is less than
<=		is less than or equal to
=		is equal to
<>		is not equal to
>=		is greater than or equal to
>		is greater than
AND		Boolean conjunction
OR		Boolean inclusive disjunction
NOT		Boolean negation
IN		test set membership
:=		becomes
,		separates items in a list
;		separates statements
:		separates variable name and type; separates case label and statement; separates statement label and statement
'		delimits character and string literals
.		decimal point, record selector and program terminator
..		subrange specifier
↑	@	file and pointer variable indicator
(		starts parameter list or nested expression
)		ends parameter list or nested expression
[	(.	starts subscript list or set expression
(*	{	starts a comment
*)	}	ends a comment
]	.)	ends subscript list or set expression

APPENDIX D PRECEDENCE OF OPERATORS

NOTE: 1. Parentheses can be used to change the order of precedence.
2. When operators of equal precedence are used, they are executed in left to right order.

NOT	Highest precedence
* / DIV MOD AND	
+ − OR	
< <= = >= > <> IN	Lowest precedence

APPENDIX E SYNTAX DIAGRAMS

PROGRAM

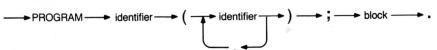

IDENTIFIER

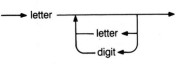

BLOCK

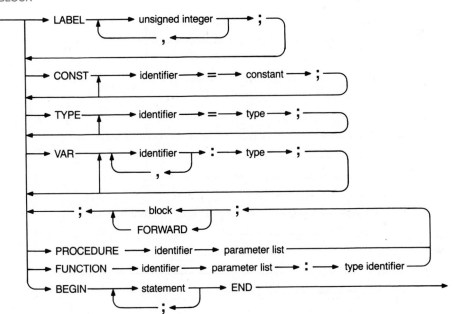

CONSTANT

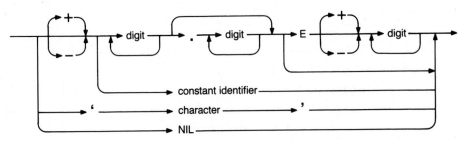

TYPE

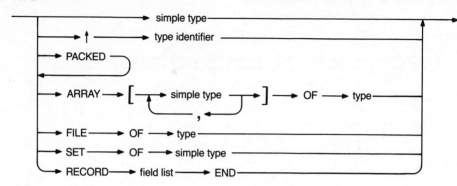

SIMPLE TYPE

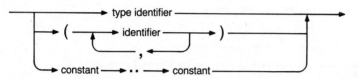

FIELD LIST

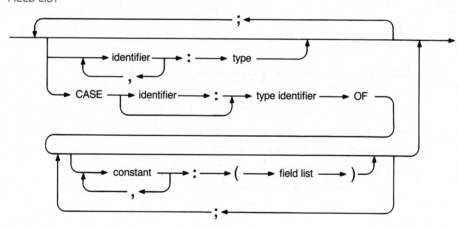

PARAMETER LIST

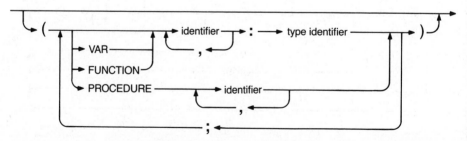

STATEMENT

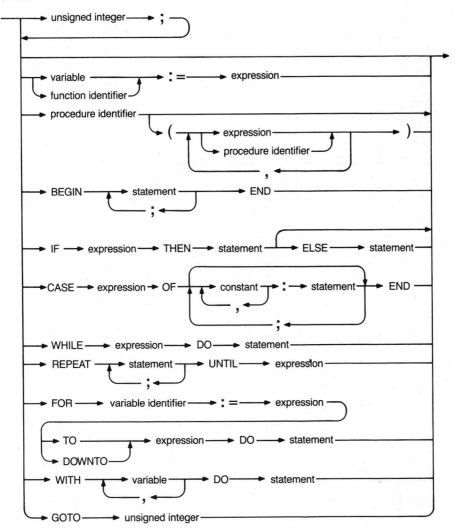

VARIABLE

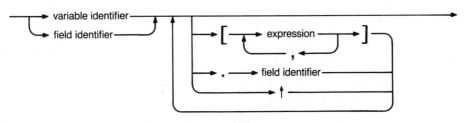

EXPRESSION

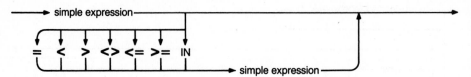

SIMPLE EXPRESSION

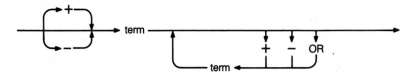

TERM

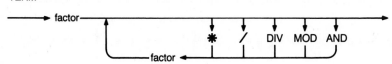

FACTOR

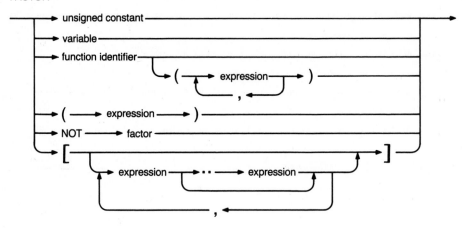

APPENDIX F PROGRAM FORMATTING*

These suggestions will lead to more readable programs.

1. Each statement must begin on a separate line.
2. Each line shall be less than or equal to 72 characters.
3. At least one space must appear before and after ':=' and '='. At least one space must appear after ':'.
4. At least one blank line (or other recognizable dividing line) must appear before PROCEDURE and FUNCTION declarations.
5. PROGRAM, PROCEDURE, and FUNCTION headings must begin at the left margin. However, nested procedures and functions should be indented according to the level of nesting.
6. The keywords REPEAT, BEGIN and END must stand on a line by themselves.
7. The main BEGIN-END block for programs, procedures and functions shall be lined up with the corresponding heading.
8. Each statement within a BEGIN-END, REPEAT-UNTIL or CASE statement must be aligned. The bodies of CONST, TYPE and VAR declarations and BEGIN-END, FOR, REPEAT, WHILE, CASE and WITH statements must be indented from the corresponding header keywords. Be consistent with indenting.
9. An IF-THEN-ELSE statement must be displayed as:

```
        IF expression
          THEN statement
          ELSE statement
```

Of course <statement> can be a compound statement:

```
        IF expression
          THEN
                BEGIN
                    statements
                END
          ELSE
                BEGIN
                    statements
                END
```

An exception is allowed for multiple nesting (generalized case statement):

```
        IF expression THEN
            statement
        ELSE IF expression THEN
            statement
                    .
                    .
                    .
        ELSE
            statement
```

---

* Reprinted with permission of Hayden Book Company from *Pascal With Style: Programming Proverbs*, by Henry F. Ledgard, Paul A. Nagin, and John F. Huares. Copyright © 1978.

APPENDIX G ADDITIONAL FEATURES OF PASCAL

Standard Pascal has some additional features not usually covered in a first course. The syntax diagrams in APPENDIX E describe the complete Pascal language and show some of these additional features.

For the sake of completeness, the additional features which we have used in this text are described in this appendix. They include another structuring option for records (variant records), the use of functions and procedures as parameters, and a mechanism for forward referencing procedures and functions.

Variant Records

Within a record type, there may be some fields which are mutually exclusive. That is, fields A and B may never be in use at the same time. Instead of declaring a record variable large enough to contain all the possible fields, you can use the variant record provided in Pascal.

The variant record has two parts: the fixed part where the fields are always the same and the variant part where the fields will vary. Since only a portion of the variant fields are in use at any one time, they may share space in memory. The compiler need allocate only enough space for the record variable to include the largest variant.

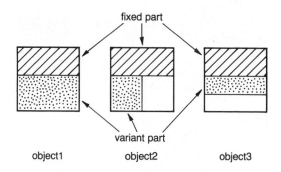

object1   object2   object3

If a record has both a fixed part and a variant part, the fixed part must be defined first. The following is an example of a record definition that contains a variant part.

```
TYPE ITEM = (ASSEMBLY, NUT, BOLT, WASHER, LOCK);

     PARTTYPE = RECORD
               ID  : PACKED ARRAY[1..10] OF CHAR;
               QTY : INTEGER;
               TAG : ITEM;
               CASE ITEM OF
                  ASSEMBLY : (DRAWINGID : PACKED ARRAY
                                            [1..5] OF CHAR;
```

```
        CODE : 1..12;
        CLASS : (A, B, C, D) );

   NUT, BOLT, WASHER : ();

     LOCK : (KEYNO : INTEGER)
END;    (* record *)
```

```
VAR PART : PARTTYPE;
```

When using a variant record variable, the user is responsible for accessing fields that are consistent with the TAG field. For example, if the TAG field is NUT, BOLT, or WASHER, only the fixed fields can be accessed. If the TAG field is LOCK, PART.KEYNO is a legal field reference. If the TAG field is ASSEMBLY, PART.DRAWINGID, PART.CODE, and PART.CLASS are all legal references.

Several points should be made about defining and using variant records. We will use the above definition to illustrate.

1. A record definition may contain only one variant part, although field lists in the variant part may contain a variant part (nested variant).

2. All field identifiers within a record definition must be unique.

3. The tag field (TAG) is a separate field of a record (if present).

4. The tag field is used to indicate the variant used in a record variable.

5. The case clause in the variant part is not the same as a CASE statement.
   (a) There is no matching END for the CASE; the END of the record definition is used.
   (b) The case selector is a type (ITEM).
   (c) Each variant is a field list labeled by a case label list. Each label is a constant of the tag type (ITEM).
   (d) The field lists are in parentheses.
   (e) The field lists define the fields and field types of that variant.

6. The tag type can be any ordinal type, but it must be a type identifier.

7. Several labels can be used for the same variant (NUT, BOLT, WASHER).

8. A field list can be empty, which is denoted by "()".

9. The variant to be used is assigned at run-time. The variant can be changed by assignments to other variant fields and the tag field. When a variant is used, data (if any) in a previous variant is lost.

10. The tag field does not appear in the field selectors for the variant fields.

11. It is an error to access a field that is not part of the current variant.

The case clause in the variant part of the record definition is often matched by a CASE statement in the body of the program. For example, the following program fragment could be used to print data about a record.

```
WRITELN('PART ID - ', PART.ID);
WRITELN('QTY - ', PART.QTY:1);
CASE TAG OF
   ASSEMBLY : WRITELN('ASSEMBLY : ', PART.DRAWINGID);
   NUT      : WRITELN('NUT');
   BOLT     : WRITELN('BOLT');
   WASHER   : WRITELN('WASHER')
   LOCK     : WRITELN('LOCK, KEY ATTACHED')
END;  (* CASE *)
```

Functions and Procedures as Parameters

In addition to variable and value parameters, Pascal allows procedures and functions to be passed as parameters. That is, the actual parameter is a procedure or function identifier. The only restriction is that procedures and functions used as parameters may only have value parameters themselves.

This is a syntax diagram for a formal parameter list:

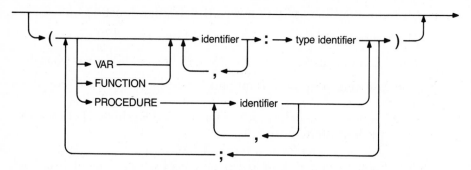

As an example, suppose we need a procedure that will find the minimum and maximum values of various functions within a specified range. The functions can be passed as a parameter to the procedure which can check the function's value at specified intervals.

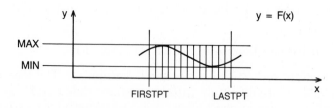

The following procedure will evaluate the function F at intervals between FIRSTPT and LASTPT and return the minimum and maximum values in MIN and MAX.

```
PROCEDURE MINMAX (FUNCTION F : REAL;              (* function name *)
                        FIRSTPT,                  (* first point to evaluate *)
                        LASTPT,                   (* last point to evaluate *)
                        INTERVAL : REAL;          (* interval between points *)
                                                  (* to be evaluated *)
                    VAR MIN,                  (* minimum value returned by F *)
                        MAX : REAL;           (* maximum value returned by F *)

VAR   RESULT,                                 (* value returned from function F *)
      EVALPT : REAL;                          (* point to be evaluated *)

BEGIN
    (* initialize MIN and MAX to first function value *)
    MIN := F(FIRSTPT);
    MAX := MIN;
    EVALPT := FIRSTPT + INTERVAL;

    WHILE EVALPT <= LASTPT DO
      BEGIN
        RESULT := F(EVALPT);              (* evaluate function F at EVALPT *)
        IF RESULT < MIN
            THEN MIN := RESULT;
        IF RESULT > MAX
            THEN MAX := RESULT;
        EVALPT := EVALPT + INTERVAL
      END
END;
```

The procedure calls the function specified for F in the call to MINMAX.
For example, the calls

```
MINMAX (SIN, 0.5, 0.9, 0.01, MIN, MAX);
MINMAX (RESPONSE, A, B, T, MIN, MAX);
MINMAX (POLY, D1, D2, S, MIN, MAX)
```

are all valid calls to the procedure if RESPONSE and POLY are declared
real functions, with one real formal parameter each (must be a value parameter). The other actual parameters must be real—all parameters must match
in type.

The call to function F within MINMAX would substitute the function
specified in the call to MINMAX. For example,

```
RESULT := F(EVALPT)
```

within MINMAX would be evaluated as

```
RESULT := RESPONSE(EVALPT)
```

if RESPONSE was specified in the call to MINMAX.

The syntax diagram and the following example adhere to the Jensen and
Wirth standard. However, several popular implementations require that
the entire procedure or function heading be repeated in the formal parame-

ter list. The implementation that was used to test the mailing label program was one of these. On page 235, Function XCOMPARE is defined in the formal parameter list of Procedure INSERT. On pages 237 and 238, Procedure INSERT is called with Function COMNAME or Function COMZIP as actual parameters.

Forward Statement

Identifiers in Pascal must be defined before being used (the type identifier in the pointer type definition is an exception). Recursion was defined as a procedure or function calling itself. There are recursive situations where one procedure or function calls another which in turn calls the first. This is called mutual recursion.

```
.
.
(*******************************************************)
PROCEDURE ONE (VAR A : ATYPE);
BEGIN
   .
   .
   TWO(X);
   .
   .
END;
(*******************************************************)
PROCEDURE TWO (VAR B : BTYPE);
BEGIN
   .
   .
   ONE(Y);
   .
   .
END;
(*******************************************************)
.
.
.
```

In the above example, the call to procedure TWO in the body of procedure ONE is not allowed because procedure TWO has not yet been defined. The solution to this problem is to make a forward reference to procedure TWO by using the FORWARD statement.

```
.
.
(*******************************************************)
PROCEDURE TWO (VAR B : BTYPE);
FORWARD;
(*******************************************************)
PROCEDURE ONE (VAR A : ATYPE);
```

```
BEGIN
    .
    .
    TWO(X);
    .
    .
END;
(*******************************************************)
PROCEDURE TWO;
BEGIN
    .
    .
    ONE(Y);
    .
    .
END;
(*******************************************************)
    .
    .
    .
```

Notice that the parameter list (and the result type for a function) is written in the forward reference; it is *not* repeated in the actual declaration of the procedure (or function). The compiler "remembers" the parameter declarations when it encounters the actual procedure.

APPENDIX H CHARACTER SETS

The following charts show the ordering of the most common character sets: ASCII (American Standard Code for Information Interchange), EBCDIC (Extended Binary Coded Decimal Interchange Code) and CDC Scientific. Only printable characters are shown. The ordinal number for each character is shown in decimal. The blank character is denoted by a "□".

Left Digit(s) \ Right Digit	ASCII									
	0	1	2	3	4	5	6	7	8	9
3			□	!	"	#	$	%	&	'
4	(	)	*	+	,	−	.	/	0	1
5	2	3	4	5	6	7	8	9	:	;
6	<	=	>	?	@	A	B	C	D	E
7	F	G	H	I	J	K	L	M	N	O
8	P	Q	R	S	T	U	V	W	X	Y
9	Z	[	\	]	∧	−	`	a	b	c
10	d	e	f	g	h	i	j	k	l	m
11	n	o	p	q	r	s	t	u	v	w
12	x	y	z	{			}	-			

Codes 00-31 and 127 are nonprintable control characters.

Left Digit(s)	Right Digit	EBCDIC								
---	0	1	2	3	4	5	6	7	8	9
6					□					
7					¢	.	<	(	+	|
8	&									
9	!	$	*	)	;	¬	–	/		
10							^	,	%	—
11	>	?								
12			:	#	@	'	=	"		a
13	b	c	d	e	f	g	h	i		
14						j	k	l	m	n
15	o	p	q	r						
16			s	t	u	v	w	x	y	z
17								\	{	}
18	[	]								
19				A	B	C	D	E	F	G
20	H	I								J
21	K	L	M	N	O	P	Q	R		
22							S	T	U	V
23	W	X	Y	Z						
24	0	1	2	3	4	5	6	7	8	9

Codes 00-63 and 250-255 are nonprintable control characters.

Left Digit(s)	Right Digit	CDC								
---	0	1	2	3	4	5	6	7	8	9
0		:	A	B	C	D	E	F	G	H	I
1		J	K	L	M	N	O	P	Q	R	S
2		T	U	V	W	X	Y	Z	0	1	2
3		3	4	5	6	7	8	9	+	−	*
4		/	(	)	$	=	□	,	.	≡	[
5		]	%	≠	↦	∨	∧	↑	↓	<	>
6		⩽	⩾	¬	;						

APPENDIX I SETS

SET

A structured data type composed of a collection of distinct elements (members) chosen from the values of the base type.

```
TYPE LETTERSET = SET OF 'A'..'Z';
VAR VOWELS, CONSONANTS : LETTERSET;
```

To declare a set type you use the following syntax:

SET OF base type

The type LETTERSET in the example above describes a set type in which the base type is the letters of the alphabet. The statement

```
VAR VOWELS, CONSONANTS : LETTERSET;
```

actually creates two set variables of this type. VOWELS and CONSO-NANTS are undefined (like all variables) until you initialize them in your program. Be careful; each is a structure that can contain none, one, or a combination of alphabetic characters. The set variables do not start out with the letters in them.

To put elements into a set, you must use an assignment statement.

```
VOWELS := ['A', 'E', 'I', 'O', 'U']
```

puts the elements 'A', 'E', 'I', 'O', 'U' into the set variable VOWELS. Notice that []s are used here, not ()s.

You cannot access the individual elements of a set, but you can ask if a particular element is a member of a set variable. You can also do the standard set operations: union, intersection, and difference.

- \+ (Union): the union of two set variables is a set made up of those elements that are in either or both.
- * (Intersection): the intersection of two set variables is a set made up of those elements occurring in both set variables.
- − (Difference): the difference between two set variables is a set made up of the elements that are in the first set variable but not in the second.

The relational operators (=, <>, > = , < = , <, >) can all be applied to sets. In addition, there is a test for set membership.

Expression	Returns TRUE if
SET1 = SET2	SET1 and SET2 are identical
SET1 <> SET2	there is at least one element in SET1 not in SET2 or there is at least one element in SET2 not in Set 1
SET1 <= SET2	all the elements in SET1 are in SET2
SET1 < SET2	all the elements in SET1 are in SET2 and there is at least one element in SET2 not in SET1
SET1 >= SET2	all the elements in SET2 are in SET1
SET1 > SET2	all the elements in SET2 are in SET1 and there is at least one element in SET1 not in SET2
element IN SET1	element is a member of SET1

Since IN is a new operator, let's look at it a little more closely. The statement

```
IF CH IN ['A', 'E', 'I', 'O', 'U']
    THEN ...
```

is equivalent to the statement

```
IF (CH='A') OR (CH='E') OR (CH='I') OR (CH='O') OR (CH='U')
    THEN ...
```

We could also have used the statement

```
IF CH IN VOWELS
    THEN ...
```

if VOWELS had been initialized to ['A', 'E', 'I', 'O', 'U']. Testing for set membership is a much faster operation than evaluating a long expression in an IF statement, and it certainly is easier to read.

Ordering has no meaning in sets. The assignment

```
VOWELS := ['A', 'E', 'I', 'O', 'U']
```

is the same as

```
VOWELS := ['E', 'O', 'A', 'U', 'I']
```

so it doesn't matter how you list values within the set brackets.

We've used subranges to assign values to sets. As usual, the second value must be greater than the first. For example,

```
LET1 := ['C'..'A']
```

actually makes LET1 the empty set. This is what we wanted:

```
LET1 := ['A'..'C']
```

Since ordering has no meaning, we could have

```
LET1 := ['P'..'T', 'A'..'C', 'Z', 'K'..'M']
```

although it makes better sense to list the values in a more readable order.

Just like variables of other types, you need to initialize the value of a set variable before you manipulate it. If you want a set to be empty before adding elements to it, the assignment to the empty set,

```
LET1 := []
```

should be used.

APPENDIX J FILES

> **FILE**
>
> A data structure consisting of a sequence of components all of the same type.

The definition of a file does not limit the type of the file components. You can have files of any type, simple or structured.* Only INPUT and OUTPUT are predeclared as file variables (of type TEXT). All other file variables must be declared in the program. The following declarations are all valid.

```
TYPE STRING = PACKED ARRAY[1..40] OF CHAR;
     PART = RECORD
                DESCR : STRING;
                ID : INTEGER;
                COST : REAL
            END;   (* record *)
     NAME = ARRAY[1..20] OF CHAR;

VAR INFILE, OUTFILE : TEXT;
    MAIL : FILE OF NAME;
    WORDS : FILE OF STRING;
    INVTRY : FILE OF PART;
    LETTER : NAME;
    WORD : STRING;
    APART : PART;
```

Notice that INFILE is a text file, MAIL is a file of arrays, WORDS is a file of strings, and INVTRY is a file of records. Also declared are variables of the component types in order to manipulate a component of each file.

File Buffers

You have access to only one component of a file at any one time. Whenever you declare a file variable, you automatically create another variable known as the file buffer variable. The buffer variable is denoted by the file name followed by an up-arrow (↑). For example, the buffer variable for file INFILE is written as

```
INFILE↑
```

---

*A file of files is not generally allowed. There may also be restrictions on the use of files as elements of other structured types.

This buffer variable is the "window" through which you can either inspect (read) or append (write) file components.

Whenever you do a READ or WRITE operation, you are actually manipulating the file buffer variable. In Figure J-1(a) the character 'F' was read last. The buffer variable, INFILE↑, contains the next component to be read—in this case the character 'G'. The statement

```
READ(INFILE, CH)
```

actually assigns the value in INFILE↑ to CH, and INFILE↑ gets the next component in the file. [See Figure J-1(b).] INFILE↑ now contains a blank because it is accessing the <eoln> marker and the <eoln> character is stored as a blank. EOLN is currently TRUE. The statement

```
READLN(INFILE)
```

would move the window to the component past the <eoln> marker, and EOLN would be FALSE. [See Figure J-1(c).]

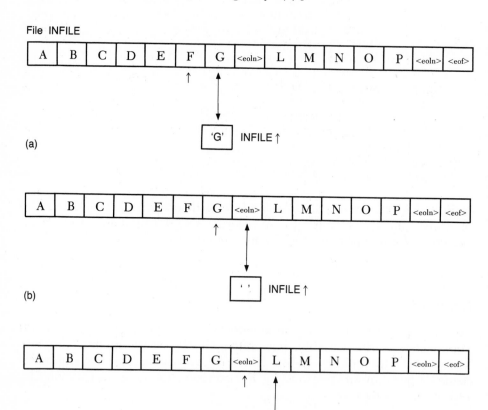

Figure J-1.

Pascal provides the standard procedures GET and PUT to manipulate the buffer variable directly.

GET(F)   advances the current position of file F to the next component and assigns the value of the component to the buffer variable F ↑.

PUT(F)   appends the value of the buffer variable F ↑ to the file F.

In fact, these two procedures are the primitive operators out of which the procedures READ and WRITE are built. The statement

```
READ(INFILE, CH)
```

is equivalent* to

```
CH := INFILE↑;
GET(INFILE)
```

If a

```
READ(INFILE, CH)
```

is done when INFILE ↑ is accessing the last <eoln> marker, CH is assigned a blank, EOF becomes TRUE, and INFILE ↑ becomes undefined (no next component exists).

The statement

```
WRITE(OUTFILE, CH)
```

is equivalent to

```
OUTFILE↑ := CH;
PUT(OUTFILE)
```

When OUTFILE is initialized by using REWRITE, the file is empty, EOF is TRUE, and OUTFILE ↑ is undefined. [See Figure J-2(a).] The statement

```
OUTFILE↑ := CH
```

assigns a value to the buffer (assume CH contains the character 'C'). [See Figure J-2(b).] Then the statement

```
PUT(OUTFILE)
```

---

*Note that this equivalence holds only if the variable CH is of the type CHAR.

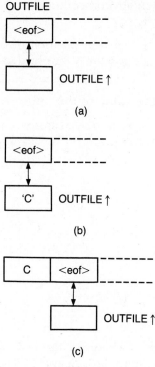

OUTFILE

(a)

(b)

(c)

Figure J-2.

would append the value in OUTFILE ↑ to the file OUTFILE. [See Figure J-2(c).] After the PUT operation, OUTFILE ↑ is again undefined. Notice that EOF is always TRUE for an output file. The foregoing example is identical to what would have happened if the statement

```
WRITE(OUTFILE, CH)
```

had been used instead.

Before introducing GET and PUT and the file buffer, we had to declare a separate variable of the same type as the file component to use in our READ and WRITE statements. We can dispense with this extra variable now and use the file buffer directly with GET and PUT. In the following example, the routine on the left which copies a file can be rewritten as shown on the right with GET and PUT.

```
(* uses READ & WRITE *)                     (* uses GET & PUT *)


WHILE NOT EOF(FILE1) DO            WHILE NOT EOF(FILE1) DO
  BEGIN                             BEGIN
    WHILE NOT EOLN(FILE1) DO          WHILE NOT EOLN(FILE1) DO
      BEGIN                            BEGIN
```

```
        READ(FILE1, CH);              FILE2↑ := FILE1↑;
        WRITE(FILE2, CH)                PUT(FILE2);
      END;                              GET(FILE2)
    READLN(FILE1);                    END;
    WRITELN(FILE2);                   GET(FILE1);
  END;                                WRITELN(FILE2)
                                    END;
```

We still need the WRITELN to generate the <eoln> marker when dealing with text files. However, the <eoln> marker does not exist for nontext files, so, if FILE1 and FILE2 are nontext files, the above code reduces to

```
WHILE NOT EOF(FILE1) DO
    BEGIN
      FILE2↑ := FILE1↑;
      PUT(FILE2);
      GET(FILE1)
    END
```

The procedures READ and WRITE are not defined in standard Pascal for nontext files, though some implementations do support this. So, for nontext files, you must use GET and PUT and the file buffer variable. For example, if INVTRY is a file of parts records, INVTRY ↑ represents a record in INVTRY, and

```
GET(INVTRY)
```

would assign the next record in INVTRY to INVTRY ↑. We can access components (fields) of INVTRY ↑ in the usual way with a field selector.

```
IF INVTRY↑.ID > 999
    THEN ...
```

Exercise Answers

CHAPTER 1

1. This program will read in a series of student records, sort them by GPA, and print out a listing of the student records by descending class rank.
   Input:
   The data for each student is free format, with each field separated by at least one blank.
   The fields for each record are in the following order:

LAST NAME	1 to 20 characters terminated by a comma (may include embedded blanks, hyphens, etc.; e.g., DE GAULLE, SMITH-PETERSON)
FIRST NAME	1 to 20 characters terminated by a colon (may include embedded blanks, hyphens, etc.; e.g., BILLY JOE)
SEX	M (male) or F (female)
DEPARTMENT (major)	2- or 3-letter abbreviation terminated by a blank (e.g., CS, PSY)
CLASS	integer: 1 = freshman; 2 = sophomore; 3 = junior; 4 = senior.

   Following the last record is a single 0 (in place of the next ID number), to designate the end of the file.
   Output:
   The sorted listing should be output in the following format, ordered by descending class rank, with appropriate headings:

   ```
   COL. 1 2–6 7    8–27      28 29    30–49     50–54   55  56–59 60–62
        ЂX.XXXЂ   X···X     ,  Ђ     X···X     ЂЂЂЂЂ   X   ЂЂЂЂЂ XXX
           GPA  LASTNAME      FIRSTNAME       CLASS       DEPT
   ```

The sex field is not printed.

Assumptions:

1. This program will be run as a batch job at night, so it does not have to be extremely efficient in its sorting algorithm.
2. You cannot assume that the records for all the students will fit in memory at the same time.
3. You may assume that input fields are of the correct size (e.g., there will not be 21-character last names).

Testing:

The student data is located on file DATA1.

2. Clarification of problem, documentation

3. Defer details as long as possible.

4. Outline.

5. Step-wise refinement is a synonym for top-down design. The original problem is broken down into subproblems. Each subproblem is further broken down into subproblems. This process continues until each subproblem or subtask is small enough that it is possible to directly code the solution in a programming language.

6. **MAIN MODULE** **LEVEL 0**

```
GET UP
GET DRESSED
IF HUNGRY
    GET BREAKFAST
GO TO CLASS
```

GET UP **LEVEL 1**

```
WHILE NOT AWAKE
    ALARM RINGS
TURN OFF ALARM
GET OUT OF BED
```

GET DRESSED **LEVEL 1**

```
TAKE SHOWER
GET CLOTHES
PUT ON CLOTHES
```

GET BREAKFAST   **LEVEL 1**

```
GO TO KITCHEN
GET CEREAL
PUT CEREAL IN A BOWL
GET MILK
PUT MILK ON CEREAL
WHILE MORE CEREAL IN BOWL
    EAT
CLEAN UP MESS
```

GO TO CLASS   **LEVEL 1**

```
LEAVE HOUSE
GO TO BUS STOP
WHILE NO BUS
    WAIT
GET ON BUS
WHILE NOT THERE
    STAY ON BUS
WALK TO CLASS
```

Each of the tasks listed in the level 1 modules must be further subdivided. We will leave that to your imagination. You should have the idea by now.

7. Main program

8. The top-down method takes a problem and breaks the solution into smaller and smaller modules. Each of these modules can be naturally coded into procedures or functions.

9. F   10. F   11. T

12. A program that makes use of meaningful constants and identifiers and is formatted properly is said to be self-documenting.

13. The documentation for a program should begin when you start working on the problem.

14.
```
CONST   PI = 3.1416;

VAR     RADIUS,                         (* radius of the circle *)
        NUMCIRCLES,                     (* number of circles *)
        TOTALAREA : REAL;
                        (* total area in NUMCIRCLES of radius RADIUS *)
   .
   .
TOTALAREA := NUMCIRCLES * PI * SQR(RADIUS);
```

15. Logic errors are errors in the problem solution. These errors are found during run time when your program either fails to run to completion or gives the wrong answer.

    Syntax errors are errors made in coding your solution in a programming language. These errors are usually found during compile time.

16. F

17. Error 1: The parameter for Procedure INCREMENT should be a VAR parameter.
    Error 2: The BEGIN-END pair has been left off the body of the WHILE loop. Only the WRITELN statement is actually within the WHILE statement.
    Error 3: The call to Procedure INCREMENT is within the comment.

18. Top-down testing makes use of stubs. Stubs are dummy procedures or functions that stand in for procedures or functions that have not been coded yet. You test the top levels of a program by running the program with these stubs. At the next level of testing, you substitute the actual procedures or functions for the stubs.

    Drivers are used in bottom-up testing. Each procedure or function is tested within a special program that invokes the procedure or function with appropriate parameters and prints the results. These special programs are called drivers.

19. This program will read in a set of records, each containing a name, a city, and a zip code.

    Sort the records in ascending order by last name, and print out the information in table form.

    Input:
    The input data is in semifixed format, with one record per line. The fields are:

col. 1–9	FIRSTNAME	The name may begin anywhere in the field. There may be embedded blanks, hyphens, periods, etc.
col. 10	blank	
col. 11–19	LASTNAME	The name may begin anywhere in the field. There may be embedded blanks, hyphens, periods, etc.
col. 20	blank	
col. 21–34	CITY	Begins in col. 21. May include embedded blanks or periods.
col. 35	blank	
col. 36–40	ZIPCODE	

    You may assume that the input correctly conforms to this format.
    The last line of the input has NOMORE beginning in col. 1 to designate the end of the file.
    Output:
    The sorted records are to be printed in ascending order in the following table format:

```
col. 1          2-21              22  23-37 38  39-43
                X···X                 XXXXX     XXXXX
        ƀ FIRSTNAMEƀLASTNAME    ƀ CITY ƀ ZIPCODE
```

If the input for FIRSTNAME or LASTNAME contained leading blanks in
the field, the blanks should be omitted. Trailing blanks at the end of
FIRSTNAME should be deleted; only one blank should separate first and
last names.

The NOMORE record should not be printed.

Assumptions:
1. You may assume that all the data will fit in memory at one time.
2. There will be a maximum of 200 records.
3. You do not need to use a very fast sorting routine.

20.
```
PROGRAM GOODSTYLE (INPUT, OUTPUT);

CONST   NUMLET = 16;                    (* number of letters in a word *)
        NUMWORDS = 25;                          (* number of words *)

TYPE    WORDTYPE = PACKED ARRAY[1..NUMLET] OF CHAR;
        WORDS    = ARRAY[1..NUMWORDS] OF WORDTYPE;

VAR     WORD       : WORDTYPE;
        WORDLIST   : WORDS;
        CH         : CHAR;   (* temporary character used in reading *)
        WORDCT     : 1..NUMWORDS;
                            (* loop control variable for words *)
        LETCT      : 1..NUMLET;
                            (* loop control control variable for letters *)
PROCEDURE SORT (VAR WORDLIST : WORDS);
(* Code for SORT goes here. *)
        .
        .
        .
BEGIN   (* main program *)

    (* Read in list of NUMWORDS words. *)
    FOR WORDCT := 1 TO NUMWORDS DO
      BEGIN

          (* Read in and store one word. *)
          FOR LETCT := 1 TO NUMLET DO
            BEGIN
              READ(CH);
              WORD[LETCT] := CH
            END;
          READLN;
          WORDLIST[WORDCT] := WORD
      END;

    (* Sort the list of words. *)
    SORT(WORDLIST);
```

```
(* Print sorted list of words. *)
    FOR WORDCT := 1 TO NUMWORDS DO
        WRITELN(WORDLIST[WORDCT])
END,    (* main *)
```

CHAPTER 2

1.  ```
    CONST   ARRAYLIMIT = 40;
    TYPE    ARRAYTYPE = ARRAY[1..ARRAYLIMIT] OF REAL;
    VAR     ONED : ARRAYTYPE;
    ```

2. The accessing function of a one-dimensional array consists of two parts: the name of the collection of elements and an index that determines which element in the collection is to be accessed.

    For example, ONED[I] accesses the Ith element in the array defined in question 1.

3. (a) 5
    (b) 26
    (c) 11

4. | | |
    |---|---|
    | NUM[1] | 0 |
    | NUM[3] | 2 |
    | NUM[5] | 4 |
    | LET['A'] | 5 |
    | LET['N'] | 18 |
    | LET['Z'] | 30 |
    | FP[− 4] | 31 |
    | FP[0] | 35 |
    | FP[6] | 41 |

5.  ```
    TYPE TWOD1TYPE = ARRAY[1..10,'A'..'Z'] OF CHAR;
    VAR  TWOD1 : TWOD1TYPE;
    ```

6.  ```
    TYPE VECTOR = ARRAY['A'..'Z'] OF CHAR;
         TWOD2TYPE = ARRAY[1..10] OF VECTOR;
    VAR  TWOD2 : TWOD2TYPE;
    ```

7. The accessing function consists of three parts: the name of the collection of elements, an element's place in the first dimension, and an element's place in the second dimension.

    For example, TWOD2[I, J] accesses the element in the collection named TWOD2 whose place in the first dimension is designated as I and whose place in the second dimension is designated as J.

8. (a) 30
    (b) 9
    (c) 78

9. | | |
    |---|---|
    | VALU[1, 1] | 1000 |
    | VALU[5, 2] | 1025 |
    | VALU[5, 6] | 1029 |
    ```

TABLE[L, −2]   1030
TABLE[2, 1]   improper reference
TABLE[3, 0]   1038
BOX['A', 1]   1039
BOX['Z', 2]   1115
BOX['N', 3]   1080

10. A record is a collection of not necessarily homogeneous elements called fields.

11. The accessing function is made up of two parts: the name of the collection of fields and the name of the specific field to be accessed. For example, PEOPLE.BDATE accesses the BDATE field of the record PEOPLE.

12. NAME   20
    BDATE   1
    AGE   1
    ADDRESS   15

13. PERSON.NAME   50–69
    PERSON.BDATE   70
    PERSON.ADDRESS   72–86
    PERSON.AGE   71

14. CROWD[1].NAME   10–29
    CROWD[1].NAME[1]   10
    CROWD[5].BDATE   178
    CROWD[4].AGE   142
    CROWD[10].ADDRESS[6]   370
    CROWD[1].NAME[20]   29

15. See text for definitions of abbreviations.

    BASE
    + (ORD(UB1) − ORD(LB1) + 1)   (* number of elements per column *)
    * SIZE   (* number of cells per element *)
    * (ORD(I2) − ORD(LB2))   (* columns to be skipped *)
    + ((ORD(I1) − ORD(LB1)) * SIZE)   (* correct cell in column *)

16. A three-dimensional array is a structured data type made up of a finite collection of elements, all of which are of the same data type. Each element is ordered on three dimensions. Accessing is done by specifying an element's place in each of the three dimensions.

17. UB3 = upper bound of third dimension
    LB3 = lower bound of third dimension
    I3 = third dimension index

    BASE
    + (ORD(UB2) − ORD(LB2) + 1)   (* number of elements per row *)
    * (ORD(UB3) − ORD(LB3) + 1)   (* number of elements per plane *)
    * SIZE   (* number of cells per element *)
    * (ORD(I1) − ORD(LB1))   (* number of upper boxes to skip *)
    + (ORD(UB3) − ORD(LB3) + 1)   (* number of elements per plane *)

```
*    (ORD(I2) − ORD(LB2))              (* number of partial planes to skip *)
*    SIZE
+    ((ORD(I3) − ORD(LB3))*SIZE)       (* correct cell *)
```

18. SEARCH: Data should test the following conditions:
    STRING should contain SUBSTR exactly once.
    STRING should contain SUBSTR more than once.
    STRING should contain SUBSTR beginning at the first position.
    STRING should contain SUBSTR ending at the last position in
        STRING.
    STRING should be empty.
    SUBSTR should be empty.
    All of the nonerror conditions should be tried with STRING equal to
        MAXLENGTH, 1, and something in between.
    SUBSTR should be longer than STRING.
    SUBSTR is not in STRING.

    SUBSTRING: Data should test the following conditions:
    STARTPOS + NUM − 1 should be greater than STRING.LENGTH.
    STARTPOS + NUM − 1 should be less than STRING.LENGTH.
    STARTPOS + NUM − 1 should be equal to STRING.LENGTH.
    STARTPOS should be 1 and NUM should be 1.
    STARTPOS should be MAXLENGTH and NUM should be 1.

CHAPTER 3

1. (a) 4   (b) 5   2. (a) 2   (b) 36
       2   X = 1   4   25
       3   Y = 5   6   16
       5   8   9
       3   10   1

3. OVERFLOW? __   UNDERFLOW? __

   S | 'A' | 'B' | 'C' | 'F' | 'E' | TOP = __4__
       [1]   [2]   [3]   [4]   [5]   C = __'F'__

4. OVERFLOW? __   UNDERFLOW? __

   S | 'S' | 'T' | 'U' | 'M' | 'X' | TOP = __5__
       [1]   [2]   [3]   [4]   [5]   C = __'A'__

5. OVERFLOW? __   UNDERFLOW? __

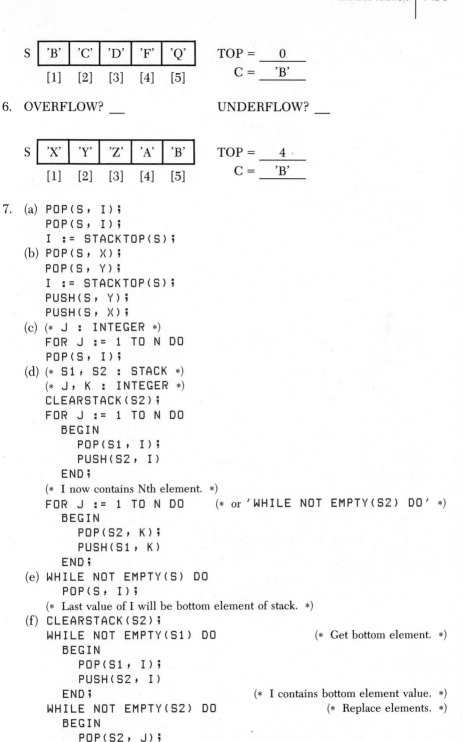

S	'B'	'C'	'D'	'F'	'Q'
	[1]	[2]	[3]	[4]	[5]

TOP = _____0_____

C = _____'B'_____

6. OVERFLOW? __   UNDERFLOW? __

S	'X'	'Y'	'Z'	'A'	'B'
	[1]	[2]	[3]	[4]	[5]

TOP = _____4_____

C = _____'B'_____

7. (a) POP(S, I);
       POP(S, I);
       I := STACKTOP(S);
   (b) POP(S, X);
       POP(S, Y);
       I := STACKTOP(S);
       PUSH(S, Y);
       PUSH(S, X);
   (c) (* J : INTEGER *)
       FOR J := 1 TO N DO
       POP(S, I);
   (d) (* S1, S2 : STACK *)
       (* J, K : INTEGER *)
       CLEARSTACK(S2);
       FOR J := 1 TO N DO
         BEGIN
           POP(S1, I);
           PUSH(S2, I)
         END;
       (* I now contains Nth element. *)
       FOR J := 1 TO N DO   (* or 'WHILE NOT EMPTY(S2) DO' *)
         BEGIN
           POP(S2, K);
           PUSH(S1, K)
         END;
   (e) WHILE NOT EMPTY(S) DO
         POP(S, I);
       (* Last value of I will be bottom element of stack. *)
   (f) CLEARSTACK(S2);
       WHILE NOT EMPTY(S1) DO   (* Get bottom element. *)
         BEGIN
           POP(S1, I);
           PUSH(S2, I)
         END;   (* I contains bottom element value. *)
       WHILE NOT EMPTY(S2) DO   (* Replace elements. *)
         BEGIN
           POP(S2, J);
           PUSH(S1, J)
         END;

8. Two elements are PUSHed and three are POPed. POP (S, Y − 2) is illegal because the second parameter is a VAR parameter.

9.
```
VAR S1, S2 : STACKTYPE;
    CH1, CH2 : CHAR;
    COUNT : 0..100;
    MATCHING : BOOLEAN;
    I, HALFCT : 0..50;
  .
  .
CLEARSTACK(S1);                              (* Initialize stacks. *)
CLEARSTACK(S2);
COUNT := 0;
READ(CH1);                                   (* Read data into S1. *)
WHILE CH1 <> ',' DO
  BEGIN
    PUSH(S1, CH1);
    COUNT := COUNT + 1;                      (* Count number of letters. *)
    READ(CH1)
  END;
HALFCT := COUNT DIV 2;
FOR I := 1 TO HALFCT DO
  BEGIN
    POP(S1, CH1);                            (* Put half of the chars on S2. *)
    PUSH(S2, CH1)
  END;
IF COUNT MOD 2 = 1              (* If COUNT is odd, POP S1 again. *)
    THEN POP(S1, CH1);
MATCHING := TRUE;
WHILE NOT EMPTY(S1) AND MATCHING DO
  BEGIN
    POP(S1, CH1);
    POP(S2, CH2);
    IF CH1 <> CH2
        THEN MATCHING := FALSE
  END;
IF MATCHING
    THEN WRITELN('YES')
    ELSE WRITELN('NO')
```

CHAPTER 4

1.	2.
8	5
5	7
7	2
6	5
	5

3. An inefficient DEQ would be acceptable in an application in which the length of the queue was known to remain short.

4. (a) E becomes F, FRONT = 1, REAR = 5
   (b) OVERFLOW, nothing changed
   (c) A becomes H, FRONT = 4, REAR = 1
   (d) FRONT = 3, REAR = 1, X = C
   (e) UNDERFLOW, X is undefined, nothing changed
   (f) FRONT = 1, REAR = 3, X = A

5. CLEAR
   ENQ 2 ⎱
   ENQ 3 ⎮
   ENQ 3 ⎮ fill the queue
   ENQ 4 ⎰
   PRINTALL
   ENQ 5 ⎱ try to add to full queue
   PRINTALL
   DEQ ⎱
   DEQ ⎮
   DEQ ⎮ remove every element
   DEQ ⎰
   PRINTALL
   DEQ ⎱ try to remove element from empty queue
   PRINTALL

6. (a)
```
PROCEDURE TESTENQ (VAR QUEUE   : QTYPE;
                       NEWVAL : ELTYPE;
                   VAR OFLOW   : BOOLEAN);
```

   (* See question for proper documentation. *)
```
BEGIN
  OFLOW := FULLQ(QUEUE);
  IF NOT OFLOW
    THEN
      BEGIN
        IF QUEUE.REAR = MAXQUEUE
          THEN  QUEUE.REAR := 1
          ELSE  QUEUE.REAR := QUEUE.REAR + 1;
          QUEUE.ELEMENTS[QUEUE.REAR] := NEWVAL
      END
END;
```
   (b)
```
PROCEDURE TESTDEQ (VAR QUEUE  : QTYPE;
                   VAR DEQVAL : ELTYPE;
                   VAR UFLOW  : BOOLEAN);
```

   (* See question for proper documentation. *)

```
BEGIN
  UFLOW := EMPTYQ(QUEUE);
  IF NOT UFLOW
    THEN
      BEGIN
        IF QUEUE.FRONT = MAXQUEUE
          THEN QUEUE.FRONT := 1
          ELSE QUEUE.FRONT := QUEUE.FRONT + 1;
        DEQVAL := QUEUE.ELEMENTS[QUEUE.FRONT]
      END
END;
```

7. The procedures and functions are given below without comments unless the code is not self-documenting. QUEUE.FRONT points to the front element.

```
PROCEDURE CLEARQ (VAR QUEUE : QTYPE);

BEGIN
  QUEUE.FRONT := 1
  QUEUE.REAR  := MAXQUEUE;
  QUEUE.COUNT := 0
END;

(*********************************************)

FUNCTION FULLQ (QUEUE : QTYPE);

BEGIN
  FULLQ := QUEUE.COUNT = MAXQUEUE
END;

(*********************************************)

FUNCTION EMPTYQ (QUEUE : QTYPE);

BEGIN
  EMPTYQ := QUEUE.COUNT = 0
END;

(*********************************************)

PROCEDURE ENQ (VAR QUEUE  : QTYPE;
                   NEWVAL : ELTYPE);

BEGIN
  IF QUEUE.REAR = MAXQUEUE
    THEN QUEUE.REAR := 1
    ELSE QUEUE.REAR := QUEUE.REAR + 1;
  QUEUE.ELEMENTS[QUEUE.REAR] := NEWVAL;
  QUEUE.COUNT := QUEUE.COUNT + 1
END;
```

```
( * * * * * * * * * * * * * * * * * * * * * * * * * * * * * * * * * * * * * * * * * * * * )

   PROCEDURE DEQ (VAR QUEUE   : QTYPE;
                  VAR DEQVAL : ELTYPE);

   BEGIN
     DEQVAL := QUEUE.ELEMENTS[QUEUE.FRONT]
     QUEUE.COUNT := QUEUE.COUNT - 1;
     IF QUEUE.FRONT = MAXQUEUE
        THEN QUEUE.FRONT := 1
        ELSE QUEUE.FRONT := QUEUE.FRONT + 1
   END;
```

8. (a)
```
CONST MAXDEQUE = 100;

    TYPE  DEQUE = RECORD
                    ELEMENTS = ARRAY[INDEXTYPE] OF ELTYPE;
                    COUNT : INTEGER;
                    REAR, FRONT : INDEXTYPE
                  END;   (* record *)
```

(b)
```
PROCEDURE INDEQUEFRONT (VAR DEQUE   : DEQTYPE;
                        NEWVAL : ELTYPE);

    BEGIN
      IF DEQUE.FRONT = 1
         THEN DEQUE.FRONT := MAXDEQUE
         ELSE DEQUE.FRONT := DEQUE.FRONT - 1;
      DEQUE.ELEMENTS[DEQUE.FRONT] := NEWVAL;
      DEQUE.COUNT := DEQUE.COUNT + 1
    END;
```

(c) PROCEDURE INDEQUEREAR is the same as the ENQ routine for question 7.

(d) PROCEDURE OUTDEQUEFRONT is the same as the DEQ routine for question 7.

(e)
```
PROCEDURE OUTDEQUEREAR (VAR DEQUE   : DEQTYPE;
                        VAR DEQVAL : ELTYPE);

    BEGIN
      DEQVAL := DEQUE.ELEMENTS[DEQUE.REAR];
      DEQUE.COUNT := DEQUE.COUNT - 1;
      IF DEQUE.REAR = 1
         THEN DEQUE.REAR := MAXDEQUE
         ELSE DEQUE.REAR := DEQUE.REAR - 1
    END;
```

(f) Deque applications are usually generalizations of queue operations. For example, the data structure used to simulate a terminal input is a modified deque. Characters are entered into the deque as they are typed, but they can be removed from the front by the read operation or from the rear by the rubout or delete operation.

```
9.  TYPE JOBTYPE = ARRAY[1..9] OF QTYPE;
   (a) PROCEDURE ADDJOB (VAR JOBS  : JOBTYPE;
                             ID    : INTEGER;
                             TOKEN : ELTYPE);
       BEGIN
         ENQ (JOBS[ID DIV 100], TOKEN)
       END;
   (b) PROCEDURE GETNEXTJOB (VAR JOBS  : JOBTYPE;
                             VAR TOKEN : ELTYPE;
                             VAR ERROR : BOOLEAN);

       (* Error is set to TRUE if there are no jobs to be run. *)

       VAR  COUNTER : INTEGER;              (* loop control counter *)
            FOUND   : BOOLEAN:

       BEGIN
         FOUND := FALSE;
         COUNTER := 1;
         WHILE NOT FOUND AND COUNTER <= 9 DO
           BEGIN
             FOUND := NOT EMPTYQ(JOBS[COUNTER]);
             IF FOUND
                THEN DEQ(JOBS[COUNTER], TOKEN)
                ELSE COUNTER := COUNTER + 1
           END;
         ERROR := NOT FOUND
       END;
   (c) PROCEDURE CLEANUPJOBS (JOBS : JOBTYPE);

       VAR  COUNTER : INTEGER;              (* loop control counter *)
            TOKEN : ELTYPE;

       BEGIN
         FOR COUNTER := 1 TO 9 DO
           WHILE NOT EMPTYQ(JOBS[COUNTER]) DO
             BEGIN
               DEQ(JOBS[COUNTER], TOKEN);
               NOTIFY(TOKEN, MESSAGE7)
             END
       END;
```

CHAPTER 5

1. (a) [3].INFO becomes 17   (b) [3].NEXT becomes 0
       [3].NEXT becomes 6   [10].NEXT becomes 2
       [10].NEXT becomes 3   AVAIL becomes 10
       AVAIL becomes 2

(c) [3].NEXT becomes 8
[7].NEXT becomes 10
[8].INFO becomes 42
[8].NEXT becomes 6
LIST becomes 2
AVAIL becomes 7

2. (a)
```
P := LIST;
WHILE P <> NULL DO
   BEGIN
      WRITE(NODES[P].INFO:2);
      P := NODES[P].NEXT
   END;
```
(b) B D G I K V W

3.
```
P := START;  (* P : PTR *)
START := NODES[P].NEXT;
FREENODE(P);
```

4.
```
(* N : INTEGER *)
Q := GETNODE;
NODES[Q].INFO := N;
NODES[Q].NEXT := NULL;
IF START = NULL
   THEN START := Q
   ELSE
      BEGIN
         P := START;
         WHILE NODES[P].NEXT <> NULL DO
            P := NODES[P].NEXT;
         NODES[P].NEXT := Q
      END;
```

5.
```
P := START:                                    (* Initialize. *)
COUNT := 1;
IF I = 1                          (* If we need to delete first element. *)
   THEN
      BEGIN
         START := NODES[P].NEXT;
         FREENODE(P)
      END
   ELSE
      BEGIN
         WHILE (COUNT < I - 1) AND (NODES[P].NEXT <> NULL) DO
            BEGIN
               COUNT := COUNT + 1;
               P := NODES[P].NEXT
            END;
         IF (COUNT = I - 1) AND (NODES[P].NEXT <> NULL)
            THEN
               BEGIN
                  Q := NODES[P].NEXT;
                  NODES[P].NEXT := NODES[Q].NEXT;
```

```
                    FREENODE(Q)
                END
                ELSE WRITELN('NO ITH ELEMENT');
```

6.

```
PROCEDURE INSERT (VAR START : PTR; Q : PTR);

VAR P : PTR; PLACEFOUND : BOOLEAN;

BEGIN
  P := START;
  IF NODES[P].INFO > NODES[Q].INFO
```
                                        (* If Q goes before first node. *)
```
      THEN
        BEGIN
          NODES[Q].NEXT := START;
          START := Q
        END
      ELSE
        BEGIN
          PLACEFOUND := FALSE;
          WHILE (NODES[P].NEXT <> NULL) AND NOT PLACEFOUND DO
            IF NODES[NODES[P].NEXT].INFO < NODES[Q].INFO
              THEN P := NODES[P].NEXT
              ELSE PLACEFOUND := TRUE;
          NODES[Q].NEXT := NODES[P].NEXT;
          NODES[P].NEXT := Q
        END
END;   (* insert *)
```

7. (* P, TEMP : PTR *)
```
    TEMP := START;
    START := NODES[START].NEXT;
```
                                (* Initialize TEMP with first node from START *)
```
    NODES[TEMP].NEXT := NULL;
    WHILE START <> NULL DO                   (* while more elements in list *)
      BEGIN
        P := START;                          (* Put them in sorted list TEMP. *)
        START := NODES[START].NEXT;
        INSERT(TEMP, P)
      END;
    START := TEMP;                           (* TEMP pointed to sorted list. *)
```

8. Algorithm: Traverse both lists, comparing the first nodes in each list.
    MOVE the node with the smaller INFO field to NEWLIST. We must add
    to the *end* of NEWLIST. (Let LASTNODE be a pointer to the last node in
    NEWLIST.) When one list is empty, move the rest of the other list to the
    end of NEWLIST. It would be convenient to have a short procedure that
    would move the designated node from the beginning of its list to the end
    of NEWLIST. Let us call it MOVE:

```
PROCEDURE MOVE (VAR P, NEWLIST, LASTNODE : PTR);

BEGIN
   IF NEWLIST = NULL              (* If it will be first node in NEWLIST. *)
      THEN NEWLIST := P
      ELSE NODES[LASTNODE].NEXT := P;
    LASTNODE := P;
    P := NODES[P].NEXT
END;   (* move *)
(* Assumes at least one element in each list. Saves duplicate nodes. *)
   ,

   ,
NEWLIST := NULL:                   (* Initialize NEWLIST pointer. *)
LASTNODE := NULL;
WHILE (START1 <> NULL) AND (START2 <> NULL) DO
   IF NODES[START1].INFO > NODES[START2].INFO
      THEN MOVE(START2, NEWLIST, LASTNODE)
      ELSE MOVE(START1, NEWLIST, LASTNODE);
   IF START1 <> NULL                       (* more nodes in START1 *)
      THEN NODES[LASTNODE].NEXT := START1
      ELSE NODES[LASTNODE].NEXT := START2;
                                            (* more nodes in START2 *)
```

9. Both linked lists (LIST and AVAIL) end in the same place. Is NODE[7] on the available space list or on the ordered linked list pointed to by LIST?

10. We need one NULL value to denote the last node in each linked list. This array contains two linked lists: LIST and AVAIL.

11.
```
PROCEDURE PRINTPOS (LIST : PTR);

VAR P : PTR;
    POS : BOOLEAN;

BEGIN
   P := LIST;
   POS := FALSE;
   IF P = NULL
      THEN WRITELN('EMPTY LIST')
      ELSE REPEAT
              P := NODES[P].NEXT;
              IF NODES[P].INFO > 0
                 THEN
                    BEGIN
                       WRITELN(NODES[P].INFO);
                       POS := TRUE
                    END
           UNTIL P = LIST;
    IF NOT POS THEN WRITELN('NO POSITIVE ELEMENTS')
END;
```

12.
```
PROCEDURE ENQ (VAR Q : PTR; X : ELTYPE);

    VAR P : PTR;

    BEGIN
      GETNODE(P);
      NODES[P].INFO := X;
      IF  Q = NULL                                    (* If Q is empty. *)
         THEN NODES[P].NEXT := P
         ELSE
            BEGIN
               NODES[P].NEXT := NODES[Q].NEXT;
               NODES[Q].NEXT := P;
            END;
      Q := P
    END;
```

13.
```
PROCEDURE DEQ (VAR Q : PTR; VAR X : ELTYPE);

    VAR P : PTR;

    BEGIN
      P := NODES[Q].NEXT;
      X := NODES[P].INFO;
      IF  P = Q                                       (* Only one node in queue. *)
         THEN Q := NULL
         ELSE NODES[Q].NEXT := NODES[P].NEXT;
      FREENODE(P)
    END;   (* deq *)
```

CHAPTER 6

1. (a) P := P↑.NEXT

   (b) Q := P

   (c) R := P↑.NEXT

   (d) P↑.INFO := Q↑.INFO

   (e) P↑.INFO := Q↑.NEXT↑.INFO

(f) R↑.NEXT := P

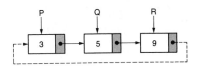

2. (a) P↑.NEXT := P↑.NEXT↑.NEXT;
   (b) R↑.NEXT := S;
   (c) LIST := P↑.NEXT;
   (d) P↑.NEXT↑.NEXT := LIST;

3. (a) 1   1
   (b) 2   NULL

4. F

5. NULL   NULL

6. (a) Employees are assigned EMPNOs from 1 to 1000. Use zero in header
   node.

```
NEW(P);
P↑.EMPNO := 0;
P↑.NEXT := NIL;
EMPLOYEES := P;
```

   (b)
```
VAR I : INTEGER;
    CH : CHAR;
    DEPT : 1..20;
    EMPNO : 1..1000;
    NAME : ARRAY[1..25] OF CHAR;
    SALARY : INTEGER;

    .
    .
    .
NEW(P);
FOR I := 1 TO 25 DO
  BEGIN
    READ(CH);
    NAME[I] := CH
  END;
P↑.NAME := NAME;
READ(DEPT);
P↑.DEPTNO := DEPT;
READ(EMPNO);
P↑.EMPNO := EMPNO;
READ(SALARY);
P↑.SAL := SALARY;
```

   (c)
```
PROCEDURE INSERT (EMPLOYEES, EMP : PTR);

VAR P, BACK : PTR;
    PLACEFOUND : BOOLEAN;

BEGIN
  PLACEFOUND := FALSE;
```

```
BACK := NIL;
P := EMPLOYEES;                          (* Initialize pointers. *)
WHILE (P <> NIL) AND NOT PLACEFOUND DO

    (* Find place to insert. *)
    (IF EMP↑.EMPNO > P↑.EMPNO
        THEN
            BEGIN
                BACK := P;
                P := P↑.NEXT
            END
        ELSE PLACEFOUND := TRUE;

    (* Insert the node. *)
    EMP↑.NEXT := P;
    BACK↑.NEXT := EMP
END;  (* insert *)
```

7. (a) P : ↑NODE is illegal in a parameter list. You must declare TYPE PTR
       = ↑NODE and use PTR in your function heading.
   (b) The condition on the loop checks for P ⟨⟩ NIL, but the code accesses
       P↑.NEXT↑.INFO. To correct this, change the condition on the loop to
       P↑.NEXT ⟨⟩ NIL.
   (c) You cannot reference LIST↑ after you DISPOSE(LIST). Make a copy of
       LIST before you change it and DISPOSE the copy.

DELETE P

8. We need to consider four cases:
   (1) NODE(P) is the *only* node in the list. In this case,
       ```
       LIST := NIL;
       DISPOSE(P)
       ```

   (2) NODE(P) is the *first* node in the list. In this case,
       ```
       P↑.NEXT↑.BACK := NIL;
       LIST := P↑.NEXT;
       DISPOSE(P)
       ```

   (3) NODE(P) is the *last* node in the list. In this case,
       ```
       P↑.BACK↑.NEXT := NIL;
       DISPOSE(P)
       ```

   (4) NODE(P) is in the *middle* of the list (general case). In this case,
       ```
       P↑.NEXT↑.BACK := P↑.BACK;
       P↑.BACK↑.NEXT := P↑.NEXT;
       DISPOSE(P)
       ```

Since we are not using a header node, it is possible that we will try to
delete the first—or only—node in the list. So we will need to pass the
external pointer to the list as a parameter.

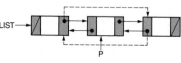

```
PROCEDURE DELETE (VAR LIST : PTR; P : PTR);
```

```
BEGIN
   IF (P↑.BACK = NIL) AND (P↑.NEXT = NIL)        (* only node *)
      THEN LIST := NIL
      ELSE IF P↑.BACK = NIL                      (* first node *)
              THEN
                 BEGIN
                    LIST := P↑.NEXT;
                    LIST↑.BACK := NIL
                 END
              ELSE IF P↑.NEXT = NIL               (* last node *)
                      THEN P↑.BACK↑.NEXT := NIL
                      ELSE                        (* middle node *)
                         BEGIN
                            P↑.NEXT↑.BACK := P↑.BACK;
                            P↑.BACK↑.NEXT := P↑.NEXT
                         END;
   DISPOSE(P);
END;   (* delete *)
```

Another version, which is less clear but has less code:

```
PROCEDURE DELETE2 (VAR LIST : PTR; P : PTR);

BEGIN
   IF P↑.BACK = NIL                              (* first or only node *)
      THEN
         BEGIN
            LIST := P↑.NEXT;
            IF LIST <> NIL THEN LIST↑.BACK := NIL
         END
      ELSE                                        (* middle or last node *)
         BEGIN
            P↑.BACK↑.NEXT := P↑.NEXT;
            IF P↑.NEXT <> NIL
               THEN P↑.NEXT↑.BACK := P↑.BACK
         END;
      DISPOSE(P)
END;   (* delete2 *)
```

9. (a) A↑.INFO   (b) C↑.NEXT↑.INFO   (c) B↑.NEXT↑.NEXT
   (d) C↑.BACK↑.NEXT   (e) B↑.BACK↑.BACK   (f) B↑.BACK
   (g) B↑.BACK↑.BACK

10. ```
PROCEDURE LAYOFF (VAR EMPLIST : PTR);

CONST FULLTIME = 40;
VAR   P, B : PTR;

BEGIN
   P := EMPLIST;
   B := NIL;
```
```

```
WHILE P <> NIL DO
  IF P↑.WEEKHRS < FULLTIME
    THEN IF B = NIL                              (* Deletes first node. *)
           THEN
             BEGIN
               EMPLIST := P↑.NEXT;
               DISPOSE(P);
               P := EMPLIST
             END
           ELSE                                  (* Deletes node. *)
             BEGIN
               B↑.NEXT := P↑.NEXT;
               DISPOSE(P);
               P := B↑.NEXT
             END
    ELSE
      BEGIN
        B := P;
        P := P↑.NEXT
      END
END;   (* layoff *)
```

11. Since the list is doubly linked, we do not need to keep a back pointer as
    we search for the insertion place. Since there is a header and a trailer, we
    need only consider the case of inserting into the middle of the list.

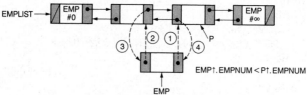

```
PROCEDURE INSERT (EMPLIST, EMP : PTR);
(* Insert node (EMP) into list pointed to by EMPLIST. *)

VAR P : PTR;

BEGIN
  P := EMPLIST;
  WHILE EMP↑.EMPNUM > P↑.EMPNUM DO
    P := P↑.NEXT;                                 (* Finds insert place. *)

  (* Inserts node (EMP) before node (P). *)
  EMP↑.NEXT := P;                                 (* 1 *)
  EMP↑.BACK := P↑.BACK;                           (* 2 *)
  EMP↑.BACK↑.NEXT := EMP;                         (* 3 *)
  P↑.BACK := EMP                                  (* 4 *)
END;   (* insert *)
```

CHAPTER 7

1.
```
FUNCTION LESSTHAN (EL1, EL2 : ETYPE) : BOOLEAN;

BEGIN
   IF SUCC(EL1) = EL2
      THEN LESSTHAN := TRUE
      ELSE IF SUCC(EL1) = LASTEL
              THEN LESSTHAN := FALSE
              ELSE LESSTHAN := LESSTHAN(SUCC(EL1, EL2))
END;   (* lessthan *)
```

2.
```
PROCEDURE ORDERPRINT (LIST : PTR);

BEGIN
   IF LIST <> NIL
      THEN
         BEGIN
            WRITELN(LIST↑.INFO);
            ORDERPRINT(LIST↑.NEXT)
         END
END;
```

3.
```
FUNCTION SUMSQRS (LIST : PTR) : INTEGER;

BEGIN
   IF LIST = NIL
      THEN SUMSQRS := 0
      ELSE SUMSQRS := SQR(LIST↑.INFO)
                        + SUMSQRS(LIST↑.NEXT)
END;   (* sumsqrs *)
```

4. (a) Will not work. A "smaller" case is called, but TEMP is reinitialized each time to LIST. Therefore TEMP will never be nil.
   (b) Calculates the product of the positive elements in the list.
   (c) Works but does nothing. It always returns FALSE.
   (d) Will not work. No trivial nonrecursive case exists.

5. (a) 4   (b) 0   (c) 1

6. (a) Trivial case: POWER := 1
      Recursive call: POWER(M, N − 1)
   (b) Trivial case: P = NIL (* Nothing is done. *)
      Recursive call: PRINT(P ↑.NEXT)
   (c) Trivial case: FACT := 1
      Recursive call: FACT(N − 1)
   (d) Trivial case: LL = UL (* Do nothing. *)
      Recursive call: SORT(A, LL, UL − 1)

CHAPTER 8

1. (a) 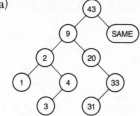   (b)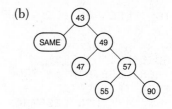

(c) 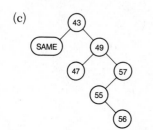   (d)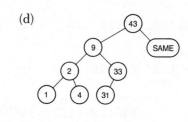

(e) 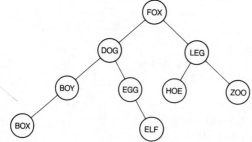   (f)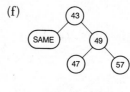

(g) 20, 9, 43   (h) 33, 31
(i) 1, 4, 2, 31, 33, 20, 9, 47, 55, 57, 49, 43
(j) 43, 9, 2, 1, 4, 20, 33, 31, 49, 47, 57, 55
(k) 1, 2, 4, 9, 20, 31, 33, 43, 47, 49, 55, 57
(l) 8   (m) 16   (n) 31

2.

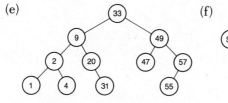

3. If the data were ordered in ascending order, the tree would have no left branches. If the data were ordered in descending order, the tree would have no right branches. For example: 1 2 3 4 5 6 ...

4. PROCEDURE STANDING (ROOT : TPTR);

```
BEGIN
  IF ROOT <> NIL THEN
      BEGIN
        STANDING(ROOT↑.RIGHT);
        WRITE(ROOT↑.GPA : 4 : 2);
        WRITE(FIRSTNAME);
        WRITE(LASTNAME);
        STANDING(ROOT↑.LEFT)
      END
END;
```

5. PROCEDURE FEMPRINT (ROOT : TPTR);

```
BEGIN
  IF ROOT <> NIL THEN
      BEGIN
        FEMPRINT(ROOT↑.LEFT);
        IF ROOT↑.SEX = FEMALE
            THEN WRITELN(ROOT↑.FIRSTNAME, ROOT↑.LASTNAME);
        FEMPRINT(ROOT↑.RIGHT)
      END
END;
```

6. FUNCTION SUMSQRS (ROOT : PTR) : INTEGER;

```
BEGIN
  IF ROOT = NIL
      THEN SUMSQRS := 0
      ELSE SUMSQRS := SQR(ROOT↑.INFO.)
                      + SUMSQRS(ROOT↑.LEFT)
                      + SUMSQRS(ROOT↑.RIGHT)
END;
```

7. VAR P : PTR;

```
BEGIN
  P := ROOT;
  WHILE P↑.INFO <> NUM DO
    BEGIN
      WRITELN(P↑.INFO);
      IF NUM > P↑.INFO
```

```
                THEN P := P↑.RIGHT
                ELSE P := P↑.LEFT
         END
    END;
```

8. (a)
```
    BEGIN
       IF P↑.INFO <> NUM THEN
          BEGIN
             WRITELN(P↑.INFO);
             IF NUM > P↑.INFO
                THEN ANCESTOR(P↑.RIGHT, NUM)
                ELSE ANCESTOR(P↑.LEFT, NUM)
          END
    END;
```
   (b) ANCESTOR(ROOT, 14);

9.
```
    BACK ← P
    TEMP ← RIGHT(P)                         (* MOVE to the right. *)
                                            (* Move as far left as possible. *)
    WHILE LEFT(TEMP) <>NULL DO
       BACK ← TEMP
       TEMP ← LEFT(TEMP)
    INFO(P) ← INFO(TEMP)
    IF P = BACK                    (* P's right child has no left child. *)
       THEN RIGHT(BACK) ← RIGHT(TEMP)
       ELSE LEFT(BACK) ← RIGHT(TEMP)
```

CHAPTER 9

1. (a) Preorder: $+ * a b / + c d e$
       Inorder: $(a * b) + ((c + d) / e)$
       Postorder: $a b * c d + e / +$
   (b) Preorder: $* / + a b c d$
       Inorder: $((a + b) / c) * d$
       Postorder: $a b + c / d *$

2. 5

3.

4. ```
PROCEDURE PREORDERPRINT (TREE : TREEPTR);

   BEGIN
     IF TREE <> NIL
        THEN
           BEGIN
              IF TREE↑.CONTENTS = OPERAND
                 THEN   WRITE(TREE↑.VAL)
                 ELSE   WRITE(TREE↑.OPER);
              PREORDERPRINT(TREE↑.LEFT);
              PREORDERPRINT(TREE↑.RIGHT)
           END
   END;
```

5. (a) Neither    (b) Full    (c) Complete

6.

| W | L | T | G | B | P | S | F | D | A |
|---|---|---|---|---|---|---|---|---|---|
| [1] | [2] | [3] | [4] | [5] | [6] | [7] | [8] | [9] | [10] |

7.

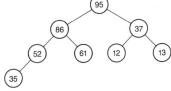

8. (a) Add dummy nodes containing some "impossible" INFO field to noncomplete binary tree to make it complete.
   (b) 0 is an impossible value.

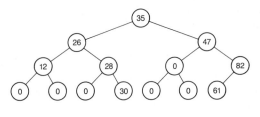

| 35 | 26 | 47 | 12 | 28 | 0 | 82 | 0 | 0 |
|---|---|---|---|---|---|---|---|---|
| [1] | [2] | [3] | [4] | [5] | [6] | [7] | [8] | [9] |

9.

| 80 | 45 | 55 | 31 | 27 | 20 | 33 | 14 | 29 |
|---|---|---|---|---|---|---|---|---|
| [1] | [2] | [3] | [4] | [5] | [6] | [7] | [8] | [9] |
```

10.

	[1]	[2]	[3]	[4]	[5]	[6]	[7]	[8]	[9]	[10]
Original	W	L	T	G	B	P	S	F	D	A
1 value in place	A	L	T	G	B	P	S	F	D	W
Reheap	T	L	S	G	B	P	A	F	D	W
2 values in place	D	L	S	G	B	P	A	F	T	W
Reheap	S	L	P	G	B	D	A	F	T	W
3 values in place	F	L	P	G	B	D	A	S	T	W

11. (a)

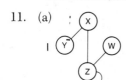

(b)

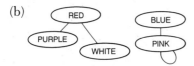

12. (a)

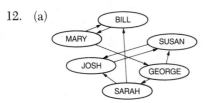

(b)

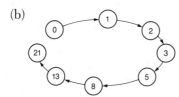

13. (a)

	MA	BI	SU	GE	JO	SA
MARY	0	1	0	1	0	0
BILL	1	0	1	0	0	0
SUSAN	0	0	0	0	1	0
GEORGE	0	0	1	0	0	1
JOSH	1	0	0	0	0	0
SARAH	0	1	0	0	1	0

(b)

	0	1	2	3	5	8	13	21
0	0	1	0	0	0	0	0	0
1	0	0	1	0	0	0	0	0
2	0	0	0	1	0	0	0	0
3	0	0	0	0	1	0	0	0
5	0	0	0	0	0	1	0	0
8	0	0	0	0	0	0	1	0
13	0	0	0	0	0	0	0	1
21	0	0	0	0	0	0	0	0

14. (a) SARAH—JOSH—SUSAN
(b) SARAH—BILL—MARY—GEORGE—SUSAN

CHAPTER 10

1. $\{I = 4\}$
$\{K = 9\}$
$\{N = 1\}$
$\{DATA[I] = J\}$

2.
```
{TRUE}
IF   X <   Y
        THEN                        {X <   Y}{X = MIN(X, Y)}
            MIN :=   X              {MIN   = MIN(X, Y)}
        ELSE                        {X >= Y}{Y = MIN(X, Y)}
            MIN :=   Y              {MIN   = MIN(X, Y)}
{MIN = MIN(X, Y)}
```

3.
```
VALU := 1;
I := 2;
WHILE I <= N DO
    BEGIN
        VALU := VALU * DATA[I];
        I := I + 1
    END;
```

4. At initialization, at termination, and at the top of the loop (i.e., invariant preserved)

5.
```
{A = 5 AND B = 4}
    BEGIN
        TEMP := A;           {B = 4 AND A = 5 AND TEMP = 5}
        A := B;              {B = 4 AND TEMP = 5 AND A = 4}
        B := TEMP            {B = 5 AND TEMP = 5 AND A = 4}
    END;
```

CHAPTER 11

1. **Inner loop of SELECTSORT:**

   DATA[MINDEX] <= DATA[I]..DATA[J − 1] and J <= N + 1

   Initialization: MINDEX is initialized to I, and J is initialized to I + 1. This gives DATA[I] <= DATA[I]..DATA[I], which is true. To show that J <= N + 1, we again substitute for J and get I + 1 <= N + 1. To show that this is true, we must know that I <= N. This is part of the outer loop invariant, so we will assume it as a precondition.

   Termination: The loop condition is no longer true; therefore we know that J > N. Since our loop invariant says that J <= N + 1, J must be equal to N + 1. Substituting this in our loop invariant, we have DATA[MINDEX] <= DATA[I]..DATA[N], which is just what we want.

   Preservation: We know that DATA[MINDEX] <= DATA[I]..DATA[J − 1] because it is the loop invariant. If DATA[J] is less than DATA[MINDEX], then MINDEX becomes J and we now know that DATA[MINDEX] <= DATA[I]..DATA[J]. If DATA[J] is not less than DATA[MINDEX], we also can say that DATA[MINDEX] <= DATA[I]..DATA[J].

   J is incremented by 1. Using the assignment rule, we have our loop invariant back: DATA[MINDEX] <= DATA[I]..DATA[J − 1].

   Outer Loop of SELECTSORT:

   DATA[1]..DATA[I − 1] is sorted.
   DATA[1]..DATA[I − 1] <= DATA[I]..DATA[N]
   I <= N + 1

   Initialization: I is initialized to 1. Substituting that value into the loop invariant, we get the following relationships:

   1. DATA[1]..DATA[0] is sorted.
      This is true because the set of values is empty.
   2. DATA[1]..DATA[0] < DATA[1]..DATA[N]
      Since there are no values in DATA[1]..DATA[0], this statement is true.
   3. 1 <= N + 1
      This statement is true provided N is greater than zero. This must be added as a precondition to the selection sort.

   Termination: On termination of the loop, we know that I > N. Since our loop invariant says that I <= N + 1, we know that I must be equal to N + 1. Substituting that value in our loop invariant, we have the following:

   1. DATA[1]..DATA[N] is sorted.
      This is exactly what we wanted to prove.
   2. DATA[1]..DATA[N] < DATA[N + 1]..DATA[N]
      This is true because DATA[N + 1]..DATA[N] contains no values.
   3. N + 1 <= N + 1

Preservation: The body of the outer loop contains three parts: the inner loop, a call to a swapping procedure, and the statement that increments the loop control counter. Since we have proved the inner loop, we can take its terminating condition as an assertion here. Since the swapping algorithm was proven as an exercise in Chapter 10, we will assume that it does what we expect. (In later courses when you go into more depth on program verification, you will learn rules about verifying procedures.)

Let us summarize what we know on exit from the inner loop:

DATA[1]..DATA[I − 1] is sorted. (outer loop invariant)
DATA[MINDEX] <= DATA[I]..DATA[N] (terminating condition of inner loop)
DATA[1]..DATA[I − 1] <= DATA[I]..DATA[N] (outer loop invariant)

The next statement swaps the contents of DATA[MINDEX] and DATA[I]. So now we can say that DATA[I] <= DATA[I]..DATA[N]. Since DATA[I] is less than or equal to any value in DATA[I]..DATA[N], yet is greater than or equal to any value in DATA[1]..DATA[I − 1], the following statements are true:

DATA[1]..DATA[I] <= DATA[I + 1]..DATA[N]
DATA[1]..DATA[I] is sorted.

The final statement in the loop increments I by 1. Applying the rule of assignment statements, we have just what we want:

DATA[1]..DATA[I − 1] <= DATA[I + 1]..DATA[N]
DATA[1]..DATA[I − 1] is sorted.

2. $O(N^2)$: insertion, selection, bubble
   $O(N \log_2 N)$: quicksort, heapsort

3. (1) Size of N: If the number of elements is small, an $O(N^2)$ sort may run faster than an $O(N \log_2 N)$ sort because of the overhead involved in a more complex algorithm.
   (2) Original order of the elements: Some sorts vary widely in time required depending on the original order of the data. For example, if the elements are already in sorted order, the bubble sort, which recognizes when elements are sorted, will be only $O(N)$, but quicksort will be $O(N^2)$.

4. (a) Selection
   (b) Bubble
   (c) Insertion (Remember that the outer loop is initialized to 2, so the first three elements are sorted among themselves after the second iteration.)

5. (a) 20   31   41   56   59   15
   (b) 15   20   31   41   56   59
   (c) 15   20   31   56   59   41

6. The selection sort given in this chapter sorts from lowest to highest. You can sort from highest to lowest by looking for the maximum element left in the unsorted portion of the array each time instead of looking for the minimum element.

In this problem, after the data have been read into an array of records, use a selection sort ordering the data in decreasing order. When you have gone through the outer loop 10 times, you will have the 10 winners.

7.

	INSSORT	SELECTSORT	BUBBLE1	BUBBLE2	QUICKSORT	HEAPSORT
Data are in completely random order.		DM	DM		BEST	DM
Data are ordered from lowest to highest	BEST	DM	DM	BEST	WORST	DM
Data are ordered from highest to lowest	WORST	DM	DM	WORST	WORST	DM

8. The strategy here is to use the percentile as an index into an array where a count is kept of the number of times that percentile has occurred. Since only the percentiles are needed, the rest of the data record can be ignored.

```
PROCEDURE PERCENTILELIST;

VAR DATA : TEXT;                                    (* input file *)
    COUNTS : ARRAY[0..100] OF INTEGER;   (* array of counters *)
    CT : INTEGER;                        (* loop control counter *)
    ID,                    (* ID will have to be read to reach percentile. *)
    SAT : INTEGER;                       (* percentile SAT score *)

BEGIN
    (* Initialize counters to zero. *)
    FOR CT := 0 TO 100 DO
        COUNTS[CT] := 0;
    (* Read and count SAT percentile scores. *)
    WHILE NOT EOF(DATA) DO
        BEGIN
            READLN(DATA, ID, SAT);
            COUNTS[SAT] := COUNTS[SAT] + 1
        END;
    (* Prints the SAT percentile scores including duplicates. *)
    FOR SAT := 100 DOWNTO 0 DO
        FOR CT := 1 TO DATA[SAT] DO
            WRITELN(SAT)
END;
```

9. $N^3 + 100 = O(N^3)$
   $3N^2 + N + 500 = O(N^2)$
   $O(N^2)$ is more efficient than $O(N^3)$.
   See answer to question 4.

10. Encapsulating frequently used code within a routine hides details and makes the code easier to read and understand. However, execution time is shorter when the code is expanded inline.

11. When determining efficiency, there are three resources to consider: memory space, execution time, and programmer time.
    It will take a programmer longer to write and debug a complex algorithm. If the code is to be executed many times, the investment in a more efficient algorithm may be worthwhile. If the code is to be executed only once or twice, a simple algorithm that takes more time to run but less time to write and debug would be more efficient.

CHAPTER 12

1.

KEYVAL	NUMBER OF COMPARISONS		
	Sequential Ordered Search	Sequential Unordered Search	Binary Search
26	1	1	3
2	1	9	3
96	3	3	3
98	4	9	4
103	6	9	3
243	9	9	4
244	9	9	4

2.

197		101	25	102	201			96	42	162
[0]	[1]	[2]	[3]	[4]	[5]	[6]	[7]	[8]	[9]	[10]

3. Remember that the KEY in the rehash function is the hash address from the previous hash function.

162	197	101	25	201		102		96	42	
[0]	[1]	[2]	[3]	[4]	[5]	[6]	[7]	[8]	[9]	[10]

4.
```
   PROCEDURE MOVE1 (VAR DATA : ARRAYTYPE
                        NUMEL,
                        KEYVAL : INTEGER;
                    VAR FOUND : BOOLEAN);

   VAR CT : INTEGER;                          (* loop control counter *)

   BEGIN
     FOUND := FALSE;
     CT := 1;
     WHILE (CT <= NUMEL) AND NOT FOUND DO
       IF DATA [CT] = KEYVAL
          THEN FOUND := TRUE
          ELSE CT := CT + 1;
     IF FOUND
        THEN
          BEGIN
            FOR CT := CT DOWN TO 2 DO
              DATA[CT] := DATA[CT - 1];
            DATA[1] := KEYVAL
          END
   END;
```

5.
```
   PROCEDURE HASHFIND (VAR LIST : ARRAYTYPE;
                           KEYVAL : INFOTYPE;
                       VAR FOUND : BOOLEAN);

   VAR CT : INTEGER:                    (* loop control counter *)
       STARTPLACE,                      (* initial hash address *)
       TRYPLACE : INDEXTYPE;            (* succeeding hash addresses *)

   BEGIN
     STARTPLACE := HASH(KEYVAL);
     TRYPLACE := STARTPLACE;
     FOUND := FALSE;

     REPEAT
       IF LIST[TRYPLACE] = KEYVAL
          THEN FOUND := TRUE
          ELSE TRYPLACE := (TRYPLACE + 1) MOD MAXLIST
     UNTIL FOUND OR (TRYPLACE = STARTPLACE)
   END;
```

Glossary

ACM Association for Computing Machinery, a professional society of computer scientists, programmers, and others interested in computers and data processing.

actual parameter A variable or expression contained in a procedure or function call and passed to that procedure or function.

actual parameter list The list of actual parameters contained in a procedure or function call.

Ada High-level programming language commissioned by the Department of Defense; created to provide a single language in which to implement the many large and complex Department of Defense programming projects.

address A label (name, number, or symbol) designating a location in memory.

adjacency list Linked lists, one for each node in a graph, that contain the names of the nodes to which each node is connected.

adjacency matrix For a graph with N nodes, an N × N table that shows the existence (or weights) of all edges in the graph.

adjacent nodes Two nodes in a graph that are connected by an edge.

algorithm A step-by-step procedure for solving a problem in a finite amount of time.

allocate To set aside space in memory. See dynamic and static allocation.

alphanumeric A general term for human-readable alphabetic letters, numeric digits, and special characters that are machine processable.

ANSI American National Standards Institute, an organization that promotes voluntary standards in the United States.

argument See parameter.

arithmetic logic unit (ALU) The computer component that performs arithmetic operations (addition, subtraction, multiplication, division) and logical operations (comparison of two values).

arithmetic operator A symbol used in a numeric expression whose operation results in a numeric value.

array A structured data type composed of a fixed number of components of the same type, with each component directly accessed by the index.

ASCII American Standard Code for Information Interchange, a widely used encoding scheme for a character set composed of printable and control characters.

assembler A program that translates an assembly language program into machine code.

assembly language A language, similar to machine code, that uses mnemonics to represent operations and identifiers to represent addresses.

assignment operator The Pascal symbol ":=" used in an assignment statement.

assignment statement A statement that uses the assignment operator to assign a value to a variable or function.

base The number of digits used in a number system (e.g., decimal uses 10, binary uses 2).

base type The set of allowable values that a variable may take.

batch processing A technique for executing programs and data without intermediate user interaction with the computer.

binary expression tree Binary tree in which each nonleaf node contains a binary operator and each leaf node contains one of the operands of its parent node.

binary operator An operator requiring two operands. See arithmetic operator, logical operator, relational operator.

binary search tree Binary tree in which the left child, if any, of each node contains a smaller value and the right child, if any, contains a larger value than the parent node.

binary tree A tree data structure in which each node has at most two offspring. See tree.

bit A BInary digiT (1 or 0) often used to represent information in a computer. Several bits make up a byte. See byte, word.

block A program unit consisting of an optional declarations part and a compound statement; program and procedure/function declarations consist of a heading and a block. Pascal is known as a block-structured language.

Boolean operator See logical operator.

branch See selection.

breadth-first search Searching strategy of visiting nodes one level at a time.

buckets Collection of records associated with a particular hash address.

buffer An intermediate data storage area usually used to balance the different operating speeds of computer components (e.g., slow I/O and the faster CPU).

buffer variable See file buffer variable.

bug An error in a program that prevents compilation or execution or causes incorrect results.

byte A sequence of bits (often 8) used to encode a character within a computer. See word.

call A transfer of control from one portion of a program to a named subroutine (procedure or function).

cancellation error A loss in accuracy during addition or subtraction of numbers of widely differing sizes, due to limits of precision. See representational error.

cardinality The number of values contained in an ordinal type.

case statement A selection control structure that provides for multi-way selection of different courses of action; a generalization of the IF statement equivalent to nested IF-THEN-ELSE statements.

cathode ray tube (CRT) screen An electronic tube with a screen upon which visual information may be displayed (used in computer video terminals and television sets).

central processing unit (CPU) The "brain" of a computer, which interprets and executes instructions; the combination of the control unit and the arithmetic logic unit.

character set The set of machine-representable characters encoded according to a specific coding system. See collating sequence.

character string A string of alphanumeric characters. See string.

circular list List in which the last element is followed by the first element.

code All or part of a program. To write all or part of a program in a programming language. See programming language.

coding Writing code. See computer programming.

collating sequence The ordering of a computer's character set.

collision Condition resulting when two or more keys produce the same hash address.

comment A note in a program intended for human understanding but ignored by the compiler.

comparison operator See relational operator.

compile To translate a program in a high-level language into machine language, using a compiler.

compile-time The phase of program translation (as opposed to the phase of program execution known as run-time).

compiler A program that translates a high-level language program (source code) into machine code (object code).

compiler options Selectable options chosen through command lines or program comment lines directing the compiler to perform compilation in certain ways.

complete binary tree Binary tree that is either full or full through the next-to-last level, with the leaves on the last level as far left as possible.

complete graph Graph in which every node is connected to every other node.

component A logical part or element of a data structure.

component type See base type.

compound statement A group of statements between the Pascal reserved words BEGIN and END that are treated as a single statement.

computer A programmable electronic device that can store, retrieve, and process data.

computer program A sequence of instructions outlining the steps to be performed by a computer.

computer programming The process of planning a sequence of instructions for a computer to perform.

condition A Boolean expression used to determine the action of a selection or looping control structure.

conditional See selection.

constant A location in memory, referenced by a program constant name (identifier), where a data value is stored (this value cannot be changed).

control structure A construct that determines the flow of control in part of a program and is usually represented by a statement, with the basic types being the sequence, selection, and loop.

control unit The computer component that controls the actions of the other components in order to execute instructions (your program) in sequence.

data abstraction The separation of the logical properties of the organization of a program's data from its implementation, ignoring inessential details.

data encapsulation Separation of the representation of data from the applications that use the data at a logical level.

data structure A collection of data elements whose organization is characterized by accessing functions that are used to store and retrieve individual data elements.

data type See type.

debugging The task of removing errors, or "bugs," from a computer program.

declaration section The part(s) of a Pascal program where identifiers to be used in a procedure or program are specified.

default value An assumed value used by a system or compiler when no specific choice is given by the program or the user.

depth-first search Searching strategy of going down a branch to its deepest point before examining other nodes on the same level.

direct access See random access.

directed graph Graph in which each edge is directed from one node to one (may be the same) node; sometimes called digraph.

disk A secondary mass storage medium providing a large amount of permanent storage; a rotating magnetic disk used to store and retrieve magnetically encoded data through a read/write head that is in close proximity to the surface of the disk.

documentation Written descriptions, specfications, design, code, and comments (internal and external to a program) which make a program readable, understandable, and more easily modified; also, a user's manual for a program. See self-documenting code.

doubly linked list Linked list in which each node has pointers to both the next and previous nodes.

dynamic allocation Creation of storage space in memory for a variable during run-time (as opposed to static allocation during compile-time). See referenced variable.

dynamic data structure A data structure that may expand and contract during run-time.

dynamic storage See dynamic allocation.

dynamic variable See referenced variable.

edge Connection between two nodes in a graph; sometimes called arc.

editor An interactive program that allows the user to create and alter text files such as data, programs, manuscripts, etc.

empty set The set with no members at all.

empty statement An allowable Pascal syntax, implying no action, that is created when two statement separators (such as a semi-colon and END) are used consecutively. Sometimes needed when no action is required after a case label list.

end-of-file (eof) marker The mechanism for indicating the end of a file.

end-of-line (eoln) marker The mechanism for indicating the end of a line. (Pascal returns a blank when this marker is read.)

enumerated type See user-defined type.

error checking Explicit checking for invalid and error conditions in a program.

execute To carry out the instruction(s) in a statement or program; to run a program.

execution-time See run-time.

exponential notation See scientific notation.

expression A sequence of identifiers and/or constants, separated by compatible operators, that is evaluated at run-time.

external documentation Program specification, design, and development history that are external to the body of executable code.

external file A permanently stored file separate from the executing program.

field identifier The name of a component in a record.

field selector The expression used to access components of a Pascal record variable, consisting of the record variable name and the field identifier separated by a period.

fieldwidth specification In Pascal, a colon and integer value following a parameter in a WRITE statement, specifying the number of columns in which that parameter will be printed and right-justified.

file A data structure consisting of a sequence of components that are all of the same type; a collection of related data, usually stored on disk or tape, and referenced by a single name.

file buffer See file buffer variable.

file buffer variable A variable of the same type as the components of the file with which it is associated, and used as a "window" through which we can read or write file components.

floating point representation Also known as floating point notation. See scientific notation.

flow of control The order in which statements are executed in a program. See control structure.

FOR statement A looping control structure similar to a WHILE loop but with predefined initial and final values for the loop control variable, as well as automatic incrementing (or decrementing) of the loop control variable.

formal parameter A variable, declared and used in a procedure or function declaration, that is replaced by an actual parameter when the procedure or function is called.

formal parameter list The list of formal parameters contained in a procedure or function heading.

free format An allowable formatting of program statements characterized by no rules governing the indentation or number of syntax elements that may appear on a line of code.

full binary tree Binary tree in which all the leaves are on the same level and every nonleaf node has two children.

function A subroutine that returns a value when called. See subroutine, parameter.

global identifier An identifier declared in the outermost block (main program); an identifier that is not local to a block but whose scope includes that block.

GOTO Unconditional branch to a statement in a program; almost never seen in structured programs.

graph Data structure that consists of a set of nodes and a set of edges that relate the nodes to each other.

hardware The physical components of a computer.

hash function Function used to manipulate the key of a record in a list to produce a unique location.

hashing Technique used for ordering and accessing elements in a list in a relatively constant amount of time by manipulating the key to produce a (hopefully) unique location.

header node Dummy node at the beginning of a list; used to simplify list processing and/or to contain information about the list.

heap A complete binary tree in which the value in each node is greater than or equal to the value in each of its children.

high-level language A programming language that is closer to natural language than assembly language and whose statements each translate into more than one machine language instruction.

identifiers Names that are associated with processes and objects and used to refer to those processes and objects. Pascal identifiers are made up of letters and numbers but must begin with a letter.

implementation The representation of a programming language on a particular computer system; a specific compiler and associated run-time support subroutines.

index An ordinal value identifying a particular component of a data structure such as an array.

infinite loop A loop whose terminating condition would never be reached; the loop would (theoretically) execute indefinitely and the program would never terminate.

infix notation Notation for expressions in which the binary operator is placed between its operands.

information hiding Principle of making details of a function or data structure inaccessible to other parts of the program.

initialize To assign an initial value to a variable.

inorder traversal Traversal of a binary tree in which each node is visited between its left and right subtrees.

input Any external data used by a program, from whatever source, such as a keyboard or disk file.

input/output (I/O) Media and devices used to achieve human/machine communication.

interactive processing Use of an interactive program; user interaction with a program usually by prompts, data entry, and commands made through a terminal.

interactive programming Use of an interactive system to create and compile programs through the use of an editor, compiler, debugger, and other tools.

interactive system Direct communication between the user and the computer; a terminal/computer connection allowing direct entry of programs and data and providing immediate feedback to the user.

interface A shared boundary where independent systems meet and act on or communicate with each other.

internal documentation Features within the executable code that make a program easy to read and understand; includes comments, prettyprinting, and self-documenting code.

interpreter A program that translates each statement of a (usually) high-level language source program into a sequence of machine code instructions which are executed before the next statement of the source program is translated.

invoke See call.

ISO International Organization for Standardization, an organization that promotes voluntary standards.

key Field in a record whose value is used to order the records in a list or file.

label A name used in a computer program to identify an instruction, statement, data value, record, or file; an integer in the range 1 to 9999 declared in a Pascal label declaration and used to mark a particular statement, usually as the destination of an unconditional jump (GOTO).

leaf Node in a tree that has no children.

left child Node to the left of a given node in a binary tree; sometimes called left son.

left subtree All the nodes to the left of a given node in a binary tree.

linked list List in which the order of the elements is determined by an explicit link field in each element rather than sequential order in memory.

listing See source listing.

literal A symbol that defines itself; a constant value such as a literal string or number.

local identifier An identifier declared in the block where it is used. See name precedence.

logical operator A symbol used in a Boolean expression whose operation results in a Boolean value of TRUE or FALSE.

loop A control structure that allows a statement(s) to be executed more than once (until a termination condition is reached).

loop control variable A variable (usually ordinal) used to control the number of times the body of a loop is executed.

machine code See machine language.

machine language The language used directly by the computer and composed of binary coded instructions.

main storage Also main memory. See memory.

memory The ordered sequence of storage cells (locations, words, places) in a computer that are accessed by address and used to temporarily hold the instructions and variables of an executing program. See secondary storage.

memory unit The internal data storage of a computer. See memory.

module An independent unit that is part of a whole; a logical part of a design or program, such as a procedure.

multi-dimensional array An array of one or more arrays.

name precedence The priority of a local identifier over a more global identifier, where the identifiers have the same name. See scope.

nested logic A control structure contained within another control structure.

NIL A constant in Pascal that can be assigned to a pointer variable, indicating that the pointer points to nothing.

node Element in a list or tree.

object code The machine code producd by a compiler or assembler from a source program. Also called object program.

operating system The set of programs that manage computer resources.

operator A symbol that indicates an operation to be performed.

operator precedence See precedence rules.

order of magnitude Way of expressing relationships between large numbers by using formal approximation. Used in computing to express amount of work done.

ordinal type A set of distinct values that are ordered such that each value (except the first) has a unique predecessor and each value (except the last) has a unique successor; any scalar type except REAL.

output Data produced by a program and sent to an external file or device.

overflow A condition where the results of a calculation are too large to represent on a given machine. See precision.

packed array An array which occupies as little memory space as possible by having as many array components as possible packed into each memory word.

packed option A Pascal feature allowing more efficient storage of records and arrays.

palindrome String that reads the same backward or forward (e.g., RADAR).

parameter An expression passed in a procedure or function call. See actual parameter, formal parameter.

parameter list See actual parameter list, formal parameter list.

path Sequence of vertices that connects two nodes in a graph.

peripheral device An input, output, or auxiliary storage device of a computer.

pointer A simple data type, consisting of an unbounded set of values, which addresses or otherwise indicates the location of a variable of a given type.

portability The ability of software written for one computer to run successfully on different machines.

postconditions Output specifications of a routine which describe the transformed data; tell what is true on exit from a subprogram.

postfix notation Notation for expressions in which the binary operator follows its operands.

postorder traversal Traversal of a binary tree in which each node is visited after its left and right subtrees.

powerset See universal set.

precedence rules The order in which operations are performed in an expression.

precision The maximum number of significant digits.

preconditions Input specifications and allowable assumptions for a routine; tell what is true on entry to a subprogram.

prefix notation Notation for expressions in which the binary operator precedes its operands.

preorder traversal Traversal of a binary tree in which each node is visited before its right and left subtrees.

prettyprinting Program formatting to make a program more readable.

procedure A subroutine that is executed when called. See subroutine, parameter.

procedure call See call.

program verification Demonstration of a program's correctness by formal proof or logical argument.

programming The planning, scheduling, or performing of a task or an event. See computer programming.

programming language A set of rules, symbols, and special words used to construct a program.

pseudo-code A mixture of English and Pascal-like control structures used to specify a design.

queue A data structure in which elements are entered at one end and removed from the other; a "first in, first out" (FIFO) structure.

queuing system   System made up of servers and queue(s) of objects to be served.

random access   The process of retrieving or storing elements in a data structure where the time required for such access is independent of the order of the elements.

range   The smallest and largest allowable values.

range-checking   The automatic detection of an out-of-range value being assigned to a variable.

real number   One of the numbers that has a whole and a fractional part and no imaginary part.

record   A structured data type with a fixed number of components (not necessarily of the same type) that are accessed by name (not subscript).

recursion   The ability of a procedure or function to call itself.

referenced variable   A variable accessed not by name but through a pointer variable; a dynamic variable; a variable created by the procedure NEW in Pascal.

regression testing   Re-execution of program tests after modifications have been made in order to ensure that the program still works correctly.

relational operator   A symbol that forms an expression with two values of compatible types, and whose operation of comparing these values results in a Boolean value of TRUE or FALSE.

repeat statement   A looping control structure similar to a WHILE loop, except that there will always be at least one execution of the loop since the loop condition is tested after the body of the loop.

representational error   An arithmetic error that occurs when the precision of the result of an arithmetic operation is greater than the precision of a given machine.

reserved word   An identifier that has a specific meaning in a programming language and may not be used for any other purpose in a program.

right child   Node to the right of a given node in a binary tree; sometimes called right son.

right subtree   All the nodes to the right of a given node in a binary tree.

robustness   The ability of a program to recover to a known state following an error.

root node   The external pointer to a tree data structure; the top or base node of a tree.

round off   To truncate (or make zero) one or more least significant digits of a number, and to increase the remaining least significant digit by one if the truncated value is more than half of the number base. Pascal provides a function to round off a real value to the nearest integer.

run-time   The phase of program execution during which program instructions are performed.

scalar data type   A set of distinct values (constants) that are ordered.

scientific notation   A method of representing a number as an expression consisting of a number between 1 and 10 multiplied by the appropriate power of 10. Also called floating point notation.

scope   The range or area within a program in which an identifier is known.

searching   The locating of a particular element in a data structure.

secondary storage   Backup storage for the main storage (memory) of a computer, usually permanent in nature (such as tape or disk).

seed   Global variable that initializes a random number generator.

selection   A control structure that selects one of possibly several options or paths in the flow of control, based upon the value of some expression.

self-documenting code   A program containing meaningful identifier names, as well as the judicious use of clarifying comments.

semantics   The set of rules which give the meaning of a statement.

sentinel   A special data value used to mark the end of a data file.

sequential access   The process of retrieving or storing elements in a fixed order in a data structure where the time required for such access is dependent on the order of the elements.

set   A structured data type composed of a collection of distinct elements (members) chosen from the values of the base type.

siblings   Nodes in a tree that have the same parent node; sometimes called brothers.

side effects   A change, within a procedure or function, to a variable that is external to, but not passed to, the procedure or function.

significant digits   Those digits that begin with the first non-zero digit on the left and end with the last non-zero digit on the right (or a zero digit that is exact).

simple type   A scalar type; a type that is not structured; any of the Pascal types INTEGER, REAL, BOOLEAN, CHAR or any user-defined (ordinal) type.

software   Computer programs; the set of all programs available to a computer.

software engineering   Disciplined approach to the design and maintenance of computer programs using tools that help manage the size and complexity of the resulting software products.

sorting   Arrangement of elements in a list according to the increasing (or decreasing) values of some key field of each element.

source code   Also called source program; a program in its original form, in the language in which it was written, prior to any compilation or translation.

source listing   A printout of a source program processed by a compiler and showing compiler messages, including any syntax errors in the program.

stack   A data structure in which elements are entered and removed from only one end; a "last in, first out" (LIFO) structure.

stack overflow   The condition resulting from trying to push an element onto a full stack.

stack underflow   The condition resulting from trying to pop from an empty stack.

statement   An instruction in a programming language.

statement separator   A symbol used to tell the compiler where one instruction ends and another begins in a program, such as the semi-colon in Pascal.

static allocation Creation of storage space in memory for a variable at compile-time (cannot be changed at run-time).

static data structure A data structure fixed in size at compile-time. See static allocation.

step-wise refinement A design method in which an algorithm is specified at an abstract level and additional levels of detail are added in successive iterations throughout the design process. See top-down design.

storage See memory.

string A collection of characters interpreted as a single data item; a packed character array.

structured design A design methodology incorporating a high degree of modularity, and employing generic control structures having only one entry and one exit. See top-down design.

structured programming The use of structured design and the coding of a program that parallels the structure of the design. See top-down programming.

structured type A type composed of more than one element, which at its lowest level is a simple type; any of the Pascal types ARRAY, RECORD, SET, and FILE.

stub Dummy procedure or function that is used to stand in for a lower-level subprogram in a top-down testing approach.

subprogram See subroutine.

subrange type A data type composed of a specified range of any standard or user-defined ordinal type.

subroutine A collection of statements in a program, but not part of the main program, that is treated as a named entity, performs a specific task, and is capable of being called (invoked) from more than one point in the program; a function or procedure in Pascal.

subscript See index.

subscripted variable See array.

subset The set A is a subset of the set B if each element of A is an element of B.

symbol table Table, defined by the compiler, that maps variables to memory locations.

syntax The formal rules governing the construction of valid statements in a language.

syntax diagram A pictorial definition of the syntax rules of a programming language.

system software The set of programs that improves the efficiency and convenience of using a computer, such as the operating system, editor, and compiler.

tag field Field in a variant record that determines which set of variant fields will be included in a particular instance of the record.

tail recursion Condition when a subprogram contains a single recursive invocation that is the last statement in the subprogram.

tape A secondary mass storage medium providing a large amount of permanent storage; a thin plastic strip having a magnetic surface used to store and retrieve magnetically encoded data through a read/write head that is in close proximity to the surface of the tape.

test driver Program that sets up the testing environment by declaring and assigning initial values to variables, then calls the procedure to be tested.

text file A file of characters that is also divided into lines.

time sharing A method of operation in which a computer is shared by several users simultaneously.

top-down design A design methodology that works from an abstract functional description of a problem (top) to a detailed solution (bottom); a hierarchical approach to problem solving that divides a problem into functional sub-problems represented by modules, which are easier to solve and which may themselves be further broken down into modules. The design consisting of a hierarchy of separate modules (solutions), with lower level modules containing greater detail than higher level modules. See structured design.

top-down programming Programming that incorporates top-down design, and, through the use of procedures, functions, and control structures, maintains in the program the modularity and structure of the design.

top-down testing A technique for testing the modules (procedures and functions) of a program, as they are written, by calling them with actual parameters and providing stub (dummy) modules for those modules not yet written but referenced in the program.

trace To follow the logical flow of a program and determine the value of variables after each instruction. Also known as code walk-through and playing computer.

trailer node Dummy node at the end of a list used to simplify list operations.

translator A program that translates from one programming language to another (usually machine code). See assembler, compiler, interpreter.

tree A data structure composed of a root node having offspring that are also nodes that can have offspring, and so on.

tree diagram A hierarchical chart showing the relationships of modules in a top-down design.

truncation The decrease in precision of a number by the loss or removal of one or more least significant digits.

type A formal description of the set of values that a variable of a given type may take or to which a datum of that type must belong.

type definition A definition of a data type in Pascal in the type declaration of a block, with the type identifier on the left of the equal sign ("=") and the definition on the right.

unary operator An operator requiring only one operand such as the logical operator NOT.

underflow A condition that occurs when the results of a calculation are too small to represent in a given machine.

universal set The set consisting of all values of the base type.

user-defined (enumerated) type The ordered set of distinct values (constants) defined as a data type in a program. See ordinal type.

value parameter A formal parameter that is a local variable of a procedure or function, but whose value is initialized to the value of an actual parameter in a call to the procedure or function.

variable A location in memory, referenced by a program variable name (identifier), where a data value can be stored (this value can be changed during program execution).

variable declaration The creation of a variable in Pascal in the variable declaration section of a block with the variable identifier on the left of the colon (":") and the type definition or identifier on the right.

variable parameter A formal parameter that is replaced by an actual parameter in a call to a procedure or function.

variant record Record type which may contain different collections of fields, according to the value of a tag field.

vertex (pl. vertices) A node in a graph.

weighted graph Graph in which each edge carries a value.

window See file buffer variable.

word A group of bits, one or more bytes in length, treated as a unit or location in memory, and capable of being addressed.

word size The number of bits comprising a word or location in memory.

Programming Assignments

A collection of programming assignments, each much altered over time, is part of the folklore of every department. In the assignments that follow we have tried to attribute ones we didn't write ourselves to their original authors. If you recognize one of your own and we didn't credit you, forgive us; it was unintentional.

Chapter 1

The programming assignments for Chapter 1 require only a knowledge of arrays and records; in some cases, a knowledge of packed arrays would be useful, but is not essential. The assignments vary in difficulty, with the more difficult problems marked with an asterisk.

1. Your assignment is to write a program for a computer dating service. Clients will give you their names, phone numbers, and a list of interests. It will be your job to maintain lists of men and women using the service and to match up the compatible couples.

   Data structures: The problem requires you to maintain two lists, men and women. The lists must include the following information: name (20 characters), phone number (8 characters), number of interests (maximum number is 10), interests (10 characters; must be in alphabetical order), and a variable that gives the position of the client's current match (will be 0 if not matched). When a new client is added to the list, he or she is added to the bottom of the appropriate list. (You do not keep the names of the clients in alphabetical order.)

   Input: The first part of the input file contains the data base of current clients.

   1. Number of current clients
   2. For each current client, a record containing the following: sex (7 characters), name (20 characters), phone number (8 characters), number of interests, list of interests (10 characters for each one; must be sorted; interests are separated by commas with a period after the final interest.)

   The rest of the file will include commands to the dating service. Each command will begin with a 10-character command word, on a new line of input.

Commands:

NEWCLIENT ⅄ ⟨sex⟩ ⟨name⟩ ⟨number of interests⟩ ⟨interests⟩

If the key word NEWCLIENT occurs, you should add the client to the appropriate list by storing the appropriate information. Match him or her with a member of the opposite sex. (A match occurs when three or more of the interests are the same. Use the fact that interests are sorted to make the match process easier.) Make sure you then designate both persons as matched, as described above. Print the name of the new client, his or her match, and both phone numbers. If no match is found, print an appropriate message.

OLDCLIENT ⅄ ⟨name⟩

Unmatch this name with his (or her) current match by setting the MATCH variables for this name and his (or her) match to 0.

PRINTMATCH

Print a list of all matched pairs.

PRINTOOT ⅄⅄

Print the names and phone numbers of clients who are not currently matched.

STOPPROG ⅄⅄

This will be the last line in the input.

Output: Print information as described above with appropriate labels.

Original by Jim Bittner;
modified by Joyce Brennan

2. Although many people think of computers as large number-crunching devices, much of computing deals with alphanumeric processing. For example, the compiler reads your program as alphanumeric data. To let you get a taste of this type of processing, we will use a Pascal program as the input data for this problem.

   The assignment is to read a Pascal program and find all of the assignment statements. From each of these you will extract the variable getting a value (the one before the := operator) and all of the variables in the expression on the right-hand side. You may assume that no variable contains an embedded blank and that each statement is on a line by itself.

   Input: A Pascal program.

   Output: Print out each assignment statement and next to it the variables that you have extracted. The output should be labeled.

   Example:

```
ASSIGNMENT STATEMENTS              LEFT     RIGHT

X := B                             X        B
X := 5.6                           X
TEST := SQR(X + 5.4) + Y/A         TEST     X        Y        A

X := REC + NUM * (AGE - 10)        X        REC      NUM      AGE
```

*3. A small trucking firm acts as a broker between people who want things shipped and independent drivers who own their own trucks. The company receives requests from customers who want goods shipped from city A to city B. When truckers are free, they call the company and give their location and the mile radius they are willing to travel to pick up goods. The company looks at its requests and arranges for as full a load as possible.

Input: 1. Mileages between the cities served by this trucking firm.

⟨city⟩ ⟨city⟩ ⟨miles between⟩

These entries are repeated, one per line. An asterisk (*) ends these entries.
2. A mixture of shipper and driver requests.

SHIPPER ⟨name⟩ ⟨city⟩ ⟨city⟩ ⟨pounds⟩ ⟨cost⟩
DRIVER ⟨name⟩ ⟨city⟩ ⟨mile radius⟩ ⟨truck capacity⟩

where ⟨name⟩ and ⟨city⟩ are character strings of up to ten characters with no embedded blanks. There may be multiple blanks between components of each individual request.
⟨pounds⟩, ⟨mile radius⟩, and ⟨truck capacity⟩ are integer numbers.
⟨cost⟩ is a real number (i.e., dollars and cents).
There will be at least one blank following the key words SHIPPER and DRIVER.

Output: 1. Echoprint the mileage table.
2. Echoprint each shipper request.
3. For each driver request,
   (a) Echoprint the driver request.
   (b) Print a list of the shippers who have goods to be shipped from the city where the driver is and from cities within the radius designated as acceptable by the driver. This list should be printed in order by cost. That is, the shipper whose load will cost the most should be printed first.
   (c) The names of those shippers whom the driver should service, along with their locations and the destinations of their goods. This list will be made up of as many of those shippers as the driver can handle with his or her particular truck. That is, the combined pounds must be within the capacity of the driver's truck.
4. After all the shipper and driver requests have been processed, print a list of those shipper requests still not picked up.
5. If a driver request comes in and there are no shipper requests for a pick-up within the designated radius, or the driver's truck does not have the capacity to service the requests that do exist, print a message to the driver to take a day off.

Data structures: 1. A two-dimensional array representing mileages. A city's place in the array of city names is used as an index into this mileage table.
2. An array of records that represent shipper requests.

Assumptions: 1. Intra-city shipper requests are legal.

    2. The distance between cities is symmetric. That is, the distance between city A and city B is the same as between city B and city A. The distance between a city and itself is 0.

4. Simplify Assignment 3 above by allowing city designations and names to be integer numbers. The definitions of ⟨city⟩ and ⟨name⟩ should simply be integer numbers within a specified range.

5. Add to Assignment 3 above the requirement that summary statistics be kept for each driver. You will need one more item in the output specification, one more data structure, and one more assumption.

Output: After all shipper and driver requests have been processed, print summary statistics for all drivers, showing the driver's name, the number of pounds hauled, and the total cost.

Data structure: A one-dimensional array of records, in which each record represents a driver.

Assumption: A driver's name is not entered into the list of drivers until he or she has actually picked up a shipment.

                                            Gael Buckley

*6. Your cousin—the noisy one—has been sitting in the corner for hours, quietly absorbed with a new game. Being a little bored (and curious), you ask if you can play. The game consists of a 2-dimensional black box with numbers between 0 and 39 on all sides.

    There are five obstructions, called *baffles*, which you cannot see, placed in the box. The object of the game is to find the baffles. You select a number between 0 and 39, which activates a laser beam originating at that location. You are then told where the beam leaves the box. If the beam does not encounter a baffle, it will exit directly opposite where it entered. If the beam encounters a baffle, it will be deflected at right angles, either right or left, depending on the direction of the baffle. You can locate the baffles by shooting beams into the box, using the deflections of the beams as hints to the placement and direction of the baffles.

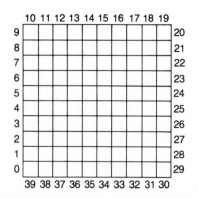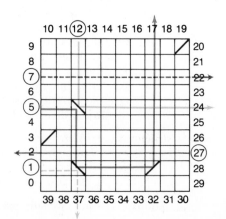

Given the box on the preceding page, a beam shot from 7 comes out at 22. A beam shot from 1 is deflected once and exits at 37. A beam shot from 27 exits at 2 without being deflected. A beam shot from 5 comes out at 17 after three deflections. A beam shot from 12 is deflected once, exiting at 24.

The game is scored by giving one point for each laser shot and two points for each guess. A lower score, obviously, is more desirable.

When your cousin demands his game back, you decide to write a computer program to simulate the game. (*Note:* Your program is not supposed to *solve* the baffles problem; it is supposed to present the game to be played.) This clearly ought to be an interactive program, where the baffles are set by a random number generator, and a player either fires a laser beam or makes a guess as to the position of a baffle. However, you decide to write the program and test it first. You can add the prompts for interactive play later.

Input/output: 1. In our interactive game, the baffles will be set by a random number generator. To test this program, however, we will read in the coordinates from an input file. The information for each baffle will be one line of input in the format

⟨X⟩ ⟨Y⟩ ⟨dir⟩

where ⟨X⟩ is an integer between 0 and 9
⟨Y⟩ is an integer between 10 and 19
⟨dir⟩ is either an R or an L

⟨X⟩, ⟨Y⟩, and ⟨dir⟩ are separated by at least one blank, maybe more.

Example:

5   12   L   sets   5

9   19   R   sets   9

Error checking: You are not assured that each line of input will be unique (just as the random number generator may coincidentally come up with the same coordinates for two baffles). You can only get a baffle in a "free" position, i. e., one that has not been previously set. You need to set a total of five unique baffles.

When you have set five unique baffles, skip all input until you encounter a *.

2. Input for playing the game follows the *. Each command to the game will be on a separate line in the input file. Echoprint each command before the specified output. The format for the command input will be the following:

Col. 1	Col. 2	Meaning
P		Print the box, showing the locations and directions of all the baffles that have already been found.
L	integer (0–39)	Laser shot. Shoot the laser, with the beam entering the box at the designated location. **Output:** `LASER SHOT #____ EXITED THE BOX AT ____.`
G	⟨X⟩ ⟨Y⟩ ⟨dir⟩ (same format as part 1)	Guess the location of one baffle. ⟨X⟩, ⟨Y⟩, and ⟨dir⟩ refer to the coordinates and direction of the baffle. **Output:** `THIS IS GUESS NUMBER ____.` If guess is correct, print `CONGRATULATIONS, YOU HAVE NOW FOUND ____ BAFFLES.` If guess is correct but baffle was found on a previous guess, print `YOU HAVE ALREADY FOUND THIS BAFFLE.` If guess is incorrect, print `SORRY, BETTER LUCK NEXT TIME.`
S		Score. **Output:** `NUMBER OF SHOTS: ____` `NUMBER OF GUESSES: ____` `CURRENT SCORE: ____`

Continue processing until all five baffles are found. Output message of congratulations and calculated score. Print the box showing the location and direction of all the baffles.

Error checking: In addition to the specific error checking mentioned above, you must check *all input*. If an error is found in any line, that line is not used, and an appropriate warning should be printed. (Use your imagination.) You may assume that the number of items on a line and their respective types *are* correct.

Example:

```
L   40  *** LASER SHOT OUT OF BOUNDS -- TRY AGAIN ***
B    5  12 2 *** ILLEGAL COMMAND -- TRY AGAIN ***
```

Sample game:

Input:

```
5       12      L
9   19          R
```

```
2  17  J
3              10        R
9       19       L
14      3    R
1       12   L
           1   17        R
   3  13      R
   9              11   L
*
L8
L12
G 5 12 L
P
L 30
G     30 20 R
G   9   19              R
R      17
L  17
G         5 12           L
S
.
.
.
G    1 10 R
L 1
G     1 12          L
```

Output:

```
***  SET  BAFFLES  ***
      5      12    L       BAFFLE  1  SET
      9      19    R       BAFFLE  2  SET
      2      17    J          *** error message ***
      3      10    R       BAFFLE  3  SET
      9      19    L       *** error message ***
     14       3    R       *** error message ***
      1      12    L       BAFFLE  4  SET
      1      17    R       BAFFLE  5  SET
```

Ignore the rest of the input until '*' is encountered.

```
***  PLAY  GAME  ***

L     8
      LASER  SHOT  #1  EXITED  THE  BOX  AT  21.

L     12
      LASER  SHOT  #2  EXITED  THE  BOX  AT  24.

G   5    12    L
      THIS  IS  GUESS  #1.
      CONGRATULATIONS,  YOU  HAVE  NOW  FOUND  1  BAFFLE(S).
```

P

```
              10 11 12 13 14 15 16 17 18 19
            9 -+--+--+--+--+--+--+--+--+--+- 20
            8 -+--+--+--+--+--+--+--+--+--+- 21
            7 -+--+--+--+--+--+--+--+--+--+- 22
            6 -+--+--+--+--+--+--+--+--+--+- 23
            5 -+--+--L--+--+--+--+--+--+--+- 24
            4 -+--+--+--+--+--+--+--+--+--+- 25
            3 -+--+--+--+--+--+--+--+--+--+- 26
            2 -+--+--+--+--+--+--+--+--+--+- 27
            1 -+--+--+--+--+--+--+--+--+--+- 28
            0 -+--+--+--+--+--+--+--+--+--+- 29
              39 38 37 36 35 34 33 32 31 30
```

L   30
     LASER SHOT #3 EXITED THE BOX AT 20.

G   30   20   R

     *** OPERANDS OUT OF BOUNDS -- TRY AGAIN ***

G   9   19   R
     THIS IS GUESS #2.
     CONGRATULATIONS, YOU HAVE NOW FOUND 2 BAFFLE(S).

K   17
     *** ILLEGAL COMMAND -- TRY AGAIN ***

L   17
     LASER SHOT #4 EXITED THE BOX AT 5.

G   5   12   L
     THIS IS GUESS #3.
     YOU HAVE ALREADY FOUND THIS BAFFLE.

S

     NUMBER OF SHOTS: 4
     NUMBER OF GUESSES: 3
     CURRENT SCORE: 10

        .
        .
        .

G   1   10   R
     THIS IS GUESS #15.
     SORRY, BETTER LUCK NEXT TIME.

L   1
     LASER SHOT #26 EXITED THE BOX AT 37.
```
```

```
G   1   12   L
    THIS IS GUESS #16.
    CONGRATULATIONS, YOU HAVE NOW FOUND 5 BAFFLE(S).

************* YOU FOUND ALL THE BAFFLES ***************

    NUMBER OF SHOTS: 26
    NUMBER OF GUESSES:   16
    CURRENT SCORE:   58

            10 11 12 13 14 15 16 17 18 19
         9 -+--+--+--+--+--+--+--+--+--R- 20
         8 -+--+--+--+--+--+--+--+--+--+- 21
         7 -+--+--+--+--+--+--+--+--+--+- 22
         6 -+--+--+--+--+--+--+--+--+--+- 23
         5 -+--+--L--+--+--+--+--+--+--+- 24
         4 -+--+--+--+--+--+--+--+--+--+- 25
         3 -R--+--+--+--+--+--+--+--+--+- 26
         2 -+--+--+--+--+--+--+--+--+--+- 27
         1 -+--+--L--+--+--+--+--R--+--+- 28
         0 -+--+--+--+--+--+--+--+--+--+- 29
            39 38 37 36 35 34 33 32 31 30
```

Your output may differ in minor details from this example. (Different error messages, slight format differences, etc.)

7. You are the manager of a team of ten programmers who have just completed a seminar in structured programming and top-down design. To prove to your boss that these techniques pay off, you decide to run the following contest: You number the programmers 1 .. 10 based on their performance in the seminar (1 is poorest, 10 is best) and monitor their work. As each does his or her part of your project, you keep track of the number of lines of debugged code turned in by each programmer. You record this number as a programmer turns in a debugged module. The winner of the contest is the first person to reach 1000 lines of debugged code. (You hope this will be programmer #9 or #10.) As further proof of the the value of these new techniques, you want to determine how many poor programmers it takes to surpass the winner's figure; that is, find the smallest k such that programmers 1 .. k have turned in more lines than the winner.

Input: The input consists of a sequence of pairs of integers. The first integer in each pair is the programmer's number (an integer from 1 to 10), and the second is the number of lines of code turned in. The pairs occur in the same order as that in which the modules were turned in. (Incidentally, there will be two integers per line, but this should make no difference.)

Output: Read in pairs of integers until someone's total goes over 1000. Print out (echoprint) each pair as you read it. Ignore any input after someone's total exceeds 1000. Then print out a table listing the ten programmers and their totals, with the winner flagged as shown in the example below. Finally, find the smallest k such that the sum of programmers

1 .. k totals exceeds the winner's total. Print k in a sentence describing k's meaning.

Sample:

Input:

10	230	Note: To keep it short, we made these
8	206	numbers unrealistically big.
7	111	
3	159	
9	336	
1	51	
10	250	
4	101	
9	341	
2	105	
8	256	
10	320	
3	150	
5	215	
7	222	
9	400	← #9 goes over 1000.
8	321	} Ignore these.
5	56	

Output:

```
      10          230  ⎫
              ·         ⎬  Echo the first 16 pairs.
              ·         ⎪
       9          400  ⎭
```

```
Programmer #  Lines
    1           51
    2          105
    3          309
    4          101
    5          215
    6            0
    7          333
    8          462
    9         1077 *** THE WINNER
   10          800

IT TOOK PROGRAMMERS 1 THROUGH 7 TO
PRODUCE MORE THAN THE WINNER.
```

Chapter 2 ─────────────────────────────

Since no new structures are introduced in Chapter 2, the programming assignments for Chapter 1 are also appropriate for Chapter 2.

1. Complete the command-driven tester described in this chapter and test the string routines. (Let us know if you find an error!)

2. You have just bought a personal computer to use for writing your term papers. It has a text editor, but it does not have a text formatter. You decide to write one that will recognize a simple set of formatting commands.

Input: There are two kinds of inputs to your formatter. One consists of commands to the formatter and the other is the text to be formatted. Formatting commands all begin with a period in the first character position of a line. Formatting commands and the text to be formatted are interspersed on the same file.

Commands:

.L ⟨integer⟩   Set line length to ⟨integer⟩ characters

.B ⟨integer⟩   Write ⟨integer⟩ blank lines.

.J   The text to be formatted begins on the next line and continues until another formatting command is encountered. The text should be both left and right justified within the line length specified.

.Q   Quit processing.

Output: The text formatted as described by the embedded formatting commands.

Assumptions:
1. A .L command setting the line length will be encountered before any text that is to be formatted is encountered.
2. The line length may be reset at any time.
3. When a command line is encountered, finish processing the current output line before executing the formatting command. The current line may not be right justified in this case.
4. Each formatting command is on a line by itself.
5. .J will appear immediately before any text that is to be formatted.

Sample input:

```
.L80
.B2
.J
text to be formatted
.B2
.J
text to be formatted
.Q
```

Prints two blocks of text with 2 blank lines between; the lines in each block are both right and left justified within 80 columns; the last line of each block may be less than 80 columns.

*3. Your assignment is to write a pattern-matching program that responds to a sequence of inquiries concerning the meanings of certain words in a given dictionary. Each inquiry specifies a pattern of characters along with a restriction regarding the pattern's relative position within the required word. The pattern may be found at the beginning, end, or middle of the word, according to the request. For each inquiry, either no such word exists in the given dictionary, exactly one such word exists, or more than one is found to satisfy the requirement specified by the inquiry. Corresponding to each of these three cases should be an appropriate response from your program (see output section below).

Input: The first part is in fixed format, and its purpose is to define the dictionary; the second part is in free format, and it contains the sequence of inquiries.

Part 1 is composed of a series of lines, each containing a word terminated by a colon, followed by its meaning. There may be blanks following the colon and preceding the meaning. The last line in this part is recognized by an asterisk in column 1.

The words begin in column 1, and their corresponding meanings may be stored and printed out, whenever required, in the same format as they appear in the input file, with leading blanks removed.

Part 2 is composed of a sequence of four possible inquiries appearing in any order. In each inquiry, ⟨pattern⟩ is a string of alphanumeric characters terminated by a period.

STARTING	⟨pattern⟩	Find the meaning of the word that starts with the given pattern.
ENDING	⟨pattern⟩	Find the meaning of the word that ends with the given pattern.
CONTAINING	⟨pattern⟩	Find the meaning of the word that contains the given pattern (including the beginning or the end of the word).
STOP	⟨pattern⟩	Stop all processing immediately.

Data structure: The dictionary of words and their meanings must be stored in an appropriate data structure.

Output: Echoprint all the input. For each inquiry there are three possible outputs:

1. If no word in the dictionary satisfies the inquiry, print an appropriate message.
2. If exactly one such word exists, the meaning of this word should be printed out.
3. If more than one word satisfies the inquiry, list these words without their meanings.

Assumptions: You may assume that there are no more than 30 words in the dictionary for testing this program.

*4. Groucho Marx used to have a game show called "You Bet Your Life" in which he would have a conversation with the contestant and would try to get him or her to say a specified "magic word." If the contestant said the magic word, a duck would drop down, signaling that the contestant had won a prize. This problem deals with a similar game (we could call it "You Bet Your Grade"), which will have a specified *set* of magic words. The input will consist of several passages of text. You will read in each passage, see if it includes all the magic words, and then print whether or not the person wins the prize.

Input: The input is divided into sections. The last section is terminated by a $. All other sections are terminated by a *. You may assume the $ and all the *s are preceded by a blank.

A section is divided into words. A *word* is a sequence of letters and is terminated by any nonalphabetic character. Words are at most ten characters long. All nonalphabetic characters are completely ignored; their only purpose is to terminate words and (for * and $) mark the end of a section.

The first section gives all the magic words. The remaining sections give the text for each contestant. The first two words in each section give the contestant's name.

Output: Initially, print out the list of magic words, then echo each section as it is read. Test for end-of-line so that the output will have its end-of-lines in the same place as the input. For each section, keep track of which magic words were said, and at the end of the section, print out a message indicating whether the contestant won the prize. Suitable messages are

CONGRATULATIONS ⟨name⟩, YOU HAVE WON THE PRIZE

SORRY, ⟨name⟩, YOU FAILED TO SAY THE FOLLOWING MAGIC WORDS:
⟨list of unsaid magic words⟩

Note that you must print out the name and the list of unsaid magic words if the contestant loses.

Jim Bitner

Chapter 3

1. You are to write a set of utility routines to manipulate a group of three stacks. The specifications for these routines are given in terms of preconditions and postconditions. The preconditions to each routine tell you what the routine may assume to be true on entry to the routine. The postconditions state what the routine guarantees to be true on exit from the routine. The notation is as follows:

S	the specified stack
S′	the stack before the last operation on it
first(S)	the most recent element put in S
length(S)	the number of elements in S
‖	concatenated with

Stack operations:

```
PROCEDURE PUSH (VAR S : STACKTYPE;
                X : ETYPE;
                VAR OVERFLOW : BOOLEAN);
```

preconditions: TRUE
postconditions: S = X ‖ S′ AND OVERFLOW = NOT FULL(S′)
    OR S = S′ AND OVERFLOW = FULLS(S)

```
PROCEDURE POP (VAR S : STACKTYPE;
                VAR X : ETYPE;
                VAR UNDERFLOW : BOOLEAN);
```

preconditions: TRUE
postconditions: S′ = X ‖ S AND UNDERFLOW = EMPTYS(S)

```
PROCEDURE CLEARS (VAR S : STACKTYPE);
```

precondition: TRUE
postconditions: S = emptystack

```
PROCEDURE STACKTOP (S : STACKTYPE;
                    VAR UNDERFLOW : BOOLEAN;
                    VAR TOP : ETYPE);
```

preconditions: TRUE
postconditions: S = S′ and TOP = first(S) AND UNDERFLOW =
            NOT EMPTYS(S)
        OR S = S′ AND UNDERFLOW = EMPTYS(S) AND TOP
        IS UNDEFINED

```
FUNCTION EMPTYS (S : STACKTYPE) : BOOLEAN;
```

precondition: TRUE
postconditions: FULLS = (length(S) = MAXSTACK);

Testing: The input data consist of a series of commands to test your routines.
There are an arbitrary number of blanks between commands. Be sure
to echoprint each command before you execute it.

Stacks will be designated by the integers 1 through 3. Elements will be
strings of 1 to 20 characters, including embedded blanks, delimited by a period.
(The period is *not* part of the element.)

Commands:

PUSH ⟨stacknumber⟩ ⟨element⟩
Execute Procedure PUSH, using ⟨element⟩ as the value to be put on the designated stack. If an error condition occurs, print an appropriate message.

POP ⟨stacknumber⟩
Execute Procedure POP, using the designated stack, and print the value returned. If an error condition occurs, print an appropriate message.

STACKTOP ⟨stacknumber⟩
Execute Procedure STACKTOP, using the designated stack, and print the value
returned. If an error occurs, print an appropriate error message.

CLEARS ⟨stacknumber⟩
Execute Procedure CLEARS, using the designated stack.

EMPTYS ⟨stacknumber⟩
Execute Function EMPTYS, using the designated stack, and print the result.

FULLS ⟨stacknumber⟩
Execute Function FULLS, using the designated stack, and print the result.

PRINT ⟨stacknumber⟩

Print the elements in the designated stack. The stack must be returned to its original state. (*Hint:* Use a temporary stack.)

DUMP

Print the elements in *all* the stacks.

STOP

Stop executing.

Note that all the preconditions are TRUE. This means that all the testing for full and/or empty is being done in the utility routines themselves. If the testing were done in the *calling* routine, this would be stated in the preconditions. Which routines would this change? What would the preconditions look like?

Sample data:

```
CLEARS 2
PUSH         2 SALLY.
CLEARS       1
    CLEARS 5
PUSH 1 GEORGE.    PUSH      2
 JO ANN.
     PUSH
5 SUSAN.          CLEARS         3
CLEARS      4 POP 5 TOP 2    PUSH 5 JOE. PUSH 5
TOM.   PUSH 5    MARY    JO. PUSH    3 HENRY. PUSH 3        HARRY.
PUSH 5 DICK.
TOP 5   EMPTYS                  2 EMPTYS 4 PUSH
4    ELLEN. PUSH 3 JANE.POP   2 POP 2 POP 2 DUMP
PUSH 1 HARRIET.
PUSH 1 STANLEY.
PUSH 1 LIVINGSTON.
FULLS 1
TOP 4
POP         5
CLEARS 2
PUSH 2 LIZZIE.PUSH 1 JOSEPH.PUSH      1 ELLEN. TOP 4
     PUSH 1 SALLY ANN. PUSH 2 JOHN. PUSH    5 HARRY. POP
4
PUSH 1 GEORGE II.PUSH 1              ELIZABETH. PUSH   1 SALLY.
PUSH 1 DICK.      POP 5
PUSH 1      WILLIAM. EMPTYS 5 TOP 1 EMPTYS 4 FULLS 1
CLEARS 5
   DUMP
PUSH 1 TOM. PUSH 1 JO ANN. POP 3 POP 3
PUSH 1 JAMIE. PUSH 1 DANIEL. TOP 1       PUSH 1
ELLEN. TOP 4     DUMP
CLEARS    2   CLEARS 3    PUSH   1 JOHN. PUSH 1 LIZZIE.
PUSH 1 RICKIE.
FULLS 1
FULLS 2
EMPTYS 1
```

```
CLEARS 3
EMPTYS 2      PUSH 1     JULIE.                    DUMP
STOP
```

2. Alter the maze program given in this chapter so that it prints out the path used to exit the maze if a path is found.

*3. This problem requires you to write a program to convert an infix to a postfix expression. The evaluation of an infix expression like A + B * C requires knowledge of which of the two operations, + or *, should be performed first. In general, A + B * C is to be interpreted as A + (B * C) unless otherwise specified. We say that multiplication takes *precedence* over addition. Suppose that we would now like to convert A + B * C to postfix. Applying the rules of precedence, *we first convert the portion of the expression that is evaluated first,* namely the multiplication. Doing this conversion in stages, we obtain:

A + B * C	Given infix form
A + BC *	Convert the multiplication
ABC * +	Convert the addition

The major rules to remember during the conversion process are that the operations with highest precedence are converted first and that after a portion of an expression has been converted to postfix it is to be treated as a single operand. Let us now consider the same example with the precedence of operators reversed by the deliberate insertion of parentheses.

(A + B) * C	Given infix form
AB + * C	Convert the addition
AB + C *	Convert the multiplication

Note that in the conversion from AB + * C to AB + C *, AB + was treated as a single operand. The rules for converting from infix to postfix are simple, provided that you know the order of precedence.

We consider four binary operations: addition, subtraction, multiplication, and division. These operations are denoted by the usual operators, +, −, *, and /, respectively. There are two levels of operator precedence. Both * and / have higher precedence than + and −. Furthermore, when unparenthesized operators of the same precedence are scanned, the order is assumed to be left to right. Parentheses may be used in infix expressions to override the default precedence.

As we discussed in this chapter, the postfix form requires no parentheses. The order of the operators in the postfix expressions determines the actual order of operations in evaluating the expression, making the use of parentheses unnecessary.

Input: A collection of *error-free* simple arithmetic expressions. Expressions are separated by semicolons, and the final expression is followed by a period.

The input is free format; an arbitrary number of blanks and end-of-lines may occur between any two symbols. A symbol may be a letter (A . . Z), an operator (+, −, *, or /), a left parenthesis, or a right parenthesis.

Each operand is composed of a single letter. The input expressions are in infix notation.

Example: A + B − C ;
          A + B * C ;
          (A + B)/(C − D) ;
          ((A + B) * (C − D) + E)/(F + G) .

Output: Your output should consist of each input expression, followed by its corresponding postfix expression. All output (including the original infix expressions) must be clearly formatted (or reformatted) and also clearly labeled.

Example: (Only the four postfix expressions corresponding to the above sample input are shown here.)
          AB + C −
          ABC * +
          AB + CD − /
          AB + CD − * E + FG + /

Discussion: In converting infix expressions to postfix notation, the following fact should be taken into consideration: The order of applying operators in infix form is governed by the possible appearance of parentheses and the operator precedence relations; however, in postfix form the order is simply the "natural" order, i.e., the order of appearance from left to right.

    Accordingly, subexpressions within innermost parentheses must first be converted to postfix, so that they can then be treated as single operands. In this fashion, parentheses can be successively eliminated until the entire expression is converted. The *last* pair of parentheses to be opened within a group of nested parentheses encloses the *first* subexpression within that group to be transformed. This last-in, first-out behavior should immediately suggest the use of a stack.

    Your program should utilize all the basic stack utility routines. (When writing these utility routines you must exercise extra care in making style and implementation decisions—i.e., choice of data structure and parameter lists.) You will need to CLEAR the stack, PUSH certain symbols on the stack, POP symbols, test if the stack is EMPTY, and look at the top symbol of the stack—STACKTOP—without changing the state of the stack.

    In addition, you must devise a BOOLEAN function that takes two operators and tells you which has higher precedence. This will be helpful because in Rule 3 below you need to compare the next input symbol to STACKTOP. Question: What precedence do you assign to "("? You need to answer this question since (may be the value of STACKTOP.

    You should formulate the conversion algorithm using the following six rules:

Rule 1:   Scan the input string (infix notation) from left to right. One pass is sufficient.

Rule 2:   If the next symbol scanned is an operand, it may be immediately appended to the postfix string.

Rule 3:   If the next symbol is an operator,
      (a) Pop and append to the prefix string every operator on the stack that
          (i) is above the most recently scanned left parenthesis, and
          (ii) has higher precedence than the new operator symbol.
      (b) Then push the new operator symbol onto the stack.

Rule 4: When an opening (left) parenthesis is seen, it must be pushed onto the stack.

Rule 5: When a closing (right) parenthesis is seen, all operators down to the most recently scanned left parenthesis must be popped and appended to the postfix string. Furthermore, this pair of parentheses must be discarded.

Rule 6: When the infix string is completely scanned, the stack may still contain some operators. (No parentheses at this point. Why?) All these remaining operators should be popped and appended to the postfix string.

Examples: Here are two examples to help you understand how the algorithm works. Each line below demonstrates the state of the postfix string and the stack when the corresponding next infix symbol is scanned. The rightmost symbol of the stack is the top symbol. The rule number corresponding to each line demonstrates which of the six rules was used to reach the current state from that of the previous line.

Example 1: Input expression is A + B * C / D − E.

Next symbol	Postfix string	Stack	Rule
A	A		2
+	A	+	3
B	A B	+	2
*	A B	+ *	3
C	A B C	+ *	2
/	A B C *	+ /	3
D	A B C * D	+ /	2
−	A B C * D / +	−	3
E	A B C * D / + E	−	2
	A B C * D / + E −		6

Example 2: Input expression is (A + B * (C − D))/E.

Next symbol	Postfix string	Stack	Rule
(		(	4
A	A	(	2
+	A	(+	3
B	A B	(+	2
*	A B	(+ *	3
(	A B	(+ * (	4
C	A B C	(+ * (	2
−	A B C	(+ * (−	3
D	A B C D	(+ * (−	2
)	A B C D −	(+ *	5
)	A B C D − * +		5
/	A B C D − * +	/	3
E	A B C D − * + E	/	2
	A B C D − * + E /		6

4. This problem requires you to write a program to convert a prefix to a postfix expression.

Input: The input consists of a series of error-free, simple arithmetic expressions in prefix notation. Expressions are separated by semicolons, and the final expression is followed by a period.

The input is free format; an arbitrary number of blanks and end-of-lines may occur between any two symbols. A symbol may be a letter (A . . Z) or an operator (+, =, *, or /).

Each operand is composed of a single letter.

Example: + * A B / C D;
       * A + B / C D;
       - * A + B / C D E;
       * + A B - C D.

Output: Your output should consist of the list of input expressions along with the corresponding converted postfix forms. All output should be clearly formatted and labeled.

Example: (These expressions correspond to the above input.)

Prefix	*Postfix*
+ * A B / C D	A B * C D / +
* A + B / C D	A B C D / + *
- * A + B / C D E	A B C D / + * E -
* + A B - C D	A B + C D - *

Note: Although your program does not process or print infix, here are the four infix expressions that correspond to the above forms:

A * B + C / D
A * (B + C / D)
A * (B + C / D) - E
(A + B) * (C - D)

Discussion: The key idea here is that after a portion of an expression has been converted, it is to be treated as a single operand.

Assume that every operator is associated with a flag. The flag is initially off to signal that neither of the two operands corresponding to the given operator has been processed yet. When the first operand is processed, the flag is switched on. When the second operand is processed, the given operator may be immediately appended to the output string.

Below is a description of a simple prefix-to-postfix conversion algorithm that works on one input expression:

1. Initialize the input string, the output string, and the operators stack.
2. Repeat steps 3–5 until there are no more input symbols.
3. Get the next input symbol.

4. If it is an operator, put it on the stack with its associated flag off.
5. If it is an operand, append it to the output string. Furthermore, the operand must correspond to the top operator on the stack. (Why?) Of course, the stack cannot be empty at this point. (Why?) Finally, here is the important question: Is the operand just processed the first or the second operand associated with the top operator? If it is the second, it is time to append the top operator to the output string. Now, remembering the key idea at the beginning of this section, determine what happens to the remaining operators on the stack.

Examples: Here is a hand simulation of the first and third sample input expressions given above. The rightmost symbol under *Stack* is the top operator. Parentheses around an operator denote that the associated flag is on. The *Stack* and *Out so far* columns show the relevant information *after* the next prefix symbol given on the same line has been processed.

Next prefix symbol	Stack	Out so far
+	+	
*	+ *	
A	+(*)	A
B	(+)	A B *
/	(+)/	A B *
C	(+ /)	A B * C
D		A B * C D / +
-	-	
*	- *	
A	- (*)	A
+	- (*)+	A
B	- (* +)	A B
/	- (* +)/	A B
C	- (* + /)	A B C
D	(-)	A B C D / + *
E		A B C D / + * E -

Munjid Musallam

Chapter 4

1. You are to write a set of utility routines to manipulate a queue. The specifications you are given are in terms of preconditions and postconditions, just as in assignment 1, Chapter 3. The following notation is used in the description of the routines:

Q — The current queue

Q' — The queue before the last operation on it

first(Q) — The element that has been in the queue for the longest time

length(Q) — The number of elements in the queue

‖ — concatenation

Queue operations:

```
PROCEDURE ENQ (VAR Q : QUEUETYPE; X : ETYPE;
               VAR ERROR : BOOLEAN)
```
  precondition: TRUE
  postcondition: $(Q = Q' \| <X>$ AND ERROR = FALSE)
           or $(Q = Q'$ AND ERROR = TRUE)

```
PROCEDURE DEQ (VAR Q : QUEUETYPE; VAR X : ETYPE;
               VAR ERROR : BOOLEAN)
```
  precondition: TRUE
  postcondition: $(Q' = <X> \| Q$ AND ERROR = FALSE)
           or $(Q' = Q$ AND ERROR = TRUE AND X = ?)

```
PROCEDURE CLEARQ (VAR Q : QUEUETYPE)
```
  precondition: TRUE
  postcondition: Q' = empty queue

```
PROCEDURE LOOK (Q : QUEUETYPE; VAR NEXT : ETYPE;
               VAR ERROR : BOOLEAN)
```
  precondition: TRUE
  postcondition: (NEXT = first(Q) AND $Q = Q'$ AND ERROR = FALSE)
           or $(Q' = Q$ AND ERROR = TRUE AND NEXT = ?)

```
FUNCTION EMPTYQ (Q : QUEUETYPE) : BOOLEAN
```
  precondition: TRUE
  postcondition: EMPTYQ = $(Q = <>)$

```
FUNCTION FULLQ (Q : QUEUETYPE) : BOOLEAN
```
  precondition: TRUE
  postcondition: FULLQ = (length(Q) = MAXQUEUE)

Note that all the preconditions are simply the one word TRUE, which means that there are no preconditions and that all error checking must be done in the procedures and functions themselves. The actual tests for full and empty queues must be coded only once. If you need to make that test in another procedure, call the appropriate functions.

Testing: Test your queue routines with a command-driven tester.

Commands:

ENQ ⟨letter⟩   Execute Procedure ENQ using ⟨letter⟩ as the value to be entered into the queue. If the error flag was set, print an appropriate error message.

DEQ   Execute Procedure DEQ. If the error flag was set, print an appropriate error message. Otherwise, print the value returned.

LOOK   Execute Procedure LOOK. If the error flag was set, print an appropriate error message. Otherwise, print the value returned.

CLEARQ   Execute Procedure CLEARQ.

EMPTYQ   Execute Function EMPTYQ.

FULLQ   Execute Function FULLQ.

PRINT   Print the elements of your array that are in the queue.

Be sure to echoprint each command before you execute it.

2. The application in this chapter is a simulation of a one-teller drive-in bank where the average transaction was fixed. Extend the simulation by varying transaction times as follows:

   20% of the customers take 2 minutes
   50% of the customers take 4 minutes
   30% of the customers take 7 minutes

3. In the discussion following the simulation of the one-teller drive-in bank, the technique of time stamping was described. Rewrite the simulation using time stamping.

*4. The local medical clinic has decided to automate its scheduling services. You have been assigned to design the initial version of the schedules. The basic functions that the clinic has in mind are doctor check-in and check-out and patient check-in and check-out.

   When a doctor checks in, he or she tells the scheduler his or her name, an examination room number, and a specialist code that tells what kind of doctor he or she is. Each doctor has a favorite room. The scheduler checks to see whether the room is free. If so, it assigns this doctor to the room; if not, it rejects the request with a message, and the doctor can try again to check in. When a doctor checks out, the examination room is freed.

   A patient checking in gives a name, age, specialist code, and emergency indication. The scheduler will try to match up the patient with a doctor according to a set of rules which will be described below. If there is a match, the patient is seen by the assigned doctor. If this doctor is currently seeing a patient, the new patient is queued to see the doctor according to the emergency indicator. Usually there is no emergency, and the patient is put at the end of the doctor's waiting list; if there is an emergency, however, the patient is put at the front of the waiting list ahead of any other patients.

   The rules for assigning doctors to patients are as follows:

   1. Any patient under age 16 is assigned to see a pediatrician.
   2. To patients age 16 and older, a doctor is assigned according to his or her specialty. If there is no doctor in the clinic with the requested specialty, the patient is assigned to a general practitioner (GP). If there is no GP, the patient can be assigned to any doctor.
   3. If there is more than one doctor of the requested specialty, the patient is assigned to the doctor with the shortest waiting list.

   When a patient checks out, the doctor he or she was assigned to is available to see the next patient if there is anyone in the waiting list.

   Input: Since this will be an interactive system, your program should prompt the users to input the correct information.

   The initial prompt is

   'TYPE D FOR DOCTOR OR P FOR PATIENT:'

The next prompt is

```
'TYPE I FOR CHECKIN OR
    O FOR CHECKOUT:'
```

According to the request, your program should prompt the user for any other needed information.

Doctor check-in: doctor name
                              room number
                              specialty code
Doctor check-out: doctor name
Patient check-in: patient name
                              age
                              specialty (code requested)
                              emergency flag
Patient check-out: patient name
                              room number

You may define the format for the input processed by your program.

Output: The output for each request is in the form of messages to the user according to the request.

Doctor check-in: confirmation that room is available *or* error message if room is in use
Doctor check-out: goodbye message
Patient check-in: Message telling patient which room to go to and which doctor has been assigned. If no doctor available, apologetic message.
Patient check-out: goodbye message. At a later time we may add billing information at this point.

Details and assumptions: 1. There are 100 examination rooms at the clinic, each with a waiting room attached.
                                    2. Specialty codes are:

PED	Pediatrics
GP	General practice
INT	Internal medicine
CARD	Cardiology
SUR	Surgeon
OBS	Obstetrics
PSY	Psychiatry
NEUR	Neurology
ORTH	Orthopedics
DERM	Dermatology
OPTH	Opthomology
ENT	Ear, Nose, and Throat

3. You may assume that no patient leaves without checking out. (That is, every doctor becomes free eventually.)
4. No one leaves before he or she sees the assigned doctor. (That is, no one has to be taken out of the waiting queue.) The clinic is open 24 hours a day, 7 days a week.
5. If a doctor checks out while there is still a waiting list of patients assigned to him or her, the patients must be reassigned to other doctors.

Data structures: The basic data structure is a list of examination rooms with waiting lists attached to each. Since the number of rooms is fixed, you may use an array of records to represent it. It is the waiting list attached to each examination room that is of interest to us. We have seen that patients are seen in the order in which they are added to the list (a simple queue), with one exception: emergency patients are "popped" onto the front of the queue. What we have here is a special data structure, kind of a dequeue, in which additions may be made to either end and deletions are always made at the front of the list.

Use the kind of data design process described in Chapter 4 to figure out how to best represent this structure. However you decide to implement it, you should encapsulate the details by creating utility routines to make the necessary additions and deletions to the waiting lists. (Consider, for instance, that you may have to find the shortest waiting list for a given specialty code, so the number of elements in the list is important.)

Chapter 5

1. This program illustrates the benefits of pushing implementation details into low-level subprograms. You are to revise Programming Assignment 1 of Chapter 3 to implement the stacks as linked lists. Use the array of records implementation for the linked lists. All five LISTS (and AVAIL) should be kept in the same array. You may assume in testing the routines that the number of elements in all the stacks together will not exceed 30, although they may all be in one stack. You should use the following declarations:

```
CONST MAXNODE = 30;
TYPE ETYPE = PACKED ARRAY[1..10] of CHAR;
     NODE = RECORD
                INFO : ETYPE;
                NEXT : 0..MAXNODE
            END; (* record *)

VAR NODES : ARRAY[1..MAXNODE] OF NODE
```

You will need to modify the stack operation procedures and functions. Since the number of elements in all the stacks together will not exceed 30, a stack can never be full. Hence the result of Command FULLS and Function FULLS under this implementation would always be FALSE. If there is danger of running out of storage space, the error checking should be within the system routine GETNODE. What should be done in such a case is an interesting question, but not one this problem is designed to examine.

2. Rewrite the queue routines described in Chapter 4 using a linked-list representation. Test these routines using the driver in Assignment 1 of Chapter 4.

3. Modify the mailing label program as suggested in the discussion following the program.

4. You know that your next program is going to be large. You can guess that it will use linked lists. To get ahead of the rest of the class, you decide to write some utility routines and have them debugged and ready to use. The utility routines that you decide to write are listed below:

INSERT FIRST
This routine will take a LIST and an element, and insert the element as the first element in the LIST.

REMOVE FIRST
This routine will take a LIST and a variable name, remove the first element of the LIST, and return its value in the variable.

PRINT LIST
This routine will take a LIST and print the elements.

SEARCH & DELETE
This routine will take a LIST and an element. If the element is on the LIST, it will delete it. A Boolean variable will record whether or not the element was found.

EXCHANGE RIGHT
This routine will take a LIST and an element. If the element is not the last element, it will change places with the element to its right in the list (that is, move it down in the list). You may assume that the element is there.

EXCHANGE LEFT
This routine will take a LIST and an element. If the element is not the first element, it will change places with the element to its left in the list (that is, move it up in the list). You may assume that the element is there.

INSERT IN PLACE
This routine will take a LIST and an element, and insert the element in its place so that the element to its left is less than it and the element to its right is equal to or greater than it.

IS THERE
This routine takes a LIST and an element, and returns TRUE if the element is in the LIST and FALSE otherwise.

Since you do not know whether singly linked lists or doubly linked lists will be better for this program, you decide to write these routines for both. That is, each task will have two routines, one for a list with a forward link only and one for a list with both a forward and a backward link.

Testing: You should test your routines in two runs: one for the singly linked list and one for the doubly linked version. To create your list, insert the characters 'A' .. 'Z'.

Part of this assignment is to determine what test cases must be run to completely test the routines you have written. For instance, to test the exchange left routine, you should call it with a letter from the middle of the list, like 'D', and with the letter from the beginning of the list. Run enough test cases to completely demonstrate the function of your routines and any error conditions.

Use your print routine to print the contents of the list after each of the tests has been done.

*5. Your assignment is to track the corporate careers of some up-and-coming executives who are busily changing jobs, being promoted and demoted, and, of course, getting paid.

In this version of the corporate world, people either belong to a company or are unemployed. The list of people the program must deal with is not fixed; initially there are none, and new people may be introduced by the JOIN command (see below).

Executives within a company are ordered according to a seniority system and are numbered from 1 to N (the number of people in the company) to indicate their rank: 1 is the lowest rank and N is the highest. A new employee *always* enters at the bottom of the ladder and hence will always start with a rank of 1. When a new person joins a company, the rank of everyone in the company is increased by one, and when an employee quits, the rank of employees above him or her in that company is decreased by one. Promotions can also occur and affect the ranks in the obvious way.

Naturally, salaries are based on rank. An employee's salary is RANK * $1000. Unemployed people draw a $50 "salary" in unemployment compensation.

Input: The input consists of a list of all possible companies, followed by the word END, followed by a list of commands (see below), followed by the word END.

The input is free format; an arbitrary number of blanks and end-of-lines may occur between any two input words. There will be at most 20 companies. The name of every company and person will be at most ten characters long. Names consist of letters only and do not have embedded blanks.

Commands and output: Execution consists of two phases—processing the commands and then printing out the total amount each person has earned during execution of the program. The seven commands are listed below, along with the required output. Note that if a person is currently employed, the command does not tell you his or her current company, so you will have to search your data structure to find the person.

JOIN ⟨person⟩ ⟨company⟩

The given person joins the specified company. This may be the first reference to this person, or he or she may be unemployed. The person will not currently belong to another company. Remember that when a person joins a company he or she always starts at the bottom.

QUIT ⟨person⟩

The given person quits his or her job and becomes unemployed. You may assume that the person *is* currently employed.

CHANGE ⟨person⟩ ⟨newcompany⟩

The given person quits his or her job and joins the specified company. You may assume that the person *is* currently employed.

PROMOTE ⟨person⟩

The given person is moved up one step, ahead of his or her immediate superior. If the person has highest rank within the company, no change occurs.

DEMOTE ⟨person⟩

The given person is moved one step down, below his or her immediate subordinate. If the person has lowest rank within the company, no change occurs.

PAYDAY

Each person is paid his or her salary as specified above. (You will have to keep track of the amount each person has earned from the start of the program.)

DUMP

The current list of employees should be printed for each company. The employees must be printed in order of rank; either top to bottom or bottom to top is appropriate. The list of unemployed people should also be printed. (Note that DUMP may be very useful in debugging.)

After all the commands have been processed, print out one list consisting of all the people who have been mentioned in any command and the total amount of money they have accumulated. The list should be sorted by decreasing order of total salary accumulated.

Testing: You may want to test your program on the following sample data:

```
UNIVEGA    REYNOLDS    ECLIPSE    TREK    MOTOBECANE
    PEUGEOT  PINTO  END  JOIN
    EVEL
PINTO JOIN
    MARIO
    PINTO
JOIN JOHN TREK
JOIN FRED TREK
JOIN PHIL ECLIPSE
CHANGE FRED PEUGEOT
JOIN SUE TREK
JOIN SHARON REYNOLDS
JOIN HARV TREK
CHANGE SUE UNIVEGA
        PAYDAY          DUMP
JOIN MARGE UNIVEGA
JOIN LESLEY REYNOLDS
JOIN SAM TREK
JOIN GEORGE PEUGEOT
```

```
JOIN BOB UNIVEGA
JOIN SHARLEENA ECLIPSE
JOIN DAVE TREK
JOIN MAX PEUGEOT
        PAYDAY DUMP
JOIN TIM ECLIPSE
DEMOTE HARV
PROMOTE MAX
DEMOTE MARGE
CHANGE MARGE ECLIPSE
QUIT JOHN
        DUMP      PAYDAY     DUMP
QUIT MARIO
QUIT EVEL
PROMOTE MARGE
PROMOTE MARGE
        PAYDAY    DUMP
JOIN JOHN MOTOBECANE
JOIN RALPH MOTOBECANE
QUIT PHIL
JOIN PHIL MOTOBECANE
          DUMP
CHANGE MARGE MOTOBECANE
CHANGE SUE MOTOBECANE
CHANGE FRED MOTOBECANE
CHANGE SHARLEENA MOTOBECANE
QUIT TIM
          PAYDAY    DUMP
JOIN MARIO PINTO
JOIN EVEL PINTO
JOIN TIM MOTOBECANE
PROMOTE TIM
PROMOTE FRED
DEMOTE SUE
        DUMP
JOIN LASZLO TREK
PROMOTE LASZLO
CHANGE DAVE MOTOBECANE
        PAYDAY    DUMP
PROMOTE SHARON
DEMOTE LESLEY
PROMOTE BOB
DEMOTE BOB
DEMOTE JOHN
          PAYDAY    DUMP
END
```

Jim Bitner

*6. The problem is to keep track of the lists of members in a set of clubs as members join, quit, and change clubs, as given by the input. Periodically, the input will ask you to print all the members in a given club or to find all the clubs to which a given person belongs.

Input: A list of all possible clubs, followed by the word END followed by a list of commands (see next section), followed by the word END. The input is free format; an arbitrary number of blanks and end-of-lines may occur between any two input words.

Example:

```
KIWANIS LIONS ELKS YMCA END
JOIN SMITH YMCA
JOIN FIXX YMCA
END
```

There will be at most 20 clubs. The name of every club and person will be at most 10 characters.

Commands and output: The six possible commands are listed below, together with their semantics and required output.

JOIN   ⟨person⟩ ⟨club⟩

Add the given person to the given club. (If the person is already in it, do nothing.)

Output: Either "⟨person⟩ has been added to ⟨club⟩" or "error— ⟨person⟩ is already in ⟨club⟩", whichever is appropriate.

QUIT   ⟨person⟩ ⟨club⟩

Delete person from club.

Output: Either " ⟨person⟩ has been deleted from ⟨club⟩" or "error— ⟨person⟩ is not in ⟨club⟩".

CHANGE   ⟨person⟩ ⟨club1⟩ ⟨club2⟩

Delete person from club1, then add person to club2.

Output: First print the appropriate deletion message (see QUIT), then the appropriate insertion message (see JOIN).

PRINT   ⟨club⟩

Print all the members in the club.

Output: "The member(s) in club are:", followed by the list of members in sorted order, one per line.

FIND   ⟨person⟩

Find and print all the clubs to which the person belongs.

Output: " ⟨person⟩ belongs to the following club(s):" followed by the list of clubs, in any order, one per line.

MERGE   ⟨club1⟩ ⟨club2⟩

Merge the list of members for the two clubs. If a person is in both clubs, the name should occur only once in the merged list. From now on, the merged club can be referred to by either club name (!)

Output: "club1 and club2 have been merged."

Suggested data structure: The only requirement placed on your data structure is that you *must* store the members of each club in a linked list. The list can be doubly linked or circular if you think that will make things easier.

One suggested data structure consists of an array, TABLE, of records that have one field, NAME, to store the club name, and another field, NEXT, to point to a list of members of this club. A suitable declaration is

```
TYPE NAMETYPE  = PACKED ARRAY (1..10) OF CHAR;
     PTRTYPE   = 0..20;
     BLOCK     = RECORD
                     NAME: NAMETYPE;
                     NEXT: PTRTYPE
                 END; (* record *)
     TABLETYPE = ARRAY (1..20) of BLOCK;

     VAR TABLE:  TABLETYPE;
```

Each club can be stored as a linked list (whose components are of type BLOCK) that has a header (whose name is ignored) and a trailer (whose name is ZZZZZZZZZZ, which you can assume is *not* the name of any person). The linked list should be sorted so that the PRINT operation is easily done.

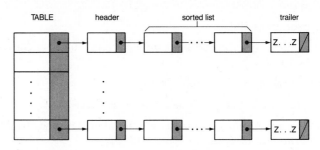

The header will make the insert, delete, and merge operations easier, and the trailer will simplify insertion into the sorted list.

A note on the merge operation: After the two lists are merged together, the pointers for both clubs must be set to the header of the merged list. In this way, we access the merged list of members when the name of either club is mentioned. If this club is merged with another club, *both* these pointers will have to be changed again.

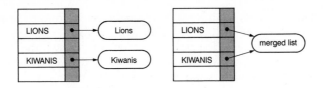

Jim Bitner

*7. A friend of yours is opening a small grocery warehouse. He has offered you 10% of the first year's profits if you will write an accounting system for the warehouse. What can you lose?

Input:

Inventory master file (maximum of 20 items):

⟨item name⟩ ⟨L / F⟩ ⟨quantity price⟩,
⟨quantity price⟩ ... *

⟨item name⟩	A character string of up to ten characters ending with a blank. (There are no embedded blanks.)
⟨L / F⟩	Either the letter L (for LIFO) or the letter F (for FIFO). There will be at least one blank before this letter (the blank that ended the item name); there may be more than one.
⟨quantity price⟩	The quantity will be a three-digit integer followed by at least one blank; the price will be a real value representing the cost per unit of the item followed by at least one blank. The end of the information for an item name is an asterisk in place of the comma. Both the asterisk and the comma may have one blank or multiple blanks around them.

The last item on the INVENTORY FILE has a $ in place of the asterisk.

Transaction file:

BOUGHT	⟨item name⟩ ⟨quantity price⟩	Item delivered to warehouse.
SOLD	⟨item name⟩ ⟨quantity⟩	Item removed from warehouse
LOSS	⟨item name⟩ ⟨reason⟩ ⟨quantity⟩	Item removed from warehouse
ENDDAY	⟨date⟩	
STOP		

⟨item name⟩ and ⟨quantity price⟩ are defined as above. ⟨reason⟩ and ⟨quantity⟩ are the same syntactically as ⟨item name⟩. ⟨reason⟩ is the one-word explanation of the loss, and ⟨date⟩ is the day's date. There is only one ⟨quantity price⟩ per BOUGHT or SOLD command. The transaction file is ended with the command STOP.

Processing: (See OUTPUT for required statistics.)

BOUGHT This ⟨quantity price⟩ pair will be added to the list of ⟨quantity price⟩ pairs associated with this ⟨item name⟩. This transaction will be recorded on the daily report. When an item is bought, the backorder list must be checked to see if there is an unfilled order for this item.

SOLD   This ⟨quantity⟩ will be removed from the list of the ⟨item name⟩ and the transaction will be recorded. If the item is a LIFO item, the ⟨quantity⟩ will be recorded at the last purchase price. If the item is a FIFO item, the ⟨quantity⟩ will be recorded at the earliest purchase price.

          If the ⟨quantity⟩ sold is more than is currently in inventory, fill as much of the order as you can and backorder the rest. This means putting the item name and the quantity left to be filled into the list of backordered items. This list should be kept in alphabetical order by item name.

LOSS   Remove from inventory as if it were sold. The quantity lost, the cost of the loss, and the reason for the loss should be recorded on the daily report.

ENDDAY   Write the date and summary statistics for the day as specified under OUTPUT.

STOP   Write out the updated INVENTORY MASTER file to be used for the next update run. The STOP will always follow the last ENDDAY.

Output: A daily report on OUTPUT showing the following information:

   1. Value of the inventory at the beginning of the day.
   2. Each transaction recorded as specified.
   3. The following summary statistics:
      (a) Dollar volume of items BOUGHT that day
      (b) Dollar volume of items SOLD that day
      (c) Dollar volume of LOSS that day
      (d) Value of inventory at the end of that day

Data structures: 1. An array of records. Each record contains the item name, whether it is LIFO or FIFO, and a pointer to a linked list of nodes, each of which contains an amount and a price per amount.

           2. A linked list of backordered items and quantity kept, ordered by item name.

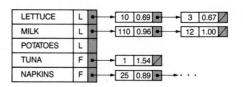

Note: You might find it useful to carry a pointer to the end of the list as well.

Assumptions: 1. You may assume that the master file is correct.
           2. You may not assume that the transaction file is correct. It may have invalid commands or misspelled item names. If you encounter an unknown ⟨item name⟩ or command, print an error message on the daily report and skip to the next command. You may assume that the ⟨quantity price⟩ is correct (i.e., you may use a numeric read).
           3. An item name will appear only once on the INVENTORY MASTER file.
           4. There will be no more than 20 item names.

Special cases: 1. Two nodes with the same price side by side can be combined.

2. If the amount sold is more than the quantity in the node to be removed first, you may have part of the order filled at one price and part at another.

*8. Your neighbor is an agent for a group of magicians. People call her to book magicians for holidays. She would like to use her new computer to keep track of the jobs she schedules for the magicians she manages, so she hires you to write the program.

Input: The input comes in three parts. The first part is a list of magicians. The names are in free format, separated by blanks and terminated by a *. You may assume that none of the magicians has a name longer than ten characters.

The second part of the input is a list of holidays. Again, the names are in free format, separated by blanks and terminated by a *. Assume none of the holidays has a name longer than ten characters.

The third part of the input is a series of commands (see below). Commands are in free format. Names in a command are at most ten characters long.

SCHEDULE ⟨person⟩ ⟨holiday⟩

The given person wants to book a magician for the given holiday. Check to see if there is a magician free for this holiday. You should sequence through the magicians in the order in which you read them in. If a magician is available, book the magician and print out the name of the magician, the holiday, and the name of the person. If a magician is not available, put the person on a waiting list, and print out a message indicating that the person and holiday have been put on a waiting list.

CANCEL ⟨person⟩ ⟨holiday⟩

The given person has canceled his or her booking of a magician for the listed holiday. Delete the reservation for that holiday. Update the schedule of the magician who was going to perform for the occasion. This may allow someone on the waiting list to be serviced. Sequence through the waiting list to see if someone wanted a booking on that holiday. If someone did want a magician on that holiday, schedule the booking and print a message. If this person is on the waiting list, delete the name from the waiting list.

QUIT ⟨magician⟩

Occasionally a magician quits. When that happens, you have to try to redistribute that magician's bookings to other magicians. If you reschedule a booking, print a message. If you can't, print out a message and add the request to the front of the waiting list.

STATUS ⟨magician *or* holiday⟩

Print out either the schedule of the named magician or the schedule for a given holiday.

END

End of input; quit processing.

Data structures: You will need data structures for storing each of the following:

1. a list of bookings for each holiday. There are at most ten holidays you need to worry about, so use an array of ten lists. Each list is the schedule on some holiday. Each record in a list gives the name of the person who made the booking and the name of the magician. Each list should be stored in alphabetical order according to the person who made the booking.

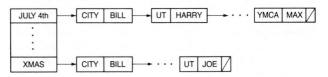

2. a list of bookings for each magician. There are at most ten magicians. Use an array of ten lists. Each list is the schedule of some magician. Each record in a list gives the name of the person who made the booking and the holiday. Each list should be stored in alphabetical order according to the holiday.

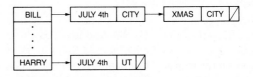

3. a waiting list. You will need to be able to add to either end of the waiting list. You add to the front of the waiting list if you are rescheduling someone who had a booking but lost it when a magician quit. You add to the back of the waiting list if someone requests an appointment and there are no free magicians.

Each of the lists should be a linked list, represented using arrays.

Output: 1. If a booking is made, print

⟨person⟩ ⟨holiday⟩ ⟨magician⟩

Example:

YMCA JULY4th HOUDINI

2. If you put someone on the waiting list, print

I'VE PUT ⟨person⟩ ⟨holiday⟩ ON THE WAITING LIST.

3. If you cancel an appointment, print

I'VE CANCELED ⟨person⟩ ⟨holiday⟩ ⟨magician⟩.

4. If a magician quits and you put someone on the waiting list, print

   I'VE PUT ⟨person⟩ ⟨holiday⟩ AT THE FRONT OF THE
   WAITING LIST.

5. If a status report of a magician is asked for, print

   ⟨magician⟩'s SCHEDULE:
   ⟨holiday1⟩ ⟨person1⟩   ← alphabetical order by
   ⟨holiday2⟩ ⟨person2⟩   holiday

6. If a status report for a holiday is asked for, print

   ⟨holiday⟩ SCHEDULE:
   ⟨person⟩ ⟨magician⟩   ← alphabetical order by
   ⟨person⟩ ⟨magician⟩   person who made the
                                 booking

Rick Alterman

Chapter 6

Any of the programming assignments for Chapter 5 may be written using Pascal pointer variables instead of an array implementation.

*1. This is a program for the local libraries. It contains the fiction books available at each of several branches. Each branch keeps its books in a linked list arranged in alphabetical order by the author's name. Books by the same author are arranged alphabetically by title. There may be several copies of the same book in a branch.

When a book is checked out from a branch, it is deleted from the linked list for that branch. When it is returned to a branch, it is inserted in the appropriate position in the list by its author and title. Patrons can ask the library to find the number of copies of a book available at a particular branch at the present time.

Occasionally remodeling is done, and the library moves all the fiction books from branch A to branch B, where branch B never has been and never will be remodeled. When this happens, the list of books from the branch to be remodeled should be merged with the list of books at the branch that will now contain those books. If a customer should try to return a book or check out a book from the branch being remodeled, he or she will want to go to the branch now housing the remodeled branch's books. Hence, you should keep a pointer from the branch being remodeled to the branch that its books were moved to. (We will not ask you to reopen a remodeled branch.)

The list structure can be one of three major designs:

1. BRANCH

2. BRANCH

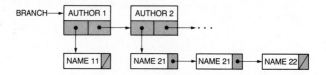

3. Either 1 or 2 with a num-of-copies field rather than two separate NAME21 nodes.

The list structure under option 2 performs the operations requested more efficiently than the others. However, you may use any one of the three.

The program is horribly inefficient if it starts scanning at Adams when looking for a book by Stevenson. To avoid this problem, you can create an array (LETARRAY) of 26 pointers, each of which points to the first author in the list whose name starts with that letter. Create the array so the indices are A through Z. Hence, when looking for Stevenson, start with the pointer at LETARRAY['S']. You can keep one LETARRAY for each branch, or you can have one element in LETARRAY store a pointer for each branch, in which the first points to the position of the letter for the first branch, the next for the second branch, etc.

You must use Pascal pointers for this program!

Input: Every input string (the strings for ⟨title⟩, ⟨author⟩, and ⟨branch⟩) is a maximum of 10 alphabetic characters ended with a blank. There may be multiple blanks between strings. Every command appears on a single line of input.

To set up each branch of the library:

```
BRANCH ⟨branch⟩
BOOK ⟨author⟩ ⟨title⟩
ENDBRANCHES
```

Several books will be read in after each branch command. There will be at most 10 branches and 200 books total. ENDBRANCHES separates the initialization from the requests.

A customer can make one of the following requests:

```
RETURN ⟨author⟩ ⟨title⟩ ⟨branch⟩
CHECKOUT ⟨author⟩ ⟨title⟩ ⟨branch⟩
NUMBER ⟨author⟩ ⟨title⟩ ⟨branch⟩
```

The building committee can issue the following command:

```
REMODEL ⟨branch1⟩ TO ⟨branch2⟩
```

These last four commands can come in any order and are terminated by an end-of-file.

Output: 1. Echoprint the input.

2. For CHECKOUT: If the branch is being remodeled, print the message, "This branch is temporarily closed and please go to branch ⟨branch2⟩." If there is no copy of the book at that branch, print the message "Sorry, ⟨title⟩ by ⟨author⟩ is not in stock at branch ⟨branch⟩." If there is a copy available, print the message that "Book ⟨title⟩ by ⟨author⟩ is available at branch ⟨branch⟩."

3. For RETURN: If the branch is being remodeled, print the message "Please return book ⟨title⟩ by ⟨author⟩ to branch ⟨branch2⟩." Otherwise, accept the book and print "Book ⟨title⟩ by ⟨author⟩ was returned to branch ⟨branch⟩."

4. For NUMBER: If the branch is being remodeled, print "Branch ⟨branch1⟩ is being remodeled; please check with branch ⟨branch2⟩." Otherwise, find the number of books at the branch and print "Branch ⟨branch⟩ has ⟨number⟩ copies of ⟨title⟩ by ⟨author⟩."

5. For REMODEL: Print "Branch ⟨branch1⟩'s books have been moved to ⟨branch2⟩. Branch ⟨branch2⟩ now contains: (and print the list of books at ⟨branch2⟩ in alphabetical order by author's name)."

6. At the end of the input, print out the books in each branch in the order in which the branches were read in, the books arranged in alphabetical order by author, with the number of books at each branch. If the branch is being remodeled, state where the books are now kept.

Sample:

Input:

```
BRANCH          BURNET
BOOK            ADAMS       LIFE
BOOK            ADAMS       LIFE
BOOK            ADAMS       WORKS
BRANCH          MANCHACA
BOOK            BURNS       POEMS
BOOK            WIRTH       PROGRAMS
BOOK            FLON        STRUCTURES
BRANCH          MLK
BOOK            AHO         ALGORITHMS
BOOK            ROUSSEAU    LIFE
BRANCH          RESEARCH
BOOK            YEH         CHEERS
ENDBRANCHES
RETURN          EVANS       DANCES      MANCHACA
CHECKOUT        AHO         ALGORITHMS  MLK
CHECKOUT        AHO         ALGORITHMS  MLK
NUMBER          AHO         ALGORITHMS  MLK
REMODEL         BURNET      TO RESEARCH
```

Output: Without echoprinting, output is as follows:

```
Book DANCES by EVANS was returned to branch MANCHACA.
Book ALGORITHMS by AHO is available at branch MLK.
```

```
Sorry, ALGORITHMS by AHO is not in stock at branch MLK,
Branch MLK has 0 copies of ALGORITHMS by AHO,
Branch BURNET's books have been moved to RESEARCH, Branch
RESEARCH now contains:

                    ADAMS, LIFE, 2 copies
                    ADAMS, WORKS, 1 copy
                    YEH, CHEERS, 1 copy

The books in each of the branches are:
BURNET: All books moved to RESEARCH

MANCHACA:           BURNS, POEMS, 1 copy
                    EVANS, DANCES, 1 copy
                    FLON, STRUCTURES, 1 copy
                    WIRTH, PROGRAMS, 1 copy

MLK:                ROUSSEAU, LIFE, 1 copy

RESEARCH:           ADAMS, LIFE, 2 copies
                    ADAMS, WORKS, 1 copy
                    YEH, CHEERS, 1 copy
```

Gael Buckley

*2. During the holiday season last winter, you spent hours standing in line at the cosmetics counter of your favorite department store. You marched right up to the president and complained. She apologized and asked if you had any suggestions of a better way to handle the crowds at peak periods, such as Christmas, Valentine's Day, Father's Day, and Mother's Day.

Being a good computer science major, you decided to take the challenge. Here is the scheme you suggested:

When customers come into the cosmetics department of the store at peak times, have them sign in, stating which cosmetic line they are interested in. If that counter is free, they go right up to it. If it is not free, they put their name on a waiting list for that cosmetic line. They then can do other shopping or browse around until they are paged. Customers who say that any cosmetics line will do are put on the waiting list for all the men's or all the women's lines, whichever they stipulate. They will be paged for the first opening. (They will of course have to be removed from all other lines when they are serviced at one.)

You convince the president that this plan not only will work but will increase sales, because people will buy while they are waiting, rather than fume. However, before instituting this scheme, the president wants you to do a computer simulation of this process.

This will be a simulation of a queuing system. Such a system has servers and queues. The servers are the cosmetic counters; the queues are the people on the waiting lists.

What we want to find out from the simulation is the average waiting time and the average queue length for each cosmetic line.

The parameters of the system are as follows:

1. The number of servers: This store carries no more than 20 lines of cosmetics. Some are for women and some are for men (but not both).
2. The events of the simulation and their effect on the system:

    (a) A customer arrives: A customer signs in and is serviced immediately if the requested counter is free. Otherwise, the customer's name is put on the appropriate queue.

    (b) A customer leaves the counter: When a customer leaves, the next one on the queue is paged, i.e., served.

3. Distribution of arrival time: For this simulation, this parameter will be given as time marks (#) in the input.

4. Expected service time: After talking with the sales personnel, you determine that most customers (50%) take about three minutes. A few (20%) take a minute or less. A few more (30%) take about ten minutes.

Input: 1. The names of the cosmetics companies (lines).

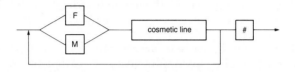

2. A sequence of names and cosmetic lines followed by a time marker. These are repeated until an end-of-simulation marker (a period) is encountered.

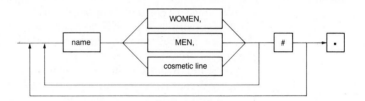

⟨name⟩   is a string of 10 or fewer characters, terminated by a blank.
⟨cosmetic line⟩ is a string of twenty or fewer characters, terminated by a comma or a pound sign (#).

Output: 1. Echoprint the input.

2. Every time a time mark (#) is encountered, print the names of the customers being served at each cosmetic counter and the number of customers in the queue.

3. When the end-of-simulation mark is encountered, print the average queue length for each cosmetic counter and the average wait time for people who reached the counter. The service time is not included in the average wait time.

4. Print out an alphabetical list of those people who have been serviced.

Processing: Repeat the following until a time mark is encountered:

1. Get a customer. Use a random number generator to determine how long this customer will take once he or she reaches the counter. (If the number generated is less than .20, the customer will take one minute; if it is between .20 and .50, the customer will take ten minutes; if it is between .50 and 1.00, the customer will take three minutes.)

2. If the desired counter is empty, assign the customer to it. If the counter is busy, enter the customer's name in the queue.

3. If the customer's preference is WOMEN or MEN, put the customer at any open WOMEN's or MEN's counter. If there are no open counters, put the customer in every appropriate queue.

4. When a time marker is encountered, do the following:

   (a) Decrement the service time of the customer being served at each counter.

   (b) When the service time of a customer becomes 0, that customer is finished being served. The customer's name is inserted into the alphabetical list of customers, and the person at the front of the queue becomes the customer being serviced.

   (c) If the person leaving the queue (starting to be serviced) had no counter preference, that customer must also be removed from the remaining queues.

   (d) Print out the name of the person being served at each counter and the number of people in the queue for each counter.

5. When the end-of-simulation marker is encountered, print the average wait time for each counter, then the average queue length. This time will be measured in minutes; i.e., each time mark is one minute.

Data structures: A suggested data structure is an array of records. Each record should contain a cosmetic company name, a pointer to the next MEN company or WOMEN company, an external pointer to the queue for that company, and any other fields necessary to process the required information.

MEN and WOMEN should be external pointers to lists of companies that carry the appropriate products.

A linked list of all the customers who have been served should be kept in alphabetical order.

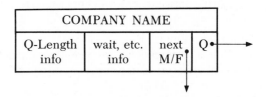

Tips: 1. Average Queue Length: There is one such value for each cosmetic line. To obtain this value, sum up the queue lengths at each hash mark (#) and then divide this sum by the number of hash marks.

2. Average Wait Time: There is one such value for each cosmetic line. This is only for those customers who have left the service counter. To obtain this value, sum up the wait times of the customers who left the service counter and then divide this sum by the number of customers who left the counter.

3. Service Time Wait Time: Service time for each customer is obtained using the random number generator. Wait time is the time each customer spent in a queue before entering a service counter. At each hash

mark, decrement the "time left" at each service counter by 1 and increment the wait time of each customer in the queue by 1.

4. Time Interval Between Two Consecutive Hash Marks Is 1 Minute: If a customer (service time = 5 minutes) has just reached a counter, the customer in the front of the queue can reach this counter only after five hash marks.

Sample data:

```
F    ELIZABETH ARDEN,        M HALSTON,
F    ESTEE LAUDER,
M    ARAMIS, M PALO,      F
CHRISTIAN DIOR, F LANCOME, M
PACO RABANNE,      M OSCAR DE LA RENTA,
F    GERMAINE MONTEIL#

MISSPIGGY     ESTEE LAUDER, KERMIT
   PACO RABANNE,       GONZO     ARAMIS,
   RIGGINS   OSCAR DE LA RENTA#    TAMMY
WOMEN,      HAWKEYE    PALO, RADAR    MEN,
 FELIXUNGER   HALSTON# OSCARMADISON PALO, FREDDY
 OSCAR DE LA RENTA,    MR, ED PACO RABANNE,
    WATCH:OUT? MEN#  DIANA   ELIZABETH ARDEN,    BEEJAY MEN,
BARDOT WOMEN#   MONROE WOMEN,   NONAME   WRONGLINE,
 KLINGER PALO,   DORSET WOMEN,   GARGOYLE  GERMAINE MONTEIL#
TOMMY MEN,    DR.WHO   PACO RABANNE, PINK-FLOYD MEN,
   MS.GOGOS   WOMEN#    DIAMOND   ARAMIS,  BOBDYLAN PALO,
EVERT   ESTEE LAUDER,   KEATON   GERMAINE MONTEIL,
 WINNIE HALSTON, THEPOOH   WOMEN, POTTER PALO#    ,
 ,,,,, STOP IT RIGHT HERE !!!!!
```

*3. You have been hired to write a program to manage the ticket office of a theater. Your program will sell tickets and assign people seats, based on input containing ticket requests and cancellations of ticket orders. Periodically, you are asked to display the current status of all tickets and customers.

Input/output: The input consists of two different parts. The first part consists of two numbers—the number of rows in the theater and the number of seats per row. The rows are numbered starting at 1. You may assume there are at most 100 rows. Seats are numbered from left to right. You may not assume any bound on the number of seats per row.

The second part of the input contains ticket requests and cancellations. There are four different commands (see below). Commands are free format; an arbitrary number of blanks and end-of-lines may occur between fields in a command. Names in a command are at most 10 characters long.

Commands:

REQUEST   ⟨person⟩ ⟨number⟩

The given person requests the indicated number of tickets. Further, our theater-goers are a little finicky; they require that all tickets in each particular request be for *consecutive seats* in the *same row*. In addition, they must be given the row with the smallest possible number. If there are several blocks in the row that are large enough, the theater-goers must be given the seats that are as far to the left as possible (see an example later). You must follow this seat allocation policy. If there is no block of available seats large enough, the person's request goes onto a waiting list. It is possible that later cancellations will free up a suitable block of seats. After processing the person's request, print a message indicating which seats (if any) he or she was allocated or whether the request was put on the waiting list.

CANCEL 〈person〉

The given person cancels a ticket request. If this person has made several requests, all of them are canceled. If this person is on the waiting list, his or her name is crossed off the list. If this person has been allocated a block of tickets, the tickets are freed. This may allow people on the waiting list to be serviced. Before reading in any more requests, we go down the waiting list, allocating tickets until someone cannot be serviced (or until we reach the end of the list). If someone cannot be serviced, we do not skip over him or her and look at people lower on the list; we read in the next request instead. After processing the cancellation, print out a message that the person's order was canceled and which (if any) people were allocated seats.

STATUS

Print out in a readable format: (1) the names of the people who have been allocated seats and which seats they were allocated. (This list does not have to be sorted; the people can occur in any order. If a person has several blocks of tickets, they do not have to be printed out consecutively.) (2) the names of people on the waiting list and the sizes of their requests.

END

End of input; quit processing.

Data structures: You will need data structures for storing:

1. what people have been given which tickets,
2. what seats are available, and
3. the waiting list.

(Note that Pascal pointers must be used.) This section suggests possible data structures and outlines some restrictions on the data structures you may use.

1. *Storing what people have been given which tickets.* You *may not* use an array for this. Use a linked list in which each block in the list contains the person's name, the row number of his or her tickets, the number of the first and last seat in the block, and a pointer to the next block in the list. If a person has made several requests, just have separate blocks for each. A more complicated structure in which the person only occurs once is not necessary (but may be used).
2. *Storing what seats are available.* For this you may *not* use a big two-dimensional array or any other structure requiring an excessive amount of space. A

possible structure is an array of 100 lists, in which the ith list describes the seats available in row i. However, a list may not have one entry per seat (this would be as bad as using a two-dimensional array). Seats must be grouped together into blocks of adjacent seats as shown below.

THEATER   DATA STRUCTURE

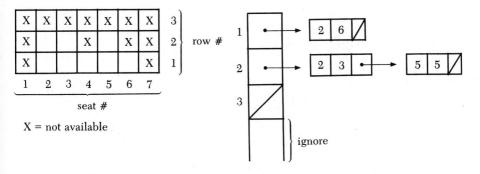

X = not available

Each record in the ith list describes a block of available adjacent seats in that row. For example, the first block in the list for row 1 says that seats 2 through 6 are available. Each list is sorted in order of increasing seat number. You may find it useful to use a doubly linked list and/or headers and trailers.

3. *Storing the waiting list.* You may use an array to store the waiting list (which is actually a queue) in sequential allocation. If you do, you *must* check for overflow. You may use another linked list instead if you wish.

Sample:

Input:

```
   3   7
REQUEST WAGNER 4
REQUEST BRAHMS 5
REQUEST WAGNER 4
REQUEST BEETHOVEN 1
REQUEST HANDEL 3
REQUEST LISZT 7
REQUEST WAGNER 4
REQUEST BERLIOZ 3
STATUS
CANCEL WAGNER
STATUS
REQUEST VIVALDI 2
CANCEL BEETHOVEN
REQUEST BACH 4
STATUS
CANCEL BRAHMS
STATUS
END
```

Selected output: The output of the STATUS commands is shown below. (The diagrams of the theater are for purposes of illustration; you are not required to print them.)

Output of the first STATUS command:

```
TICKETS:
WAGNER          ROW 1      SEATS 1    THROUGH 4
BRAHMS          ROW 2      SEATS 1    THROUGH 5
WAGNER          ROW 3      SEATS 1    THROUGH 4
BEETHOVEN       ROW 1      SEATS 5    THROUGH 5
HANDEL          ROW 3      SEATS 5    THROUGH 7
```

	1	2	3	4	5	6	7
3	X	X	X	X	X	X	X
2	X	X	X	X	X		
1	X	X	X	X	X		

```
WAITING LIST:
LISZT           7
WAGNER          4
BERLIOZ         3
```

Output of the second STATUS command:

```
TICKETS:
BRAHMS          ROW 2      SEATS 1    THROUGH 5
BEETHOVEN       ROW 1      SEATS 5    THROUGH 5
HANDEL          ROW 3      SEATS 5    THROUGH 7
```

	1	2	3	4	5	6	7
3					X	X	X
2	X	X	X	X	X		
1					X		

```
WAITING LIST:
LISZT           7
BERLIOZ         3
```

Output of the third STATUS command:

```
TICKETS:
BRAHMS          ROW 2      SEATS 1    THROUGH 5
HANDEL          ROW 3      SEATS 5    THROUGH 7
```

```
VIVALDI      ROW 1      SEATS 1   THROUGH 2
BACH         ROW 1      SEATS 3   THROUGH 6
```

	1	2	3	4	5	6	7
3					X	X	X
2	X	X	X	X	X		
1	X	X	X	X	X	X	

```
WAITING LIST:
LISZT        7
BERLIOZ      3
```

Output of the fourth STATUS command:

```
TICKETS:
HANDEL       ROW 3      SEATS 5   THROUGH 7
VIVALDI      ROW 1      SEATS 1   THROUGH 2
BACH         ROW 1      SEATS 3   THROUGH 6
LISZT        ROW 2      SEATS 1   THROUGH 7
BERLIOZ      ROW 3      SEATS 1   THROUGH 3
```

	1	2	3	4	5	6	7
3	X	X	X		X	X	X
2	X	X	X	X	X	X	X
1	X	X	X	X	X	X	

```
WAITING LIST:
empty
```

Jim Bitner

*4. You are to write a genealogy program that will accept data about the various relations among a set of people and, when requested, print out information about the relations.

Input/output: The input file consists of statements and commands as listed below. The statements and commands are free format; any number of blanks and ends-of-lines can occur between words. Words and names are terminated by blanks and hence cannot contain blanks. Names are at most 20 characters long. The possible statements and commands and their meanings are described below. You should echoprint each statement or command as it is read in. In addition, the PRINT command will cause you to output information.

```
MALE ⟨name⟩ EXISTS
```
⟨name⟩ is man, but we know nothing about his parentage.

```
FEMALE ⟨name⟩ EXISTS
```
⟨name⟩ is a woman, but we know nothing about her parentage.

```
⟨name1⟩ AND ⟨name2⟩ BEGET SON ⟨name3⟩
```
Same as above except that ⟨name3⟩ is a female.

Note: In the statements above, you may assume no one with the same name as the new person already exists.

```
⟨name1⟩ MARRIES ⟨name2⟩
```
You may assume that ⟨name1⟩ and ⟨name2⟩ are people of the opposite sex and that neither is already married. Either ⟨name1⟩ or ⟨name2⟩ may be the male, however. Both ⟨name1⟩ and ⟨name2⟩ have already been referred to by an EXISTS or BEGET command.

```
PRINT ⟨name⟩'S RELATION
```
All of ⟨name⟩'s relatives satisfying the given relation are to be printed in any order. ⟨name⟩ has already been referred to by an EXISTS or BEGET command. RELATION may be any of the following words:

```
SIBLINGS, SISTERS, BROTHERS, CHILDREN, DAUGHTERS,
SONS, PARENTS, GRANDPARENTS, AUNTS, UNCLES,
```

For simplicity, you do not have to consider relations by marriage; if someone marries your sister, he does not become your brother.

If any of the information requested by a PRINT command is not known (i.e., if we are only told X EXISTS and then are asked to PRINT X'S FATHER), the phrase UNKNOWN should be printed at least once. You may print it several times if that's convenient. If X has no relatives satisfying the specified relation, nothing need be printed. If you are unfamiliar with any of these terms, don't hesitate to look them up to make sure of their meaning.

Note: The statements and commands above may be intermixed in any order.

```
END
```
Stop processing.

Sample output: The output below reflects the input statements and commands by echoprinting the input. The information output as a result of PRINT is indented below the command.

```
MALE ADAM EXISTS
FEMALE EVE EXISTS
ADAM MARRIES EVE
ADAM AND EVE BEGET SON FRITZ
EVE AND ADAM BEGET DAUGHTER ROSY
FEMALE LILLIAN EXISTS
ADAM AND EVE BEGET SON TOM
MALE JOHN EXISTS
LILLIAN MARRIES JOHN
JOHN AND LILLIAN BEGET SON JIMMY
```

```
LILLIAN AND JOHN BEGET SON BILL
JIMMY MARRIES ROSY
FEMALE SALLY EXISTS
SALLY MARRIES BILL
FEMALE JANE EXISTS
FEMALE BARB EXISTS
JANE MARRIES FRITZ
BARB MARRIES TOM
JIMMY AND ROSY BEGET SON KEVIN
TOM AND BARB BEGET SON MARVIN
BARB AND TOM BEGET DAUGHTER MARY
ROSY AND JIMMY BEGET DAUGHTER AMY
JIMMY AND ROSY BEGET SON CYRUS
BARB AND TOM BEGET DAUGHTER MARLA
PRINT CYRUS'S SIBLINGS
     KEVIN
     AMY
PRINT CYRUS'S SISTERS
     AMY
PRINT AMY'S BROTHERS
     KEVIN
     CYRUS
PRINT AMY'S SISTERS
PRINT JIMMY'S CHILDREN
     KEVIN
     AMY
     CYRUS
PRINT ROSY'S CHILDREN
     KEVIN
     AMY
     CYRUS
PRINT EVE'S SONS
     FRITZ
     TOM
PRINT BILL'S PARENTS
     LILLIAN
     JOHN
PRINT ADAM'S PARENTS
     UNKNOWN
PRINT ADAM'S GRANDPARENTS
     UNKNOWN
PRINT MARVIN'S GRANDPARENTS
     ADAM
     EVE
     UNKNOWN
PRINT AMY'S GRANDPARENTS
     LILLIAN
     JOHN
     ADAM
     EVE
```

```
PRINT CYRUS'S UNCLES
    FRITZ
    TOM
    BILL
PRINT CYRUS'S AUNTS
PRINT MARLA'S AUNTS
    ROSY
END
```

Jim Bitner

*5. Your assignment is to write a program for a computer dating service. (Assignment 1, Chapter 1, is a simplified version of this problem.) Each customer will give you his or her name and a list of phrases (which we will call attributes) that describe the person and his or her interests. It will be your job to maintain lists of men and women using the service and to match up compatible people (those with similar qualities and interests).

Data structures: The problem requires you to maintain three lists: one of unmatched men, one of unmatched women, and a third of pairs of people who have been matched. (Actually, it may be simplest to store the pairs as two parallel lists.) When a person starts using your service, he or she is put on one of the unmatched lists. Later, he or she may be put on the list of matched pairs (if a match is found). For simplicity, you will assume that once a person is put on the list of matched pairs, he or she remains there forever. (The list of matched pairs is maintained so that you can give prospective clients a list of satisfied customers.)

Important: The lists do not have to be sorted.

Input/output: The input consists of a list of commands to manipulate the database. Input is free format; an arbitrary number of blanks are permitted at any time. Several syntax diagrams are attached at the end of this assignment. Please refer to them as you read the following.

Basic Components of the commands: The basic components of the input file are words, strings and lists of attributes. These are defined as follows:

1. A *word* is a sequence of letters. (Words are like reserved words in Pascal and tell us what kind of data is coming.) A word is at most 20 characters long.
2. A *string* is a sequence of letters, digits, and blanks. It must start with a letter, and therefore any blanks before the string are not part of the string. It can, however, have embedded blanks, which are considered significant (i.e., "JOE GREEN" is different from "JOE   GREEN"). Each name and attribute will be a string. The maximum length for a string is 20 characters.
3. A *list of attributes* is a sequence of strings separated by commas and terminated by a period. A list is at most ten items long and will contain no duplicate attributes.

Important: The list of attributes *will* be sorted to make it easier to tell if two people are compatible.

Commands: The following describes the seven possible commands to the system. Commands are separated by an arbitrary number of blanks and end-of-lines. The syntax diagrams at the end of the assignment indicate the parameters of each command.

In addition to providing the output described below, you must echoprint each command as it is read in. A blank line should be output after each command to improve readability.

ADD
The specified person should be added to either the list of men or the list of women, whichever is appropriate. You may assume no two people will have the same name.

DELETE
The specified person has become dissatisfied with our service, and his or her name should be deleted from the appropriate list. You are guaranteed that the person is actually in the list.

MATCHUP
This command requires you to find all compatible pairs of unmatched people in the database and put them on the pairs list. (People must be of opposite sex.) A pair is compatible if they have at least three attributes in common. If there are several ways of pairing up compatible people, you may choose any way you like as long as two compatible people are not left on the unpaired lists after the matching has been done. (Remember that the attribute lists are sorted. Therefore, testing to see if two people are compatible can be done much more quickly.)

PRINT
Print the names and attributes of all the unmatched people of the given sex who match the given list of attributes. (This service is provided to people for an extra charge.) Of course, *match* means having at least three attributes that are on the list. The list of attributes can be printed in any format (vertically or horizontally), as long as it is understandable.

PRINTALL
Print the names and attributes of all men, women, or matched people (depending on the word after PRINTALL). The list of pairs may be printed with the men first, followed by all the women (or vice versa), or with the men and women interleaved.

DUMP
Print the names and attributes of all people in the database. Label each list you output so that it is clear to which class people belong. (*Note:* This is useful for debugging.)

END
Stop processing.

Sample output: The upper-case letters show the original input file. They have been echoprinted.

```
ADD MALE SPORTY PETE: BADMINTON,   BASEBALL,   CANOEING,
                GETS C IN CS COURSE, LIKES RED, SAILING.
ADD MALE SMART SAM: GETS A IN CS COURSE,
                IS A BRAIN SURGEON, LIKES READING,
                LIKES INTEGRAL CALC, LINEAR ALGEBRA,
                NUCLEAR PHYSICS.
ADD FEMALE DELIGHTFUL DORIS: TELLS JOKES, MAKES BAD PUNS,
                LOOKS GOOD IN RED, SPARKLING WIT, VIVACIO
ADD FEMALE WONDER WOMAN: GETS A IN CS COURSE, LIKES READING,
                NUCLEAR PHYSICS, LIKES FAST CARS.
PRINTALL MEN
  LIST OF ALL UNMATCHED MEN:
        SPORTY PETE
                BADMINTON
                BASEBALL
                CANOEING
                GETS C IN CS COURSE
                LIKES RED
                SAILING
        SMART SAM
                GETS A IN CS COURSE
                IS A BRAIN SURGEON
                LIKES INTEGRAL CALC
                LIKES READING
                LINEAR ALGEBRA
                NUCLEAR PHYSICS
PRINT MEN BADMINTON, CANOEING, LIKES RED, WRESTLING.
    sporty pete
            badminton
            baseball
            canoeing
            gets c in cs course
            likes red
            sailing
MATCHUP
DELETE MALE SPORTY PETE.
DUMP
    list of all unmatched men:
    list of all unmatched women:
            delightful doris
                    tells jokes
                    makes bad puns
                    looks good in red
                    sparkling wit
                    vivacious
        list of all matched men:
            smart sam
                    gets a in cs courses
                    is a brain surgeon
                    likes reading
                    likes integral calc
```

```
            linear algebra
            nuclear physics
    list of all matched women:
        wonder woman
            gets a in cs courses
            likes reading
            nuclear physics
            likes fast cars
END
```

Syntax diagrams:

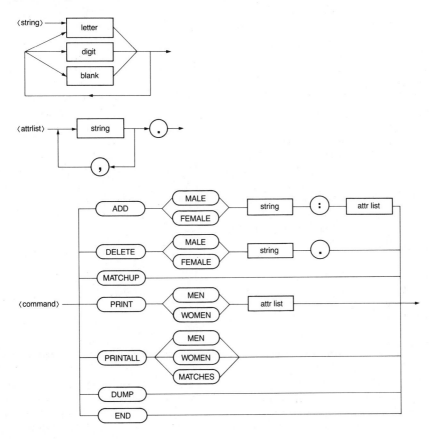

Sample input:

```
ADD MALE GREGORY GREEN:CYCLIST,GOOD LOOKING,
            GREASY SPOON GOURMET,LIKES HORSES,
            SKINNY,SMART    NO DEGREE.
PRINTALL WOMEN
ADD FEMALE MARILYN MORRIS:ALLERGIC TO CATS,ARTISTIC,
            AUTO NUT,GOOD LOOKING,LIKES HORSES,
            MEAT AND POTATOES. MATCHUP
PRINTALL MEN
```

```
DUMP ADD MALE SAM SMITH:ALLERGIC TO CATS,AUTO NUT,
              BACKGAMMON,GOOD LOOKING, MEAT AND POTATOES.
MATCHUP PRINTALL MATCHES
ADD FEMALE MARY JONES:BACKGAMMON,BRIDGE PLAYER,
              FAT,GREASY SPOON GOURMET,MORON NO DEGREE,
              SHORT, LIKES DOGS.
ADD FEMALE ROSE MARTIN:BRIDGE PLAYER,MEAT AND POTATOES,
              SKINNY,TECHNICALLY ORIENTED.
ADD MALE HARVEY HALES:MORON NO DEGREE,SHORT,LIKES DOGS,
              VEGETARIAN.
ADD MALE CITIZEN KANE:ALLERGIC TO CATS,BRIDGE PLAYER,
              FAT,LIKES HORSES,MEAT AND POTATOES,
              MORON PHD,SHORT,TECHNICALLY ORIENTED,
              TENNIS, LIKES DOGS.
PRINT MEN ARTISTIC,BRIDGE PLAYER,GOOD LOOKING,
          LIKES HORSES,MEAT AND POTATOES,SMART    NO DEGREE
PRINT WOMEN ARTISTIC,BRIDGE PLAYER,GOOD LOOKING,
          LIKES HORSES,MEAT AND POTATOES,SMART    NO DEGREE
DELETE MALE GREGORY GREEN. PRINTALL WOMEN PRINTALL MATCHES
ADD FEMALE SUZY TURNER:ARTISTIC,BRIDGE PLAYER,
              GOOD LOOKING,SMART    NO DEGREE,TALL,
              TECHNICALLY ORIENTED,TENNIS,VEGETARIAN.
ADD FEMALE SCARLET SLADE:ARTISTIC,GOOD LOOKING,
              LIKES HORSES,MEAT AND POTATOES.
ADD MALE LAWRENCE LARSEN:ARTISTIC,BRIDGE PLAYER,
              GOOD LOOKING,INTELLECTUAL MA,LIKES HORSES,
              TALL,VEGETARIAN.
MATCHUP DUMP
END
```

Jim Bitner

Chapter 7

*1. A toy that many children play with is a base with three pegs and five disks of different diameters. The disks begin on one peg, with the largest disk on the bottom and the other four disks added on by order of size. The idea is to move the disks from the peg they are on to another peg by moving only one disk at a time and without ever putting a larger disk on top of a smaller one.

This child's toy is actually an example of a classic mathematical puzzle called the Towers of Hanoi problem.

Write a recursive solution to this problem. Yes, one exists. It may take you a while to see the solution, but the program itself is quite short.

*2. Another classic problem that lends itself to a recursive solution is the Eight Queens problem. The problem is to place eight queens on a chess board in such a way that no queen is attacking any other queen.

Represent a chess board as an 8×8 array of Boolean. If a square is occupied by a queen, the position is TRUE. Otherwise the square is FALSE. The status of the chess board when all eight queens have been placed is the solution.

3. The maze problem in Chapter 3 illustrated the use of the stack data structure. Rewrite the same problem using a recursive algorithm.

*4. In this program you will write a function that computes an approximation to a definite integral that is within a given tolerance of the exact answer. You will also write a sorting procedure that will help monitor the behavior of the integration function. You will then test your function on several prescribed integrals.

Method: The integration function implements an adaptive algorithm based on the trapezoid rule of integration and its associated error estimate. The trapezoid rule for integration is

$$\int_a^b f(x)\ dx = (f(a) + f(b))*(b - a)/2$$

If the interval [a,b] is divided into two equal subintervals, another estimate of the integral can be obtained by applying the trapezoid rule to each half interval and adding the two results. This new result is normally more accurate, and an estimate of the error in the better result is given by

$$error = (T(a,b) - (T(a,c) + T(c,b)))/3.0$$

where $c = (a + b)/2$ and $T(x,y)$ is the result of applying the trapezoid rule to f on the interval [x,y].

The integral is to be computed to within a given accuracy by a divide-and-conquer strategy. With the above formulas, the integral can be approximated and the error in the approximation can be estimated. If the absolute value of the error is small enough, the program terminates. Otherwise, the integral is computed on each half interval separately with an error tolerance that is half the original one.

All the real numbers at which the function is evaluated are to be stored in an array. After the integration routine terminates, these values should be sorted and printed out. The sorting procedure will implement the quicksort algorithm to sort the array of values in increasing order. This will help monitor the behavior of the integration algorithm by showing where the function f was evaluated. The evaluations should be concentrated where the function is badly behaved (i.e., poorly approximated by straight-line pieces).

Specification: The integration function should be

FUNCTION Q ⟨f, A, B, EPS, MAXFUN, ERR⟩

where

f	is the name of the function to be integrated.
A	is the left endpoint of the interval.
B	is the right endpoint of the interval.
EPS	is the maximum allowed absolute value of the error.
MAXFUN	is the maximum number of function evaluations to be used.
ERR	is a Boolean error flag: ERR is true if more than MAXFUN function values would be needed to satisfy the error test.
Q	is returned as the estimate of the integral.

Implementation details:

1. The name of the function f, which is to be integrated, should be passed by the main program as a parameter to the integration function Q. One execution of the main program should call the integration function for each of the functions whose integrals are to be estimated. It is not acceptable to include the code of a function to be integrated inside the integration function Q.

2. To prevent the possibility of infinite recursion, the integration function should terminate if the function f is called MAXFUN times. In this case, the best available approximation to the integral should be returned and an error flag should be set.

3. The primary cost of using an integration routine is in the cost of evaluating the function f. Write your code so that it never evaluates the function twice at the same point.

4. The divide-and-conquer approach should be implemented by a recursive function. This recursive function is not called directly, but is called by the nonrecursive driver function Q, described above.

5. The straightforward way to compute the midpoint of an interval is not the best. To ensure that the computed midpoint of an interval [a,b] is not outside the interval, the formula a + (b − a)/2 should be used.

6. The main program should do the following, once for each function in the test data:
   (a) Call Q with the appropriate arguments.
   (b) Print the estimate of the interval.
   (c) Print an error message if ERR is true.
   (d) Sort the array of real numbers at which the function f was evaluated using a quicksort routine.
   (e) Print the sorted values.

Test data: Test your integration function by computing the following integrals:

f	A	B	EPS	$MAXFUN$
1	0.0	1.0	10^{-3}	5
x	−1.0	3.0	10^{-5}	3
x	−1.0	3.0	10^{-5}	2
e^{-x*x}	0.0	5.0	10^{-3}	1000
$(\frac{1}{3}-x)^{1/3}$	0.0	1.0	10^{-2}	10
$(\frac{1}{3}-x)^{1/3}$	0.0	1.0	10^{-3}	1000
$\dfrac{4}{(1 + x^2)}$	0.0	1.0	10^{-3}	1000

Note: Standard Pascal does not require that an exponential function be provided. If your version of Pascal does not include an exponential function, you should enter the code for an exponential function as a procedure in the main program or as an external function.

Also, most exponential functions will not allow you to raise a negative number to a real number power. This problem occurs with the fifth and sixth functions above. However, you can take the absolute value of the base, raise it to a power, and then append the correct sign.

Alan Cline and
David Scott

Chapter 8

Many of the programming assignments in previous chapters are also appropriate for this chapter. Any problem that uses a one-dimensional array as its main data structure can be rewritten using a binary search tree in place of the array. Listed below are programs from other chapters that particularly lend themselves to use of a binary tree as the major data structure.

1. Rewrite Programming Assignment 4, Chapter 2 (Groucho Marx magic word problem).
2. Rewrite Programming Assignment 5, Chapter 5 (corporate careers problem).
3. Rewrite Programming Assignment 6, Chapter 5 (club membership problem).
4. Rewrite Programming Assignment 7, Chapter 5 (grocery warehouse inventory problem).
5. Rewrite Programming Assignment 8, Chapter 5 (magicians' booking agency problem).
6. Rewrite Programming Assignment 5, Chapter 6 (dating service problem).
7. Creating a set of routines in preparation for a big programming assignment has worked so well in the past that you decide to do the same thing in preparation for the next program, which will also be large. Since trees are coming up next, you guess that you will need to use trees for the next programming assignment. You therefore write the following set of utility routines to manipulate trees.

INSERT IN PLACE   This routine takes a pointer to a binary tree and an element, and inserts the element in its proper place in the tree.

COPY A TREE   This routine has two parameters: a pointer to the tree to be copied and a pointer to the copy. The routine makes a copy using the second parameter as the pointer to the copy.

DELETE   This routine takes a pointer to a node in a binary tree and deletes the node from the tree. If your algorithm requires a back pointer, you may make it a parameter as well.

TESTNODES   This routine takes a pointer to a binary tree and a letter. The tree should be traversed in postorder, calling DELETE for every node in which the letter appears in the information portion of the node. Since the information portion is a STRING20, you will have to search the string for the letter.

PRINT   This routine takes a binary tree and prints the contents of the nodes in order.

Testing: Test data consist of strings of up to 20 characters. You are to read a string and insert it in place. You continue reading and inserting until you encounter an asterisk (*).
Following this set of strings is a set of commands.

Commands:

TESTNODES ⟨letter⟩   Delete each node in the tree that contains ⟨letter⟩
INSERT ⟨string⟩   Insert ⟨string⟩ into your tree
PRINT   Print the tree as it is at that time

where ⟨string⟩ is a string of up to 20 characters. You should continue reading commands and doing what they ask until you encounter an asterisk (*). When the asterisk is encountered, you should make a copy of the tree as it is at that time and print the copy.

8. You are to write a program that creates and maintains a pair of binary trees, OAK and ELM.

Data structures: You will need two binary trees, OAK and ELM. Each node on the trees contains the following information: name, phone number, and pointer fields. The nodes on each tree are to be ordered by name.

Input: The input to the program is a series of commands. All input is free format, with an arbitrary number of blanks and end-of-lines occurring anywhere.

Basic command components:

1. A *word* is a sequence of at most 10 nonblank characters, delimited by a blank. Words include phone numbers (e.g., 438-5555) and tree names (OAK or ELM).
2. A *string* is a sequence of at most 20 characters, delimited by a period or comma, including blanks, beginning with a letter. Leading blanks should be skipped, but embedded blanks are considered to be significant. Names are strings.

Commands:

These are the commands to the system. In addition to generating the specific output required, you must echoprint each command as it is read in. A blank line should be output after each command to improve readability.

ADD ⟨treename⟩ ⟨name⟩, ⟨phonenumber⟩

The specified person should be added to the tree designated by ⟨treename⟩. You may assume that no two people have the same name.

DELETE ⟨treename⟩ ⟨name⟩

Delete the specified ⟨name⟩ from the designated tree. You may assume that the person is actually on the tree.

CHECK ⟨treename⟩ ⟨name⟩

Check whether the specified ⟨name⟩ is on the designated tree, and print an appropriate message.

MATCHCHECK ⟨name1⟩, ⟨name2⟩

Check to see if ⟨name1⟩ (in the ELM tree) and ⟨name2⟩ (in the OAK tree) have the same phone number. If so, delete them both from their respective trees. You cannot assume that the names are in the tree. If one or the other is not found, print an appropriate message.

PRINT ⟨treename⟩

Print the names and phone numbers of all the nodes in the designated tree. The names should be ordered alphabetically.

DUMP

Print all the names and phone numbers in both trees. Each tree should have an appropriate heading and have its names in alphabetical order.

END

Stop processing.

Input syntax diagram:

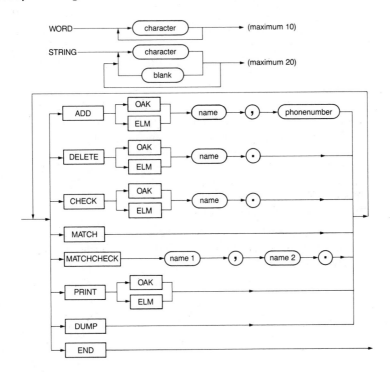

Sample data:

```
ADD ELM RONNIE ROSE,    345-4521
ADD ELM DAISY MAE CLAMPET,  267-4210
   ADD ELM WILL O'WISP, 432-4321
ADD OAK MILKWEED JONES, 562-0562
CHECK OAK RONNIE ROSE, PRINT ELM
ADD OAK CACTUS PRYOR,    671-0711
ADD OAK BRAMBLE PATCH, 430-1234
CHECK OAK CACTUS PRIOR, CHECK OAK CACTUS PRYOR,
PRINT OAK
MATCHCHECK DAISY MAE CLAMPET, RONNIE ROSE,
ADD ELM PETER PETUNIA, 471-4353
ADD ELM RANDY ROSE, 263-0563
ADD OAK YELLOW ROSE OF TEXAS, 263-0563
ADD ELM PRETTY PRIMROSE, 261-0625
DELETE ELM RONNIE ROSE,
```

```
CHECK ELM PRETTY PRIMROSE.
MATCHCHECK RANDY ROSE, MILKWEED JONES.
ADD OAK PANSY PERKINS, 561-8573
ADD OAK GARY GARDENIA, 267-4201
PRINT OAK
MATCHCHECK DAISY MAE CLAMPET, GARY GARDENIA.
CHECK ELM PETER PETUNIA.
CHECK OAK GARY GARDENIA.
ADD OAK ANN EMONIE, 253-0325
DELETE OAK BRAMBLE PATCH.
CHECK ELMER WILL O'WISP. CZECH OAK CACTUS PRYOR.
CHECK OAK  ANN EMONIE.
DUMP    END
```

*9. Your assignment is to write a program for a police department that has collected a database of information on various suspects for a given crime. (Luckily for you, the department is only investigating one crime at a time.) Each suspect has a set of attributes, such as shifty eyes, a limp, a parrot on shoulder, etc. The maximum number of such attributes for any suspect is not known. Your program will accept commands to manipulate the database in order to narrow down the list of suspects, in the hope of pinpointing the villain.

Input: The input consists of the initial database followed by *, then a set of inquiries, each separated by *, and finally terminated by *. This is shown in the following diagram:

initial database

*

inquiry 1

*

inquiry 2

*

.

.

.

*

inquiry N

*

An inquiry consists of a set of commands about a single crime. At the end of each inquiry, the crime is assumed to be solved. We begin working on a new crime with the next inquiry. Therefore, we start over with the entire original list of suspects (as given in the initial database).

Assume that each * is preceded by at least one blank space. The syntax of the initial database and of the inquiries is given in the subsequent sections.

Initial database: The initial database consists of the attributes for a list of suspects.

⟨attribute⟩ = sequence of 20 or less nonblank characters.
⟨name⟩   = sequence of 20 or less nonblank characters. (You may assume that no name is the same as any attribute.)

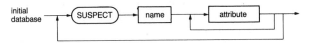

The set of attributes for each suspect starts with SUSPECT, followed by the suspect's name and attributes.

Inquiry:

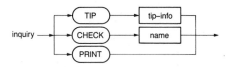

An inquiry is a set of commands. Each command is either TIP, CHECK, or PRINT. The PRINT command prints the set of suspects who have not been eliminated so far. The CHECK command checks if the person with that name is currently a suspect. The TIP command is used to reduce the list of suspects by the process of elimination. Tip-info (whose syntax is given later) is some information about the attributes of the suspect (for example, has shifty eyes, but does not walk with a limp). Any suspect who does not fit this description is eliminated, thereby narrowing down the list of suspects.

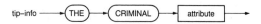

Examples of a tip-info:

```
THE CRIMINAL WALKS-WITH-LIMP
THE CRIMINAL EATS-CARROTS
```

Output: 1. Echoprint the database.
2. Echoprint each command.
3. For each CHECK command, print whether the given person is still a suspect in this inquiry.
4. For each PRINT command, print all the people who are still suspects in this inquiry.

Assumptions: 1. There is no upper bound to the number of suspects or number of attributes for a given suspect. You cannot use an array to store the suspects or the attributes for a given suspect. You must use a dynamic, linked structure.

2. The CHECK operation must be very efficient, since suspects are constantly being pulled off the street for questioning, and we must decide whether to let them go or ruthlessly interrogate them. Using a simple linked list to store the suspects will not be sufficient. You must use a binary search tree. Suspects must be actually deleted from the structure when they are eliminated by TIP information. Using a BOOLEAN to mark the suspects who have been eliminated is not sufficient. Since you will be destroying the list of suspects, a copy of the original database must be made at the beginning of each inquiry.

3. TIP does not need to be very efficient. TIP is executed much less often than CHECK, and hence can be less efficient. It is acceptable if processing a TIP command requires searching the whole database of (active) suspects. Thus, a list of attributes can be stored with each suspect. You do not have to link all the suspects with the same attributes together. (This could potentially make for a much faster TIP operation.) You may do this if you want, but it will complicate things.

Sample data:

```
SUSPECT
QUICKDRAW-MCGRAW   TALKS-WITH-DRAWL   WALKS-WITH-LIMP
HAS-LONG-HAIR
SUSPECT
TWINGUN-MORGAN   TALKS-WITH-LISP   IS-BEARDED   SMOKES-CIGARS
SUSPECT
JACKDA-RIPPER   WALKS-WITH-LIMP   BITES-FINGERNAILS
CARRIES-KNIFE   HAS-LONG-HAIR
SUSPECT
SON-OF-SAM   TALKS-WITH-LISP   IS-BEARDED   EATS-FRITOS
SMOKES-CIGARS
SUSPECT
SLOWDRAWL-RAUL   TALKS-WITH-DRAWL   CARRIES-KNIFE
HAS-LONG-HAIR   EATS-FRITOS
SUSPECT
SLOAN-DE-UPTAKE   WALKS-WITH-LIMP   IS-BEARDED
BITES-FINGERNAILS   HAS-LONG-HAIR
*
TIP   THE CRIMINAL TALKS-WITH-LISP
TIP   THE CRIMINAL HAS-LONG-HAIR
CHECK   QUICKDRAW-MCGRAW
CHECK   SON-OF-SAM
PRINT
*
TIP   THE CRIMINAL SMOKES-CIGARS
PRINT
TIP   THE CRIMINAL IS-BEARDED
```

```
CHECK TWINGUN-MORGAN
TIP   THE CRIMINAL TALKS-WITH-LISP
PRINT
*
TIP   THE CRIMINAL TALKS-WITH-DRAWL
CHECK SLOWDRAWL-RAUL
TIP   THE CRIMINAL HAS-LONG-HAIR
CHECK  SLOAN-DE-UPTAKE
PRINT
*
TIP   THE CRIMINAL BITES-FINGERNAILS
CHECK TWINGUN-MORGAN
TIP   THE CRIMINAL WALKS-WITH-LIMP
CHECK SLOWDRAWL-RAUL
TIP   THE CRIMINAL HAS-LONG-HAIR
PRINT
*
PRINT
TIP   THE CRIMINAL SMOKES-CIGARS
PRINT
TIP   THE CRIMINAL IS-BEARDED
PRINT
TIP   THE CRIMINAL BITES-FINGERNAILS
PRINT
*
```

Jim Bitner

10. There is a real program developed by a computer company that reads in written reports, issues warnings on bad style, and partially corrects the style. This assignment is to create a simplified version of this program. It will contain a tree of words that can be annoying if used in a report. The program will caution the writer on these tendencies, and then correct the report. The output will be the original text, the corrected text, a list of slight tendencies the writer has (1 to 4 occurrences of an annoying word), and a list of extreme tendencies that the author should avoid (5 or more occurrences of an annoying word). These last two lists will be printed in alphabetical order.

After an author sees which words the program has changed, the author may decide to tell the program not to change certain words using DELETEWORD ⟨badword⟩. This command will remove ⟨badword⟩ from the search tree so that all future input paragraphs will not have this word replaced in the paragraph. The author may also find other words annoying, and will tell the program to add them to the list by ADDWORD ⟨word⟩, followed on the same line by several synonyms to insert in place of this word. ADDWORD ⟨badword⟩ ⟨syn1⟩ ⟨syn2⟩ . . . . adds the new ⟨badword⟩ to the search tree, and the computer will replace any occurrence of that word in a future input paragraph with some synonym given for that word.

The program has a main data structure of annoying bad words and is arranged as a search tree (we term this BADTREE). BADTREE is complicated by the fact that when the program finds an annoying word in the text, it must replace it by a more acceptable synonym. It is nearly as annoying to have the same word repeated every time for the annoying word, and so the program has a list of several synonyms to use for every node in BADTREE (to a maximum of 5 synonyms). These are arranged in a circular list, so that the program cycles the words around for every occurrence of a particular annoying word (see example). There are at most 20 annoying words in BADTREE at any one time.

Input:

1. A list of annoying words, in which the first word on each line is the annoying word, followed by a maximum of 5 synonyms. Each word is a maximum of 15 characters and is terminated by a blank. There may be multiple blanks between words. The entry for an annoying word is ended by an EOLN.

   ENDWORDS ends the initialization of BADTREE.

2. A paragraph of text over several lines, in which each word is separated from each other by blanks, commas, periods, or quotes. There need not be a blank before the word at the beginning of the line. ENDPARAGRAPH appears on a separate line to end the paragraph.
3. Any number of the following two commands in any order, one per line (a blank ends the command):

ADDWORD annoying word followed by up to 5 synonyms.
DELETEWORD annoying word followed by up to 5 synonyms.
ENDALTER appears on a separate line to end the commands to alter BADTREE.

Output: 1. After BADTREE has been initialized, print out the badwords and their synonyms in alphabetical order by badword.
2. For a paragraph of text:
   (a) Echoprint the input text.
   (b) Print the corrected output text.
   (c) Print
       SLIGHT TENDENCIES TO USE ANNOYING WORDS:
       (a list in alphabetical order of the words used 1 to 5 times)
       EXTREME OVERUSE OF ANNOYING WORDS:
       (a list in alphabetical order of the words used more than 5 times)
3. For the list of commands altering BADTREE, echoprint the input.

Sample:

Input:

```
grungy dirty soiled grimy encrusted
awesome amazing incredible
teeny small tiny
ENDWORDS
The apartment was so grungy it was totally awesome. The sofa
was grungy, the floor was grungy, the fridge was grungy, and
even the grass outside was grungy. When I think that could
have been where I would live this year, all I could say was,
'Totally awesome.'
```

```
ENDPARAGRAPH
ADDWORD fridge refrigerator
DELETEWORD awesome
ENDALTER
The apartment was so grungy it was totally awesome. The sofa
was grungy, the floor was grungy, the fridge was grungy, and
even the grass outside was grungy. When I think that could
have been where I would live this year, all I could say was,
'Totally awesome.'
ENDPARAGRAPH
```

Output:

Annoying words and synonyms:

```
awesome amazing incredible
grungy dirty soiled grimy encrusted
teeny small tiny
```

(echoprint of input paragraph)

```
The apartment was so dirty it was totally amazing. The sofa
was soiled, the floor was grimy, the fridge was encrusted,
and even the grass outside was dirty. When I think that could
have been where I would live this year, all I could say was
'Totally incredible.'
SLIGHT TENDENCIES TO USE ANNOYING WORDS:
awesome
EXTREME OVERUSE OF ANNOYING WORDS:
grungy
ADDWORD fridge refrigerator
DELETEWORD awesome
```

(echoprint of input paragraph)

```
The apartment was so dirty it was totally awesome. The sofa
was soiled, the floor was grimy, the refrigerator was
encrusted, and even the grass outside was dirty. When I think
that could have been where I would live this year, all I could
say was, 'Totally awesome.'

SLIGHT TENDENCIES TO USE ANNOYING WORDS:
fridge

EXTREME OVERUSE OF ANNOYING WORDS:
grungy
```

Gael Buckley

Chapter 9

1. Rewrite the expression evaluator in this chapter so that it is robust.
2. Write a program that reads in the nodes in a graph and the edges and does a depth-first search of the graph.

Input: 1. The nodes in the graph in the following form:

⟨string⟩, ⟨string⟩, . . . ⟨string⟩.

2. The edges in the graph in the following form:

((⟨string⟩, ⟨string⟩), ((⟨string⟩, ⟨string⟩),
((⟨string⟩, ⟨string⟩), . . . ((⟨string⟩, ⟨string⟩).

where a string is a series of alphanumeric characters. A comma ends each string except for the last one, which is terminated by a period. The string pairs are enclosed in parentheses, with a period following the last pair.

Following the definition of the graph itself will be a series of pairs of strings, one pair per line. After each pair, print the path from the first of the pair to the second of the pair if a path exists. Use a depth-first strategy.

3. Write a program to perform the same task as in the previous problem but using a breadth-first search strategy.

4. Rewrite Programming Assignment 7, Chapter 8, using the array representation of a binary tree as described in this chapter.

*5. Write a program that differentiates and simplifies an expression with respect to a variable. You do not need to know how to differentiate to solve this program; we will give you a set of rules to apply to the data.

The main function in the program will be the routine that performs the differentiation. This task is fairly trivial if you have stored the expression as a binary expression tree.

Input: The input to this program will be a series of pairs of strings, each consisting of

1. a string representing the fully parenthesized infix expression to be differentiated. The expression is composed of integers, variable names (single character), and the binary operators +, −, *, /, and # (exponentiation). You may assume that the expression is fully and correctly parenthesized. The string is terminated by a semicolon (;).
2. a single character representing the variable with respect to which you are differentiating.

The final input will be a pair of zeros.

Output: Echoprint each pair of inputs, and print out the result of the differentiation or any appropriate error message.

Discussion: The rules for differentiating the expression are given below: Assume:

C is a constant number.
S and T are expressions that include the variable X.
X is the variable with respect to which you are differentiating.

`DIFF(C) = 0`

Rule 1: The derivative of a constant is zero.

```
DIFF(X) = 1
```

Rule 2: The derivative of the variable with respect to which you are differentiating is 1.

```
DIFF(S+T) = DIFF(S) + DIFF(T)
```

Rule 3: The derivative of the sum of expressions S and T is the sum of the derivative of expression S plus the derivative of expression T.

```
DIFF(S-T) = DIFF(S) - DIFF(T)
```

Rule 4: The derivative of the difference between expressions S and T is the derivative of expression S minus the derivative of expression T.

```
DIFF(S*T) = S * DIFF(T) + T * DIFF(S)
```

Rule 5: The derivative of the product of expressions S and T is equal to the product of expression S and the derivative of expression T plus the product of expression T and the derivative of expression S.

```
DIFF(S/T) = ((T * DIFF(S)) - (S * DIFF(T)))/SQR(T)
```

Rule 6: The derivative of the division of expression S by expression T is equal to the product of expression T and the derivative of expression S minus the product of expression S, and the derivative of expression T, divided by the square of expression T.

Assuming that X is not contained in expression T,

```
DIFF(S#T) = T * (S#(T - 1)) * DIFF(S)
```

Rule 7: The derivative of expression S raised to the expression T power is expression T times expression S raised to the T − 1 power times the derivative of expression S. You may assume that the variable with respect to which you are differentiating will not appear in the expression representing the exponent.

Example 1
expression = (X + 1)
variable = X

DIFF (X + 1) = DIFF(X) + DIFF(1)	*by Rule 3*
= 1 + 0	*by Rules 2 and 1*
= 1	

Example 2
expression = ((3 * X) − 5)
variable = X

DIFF((3 * X) − 5) = DIFF(3 * X) − DIFF(5)	*by Rule 4*
= 3 * DIFF(X) + X * DIFF(3)) − 0	*by Rules 5 and 1*
= (3 * 1 + X * 0) − 0	*by Rules 2 and 1*
= 3	

You can see that this is a recursive process, since DIFF is defined in terms of other uses of DIFF. The base cases are DIFF(C) = 0 and DIFF(X) = 1 (when X is the variable with respect to which you are differentiating).

If the expression you are differentiating is stored in a binary expression tree, applying these rules to the expression is really simple. Consider the binary expression tree that represents Example 2:

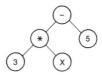

To differentiate the expression, we evaluate

DIFF (expression in LEFT(TREE)) − DIFF (expression in RIGHT(TREE))

The recursive DIFF function itself is similar to the function that evaluates an expression stored in a binary expression tree. The basic processing, given a pointer to a node in the tree, PTR, and a variable with respect to which we are differentiating, V, is:

```
IF INFO (PTR) = V
    THEN
        DIFF←1    (* Rule 1 *)
    ELSE
        IF INFO (PTR) = a constant OR
            INFO (PTR) = another variable
        THEN
            DIFF←0    (* Rule 2 *)
        ELSE

            (* Case on operator type *)
            CASE INFO (PTR) OF
                '+' : (* apply Rule 3 *)
                        i.e., DIFF←DIFF(LEFT(PTR)) +
                                DIFF(RIGHT(PTR))
                '−' : (* apply Rule 4 *)
                '*'  : (* apply Rule 5 *)
                '/'  : (* apply Rule 6 *)
                '#' : (* apply Rule 7 *)
            END CASE
```

You have one other task in evaluating the derivative of the expression: simplifying it as much as possible. Following are some rules for simplifying. You should choose the best place(s) in your program to apply the simplification rules. S is an expression.

$$S + 0 = S$$
$$0 + S = S$$
$$S - 0 = S$$
$$S * 0 = 0$$
$$0 * S = 0$$
$$S * 1 = S$$
$$0 / S = 0$$
$$S \# 0 = 1$$

S # 1 = S
S − S = 0
S / S = 1

Subexpressions involving only constants and the +, −, or * operators must be evaluated (e.g., 2 + 3 becomes 5).

There are two error conditions that you must note:

S / 0 = 'DIVISION BY ZERO'
0 / 0 = 'UNDEFINED'

Basically your program has three main tasks per expression/variable pair.

1. Build a binary expression tree representing the expression.
2. Differentiate the expression in the tree with respect to the variable.
3. Simplify the expression representing the derivative and print result.

Chapter 10

Programming assignments are not appropriate for this chapter.

Chapter 11

1. The object of this programming assignment is twofold. First, you are to compare the relative performance of different sorting algorithms on the same data set. Second, you are to compare the relative performance of the same algorithm on two different data sets.

   Five sorting algorithms are to be tested. You are to code and run the following sorts:

   1. Insertion sort. You are to run two different versions of the standard insertion sort. One will use a singly linked list and the other will use an array implementation with elements being shifted down as necessary.
   2. Binary tree sort.
   3. Quicksort. You may use either a recursive or a nonrecursive version of quicksort. Be sure to indicate which it is on the output.
   4. Any sort of your choice. This can be any sort you choose. It can even be the other version of quicksort if you wish.

You must include a counter in the inner loop of each sort which counts comparisons.

   Input: Two files of integers to be sorted. A maximum of 100 integers in the first data set and a maximum of 1000 integers in the second data set.

   Output: The following output should be repeated for each sort:

   1. The name of the sort
   2. Echoprint of the input

3. The sorted file
4. The number of comparisons required

Your final output should be a summary table that lists the type of sort and number of comparisons, by data set.

Chapter 12

1. The object of this assignment is twofold. First, you are to compare the relative performance of different searching algorithms on the same data set. Second, you are to compare the performance of the same algorithm on data sets of different sizes.

   Code the following three search strategies:

   1. linear search in an unordered list
   2. linear search in an ordered list
   3. binary search

   In each routine, keep track of how many comparisons are made.

   INPUT: Create a data set of 100 integers. Do ten searches with each algorithm. Be sure the searches include values not in the list as well as those in the list.

   Create a second data set made up of three different sets of data to be searched. The first set of data should have 6 values, the second 50, and the third 150. Run each routine with five searches within each of the three data sets.

2. Take the data from the previous assignment and use the division method of hashing to store the data values. Use table sizes of 7, 51, and 151. Use the linear method of collision resolution. Print out the tables after the data have been stored. Run the same five searches within each of the three data sets, counting the number of comparisons necessary. Print out the number of comparisons necessary in each case.

   OUTPUT: The following should be printed for each data set.

1. Echoprint the input data.
2. For each search request,
   (a) print the value being searched for.
   (b) In each algorithm print
       (i)   the algorithm name.
       (ii) 'YES' if the search is successful; 'NO' otherwise.
       (iii) the number of comparisons made.

Note: The input will have to be sorted before algorithms 2 and 3 can be run.

Index